Handbook of Research on Agent-Based Societies:
Social and Cultural Interactions

Goran Trajkovski
Laureate Education Inc., USA

Samuel G. Collins
Towson University, USA

Information Science
REFERENCE

INFORMATION SCIENCE REFERENCE

Hershey · New York

Director of Editorial Content:	Kristin Klinger
Assistant Development Editor:	Heather Probst
Director of Production:	Jennifer Neidig
Managing Editor:	Jamie Snavely
Assistant Managing Editor:	Carole Coulson
Typesetter:	Carole Coulson
Cover Design:	Lisa Tosheff
Printed at:	Yurchak Printing Inc.

Published in the United States of America by
Information Science Reference (an imprint of IGI Global)
701 E. Chocolate Avenue, Suite 200
Hershey PA 17033
Tel: 717-533-8845
Fax: 717-533-8661
E-mail: cust@igi-global.com
Web site: http://www.igi-global.com

and in the United Kingdom by
Information Science Reference (an imprint of IGI Global)
3 Henrietta Street
Covent Garden
London WC2E 8LU
Tel: 44 20 7240 0856
Fax: 44 20 7379 0609
Web site: http://www.eurospanbookstore.com

Library of Congress Cataloging-in-Publication Data

Library of Congress Cataloging-in-Publication Data

Handbook of research on agent-based societies : social and cultural interactions / Goran Trajkovski and Samuel G. Collins, editors.
     p. cm.
  Includes bibliographical references and index.
  Summary: "This volume addresses a variety of issues, in particular the emergence of societal phenomena in the interactions of systems of agents (software, robot or human)"--Provided by publisher.
  ISBN 978-1-60566-236-7 (hardcover) -- ISBN 978-1-60566-237-4 (ebook)
  1. Social systems--Computer simulation. 2. Social evolution--Computer simulation. 3. Intelligent agents (Computer software) 4. Human-computer interaction. 5. Artificial intelligence--Social aspects. I. Trajkovski, Goran, 1972- II. Collins, Samuel Gerald. III. Title: Agent-based societies : social and cultural interactions.
  HM701.H36 2009
  303.48'330113--dc22
                          2008024389

British Cataloguing in Publication Data
A Cataloguing in Publication record for this book is available from the British Library.

List of Reviewers

Shah Jamal
Alam Centre for Policy Modelling, UK

Costin Badica
University of Craiova, Romania

Susanne Barber
The University of Texas, USA

Olivier Boissier
Ecole Natiionale Superieure des Mines de Saint-Etienne, France

Jeffrey M. Bradshaw
Florida Institute for Human and Machine Cognition (IHMC), USA

James Braman
Towson University, USA

Joseph Bullington
Georgia Southern University, USA

Marco Campenni
ISTC/CNR, Italy

Paul Davidsson
Blekinge Institute of Technology, Sweden

Stefano DeLuca
Evodevo, Italy

Deborah Duong.
Office of the Secretary of Defense, USA

Adrian Gardner
Georgia Southern University, USA

Paolo Giorgini
University of Trento, Italy

Daniela Godoy
ISISTAN, UNICEN University, Argentina

David Newlin
RTI International, USA

Ann Nowe Vrije
Universiteit Brussel, Belgium

Gregory M.P. O'hare
University College Dublin, Ireland

Mario Paolucci
CNR, Italy Italy

Michal Pechoucek
Czech Technical University in Prague, Czech Republic

Oliver Popov
Mid Sweden University, Sweden

Wilhem Rossak
FSU Jena, Germany

Josefina Sierra
Universidad Politécnica de Cataluña, Spain

John Symons
University of Texas at El Paso, USA

Maksim Tsvetovat
George Mason University, USA

Giovanni Vincenti
Gruppo Vincenti, S.r.l. , Italy

Vern Walker
Hofstra University, USA

List of Contributors

Table of Contents

Section III
Second Order Emergences

Detailed Table of Contents

Section I
Initial States

The chapter critically examines the sociology of emergence, developing an often-ignored, Durkheimian heritage into what amounts to a manifesto for a social science of emergence resting on a complex understanding of agents

This chapter builds on Sawyer's insights, interrogating the movement from agential properties to social emergence, and using an enactivist perspective to critique questions of structure and agency in sociology and to explore the challenge of modeling a social emergence that builds from cognitive to social levels.

This chapter takes up the genealogical task from the perspective of social psychology and ethology, the other two disciplines MAS research has most often drawn from. In particular, asking how different agents (human and non-human) interact together and how insights from these studies can help researchers build more "life-like" agents to interact with us, including some of our more emergent properties (emotion, empathy and inference).

This chapter takes the interdisciplinary legacies from the previous chapters into the area of simulations.

This chapter takes aforementioned interdisciplinary legacies into e-business, respectively—and, in the process, bridges the theoretical and conceptual configurations of this section with the emergent organizations in the next.

Section II
Emergences

This chapter critiques the one-dimensional, temporal assumptions built into extant simulations (and, synedochically, Conway's "Game of Life") and suggests the possibility of introducing heterogeneous temporalities into simulation design.

This chapter exploits some of the diverse temporalities from the previous chapter, in order to build scalable models of agent communications based in part on biofeedback.

Zhang et al. look to interactionist models of social cognition in order to build MAS where decision-making emerges from the interactions between agents rather than through the more autonomous models of decision making in classic rational choice theory.

This chapter looks to social interactionism, networking, and community in order to build "socially interactive virtual agents" for the creation of virtual learning environments.

This chapter underscores the problem and promise of communicative models in MAS. Tacking back and between ethological examples and AI simulation, Takác proposes interactionist communications premised on models of evolutionary adaptation.

This chapter examines the ways agents might build on models of teamwork in order to coordinate with other agents to fulfill the needs of human agents.

This chapter looks to one of the relatively undeveloped directions in agent perception in order to build new models for the emergent of MAS socialities.

This chapter explores the possibility for emergent socialities between diverse agents based on almost sui generis communicative models where syntactical structures emerge in the space of agent interaction.

This chapter on the other hand explores the possibilities latent in more affective communications: What advantages might an "emotion-based agent" have over other kinds of social agents? Could emotion-based agents couple more effectively with human agents?

This chapter inverts the usual assumptions implicit in MAS by suggesting that it is the human agents who may be emulating non-human agents, and that the task for the researcher is as much to develop different human behaviors as it is as different models for non-human agents. In the process, the authors draw a much richer (and more ambiguous) picture of agent communication (including the possibilities in miscommunication). Fittingly, the application of some of these ideas leads us to questions of second-order emergence.

Section III
Second Order Emergences

This chapter takes the social theories elaborated in Part I in the designs of Virtual Learning Environments designed to reduce the incidence (as well as mitigate the effects) of school bullying. In these hybrid agent interactions, "believability" is an emergent category—non-human agents can be "too believable" (and hence unbelievable), as are ideas about empathy and engagement.

This chapter looks at reputation as the "meta-belief" enabling other beliefs and, in the process, generates other, emergent socialities: cooperation, altruism, and other reciprocal behaviors.

In this chapter, the forms emerging from temporal variance in a MAS are exploited by agents who attempt to influence each other's beliefs, in the process stretching Conway's cellular automata to new (and emergent) applications in both simulations and future, hybrid MAS.

This chapter applies MAS to neurophysiology, and in the process introduces a tantalizing example of second-order emergence in the self-reflexive monitoring of oneself facilitated by the imitative impulse structured into our frontal-parietal mirror neuron system.

This chapter also incorporates emergent cognition into its models; in this case what the authors terms an "abstraction-emergence loop" that captures the way agents generalize on their experience and thereby influence the behavior of subsequent local behaviors.

In this chapter's applications of a "Default-Logic" framework result in MAS capable of both rendering legal decisions as well as deliberating on the structure of legal reasoning itself, in the process implicating both human- and non-human agents in the future of the legal process itself.

This chapter develops a model network intrusion where "malicious" and "normal" traffic are (secondarily) emergent concepts arising from an emergent MAS consensus.

Chapter XXIII

This chapter details search tools for emergent agents. As new properties emerge in MAS, the relationship of the observer changes—that is, new kinds of properties are sought after and search engines represent the boundary between one kind of emergence (emergent properties of agents) and another emergence (new foci emerges from the consciousness of emergent properties).

Foreword

As a genuine believer in strong emergence, I guess it would be self-defying if not outright contradictory, for me to say that this edited volume will have such and such effects in the field or on the readers.

On the other hand, I can confidently say that in these times of Kurzweilian acceleration and Clarkian "tools-r-us" adage, yet another book-object to think with and about multi-agent systems and emergent phenomena will certainly help us catch up with the pace of "reality" changes. Who could have predicted the emergence of micro-crediting schemes made possible by the ubiquity of cell phones? Or the effects of sites hosting user generated videos on the U.S. presidential campaign and on politics in general,or the crowd sourcing phenomenon as well as the economy of the niche.

As our tools get more and more complex, so do we, as well as our relations with others. The editors' efforts invested into this edited volume resulted in something that will certainly help understand ourselves better by supporting the "extrospective" processes. An explanation of this neologism would be in order here: if we adopt the *distributed mind/cognition* theory, then I believe that (at least in this transitory phase of getting used to it) *extrospection* may a better word to describe what was once (during the *mind-does-not-go-beyond-our-skin-bag* era) called introspection.

The three sections of the volume—Initial States, Emergences, and Second Order Emergences—make for a new organic whole. The first section covers foundations of MAS (sociology of emergence, enactivist critique of questions of structure and agency in sociology, and issues of heterogeneous societies). In the second, we find a concentrate on emergences, where at least two levels of emergence are treated. First, there is the simultaneous focus on the three components of MAS, agents, their interactions, and properties of the groups. Second is the wide acceptance that MAS theories and tools do offer practical solutions in the world of today. Finally, the last part offers insights into the behavior of agents that become aware of emergent behaviors or emergent phenomena.

I am positive that even non-specialists will find this volume informative, and that every reader will get the update of latest on-goings in the field. The introduction by the editors gives an excellent *advance organizer* for what's ahead, and definitely helps the assimilation of the chapters.

What tags would I use for this book? Multi Agent Systems, emergence, second order cybernetics, heterogeneous societies, mixed realities, distributed cognition … in one word? Del.icio.us!

Georgi Stojanov
Paris, May, 2008

Georgi Stojanov *received his master's degree in 1993 and his PhD degree in computer science from the Faculty of Electrical Engineering, "SS Cyril and Methodius" University in Skopje, Macedonia in 1997. His main research interest is in developmental robotics and modeling of higher cognitive processes (learning, anticipation, curiosity and analogical and metaphorical reasoning). Currently he is with the American University of Paris where he teaches several courses in computer science. Dr. Stojanov has been a member of organizing and program committees of numerous internationally recognized workshops and conferences. He has published extensively in the above mentioned fields. Dr. Stojanov has collaborated with many universities and research institutions among which: University of California in San Diego, University of Geneva, Lehigh University, University of Trieste, Paris V. His research projects and visiting researcher/professor posts have been funded by several institutions including: European Commission, US Academies Offices of Central Europe and Eurasia, Macedonian Academy of Arts and Sciences, SOROS Foundation.*

Preface

TOWARDS MORE LIVELY MACHINES

If there is one thing anthropology (and archaeology) teaches, it is that our tools are key to our identity as humans. In fact, this was one of the earlier—though now discarded—definitions of human (qua Carlyle). But, despite numerous other ethological examples of tool-use, we still tend to think of ourselves as ontologically grounded in the tools we use. Homo habilis is, after all, a "tool using man."

Certainly, anthropologists like Mead and Bateson (anticipating what would later become distributed cognition), have noted our embeddedness in systems composed of humans and their material culture (Bateson 1972). But, in the millennia since Acheulian hand-axes, we have not only developed more and more complex tools (and relied on them more), but, the tools themselves have begun to take on a life of their own. As Haraway wrote (in a style at once half ethnographic and half prognostication), our "machines are disturbingly lively, and we ourselves frighteningly inert" (Haraway 1985).

The fear of non-human agency is a theme in 20th century dystopian fiction—aliens, monstrous forces awakened by nuclear blasts ("The Thing," "Gojira"), robots carefully hemmed by laws hard-wired into their programming (Asimov's I, Robot), Draconian supercomputers orchestrating the end of humanity ("War Games," "Terminator"). And yet, just as compelling a case could be made that the possibility of non-human agency and intelligence represents the culmination of our human potential (Heckman 2008; Collins 2008).

If the 20th century suggested fear and unease with non-human agents, the 21st century adds a utopian edge, particularly in the hopes we have for Multi-Agent Systems (MAS). Whether optimizing resource allocation, organizing complex systems, or simulating human behaviors, the hope is that non-human agents may prove a palliative to the kinds of alienation we face in a society characterized by high degrees of mobility, tenuous relationships with place and people, and in general, unremitting complexity (Allison 2006). Thus, navigating news coverage, financial systems, traffic, internet searches, and so forth, are all thought to be assisted by systems of agent proxies (self)-organized about our individuated needs. From the fears of "Terminator" (being replaced by the robot), we all become hopeful cyborgs, variously hybrid agents embedded in our machines (Clark 2003).

Traditionally, multi-agent systems are composed of either software or robot agents, although many researchers have utilized "human agents" as a baseline in their development of non-human agents. Woolridge (2002:11) adds that they are:

at least to some extent capable of autonomous action—of deciding for themselves what they need to do in order to satisfy their design objectives. Second, they are capable of interacting with other agents, not simply by exchanging data, but, by engaging in the analogues of the kind of social activity that we all engage in every day of our lives—cooperation, coordination, negotiation, and the like.

Although Woolridge's work grounds the articles in this volume in a common vision of MAS, we also go beyond this more engineering-inflected vision of MAS.

In Disney's retelling of *The Sorcerer's Apprentice* in its 1940 *Fantasia*, Mickey Mouse is overwhelmed by a material world over which he loses control. His broom, split into pieces, continues the (multi-agent) work of carrying (and dumping) water without Mickey, to the extent that the house floods. And yet, in MAS, the hope is exactly that—programmers and roboticists look (in some way) to lose control over the systems they've engineered, with the hope that some different kind of solution will emerge. For some, this is an adaptation to the world around us. For example, for Serugeno et al (2006: 45):

The complexity of today's applications is such (e.g., world scale) that no centralized or hierarchical control is possible. In other cases, it is the unforeseeable context, in which the application evolves or moves, which makes any supervision difficult.

In other words (qua "*The Sorcerer's Apprentice*"), we've already "lost control" in any deterministic, more Newtonian sense: financial markets, ecological catastrophe, refugee flows, and Internet traffic. Our problems are increasingly non-linear; traveling salesman-type (NP) problems are more and more the rule than the exception. The solution cannot be the reinstatement of patriarchical authority (the return of the sorcerer), but it's opposite—the manumission of control. The hapless apprentice, after all, had only granted the broom limited autonomy (to carry water and nothing else). If he had granted the broom the freedom to decide when there was enough water, than the problem could, literally, have solved itself.

This was certainly the hope embodied in something like Rodney Brooks-style reactive architectures, where the scientist looked to what kinds of behavioral phenomena might emerge from autonomous, multi-agent systems in way not reducible to individual agents or local rules. These kinds of hopes take on an almost mystic quality in something like artificial life, where emergence literally animates local rules, investing them with an elusive, black-box quality: life itself (Helmreich 1998). Although none of the contributors to this volume invest the same kind of religiosity in emergence, we nevertheless believe that MAS may be generative of novel adaptations with ultimately salutary effects for the humans who rely upon them.

This volume aims to address all of these issues and the emergence of societal phenomena in the interactions of systems of agents (software, robot or human) in particular. In a given environment, agents interact with each other, imitating, communicating, exchanging, and competing. Based on these heterogeneous modalities of interaction, a variety of socialities may emerge: language and communication, identities, economies, cultures. Tracking those emergences not only allows us to program more realistic simulations of biologies (human and otherwise), but may allows us to more effectively combine (qua hybrid agents) with our lively machines to form new socialities that are, themselves, doubly emergent—self-reflexively emergent.

We know (or, at least, think we know) what our non-human agents want. But what kinds of agency and intentionality emerge in hybrid systems composed of humans embedded in machine assemblages of non-human agents? The articles here go well beyond describing the next generation of MAS in simulations and system engineering; they gesture to the novel systems that we form (and that we might form) with our varied, lively tools. That is, the contributors to the present work are not only describing their research in the present, they are also gesturing to the kinds of MAS (with their own, attendant emergences) that may exist in the future. It is our belief that this meeting of AI research, cognitive science, and the social sciences, may constitute a novel direction for MAS that not only describes our lives in information society, but also intervenes in future assemblages of hybrid agents and agencies.

In other words, we hope the book acts as an agent in itself, in particular, what Michel Serres terms a "quasi-object," that is, an object that not only takes on agential properties, but also catalyzes agencies in others. Just as we now emulate the non-human agents we originally developed to simulate us, so the analysis of extant MAS may stimulate the development of new multiagencies, heretofore undiscovered conurbations of human and non-human, information and social sciences.

Accordingly, we have divided the books into three sections that attempt to structure this dialectic of revelation and evocation. We have tried to resist the power of the text (as an agent in its own right) to dictate the course of chapters. As artifacts of a particular way of seeing and ordering the world, texts present us with linear teleologies (in Aristotelian terms, the necessity of a "beginning, "middle" and "end"): things begin, develop according to their narrative logic, then culminate. Someone has the first word (an introduction), and someone, the last (a conclusion). We have tried to avoid characterizing this work (as well as MAS in general) as linear and have therefore ordered the book along principles which, in first-generation cybernetics, were called "circular causality": accordingly, the end of the book takes us back to the beginning, and the cascade of emergent phenomena and organizations described herein refer back and forth to teach other in a temporally chiasmic (if not emergent) fashion. Of course, we have not entirely succeeded. As Bruno Latour has pointed out of non-human "actants," our tools make reciprocal demands upon us, and to escape the kind of consciousness demanded of us by the text, we would need to leave the text behind all together.

SECTION I: INITIAL STATES

In Conway's now-apocryphal Game of "Life," "initial states" describe the configuration of cellular automata (and the rules for successive turns). Here, contributors offer insights into the foundations of MAS. But these states are themselves hardly given—they "emerge" out of the play of different disciplines, many of which come together in the space of this volume, and which we, in turn, hope may spur subsequent emergences. Along with these disciplines come diverse assumptions about psychology, social interaction, language, cognitive development, and culture, all of which form what Hegel might have called the "second nature" of MAS (Helmreich 1998). The first chapter, Sawyer's "The Science of Social Emergence," critically examines the sociology of emergence, developing an often-ignored, Durkheimian heritage into what amounts to a manifesto for a social science of emergence resting on a complex understanding of agents. Goldspink's and Kay's "Agentive Cognitive Capabilities and Orders of Social Emergence," builds, in many ways, on Sawyer's insights; interrogating the movement from agential properties to social emergence, and using an enactivist perspective to critique questions of structure and agency in sociology and to explore the challenge of modeling a social emergence that builds from cognitive to social levels. Bullington's "Agents in Social Interaction" takes up the genealogical task from the perspective of social psychology and ethology, the other two disciplines MAS research has most often drawn from, in particular, asking how different agents (human and non-human) interact together, and how insights from these studies can help researchers build more "life-like" agents to interact with us, including some of our more emergent properties (emotion, empathy and inference). Upal's "Predictive Models of Cultural Information Transmission" and Romero's "Interaction of Agent in E-Business" each take these interdisciplinary legacies into two applications—simulation and e-business, respectively—and, in the process, bridging the theoretical and conceptual configurations of this section with the emergent organizations in the next.

SECTION II: EMERGENCES

There are at least two levels of emergence at play in this section of the book. The first, as Sawyer writes, involves applications of the central premise of social emergence, the "simultaneous focus on three levels of analysis: individuals, their interactional dynamics, and the socially emergent properties of the group."

The second is the growing awareness among people within and without the information and computing sciences regarding the utility of MAS for "solving" (keeping in mind that only sub-optimal solutions may be possible) the problems of today's world. This section is witness to the varied contexts to which MAS have been applied, and to the possibilities for their applications in areas rather far removed from areas usually associated with MAS.

These two directions mirror the general dynamics of emergence itself—the social sciences, cognitive sciences, and AI suggest the properties non-human agents might emulate, and influence the scope of simulations produced. At the same time, developments in MAS simulations suggest answers to old problems bedeviling social theory (e.g., structure versus agency) and gesture towards new opportunities for human-non-human interaction, hybrid MAS facilitated by these human/animal behavior emulating agencies.

Conover's "A simulation of Temporally Variant Agent Interaction via Passive Inquiry" critiques the one-dimensional, temporal assumptions built into extant simulations (and, synedochically, Conway's "Game of Life") and suggests the possibility of introducing heterogeneous temporalities into simulation design. Schilling's "Agent Feedback Messaging: A Messaging Infrastructure for Distributed Message Delivery" exploits some of those diverse temporalities in order to build scalable models of agent communications based in part on biofeedback.

Zhang et al. look to interactionist models of social cognition in order to build MAS where decision-making emerges from the interactions between agents rather than through the more autonomous models of decision making in classic rational choice theory. Similarly, in Part 1 of their "Developing Relationships between Autonomous Agents: Promoting Pro-Social Behaviour through Virtual Learning Environments," Watson et al. look to social interactionism, networking, and community, in order to build "socially interactive virtual agents" for the creation of virtual learning environments (VLEs), while Takác's "Construction of Meanings in Biological and Artificial Agents" underscores the problem and promise of communicative models in MAS. Tacking back and between ethological examples and AI simulation, Takáč proposes interactionist communications premised on models of evolutionary adaptation.

Abramson's "Training Coordination Proxy Agents Using Reinforcement Learning" examines the ways agents might build on models of teamwork in order to coordinate with other agents to fulfill the needs of human agents. Likewise,

Duong's "The Generative Power of Signs: The Importance of the Autonomous Perception of Tags to the Strong Emergence of Institutions" looks to one of the relatively undeveloped directions in agent perception in order to build new models for the emergent of MAS socialities.

Sierra's and Santibáñez's "Propositional Logic Syntax Acquisition Using Induction and Self-Organisation" explores the possibility for emergent socialities between diverse agents based on almost sui generis communicative models where syntactical structures emerge in the space of agent interaction. In their "Hybrid Emotionally Aware Mediated Multiagency," on the other hand, Vincenti and Braman explore the possibilities latent in more affective communications: what advantages might an "emotion-based agent" have over other kinds of social agents? Could emotion-based agents couple more effectively with human agents? Finally, Collins's and Trajkovski's "Mapping Hybrid Agencies through Multiagent Systems" inverts the usual assumptions implicit in MAS by suggesting that it is the human agents who may be emulating non-human agents, and that the task for the researcher is as much to develop different human behaviors as much as it is different models for non-human agents. In the process, they draw a much richer, and more ambiguous, picture of agent communication (including the possibilities in miscommunication). Fittingly, the application of some of these ideas leads us to questions of second-order emergence.

SECTION III: SECOND ORDER EMERGENCES

Second order emergences describe the agents changing their behaviors according to their awareness of emergent phenomena or behaviors. Here, we include not only a host of reflexively understood human phenomena, which, strictly speaking, gives rise to a recursive chain of emergences, but also to the possibility that our awareness of the possibilities inherent in MAS may catalyze new combinations of hybrid agents and new applications for those combinations. "Second order emergence" also refers to the state of MAS research in general. Now almost two decades old, MAS research has moved into a new stage involving new sites of application as well as new hybridities linking together not only different systems, but also human and non-human agents in new ways—all enabled by our growing consciousness of both the usefulness of MAS as well as their (always already) ubiquity in our lives.

In Part II of "Developing Relationships between Autonomous Agents," Watson et al. take the social theories they elaborate in Part I in their designs of Virtual Learning Environments designed to reduce the incidence (as well as mitigate the effects) of school bullying. In these hybrid agent interactions, "believability" is an emergent category—non-human agents can be "too believable" (and hence unbelievable), as are ideas about empathy and engagement. In "Reputation: Social Transmission for Partner Selection," however, Paolucci and Conte look at reputation as the "meta-belief" enabling other beliefs and, in the process, generating other, emergent socialities—cooperation, altruism, and other reciprocal behaviors. Finally, in part II of Conover's "A Simulation of Temporally Variant Agent Interaction via Belief Promulgation," the forms emerging from temporal variance in a MAS are exploited by agents who attempt to influence each other's beliefs in the process stretching Conway's cellular automata to new, and emergent, applications in both simulations and future, hybrid MAS.

Newlin applies MAS to neurophysiology, and in the process introduces a tantalizing example of second-order emergence in the self-reflexive monitoring of oneself facilitated by the imitative impulse structured into our frontal-parietal mirror neuron system. In their "Relationship Between the Processes of Emergence and Abstraction in Societies" Baumer and Tomlinson also incorporate emergent cognition into their models, in this case what the authors terms an "abstraction-emergence loop" that captures the way agents generalize on their experience and thereby influence the behavior of subsequent local behaviors. But MAS cannot only be confined to applications in what might be called "lower-levels" of cognition. In Walker's "Emergent Reasoning Structures in Law," applications of a "Default-Logic" framework result in MAS capable of both rendering legal decisions as well as deliberating on the structure of legal reasoning itself, while in the process implicating both human- and non-human agents in the future of the legal process itself.

The final articles consider reflexivity in MAS, agents examining each other for new (wanted or unwanted) properties. Richardson's "Agents in Security: a Look at the Use of Host-Based Monitoring and Protection and Network Intrusion Detection" develops a model network intrusion where "malicious" and "normal" traffic are (secondarily) emergent concepts arising from an emergent MAS consensus. North et al. detail search tools for emergent agents. As new properties emerge in MAS, the relationship of the observer changes, that is, new kinds of properties are sought after and search engines represent the boundary between one kind of emergence (emergent properties of agents) and another emergence (new foci emerges from the consciousness of emergent properties).

Recursively, that search for new properties leads us looping back to the kinds of assumptions we held about MAS and their possibilities to begin with. Hence, back to the beginning of the book!

REFERENCES

Allison, Anne (2006). *Millennial monsters.* Durham, NC: Duke University Press.

Bateson, Gregory (1972). *Steps to an ecology of mind.* NY: Ballantine.

Clark, Andy (2003). *Natural-born cyborgs.* NY: Oxford University Press.

Collins, Samuel Gerald (2008). *All tomorrow's cultures.* NY: Berghahn.

Haraway, Donna (1985). *Simians, cyborgs, and women.* NY: Routledge.

Heckman, Davin (2008). *A small world.* Durham, NC: Duke University Press.

Helmreich, Stefan (1998). *Silicon second nature.* Berkeley: University of California Press.

Serugeno, Giovanna Di Marzo, Marie-Pierre Gleizes & Anthony Karageorgos (2006). "Self-Organisation and Emergence in MAS." *Informatica, 30,* 45-54.

Woolridge, Michael (2002). *An introduction to multisgent systems.* NY: Wiley and Sons.

Section I
Initial States

Chapter I
The Science of Social Emergence

R. Keith Sawyer
Washington University in St. Louis, USA

ABSTRACT

Sociology should be the foundational science of social emergence. But to date, sociologists have neglected emergence, and studies of emergence are more common within microeconomics. Moving forward, I argue that a science of social emergence requires two advances beyond current approaches—and that sociology is better positioned than economics to make these advances. First, consistent with existing critiques of microeconomics, I argue that we need a more sophisticated representation of individual agents. Second, I argue that multi-agent models need a more sophisticated representation of interaction processes. The agent communication languages currently used by multi-agent systems researchers are not appropriate for modeling human societies. I conclude by arguing that the scientific study of interaction and emergence will have to migrate out of microeconomics and become a part of sociology. Sociologists, for their part, should embrace multi-agent modeling to pursue a more rigorous study of these traditional sociological issues.

INTRODUCTION

Social emergence is the central phenomenon of the social sciences. The science of social emergence is the basic science underlying all of the social sciences, because social emergence is foundational to all of them. *Political science, economics, education, history, and sociology* study phenomena that socially emerge from complex systems of individuals in interaction. In this chapter, I argue that sociology should become the basic science of social emergence, and I outline a theoretical framework to guide this study.

But this is not the sociology we see today; few sociologists study social emergence. In the second half of the twentieth century, economics has made the best case for being the foundational social science, by making social emergence central to its theory and practice. Perhaps the most important strength of the *neoclassical economic* approach is that it has rigorous formalisms for modeling the ways that individual action generates aggregate outcomes at the level of an entire population (Bowles, 2001; Durlauf & Young, 2001). Because social emergence is the central phenomenon of the social sciences, and economics has developed the most successful model of social emergence, this has naturally led to "*economic imperialism*," with neoclassical economists beginning to analyze non-economic phenomena traditionally associated with sociology (Boulding, 1969, p. 8; Hirshleifer, 1985; Radnitzky & Bernholz, 1987; Tullock, 1972). These imperialists argue that economics is "the universal grammar of social science" (Hirshleifer, 1985, p. 53), and that it simply represents "straight thinking" applied to social science (Radnitzky, 1992, p. 15). And, in fact, microeconomics has been the only game in town for those interested in studying social emergence.

However, there are many problems with the models of social emergence dominant in microeconomics. Critics such as the "*New Economic Sociologists*" (see Krier, 1999; Zafirowski, 1999) claim that the microeconomic account of social emergence is empirically unfounded, methodologically individualist, neglects the *social embeddedness* of actors, neglects the importance of *institutions* and *social networks*, and neglects the unavoidable inefficiencies introduced by institutions, power, and *path dependence*. I focus on two specific critiques in this chapter. The first one is well known: many critics of microeconomics have called for a more sophisticated representation of the individual agents. Some agent models have begun to develop more accurate agent representations by drawing on the field of *cognitive psychology*, and occasionally on sociological theories of agency.

My second critique is less widely acknowledged: I argue that *microeconomics* radically simplifies important elements of social *emergence*—particularly, the key role played by *symbolic interaction*. Microeconomics uses formalisms that impose a simplistic representation of individual agents, and a simplistic representation of agent interaction. Some microeconomists have begun to use *multi agent system models*, but when they do, they tend

to reproduce the overly simplistic models of agents and agent interaction associated with the optimizing mathematics of *rational choice*. Multi-agent models, whether developed by economists or by sociologists, need a more sophisticated representation of interaction processes. The most sophisticated of these are modeled using what is called an *Agent Communication Language (ACL)*, but the ACLs developed to date in the MAS research community are not appropriate for modeling human societies. Social modelers can develop better representations of interaction by drawing on the science of micro-interaction within sociology. I have done several empirical studies of emergence in conversation, and I have shown that different communication mechanisms change the processes of social *emergence* (e.g. Sawyer, 2003b). This leads to a second critique of rational choice models: such models of social emergence have a radically simplified account of *human interaction*.

To respond to these two critiques, and develop a science of social emergence, the social sciences must bring together studies of interaction and studies of emergence. Despite the weaknesses of existing ACLs, I nonetheless believe that multi-agent simulations have the potential to enable the study of interaction in emergence processes (Hedström, 2005; Sawyer, 2005). In this paper, I begin by summarizing the two dominant paradigms in sociological research, and providing a historical account that shows why sociology has not yet brought together studies of interaction and emergence. Then, I present a theoretical framework that I call *the emergence paradigm* that brings together interaction and emergence, and I discuss the potential explanatory scope of this paradigm. I conclude by discussing some of the implications for the social sciences at large.

BACKGROUND

Twentieth century sociology did not focus on social emergence; sociology as a discipline has failed to recognize the importance of social emergence to the foundational issues facing the discipline (Coleman, 1987; Saam, 1999). In some cases, an expressed interest in emergence is seen as synonymous with *methodological individualism*, because it is primarily methodological individualists who have emphasized the importance of emergence to sociology. For example, Coleman's emphasis on "foundations" was an attempt to address the failure of sociologists to develop models of social emergence (Coleman, 1987, p. 171); and *social mechanists* have also proposed methodologically individualist versions of emergence (see Sawyer, 2004a).

Sociology has devoted a lot of attention both to interaction and to emergence, but unfortunately not to both at the same time. In the last chapter of my book *Social emergence* (Sawyer, 2005), I give an account of the history of 20th century sociology that explains this neglect, which I briefly summarize here. The study of interaction has been a strong trend in sociology since Georg Simmel's 19th century writings, but it became a significant component in academic sociology in the 1950s, 1960s, and 1970s, with the rise of *symbolic interactionism*, ethnomethodology, and conversation analysis. But because these sociologists in part defined themselves in opposition to structural functionalism, they resisted attributing any autonomous causal power to the macrosocial or structural level. As a result of this neglect of macrosocial phenomena, interactionist sociology contributed very little to the science of emergence—even though it pointed the way to a new science of social emergence by demonstrating how one could empirically study human interactional mechanisms.

In contrast to interactionism, mainstream sociology had always considered emergence to be an important phenomenon to be explained, from Durkheim's early writings (Sawyer, 2005) to Blau's structural sociology (1977). But the focus on very large-scale macrosocial phenomena made it impossible to closely focus on the interactions among agents that are the mechanisms of emergence processes. Most sociologists assume that communication is not central to sociology's main concerns, and that its study can be safely tucked away into the subfield of microsociology (*symbolic interactionism, conversation analysis, sociolinguistics*). In general, sociology assumes that all social constraint must be institutional; the implicit assumption is that communication is epiphenomenal—that it has no causal consequences, either for emergent macro phenomena or for individuals. Instead, the ultimate causal forces in social life are either *institutions*, networks, and group properties (for the collectivist), or rational actions taken in the context of pairwise game-like encounters (for the individualist). Consequently, for different reasons, both collectivists and individualists implicitly assume that interaction is of only marginal concern to the sociologist.

If sociology becomes the science of social emergence, it will be different from the sociology that we have today. The study of social emergence requires a simultaneous focus on three levels of analysis: individuals, their *interactional dynamics*, and the socially emergent macro properties of the group. In this chapter, I describe what a new sociology of *social emergence* might look like; I explain how this new sociology would relate to past

Figure 1. The emergence paradigm

Social Structure (Level E) Written texts (procedures, laws, regulations); material systems and infrastructure (architecture, urban design, communication and transportation networks)
Stable emergents (Level D) Group subcultures, group slang and catchphrases, conversational routines, shared social practices, collective memory
Ephemeral emergents (Level C) Topic, context, interactional frame, participation structure; relative role and status assignments
Interaction (Level B) Discourse patterns, symbolic interaction, collaboration, negotiation
Individual (Level A) Intention, agency, memory, personality, cognitive processes

sociological theory and practice; and I outline how this reformulated sociology could transform the disciplinary boundaries of the social sciences, with a particularly strong impact on *economics*.

THE EMERGENCE PARADIGM

To bring together both interaction and emergence, one must integrate two paradigms in sociological research that have, for the most part, remained independent. One paradigm, *microsociology*—which studies interactions between individuals—includes ethnomethodology, symbolic interactionism, conversation analysis, and to some extent, sociolinguistics. The other paradigm, *macrosociology*, studies large-scale social phenomena such as *institutions* (schools, governments, economies, corporations, markets) and *roles* and *statuses* (social class, gender, race).

Integrating symbolic interaction into the study of emergence requires that we consider two intermediate levels of social reality: *stable emergents* and *ephemeral emergents* (see Figure 1). In any social situation, there is a continuing dialectic: social emergence, where individuals are co-creating and co-maintaining ephemeral and stable emergents; and *downward causation* from those emergents. The new, modified versions of the emergents at Levels C and D continually constrain the flow of the interaction. During conversational encounters, *interactional frames* emerge, and these are collective social facts that can be characterized independently of individual's interpretations of them. Once a frame has emerged, it constrains the possibilities for action. Although the frame is created by participating individuals through their collective action, it is analytically independent of those individuals, and it has causal power over those individuals. I refer to this process as *collaborative emergence* (Sawyer 2003a), to distinguish it from models of emergence that fail to adequately theorize interactional processes and emergence *mechanisms*. The emergence paradigm emphasizes the identification of the *mechanisms* of collaborative emergence that lead to ephemeral and stable emergents. By introducing these intermediate levels, and the corresponding notion of collaborative emergence, my goal is to move beyond various

undeveloped conceptions of emergence in sociology, which try to make too large a jump from the individual to the structural level.

In the philosophy of science, accounts of *emergence* focus on properties of systems or properties of specific events in time, rather than focusing on the systems themselves. The debate focuses on which properties of a system at a specific event in time are emergent, and which properties are not emergent—merely aggregative or *resultant* from the properties of the system's components. From this perspective, one would not claim, for example, that the Catholic church is an *emergent phenomenon*; rather, the debate would focus on specific properties of the Catholic church—for example, the centralized nature of doctrinal authority in the Catholic church. A property is said to be emergent when it cannot be *predicted* from a complete knowledge of the system's components and their interactions; and when that system property is *novel*, not possessed by any of the system's components. Some philosophers go further and argue that an emergent property cannot be *explained* by analyzing the system's components and their interactions, although this claim is controversial, and in fact most multi agent system developers would claim that their simulations provide *explanations* of emergent system properties (see Sawyer, 2004b).

In much of traditional sociological theory, lower levels represent smaller groups of people, and higher levels represent larger groups—the Catholic church is the highest level of analysis, and progressively lower levels would be administrative units such as the diocese and the individual parish. In contrast, the emergents at Levels C and D are not structures in the traditional sociological sense of organizations and networks. They are emergent properties of sociological events, and have an existence independent of any particular configuration of individuals. Although levels C and D are at lower levels of analysis than the social structures of Level E, they do not necessarily correspond to smaller groups. Rather, they represent emergent properties of groups of any size.

The *emergence paradigm* accepts an important role for *methodological individualism* in sociology; it can play an important role in identifying the *mechanisms* and processes of social emergence in specific token instances. But *methodological individualism* is incomplete, because the *emergence paradigm* supports a *social realism* in which emergents have autonomous causal powers. Due to social emergence, social life cannot be fully explained by analyzing the actions or mental states of the participant individuals, and then by analyzing the interactions of these individuals, working "upwards" to an *explanation* of the emergents. This sort of analysis can partially explain the *collaborative emergence* of ephemeral interactional *frames*, but cannot adequately represent the analytic independence of emergents, and the ways that they causally constrain and enable participants.

My argument for *social realism* is based in somewhat complex arguments in the philosophy of science; I will briefly summarize the argument that I present in (Sawyer, 2005). Just as social simulators claim, I grant that a social simulation may be a valid representation of the *mechanism* underlying a given instance of a macrosocial phenomenon. For example, Hedström (2005) describes an elaborate simulation of unemployment in Stockholm, Sweden, which contains a separate agent for every unemployed individual. But if the macrosocial phenomenon (unemployment, in this case) has many different potential underlying *mechanisms*, any one social simulation would only explain one instance of it. Perhaps the mechanisms that account for urban unemployment are different in every major city; if so, a simulation of Stockholm would not be of use in explaining the broader macrosocial phenomenon of urban unemployment. But even in such a situation of what philosophers call "*multiple realizability*," it might nonetheless be possible to develop social laws, that do not refer to specific individuals, that provide explanations of urban unemployment. If such a situation holds, I then argue that attributing causal powers to the system property "unemployment rate" is warranted.

The *emergence paradigm* generally focuses on even lower levels of analysis than a macrosocial property like the unemployment rate. Instead, it advocates a focus on the causal forces that originate in an emergent that was created by the participants in a given encounter—to continue with the Stockholm unemployment example, one might study specific practices that emerge among unemployed youths in Stockholm, such as preferred leisure activities or distinctive slang and ways of talking. *Emergence paradigm* research focuses on the microinteractional *mechanisms* whereby shared social phenomena emerge, and how those emergents constrain those mechanisms.

Level C: Ephemeral Emergents

Level C includes the *interactional frames* of conversation analysis. In conversation, an interactional frame emerges from collective action and then constrains and enables collective action. These two processes are always simultaneous and inseparable. They are not distinct stages of a sequential process—emergence at one moment, and then constraint in the next; rather, each action contributes to a continuing process of *collaborative emergence*, at the same time that it is constrained by the shared emergent frame that exists at that moment. The collaborative emergence of frames has been studied by several researchers in interactional sociolinguistics and conversation analysis, including Deborah Tannen, Alessandro Duranti, and Charles Goodwin (Duranti & Goodwin, 1992; Tannen, 1993).

The emergent *frame* is a dynamic structure that changes with each action. No one can stop the encounter at any one point and identify with certainty what the frame's structure is. It is always subject to continuing negotiation, and because of its irreducible ambiguity, there will always be intersubjectivity issues, with different participants having different interpretations of the frame's constraints and affordances.

Level D: Stable Emergents

The second form of *collaborative emergence* is from Level B to Level D, with a complicated mediation through Level C. Level D represents the shared, collective history of a group. Stable emergents of small groups include group learning, group development, peer culture, and collective memory. Stable emergents of an entire society include its culture and its language; their *collaborative emergence* has been studied by cultural and linguistic anthropology.

The line between stable and ephemeral emergents is a fine one; for purposes of definition, I consider an emergent to be stable if it lasts across more than one encounter. Stable emergents have different degrees of stability; some are stable over generations, and others are stable only for weeks or months. From most to least stable, examples of stable emergents include language, catchphrases, trends and tastes, cohort private jokes and stories, the ensemble feel of a theater group during a month-long run of a play. Under this definition, distinctive slang used by unemployed youths in Stockholm would be stable emergents, because they are used in many different encounters, but would be relatively unstable. The issue of how stable emergents are related to ephemeral emergents is still unresolved within social science. In different ways, the issue is central to folkloristics, ethnomusicology, popular culture studies, the study of peer cultures and subcultures, and collective behavior studies of rumors and fads.

Ephemeral emergence occurs within a single encounter. Most sociological discussions of emergence have focused on the broader macrostructures that emerge and how those emergent patterns constrain future interaction. Yet, these studies have not had much success in tracing the exact details of the moment-to-moment emergence processes whereby macrostructures are collectively created. In contrast, various strands of *microsociology* have focused exactly on the moment-to-moment details of how ephemeral emergents result from interaction. However, in shifting their focus to interactional process, they have tended to neglect the nature of what emerges, and of what perdures across repeated encounters.

The collaborative emergence of stable emergents is the concern of the field known as *collective behavior*, the study of phenomena such as mob actions, riots, mass delusions, crazes, fads, and fashions. Park and Burgess (1921) first noted a special kind of behavior that they called "collective behavior." Lang and Lang (1961) called it "collective dynamics." They were also concerned with how collective action transforms into stable emergents; and during the 1960s, this became the concern of social movements researchers (Evans, 1969, p. 10).

But these classic theories of collective behavior went from the individual to the emergents directly, without an examination of the *mechanisms* of interaction. These theorists used extremely simplistic notions of interaction such as "social contagion" (Blumer, 1939) or "milling" (Park & Burgess, 1921); historically, this is because these writings on *collective behavior* predated the development of sophisticated methodologies for analyzing interaction. The sociology of *collective behavior* never made connections to the study of how stable emergents are created over time—oral culture, ritual change, and related subjects from linguistic anthropology. It's time to revisit these phenomena of collective behavior, with the additional power provided by multi agent system techniques.

Several social theorists have recognized the theoretical benefits of introducing stable emergents as a mediator between individual and macrostructure. These include Collins's *repetitive patterns of behavior* (1981), Giddens' *situated social practices* (1984), and Lawler, Ridgeway, and Markovsky's *microstructures* (1993). For Lawler, Ridgeway, and Markovsky, microstructures "emerge from and organize particular encounters" (1993, p. 272). Stable emergents are symbolic phenomena that have a degree of intersubjective sharing among some (more or less stable) group of individuals.

Some network analysts have argued that in many cases, *institutions* are crystallizations of emergent activity patterns and personal networks. Granovetter (1990) cited two historical examples of such institutional emergence: the development of the electrical utility industry in the United States between 1880 and 1930, and the professionalization of psychiatric practice. In both cases, the original institutions were "accretions of activity patterns around personal networks" (p. 105). Empirical and historical study suggests that these economic institutions emerged from the same processes as other social institutions. This sort of historical analysis of institutional emergence demonstrates that institutions are contingent and are socially constructed; the processes of their emergence must be studied empirically, and they cannot be predicted from neoclassical economic theory. As Granovetter (1990) concluded, *explanations* of institutions that do not incorporate the contingencies of social emergence "fail to identify causal *mechanisms*; they do not make an adequate connection between micro and macro levels, and so explain poorly when historical circumstances vary from the ones under which they were formulated" (p. 106).

Downward Causation

As levels of reality, stable and ephemeral emergents have an independent ontological status, and they have causal powers. These causal powers result in constraining and enabling effects on individuals. For example, in a conversation, once an *interactional frame* has emerged, it then constrains the future interaction of the participants, constraining both interaction (at Level B) by acting directly on the interactional semiotics of the interaction, and also constraining individuals directly (at Level A). Numerous examples of both forms of causation are documented in (Sawyer, 2003b).

Emergents Constrain Individuals

Participants are constrained by stable and ephemeral emergents. For example, the strategic options that the ephemeral emergent *frame* makes available are limited; and that limiting of the selection set is a form of constraint, although not a strictly deterministic one. Social encounters are often *improvisational*, and in improvisational encounters, there is always contingency, and actions are never fully constrained.

There are four distinct types of *downward causation* operating on individuals:

- Structures constraining individuals (E→A)
- Stable emergents constraining individuals (D→A)
- Ephemeral emergents constraining individuals (C→A)
- Properties of interaction constraining individuals (B→A)

Many sociologists have observed (beginning with Weber, 1968) that complex social systems have a unique feature not held by any other complex system: individuals are aware of the social products that emerge from their encounters. In no other complex system do the components internalize representations of the emergents that they participated in creating. When sociologists have considered social causation, they have largely limited their analysis to this form of "interpretivist" *downward causation*.

However, many complex systems manifest *downward causation* (Andersen et al., 2000); for example, philosophers of mind generally accept that mental states are emergent from the physical brain and yet have causal powers over the physical brain. Note that this downward causation does not require that neurons have awareness or agency; by analogy, there is no reason why individuals could not be constrained even when they are not aware of it.

Structural sociology does not recognize interaction as an autonomous level of reality, and the first three forms of downward causation are conflated within most macrosociology, which places Levels C and D at the structural level. Because *macrosociology* does not distinguish these types of emergents, it has difficulty accounting for the mechanisms whereby emergent properties constrain individuals. Microsociologists who study interaction do not recognize *downward causation* because they deny that levels C, D, and E have ontological status apart from interaction.

Anthropologists—both French structuralist anthropologists of the 1960s and Chicago-style symbolic anthropologists of the 1970s—have argued that cultures provide *emblems* or *ready-mades* to individuals, and that these combine to form a shared system of knowledge which individual actors can then use in interaction. This is a downward causal force from the stable emergents that make up culture. These emblems and ready-mades are stable emergents from prior interaction. Anthropologists have not adequately examined the historical processes of collaborative emergence, typically considering that the symbolic structures of the culture are relatively stable and pre-exist any given encounter.

Emergents Constrain Interaction

Because interaction is an autonomous level of analysis, there is downward causation onto Level B that is not mediated through individual representations at Level A.

- Structures constrain interaction (E→B) (this was a focus of Althusserian discourse analysis)
- Stable emergents constrain interaction (D→B) (the focus of much of linguistic anthropology)
- Ephemeral emergents constrain interaction (C→B) (the focus of Sawyer, 2003b)

Emergents constrain the kinds of discursive patterns that can occur, and this is a strictly semiotic, interactional phenomenon, independent of human agency. Linguistic anthropologists and sociolinguists have demonstrated a wide range of situations where interaction patterns are directly constrained by the situation, even in cases where that situation has been collaboratively negotiated by the participants. This causal arrow is analytically distinct from any participating individual—their strategic intentions or agency—because it operates directly on interaction processes themselves. Examples include studies of politeness and formality (Brown & Levinson, 1978), greeting rituals (Irvine 1974), and collaborative joke-telling (Brenneis, 1984). Accounting for the dialectic between emergence and downward causation requires a semiotic argument about the nature of interaction (e.g., Sawyer, 2003a).

INTERACTION AND EMERGENCE

In (Sawyer, 2005), I argued that *interaction* is central to studies of *emergence*, because different interaction languages and mechanisms result in different emergence mechanisms and outcomes. I began by comparing the interaction mechanisms of reactive agent societies (evolved from artificial life research), cognitive agent societies (evolved from intelligent agent research), and collaborative systems (evolved from distributed artificial intelligence research).

Collaborative systems represent the current leading edge of social simulation research—with the most complex agent models and the most complex communication languages. These researchers study how teams *improvisationally* respond to unexpected developments, as agents operate in complex and changing environments, and individual agents possess only partial information about the environment and about other agents. In such environments, plans cannot be developed in advance, with subtasks parceled out to team members; rather, the distribution of the task must emerge dynamically as the team proceeds. Agents must be able to communicate when they realize they cannot complete a task that they've previously committed to; this also requires that agents be able to perceive the impact of this difficulty on the overall group plan, and decide what information is necessary to communicate to

its partners (also see Levesque, Cohen, & Nunes, 1990). Team members must be jointly committed to such plan "repair," and this process requires sophisticated inter-agent communication. Emergence in these systems is found in the dynamically changing configurations of agents, responding in distributed team-like fashion to unexpected developments as the task proceeds.

In some of these *collaborative systems*, disagreements are resolved by a team or subteam leader, rather than by negotiation among team members. Yet researchers remain keenly interested in modeling *"distributed leadership"* in such systems, so that agents can negotiate their plans without a leader (Tambe, 1997, p. 115); this is thought to require further as-yet untheorized enhancements to agent communication languages. In a situation in which people do not share a mental state of joint intention, they can still collaborate and improvisationally generate emergent properties. But this can only happen when *metapragmatics* are introduced to the communication language. In an empirical study of *improvised dialogues* (Sawyer, 2003b), I demonstrated that the *metapragmatic* features of human communication lead to unintended emergent effects, and that these emergent effects have causal consequences for the future flow of the encounter. Yet metapragmatics have not yet been implemented in agent communication languages.

Speakers use the metapragmatic function of language to reflexively communicate about the emergent process and flow of the encounter, or about the ground rules and the communication language itself. In a simple everyday conversation, when no dialogue or topic is selected in advance, how do agents determine the variables of the interactional frame? In my study of *emergence* in *improvising* theater dialogues (Sawyer, 2003b), I found that the *interactional frame* emerged from the metapragmatic properties of the discourse.

In small group encounters, no single agent creates the frame; it emerges from the give and take of interaction. The *interactional frame* includes all of the pragmatic elements of the encounter: the socially-recognized *roles* and practices enacted by each agent, the publicly shared and perceived motives of those agents, the relationships among them, and the collective definition of the joint activity they are engaged in. The *frame* is constructed turn by turn; one agent proposes a new development for the frame, and others respond by modifying or embellishing that proposal. Each new proposal for a development in the frame is the creative inspiration of one agent, but that proposal does not become a part of the frame until it is evaluated by the others. In the subsequent flow of dialogue, the group collaborates to determine whether to accept the proposal, how to weave that proposal into the frame that has already been established, and then how to further elaborate on it.

The *metapragmatic* properties of interaction are not represented in current *agent communication languages*, and this may prevent them from being used to fully understand the relationships between *interaction* and *emergence*. As the cutting edge of *multi agent simulation* research implements increasingly complex agents, and as it increases the number of agents and the task complexity, empirically accurate simulations of human interaction will require more sophisticated *ACLs*. Of particular relevance will be studies of *improvised dialogues*, and how different dialogues result in different emergence processes and outcomes.

LIMITATIONS OF A SCIENCE OF SOCIAL EMERGENCE

The study of emergence incorporates a wide range of phenomena that are studied across the social sciences. But the potential scope of the science of emergence is logically limited, both at the macro level and at the individual level.

Limitations at the Macro Level

Level E represents stable emergents that have become fixed in objective material form. These include the technological and material systems of a society—communication networks, systems of highways and rail lines, residential population distributions, urban architecture, physical locations of goods and services, distribution networks for goods and services, and many other such features (Collins, 1981, pp. 994-995). Level E also includes those stable emergents that have become codified externally through writing technology: schedules,

project plans, organizational charts, procedural and operations manuals, audit procedures, legal codes, constitutions.

Many Level E phenomena are already the purview of other social sciences:

- Political systems are fixed by the documents and records that support institutions. These systems are studied by political science.
- Economic systems are fixed by patterns and technologies of distribution of goods, the status of contemporary technology (the means of production), locations of factories, and financial communication technologies that make possible international interbank transfers and letters of credit that, in turn, make international trade possible. These systems are studied by economics.
- Educational systems are fixed by the locations of schools, by their classroom architectures, by the documents and records that support the institutions of schooling, by the textbooks that encode knowledge. These systems are studied by education researchers.

The physical world is fixed in a way that stable emergents are not. Level E phenomena are not subject to normal social emergence, and they fall outside of the scope of *the emergence paradigm*—with its emphasis on *symbolic interaction*—because their emergence from interaction is lost to history, and their continued existence does not depend on interactional phenomena at Level B. For the most part these material phenomena are resistant to explanation in terms of social emergence. Level E phenomena always socially emerge from historical processes, although their emergence is often too distant in the historical past to be of empirical interest to sociologists, and as a result they are usually studied by historians rather than sociologists.

Modern transportation infrastructures are examples of Level E phenomena. Before the industrial era in the United States, shipping and travel tended to follow inland waterways. In the 19th century, rail lines—materialized social emergents—increasingly influenced the development of the United States. They influenced the settlement patterns of the American West, and determined the rise and fall of many Midwestern cities. Once established, these transportation networks had causal power over individuals. In the second half of the 20ᵗʰ century, another complex set of materialized social facts emerged: the automobile, interstate highways, and cheap fossil fuel. Because these material facts exist at Level E, they cannot be explained by studying interaction and emergence processes occurring today. Generally it is historians, rather than sociologists, who explain these historical cases of emergence. The emergence paradigm could be combined with social history to help us explain the emergence of Level E structures through historical time. But questions within the circle of emergence are more central to sociology, and sociology proper should focus on the empirical study of contemporary processes of social emergence.

Sociologists often conflate Levels C, D, and E into "macrostructure" and Levels A and B into the "microlevel." Introducing the distinction between Levels D and E results in a rethinking of the notion of social structure, because many conceptions of structure include Level D phenomena. From the perspective of *the emergence paradigm*, it is critical to clarify the divide between levels D and E, because Level D phenomena fall under the purview of the emergence paradigm whereas Level E phenomena do not.

Limitations at the Lower Levels

To the extent that the individual can be studied outside of the circle of emergence, the individual will be the subject of the discipline of psychology. This psychology will be much more limited in scope than the current discipline, because much of what we think of as "the individual" is subject to *emergence* processes—for example, the personality forms, language is acquired, and early concepts are learned during childhood interactions with parents and peers—and these aspects of the individual must be studied via social emergence.

Individual brains have properties that are not subject to *downward causation* from the upper levels, and the task of psychology is to identify those properties of individual brains that are universal across sociocultural context and across individuals. These properties include such things as memory capacity, processing speed, abilities to multitask,

factors of personality, and cognitive developmental pathways. All of these things may, at least in principle, be ultimately tied to the genotype of the organism and to its expression during development. To that extent, they are not subject to *downward causal* forces, and as such, would fall outside the realm of *social emergence*.

The emergence paradigm is of interest whenever properties of Levels B, C, or D begin to influence or constrain the way individuals think, solve problems, or behave. *Social causation* is significant during socialization; contemporary sociocultural research has found that a large part of the child's development depends on social and cultural context (Rogoff, 2003). Social causation also plays a significant role throughout adult life when situations influence individual behavior; many such cases have been documented by both social psychologists and sociologists.

To the extent that individuals are influenced and constituted by their social situation, the study of the individual will be a part of *the emergence paradigm*. For example, to the extent that developing individuals can change during development to reflect the society or culture that they live in, the study of individual development would fall within the emergence paradigm. This study is currently the purview of psychologists, but only of psychologists of a certain persuasion—sometimes known as "cultural psychologists" or "sociocultural psychologists"; the mainstream of psychology is still focused on those universal, biologically based behavioral phenomena that are constant across the situation.

If *the emergence paradigm* takes hold, psychology will split into two distinct disciplines. The first, the study of biologically based universal properties of human brains, will increasingly merge with neuroscience. The second, those phenomena that cannot be explained by reduction to neuroscience, will migrate into the new sociology of social emergence. Alternatively, as the universalist elements of psychology merge with neuroscience, the discipline of psychology may give itself new life by reformulating itself as emergence psychology, a psychology broken free from its reductionist theoretical assumptions.

SOCIOLOGY AND THE SOCIAL SCIENCES

I have argued that sociologists should attempt to re-make sociology as the foundational science of *social emergence*. A science of social emergence must be heavily based on studies of *symbolic interaction* and of communication processes. If sociology indeed becomes the science of *social emergence*, there are ramifications for many other social sciences as well, because the science of *social emergence* would provide foundational theoretical frameworks and *explanations* for all of the social sciences.

The emergence paradigm suggests that the social sciences are currently misconfigured in three ways that result from the failure of sociology to define itself as the foundational study of social emergence. First, much of what is currently considered to be part of psychology requires emergentist and interactionist explanation; but only rarely have psychologists collaborated with, or even become familiar with, sociologists. Second, sociology has an important role to play in explaining collective symbolic products, such as those studied by cultural anthropology, folkloristics, and popular culture studies—again, disciplines that rarely turn to sociology for theory or methodology. These disciplines study stable emergents; yet none of these disciplines have adequate theoretical foundations of how their objects of study emerge, maintain themselves, and change over time. A sociology centered on social emergence would provide theoretical foundations to these social sciences.

And third, the *microeconomic* study of social emergence should be located in the discipline of sociology. My argument here is consistent with a long history of scholars who have argued that economics is a subdiscipline of sociology, because the economic system is part of the social system (scholars making such an argument include Comte, Weber, Mises, and other Austrian school economists). Based on the argument I make in this chapter, the main reason that the study of emergence belongs in sociology rather than economics is because of the importance of incorporating a sophisticated analysis of *symbolic interaction*, and sociology is a more appropriate discipline than economics for the incorporation of the science of interaction with the science of emergence.

Since the 1980s, there has been increasing discussion about the relation between *economics* and sociology. *Economic sociologists* (e.g., Smelser & Swedberg, 1994) and social economists (e.g., Durlauf & Young, 2001) disagree about what the new division of labor between economics and sociology should be. I add to this debate my proposal that the sociology of social emergence should be the foundational, basic science, and economics should be one of the applied social sciences. Economics is the science of economic institutions, but the study of how they emerge is a question for this reformulated sociology.

The emergence paradigm is consistent with the foundational assumptions of *economic sociology*: economic action is a form of social action, economic action is socially situated, and economic institutions are social institutions (Granovetter & Swedberg, 1992). Both are positivist and reject interpretivism (Krier, 1999). I accept the criticisms of *neoclassical microeconomics* made by the economic sociologists: the rejection of neoclassical assumptions regarding market efficiency, and individual optimization or utility maximization (Etzioni, 1991). The social emergence of economic institutions is no different from the social emergence of any other institution (Granovetter & Swedberg, 1992); all social phenomena emerge from individual collective action, and there is no reason to believe that there are different emergence processes for different social phenomena. Economic action is a form of social action, and economic institutions are social institutions. Economists who import rational choice models into sociological problems agree with this, but assume that rational economic action is the fundamental form of social action. However, empirical evidence has made this assumption increasingly difficult to maintain.

One claim *microeconomics* makes vis-à-vis sociology is the rigor of its mathematical method. The claim is that without mathematics, sociology is not a science, because it can only provide discursive accounts of single phenomena: historicism or story telling, rather than a lawful science of regularities. But the sociology of *social emergence* now has an equally powerful and equally rigorous methodology: *multi-agent based simulation*. The power and rigor of sociology's new methodology will replace the mathematics of utility maximization, because those formalisms cannot be expanded to model symbolic interaction and how it contributes to emergence. Empirically grounded, theoretically rich, sociological models of action, simulated using multi agent systems, will result in models of social emergence that will then become foundational to economics, replacing the mathematical formalisms of rational choice.

If *the emergence paradigm* takes hold, then academic departments are currently configured in a theoretically unstable fashion, because to the extent that *microeconomics* studies emergence processes in general and how they give rise to stable emergents, should be a part of sociology. This disciplinary reconfiguration leaves to economics the study of emergent economic phenomena, just as it leaves to political science the study of emergent political systems, to education the study of emergent educational systems, and so on. However, it removes a chunk of microeconomics as currently practiced: the use of rational choice models of individuals, combined with simple aggregation assumptions as the interaction mechanism, to develop *micro-explanations* of macroeconomic phenomena. The study of social emergence has taken place largely in microeconomics because sociology has not been receptive to studies of social emergence; those scholars interested in emergence *mechanisms* have had no choice but to affiliate with microeconomics. But its models of social emergence are simplistic, empirically ungrounded, and have largely failed (see the critiques of Granovetter, 1985, and Etzioni, 1991). They persist in the face of such problems because social science needs a foundation in *social emergence*, and at present *microeconomics* has the only one.

It is frequently observed that *microeconomics* has a radically simplified theory of both the individual and of the social. *Neoclassical microeconomics'* model of the individual is a *homo economicus* who has complete, certain information, and rationally maximizes exchange value. This simplified model of the individual has allowed the study of social emergence to operate within economics. However, toward the end of the 20th century experimental economists and behavioral economists began to challenge assumptions of rationality, certainty, and complete information, drawing on experimental findings from psychology that show that individuals operate

with bounded rationality, bounded willpower, and bounded self-interest. Social economists (Durlauf & Young, 2001) have introduced heterogeneity in individuals, direct interaction as well as interaction mediated by market prices (peer groups, social networks, and role models), individual preferences that are influenced by these interactions, and the use of dynamical systems theory and models. As these challenges continue and expand, it will become increasingly obvious that the study of social emergence belongs within sociology.

Sociologists have focused their critiques of *microeconomics* on its inadequate model of the individual, rather than on its simplistic approach to *interaction* and aggregation—exchange of goods, price, and the interaction between demand and supply. Rather than focus my critique on its assumptions of rational action, I think economics has a more significant weakness vis-à-vis sociology: the forms of *symbolic interaction* that give rise to the emergence of social phenomena are not amenable to study using economic concepts. As Coleman (1986) observed, sociologists have not realized that "the major theoretical obstacle to social theory built on a theory of action is not the proper refinement of the action theory itself, but the means by which purposive actions of individuals *combine* to produce a social outcome" (p. 1321). Before the approaches to *social emergence* found in *neoclassical micro-economics* can expand to incorporate an empirically valid theory of interaction and emergence, they will have to merge with the sociological study of human *symbolic interaction*.

Unlike economics, sociology has a long history of studying *situated symbolic interaction*. For economics to model *social emergence* as I have described it, economics would have to import whole subdisciplines of sociological theory and practice, subdisciplines whose object of study has no obvious relation to rational economic action—conversation analysis, symbolic interaction, interactional socio-linguistics. Such a disciplinary redefinition would make no sense for economics. Yet for sociology, the redefinition required to incorporate the study of social emergence is a natural development, a synthesis of the two dominant 20th century sociological paradigms—the focus on emergence in macrosociology and in methodological individualism, and the focus on interaction found in interactionist sociology.

CONCLUSION

Social emergence is one of the big questions that sociology was founded to answer over 100 years ago. The appropriate methodology to study social emergence has only recently become available: *multi-agent simulations* that combine the close focus on interaction associated with conversation analysis with the independent analysis of the ephemeral and stable emergents that result. *The emergence paradigm* doesn't propose any definite answers to longstanding sociological questions, but it has significant implications for how sociological theory and methodology should proceed.

The emergence paradigm shows that we cannot answer the fundamental question of the social sciences—How do individuals and collectivities mutually make each other up?—without close analysis of the bidirectional mechanisms interacting between these three intermediate levels. Most micro-macro debate neglects the most important components of the *mechanism*—the interactional phenomena at the center of the circle of emergence.

The study of emergence without sophisticated representations of interaction will always have limited value to sociology. Several decades of microsociological research have demonstrated the causal role played by interaction in social life. Inversely, studying interaction without also examining the role it plays in emergence processes is also of limited value. Several decades of macrosociological research have demonstrated that collective action does indeed give rise to apparently autonomous macrosocial phenomena. A science of social emergence requires a joint focus on both interaction and emergence; bringing these two longstanding strands of sociological research together can result in a unified science of social emergence, one that is empirically accurate and theoretically sophisticated.

FUTURE RESEARCH DIRECTIONS

In the near term, the science of social emergence needs a better understanding of two foundational topics: representations of individual agents, and representations of interaction. To increase our understanding of individual agents, the science of *social emergence* can draw on the fields of cognitive psychology and of behavioral economics. To increase our understanding of interaction, the science of social emergence can draw on empirical studies of microinteraction within sociology, and theoretical analyses of interaction in sociology, anthropology, and linguistics.

If sociology begins to reformulate itself as the foundational study of *social emergence*, and if *microeconomists* who study social emergence increasingly modify their models to incorporate interaction and emergence *mechanisms*, the two strands of social emergence study will begin to converge. And as *microeconomists* increasingly address the flaws in their models of social emergence, they will find it increasingly inappropriate to be housed in departments of economics—because economic institutions emerge from the same human actions, and through the same emergence processes, as all other social institutions. Sophisticated models of emergence from communicative interaction are not likely to rest comfortably in a department of economics.

It is a historical accident that many such studies are now conducted by economists. Economics was the first discipline to develop rigorous formalisms with which to model emergence; and because these models were consistent with economic assumptions and not with sociological ones, the discipline of sociology has never been completely comfortable with them (in spite of notable attempts such as Coleman, 1990). Eventually, studies of social emergence will be grouped in a single discipline, and that discipline is more likely to be sociology. The emergence of macro phenomena cannot be explained with a narrow focus on maximizing utility—not even the emergence of macro economic phenomena can be explained this way.

This reconfiguration will happen only after many years, perhaps decades: after sociology reconfigures itself as the basic science of social emergence, develops appropriately sophisticated methods for simulating human symbolic interaction, and begins to have demonstrable successes, and after microeconomics responds by revamping its models to incorporate socially embedded individuals, interacting using complex communication systems. This new unified discipline will study ephemeral and stable emergents as symbolic emergents of interaction, combining empirical rigor and theoretical foundations.

REFERENCES

Blau, P. M. (1977). A macrosociological theory of social structure. *American Journal of Sociology, 83*(1), 26-54.

Blumer, H. (1939). Collective behavior. In R. E. Park (Ed.), *An outline of the principles of sociology* (pp. 219-280). New York: Barnes & Noble.

Boulding, K. E. (1969). Economics as a moral science. *The American Economic Review, 59*(1), 1-12.

Bowles, S. (2001). Comment: Individual behavior and social interactions. *Sociological Methodology, 31*, 89-96.

Brenneis, D. (1984). Grog and gossip in Bhatgaon: Style and substance in Fiji Indian conversation. *American Ethnologist, 11*, 487-506.

Brown, P., & Levinson, S. (1978). Universals in language usage: Politeness phenomena. In E. N. Goody (Ed.), *Questions and politeness: Strategies in social interaction* (pp. 56-289). New York: Cambridge University Press.

Coleman, J. S. (1986). Social theory, social research, and a theory of action. *American Journal of Sociology, 91*(6), 1309-1335.

Coleman, J. S. (1987). Microfoundations and macrosocial behavior. In J. C. Alexander, B. Giesen, R. Münch & N. J. Smelser (Eds.), *The micro-macro link* (pp. 153-173). Berkeley, CA: University of California Press.

Coleman, J. S. (1990). *Foundations of social theory.* Cambridge: Harvard University Press.

Collins, R. (1981). On the microfoundations of macrosociology. *American Journal of Sociology, 86*(5), 984-1014.

Duranti, A., & Goodwin, C. (Eds.). (1992). *Rethinking context: Language as an interactive phenomenon.* New York: Cambridge University Press.

Durlauf, S. N., & Young, H. P. (2001). The new social economics. In S. N. Durlauf & H. P. Young (Eds.), *Social dynamics* (pp. 1-14). Cambridge: MIT Press.

Etzioni, A. (1991). Socio-economics: A budding challenge. In A. Etzioni & P. R. Lawrence (Eds.), *Socio-economics: Toward a new synthesis* (pp. 3-7). Armonk, NY: M. E. Sharpe, Inc.

Evans, R. R. (Ed.). (1969). *Readings in collective behavior.* Chicago: Rand McNally & Company.

Giddens, A. (1984). *The constitution of society: Outline of the theory of structuration.* Berkeley: University of California Press.

Granovetter, M. (1985). Economic action and social structure: The problem of embeddedness. *American Journal of Sociology, 91*(3), 481-510.

Granovetter, M. (1990). The old and the new economic sociology: A history and an agenda. In R. Friedland & A. F. Robertson (Eds.), *Beyond the marketplace: Rethinking economy and society* (pp. 89-112). New York: Aldine de Gruyter.

Granovetter, M., & Swedberg, R. (Eds.). (1992). *The sociology of economic life.* Boulder, CO: Westview.

Hedström, P. (2005). *Dissecting the social: On the principles of analytic sociology.* Cambridge, UK: Cambridge University Press.

Hirshleifer, J. (1985). The expanding domain of economics. *American Economic Review, 75*(6), 53-68.

Irvine, J. T. (1974). Strategies of status manipulation in the Wolof greeting. In R. Bauman & J. Sherzer (Eds.), *Explorations in the ethnography of speaking* (pp. 167-191). New York: Cambridge University Press.

Krier, D. (1999). Assessing the new synthesis of economics and sociology: Promising themes for contemporary analysts of economic life. *American Journal of Economics and Sociology, 58*(4), 669-696.

Lang, K., & Lang, G. E. (1961). *Collective dynamics.* New York: Thomas Y. Crowell Company.

Lawler, E. J., Ridgeway, C., & Markovsky, B. (1993). Structural social psychology and the micro-macro problem. *Sociological Theory, 11*(3), 268-290.

Levesque, H. J., Cohen, P. R., & Nunes, J. H. T. (1990, July 29-August 3). *On acting together.* Paper presented at the Eighth National Conference on Artificial Intelligence (AAAI-90), Boston, MA.

Park, R. E., & Burgess, E. W. (1921). *Introduction to the science of sociology.* Chicago: University of Chicago Press.

Radnitzky, G. (1992). The economic approach. In G. Radnitzky & A. M. Weinberg (Eds.), *Universal economics: Assessing the achievements of the economic approach* (pp. 1-68). New York: Paragon House.

Radnitzky, G., & Bernholz, P. (Eds.). (1987). *Economic imperialism: The economic approach applied outside the field of economics.* New York: Paragon House Publishers.

Saam, N. J. (1999). Simulating the micro-macro link: New approaches to an old problem and an application to military coups. *Sociological Methodology, 29,* 43-79.

Sawyer, R. K. (2003a). *Group creativity: Music, theater, collaboration.* Mahwah, NJ: Erlbaum.

Sawyer, R. K. (2003b). *Improvised dialogues: Emergence and creativity in conversation.* Westport, CT: Greenwood.

Sawyer, R. K. (2004a). The mechanisms of emergence. *Philosophy of the Social Sciences, 34*(2), 260-282.

Sawyer, R. K. (2004b). Social explanation and computational simulation. *Philosophical Explorations, 7*(3), 219-231.

Sawyer, R. K. (2005). *Social emergence: Societies as complex systems.* New York: Cambridge.

Smelser, N. J., & Swedberg, R. (Eds.). (1994). *The handbook of economic sociology.* Princeton, NJ: Princeton University Press.

Tambe, M. (1997). Towards flexible teamwork. *Journal of Artificial Intelligence Research, 7,* 83-124.

Tannen, D. (Ed.). (1993). *Framing in discourse.* New York: Oxford University Press.

Tullock, G. (1972). Economic imperialism. In J. M. Buchanan & R. D. Tollison (Eds.), *Theory of public choice: Political applications of economics* (pp. 317-329). Ann Arbor, MI: The University of Michigan Press.

Zafirovsky, M. (1999). Economic sociology in retrospect and prospect: In search of its identity within economics and sociology. *American Journal of Economics and Sociology, 58*(4), 583-627.

Additional Reading

Blau, P. M. (1977). A macrosociological theory of social structure. *American Journal of Sociology, 83*(1), 26-54.

Coleman, J. S. (1990). *Foundations of social theory.* Cambridge: Harvard University Press.

Collins, R. (1981). On the microfoundations of macrosociology. *American Journal of Sociology, 86*(5), 984-1014.

Durlauf, S. N., & Young, H. P. (2001). The new social economics. In S. N. Durlauf & H. P. Young (Eds.), *Social dynamics* (pp. 1-14). Cambridge: MIT Press.

Epstein, J. M. (2006). *Generative social science: Studies in agent-based computational modeling.* Princeton, NJ: Princeton University Press.

Epstein, J. M., & Axtell, R. (1996). *Growing artificial societies: Social science from the bottom up.* Cambridge, MA: MIT Press.

Etzioni, A. (1991). Socio-economics: A budding challenge. In A. Etzioni & P. R. Lawrence (Eds.), *Socio-economics: Toward a new synthesis* (pp. 3-7). Armonk, NY: M. E. Sharpe, Inc.

Granovetter, M. (1985). Economic action and social structure: The problem of embeddedness. *American Journal of Sociology, 91*(3), 481-510.

Granovetter, M. (1990). The old and the new economic sociology: A history and an agenda. In R. Friedland & A. F. Robertson (Eds.), *Beyond the marketplace: Rethinking economy and society* (pp. 89-112). New York: Aldine de Gruyter.

Granovetter, M., & Swedberg, R. (Eds.). (1992). *The sociology of economic life.* Boulder, CO: Westview.

Hedström, P. (2005). *Dissecting the social: On the principles of analytic sociology.* Cambridge, UK: Cambridge University Press.

Hedström, P., & Swedberg, R. (Eds.). (1998). *Social mechanisms: An analytical approach to social theory.* New York: Cambridge University Press.

Krier, D. (1999). Assessing the new synthesis of economics and sociology: Promising themes for contemporary analysts of economic life. *American Journal of Economics and Sociology, 58*(4), 669-696.

Lawler, E. J., Ridgeway, C., & Markovsky, B. (1993). Structural social psychology and the micro-macro problem. *Sociological Theory, 11*(3), 268-290.

Radnitzky, G. (1992). The economic approach. In G. Radnitzky & A. M. Weinberg (Eds.), *Universal economics: Assessing the achievements of the economic approach* (pp. 1-68). New York: Paragon House.

Radnitzky, G., & Bernholz, P. (Eds.). (1987). *Economic imperialism: The economic approach applied outside the field of economics.* New York: Paragon House Publishers.

Sawyer, R. K. (2003a). *Group creativity: Music, theater, collaboration.* Mahwah, NJ: Erlbaum.

Sawyer, R. K. (2003b). *Improvised dialogues: Emergence and creativity in conversation.* Westport, CT: Greenwood.

Sawyer, R. K. (2004a). The mechanisms of emergence. *Philosophy of the Social Sciences, 34*(2), 260-282.

Sawyer, R. K. (2004b). Social explanation and computational simulation. *Philosophical Explorations, 7*(3), 219-231.

Sawyer, R. K. (2005). *Social emergence: Societies as complex systems.* New York: Cambridge.

Smelser, N. J., & Swedberg, R. (Eds.). (1994). *The handbook of economic sociology.* Princeton, NJ: Princeton University Press.

Tullock, G. (1972). Economic imperialism. In J. M. Buchanan & R. D. Tollison (Eds.), *Theory of public choice: Political applications of economics* (pp. 317-329). Ann Arbor, MI: The University of Michigan Press.

Zafirovsky, M. (1999). Economic sociology in retrospect and prospect: In search of its identity within economics and sociology. *American Journal of Economics and Sociology, 58*(4), 583-627.

Chapter II
Agent Cognitive Capabilities and Orders of Social Emergence

Christopher Goldspink
Incept Labs, Australia

Robert Kay
Incept Labs, Australia
University of Technology, Sydney, Australia

ABSTRACT

This chapter critically examines our theoretical understanding of the dialectical relationship between emergent social structures and agent behaviors. While much has been written about emergence individually as a concept, and the use of simulation methods are being increasingly applied to the exploration of social behavior, the concept of "social emergence" remains ill defined. Furthermore, there has been little theoretical treatment or practical explorations of how both the range and type of emergent structures observed may change as agents are endowed with increasingly sophisticated cognitive abilities. While we are still a very long way from being able to build artificial agents with human-like cognitive capabilities, it would be timely to revisit the extent of the challenge and to see where recent advances in our understanding of higher order cognition leave us. This chapter provides a brief recount of the theory of emergence, considers recent contributions to thinking about orders of emergence, and unpacks these in terms of implied agent characteristics. Observations are made about the implications of alternative cognitive paradigms and the position is proposed that an enactivist view provides the most logical pathway to advancing our understanding. The chapter concludes by presenting an account of reflexive and non-reflexive modes of emergence, which incorporates this view.

INTRODUCTION

Building and working with artificial societies using the methods of multi-agent social simulation serves us in several ways: 1) It allows us to operationalize social theories and to compare simulated behaviors with those observed in the real world; and 2) it allows us to build new theory by exploring the minimal mechanisms that might explain observed social behavior. Most importantly 3) it provides a unique ability to explore the interplay between levels of phenomena and to understand dynamic properties of systems. A great deal can and has been achieved in both these areas with even the simple methods we currently have available. However, Keith Sawyer (2003) has recently reminded us that, to date, we have worked with agents with very limited cognitive capability and that this necessarily limits the range and type of behavior which can be explored. This echoes a sentiment made a decade ago by Christiano Castelfranchi (1998a) that social simulation is not really *social* until it can provide an adequate account of the implication of feedback between macro and micro which becomes possible with higher cognitive functioning of social agents.

In many respects, developments in our capacity to simulate artificial societies have led us to confront anew a long-standing issue within social theory. This is a problem that social science conducted within traditional disciplinary boundaries has become quite adept at avoiding. Indeed it can be argued that the particular form disciplinary fragmentation takes in social science is a primary strategy for avoiding it. The problem is referred to in a number of ways depending on the disciplinary tradition. This chapter begins by revisiting this most important of problems. In terms of the challenge it poses to artificial societies it can be expressed in the following three questions:

1. What are the fundamental cognitive characteristics which distinguish human agents from animal or automaton?
2. How do these characteristics influence the range and type of behaviors agents may generate and the emergent structures which they may give rise to?
3. How can we theorize about the relationship between cognitive capability and categories of emergent form?

These questions form the focus for this chapter. We begin to address them by revisiting the contribution of alternative schools of thought to our understanding of the nature and origins of emergent structure and alternative concepts of orders of emergence. We then discuss the implications of the two competing cognitive paradigms within AI—that of cognitivism and the enactive view. Finally we turn to current research on the development of human cognition and examine its implications for anticipating different orders of emergent structure—proposing what we call reflexive and non-reflexive classes of emergence.

Finally a research program for the advancement of understanding in this area is proposed.

This work has its origins in two strands of research with which the authors are currently involved. The first addresses the relationship between micro and macro levels of social behavior and organization directly. Over the past decade we have explored the characteristics of the micro-macro problem (see Chris Goldspink & Kay, 2003, 2004) in pursuit of a coherent and consistent account of the interpenetration (circular causality) between micro and macro phenomena. Our aim is to develop a theory which can provide a substantive account of fundamental social generative mechanisms. To date no such social theory exists that satisfactorily explains this dynamic.

The other strand is one author's involvement with the Centre for Research in Social Simulation and though it the European Union funded project titled Emergence in the Loop (EMIL). The aim of EMIL is to : a) provide a theoretical account of the mechanisms of normative self-regulation in a number of computer mediated communities b) specify the minimum cognitive processes agents require to behave in normative ways c) develop a simulator which can replicate the range and type of normative behavior identified by the empirical research so as to further deepen our understanding of how and under what conditions normative self-regulation is possible and the range and type of environmental factors which influence it.

A BRIEF RECOUNT OF THE THEORY OF EMERGENCE

The notion of emergence has a long history, having been invoked in a number of disciplines with varying degrees of centrality to the theoretical and methodological development of associated fields. Unfortunately the concept has largely remained opaque and ambiguous in its conceptualization, leading to the criticism that it stands as little more than a covering concept – used when no adequate account or explanation exists for some unexpected phenomena. Clayton has argued that the concept covers:

...a wide spectrum of ontological commitments. According to some the emergents are no more than patterns, with no causal powers of their own; for others they are substances in their own right... (Clayton, 2006: 14).

The origin of the concept has been attributed to George Henry Lewes who coined the term in 1875 (Ablowitz, 1939). It subsequently found wide adoption within the philosophy of science but more recently has been advanced within three distinct streams: *philosophy*, particularly of science and mind; *systems theory*, in particular complex systems; and *social science* where it has largely been referred to under the heading of the micro-macro link and/or the problem of structure and agency. Interestingly there has been relatively little cross fertilization of thinking between these streams.

The Contribution from Philosophy of Science

The philosophy of science and philosophy of mind stream is arguably the oldest – some date it back to Plato (Peterson, 2006) but the debate is widely seen as having come to focus with the British Emergentists (Eronen, 2004; Shrader, 2005; Stanford Encyclopaedia of Philosophy, 2006). This school sought to deal with the apparent qualitatively distinct properties associated with different phenomena (physical, chemical, biological, mental) in the context of the debate between mechanism and vitalism: the former being committed to Laplacian causal determinism and hence reductionism and the latter invoking 'non-physical' elements in order to explain the qualitative difference between organic and in-organic matter. This stream remains focused on explaining different properties of classes of natural phenomena and with the relationship between brains and minds (See Clayton & Davies, 2006 for a recent summary of the positions). As a consequence this has been the dominant stream within artificial intelligence. Peterson (2006: 695) summarizes the widely agreed characteristics of emergent phenomena within this stream as follows. Emergent entities:

1. Are characterized by higher-order descriptions (i.e. form a *hierarchy*).

2. Obey higher order *laws*.
3. Are characterized by *unpredictable novelty*.
4. Are *composed of* lower level entities, but lower level entities are *insufficient* to fully account for emergent entities (*irreducibility*).
5. May be capable of *top-down causation*.
6. Are characterized by *multiple realization or wild disjunction* (Fodor, 1974) (alternative micro-states may generate the same macro states).

A key concept within these discussions is that of *supervenience*: a specification of the 'loose' determinisms held to apply between levels such that *'...an entity cannot change at a higher level without also changing at a lower level'* (Sawyer, 2001: 556). Within this stream prominence of place is given to both downward and upward causation. Clayton and Davies (2006) specify downward causation as involving macro structures placing *constraint* on lower level processes hence *'Emergent entities provide the context in which local, bottom up causation takes place and is made possible'* (Peterson, 2006: 697). Davies (2006) argues that the mechanism of downward causation can usefully be considered in terms of boundaries. Novelty, he argues, may have its origin in a system being 'open'. If novel order emerges it must do so within the constraints of physics. He concludes:

...top-down talk refers not to vitalistic augmentation of known forces, but rather to the system harnessing existing forces for its own ends. The problem is to understand how this harnessing happens, not at the level of individual intermolecular interactions, but overall – as a coherent project. It appears that once a system is sufficiently complex, then new top down rules of causation emerge. (Davies 2006: 48).

For Davies then, top-down causation is associated with self-organization and may undergo qualitative transitions in form with increasing system complexity. For Davies also it is the 'openness' of some systems that 'provides room' for self-organizing process to arise, but he concludes, *'openness to the environment merely explains why there may be room for top-down causation; it tells us nothing about how that causation works.'* The devil then, is in the detail of the mechanisms specific to particular processes in particular contexts and particular phenomenal domains. Perhaps then a part of the problem with the concept is that it has been approached at too abstract a level.

The Contribution from Social Science

The micro-macro problem—the relationship between the actions of individuals and resulting social structures and the reciprocal constraint those structures place on individual agency—has long standing in social science as well as in philosophy. The problem is central to many social theories developed throughout the 19th and 20th century. Examples include: Marxian dialectical materialism (Engels, 1934) built upon by, among others, Vygotsky (1962) and Lyont'ev (1978); the social constructionism of Berger and Luckmann (1972); Gidden's structuration theory (1984); and the recent work of critical realists (Archer, 1998; Archer, Bhaskar, Ciollier, Lawson, & Norrie, 1998; Bhaskar, 1997, 1998). These alternative theories are frequently founded on differing assumptions, extending from the essentially objectivist/rationalist theory of Coleman (1994), through the critical theories of Habermas and to the radical constructivism of Luhmann (1990; 1995).

Fuchs & Hofkirchner (2005: 33) have recently suggested a four category schema for classifying social theory according to the ontological position adopted with respect to the micro-macro relationship. The majority of existing social theories, they argue, fall into one or other of two categories which they label *individualism* and *sociologism*. Neither of these 'paradigms' provides a theoretical foundation which supports exploration let alone the possibility of advancing understanding of the interplay between agency and structure, rather the problem is avoided by restricting analysis to one level or the other. A third category, *dualism*, while considering both aspects, insists on the adoption of a dichotomous stance and as a consequence does not support any understanding of the interplay between levels. Only those theories categorized as *dialectical* therefore have relevance. Even here, it is reasonable to conclude that little practical advance has been achieved,

as most positions result in a straddling of bottom up and top-down arguments and/or suffer from excessively vague conceptualization. These theories also quickly break down into a dichotomy the moment an attempt is made to make them operational.

What has been largely agreed, despite the very different theoretical and often inadequate handling of this problem, is that structure and agency come together in *activity* or in *body-hood* – the specific psycho-motor state at the instant of enaction. Both Vygotsky and Giddens, for example, focus on action as the point of intersection between human agency and social structures and it is implicit in Bourdieu's *habitus* also.

The Contribution from Systems Theory

Systems language was clearly evident in the work of the early Emergentists and in a great deal of sociology and anthropology which took seriously the structure/agency problem – notably that of Margaret Mead and Gregory Bateson. However, 'systems' as a focus of systematic research arguably took form with von Bertalanffy's attempt to establish a General Systems Theory in 1950 (Bertalanffy, 1950; Bertalanffy_von, 1968). As the science of 'wholes' systems theory stands in contrast to reductionism's concern with parts. Systems theory was put forward as a counter to what was perceived as excessive reductionism dominating scientific discourse during much of the 20th century.

In the early stages of development of the theory systems tended to be modeled as 'black boxes' effectively masking the relationship between micro and macro elements. The application of the concept to social science, in particular through the development by Ernst von Glasersfeld and Heinz von Foerster (Keeney, 1987) of social cybernetics along with soft systems approaches (Checkland, 1988) provided a theoretical lens and methods useful for describing the systemic behavior of social systems. So while the aspiration of GSM to establish a general science of systems is generally regarded to have failed (Jackson, 2000), systems approaches have contributed valuable methods for the study of the interplay between levels in a social system. The Systems view of emergence was founded on:

- Holism; the whole is greater than the sum of its parts.
- A concern with *feedback both positive and negative.*
- A concern with boundaries and boundary conditions.

More recently the development of complex systems theory and its application to natural, social and cognitive phenomena has provided additional concepts upon which much current debate about emergence draws. Many of these concepts and methods have become widely used within the multi-agent modeling community (Castelfranchi, 1998b; Conte, Hegselmann, & Terna, 1997; Gilbert, 1995; Holland, 1998).

Within contemporary debate, and in contrast to the position taken by the British Emergentists who argued that irreducibility was the *exception* (Eronen, 2004), most real world systems are now argued to be non-linear (S. Kauffman, 2000; S. A. Kauffman, 1993, 1996; Stewart, 1990) and hence irreducible. It is non-linearity which contributes to these system's capacity for novelty and unpredictability through the presence of deterministic Chaos (Lorenz, 2001; Williams, 1997) and/or equifinality. Equifinality as it is known within systems theory, or the principle of 'wild disjunction' as it is known in philosophy, refers to a system where a single high level property may be realized by more than one set of micro-states which have no lawful relationship between them (Richardson, 2002a, 2002b; Sawyer, 2001). As there is no a-priori basis by which the likely micro state can be determined, such systems are irreducible and unpredictable in principle.

Observations

The concept of emergence has led to the establishment of a number of general principles which describe the relationship between micro and macro phenomena, as well as some methods and techniques for identifying and exploring it. Specifically, we can conclude that there are systems which are:

- Inherently analytically reducible (to which the concept of emergence does not apply);
- Analytically reducible in principle but dif-

ficult to reduce in practice and/or where an advance in science/knowledge is needed for reduction to be possible because the results were 'unexpected' (Chalmers, 2006) (to which the concept of 'weak' emergence can be applied);
- Not reducible in principle (to which the principle of 'strong' emergence is relevant).

We argue that all living systems and all social systems belong to the latter class. Accordingly we agree with McKelvey (1997) that a great deal of social order may be attributable to complex organization involving non-liner relations between elements. It is for this reason that simulation methods are regarded as important but only to the extent that we can construct artificial societies which are reasonable analogues of the social systems we want to understand and this implies agent architectures which are capable of generating the range of social behaviors/structures of interest. The problem here is that we still have a very rudimentary understanding of what cognitive capabilities support or are necessary for what range and types of social structures.

In the following section we draw on the limited prior attention given to this problem and attempt to clarify what is currently known. Throughout the discussion, pointers are provided to where the mechanisms being outlined have, at least in part, been incorporated into computer simulations of artificial intelligence or artificial societies.

ORDERS OF EMERGENCE

A number of authors have identified what they refer to as orders of emergence. Gilbert, for example distinguishes between first and second order emergence. First order emergence includes macro structures which arise from local interactions between agents of limited cognitive range (particles, fluids, reflex action). By contrast, second order emergence is argued to arise *'where agents recognise emergent phenomena, such as societies, clubs, formal organizations, institutions, localities and so on where the fact that you are a member or a non-member, changes the rules of interaction between you and other agents.'* (Gilbert, 2002). This reflects high order cognition on the part of the agent. In particular it reflects a range of capabilities including but not limited to the ability to distinguish class characteristics; assess 'self' for conformity with class characteristics and/or signals from other agents which suggest acceptance or belonging; the ability to change rule associations and behavior as a function of these changes. First and second order emergence then each imply qualitatively distinct mechanisms and suggest a continuum of orders of emergence linked, in biological entities at least, to cognitive capability.

In a similar vein, Castelfranchi (1998a: 27) has distinguished what he refers to as cognitive emergence. *'Cognitive emergence occurs where agents become aware, through a given 'conceptualization' of a certain 'objective' pre-cognitive (unknown and non deliberated) phenomenon that is influencing their results and outcomes, and then, indirectly, their actions.'* This approach is based on a first generation AI (Franklin, 1998) approach to conceptualizing agents: agent cognition is assumed to involve acting on beliefs desires and intentions (BDI). Thus Castelfranchi conceives of a feedback path from macro pattern to micro behavior in much the same way as Gilbert, except that here a cognitive mechanism is specified. Castelfranchi argues that this mechanism has a significant effect on emergence and indeed *'characterises the theory of social dynamics'* – that is, it gives rise to a distinct class of emergent phenomena. In this account, the representations agents have about the beliefs, desires and intentions of other agents plays a causal role in their subsequent behavior and therefore shapes the structures they participate in generating. In this same chapter Castelfranchi argues that understanding this process is fundamental to social simulation: it is where social simulation can make its greatest contribution.

These ideas are more comprehensively reflected in the five orders of emergence suggested by Ellis (2006:99-101). These are:

1. Bottom up leading to higher level generic properties (examples include the properties of gases, liquids and solids)

2. Bottom up action plus boundary conditions leading to higher level structures (e.g. convection cells, sand piles, cellular automata)

3. Bottom up action leading to feedback and control at various levels leading to meaningful top down action - teleonomy (e.g. living cells, multi-cellular organisms with 'instinctive' – phylogenetically determined reactive capability)

4. as per 3 but with the addition of explicit goals related to memory, influence by specific events in the individuals history (i.e. learning)

5. In addition to 4 some goals are explicitly expressed in language (humans).

Ellis's framework makes clear that the range and type of emergence possible in a system depends fundamentally on the range and class of behavior agents are able to generate and that this varies depending on the properties of the agent.

If we consider Ellis' category one emergence, it is apparent that particles have fixed properties and are able to enter into a limited range of interactions (specified by physical laws) based on those properties. Swarms of particles can nevertheless demonstrate some rudimentary self-organization and hence emergence (Kennedy & Eberhart, 2001). Physics has furnished good accounts of many specific examples (Gell-Mann, 1995) but they have limited implication for our understanding of social behavior.

Category two has also recently been well explored as it is the focus of complexity theorists. Examples include the work of Per Bak (1996) on sand piles and earthquakes, Lorenz (2001) on weather systems and Prigogine (1997; 1985) on far from equilibrium systems. Many so called social simulations also belonging here– specifically those which incorporate agents which have fixed behaviors and no capacity for learning (individual or social). These include classic simulations based on swarms (Boids) and/or involving fixed decision criteria or rules such Schelling's segregation model, the cooperation models of Axelrod (1984) or the Sugarscape models of Epstein and Axtell (1996). Some may argue that these models involve agents with goals and therefore represent examples of fourth order emergence. The transition between 3rd order and fourth, as will be argued below, involves a move to agent autonomy that is missing in these models: their goals are designed in and not a result of their own operation it is for this reason that we argue they belong to order two.

It is significant that Ellis provides primarily biological examples for his category three order of emergence. The paradigmatic biological entity which illustrates the processes of reciprocal micro-macro causality and for which we have an excellent description which has been made operational both in vitro and in silico (see for example McMullin & Grob, 2001; F. Varela, Maturana, & Uribe, 1974) is the cell. While the mechanisms of autocatalysis and the metabolic pathways of cell self-production are well known, well documented and closely studied, the most concise articulation of the fundamental processes involved come with the theory of autopoiesis developed by the theoretical biologists Humberto Maturana and Francisco Varela (H. Maturana & Varela, 1980; H. R. Maturana & Varela, 1992; F. Varela, 1979; F. Varela et al., 1974). Unfortunately this account is not widely appreciated even within biology itself[1]. Varela (1997: 78) states:

Autopoiesis is a prime example of a ...dialectics between the local component levels and the global whole, linked together in reciprocal relation through the requirement of constitution of an entity that self-separates from its background.

The theory of autopoiesis provides a foundation for understanding other emergent processes, particularly those associated with biological entities. The originating authors themselves extended it to cover multi-cellular entities and to provide a more general theory of cognition. Others have gone so far as to argue that it furnishes a theory of society and/or organization (Niklas Luhmann, 1995; von_Krogh & Roos, 1995; Zeleny, 1991) although this remains controversial (Bednarz, 1988; Mingers, 2002, 2004) and we specifically reject it as incompatible with the original concept and as unnecessary (Goldspink, 2000; Kay, 1999).

Unlike the self-organizing processes which characterize the second order, the defining characteristic of biological self-organization is the attainment of 'strong autonomy' (Rocha, 1998). While Ellis does not say so directly, it would appear that it is the advent of a self-referential operational closure which demarcates third and higher orders of emergence from the lower orders.

Maturana and Varela argue that cognition is associated with this operational closure or autonomy.

Autonomy is used here to refer to a *constitutive* process rather than as a *categorical* distinction and cognition is defined as the range of behaviors the agents can generate to remain *viable* or *to retain its identity* as a self-constituting agent (Froesea, Virgo, & Izquierdo, 2007; Thompson & Varela, 2001). For those immersed in symbolic AI it may come as a surprise that a biological cell may thus be described as a cognitive entity. This theme will be developed further in a following section as it is central to the idea of enactive cognition finding increasing uptake within second generation AI, artificial life and robotics (Barandiaran, 2005; Di Paolo & Lizuka, 2007; Di Paolo, Rohde, & De Jaegher, 2007; Moreno & Etxeberria, 1995; Moreno, Umerez, & Ibanes, 1997).

In his third order category Ellis includes a range of capabilities of biological entities up to and including 'instinctive' action. These suggest that this category would pertain to single and multi-cellular organisms including those with a central nervous system. It may be that this order is too broadly cast. Multi-cellularity is arguably another threshold point as differentiated aggregates of cells display greater capacity to respond to their environment, even where they do not possess a central nervous system, than do individual cells. Furthermore those with a central nervous system enjoy even greater behavioral flexibility. As a consequence each probably originates a distinct macro phenomenology different from that of the cells that constitute them (H. R. Maturana & Varela, 1992).

The primary point of distinction between order three and order four would appear to be between (phylogenetically) fixed individual characteristics and a capacity for an individual agent to have goals and to learn. The mechanisms by which these characteristics are acquired and fixed at the level of individuals (sexual transmission and natural selection) are ignored by Ellis or seen as unimportant from the perspective of emergence. This is reasonable if our concern is with social behavior which manifests over relatively short time cycles in geological terms. When does a capacity to adjust structure in response to an environment as implied by the characteristics of Ellis' third order become the learning ability associated with the forth order?

Ellis explicitly demarcates the goal directedness of the fourth order from apparent goals implied in the teleonomic operation of living things implicit in the third. We must therefore assume he means active goal-setting : the exercise of what we commonly refer to as agency or free will. Agency results from the vastly expanded behavioral plasticity available when an organism develops an advanced nervous system. Also, to learn an agent must have some form of memory. Memory too is generally associated with the existence of a central nervous system and is often seen as involving stored representations. But the idea of 'representations' is highly problematic from a biological point of view. What is it that is represented and how? We consider this problem in the next section.

Ellis would seem to be pointing to a category here which deals with non-human animals but the transition points are not well defined from the perspective of mechanisms of emergence. Learning in animals can stretch from simple operant conditioning to complex evaluative processes involving logical reflexion. Different stages along this continuum would appear to support significantly different forms of emergent structure. Ellis makes no distinction, for example, between individual and social learning.

Ellis marks his final transition from category four to category five by moving from simple learning capability to the capacity for language. Animals such as apes have rudimentary language ability – are they included in here or is this category the human catch-all category? Unfortunately the more closely we look at the jump between fourth and fifth order the more it resembles an abyss.

There has been a considerable research effort directed at understanding the origins and developmental phases associated with the attainment of the distinctive human cognitive capabilities. These are the capabilities which seem to relate to the transition between Ellis' category four and five orders of emergence. Much of this has drawn on comparative neurology, and sociological and psychological study of non-human animals, in particular apes. Insights are available also from developmental psychology and neurology directed at understanding human ontogeny: the phases of development from infant to adult. Note that these may overlap as phylogenetically determined capabilities characteristic of some animals may correspond to early stages of human ontogenetic development. This corpus offers those

of us involved with AI two opportunities a) a capacity to aim to better stage the development of agent specifications - aiming to provide a reasonable model for simple intelligence before the more complex and b) a capacity, even before we can effectively model or simulate more advanced intelligence, to theorize about the implications it may have for emergence of social structure.

Some work has already been undertaken in this area, most notably in the area of robotics rather than computer simulation of social phenomena (although robots can be regarded as physical simulations and multi-agent software simulations as simulated robotics). Of particular note here is the work of Dautenhahn (2001; 2002), Bryson (2007; n.d) and Steels (1997; 2005; 1999) in the area of language.

Gardenfors (2006) identifies the following as needing to be explained (presented in order of their apparent evolution).

- Sensations
- Attention
- Emotions
- Memory
- Thought and imagination
- Planning
- Self-consciousness/theory of mind
- Free-will
- Language

These are present to varying degrees in different organisms and develop at different stages in humans as they develop from infancy to adulthood. The degree of interrelatedness is not, however, straight forward. Apes for example demonstrate self-awareness and theory of mind but do both without language whereas in humans language appears to play a significant role in both. For the time being then too little is known about these transitions.

It is perhaps in understanding these transitions that we find the greatest challenges for advancing artificial societies and it is here that we find philosophy may have dealt us an unhelpful turn. The advent of the central nervous system and the observation that cognitive function is correlated with brain size has contributed to a distinctive account of the function of brain and its relationship to mind (Johnson, 1990; Lakoff & Johnson, 1999). In this convention, mind and hence cognition has been argued to originate in brains and to involve symbol manipulation. As we consider the literature on what makes human cognition distinctive, we need to be mindful of the effect of this and alternative paradigms. What are these alternatives and what difference do they make to our understanding of orders of emergence in general and social emergence in particular?

TWO PARADIGMS: TWO POSSIBLE APPROACHES

Within AI there are two alternative and some argue antithetical paradigms of cognition – symbolic and connectionist. Symbolic AI assumes that it is possible to model every general intelligence using a suitable symbol system and that intelligence involves symbol manipulation (Franklin, 1998).

In their book *The Embodied Mind*, Varela & Rosch (1992) state:

The central intuition ... is that intelligence—human intelligence included—so resembles computation in its essential characteristics that cognition can actually be defined as computations of symbolic representations (F. Varela, Thompson, & Rosch, 1992: 40).

The symbolic approach inevitably constructs a duality. The environment is experienced as a facticity and acted upon directly, but is also conceived and symbolically represented in the mind. Mind and behaviour are linked as hypothesis and experiment. The mind looks for patterns in representations and tests the degree to which these accord with the outside world.

More recently, this tradition has been challenged. The advent of complexity theory has given greater impetus to connectionist models of mind such as neural networks. Here emergent structure or pattern arises from massively interconnected webs of active agents. Applied to the brain, Varela et al state:

The brain is thus a highly cooperative system: the dense interconnections amongst its components entail that eventually everything going on will be a function of what all the other components are doing (1992: 94).

It is important to note that no symbols are invoked or required by this model. Meaning is embodied in fine-grained structure and pattern throughout the network. Unlike symbolic systems, connectionist approaches can derive pattern and meaning by mapping a referent situation in many different (and context dependent) ways. Meaning in connectionist models is embodied by the overall state of the system in its context. It is implicit in the overall 'performance in some domainre'. Herein lays its major problem from the perspective of multi-agent simulation. In connectionist models the micro-states which support a given macro state is opaque – relatively inaccessible to an observer and difficult to interpret – indeed, there will often be several or many micro configurations compatible with a given macro-state (Richardson, 2002b). Several attempts have been made to address this problem. The first was to consider hybrid systems in an attempt to gain the advantage of each (Khosla & Dillon, 1998). The second has been to find a middle ground. This is apparent for example in Gardenfors' theory of conceptual spaces (Gardenfors, 2004). At the same time the practical value of connectionist systems – their capacity to categorize contexts or situations in a non-brittle way– has been seen as a significant advantage in robotics (Brooks, 1991).

Back in 1992 Varela et al noted that:

...an important and pervasive shift is beginning to take place in cognitive science under the very influence of its own research. This shift requires that we move away from the idea of the world as independent and extrinsic to the idea of a world as inseparable from the structure of [mental] processes of self modification. This change in stance does not express a mere philosophical preference; it reflects the necessity of understanding cognitive systems not on the basis of their input and output relationships but by their operational closure (1992: 139).

They go on to argue that connectionist approaches, while an advance on cognitivism are not consistent with an approach which views biological agents as operationally closed in that '...the results of its processes are those processes themselves' (1992, p. 139). They assert:

Such systems do not operate by representation. Instead of representing an independent world, they enact a world as a domain of distinctions that is inseparable from the structure embodied by the cognitive system (1992: 140).

These authors argue for an approach of cognition as 'enaction', an intertwining of experience and conceptualization which results from the structural coupling of an autonomous organism and its environment. Autopoietic theory provided a concrete and operationalizable account of the intertwining of micro and macro at the level of the cell. The enactive theory of cognition goes some way towards providing a basis for understanding this process in multi-cellular animals. Enactive cognition is currently enjoying significant attention and hence conceptual extension as well as experimental grounding in the field of robotics (see for example De Jaegher & Di Paolo, 2007; Di Paolo et al., 2007; Metta, Vernon, & Sandini, 2005). The attraction here is pragmatic – it helps to address longstanding problems within robotics, in particular the problem of symbol grounding (Harnad, 1990). To date it has seen little uptake within social simulation. The implications of enaction go well beyond pragmatics however.

The enactive turn in AI has as an explicit target a resolution of the micro-macro problem. While symbolic AI assumes the existence of an objective independent world and a mental model with some correspondence to the real world, enaction dispenses with this dichotomy. As an autonomous entity, the cognizing agent is concerned only to maintain its viability in an environment. It adjusts its structure to accommodate perturbation from the environment (which includes other cognitive agents) in order to do so. Advanced nervous systems and capabilities such as language simply extend the requisite variety available to the agent extending the range and type of environmental perturbations it can survive. As agents and environments structurally couple they co-determine one another to 'satisfice' the conditions for mutual viability. From this perspective, the importance of environment recedes from determinant to constraint. Intelligence moves from problem solving capacity to flexibility to enter into and engage with a shared world. However, McGee (2005a; 2005b) has

recently argued that despite its promise, enactive cognition is not yet sufficiently well articulated to 'speak of hypothetical mechanisms'. The limiting factor here would appear to be as much one of insufficient application as theoretical difficulty. In the final section we attempt a definition of two classes of emergence which we call reflexive and non-reflexive. These draw on the enactive paradigm and attempt to provide a concrete specification of the mechanisms which underlay each.

TOWARDS AN ENACTIVE SPECIFICATION OF ASPECTS OF COGNITION AND THEIR ASSOCIATED ORDERS OF EMERGENCE

How then do we advance our understanding of the effect of different cognitive capability on orders of emergence? A useful strategy may be to simplify the problem. By way of a mental exercise we will take simple extremes and recast the problem in terms of an enactive view. From an enactive position the critical phases of cognitive development appear to be as follows:

- Autonomy (operational closure)
- Structural Coupling
- Reflexivity/self consciousness
- Language/consensual domains

All living beings (from amoeba to humans) are distinguished by autonomy and as autonomous entities they necessarily enter into structural coupling with their environment. We take this as one pole of the continuum and identify the class of emergence which it can support as non-reflexive. This is the enactive equivalent to social order which is a product of emergence *without* the feedback loop from macro to micro which Castelfranchi (1998a) refers to as immergence. The mechanisms are, however, more sophisticated than are currently modeled in Artificial Societies as they involve autonomous agents – these are essentially what Ellis refers to in his category four – i.e. biological agents which can change their structure (learn) in response to environmental perturbation. It should be feasible to simulate this type of agent with current technology or at least to achieve a close proxy although we have not yet managed to do so beyond the most basic chemical system analogues of cell autopoiesis. If we were to achieve it how might we describe the system operation?

Non-Reflexive Social Emergence

Non-reflexive emergence arises from the mechanism of structural coupling between operationally closed (autonomous) agents. Structural coupling will arise between such agents which have sufficient cognitive range (behavioral repertoire) when they are located in a common environment. Assuming that their phylogeny and ontogeny is such that they can co-exist, through the process of recurrent mutual perturbation, each will adjust its structure so as to accommodate the other – their structures will become mutually aligned or structurally coupled. This process has been approximated in a simulation by Stoica-Kluver and Kluver (2006).

An observer may notice regularities in the resulting patterns of interaction and these may be labeled as 'norms' for example although Castelfranchi would refer to them as social functions as they 'work without being understood'. These patterns represent mutual accommodations, and an observer might attribute to those accommodations some social 'function'. The accommodations an agent makes to remain viable in one domain of interaction will need to be reconciled (within its body-hood) against accommodations being made (simultaneously) as it also participates with different agents in other domain/s in which it is simultaneously participating – agency and structure converge and are both instantiated at the point of enaction. The accommodations made will be those that allow the agent to remain viable and to maintain its organization (i.e. which 'satisfice' the constraints and allow conservation of identity) based on its unique ontogeny (structure resulting from its history of interactions in a variety of domains including the current one).

Here the emergent structure can be seen to be 'in' (i.e. internalized within its own cognitive structure) each agent to the extent that each has had to make structural adjustments to operate in the shared domain. The structural adjustment each needs to

make in order to persist will, however, be unique. In other words the structural accommodations each has made in order to contribute to the patterns, will *not* be the same. The structure, then, can also be regarded as 'in' the network, as it is the intersection of these disparate agent structures which gives it its particular form at a particular time. As any agent could leave the domain and have minimal effect on the resulting pattern, each agent's 'contribution' will be relatively small. The pattern can be thought about as like a hologram. The whole is in every part (agent) such that removal of parts (agents) reduces the resolution (coherence) but does not constitute loss of overall pattern. However, the loss of too many components may reduce the coupling to the point that the existing pattern de-coheres and transforms into something different. Each agent contributes to the pattern formation, so it is conceivable that the pattern will only be realized with some critical minimal number of agents present which have had a sufficient mutual history to have aligned their structures.

In natural systems, the local level interactions between agents are constrained by the existing structures of the agents and the state of their environment. With biological agents the system is open in that any emergent structure is possible as long as it remains consistent with the biological viability of the agents as living (autopoietic) entities. This biological constraint includes limits to environmental conditions conducive to life (i.e. not too hot or too cold, the need for energy, limitations to sensory channels, channel bandwidths and affective/psychomotor response capabilities etc). These are primarily a product of phylogeny (the evolutionary history of the organism at the level of the species) rather than ontogeny (the history of development at the level of the individual), and are therefore slow to change and not under the control of the emergent social system. As a consequence the basic dimensionality of the phase space of the social system does not change over the time frame of interest for understanding social systems. The dimensionality of the phase space is determined by the dimensions of variability possible by individuals – i.e. the plasticity of their nervous systems and by higher order dimensions which emerge from their interaction.

Reflexive Social Emergence

What changes if we now jump to the opposite pole on our hypothetical continuum? Here we attempt to outline the difference made by agents which are self aware and which can interact in language.

Biological agent's sensory surfaces are selected to be sensitive to difference in dimension of their world relevant to their survival and their cognitive apparatus is thus geared to make distinctions relevant to maintaining their viability in past environments. Once cognitive complexity exceeds a critical threshold (Gardenfors, 2006) these distinctions can be represented in language. Maturana and Varela (1980) describe language as involving the co-ordination of the co-ordination of actions – i.e. language provides a meta process by which agents orientate themselves within a world. Structural coupling can arise purely through behavioral coordination of action (as discussed above), but it can also take place in and through linguistic exchange – the mutual co-ordination of co-ordination of behaviors. This gives rise to a consensual linguistic domain characterized by a more or less shared lexicon. This process has been simulated using both shared referents and simple structural coupling in the absence of objective referents (Gong, Ke, Minett, & Wang, 2004; Hutchins & Hazlehurst, 1995; Steels, 1997, 1998; Steels, 2005; Steels & Kaplan, 1998; Steels & Kaplan, 1999), as has the emergence of a rudimentary grammar (Howell & Becker, n.d; Vogt, n.d).

The advent of language radically increases the behavioral plasticity of agents and has significant implications for the dimensionality of the phase space and of the resulting higher order structures it can generate and support. This is because language makes possible the emergence of domains of interaction which can themselves become the target for further linguistic distinction and hence new domains. In other words, language allows the agent to make distinctions on prior distinctions (to language about its prior language or to build further abstractions on prior abstractions). This supports the possibility of infinite recursion and infinite branching (there are no doubt biological constraints on this in humans). This is an intrinsically social process. Furthermore, a capacity to distinguish (label or categorize) processes supports

reification and this simplifies the cognitive handling of processual phenomena and allows the resulting reifications to be treated by the agent in the same manner as material objects.

These capabilities greatly expand the structural flexibility of the agents: they can now invent shared epistemic worlds. The phase space of agent cognition is now based primarily on constraints of ontogeny rather than phylogeny and is hence under the influence of the agent/s.

Language makes possible a further major qualitative difference in natural and human social emergence. Humans (and possibly some other primates, cetaceans and elephants)[2] have developed sufficient cognitive capacity to become self-aware and as such exhibit reflexive behavior. This occurs when the agent is capable of distinguishing 'self' and 'other' i.e. the agent can entertain the notion of 'I' as a concept and treat that concept as an object. The advent of this capacity for reflexive identity also supposes the existence of a range of conceptual operators that act on identity – identity construction and maintenance becomes a part of the agent's world creation. Exploration of this process is proceeding under the title of Neurophenomenology (Rudrauf, Lutz, Cosmelli, Lachaux, & Le Van Quyen, 2003; Thompson & Varela, 2001).

In other words, agents can now notice the patterns that arise as they interact with others and distinguish those patterns in language. Such a mechanism would be the enactive equivalent to Castelfranchi's (1998a) Cognitive Emergence. Here a reflexive agent can notice an emergent pattern of social behavior and explicitly denote it as a 'norm' for example. While this denotation may be idiosyncratic (i.e. based on the necessarily limited perception of the individual agent), the agent can nonetheless act on the basis of this denotation. Once distinguished and reified within a domain, agents can decide (on the basis of rational as well as value based or emotional criteria) how to respond – they can choose to ignore the norm or to behave in ways they believe will limit the reoccurrence of the behaviors that are outside the agreed/shared patterns of the group. Once a pattern has been distinguished in language it can make the transition to a rule: a formally stated, linguistically explicit requirement with stated conditionals and possible resources to maintain it. This suggests that an agent can form hypotheses about the relationship between a macro structural aspect of the social system in which it is a participant and then act on that hypothesis, potentially changing the structure which it participates in generating. This gives rise to a feedback path between macro and micro phenomena that is not present in any other natural phenomena.

Consistent with Castelfranchi's claim, agents possessing this cognitive complexity form the components of a social system which would exhibit a distinct class of emergence. From the emergent perspective this is argued on the basis that reflexive agents will display qualitatively different behaviors from non-reflexive through the ability to modify their own sets of behavioral change triggers. For agents which have linguistic capability, the two processes (linguistic and non-linguistic) intertwine or even become one and would not be able to be empirically disentangled. Their respective influences will only be able to be examined through simulations or by comparing agents with different (phylogenetic) capabilities (i.e. different species) and this sets some interesting methodological challenges.

The Role of the Observer

Another significant implication of the relationships described above is the observer dependant nature of emergence in social systems. In human social systems every agent is an observer and it is the process of observation and the associated distinction-making which is the reflexive engine of emergence. In natural systems, the agents of the system are unable to observe and distinguish linguistically or to distinguish external structures as separate from themselves hence the process of observation has no impact on the dynamics of the system or the way in which emergence takes place. To some extent we can see an acknowledgement of this effect in methodological discussions within ethnography, action research (Carr & Kemmis, 1986) and grounded theory (Corbin & Strauss, 1990). In each of these methodologies the impact of the researcher on the social system under study is acknowledged and seen as part of the process. The view being proposed here is that any agent that becomes a part of the system being observed has

the potential to influence that system. An agent can become a part of the system simply by being itself observed or conceived as observing by those who constitute the system. In other words, the effect of the entry of a new observing agent is to change the system boundary so as to include that agent. The boundary is itself an entity of ambiguous status – it is an epistemic distinction albeit one based on potentially ontological markers. In most social theory, positing the observer as a necessary part of the system removes any ontological privilege and threatens either infinite recursion or paradox. Based on the position advocated here, a degree of both may well be fundamental to the type of system being described (Hofstadter, 2007).

Implications for Emergence

Complex systems of all kinds demonstrate a capacity to give rise to complex macro patterns as a result of local interactions between agents in highly connected webs. This local interaction can often be characterized as involving some signaling between agents. As we have seen above, in human social systems, this signaling behavior takes on a qualitatively different form. This has three key implications for our understanding of emergence that to date have largely been ignored by the literature.

1. **Social systems will display an increased range of emergent possibilities:** The reflexive nature of social systems implies that a greater range of emergent structures should be expected and they will be subject to more rapid change.
2. **Dimensions of phase space are non-constant:** As the agents in the social system define and redefine the phase space as a function of their reflexive distinctions they will create and change the dimensions of that phase space, in order to support their own viability in that space.
3. **Phase space comes under control of the system and is dynamic:** The dimensionality of the phase space associated with ontogenetic parameters is derived through the self-distinguishing characteristics of the agents and can be influenced by their situated behavior.

Significantly the feedback path between macro and micro would add significant non-linearity to the system and it becomes important to identify and explain order producing mechanisms within the network.

CONCLUSION AND FUTURE DIRECTIONS

In this chapter we have attempted to provide an operational specification of the gap implicit in Ellis' fourth and fifth order emergence. In a sense we have demarcated the extremes using the lens of enactive cognition. Enactive cognition was selected as it provides a theoretical underpinning which avoids the dualism inherent in symbolic systems and the confusion of fundamental processes which results from this. It has been argued to be both theoretically better capable of capturing the essential mechanisms and of providing a practical way of avoiding the now well documented pitfalls of symbolic AI. From this perspective the first challenge that must be addressed to advance social simulation is to achieve some form or proxy of constitutive autonomy in our multi-agent models. Significant work is currently underway on this problem in robotics but there have been few systematic attempts within social simulation.

Once this has been achieved we then need to model autonomous closure in linguistic systems. We would seem to be a very long way from this at present. It may be possible however to achieve this first in some abstract domain – simulating perhaps Luhmann's self-referential systems of communicative acts. This is probably unlikely however.

In our sketching out the extremes many questions remain about what might lay in the middle. This middle includes very significant phases of human cognitive development – including theory of mind and narrative intelligence. There can be no doubt that these will support qualitatively distinct classes of emergent social phenomena. There is evidence from the study of apes that forms of these cognitive capabilities do not require language. These may be much more accessible to our still limited capacity to simulate than the human equivalents which appear to intertwine with linguistic capability. We probably have much to learn then from the study of primate communities and from research into cognition in species other than humans. At present these attract considerably less attention within the social simulation community and perhaps this is a mistake. We have learned a lot from ants – how much more from apes? Robotics also appears well equipped to incorporate the insights coming from situated, embodied and enactive cognition. Its more difficult to see how embodied proxies may be incorporated into multi-agent simulations but no doubt there are ways. Such systems will doubtless need to be able to bootstrap some level of operational closure and it will be behavior within the self-determining boundary that – free from the inevitable teleological hand of the designer can reveal insights into how we humans do what we seem to do so effortlessly – construct social worlds in which we can live viable and interesting lives.

REFERENCES

Ablowitz, R. (1939). The Theory of emergence. *Philosophy of Science, 6*(1), 16.

Archer, M. (1998). Realism in the social sciences. In M. Archer, R. Bhaskar, A. Collier, T. Lawson & A. Norrie (Eds.), *Critical realism: Essential readings.* London: Routledge.

Archer, M., Bhaskar, R., Ciollier, A., Lawson, T., & Norrie, A. (1998). *Critical Realism: Essential Readings.* London: Routledge.

Axelrod, R. (1984). *The evolution of cooperation.* New York: Basic Books.

Bak, P. (1996). *How nature works: The science of self-organized criticality.* New York: Copurnicus.

Barandiaran, X. (2005). Behavioral adaptive autonomy. A milestone on the ALife roue to AI? San-sebastian, Spain: Department of Logic and Philosophy of Science, University of the Basque Country.

Bednarz, J. (1988). Autopoesis: The organizational closure of social systems. *Systems Research, 5*(1), 57-64.

Berger, P. L., & Luckman, T. (1972). *The social construction of reality.* Penguin.

Bertalanffy, L. v. (1950). An outline of general systems theory. *British Journal for the Philosophy of Science, 1*(2).

Bertalanffy_von, L. (1968). *General systems theory*. New York: Braziller.

Bhaskar, R. (1997). A realist theory of science. London: Verso.

Bhaskar, R. (1998). *The possibility of naturalism*. London: Routledge.

Brooks, R. A. (1991). Intelligence without representation. *Intelligence without Reason*, (47), 569-595.

Bryson, J. J. (2007). Embodiment vs. memetics. Bath: Artificial Models of Natural Intelligence, University of Bath.

Bryson, J. J. (n.d). Representational requirements for evolving cultural evolution, *Interdiciplines.*

Carr, W., & Kemmis, S. (1986). *Becoming critical: Knowing through action research*. Deakin University.

Castelfranchi, C. (1998a). Simulating with cognitive agents: The importance of cognitive emergence. In J. S. Sichman, R. Conte & N. Gilbert (Eds.), *Multi-agent systems and agent based simulation*. Berlin: Springer.

Castelfranchi, C. (1998b). Simulating with cognitive agents: The importance of cognitive emergence. In J. S. Sichman, R. Conte & N. Gilbert (Eds.), *Lecture Notes in Artificial Intelligence*. Berlin: Springer Verlag.

Chalmers, D. J. (2006). Strong and weak emergence. Canberra: Research School of Social Sciences, Australian National University.

Checkland, P. (1988). *Systems thinking systems practice*. G.B.: John Wiley.

Clayton, P. (2006). Conceptual foundations of emergence theory. In P. Clayton & P. Davies (Eds.), *The re-emergence of emergence: The emergentist hypothesis from science to religion*. Oxford: Oxford University Press.

Clayton, P., & Davies, P. (2006). *The re-emergence of emergence: The emergentist hypothesis from science to religion*. Oxford: Oxford University Press.

Coleman, J. S. (1994). *Foundations of social theory*. Cambridge: Belknap.

Conte, R., Hegselmann, R., & Terna, P. (1997). *Simulating social phenomena*. Berlin: Springer.

Corbin, J. M., & Strauss, A. (1990). Grounded theory research: Procedures, canons, and evaluative criteria. *Qualitative Sociology, 13*(1), 18.

Dautenhahn, K. (2001). The narrative intelligence hypothesis: In search of the transactional format of narratives in humans and other social animals. In *Cognitive Technology*, (pp. 248-266). Hiedelberg, Germany: Springer-Verlag.

Dautenhahn, K. (2002). The origins of narrative. *International Journal of Cognition and Technology, 1*(1), 97-123.

Davies, P. (2006). The physics of downward causation. In P. Clayton & P. Davies (Eds.), *The Re-Emergence of Emergence: The Emergentist Hypothesis from Science to Religion*. Oxford: Oxford University Press.

De Jaegher, H., & Di Paolo, E. A. (2007). Participatory Sense-making: An enactive approach to Social Cognition. *Phenomenology and the cognitive Sciences, forthcoming.*

Di Paolo, E. A., & Lizuka, H. (2007). How (not) to Model Autonomous Behaviour. *Biosystems.*

Di Paolo, E. A., Rohde, M., & De Jaegher, H. (2007). Horizons for The Enactive Mind: Values, Social Interaction and Play. In J. Stewart, O. Gapenne & E. A. Di Paolo (Eds.), *Enaction: Towards a New Paradigm for Cognitive Science*. Cambridge MA: MIT Press.

Ellis, G. F. R. (2006). On the Nature of Emergent Reality. In P. Clayton & P. Davies (Eds.), *The Re-Emergence of Emergence: The Emergentist Hypothesis from Science to Religion*. Oxford: Oxford University Press.

Engels, F. (1934). *Dialectics of Nature*. Moscow: Progress Publishers.

Epstein, J. M., & Axtel, R. (1996). *Growing Artificial Societies*. Cambridge, Ma.: MIT Press.

Eronen, M. (2004). *Emergence in the Philosophy of Mind*. University of Helsinki, Helsinki.

Fodor, J. A. (1974). Special; Sciences or The Disunity of Science as a Working Hypothesis. *Synthese, 28*, 18.

Franklin, S. (1998). *Artificial Minds*. London: MIT press.

Froesea, T., Virgo, N., & Izquierdo, E. (2007). Autonomy: a review and a reappraisal. Brighton Uk: University of Sussex.

Fuchs, C., & Hofkirchner, W. (2005). The Dialectic of Bottom-up and Top-down Emergence in Social Systems. *tripleC 1*(1), 22.

Gardenfors, P. (2004). *Conceptual Spaces*. London: The MIT Press.

Gardenfors, P. (2006). *How Homo became Sapiens: On the evolution of Thinking*. Oxford: Oxford University Press.

Gell-Mann, M. (1995). *The Quark and the Jaguar: Adventures in the simple and the complex*. Great Britain: Abacus.

Giddens, A. (1984). *The Constitution of society: Outline of the theory of structuration*. Berkeley: University of California Press.

Gilbert, N. (1995). Emergence in Social Simulation. In N. Gilbert & R. Conte (Eds.), *Artificial Societies*. London: UCL Press.

Gilbert, N. (2002). *Varieties of Emergence*. Paper presented at the Social Agents: Ecology, Exchange, and Evolution Conference Chicago.

Goldspink, C. (2000). *Social Attractors: An Examination of the Applicability of Complexity theory to Social and Organisational Analysis*. Unpublished PhD, University Western Sydney, Richmond.

Goldspink, C., & Kay, R. (2003). Organizations as Self Organizing and Sustaining Systems: A Complex and Autopoietic Systems Perspective. *International Journal General Systems, 32*(5), 459-474.

Goldspink, C., & Kay, R. (2004). Bridging the Micro-Macro Divide: a new basis for social science. *Human Relations, 57* (5), 597-618.

Gong, T., Ke, J., Minett, J. W., & Wang, W. S. (2004). A Computational Framework to Simulate the co-evolution of language and social structure.

Harnad, S. (1990). The Symbol Grounding Problem. *Physica, 42*, 335-346.

Hofstadter, D. R. (2007). I am a Strange Loop. In: Basic Books.

Holland, J. H. (1998). *Emergence: from chaos to order*. Ma.: Addison Wesley.

Howell, S. R., & Becker, S. (n.d). Modelling Language Aquisition: Grammar from the Lexicon?

Hutchins, E., & Hazlehurst, B. (1995). How to invent a lexicon: the development of shared symbols. In N. Gilbert & R. Conte (Eds.), *Artificial Societies*. London: UCL Press.

Jackson, M. C. (2000). *Systems Approaches to Management*. London: Kluwer Academic.

Johnson, M. (1990). *The Body in the Mind: The Bodily Basis of Meaning, Imagination and Reason*. Chicago: The University of Chicago Press.

Kauffman, S. (2000). *Investigations*. New York: Oxford.

Kauffman, S. A. (1993). *The Origins of Order: Self Organization and Selection in Evolution*: Oxford University Press.

Kauffman, S. A. (1996). *At home in the Universe: The Search for Laws of Complexity*. London: Penguin.

Kay, R. (1999). *Towards an autopoietic perspective on knowledge and organisation*. Unpublished PhD, University of Western Sydney, Richmond.

Keeney, B. P. (1987). *Aesthetics of change*: Guilford.

Kennedy, J., & Eberhart, R. C. (2001). *Swarm Intelligence* (1 ed.). London: Academic Press.

Khosla, R., & Dillon, T. S. (1998). Welding Symbolic AI with Neural Networks and their applications.

IEEE Transactions on Evolutionary Computation.

Lakoff, G., & Johnson, M. (1999). *Philosophy in the flesh: The embodied mind and its challenge to Western thought.* New York: Basic Books.

Leont'ev, A. N. (1978). *Activity, Consciousness and Personality.* Engelwood Cliffs: Prentice Hall.

Lorenz, E. N. (2001). *The Essence of Chaos* (4 ed.). Seattle: University of Washington Press.

Luhmann, N. (1990). *Essays on Self Reference.* New York: Columbia University Press.

Luhmann, N. (1995). *Social Systems.* Stanford: Stanford University Press.

Maturana, H., & Varela, F. (1980). *Autopoiesis and Cognition: The Realization of the Living* (Vol. 42). Boston: D. Reidel.

Maturana, H. R., & Varela, F. J. (1992). *The Tree of Knowledge: The Biological Roots of Human Understanding.* Boston: Shambhala.

McGee, K. (2005a). Enactive Cognitive Science. Part 1: Background and Research Themes. *Constructivist Foundations, 1*(1), 15.

McGee, K. (2005b). Enactive Cognitive Science. Part 2: Methods, Insights, and Potential. *Constructivist Foundations, 1*(2), 9.

McKelvey. (1997). Quasi-Natural Organisation Science. *Organization Science, 8,* 351-380.

McMullin, B., & Grob, D. (2001). Towards the Implementation of Evolving Autopoietic Artificial Agents, *6th European Conference on Artificial Life ECAL 2001.* University of Economics, Prague.

Metta, G., Vernon, D., & Sandini, G. (2005). *The Robotcup Approach to the Development of Cognition.* Paper presented at the Fifth International Workshop on Epigenetic Robotics: Modeling Cognitive Development in Robotic Systems Lund University Cognitive Studies, .

Mingers, J. (2002). Are Social Systems Autopoietic? Assessing Luhmanns Social Theory. *Sociological review, 50*(2).

Mingers, J. (2004). Can Social Systems be Autopoietic? Bhaskar's and Giddens' Social Theories. *Journal for the Theory of Social Behaviour, 34*(4), 25.

Moreno, A., & Etxeberria, A. (1995). Agency in natural and artificial systems. San Sabastian, Spain: Department of Logic and Philosophy of Science University of the Basque Country.

Moreno, A., Umerez, J., & Ibanes, J. (1997). Cognition and Life. *Brain and Cognition, 34,* 107-129.

Oyama, S. (2000). *The Ontogeny of Information: Developmental Systems and Evolution*: Duke University Press.

Peterson, G. R. (2006). Species of Emergence. *Zygon, 41*(3), 22.

Prigogine, I. (1997). *The End of Certainty: Time, Chaos and the New Laws of Nature.* New York: The Free Press.

Prigogine, I., & Stengers, I. (1985). *Order out of Chaos: Man's New Dialogue with Nature*: Flamingo.

Richardson, K. A. (2002a). Methodological Implications of a Complex Systems Approach to Sociality: Some further remarks. *Journal of Artificial Societies and Social Simulation, 5*(2).

Richardson, K. A. (2002b). *On the Limits of Bottom Up Computer Simulation: Towards a Non-linear Modeling Culture.* Paper presented at the 36th Hawaii International Conference on Systems Science, Hawaii.

Rocha, L. M. (1998). Selected Self-Organization: and the semiotics of evolutionary systems In S. Salthe, G. Van de Vijver & M. Delpos (Eds.), *Evolutionary Systems: Biological and Epistemological Perspectives on Selection and Self-Organization* (pp. 341-358): Kluwer Academic Publishers.

Rudrauf, D., Lutz , A., Cosmelli, D., Lachaux , J.-P., & Le Van Quyen, M. (2003). From Autopoiesis to Neurophenomenology: Francisco Varela's exploration of the biophysics of being. *Biol. Res, 36,* 27-65.

Sawyer, K. R. (2001). Emergence in Sociology: Contemporary Philosophy of Mind and Some Implications for Sociology Theory. *American Journal of Sociology, 107*(3), 551-585.

Sawyer, K. R. (2003). Artificial Societies: Multiagent Systems and the Micro-macro Link in Sociological Theory. *Sociological Methods & Research, 31*, 38.

Shrader, W. E. (2005). *The Metapysics of Ontological Emergence.* University of Notre Dame.

Stanford Encyclopedia of Philosophy. (2006). Emergent Properties, *Stanford Encyclopedia of Philosophy.*

Steels, L. (1997). *Constructing and Sharing Perceptual Distinctions.* Paper presented at the European Conference on Machine Learning, Berlin.

Steels, L. (1998). *Structural coupling of cognitive memories through adaptive language games.* Paper presented at the The fifth international conference on simulation of adaptive behavior on From animals to animats 5, Univ. of Zurich, Zurich, Switzerland.

Steels, L. (2005). The emergence and evolution of linguistic structure: from lexical to grammatical communication systems. *Connection Science, 17*(3 & 4), 17.

Steels, L., & Kaplan, F. (1998). Stochasticity as a Source of Innovation in Kanguage Games. In C. Adami, R. K. Belew, H. Kitano & C. Taylor (Eds.), *Artificial Life VI.* Cambridge, MA: MIT Press.

Steels, L., & Kaplan, F. (1999). Bootstrapping grounded word Semantics. In T. Briscoe (Ed.), *Linguistic evolution through language acquisition: formal and computational models,* . Cambridge, UK: Cambridge University Press.

Stewart, I. (1990). *Does God Play Dice - The New Mathematics of Chaos*: Penguin.

Stioica-Kluver, C., & Kluver, J. (2006). Interacting Neural Networks and ther Emergence of Social Structure. *Complexity, 12*(3), 11.

Thompson, E., & Varela, F. J. (2001). Radical Embodiment: neural dynamics and consciousness. *TRENDS in Cognitive Sciences, 5*(10), 418-425.

Varela, F. (1979). *Principles of Biological Autonomy.* New York: Elsevier-North Holland.

Varela, F. (1997). Patterns of Life: Intertwining Identity and Cognition. *Brain and Cognition, 34*, 72-87.

Varela, F., Maturana, H., & Uribe, R. (1974). Autopoiesis: The Organization of Living Systems, Its Characterization and a Model. *Biosystems, 5*, 187-196.

Varela, F., Thompson, E., & Rosch, E. (1992). *The Embodied Mind.* Cambridge: MIT Press.

Vogt, P. (n.d). Group Size Effects on the Emergence of Compositional Structures in Language. Tilburg, Netherlands: Tilburg University.

von_Krogh, G., & Roos, J. (1995). *Organizational Epistemology.* London: St Martins Press.

Vygotsky, L. S. (1962). *Thought and Language.* Cambridge, Mass: MIT Press.

Williams, G. P. (1997). *Chaos Theory Tamed.* Washington D.C: Joseph Henry Press.

Zeleny, M. (1991). *Autopoiesis: A Theory of Living Organization.* New York: North Holland.

ENDNOTES

[1] Quite why this should be the case is not clear. It does challenge the dominant paradigm within molecular biology and may have been displaced by the apparent potential offered by genomics (Oyama, 2000). It may also be that its implications are most significant outside of the biology discipline.

[2] It is important to note that we can infer the existence of threshold effects here but cannot precisely specify the critical points of complexity at which self-awareness and language becomes possible. The ability for language is of course evident in species other than humans, but the degree to which their linguistic plasticity involves or enables reflexivity in the system is a subject for further research.

Chapter III
Agents and Social Interaction:
Insights from Social Psychology

Joseph C. Bullington
Georgia Southern University, USA

ABSTRACT

Social interaction represents a powerful new locus of research in the quest to build more truly human-like artificial agents. The work in this area, as in the field of human computer interaction, generally, is becoming more interdisciplinary in nature. In this spirit, the present chapter will survey concepts and theory from social psychology, a field many researchers may be unfamiliar with. Dennett's notion of the intentional system will provide some initial grounding for the notion of social interaction, along with a brief discussion of conversational agents. The body of the chapter will then survey the areas of animal behavior and social psychology most relevant to human-agent interaction, concentrating on the areas of interpersonal relations and social perception. Within the area of social perception, the focus will be on the topics of emotion and attribution theory. Where relevant, research in the area of agent-human interaction will be discussed. The chapter will conclude with a brief survey of the use of agent-based modeling and simulation in social theory. The future looks very promising for researchers in this area; the complex problems involved in developing artificial agents who have mind-like attributes will require an interdisciplinary effort.

INTRODUCTION

As our technologies become more interactive in nature, the necessity of building in a social component has become more important than ever. The present chapter will review and discuss a variety of theories that have been used to guide academic research and development in the area of multi-agent interaction. Of particular interest are those models specifying an underlying theory of the character and develop-

ment of social interaction, as well as those that have focused attention on the affective components of human-agent and agent-agent interaction.

As originally conceived (e.g., Maes, 1995), software agents were to carry out tasks on our behalf such as seeking out information that we might be interested in, or finding the best prices for products, or even carrying out negotiations on our behalf. The notion that we would have a relationship with an agent and how that relationship would unfold, and even how the agent could be designed with social capabilities in mind seemed somewhat far removed from the issues related to the design of an autonomous search agent.

In order to develop more life-like agents that are capable of interacting in a believable way with humans, it is necessary to imbue them with some of the same attributes that are thought to underlie human social interaction. Otherwise, the agents may be thought of by users as dumb or simply annoying (e.g., the Microsoft Office Paperclip). The development of simulations of an agent's interactions with humans (or with other agents) thus could be guided by some underlying theory of social interaction. If so, then which theories of human social interaction, particularly theories of mind and social cognition, could play a role in the development of multi-agent systems and in human-agent systems? The overall goal of this chapter is to introduce selected theory and research in the area of social psychology to others who may not be familiar with the concepts and theory in this field. Thus, though portions of the chapter will review instances where social psychological concepts have been applied to actual systems, the focus will be on surveying concepts and ideas, not on the practical application of such ideas to system development.

The chapter will begin with a look at the question of what guides our social interactions with others, whether they are human or artificial. Dennett's (1978, 1989) concept of the intentional stance will be examined in some detail, and will be used as a basis for understanding interaction at a basic level. The search for relevant concepts and research findings that could be applied to deepen our understanding of agent interaction will continue with a review of selected concepts from the ethological and animal behavior literatures, including the concepts of fixed action pattern, imprinting, and imitation.

The next section will include a brief review of theories and evidence from social psychology that are applicable to multi-agent systems research. Social psychology represents a rich source of theory and insights into the nature of social interaction in multi-agent systems, and the review will include the areas of social perception and impression formation, selected portions of the interpersonal relationship and social exchange literatures, as well as examples of research in the agent-human literature that have built on these underlying ideas. The aim here is not

to provide a comprehensive review of these research areas, but to point out their relevance as we go forward with research in the field of agent interaction, particularly agent-human interaction.

Affective components have played a guiding role in research in the area of human-agent interaction, as exemplified in the work of Rosalind Picard and her group at MIT. Thus, Picard's work and its application to the area of social interaction will be discussed, along with that of Cynthia Breazeal and her efforts to build interactive robots.

The final section of the chapter will include a brief survey of the work in agent-based modeling, as well as a look into the future of this research. Of particular interest is the potential contribution this research can make to our overall understanding of social interaction. For example, can it provide confirming evidence for models of social behavior emerging from the human experimental social and developmental laboratories, as well as ethnographic and field research? Also, what types of interactive systems will emerge from this research and how will they change the way we use computing technology?

ISSUES, CHALLENGES, PROBLEMS

Social Interaction Between Agents, Both Human and Artificial

What is it that seems to guide our interactions with other agents? Whether these agents are people, animals, or machines? We will turn to a variety of disciplines for insight into this question, among them social psychology, philosophy and computer science.

Among philosophers, Dennett (1978) has used the term "intentional system" to describe "...a system whose behavior can be – at least sometimes – explained and predicted by relying on ascriptions to the system of beliefs and desires" (Dennett, 1978). He is careful to note that in using the terms 'beliefs' and 'desires,' he is not suggesting that the entity *has* beliefs and desires, only that we behave towards the entity *as if* it possessed such things. An entity is an intentional system only in the case where someone is seeking to explain and predict its behavior.

To further clarify these points, Dennett uses the example of someone seeking to predict the next move of a chess-playing computer. There are three 'stances' one can take in attempting to predict the computer's behavior. First, if one knows exactly how the computer is designed – including the hardware and software, then if the computer functions as it was intended, one can predict its behavior in response to any given move. This is referred to as the *design stance*. Second, one takes a *physical stance* if one knows the actual physical state of the entity at any moment in time. For instance, with a human chess opponent, this would require knowledge of (among other things) the firing patterns of all the neurons in the brain, or in the case of the chess playing computer, the physical state of all the electrical circuitry in the processor and all connected components. From this knowledge, one could predict the system's physical state in response to a particular move. Of course, because of the complexity of the chess-playing computer system (or a chess playing human), a person could never have the kind of detailed knowledge required by the design and physical stances. Therefore, one's best strategy for predicting the computer's next chess move is to assume that it will make the most *rational* move, given that its design is optimal and that it is not currently malfunctioning. This last strategy, assuming that one is dealing with a rational entity, whether animal, human or machine, is referred to as the *intentional stance*. The implication of this stance, according to Dennett, is that we ascribe to the system the possession of certain information (beliefs), and suppose it to be directed by certain goals (desires) (Though, it should be stressed again, that Dennett is not implying that the intentional system *has* beliefs and desires). When we take an intentional stance toward a person, an animal, or a machine, we are using a *theory of behavior* in order to explain or predict the behavior of the other entity, one involving the implied rationality of the entity.

Turning to our interactions with artificial agents, the question of how humans think about the technologies that they interact with on a daily basis was investigated in a series of studies by Reeves and Nass. Their research suggests that we tend to interact with computers as if they were people (Reeves and Nass, 1996). Using such methods as brainwave monitoring, home video, and questionnaires to measure peoples' responses to media in all its forms, they found that people tended to interact with computers and other media technology in a fundamentally social and natural way, and may not even have realized that they were doing so. For example, people tend to evaluate the performance of other people more favorably when the evaluation is given to the other person face to face, as opposed to giving the evaluation of the same performance to a third party. Reeves and Nass obtained the same finding when a computer's performance was being evaluated instead of another person. The theory they proposed to explain these findings suggests that for most of our history, humans only responded both socially and naturally to other humans (and perhaps animals), so no mechanism other than a human social response for dealing with artificial entities has ever developed.

Major Types of Interactive Systems

Conversational agents. The Turing test provides a model for human-machine interaction (Turing, 1950). Turing used a parlor game as an interaction model, designed originally as a response to the question of whether machines can think. The 'imitation' game involves two unseen people, a male and a female, along with a group of interrogators. The interrogators attempt to decide which person is the male, and which is the female based on written responses alone. The male tries to convince the interrogators that he is the female, while the female attempts to convince the interrogators that she is the female and that the other person is the male. In the revised version, a computer and a human take the place of the male and female, and the decision to be made is which is the human and which is the computer, based again on written responses to questions alone. The object of the machine is to try to cause the questioner to mistakenly conclude that the machine is the other person; the object of the other person is to try to help the questioner correctly identify the machine. Turing (1950) described his hopes for the test this way:

I believe that in about fifty years' time it will be possible to programme computers, with a storage capacity of about 10⁹, to make them play the imita-tion game so well that an average interrogator will not have more than 70 percent chance of making the right identification after five minutes of questioning. ... I believe that at the end of the century the use of words and general educated opinion will have altered so much that one will be able to speak of machines thinking without expecting to be contradicted. (Turing, 1950, p. 436).

Most observers believe that Turing would be disappointed at the performance of computers in this test today, judged by performance in the Loebner Prize Competition—an annual event in which computer programs are submitted to the Turing Test. Turing's test has nonetheless provided a kind of model for the development and evaluation of programs designed to provide an interactive component for their human users. Perhaps the best-known example of a conversational agent of the type suggested by Turing is Weizenbaum's ELIZA (Weizenbaum, 1966). The program was developed using the model (Weizenbaum suggested the term parody) of a non-directive psychotherapist. Rather than offer interpretations of a client's behavior, the non-directive therapist is trained to reflect the client's statements, in order to draw out their underlying emotional components (Rogers, 1951). A typical conversation would proceed as in the following; ELIZA's responses are capitalized (from Weizenbaum, 1966):

Men are all alike.

IN WHAT WAY?

They're always bugging us about something or other.

CAN YOU THINK OF A SPECIFIC EXAMPLE?

Well, my boyfriend made me come here.

YOUR BOYFRIEND MADE YOU COME HERE

He says I'm depressed much of the time.

I AM SORRY TO HEAR YOU ARE DEPRESSED

It's true. I am unhappy

DO YOU THINK COMING HERE WILL HELP YOU NOT TO BE UNHAPPY

I need some help, that much seems certain.

WHAT WOULD IT MEAN TO YOU IF YOU GOT SOME HELP

Perhaps I could learn to get along with my mother.

TELL ME MORE ABOUT YOUR FAMILY

My mother takes care of me.

WHO ELSE IN YOUR FAMILY TAKES CARE OF YOU

My father.

YOUR FATHER

You are like my father in some ways.

WHAT RESEMBLANCE DO YOU SEE

You are not very aggressive but I think you don't want me to notice that.
...and so on.

At the time, many people who interacted with ELIZA became quite quickly and emotionally involved with the program, in part motivating Weizenbaum to write *Computer Power and Human Reason: From Judgment to Calculation*, in which he explained the limitations of computers, and argued against the anthropomorphic views people had of the system he created (Weizenbaum, 1976). Web-based implementations of ELIZA can be found in several places, so one can experience the interaction for oneself.

Robots and interactive virtual graphic charac-ters. With interactive conversational agents, as in the Turing test, the social context – social cues such as facial expressions and gestures, etc. - is taken away, so that the only information one has is the answer to a question displayed on a computer screen. The need to create software agents and robots that can interact with humans in a credible way has motivated more recent research, which has concentrated on building creature-like machines designed to provoke social responses on the part of humans (Bickmore & Picard, 2005; Breazeal, 2002a, 2003). These two types of agent-human systems will be discussed in more detail below, in the context of their use of social psychological theory.

The Place of Social Psychological Theory in the Development of Agent-Based Interaction

Social psychology can be defined as the scientific study of the way in which people's thoughts, feelings, and behaviors are influenced by the real or imagined presence of other people (Allport, 1985). This group of social scientists has had a great deal to say about human to human agent interaction, and their work could potentially make a contribution to the area of human to software/robot agent interaction. This review will not cover the whole of social psychology, as there are some areas of the field that would not provide as great a contribution as others at the present time. For example, there is a great deal of interest in the study of self-perception and self-understanding, including the mechanisms of self-awareness (Carver & Scheier, 1981; Duval & Wicklund, 1972). There are no claims on the part of any researcher in the field of robotics or software agents that these entities have any consciousness or awareness. In addition, although aggression and altruism are also important research areas within social psychology, they will also not be included in this review. We will instead concentrate on the social behavior of animals, the process of social perception, and social exchange theory and interpersonal relations. Following this section we will review work involving the use of social psychological theory in the development if interactive artificial agents.

Social Behavior in Animals

Behavior in lower species provide an interesting analog for understanding the behavior in artificial agents, whether software agents or robots. There has already been a great deal of work in the area of what has come to be called swarm intelligence (Bonabeau, et al., 1999). In this research, social insects, such as ants and bees, are viewed as collective problem solvers, where, although composed of simple interacting organisms, they are collectively able to solve complex problems. Their intelligence lies in the networks of interactions among individu-

als and between individuals and the environment. This analog has been translated into systems where software agents, acting according to simple rules in a virtual environment exhibit complex collective behavior, attempt to solve complex organizational problems (Bonabeau, 2002). This research has been largely concerned with the operation of population-level mechanisms.

Lower species also conduct social interactions at the individual level as well, and perhaps this level can provide some insights to researchers in the areas of robotics and other embodied (yet virtual) agents. Ethologists (Lorenz, Tinbergen, Hinde, and others) have studied animal social behavior both in the laboratory and the field for many years. Three major concepts are important for the purposes of the present chapter: *fixed action patterns, imprinting and imitation.*

A *fixed action pattern* is a response, thought to be innate, that occurs reliably in the presence of identifiable stimuli (called sign stimuli or releasing stimuli). These responses are distinguished from other types of behavior in that, unlike reflexes, they involve numerous muscles and parts of the body; and unlike purposive behavior, the responses are inflexible and run off in a mechanical way (Tinbergen, 1951). A classic example of a fixed action pattern is the aggressive response on the part of a male stickleback fish to the entry of another stickleback into his territory, caused by the sight of the threat posture of the encroaching stickleback. Tinbergen (1951) carried out numerous studies of this behavior and determined that the red belly in the proper orientation, even on an artificial model of a fish, was enough to trigger the response. Thus the red belly is a sign stimulus or releaser for the fixed action pattern of the aggressive response.

The remaining two concepts from ethology are part of the process of learning, particularly in young animals. Learning to distinguish your species from other, potentially harmful species is an important achievement. This can be accomplished in several ways. In some species it is attained during a very brief period in life called a *critical period.* During this early period, certain species of birds engage in a 'following-response' towards the mother. That is, they simply follow behind her because she possesses or exhibits a particular pattern of *releasers* that serves to trigger the behavior, much as the sign stimulus triggers the fixed action pattern. The releaser is composed of several attributes that the species has in common; for example an odor, shape or size, or, in the case of the greylag goose, the movement of the mother, that then triggers a response. Ethologists refer to this process as *imprinting* or the triggering of specific behaviors in the face of a pattern of releasers (Lorenz, 1961). In this case, imprinting has been explained as a primitive form of learning in which an individual finds out about the characteristics of their social group. In humans, the process of imprinting involves a strong emotional response to the mother that is referred to as *attachment*. This process is believed by some researchers to be irreversible, and important for the socialization of the child (Brown, 1965). A fictional portrayal of this process involving artificial agents was portrayed in the film "Artificial Intelligence," when the parents of the eternal child/robot "David" were given specific instructions on how to cause him to begin to perceive and behave toward the female human as "Mother." Though there is currently no actual analog for this process between humans and artificial creatures, Breazeal (2003), in developing Kismet, a sociable robot, used the idea of 'releasers' to encode and mediate the information from the robot's internal and external environments, and to generate an emotional response towards its human partner based on this information.

The final concept from ethology and the study of animal behavior that is relevant to work in agent interaction is *imitation,* which is also considered a primitive form of social learning. Though the topic remains controversial in ethology (Miklosi, 1999), there is a great deal of evidence for the role of imitation in human social learning and cognition in infants (Bandura, 1986). The evidence suggests that infants are able to model novel behaviors that they are physically capable of expressing. Meltzoff and Moore (1989) have demonstrated imitation of facial gestures in infants as young as 42 minutes.

In robotic applications such as household cleaning, building, and elderly care, which involve social interaction, robots will need to be able to coordinate their actions with their human partners. Thus, robots need to be able to recognize the actions of their human partners in order to understand the goals of the actions, and they will need to imitate their behavior as a method for learning new skills. Breazeal and

Scassellati (2002) discuss the problems associated with building robots capable of imitation. Unlike studies of imitation in animal behavior or in infants, where the main goals most often are descriptive or involve the discovery of the mechanisms responsible for producing the behavior, in robotics the goal is to create or generate a behavior with minimal underlying capabilities. Two major issues in the development of robots that are capable of imitation that are currently far from being solved involve: (1) the perception of movement or "how does a robot know *what* to imitate, and (2) representing motor movements, or "how does a robot know *how* to imitate." Although there are differences in methods and goals, Breazeal and Scassellati nonetheless believe that animal research can contribute to work in interactive robotics and vice versa, and that greater understanding of robot imitation and social learning will contribute to our understanding of robot social cognition (Breazeal & Scassellati, 2002).

Interpersonal Behavior

Theories of interpersonal behavior are perhaps the most relevant for current work in artificial agent-human interaction. Social exchange theory forms the basis for later work in this area. The basic idea behind exchange theory is that humans are rational, utility maximizing creatures. Thus, we seek to maximize the social rewards a relationship with another person can provide. Given these assumptions, social exchange theory suggests that how we feel about our relationships is a function of the perception of the rewards we receive and the costs we incur, along with our feelings about what kind of relationship we deserve and the probability of obtaining a better one (Brehm, 1992; Kelley & Thibaut, 1978). When we find ourselves in a relationship with another person (or an artificial agent?) then, we evaluate the costs and benefits of that relationship to ourselves, and if the costs outweigh the benefits we seek to dissolve the relationship.

Even though there is empirical support for social exchange theory, some have criticized its view that people are simply out to get the most reward from a relationship at the least cost. Later versions of social exchange theory have incorporated the concept of equity in a relationship; in other words, we seek fairness in the amount of reward we offer the other person in a relationship and in the costs we incur. Thus, we want to be treated equally, and to the degree that the relationship is perceived as inequitable, we will seek to end it (Walster, Walster, & Berscheid, 1978; Berscheid & Reis, 1998).

Social exchange theory can help us understand what happens after a relationship begins, but what attracts us to other people to begin with? Here the major focus of the work has been on the examination of variables that determine attraction. Among the more important variables are (Berscheid & Reis, 1998):

- **Proximity:** We are more likely to develop relationships with the people who we are physically near.
- **Physical attractiveness:** Although we tend to pair up with those who are most similar to us in attractiveness.
- **Similarity:** We are more likely to be attracted to others who share our attitudes and values.

It is clear that applications that are meant to provide assistance to people, particularly the kind of live-in robotic assistants for the elderly that are envisioned, will be a part of a person's living space for extended periods of time. It thus becomes important to understand the process of developing a long-term relationship with an artificial agent. Research conducted by Bickmore and Picard (2005) is perhaps the best example of the use of concepts from social psychology to understand the interaction between humans and artificial agents. These researchers were interested in the development of long-term relationships with an artificial 'relational' agent. They developed an interactive embodied virtual character (Laura) that would interact with and help to motivate people as they engaged in a month-long exercise program. During the study, participants interacted with the agent on a daily basis over a 30-day period for at least a few minutes, in order to encourage the development of a basic level of relationship. While interaction took place via a kind of interactive chat, the animated character also used body language and facial expression to provide additional social cues. In a 'relational' condition, additional strategies were implemented in the design of the agent to encourage a relationship. For example, in a strategy

involving *meta-relational communication,* the agent would periodically ask how things were going and would offer to make changes if needed. Periodically checking on the status of the relationship would then demonstrate concern and caring for the user (Bickmore & Picard, 2005). In a 'non-relationship' condition, these additional relationship-encouraging strategies were left off.

The results of the experiment suggested that even though there were few statistically significant differences between the experimental groups in their participation in the exercise program, the 'relational' group 'liked' the agent better, felt they had a 'good' relationship (approached statistical significance), showed an interest in continuing the relationship, and, when given the option of giving 'Laura' a sentimental farewell at the end of the program, chose to do this more often than the 'non-relational' group. In interviews conducted after the study, participants' impressions of the agent were very favorable; and they found interacting with 'Laura' very natural (Bickmore & Picard, 2005).

This study represents one of the first attempts to use concepts from the social psychological literature in the design of an artificial agent. Based on the finding of significant effects on relationship measures for the experimental condition in which these (and other) concepts were used, researchers and designers of such systems should begin to apply these techniques more widely. As we continue to explore the nature of the relationship between humans and artificial agents, perhaps the concepts from the social exchange literature might also be useful. Finally, as Bickmore and Picard suggest, agents that function in the role of 'helper' have a special obligation to develop a sense of trust in their human partners. Thus, going forward, research into the development of trust in these types of relationships will be particularly important.

Social Perception

This area of social psychology is concerned with how we form impressions of and make judgments about other people. For instance, what kinds of nonverbal cues are used in our attempts to understand another person's behavior? In addition, social perception concerns how we understand and attribute causes to another person's behavior.

Nonverbal communication. Impression formation will be important for the development of long-term relationships between humans and artificial agents. Part of our impression of another person is based, of course, on what they say to us, but an awful lot of information is derived from nonverbal channels. Work on nonverbal communication, and particularly the communication of emotion via facial expression has been an important focus for research in the area of social perception and impression formation (Ekman, 1965). Nonverbal communication refers to the way in which people communicate, intentionally or unintentionally, without words, including using facial expressions, tone of voice, and body position, among others. The most important of these, for the purposes of this chapter, is the use of facial expressions to communicate emotion. Charles Darwin (1872) is credited with beginning the work in this area with his contention that facial expressions served as a means of communicating information to others in the social group. For example, an expression of disgust may signal that the food I am eating doesn't taste very good; an angry expression may be followed by aggression, etc. Darwin believed that expressions for the so-called primary emotions (anger, happiness, surprise, fear, disgust, and sadness) were universal, that is, anyone, anywhere in the world should be capable of understanding and displaying these expressions. This view has received support, based on a great deal of cross-cultural research over a number of years conducted by Paul Ekman and his colleagues (e.g., Ekman & Friesen, 1975; Ekman, Friesen, & Ellsworth, 1982). Because of the importance of the face for communication of information about the internal state of the organism, designers of interactive systems, including robots, are taking these research findings to heart as they build new systems.

Emotion. In order to develop a complete understanding of how the mind works, most cognitive scientists and some artificial intelligence workers (e.g., Minsky, 2006) believe that it is necessary to understand emotion. In evolutionary terms, emotion may play a critical role in the allocation of cognitive and other resources to areas needed to solve environmental problems (Izard, 1977). Some theorists believe that negative emotions (anger, sadness, etc.) are a signal that some action needs to be taken to bring the organism back into a balanced state, while positive emotions (happiness) signal a more or less balanced, satisfactory state (Frijda, 1994; Plutchik, 1991). The emotion process unfolds as cognitive appraisal systems evaluate environmental conditions, and recruit resources (motor, respiratory, hormonal and other systems) to respond to the environmental appraisals. Facial expressions are also thought to perform a communicative function, giving others in the social group information on the internal state of the organism, providing input on how best to respond. The purpose of this brief explanation is not to provide the reader with a comprehensive understanding of emotion theory, but to emphasize its importance in the creation of interactive agents, and to provide context for the discussion of affective computing.

There are two threads of work in the area of human-agent interaction related to the topic of social perception with particular relevance to the expression and communication of emotion. One is Rosalind Picard's work on *affective computing* (Picard, 1997), which is concerned with the development of computing technologies that are capable of understanding and expressing emotion. Of course, whether computers *have* emotions, or whether they *truly* feel empathy for their human partners is beyond the scope of this research. The major technological difficulties involve developing systems that can understand and express emotion computationally.

Recognizing emotion. The ability on the part of an artificial agent to automatically recognize the emotion of a human agent will be critical to the development of interactive applications. Picard presents a scenario for such an application in this way:

Imagine you are seated with your computer tutor, and suppose that it not only reads your gestural input, musical timing and phrasing, but that it can also read your emotional state. In other words, it not only interprets your musical expression, but also your facial expression, and perhaps other physical changes corresponding to your emotional feelings-maybe heart rate, breathing, blood pressure, muscular tightness, and posture...Given affect recognition, the computer tutor might gauge if it is maintaining your interest during the lesson, before you quit out of frustration and it is too late to try something different. "Am I holding your interest?" it would consider. In the affirmative, it might nudge you with more challenging exercises. If it detects you are frustrated..., then it might slow things down and proffer encouraging feedback. (Picard, 1997, p. 16)

Recognizing emotion will require a variety of skills on the part of the system, each of which present technical challenges to the developers of such a system. Among these requirements are those involving vision and hearing for gathering information about facial expressions, gestures and vocal intonations, but in addition, once the sensory information has been gathered, an interpretation must be made based on knowledge about the situation and knowledge about emotion generation (Picard, 1997). Research suggests that computers are capable of recognizing videotaped actor portrayals of facial expressions of emotion with greater than chance accuracy (e.g., Cohen, et al., 2003), and in more complicated tests involving multimodal systems (Kapoor & Picard, 2005). In the latter study, the goal was to extract, process and interpret naturally occurring non-verbal behavior during natural learning situations, in order to provide personalized assistance to children engaged in learning tasks, a much greater challenge for the system. The researchers obtained data on facial features and head gestures, as well as data from a posture-sensing chair, which were then fed into feature extraction processes and the data classified as to whether interest was being expressed. The system achieved an overall accuracy rate of 86%, which was significantly better than using the individual sensory modalities alone. The challenge for this research area continues to be, as the Kapoor and Picard study suggests, being able to interpret multi-modal data in real time, in naturalistic settings, for ongoing emotional states involving constantly changing expressive states; and while an 86% accuracy rate is significantly better than chance, is it good enough for applications that seek to provide accurate and timely feedback to their human partners?

Expression of emotion. Picard (1997) has similarly developed criteria that need to be met in order for computers to be said to express emotion. These include *input,* in which the computer receives instructions about which emotion to express; *feedback,*

which concerns the fact that, in humans, affective expressions can influence an ongoing affective state, as demonstrated in several laboratory experiments (Laird & Bresler, 1992). Other criteria proposed by Picard include *social display rules* or what are the relevant social norms that determine when, where, and how emotions are expressed; and the *output from the expressive process*, including changing facial expressions, posture or gait, or vocal signals. Each of these present enormously complicated technical challenges, let alone in combination, which is why, to date we have seen few examples of such systems. One exception to this is the work of Cynthia Breazeal, and her group's work on the development of socially engaging robots. She is also greatly interested in the development of emotion sensing and expressive systems for use in the service of humans.[1*]

The Sociable Machines Project at MIT is responsible for building Kismet, an expressive, anthropomorphic robot, capable of interacting in a social way with humans (Breazeal, 2003). In a nutshell (and greatly oversimplifying the entire process), the robot is capable of expressing emotions based on a complex system of sensors, drives (e.g., being over or under stimulated by an interacting human partner), and a perceptual system that keeps track of external and internal events. There is an emotion system comprised of an appraisal subsystem, which takes the results of the perceptual system and computes a value which it then hands to an emotion activation subsystem to make a decision about which emotion would be most appropriate, based on the value handed off from the appraisal subsystem. Finally, the motor system takes the result from the emotion system and generates the appropriate facial expression and posture. The robot is capable of conducting an ongoing interaction with a human partner in real time, in which the behavior of the human influences the emotional state of the robot and where the goal of the partner is to keep the robot's *drives* satisfied. This basically takes the form of keeping the robot awake and stimulated, but not overly stimulated, in which case the robot perceives threat and responds accordingly through appropriate facial expression and posture.

Breazeal and her colleagues also conducted a series of studies in which they examined the degree to which people categorized Kismet's facial expressions into one of seven categories of emotional expression. Whether they observed the expressions on a still photograph or saw Kismet model these expressions via videotape, the participants (which consisted of a group of 12 year old children and a group of adults) were able to correctly categorize the expressions significantly more often than by chance. Further, while "scolding" the robot during interactive sessions, the robot's sad face and body posture caused some participants to report that they felt 'terrible' or 'guilty,' perhaps evidence for the human partner experiencing a sense of empathy with the robot (Breazeal, 2003).

Taken as a whole, the work of Picard and Breazeal shows a great deal of promise for the development of systems that are capable of interacting with humans in a credible way. One example of a system that would have a great deal of practical value is a Furby-like creature that could serve as a companion for elderly people. Of course, such a system would have to be extremely easy to use as well as reliable; a person would need to be able to get it up and running easily, and it should not need a team of computer scientists and mechanical engineers to keep it running. Much more likely in the near future are learning technologies of the sort discussed above, combining multi-modal feedback from the learner to the system with the ability to tailor lessons to a learner on the fly based on this feedback. The acquisition of this feedback is a problem at present, requiring special headsets and, if physiological data is required, straps and sensors that provide ways of measuring processes like blood pressure and heart rate.

Attribution theory. Attribution theory is concerned with how we attribute cause to a person's behavior. People engage in this process as they attempt to understand the relationship between social situations and behavior, and predict future outcomes based on past occurrences of behavior. For instance, when we consider why a person stole another person's wallet, are we likely to place more weight on the person as causal agent, that is, to make a *dispositional* attribution? Or are we more likely to place greater weight on the environment, which would constitute a *situational* attribution? Such questions have intrigued social psychologists for years, beginning with Heider (1958), who developed most of the basic ideas and vocabulary. Once again, rather than attempt a comprehensive review of research and theory in this area, we will

survey some of the major theoretical and empirical contributions, and then, because there has been no direct application of these ideas, we will speculate on their relevance to agent interaction.

Jones and Davis developed *correspondent inference theory* to understand the way in which we make internal (dispositional) attributions, or how we *infer* dispositions from *corresponding* behaviors (Jones, 1990; Jones & Davis, 1965). The theory is concerned with how we narrow down our choices for the dispositions that we think might have caused a particular behavior to occur. To do this, we look for what Jones and Davis call *non-common effects*, that is, effects or consequences of a particular behavior that could not be produced by another behavior or course of action. For example, suppose a friend decides to take a job at an investment bank in San Francisco. If we want to understand why this person chose this particular job we need some way of narrowing down our choices for an explanation. Correspondent inference theory suggests that we look for other choices our friend could have made, and examine the effects of the second choice. If the second choice produces effects that the first cannot, for instance, if we learn that our friend turned down a job working at a non-profit agency in rural Oklahoma, there would seem to be little overlap between the effects of the first choice and the second. In other words, there would be a large number of non-common effects. If this were the case, it would be more difficult for us to determine what caused the choice of jobs. If, on the other hand, we find out that our friend turned down a job at a consulting firm in San Francisco before accepting the job at the bank, we can narrow down the causal factors more easily, because there is more overlap between the effects. In this case there would be few non-common effects.

While correspondent inference theory focuses only on dispositional attributions, Harold Kelley's *covariation model* dealt with how people initially decide whether to make an internal (dispositional) or external (situational) attribution (Kelley, 1967). Kelley assumes that when we are in the process of forming judgments about another person, we gather information with which we can test hypotheses. We then look at the pieces of information that *covary* with other pieces, as if we are conducting a statistical test, and base our judgment on these pieces of information. Where does the information come from? There are three sources: first we call on our knowledge of or guess about the way a person has acted in similar situations (distinctiveness data), second, the way a person has acted in the same situation in the past (consistency data), and third, the way other people have acted in the same situation (consistency data). For example, in trying to decide why Jeff liked a particular movie, we consider how Jeff and others who have seen the film respond to it, and how they have responded to films like it in the past. If Jeff basically raves about all films of this type, or if others who have seen it are not enthusiastic, we are likely to attribute dispositional causes to Jeff's behavior. If Jeff rarely raves about films of this type or any other type, or if others also rave about it, we are inclined to make a situational attribution, that there was something about the film that caused his behavior. As with correspondent inference theory, there is a great deal of empirical support for Kelley's model (Ross & Nisbett, 1991).

Much of the research in social psychology tends to take place in a controlled laboratory environment, and while the theories discussed above have been confirmed in these types of settings, some interesting, somewhat contradictory findings have also emerged. Whenever you tend to find a character in a movie so compelling that you suspend disbelief and feel sadness at their misfortune for instance, you are making a mistake in judgment about this person. In reality, this person was an actor whose situation dictated that she behave in a certain way, yet we seem unable to view the person's behavior in an objective light. Though this may seem like an extreme example, results from laboratory experiments suggest that our judgment, in some cases is biased by our readiness to attribute the behavior of others to their dispositions. This tendency is referred to as the *fundamental attribution error.* In a classic experiment on this concept, groups of college students were asked to read an essay written by a fellow student that either supported or opposed the rule of Fidel Castro in Cuba. Half the participants were told that the writer had freely chosen their position before writing the paper, while the other half were told that the students had been assigned the topic beforehand. The participants were then asked to what degree the writer actually supported the position she wrote about. Logically, the participants should have concluded that being assigned the topic

would not indicate actual support for the position; instead, the participants concluded that the authors actually supported their positions, whether they had freely chosen the topic or not (Jones & Harris, 1967). Thus, in general we tend to underestimate the role of the situation when making attributions about another's behavior, however, when judging the causes of our own behavior, we tend to be biased in the other direction, towards seeing situational components as the major cause. This is referred to by social psychologists as the *actor/observer bias* (Ross & Nisbett, 1991).

It is unclear just how the findings of attribution theory will be applied to the design of agent-human interactions. Breazeal (2003) has suggested that one of the next steps in the evolution of socially interactive robots like Kismet is that they be capable of acquiring mental models of other people. Scassellati (2000) has taken an important first step in this direction by examining the processes involved in shared attention. Going beyond this level, should designers build in the same reasoning biases that humans have, like the fundamental attribution error, into the systems they build? This would presumably cause the system to make the same errors in judgment as a human. Would these errors make the system seem more human? Or would it cause a human observer to feel more negatively towards the system ("Stupid robot!"), and thus be less likely to trust it? After all, aren't computers supposed to be logical? Or would we view the system as more unfeeling if it did not occasionally make mistakes? The answer would seem to be that it depends on the purpose for which the system was constructed. For a conversational system or one designed as a companion it would seem better to have the system appear as human-like as possible. In the interpersonal attraction literature this is known as the *similarity* effect; the more similar we are, the more I may like you (Berscheid & Reis, 1998). On the other hand, for a system designed for use in dangerous environments with a human partner, biased reasoning processes when it comes to making judgments about other people or the environment could be dangerous, and so should not be built in. In short, the ability to reason about the interpersonal environment would seem to be of some importance in the design of interactive systems if what we are interested in is the construction of artificial minds.

Agent-Based Modeling and Social Psychological Theory

There are two distinct strands in the agent literature that have utilized social psychological theory. One strand in this effort has used theory and research findings to develop new technologies, so their primary purpose has been on the engineering side. We have talked at great length in this chapter about this research. Representative of this approach is the work of Bickmore and Picard (2005), discussed above, and their use of the literature on human interpersonal relationships in the development of a software agent. Also representative of the engineering approach is the work of Breazeal and her colleagues, who have utilized work on the display and communication of emotion to develop socially engaging robots, and Rosalind Picard, who has pioneered the work on machine detection of affective states in human partners.

The second strand in the agent literature, which will only be briefly described here, uses agent-based modeling methods in the study of social psychological processes. In this research, the focus has been on the emergence of patterns relevant to social phenomena from the interaction of a group of autonomous software agents, programmed with a few simple rules. The approach has been referred to as *generative* in that, a phenomenon is explained by postulating underlying mechanisms that, through their interaction, generate the phenomenon. The phenomenon is said to emerge as a result of the interaction of the underlying mechanisms (Epstein, 1999; Smith & Conrey, 2007).

The use of simulation to develop and test theories in the social sciences has a long history (Abelson, 1963). In contrast to the generative approach to theory building discussed above, these programs embody a particular theory of social and/or cognitive process. Robert Abelson (1963) was one of the first social psychologists to develop computer simulations of social cognition. One of his first efforts was the development of a program that simulated Heider's Balance Theory (Heider, 1958), which suggests that if a person holds contradictory thoughts, the person must rationalize the contradiction, or change one of the thoughts in order to bring the process into balance. For example, the statement "my simulation produced silly results" contains a thought that is positively valued in the person's belief system (my simulation) and a thought that is negatively valued (silly results). According to Heider, holding these contradictory thoughts causes discomfort until the person is able to somehow balance the values by somehow rationalizing the negatively valued thought. Abelson's program took statements that were out of balance and attempted to bring the statement into balance so that it would fit into a pre-determined simulation of a belief system.

One of the first social scientists to use a generative approach was Thomas Schelling (1978). He explored the question of whether segregation can arise from a group of agents who do not explicitly desire segregation. His program used the simple rule that if the population with your 'color' fell below a certain percentage in your neighborhood, move to an empty space on a virtual grid. The pattern that emerged upon running the simulation to completion was that the populations appeared completely segregated. Thus, the motive to not be in a minority in one's neighborhood, not a desire to be segregated appeared to cause this pattern.

Following Schelling, Robert Axelrod, a political scientist at the University of Michigan designed a series of computer tournaments, which would have the effect of evaluating strategies for winning an iterated Prisoner's Dilemma. However, he also used these results to try to answer the 'generative' question: can cooperation *emerge* from the interactions of rational self-interested individuals (Axelrod, 1984). Axelrod has continued to generate interesting research on these questions, which have some applicability to real world issues such as conflict resolution (Axelrod, 1997).

The agents in Axelrod's research represent entities stripped of everything psychological except self-interest; thus, these agents provide social scientists with tremendous control over extraneous variables like emotion, feelings of empathy, or other relationship-oriented variables that human beings possess. They represent the process of social exchange at its most fundamental level. Thus game theory is often used in this type of research because it contains simplifying assumptions about social behavior (basically that we are rational, self-interested creatures) that are appropriate for modeling the interaction between two or more human agents or between computational agents.

For those seeking more information about the generative approach in social science, Smith & Conrey (2007) have written an excellent article in which they provide a justification for the use of an agent-based approach to the development and testing of theory in social psychology. They also provide a review of the use of the generative approach in social psychology and the social sciences in general, and a comprehensive bibliography which should serve as a guide for the interested reader.

CONCLUSION

We have reviewed theories and research in social psychology that may be of interest to researchers and those engaged in the design of interactive technologies. Beginning with a detour into the philosophical literature and a summary of Dennett's concept of the intentional system, the chapter subsequently examined the Turing test, as well as conversational systems that utilize written verbal means of communication only, such as ELIZA. The contribution of social psychological (including animal social behavior) concepts was then surveyed, as well as the application of these concepts to research in agent-human interaction. We reviewed selected theories in interpersonal relations, along with their application to an understanding of long-term relations between humans and artificial agents in the work of Bickmore and Picard. The survey also included concepts from social perception, with special attention to the use of emotion as a method of communicating the state of an organism, along with applications from the work of Picard and Breazeal to artificial agents. Attribution theory, the study of how we draw conclusions about the causes of an agent's behavior - are they inside the agent (personality) or outside (environment)? - was discussed, and though there have been no direct applications of this particular set of theories to agent-human interaction to date, if agents are to seem life-like, should they be subject to the same attribution biases as a human? A different strand of research, in which artificial agents are used to simulate social processes was then examined. This area has received renewed interest from social scientists, in part because of the computational power of modern personal computing platforms, and the availability of simulation software. Smith and Con-

rey (2007) have surveyed the major contributions to the literature and argued for the use of agent-based modeling in the development and testing of theory in social psychology. Finally, though the issues of whether artificial agents are truly intelligent, or are really capable of having feelings, or attaining consciousness, though important issues, may never have a final resolution. Philosophers and scientists will continue to debate these questions, but until we have a better grasp on what it means for a *human* to be conscious, or intelligent, or have emotions, it is premature to speculate about how these processes manifest themselves in an artificial being.

It is hoped that the present chapter inspires researchers and designers concerned with researching and developing interactive technologies to investigate the literature in the field of social psychology more closely. In a review such as this, one can only scratch the surface of the concepts and issues in this field, knowing that most of the ideas that have inspired researchers for many years cannot be given the space that they deserve. The field of human-computer interaction encompasses many researchers from many different backgrounds, who have come together to solve some of the most complex problems in computer science, engineering, and psychology. It behooves researchers from these areas to learn as much as they can from each other (and from fields like ethology and animal behavior, anthropology, and linguistics), because it is only as a truly interdisciplinary field that these problems can be solved. The applications resulting from this collaboration: live-in companions who can provide a psychological dimension to their interaction, workers who are able to learn new skills from their human counterparts, tutors who are genuinely able to enrich the learning experience for both children and adults, can be a great benefit to humans.

FUTURE RESEARCH DIRECTIONS

The future for the topic of this chapter, the contribution of social psychological theory to understanding and developing systems that engage in social interactions, looks very bright. The history of research efforts along these lines lies mainly in two unrelated bodies of work; first, there is the research that has sought to develop and test social theory using agent simulation (Abelson, 1965; Axelrod, 1984, 1997; Axtell & Epstein, 1999). These efforts represent a viable alternative and a complement to the current use of laboratory, ethnographic, and survey methods, characterized by Smith and Conrey (2007) as *Variable Based Modeling* as opposed to *Agent Based Modeling*. One of the advantages of such an approach for social scientists is that they are not limited in the scope of their research. That is, one is not constrained to conduct analyses at the level of the 'individual' actor, as most social psychological research is. One can create individual agents that act as nodes in a connectionist cognitive network, or agents that simulate the social networks within a large organization; the choice is up to the ingenuity of the researcher.

For researchers and designers of interactive systems the challenges include incorporating mechanisms whereby the agents are able to learn from their human partners. The interaction between human and artificial agent is most often represented as a parent-infant form of relationship. Thus, the development of systems that are capable of some form of imitation, which is thought to be one of the more primitive forms of social learning, is an important goal of this area of research and development. In addition, the ability of an agent to begin to take an intentional stance toward their human partners, in other words, to begin to reason about the behavior of their partners, as discussed in the section on attribution theory, would be a significant milestone towards the development of artificial agents who are able to reason in a social way.

REFERENCES

Abelson, R. P. (1963). Computer simulation of 'hot' cognition. In S. S. Tomkins & S. Messick (Eds.), *Computer simulation of personality:Frontier of psychological research* (pp. 277-298). New York: John Wiley & Sons.

Allport, G. W. (1985). The historical background of social psychology. In G. Lindzey & E. Aronson (Eds.), *The handbook of social psychology* (Vol. 1, pp. 1-46). Reading, MA: Addison-Wesley.

Axelrod, R. (1984). *The evolution of cooperation.* New York: Basic Books.

Axelrod, R. (1997). *The complexity of cooperation: agent-based models of competition and collaboration.* New Jersey: Princeton University Press.

Bandura, A. (1986). *Social foundations of thought and action: a social cognitive theory.* Englewood Cliffs, New Jersey: Prentice-Hall.

Berscheid, E., & Reis, H. (1998). Attraction and close relationships. In D. Gilbert, S. Fiske & G. Lindzey (Eds.), *The handbook of social psychology* (pp. 19-281). New York: McGraw-Hill.

Bickmore, T. W., & Picard, R. W. (2005). Establishing and maintaining long-term human-computer relationships. *ACM Trans. Comput.-Hum. Interact., 12*(2), 293-327.

Bonabeau, E., Dorigo, M., & Theraulaz, G. (1999). *Swarm intelligence: from natural to artificial systems.* USA: Oxford University Press.

Bonabeau, E. (2002). Agent-based modeling: methods and techniques for simulating human systems. *Proceedings of the National Academy of Sciences, 99*, 7280-7287.

Breazeal, C., & Scassellatti, B. (2002). Robots that imitate humans. *Trends in Cognitive Sciences, 6*(11), 481-487.

Breazeal, C. (2002). *Designing sociable robots.* Cambridge, Massachusetts: MIT Press.

Breazeal, C. (2003). Emotion and sociable human robots. *International Journal of Human-Computer Studies, 59*, 119-155.

Brehm, S. (1992). *Intimate relationships.* New York: McGraw-Hill.

Brown, R. (1965). *Social psychology.* New York: Free Press.

Carver, C. S., & Scheier, M. F. (1981). *Attention and self-regulation: a control-theory approach to human behavior.* New York: Springer-Verlag.

Cohen, I., Sebe, N., Garg, A., Chen, L. S., & Huang, T. S. (2003). Facial expression recognition from video sequences: temporal and static modeling. *Computer Vision and Image Understanding, 91*, 160-187.

Darwin, C. (1872). *The expression of emotions in man and animals.* London: John Murray.

Dennett, D. (1978). *Brainstorms*. Cambridge, Massachusetts: MIT Press.

Dennett, D. (1989). *The intentional stance*. Cambridge, Massachusetts: MIT Press.

Duval, S., & Wicklund, R. A. (1972). *A theory of objective self-awareness*. New York: Academic Press.

Ekman, P. (1965). Communication through non-verbal behavior: a source of information about an interpersonal relationship. In S. S. Tomkins (Ed.), *Affect, cognition, and personality* (pp. 390-442). New York: Springer-Verlag.

Ekman, P., & Friesen, W. V. (1975). *Unmasking the face*. Englewood Cliffs, New Jersey: Prentice-Hall.

Ekman, P., Friesen, W. V., & Ellsworth, P. (1982). What are the similarities and differences in facial behavior across cultures. In P. Ekman (Ed.), *Emotion in the human face* (pp. 56-97). Cambridge, England: Cambridge University Press.

Epstein, J. M. (1999). Agent-based computational models and generative social science. *Complexity, 4*(5), 41-60.

Frijda, N. Emotions are functional, most of the time. In P. Ekman & R. Davidson (Eds.), The nature of emotion (pp. 11-122). New York: Oxford University Press.

Heider, F. (1958). *The psychology of interpersonal relations*. New York: John Wiley & Sons.

Izard, C. (1977). *Human emotions*. New York: Plenum Press.

Jones, E. E., & Davis, K. E. (1965). From acts to dispositions: the attribution process in social psychology. In L. Berkowitz (Ed.), *Advances in experimental social psychology* (Vol. 2, pp. 219-266). New York: Academic Press.

Jones, E. E., & Harris, V. A. (1967). The attribution of attitudes. *Journal of Experimental Social Psychology, 3*, 1-24.

Jones, E. E. (1990). *Interpersonal perception*. New York: Freeman.

Kapoor, A., & Picard, R. W. (2005). *Multimodal affect recognition in learning environments*. Paper presented at ACM international conference on Multimedia, Singapore.

Kelley, H. H. (1967). Attribution theory in social psychology. In D. Levine (Ed.), *Nebraska symposium on motivation* (Vol. 15, pp. 192-238). Lincoln: University of Nebraska Press.

Kelley, H. H., & Thibaut, J. W. (1978). *Interpersonal relations: a theory of interdependence*. New York: John Wiley & Sons.

Laird, J. D., & Bresler, C. (1992). The process of emotional feeling: a self-perception theory. In M. Clark (Ed.), *Emotion: Review of Personality and Social Psychology* (Vol. 13, pp. 223-234). Newbury Park, CA: Sage.

Lorenz, K. (1961). *King solomon's ring*. London: Methuen.

Maes, P. (1995). Intelligent software. *Scientific American, 273*, 84-86.

Meltzoff, A. N., & Moore, M. K. (1989). Imitation in newborn infants:exploring the range of gestures imitated and the underlying mechanisms. *Developmental Psychology, 25*, 954-962.

Meltzoff, A. N., & Decety, J. (2003). What imitation tells us about social cognition: a rapprochement between developmental psychology and cognitive neuroscience. *Philosophical Transactions of the Royal Society of London, 358*, 491-500.

Miklosi, A. (1999). The ethological analysis of imitation. *Biological Reviews, 74*, 347-374.

Minsky, M. (2006). *The emotion machine: commonsense thinking, artificial intelligence, and the future of the human mind*. New York: Simon & Schuster.

Picard, R. (1997). *Affective computing*. Cambridge, Massachusetts: MIT Press.

Plutchik, R. *The emotions*. Lanham, MD: University Press of America.

Reeves, B., & Nass, C. (1996). *The media equation: how people treat computers, television, and new me-*

dia like real people and places. Stanford, CA: Center for the Study of Language and Information.

Rogers, C. (1951). *Client centered therapy.* Boston: Houghton-Mifflin.

Ross, L., & Nisbett, R. (1991). *The person and the situation.* New York: McGraw-Hill.

Scassellati, B. (2000). *Foundations for a theory of mind for a humanoid robot.* Unpublished Ph.D. Thesis, MIT, Cambridge, Massachusetts.

Schelling, T. (1978). *Micromotives and macrobehavior* New York: Norton.

Smith, E. R., & Conrey, F. R. (2007). Agent-based modeling: a new approach for theory building in social psychology. *Personality and Social Psychology Review, 11*(1), 87-104.

Tinbergen, N. (1951). *The study of instinct.* New York: Oxford University Press.

Turing, A. (1950). Computing machinery and intelligence. *Mind, 59,* 433-460.

Weizenbaum, J. (1966). Eliza: a computer program for the study of natural language communication between man and machine. *CACM, 10,* 474-480.

Weizenbaum, J. (1976). *Computer power and human reason* W.H. Freeman & Company.

ENDNOTE

[1]   Of course, there are many other individuals in artificial intelligence and robotics engaged in the same types of research or closely related research; however, Breazeal's work is an excellent representative for the collective efforts in this field.

Chapter IV
Predictive Models of Cultural Information Transmission

M. Afzal Upal
Defence R&D, Canada

ABSTRACT

This chapter will critically review existing approaches to the modeling transmission of cultural information and advocate a new approach based on a new generation of agent-based social simulation systems. It will outline how such systems can be useful for studying the formation of patterns of widely shared cultural beliefs.

INTRODUCTION

Intuitively, most people seem to understand the term **'culture'** as it is used in everyday conversation[1]; however, it remains a notoriously difficult concept to pin down precisely. A 1952 review identified 164 definitions of **culture** (Kroeber & Kluckhohn, 1952) and the situation has not improved since. Modern cultural scientists often resort to metaphors such as an onion or an iceberg to define **culture**. The idea is that culture is a hierarchy consisting of multiple layers, many of which are hidden from view. For instance, Hofstede's cultural onion (Figure 1) consists of publicly observable symbols–gestures, pictures, words/jargon, hairstyles, and flags–as the outermost

layer. Heroes–idealized people, dead or alive, seen as possessing highly prized characteristics–form the next layer. Rituals–group activities seen as essential by the group but superfluous to the achievement of the actual goal, carried out for their own sake–form the third layer. The core of a culture consists of shared beliefs about how things should be.

Each of the layers can be further deconstructed into multiple sublayers. For instance, the privately-held widely-shared beliefs of a cultural group can be further divided into beliefs about the social world, beliefs about the physical world, and beliefs about other groups, etc. Another source of complexity is the fact that aspects at any level and sublevel are related to aspects at other levels and sublev-

Figure 1. Hofstede's cultural onion

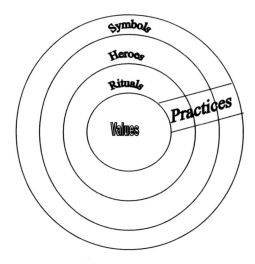

els. Elaborating this view, Bloch (2000), argues that "**culture**s form consistent wholes ... every element–wherever it came from–was moulded to fit in with the others because of a psychological need for integration which led to an organically patterned 'world view'" (p. 197).

Despite the complexity, understanding **culture** has been important for several disciplines including anthropology, sociology, and social and cross-cultural psychology. The work in these fields has contributed to our understanding of certain aspects of culture, for instance, we have several quantitative measures of cultural differences among a variety of nations (Hofstede 1994). However, this work has been criticized for failing to develop computationally predictive models of culture that would allow us to explain the macro-level cultural patterns in terms of individual level cognitive tendencies and make testable predictions about the future direction of a society (Gilbert & Conte 1995; Laland & Odling-Smee 2000). The challenge then is to design models that can not only account for multiple layers of culture and the rich connections between these layers, without abstracting away the complexity, but are also computationally predictive at the same time.

A complete theory of culture may also be able to satisfactorily explain how cultural layers come to be formed. Historically, we know that cultural

patterns seem to pass like waves on the shores of time with each new wave rearranging the lines made by the previous waves. For instance, last few centuries of Western European art history is a story of dynamism with one trend of cultural innovation following another. Any two waves that are temporally contiguous in history appear to have a paradoxical relationship with each other. The new trend is both defined in opposition to the old one and as a continuation and improvement of the old trend. Visual arts are certainly not the only aspect of culture to exhibit this pattern. Other cultural trends including religious doctrines, pop cultural trends, and patterns of political thought also appear to evolve similarly. Thus Lutheranism builds on Catholicism while it also reforms it and seems to stand in opposition to it. Postmodernist art builds on Modernist art while at the same time redefining it. Explaining these pattern of stability and change in the evolution of cultural trends is a question of central importance for the social sciences.

Several critics of traditional cultural theory have offered alternatives to the standard verbal and/or mathematical modeling approaches. The alternatives include: *memetics* **and** *agent-based social simulation*. Next, I critically examine these alternatives and suggest a new promising approach based on a multi-agent architecture specifically designed to lead to a computational model of cultural **information transmission**.

MEMETICS

Memetics is the study of culture inspired by Dawkins (1989) who coined the term *meme* to refer to a discrete unit of cultural information that is transmitted from one mind to another analogously to the way in which a gene propagates from one organism to another as a unit of genetic information. Dawkins argued that different aspects of culture, such as different tunes, catch-phrases, religious beliefs, and clothing fashions, compete to occupy mental space, similar to the competition among genes to be included in the DNA. Thus, only those ideas that are best fit for a mind are remembered and communicated to others, becoming widely-shared cultural beliefs. While the general idea has been well received, translating it into a viable research program has run into several difficulties. The first problem is finding a universally accepted way of dividing cultural information into discrete units. Cultural information seems to be too cohesive and well connected to yield to any single way of carving it up at the joints. There is also little evidence that the human mind is a replicating machine which simply makes a copy of the information it receives from others. Instead, when cultural information, such as a catch-phrase or a folk tale, spreads from one person to another, it seems to go through complex series of filters before being reproduced.

People have to integrate the new information they receive through their senses into their existing world model. The comprehension process involves a complex two-way interaction between the newly received information and the knowledge that an individual possesses prior to learning. The newly obtained information may result in revision of some of the previously held beliefs. Finally, an individual may decide to communicate this information to others if he/she believes that taking the communication actions serves the speaker's goals (Grice, 1969). Thus, sometimes there may be a causal relationship between an individual receiving a message *A* and then uttering a message *B* with *A* and *B* having some syntactic and/or semantic similarities with each other but that is not universally true. Not all messages that are received are equally likely to cause transmission of future messages. Thus informational messages are replicated with too low

fidelity to perform a gene-like role in transmission of cultural information (Sperber 2000). This makes it hard, if not impossible, to use the abstractions employed in genetic evolutionary theory or in epidemiology to devise closed form mathematical models of cultural **information transmission** of any predictive value. In fact, understanding and modeling the comprehension, belief revision, and communication biases that people have may be useful to figuring out the kind of social patterns that are likely to arise at the societal level.

One of the biases that people have is the bias to pay more attention to expectation violating objects and events (Schank 1979). Holders of this bias could have been evolutionarily favored because they may have been better able to identify gaps in their existing world model and take advantage of the learning opportunities offered to them by novel events and objects around them and build more predictive models of their environment (Upal 2005a; Upal *et al.* 2007). A number of recent studies have shown that people do in fact better remember and recall counterintuitive ideas but that the relationship between the amount of counterintuitiveness and recall is not linear; that objects and events that are too counterintuitive are actually recalled less well (Barrett & Nyhoff 2001; Boyer & Ramble 2001; Gonce *et al.* 2006). Thus the objects and events that are minimally counterintuitive i.e., they only violate expectations about one feature (such as a talking tree) are best recalled when compared with intuitive objects that do not violate any expectations (e.g., a green tree) or maximally counterintuitive concepts that violate multiple expectations (e.g., a blinking talking tree). Anthropologists (Boyer 1994; Sperber 1996) have argued that this bias results in most of the widespread religious concepts being minimally counterintuitive.

Previously, we have argued that context in which concepts are embedded plays a critical role in the memorabilty of a concept i.e., minimally counterintuitive ideas are only more memorable when the context in which they are embedded makes them expectation violating concepts (Upal 2005a; Upal *et al.* 2007). Thus concepts that are counterintuitive in one context may be intuitive in another context. To get attention in the new context then concepts have to somehow appear counterintuitive in the new context. One way for this to happen is for the new concepts to be even more counterintuitive thus ratcheting up counterintuitiveness. Hence the concepts which may have been perceived as maximally counterintuitive in the original context come to be minimally counterintuitive in the new context and exploit transmission advantages of greater memorability. Ratcheting or snowballing of counterintuitiveness may help explain why some concepts such as God which appear maximally counterintuitive to us today are still prevalent in widespread religions and how interlinked layers of beliefs come to be (Upal 2008).

My main point here, however, is that in order to have a predictive theory of cultural **information transmission**, we need to take into account people's memory biases. **Memetics**, and epidemiological models of information transmission (Watts 2002) as currently formulated to abstract away these details by appealing to mathematical evolutionary models or mathematical epidemiological models are not likely to lead to predictive models cultural information transmission.

AGENT-BASED SOCIAL SIMULATION (ABSS)

The key idea behind **agent-based social simulation (ABSS)** is to design simple bottom-up computer models of individuals using software modules (called *agents*) and allow the agents to interact with each other through a few simple interaction rules. If any social patterns emerge then it is easy to identify individual cognitive tendencies and social interactions that cause them. This allows the ABS researchers to tease apart the micro-macro causal links by carefully making one local change at a time and by analyzing its impact on the emergent social patterns. For instance, Thomas Schelling, one of the early pioneers of the ABS approach, designed 1500 agents that lived on a 500 x 500 board (Schelling 1971). The agent's cognitive structure consisted of one simple inference rule, namely, if the proportion of your different colored neighbors is above a tolerance threshold then move to a different cell, otherwise stay at your current location. He showed that even populations entirely consisting of agents

with high tolerance end up living in segregated neighborhoods. Since Schelling's pioneering work, the ABS systems have been used to discover possible explanations of a number of social patterns. Thus we now know the local interaction patterns that can give rise to the emergence of complex patterns of social networks. If individuals prefer to establish connections with well connected individuals then a society is likely to have scale free network structure with a few people having a large number of social connections while a vast majority have a small number of friends (Barabasi 2002).

As successful as the ABS strategy has been, it has not been able to explain the emergence of complex layers of cultural patterns that characterize human cultures. To understand why it is so difficult to simulate such patterns, we need to better understand the key notion of emergence better. Emergence is not magic–even though it is treated as such by some in the ABS community. Social patterns that are seen after running an **agent-based simulation** are *a direct consequence* of the internal cognitive structure of the agent's cognitive decision-making rules and agent-interaction rules even when we cannot foresee those consequences. This means that agent-structures and their interaction rules have to have certain properties to lead to the emergence of particular social patterns. Emergent social patterns are strongly constrained by the internal agent structure and agent interaction rules. For instance, if agent memory capacity is one-bit (Bainbridge 1995; Doran 1998; Epstein 2001; Bainbridge 2006) then society of such agents can never have multiple beliefs much less richly connected beliefs that make cultural patterns what they are.

In order to have societies with complex shared beliefs, individual agents need to be able to represent such beliefs and be able to acquire and modify them. The problem is that normative knowledge acquisition and belief revision are computationally intractable and simulating even a single agent that can perform these tasks in real time is not possible, hence designing cognitively-rich multiagent simulations that can be run efficiently is one of the greatest challenges facing those interested in creating simulations of layered cultural patterns. I believe that one way to address this challenge is to house the cognitively rich agents in synthetic "toy-domains" that are just complex enough to exercise the enhanced knowledge representation and reasoning capabilities of cognitively-rich agents but not too complex to make the simulation intractable. I will illustrate this approach with the help of a synthetic domain called Multiagent Wumpus World. Before, describing this domain, however, I will talk about a cognitively-rich **agent-based social simulation** architecture called the CCI-Architecture that I have designed to study the transmission of cultural information.

COMMUNICATING, COMPREHENDING, AND INTEGRATING (CCI) AGENTS

The CCI agents attempt to comprehend the information they perceive through their sensors, integrate it with their prior knowledge and take the action they perceive as best in a given situation. The possible actions an agent can undertake include comprehension actions, speech actions, and movement actions. The CCI agents are goal directed agents that plan

sequences of actions to achieve their goals. Agents attempt to build accurate models of their environment by acquiring information about cause-effect relationships among various environmental stimuli. At each instant, agents sense their environment and decide what action to take.

The CCI agents are comprehension driven. They attempt to explain their observations using their existing knowledge and their causal reasoning engine. On observing an effect *OE*, an agent searches for a cause *C* that could have produced that effect. If multiple causes are available then the agent may have to reason to eliminate some of the possible causes to select the most likely cause for the current observations. The assumed cause *AC* allows the agent to make some further predictions about the unobserved effects of the assumed cause. The assumed effects *(AEs)* deduced from *ACs* are added to the agent's world model which helps the agent form expectations about aspects of the world that the agent has not observed yet. Agent may also be able to observe causes. The observed causes *(OCs)* allow the agent to predict the effects *(PEs)* of those causes.

Figure 2. A 10 x 10 version of the Multiagent Wumpus World (MWW) domain. This version has 10 agents, 10 Wumpuses, and 10 Treasures.

Agents also sense actions performed by other agents that are in the vicinity of the observing agent and attempt to comprehend those actions. Other agents are assumed to be intentional agents and hence causes of their actions are those agent's intentions. The CCI agents ignore the information received from others if they cannot find any justification for it. Inferring these intentions allows the observing agent to make predictions about the future behavior of the agent.

An agent *A* may decide to send a message *M* to an agent *B* that happens to be within listening distance if it believes that sending *B* the message M will result in changing *B*'s mental state to cause it to perform an action *C* which can help *A* achieve some of its goals.

At every instant, agents consult their knowledge-base to form expectations about the future. If these expectations are violated, they attempt to explain the reasons for these violations and if they can find those explanations, they revise their world model.

We have embedded the CCI agents into the Multiagent Wumpus World (MWW) domain shown in Figure 2. MWW is an extension of Russell and Norvig's (2003) single agent Wumpus World and is inspired by the well known minesweeper game where an agent's objective is to navigate a minefield while looking for rewards.

Multiagent Wumpus World (MWW)

MWW has the same basic configuration as the single agent Wumpus World (WW). MWW is an *N* x *N* board game with a number of wumpuses and treasures that are randomly placed in various cells. Wumpuses emit stench and treasures glitter. Stench and glitter can be sensed in the horizontal and vertical neighbors of the cell containing a wumpus or a treasure. Similar to the single agent WW, once the world is created, its configuration remains unchanged i.e., the wumpuses and treasures remain where they are throughout the duration of the game. Unlike the single agent version, MWW is inhabited by a number of agents randomly placed in various cells at the start of the simulation. An agent dies if it visits a cell containing a wumpus. When that happens, a new agent is created and placed at a randomly selection location on the board.

The MWW agents have a causal model of their environment. They know that stench is caused by the presence of a wumpus in a neighboring cell while glitter is caused by the presence of treasure in a neighboring cell. Agents sense their environment and explain each stimulus they observe. While causes (such as wumpuses and treasures) explain themselves, effects (such as stench and glitter) do not.

Figure 3. A part of the MWW

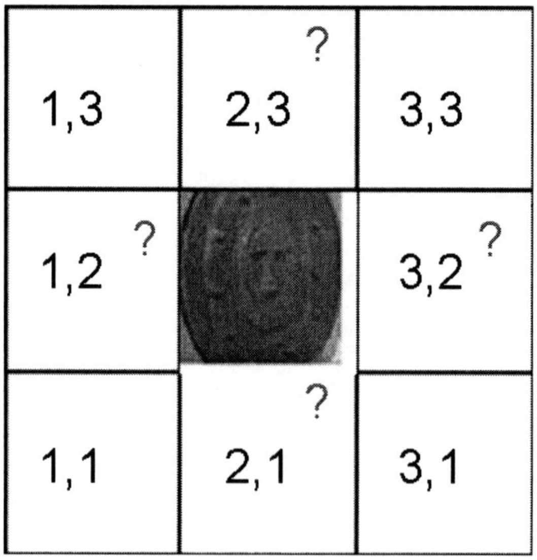

The occurrence of effects can only be explained by the occurrence of causes that could have produced the observed effects e.g., glitter can be explained by the presence of a treasure in a neighboring cell while stench can be explained by the presence of a wumpus in a neighboring cell. An observed effect, however, could have been caused by many unobserved causes e.g., the stench in cell (2, 2) observed in Figure 3 could be explained by the presence of a wumpus in any of the four cells:

- Cell (1, 2),
- Cell (3, 2),
- Cell (2, 1), or
- Cell (2, 3)

An agent may have reasons to eliminate some of these explanations or to prefer some of them over the others. The MWW agents use their existing knowledge to select the best explanation. Agent's knowledge base contains both the game rules as well as their world model. A world model contains agent's observations and past explanations. The observations record information (stench, glitter, treasure, wumpus, or nothing) the agent observed in each cell visited in the past. The MWW agents use their past observations and game knowledge to eliminate some possible explanations e.g., if an agent sensing stench in cell (2, 2) has visited the cell (1, 3) in the past and did not find sense any glitter there, then it can eliminate "wumpus at (2, 3)" as a possible explanation because if there were a wumpus at (2, 3) there would be stench in cell (1, 3). Lack of stench at (1, 3) means that there cannot be a wumpus at (2, 3). Agents use their knowledge base to form expectations about the cells that they have not visited e.g., if the agent adopts the explanation that there is a wumpus in cell (2, 1) then it can form the expectation that there will be stench in cells (1, 1) and (3, 1).

In each simulation round, an agent has to decide whether to take an action or to stay motionless. Possible actions include:

- The action to move to the vertically or horizontally adjacent neighboring cell
- The action to send a message to another agent present in the same cell as the agent, and

- The action to process a message that the agent has received from another agent.

The MWW agents are goal directed agents that aim to visit all treasure cells on the board while avoiding wumpuses. Agents create a plan to visit all treasure cells they know about. The plan must not include any cells that contain wumpuses in them.

If an agent lacks confidence in the knowledge that it currently has about a critical cell then that agent may decide to ask another agent in its vicinity for information about the cell. When an agent detects another agent in its vicinity, it ranks all the cells by how confident it is of its knowledge about a cell. It has the highest confidence in the cells that it has already visited. Next are the cells whose neighbors the agent has visited and so on. Agents also rank cells by how critical it is to find out information about that cell. The order in which the cells are to be visited determines the criticality e.g., if a cell is the next to be visited then finding information about that cell is assigned the highest priority while a cell that is not planned to be visited for another 10 rounds gets low priority. The agents then use an information seeking function that takes the two rankings (confidence and criticality) as inputs and decides what cell (if any) to seek information about.

Once the first agent has sent the request for information, the second agent may also request information about a cell from the first agent in turn. A negotiation between the two agents ensues and communication takes place only if the both agents find the communication beneficial. This way information about the presence or absence of treasure, glitter, wumpus, or stench can be transmitted throughout the population and after some time t, the shared beliefs among agents may come to have a certain pattern. I believe that designing progressively richer versions of CCI and MWW and studying the impact of each local change to see how changes in agent's internal cognitive structure cause changes in the patterns of shared beliefs is the most effective approach to developing predictive models of cultural transmission.

My students and I have conducted a number of such experiments with various versions of CCI & MWW. Upal (2006) reported that the version of a 10×10 MWW with 10-agents was most challenging for CCI agents when it contained 10 randomly distributed wumpuses and treasures compared with MWWs containing 5 or 20 wumpuses and treasures. This is the version we used in the subsequent experiments. We found that even without any communication, false beliefs generated in such a society have a particular structure to them; they are more likely to be about objects and events whose presence is harder to confirm or disconfirm. Upal & Sama (2007) reported that communication does not eliminate or even decrease the prevalence of such false beliefs. There is some evidence to suggest that in human societies, people are also more likely to have false beliefs about unconfirmable entities and events. Bainbridge and Stark (1987) made confirmability the core of their theory of religion to argue that religious beliefs are unconfirmable algorithms to achieve rewards that are highly desired by people yet cannot be obtained. Similarly, there is some evidence to suggest that many false ethnic stereotypes people have are about things that are harder to confirm or disconfirm such as the sexual practices of the neighboring tribes (Smith 2006).

CONCLUSION

After reviewing existing approaches to cultural modeling, I argue that a new approach based on building cognitively rich agent-based models is needed if we are to have any hope of building predictive models of cultural information transmission. I describe architecture of one such multiagent society in detail and describe the work we have done to this point to study the formation of cultural patterns in human societies. While agents in our model have vastly more complex knowledge representation and reasoning capabilities than any previous agent-based social simulation model and they are able to have beliefs that are linked with each other in various interesting ways, their representation and reasoning capabilities are still too limited to result in complex belief patterns such as those that characterize religious movements (Upal 2005b). To this end, we are currently working to enhance the capabilities of our model. We believe that this approach provides the best hope for the development of predictive models of cultural information transmission.

REFERENCES

Bainbridge, W. (1995). Neural network models of religious belief. *Sociological Perspectives*, 38, 483-495.

Bainbridge, W. (2006) *God from the machine: Artificial intelligence models of religious cognition*. Lanham, MD: Rowman Altamira.

Bainbridge, W., & Stark, R. (1987). *A theory of religion*. New York: Lang

Barabasi, A. L. (2003) *Linked: How everything is connected to everything else and what it means for business, science, and everyday life*. Basic Books.

Barrett, J. L. & Nyhof, M. (2001). Spreading non-natural concepts: The role of intuitive conceptual structures in memory and transmission of cultural materials. *Journal of Cognition and Culture, 1*, 69-100.

Bloch, M. (2000). A well-disposed social anthropologist's problems with memes. In *Darwinizing culture: The status of memetics as a science*, (pp. 189-203). UK: Oxford University Press.

Boyer, P. (1994). *The naturalness of religious ideas: A cognitive theory of religion*. Berkeley: University of California Press.

Boyer, P. & Ramble, C. (2001). Cognitive templates for religious concepts. *Cognitive Science, 25*, 535-564.

Dawkins, R. (1989) *The Selfish gene*. UK: Oxford University Press.

Doran, J. (1998). Simulating collective misbelieve. *Journal of Artificial Societies and Social Simulation, 1*(1).

Epstein, J. (2001) Learning to be thoughtless: Social norms and individual computation. *Computational Economics, 18*(1), 9-24.

Gilbert, N. & Conte, R. (1995) *Artificial societies: The computer simulation of social life*. London: UCL Press.

Gonce, L. Upal, M., Slone, J. Tweney, R. (2006) Role of context in the recall of counterintuitive concepts. *Journal of Cognition and Culture, 6*(3-4), 521-547.

Grice, P. (1969). "Utterer's meaning and intention". *The Philosophical Review, 78,* 147-77

Hofstede, G. (1994) *Cultures and organizations.* New York: McGraw-Hill.

Kroeber, A. L. & Kluckhohn, C. (1952) *Culture: A critical review of concepts and definitions.* Cambridge, MA: Peabody Museum.

Laland, & Odling-Smee (2000) The evolution of the meme. In *Darwinizing culture: The status of memetics as a science*, (pp. 122-141). UK: Oxford University Press.

Russell, S., & Norvig, P. (2003) *Artificial intelligence: A modern approach*, second edition. Englewood Cliffs, NJ: Prentice Hall.

Schank, R. (1979) Interestingness: Controlling inferences. *Artificial Intelligence, 12,* 273–297.

Schelling, T. (1977) Dynamic models of segregation. *Journal of Mathematical Sociology, 1,* 143-186.

Smith, L.(2006). Sects and death in the Middle East. *The Weekly Standard.*

Sperber, D. (1996). *Explaining culture: A naturalistic approach.* Malden, MA: Blackwell Publishers.

Sperber, D. (2000). An objection to the memetic approach to culture. In *Darwinizing culture: The status of memetics as a science*, (pp. 122-141). UK: Oxford University Press.

Upal, M. (2005a). Role of context in memorability of intuitive and counterintuitive concepts. In *Proceed-ings of the 27th Annual Meeting of the Cognitive Science Society,* (pages 2224-2229). Mahwah, NJ: Lawrence Earlbaum.

Upal, M. (2005b). Towards a cognitive science of new religious movements. *Cognition and Culture, 5*(2), 214-239.

Upal, M. (2007). The structure of false social beliefs. In *Proceedings of the First IEEE International Symposium on Artificial Life*, (pp. 282-286). Piscataway, NJ: IEEE Press.

Upal, M. (2008). *The layers of culture.* forthcoming.

Upal, M., Gonce, R., Tweney, R., & Slone, J. (2007). Contextualizing counterintuitiveness: How context affects comprehension and memorability of counterintuitive concepts. *Cognitive Science, 31,* 1-25.

Upal, M.A., & Sama, R. (2007). Effect of communication on the distribution of false social beliefs. In *Proceedings of the International Conference on Cognitive Modeling.*

Watts, D. (2002). A simple model of global cascades on random networks. In *Proceedings of the National Academy of Sciences,* 5766-5771.

ENDNOTE

[i] With more than 444 Million estimated hits (obtained on 12/20/2007), culture remains a widely used term in popular discourse.

Chapter V
Interaction of Agent in E-Business:
A Look at Different Sources

Jorge A. Romero
Towson University, USA

ABSTRACT

Despite the popularity of agents for the information technology infrastructure, questions remain because it is not clear what do e-business agents do for businesses and what could they do for consumers. Who benefits most from agents? Are they practical? Can we trust them? Are they as efficient as human agents? Are they already implemented in online businesses? In this chapter, we will discuss the role that agents play in e-business applications.

INTRODUCTION

Imagine this scenario: where the space on your hard drive is getting low so your computer deletes some old video files you have already watched. It is Sunday and you are low on milk, eggs, salt, and some other essentials, so your refrigerator orders more groceries; the toner in your printer is low, so it orders more toner; you receive an e-mail from your credit card company and the e-mail is replied automatically, all of this is done without any effort from you. You are probably thinking that these technologies are not yet available, but all of these

things are possible. These tasks and many more can all be performed by e-business agents. Beyond just moving an e-mail from your credit company to a folder, your agent can receive an e-mail from a new credit card company, make a folder for future emails from that company and will begin moving older e-mails to an archive folder without asking you. But your agent does not move all the e-mails from your credit card company to the archive. Your agent leaves your monthly statements from your credit card in your inbox because it knows that you would like to review your bill before you pay it. Instead of just ordering milk and eggs, your refrigerator also orders meat and some bread, anticipating your needs. An agent does not just perform the tasks you ask it to complete; an agent may make assumptions and perform tasks based on past experiences. An agent can order meals that it believes you will enjoy, or it might order a generic toner in case it knows that you do not have preference for a specific brand. One of the most common agents consumers own is Tivo[1]. Tivo can record television shows that it is programmed to record, and it also makes inferences on the shows it thinks you may want to watch.

Business agents are supposed to guide people where they need to go, and help a company make informed decisions, make recommendations, and if given the authority, hire employees, make purchases, and overall, help the company to run smoothly and efficiently. Similarly, e-business agents, sometimes referred to as digital agents, virtual agents, software agents, or intelligent agents, do many different things for people and business and must therefore be evaluated in order to determine what services they can best provide.

According to Weiss (2001), agents are a new paradigm and concept for developing software applications, and these are most prominent in e-business for agent based technology. These agents are used in many different applications, not only on a small scale but also on a large scale. Weiss (2001) states that while there is no universally accepted concept of what an agent is in terms of e-business, he identifies four widely accepted properties which are used to characterize agents: autonomy (autonomous computational entities), social ability (ability to interactive with other agents), reactivity (ability to interact with they environment), and proactiveness (ability to achieve own goals). An agent technology can also be described as a computational system that runs independently, communicates asynchronously, and can run dynamically on several processes, several machines, and can support the anonymous interoperation of agents (Helal et al., 1999).

Agents are autonomous computational devices that can interact with their environment including other agents in order to achieve their goals. Agents will have the ability to adjust to their environment and have some intelligence. Agents can represent individuals thus acting as delegates or they can act on behalf of groups thus acting as mediators.

A key difference between objects and agents is their autonomy of action (Weiss, 2001). Agents operate under their own control, can work for a long period, take initiative, react to stimuli guided by their goals, and leverage their ability to achieve their goals. A society of agents can be viewed as one that results because of agent interaction or a group of agents that operate under common restriction. A catalog of agent interaction patterns can be used to construct the agent society. The pattern of interaction may also specify constraints or policies that must be fulfilled. Policies define the constraints on the agent society. Roles are the center of agent control, and protocols reflect the pattern of behavior. This role for agents helps users by delegating time-consuming peripheral tasks. Some problems that arise are, how much discretion should be assigned to the agent, and how will the agent interact with the world? (Weiss, 2001).

E-BUSINESS

The e-business domain needs more automation for its customers, which can be facilitated through the implementation of agent technologies. Mesenbourg (2000) highlights distinctions between electronic business and electronic commerce. Electronic business is a process that a business organization conducts over computer-mediated network channels whereas commerce is any transaction conducted over computer-mediated network channels that transfers ownership of, or rights to use, goods or services. The process involves electronic marketing, electronic searching, the procurement and payment and the authentication and the processing of the payment through a financial institution.

Many current successful Web sites started off in garages or college dormitories, and were created by Web developers just for fun. In some cases, we have seen that these small companies balloon into giant corporations. A contributing factor is that a Web site is essentially no different than a corner shop, and it can easily survive by providing a service or product to a small percentage of the global population. However, ballooning can occur when a small Web site is available to over a billion people. Once a Web site, which is intended to be small, can be discovered by a billion customers, it can become a multi-million dollar company, as long as the service or product provided is basic and appealing enough to customers. Kalakota and Robinson (1999) describe the interactions between agents in e-business and how Web sites can turn into a multi-million dollar companies. Their main idea is "big dumb Web sites become big dot com companies" and they explain why and how this comes about. This study wants people to imagine a small town corner shop that only needs to be built in one city, but is somehow accessible by every city in the world and can have an unlimited number of customers within it.

Kalakota and Robinson (1999) state that the world contains over a billion Internet users and a billion cell phone users. There will only be more Internet and cell phone users in the future and this will contribute to the small Web site, big company issue. They explain how business has been traditionally conducted and how now, with e-commerce, the methodology of commerce has changed significantly. In the old methods, we had raw material suppliers selling to a supplier, and then the supplier sends to a distributor, and the distributor sells to a retailer and the retailers manage to get the product to the consumer. A good example is Walmart (www.walmart.com) and the way that it manages its supply chain network. With new e-commerce, many of these tiers are replaced or streamlined and go unnoticed. A supplier can easily become a retailer by creating a Web site and allowing customers to buy products on demand from anywhere in the world. They could also use other distributing services to ensure their products reach their customers. Instead of having a distributor, storefront and retailers, these suppliers can eliminate search costs, inventory costs and other retailer costs by allowing all customers to see stocking and inventory and create products on demand.

The e-business model has evolved and the flow is extremely simple. Kalakota and Robinson (1999) state that the world is becoming more service-oriented and they use Dell (www.dell.com) as an example. In Dell's model, if a customer wants a computer, instead of going to a retailer and buying a computer, the customer decides what kind of computer they want and Dell builds it and sends it to them. They conclude that e-commerce has changed the way we do business and changed the

way a company operates, no longer is distributing and retailing the most important aspects of a successful business, but possibly the product or service being sold, which is more important.

TECHNOLOGY

While the proliferation of technological advancement and globalization of businesses has made possible the tremendous growth of e-business applications. Helal et al. (1999) mantain that Web-based e-business applications and systems developed by individual companies are neither compatible nor interoperable with each other. Therefore, there is a need for new mechanisms and procedures that will smooth the progress of interoperability and cooperation in e-business, not only for business to business operations (B2B), but also for business to consumers operations (B2C). For instance, e-business applications need more automation and security for users, which can only be obtained through the implementation of agent technologies. In this regard, previous studies have suggested that 'agent technology' is one of the core technologies that will accommodate the growing proliferation of e-business applications.

Also, agents typically represent different users, and there may be several of them in a specific environment performing different tasks (i.e. service exchange and coordination). In the case of e-business agent communities, these consist of a large number of agents in a dynamic environment in order to offer special services for a more effective, mutually beneficial, and more appropriate interaction (Helal et al. 1999).

Helal et al. (1999) state that the global economy is the driving force for e-business to be conducted as a service-centric system. This system should offer modular services which are flexible and composed of rapidly deployable services, referred to as e-services. Because of these changes in e-business, there is a rise in the use of negotiation-based, autonomous and intelligent computing. This study suggests that in the near future it is expected that the e-services market will be created by software agents. The protocols for these agents will be based on a three-tier architecture of agents, brokers and super-brokers. This study explains what an ideal e-business agent community aims to do. It is supposed to make it easy to developer virtual enterprises, so companies can join and share resources for the purposes of producing, marketing, exchanging information, and products and services between businesses. In addition, the agents should represent a potential relationship between members and allow for interoperability amongst them. The agents should also help with the creation of relationships between agents with common interests and provide a discipline open network. Finally, the agents should accommodate solutions to the issues of trust, efficiency and credentials.

Helal et al. (1999), focusing primarily on interactions in the auto-trading community, use an example of every aspect of the auto-trading industry including the sales to customers, the infrastructure necessary for inventories and distributing to even finding new hires and determining which ones can make a dealership profitable. It uses its proposed layered agent community architecture to solve the issues of the example. The implementation of these agents has been created using Java. Each of the agents follows a specific set of commands which are defined by an XML file using a specific XML schema defining an agent. The algorithms that they have created are extremely complex and have not been tested with real data. Helal et al. (1999) conclude that they need to gain more information and knowledge on the e-services community to develop more robust and sophisticated algorithms. They also refer to the use of supply-chain management and other logistic methods which are tougher to analyze. Questions still remain, such as: what is the rationale or reason to the way each agent's algorithm was created?

The proliferation of technological advancement has made possible the phenomenon of e-Business. Information Technology has created flexibility in the business markets with the emergence of virtual enterprises or net enterprises and also the globalization of business. However, while this is true, according to Helal et al. (1999), "if we analyze the Web-based e-Business applications and systems developed by individual companies, we find that they are neither compatible nor interoperable with each other". As a result, there is a need for new mechanisms and technologies that will facilitate interoperability and

cooperation in e-Business that will support business to business (B2B) exchange.

While there is no universally accepted definition for agents, an agent technology can be described as "a computational system that operates autonomously; communicates asynchronously; and runs dynamically on different processes in different machines, which support the anonymous interoperation of agents" (Helal et al. 1999). Agents typically represent different users, and there are thus several of them in a given environment. E-business agent communities consist of a large number of agents and their dynamic environment, grouping together to offer special e-Services for a more effective, mutually beneficial, and more opportune e-business. These characteristics of agents render them useful for solving issues in information intensive e-business; which includes advertising, service exchange and coordination across services is very important.

The use of Java programming language and extensible markup language (XML) to encode information and services with meaningful structure and Semantics is becoming more common (Glushko et al., 1999). Due to the enormous amount of data that Web sites generate because of the nature of the Internet and its impact on e-commerce (e.g. tracking information and consumer behavior), new technology is needed to analyze and process this data. The introduction of XML for associating meta-content data is increasing and gaining acceptance among vendors. Companies are using XML technology to perform numerous tasks. These tasks include displaying of product catalog, placing orders and reporting financial and operation information.

HTML provides a universal standard for Web development which allows Web sites to be displayed on all browsers. This allows the companies to reach its intended customers or market share without the need for special technology. Similarly, XML technology is universally acceptable and can be used on different technologies. XML allows buyers and sellers to compare products across many vendors and catalog formats. This reduces the need to build customer interface to view different catalog formats. Also, a seller catalog can be viewed by many potential customers with different Web technology. XML may allow suppliers to differentiate products using means other than price. Agents that search catalogs on the Internet can make pricing decisions based on the availability and location of the product, therefore consumers can use shopping agents to find products with competitive prices. This is because XML allows agents to read product catalogs across the Internet and to return those products which meet the user search criteria. If a user is looking for the cheapest ticket to a baseball game, the agent can compare all the baseball price tickets and return the cheapest one to the user. Therefore, it is the need for information-exchange which brought about XML, providing an easy format for information exchange and easily analyzed by humans. One problem with this format it that it is time-consuming for the parties involved to come to an agreement (Glushko et al., 1999). Another issue with XML is that vendors usually fear making their product information readily available, because competitors with lower prices may attract those customers easily (Weiss, 2001).

Online shopping is not a personal transaction and therefore requires some level of trust, unlike a face-to-face transaction where buyer and seller make an immediate exchange of payment for product. Ensuring the quality of transactions is another pattern of agent based systems (Weiss, 2001). Currently, there is no mechanism to ensure the quality of the products sold. One method is to elicit feedback or comments from previous buyers on the quality of the product and the promptness of delivery. E-bay (www.ebay.com) has such a mechanism to rate the performance of its vendors, but a potential problem is that vendors that are rated poorly may assume new identities and continue to sell products without letting buyers be aware of their poor performance.

Consequently, agent based systems should be autonomous, and currently the dominant example for interaction with computers is direct manipulation. The user must initiate the tasks and monitor all subsequent events related to the task. For example, a user who wants get a deal on an auction that offers an item on sale must usually go to a search engine to find the auction. The user must then monitor the auction for his desired price. The monitoring of the auction price and search for the auction is peripheral to the users main objective of acquiring the item. Agents can be used as substitutes for the user performance of peripheral activities. Users

can delegate some of their tasks to agents that will perform the tasks independently. This is a cooperative process where the user and the agent both initiate communication. It allows autonomy for the agent to achieve goals without interacting with the user or another agent. The independent agent does not require approval from the user at every step of completing an action; it can complete the tasks on its own.

Similarly, autonomous agents require trust from users, and users must be able to trust that the agent will act in an unbiased manner. For example, the user would not want the agent to choose vendors for a cut in the proceeds. Users may also like to specify the degree of autonomy each agent should have. For example, the user may not want to delegate responsibilities that have financial consequences (Weiss, 2001).

Because users differ in their preferences, vendors need to adapt to each one individually, therefore agents should be able to adapt to their environment (Weiss, 2001). Tailoring information to users requires maintaining a user model, and when creating a user model two characteristics must be identified during the interaction. First, whether this is the user' first time visit and there is no information available; and second, the ability to add information of a repeat visitor. There are several solutions for this issue: one can have users register to use the site and permanently keep their profiles or one can choose to have a model during that particular time frame when the user is interacting with the site. Systems should consider both direct and indirect users, for example, the user that shops online for his daughter or some other third party. Systems should also track changes in user preferences over time. One method of gathering user information is to have each user fill out a form. This allows you to capture the information directly from the user himself and to provide a personalized profile at first contact. There may be few flaws with this approach because users may be reluctant to provide this information upfront, or because changes in user preferences will not be reflected in their profiles.

Furthermore, there may be piracy concerns when creating user profiles because it requires the disclosure of personal information (e.g. vendor preference). One can personalize information between vendors and consumers by analyzing their click stream. This process can take place without the user's knowledge and may raise privacy concerns. Users generally want to remain in control and are not likely to allow anyone monitoring their usage patterns without their consent. Users decide on what information to share on an interaction by interaction basis. Buyers that like to remain anonymous in a transactions pose serious problems to vendors that want to personalize service.

One of the possible problems in e-business that Weiss (2001) mentions is user profiling and the way it can be implemented. The problem is described as "how to capture user profiles without requiring too much explicit input from the user." Although, the idea is to track users' profiles as their behavior over time. Weiss (2001) explains that the solution includes advanced dynamic user modeling and the agents involved should be used to tailor the interaction style, providing more or less detail based on the receptiveness of the user. The user profile should best describe the user by its interactions. Custom catalogs can be created by monitoring buying patterns and preferences. An issue with the creation of user profiles is how to capture user information without requiring too much explicit information directly from the user. Such a system must be adaptable and have the ability to update changes in user preferences. User profiles can contain user interests and those interests may be rated by the degree of interest the user has in the subject. The user agent can request the user to provide demographic information which allows the agent to group the user into a class.

If limiting user input is a goal, the user profile should begin after the user has had the time to create a pattern or history. User preference can be deduced using cluster analysis. Once the user profile has been created, the system can be updated by soliciting information directly from the user. This method derives user profiles by monitoring user use. Product extractors create catalogs of product preferences listed in user profiles. Other key characteristics of the user may be deduced from the product extractor like user's age, level of expertise, and some predictive information about preferences on product features (Weiss, 2001). Agents can monitor the information source for changes in preferences by continuous

polling. Notification agents move only to a single remote location and are created with a condition that typically comprises an event and a Boolean expression on the event data. Wrapper agents are used to translate vendor specific information (Weiss, 2001). In summary, Weiss (2001) has examples that are very well thought out, but the agent concept is still a theory and there is no widely accepted definition or understanding of what an agent is. These examples help understanding the purpose and the abilities of agents; however, they do not go into detail on how to implement these agents and how they would be integrated into systems.

Another pattern discussed by Weiss (2001) is search cost. An example is that a user searches the Web for an item to purchase through an auction and iteratively monitors the state of that item. The fact that the user can only find the best deal available at the time of attempting to purchase an item limits the searching capabilities. The concept of autonomy would do this for a user, and instead of approving all tasks and forcing the user to query and control their search, an autonomous agent should execute and perform tasks automatically. These agents should also have a level of autonomy, as in, the higher the set level the more tasks that will be performed automatically, which would obviously be used for less critical concepts. There is also this concept of a need to interact. In many cases, agents cannot complete a task alone; they must rely on the capabilities of other agents to do certain tasks. All activities between the agents must be coordinated to reach a common goal; however, they must also not interfere with each other or overstep their bounds.

The dynamic features of the online marketplace cause the search for vendors to fluctuate. Consumers and vendors can enter and leave the marketplace and change their prices and requirements at any time. It becomes difficult to maintain contact lists of vendors and clients. If each user maintains his personal list of vendors, then he may not be able to get better deals from vendors that are not on their list. A solution to this is to use a mediator to match the trading parties. Mediators can maintain contact lists and alert the parties when a good deal is offered. The problem with this solution is that individual preferences cannot be tracked with a mediator since it does not represent the consumer preferences.

The consumer and the vendor need to be represented by unique identities. Identities must be tracked and authenticated. There are many ways of assigning identities including labels like a personal e-mail address or account name. Once issue with identities is the effortless process of acquiring a new identity. Therefore, tracking schemes that rely on information that can be changed quickly are unreliable. A user may have more than one email address and can seem to represent more that one user just by using an alternate email address thereby thwarting efforts to track them. There must be an incentive to have users keep the same identity for extended periods of time for this type of tracking can be useful.

INFORMATION OVERLOAD

Improvements in technology have allowed businesses accumulate enormous amount of data about buyers and their online behavior. Therefore, so much data has been generated, and information overload is another key pattern for intelligent agents where they adaptability to new information capabilities can be critical. Entities and individuals may wish to find relevant information on making deals and generating profit. However, there are many different vendors and interfaces which make it difficult to conduct transactions in the market. An answer to this issue has been to provide portal to the Web. The portal occasionally collects information from different sources and put them in a format that makes it easier for users to process. This information is then placed in a hierarchical index. A disadvantage of this index is that it is not personalized for each individual user and his preferences (Maes, 1994).

Agent based system should provide multiple interfaces. A problem with finding information is the number of interfaces used to present it. Store fronts have different organizations and many vendors do not follow the same conventions when describing their products. The product description and terms of sale may be different. Some vendors add the cost of shipping to their price and others do not. A shared vocabulary for terms of sale would be a

solution, however this must gain wide acceptance by vendors to be useful to users (Maes, 1994).

HUMAN-LIKE AGENTS

McBreen and Jack (2000) performed a series of experiments to evaluate the effectiveness of interactive agent e-commerce systems. They evaluated human-like agents and cartoon-like humanoid agents. For the human-like agents, videos, disembodied voices, and facial expressions were preferred. Most of the participants preferred human-like agents than the animated humanoid agent. Consequently, the progress of human-like agents will depend on advances in speech and voice recognition technology. So, this is an area were online business can explore and its development will depend on advances in graphics interfaces.

BUYING, SELLING, AND ONLINE AUCTIONS

Agents can perform several roles in online auctions. They could monitor auctions and keep users informed of the latest activities in the auctions. Agent can also analyze market conditions and store information on bidders in order to estimate trends and behavioral patterns. Agents can determine the auctions to bid in. Agents are more suitable to manage online auctions over human beings because there are able to perform complex activities faster than human beings He (2004).

Each agent based systems needs to provide some form of interaction. Since agents have only a partial representation of their environment, they are limited in their expertise, or access to resources. Occasionally, they have to rely on other agents to achieve goals that are outside their reach. For instance, in an online auction, a buyer or seller may have agents working as delegates, and the behavior of an agent is difficult to explain outside the context of the auction itself and the rules that exist (He, 2004). In general, agents compile user profiles that are updated regularly, and then go to the marketplace with that profile, locate a vendor, and negotiate the price.

This user profile allows the vendor to customize its offer to the agent (Weiss, 2001).

METRICS AND MEASUREMENT IN E-BUSINESS

Mesenbourg (2000) uses the United States Census Bureau to measure e-business development, and it describes the e-business framework, the strategies used and specific complexities. In today's world, consumers are heavily leveraging the use of electronic devices and other media, which instantaneously interact with each other, and the population of Internet users is expanding at exponential rates. A large number of consumers are continuously connected with Internet media devices. Clearly, improvements in technology are playing a major role in this exponential growth of use. In previous years, before the advancement of e-commerce, the measurement of the economy was simpler and most of the services in the U.S. where related to the financial industry, which most would still consider a true product. Mesenbourg (2000) explains that the problem today is that the world of e-business is much like the Wild West and very undefined, and basic examples of e-business infrastructure are: computers, routers and other telecommunication devices.

The size of something that isn't tangible is often hard to determine. Mesenbourg (2000) discusses a method for measurements of e-commerce on an economy, and specifically for the United States Census Bureau that eventually can be used in the near future. He also mentions how this would also help determine what kinds of technologies and educational facilities are necessary for a population born into an e-commerce world. This method could ultimately help in a structured development of the Internet and supplement growing e-commerce entities by affording them more information within their business community. It will also help supplement areas in development both geographically and according to their type of business.

REFERENCES

Glushko, R., J. Tenenbaum, & B. Meltzer. (1999). An XML Framework for agent-based e-commerce. *Communications of the ACM, 42*(3).

He, M. (2004). *Designing bidding strategies for autonomous trading agents.* Thesis, University of Southampton.

Helal A., A. Jagatheesan, & M. Wang. (2001). Service-centric brokering in dynamic e-business agent communities. *Journal of Electronic Commerce Research* (JECR). Baltzer Science Publishers.

Kalakota, R., & M. Robinson. (1999). E-business: Roadmap for success. *Addison-Wesley Information Technology Series.* Reading, MA: Addison-Wesley.

Maes, P. (1994). Agents that reduce work and information overload. *Communications of the ACM, 37*(7).

McBreen, H., & M. Jack. (2000). Animated conversational agents in e-commerce enterprises. In *Proceedings of the Third Workshop on Human-Computer Conversation*, (pp.112-117).

Mesenbourg, T. (2000). Measuring electronic business, definitions and underlying concepts. *United States Census Bureau*, September 2000.

Weiss, M. (2001). Patterns for e-business agent architectures: Using agents as delegates. *Pattern Languages of Programming* (PLoP-01).

ENDNOTE

[1]   Tivo is a registered brand of Tivo Inc. Tivo automatically records television programming and stores shows for later viewing.

Section II
Emergences

Chapter VI
A Simulation of Temporally Variant Agent Interaction via Passive Inquiry

Adam J. Conover
Towson University, USA

ABSTRACT

This chapter presents a description of ongoing experimental research into the emergent properties of multi-agent communication in "temporally asynchronous" environments. Many traditional agent and swarm simulation environments divide time into discrete "ticks" where all entity behavior is synchronized to a master "world clock". In other words, all agent behavior is governed by a single timer where all agents act and interact within deterministic time intervals. This discrete timing mechanism produces a somewhat restricted and artificial model of autonomous agent interaction. In addition to the behavioral autonomy normally associated with agents, simulated agents should also have "temporal autonomy" in order to interact realistically. Part I of this two-part series focuses on an exploration of the effects of incremental migration of John Conway's "Game of Life" form a simple cellular automata simulation to a framework for the exploration of spatially embedded agents.

INTRODUCTION

When we discus agents, we use the term *agent* as it is generally described in common literature (Wooldridge, 2002); (Ferber, 1999). Primarily, an agent should have attributes of autonomity, intentionality, and proactivity. However, in addition to the behavioral autonomy normally associated with agents, we add the concept of temporal autonomy to give agents the freedom to "activate" without global coordination. This includes the ability to send messages to other agents at any time, and respond to the environment (including other agents) in variable time. In our previous work, we discussed the effects of *temporal asynchronicity* on a modified version of John Conway's famous *Game of Life*. This chapter extends that research to include message-based interaction of simple agent swarms and revisits previous research into a temporally asynchronous version of *Game of Life* where relevant (Conover &

Trajkovski, 2007). By "temporal asynchronicity", we mean that agents are free to send messages or respond to their environment independently of any globally coordinated synchronization mechanism.

Experiments with a number of different models of interaction show that the variability of the rate at which certain groups of agents exchange information affects the overall state of a swarm of agents. However, these effects are not necessarily intuitively predictable. In our research, we look at the effects of this variability on the average age of agents in an environment, overall population density, and the effect of message exchange leading to unity and/or diversity of simple agent "beliefs". Here we describe the research and results behind the development of a highly multi-threaded Java™ application for the simulation of swarms of "temporally variable" autonomous agents. We will also demonstrate that measurable differences can be observed and reproduced in various agent "swarm" type simulations by varying the asynchronous variably of timing in clusters of autonomous agents.

We start by classifying two distinct behavioral models for spatially embedded swarms of agents, with each model being examined as a collection of secondary sub-models. By "spatially embedded", we mean that the agents are constrained in space within a finite *world*. Each agent communicates with a fixed set of neighboring agents throughout the duration of a simulation. The two primary behavioral groups are differentiated as follows:

- **Passive inquiry:** Each agent examines the state of its environment at periodic time intervals and updates its own state based upon an examination of agents in its immediate vicinity.
- **Belief promulgation:** Each agent periodically communicates with neighboring agents by sending simple belief messages. The recipients of the messages alter their own states based upon the type and strength of the messages received.

As an initial experiment, we have chosen to examine the effects of temporal autonomy on the well known *Game of Life* (Gardner, 1970). Though the *Game of Life* is a simulation normally asso-

ciated with cellular automata (Wolfram, 1994), diverse applications have been found in theoretical fields such as number theory and game theory (Berlekamp, Conway, & Guy, 1982), computation (Mitchell, Crutchfield, & Hraber, 1994), as well as in applied fields such a materials science (Varde et al.., 2004). For our purposes, it is reasonable to view this same simulation as a rectangular grid of *agents* where each agent is capable of limited communication with neighboring agents. Agents may be considered *active* (on) or *inactive* (off) based upon the rules of the "game" as opposed to agent states representing "live" or "dead" cells as with the *Game of Life*. Many agent simulations treat agent behavior as state changes that occur in accordance with a global clock or similar timing mechanism (Hautamäki, 1997)(Fonseca, Griss, & Letsinger, 2002)(Bordini et al.., 2006). However, if we wish simulated agents to be truly autonomous, then each agent needs the additional freedom of acting autonomously in time.

The introduction of *Temporal Autonomy* into the *Game of Life* provides a reference model for the exploration of non-deterministic temporal variability within an existing, well studied, and deterministic simulation. Though some work has been done in examining the effects of synchronous versus asynchronous updating in the *Game of Life* (Blok & Bergersen, 1998)(Schönfisch & Roos, 1999), little work has been done studying these effects as they pertain to agent interaction. To enable exploration of temporal autonomy in agent interaction, we have written a small simulation environment in Java which alters the traditional *Game of Life* behavior. In this environment each cell in the world may exist within its own independent thread of execution. Though several techniques could be employed to simulate this multi-threaded behavior, the ease of thread creation and manipulation in Java makes a truly multithreaded approach practical.

Subsequent sections of this chapter provide an overview of our continued work in the area of agent interaction in "temporally asynchronous" environments and outline preliminary results. First, we provide a brief overview of the simulation environment, and then outline the simulation methodologies and results. The experiments are divided into two distinct sets: In the first set, the *Game of Life* model is used but each cell is treated as an autonomous agent who periodically examines its environment and alters is own state accordingly. In the second set, the familiar *Game of Life* model is initially used, but all agent activity is triggered by neighboring agent event generation and message passing. This model is then evolved into a simulation where primitive agent "beliefs" are propagated through the world and variations in agent activation variance ratios affect the global behavior of the agent collective.

THE SIMULATIONS

Our first simulation re-purposes the *Game of Life* world as a grid of agents, each with eight neighbors. The grid is internally represented as a torus; the top and bottom edges of the grid are connected, as well as the left and right edges. Though our simulation platform is capable of representing the world as either a simple rectangle or a torus, the torus model has been favored since it allows all agents in the environment to have the same number of neighbors and no agent is more isolated from the "society" than any other agent. A simple two-dimensional

linked list is used to represent all cell connections. For all of the trials outlined in this chapter, a 25x25 list was used, providing a grid of 625 discrete cells. Implementation details can be found in Section "The Application Framework".

Temporal asynchronicity is achieved by establishing a mean vivification time where agents independently "awaken", momentarily interact with their environment, and then return to "sleep". Vivification is defined as the process of triggering an agent into examining or interacting with its neighboring agents. Each agent exists within its own thread of execution and will randomly vary its vivification time within predetermined limits. The vivification delay variance ratio r_{mv} is defined as the ratio between the total variance d_v and the mean vivification delay time d_m. For example, the mean vivification time for all agents in the world may be 500ms and the variance set at ± 125ms. Over the course of a given trial, each agent will examine its environment every 500ms on average, but will randomly vary this time (between each vivification) with a range of 250ms (125ms × 2), centered at 500ms. The shaded region of Figure 1 graphically depicts the range of potential vivification intervals

Figure 1. The shaded region of this figure depicts the range of the vivification intervals according to the vivification variance ratio

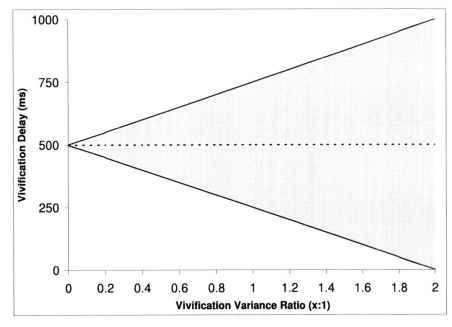

according to the vivification variance ratio.

We view each cell as a container for a single agent, where each agent is capable of two states: *active* or *inactive*. Since the objective of this experiment is to examine the effects of random time variances in asynchronously communicating agents, each agent is intentionally fixed in space and contained within a cell within the world. Each agent is capable of communication only with its adjacent neighbors by querying the neighbor's binary state (active or inactive). With each agent vivification, the agent examines the state of its adjacent neighbors, and then sets its own state as discussed below. Furthermore, we define a vivification which results in the agent adopting an *active* state to be *successful*. A vivification which causes the agent to adopt an *inactive* state is said to be *unsuccessful*. Being a standalone application designed to examine a specific phenomena in agent/swarm interaction, no formally standardized specifications—such as FIPA (Intelligent Artificial Agents, 2007)—are warranted. Inter-agent communication happens via simple direct interrogation of an agent's immediate neighborhood, or by sending simple event notifications to adjacent neighbors.

As a given simulation progresses, each agent tracks its own count of consecutive vivifications that cause it to remain in the active state. This represents the agent's *age*, which is always decoupled from "wall-time"[1]. In the trials which are synchronized to a single global clock, agents age one unit per world generation. In the trials where we eliminate the fixed global clock from the simulation, the concept of a world "generation" has no precise meaning. In generation-less modes, each agent may update its internal state without regard to the activities of neighboring agents. With every unsuccessful vivification, the age is reset to zero and the agent becomes "inactive". A dedicated monitor thread (at the world level) periodically samples all active agents in the world grid to compute the average ages, population density, etc.

To aid our understanding of the overall effects of temporal autonomy, we first take a brief look at the traditional "Conway Model" of the *Game of Life*. After studying the simulation in its traditional sense, we can then examine the effects of incrementally modifying some of the simulation's constraints;

specifically the constraint of synchronous updating. Each simulation consists of multiple trials, each with 32,000 generations or snapshots (depending on the trial type). The number of snapshots per trial was capped at 32,000 for pragmatic reasons; we wanted to graph and analyze the data in a spreadsheet or statistical package—some of which are limited to 2 rows. This number was also sufficiently high to clearly observe behavioral differences between simulation types. Section "*Rule Variations*" discusses all of the simulation types in greater detail. The remainder of this section presents a migration of simulation types ranging from synchronous to generational asynchronous to non-generational.

A Brief Overview of the Conway Model

John Conway's *Game of Life* is one of the earliest and most enduring examples of cellular automata (Wolfram, 2002). In the traditional version of this simulation, a rectangular two dimensional grid of cells is displayed where each cell exists in one of two states; "live" or "dead". The grid is synchronized to a master clock where each cell has a specific rule applied to it with each successive clock tick. The most critical aspect of this simulation is that all cells are computed and rendered *synchronously* (or "simultaneously"). In other words, *all* cells in the grid are evaluated and then updated in two separate passes. In the first pass, all cells are evaluated and their new states are determined. In the second pass, the results of the preceding evaluations are applied. The following are the rules of the traditional *Game of Life*:

- The *Game of Life* world consists of a two dimensional rectangular grid of cells, each with the potential for harboring "life" or "no life".
- All cells on the life grid are updated simultaneously in a series of successive generations.
- Life is "born" into an empty cell if the cell is bordered by exactly 3 live cells. In our revised view, an agent becomes "active" when exactly 3 neighbors are also "active".
- Existing life is sustained in any cell containing exactly two neighbors. If a cell with exactly

two neighbors is empty, it will remain empty. In the context of agents, this means that no state change is made.

- Any life within a cell with fewer than two neighbors will die. An agent with fewer than two neighbors in the "active" state will switch to the "inactive" state.
- Any life within a cell with four or more neighbors will die. An agent with more than three neighbors in the "active" state will switch to the "inactive" state.

One of the most important distinguishing characteristics of Conway's *Game of Life* is that it is purely deterministic (though often unpredictable). I.e., identical world states at time *t* produce identical world states at time *t+t'*. On an infinitely sized grid, there are three possible outcomes from any initial starting state: 1) All life is extinguished after a finite number of generations. 2) Life will expand outward from its region (or regions) of origin, ever increasing the number of live cells. 3) Life will stabilize into a static state or into an oscillating pattern between two or more repeating states[2].

Much analysis of the *Game of Life* and associated world states has been done since Martin Gardner first publicized Conway's work in *Scientific American* in 1970. William Gosper, one of the more prolific researchers on the subject, developed a technique known as *Hashlife* which—as the name suggests—uses hash tables to compute resulting world states after potentially millions of generations (Gosper, 1984). Due to the deterministic nature of the traditional simulation, in many cases it is possible to accelerate the evolution of the world grid without having to perform *all* of the intermediate calculations. Those interested in further study of the *Game of Life* in its pure synchronous cellular automata form would be well served to explore the work of Gosper. Conway himself discusses the *Game of Life* briefly in his book *On Numbers and Games* (Conway, 1976). However, for the bulk of our research, we will be looking at the simulation from an asynchronous perspective. Removing the "synchronous update" constraint effectively turns the game into a completely unique simulation.

RULE VARIATIONS

As discussed above, several factors make it difficult to perform any meaningful analysis of the *Game of Life* as a simulation of agents. The deterministic nature of the simulation coupled with a tremendous sensitivity to initial conditions (sometimes known as the "butterfly effect" (Lorenz, 1979)) makes this simulation—in its pure form—unsuitable for *agent* interaction research. This is partially due to the fact that even the slightest difference in the initial starting conditions may radically affect subsequent world states. However, with some relatively simple modifications, the *Game of Life* can be transformed into a platform and framework for studying the effects of non-deterministic agent interaction. In subsequent sections we will examine a series of simulations ranging from a traditional cellular automata approach to a version where each cell behaves autonomously and non-deterministically. Though other studies have looked at how overall population affects population survival rates (Baray, 1998), our goal here is to examine population age and density effects attributed to alterations of simple interaction dynamics.

We start by first looking at the effects of removing the synchronous update constraint from the simulation while maintaining the concept of "generations". A "generation" is defined as a finite set of agent interactions triggered by a single clock pulse. We then move onto "generation-less" interaction models, where the global "world clock" is removed and replaced with temporally autonomous agents. The remainder of this chapter details the results of four variations of agent interaction on a *Game of Life* board where each agent obeys the *life/death* rules of the traditional model, but the agent vivification methodology is altered.

We look at several traversal models which are inspired by the basic "Conway Rules" but examine the results of loosening the *Game of Life* restrictions in several different ways. In total, four distinct passive inquiry models are explored; Random Traversal, Random Selection, Continuous Interaction, and Treaded Interaction. Though each mode will be described in greater detail later, a brief description of each follows:

- **Random traversal:** This is a generation-based mode which operates via random selection *without* replacement. N unique agents are visited in a random order per generation, where N is the total number of agents. This is referred to as a "traversal" because every agent in the world is visited once and only once.
- **Random selection:** This also is a generation-based mode which operates via random selection *with* replacement. N visitations are made to randomly selected agents. In this model, it can be statistically shown that approximately $1 - e^{-1}$ agents will be visited per generation. Some agents will be visited more than once.
- **Continuous interaction:** This is the fist of the "generation-less" modes where the simulation runs by continuously selecting agents randomly for activation. In place of a "generation" which neatly subdivides the world into discrete time units, a snapshot timer is used. This snapshot timer gathers information about the world at predetermined intervals.
- **Threaded interaction:** In this final mode, each agent executes within its own thread. Updates are not synchronous or atomic; each agent acts autonomously in time, independent of the behavior or timing of any other agent in the world.

In the following sections, we examine a series of simulations ranging from a traditional cellular automata approach to a version where each cell behaves autonomously and non-deterministically. In these sections, the following designations apply: age_{avg} is the mean average age of a population of agents for all snapshots in a trial, age_{rms} is an accumulated RMS value of the average ages, pd_{avg} is the average population density across all snapshots in a trial, and pd_{rms} represents the accumulated population density RMS value for all sample points in a given trial. It is important to note that with each snapshot, all *active* agent ages are averaged together to determine the average population age per snapshot. So, age_{avg} for a trial represents the average of all snapshot averages, where each snapshot average is determined by the ages of all agents in the world at the moment of the snapshot.

Random Traversal Model

The "random traversal model" is the first model where we explore the *Game of Life* in an asynchronous updating environment. Though still generational, all agents in this model are activated in random order while guaranteeing that all agents are activated once—and only once—per generation. Thus, the algorithm is similar to a basic "card dealing" algorithm or "random selection without replacement". This mode is likely akin to a carelessly implemented version of the traditional *Game of Life* (i.e. the updates are asynchronous rather than synchronous). However, in this case, the design has been intentionally chosen to explore the effects of agent age in a non-deterministically evaluated world that still obeys the same basic inter-agent update rules as the *Game of Life*.

Though the world in the Conway model is purely deterministic, it is difficult to predict the ultimate behavior of the agents—hence, it is difficult to predict any future state of the world after a large number of generations without actually iterating though all interim generations. Ironically, random traversal provides very consistent results regardless of initial starting conditions. Each trial began with a randomly generated initial population covering 20% of the world. After several thousand generations in each trial, the average agent ages and agent population densities converge to results similar to those shown in Table 1. Figure 2a shows the graph of all data points gathered for an arbitrarily chosen trial summarized in Table 1.

It can be shown (non-trivially) that the maximum density of a *Game of Life* world is 50% world coverage in a "still-life" configuration (Elkies, 1998). A "still-life" configuration is any life board configuration where live cells exist, but no changes occur in successive generations. In other words, if S_t represents the state of the world at time t then $S_t = S_{t+n}$ for all $n > 0$. Considering that the maximum steady state density is 50% then the addition of any active agents would increase the density beyond 50%, thus disrupting the steady state. It is possible to have a *valid* configuration that exceeds a density of 50% for a single generation at time t, but this would in turn cause more agents to become inactive at time $t + 1$. This implies that the average population density

Table 1. This table represents the summary data from a random subset of trials run in random traversal mode. The ages age and population densities pd are representative of the entire population at periodic snapshot intervals over the course of an entire trial of 32,000 "generations".

age_{avg}	age_{rms}	pd_{avg}	pd_{rms}
6.1795	6.3045	0.4202	0.4206
6.2038	6.3278	0.4209	0.4214
6.2355	6.3408	0.4208	0.4212
6.2563	6.3880	0.4215	0.4218
6.2815	6.4207	0.4208	0.4211
6.2911	6.4144	0.4217	0.4220
6.3545	6.4608	0.4219	0.4221

$\hat{\sigma}_{age_{avg}} = 0.05856$	$\hat{\sigma}_{age_{rms}} = 0.05685$
$\hat{\sigma}_{pd_{avg}} = 0.00060$	$\hat{\sigma}_{pd_{rms}} = 0.00057$

Figure 2. These graphs depict the average age of all active agents at the time of the data collection snapshot for 32,000 snapshots for a randomly chosen trial of the given type. The population density can be calculated be dividing the number of active agents by 625 – the number of cells in the world.

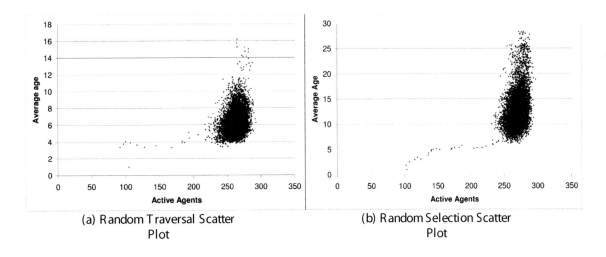

(a) Random Traversal Scatter Plot

(b) Random Selection Scatter Plot

will remain below 50% regardless of the order in which the agents are chosen for vivification. We have yet to develop a full probabilistic model for results shown in Table 1. However, we will use this data as the baseline for the discussion of the behavior of other the agent vivification/activation strategies discussed below.

Random Selection Model

Before delving into the first non-generational model, we look at another selection model that sequentially operates on agents. This model is essentially random selection with replacement. Though the *Random Selection* model is generational, it differs

Table 2. This table represents the summary data from a random subset of trials run in random selection mode. The ages age and population densities pd are representative of the entire population at periodic snapshot intervals over the course of an entire trial of 32,000 "generations". Of the data in table, the mean age_{avg} and pd_{avg} are 12.9077 and 0.4316 respectively.

age_{avg}	age_{rms}	pd_{avg}	pd_{rms}
12.6338	13.0338	0.4322	0.4325
12.6493	13.0923	0.4308	0.4312
12.7075	13.1258	0.4308	0.4312
12.7828	13.2651	0.4309	0.4313
12.9205	13.4276	0.4317	0.4320
13.0278	13.4969	0.4324	0.4327
13.6322	14.2437	0.4325	0.4328

$\hat{\sigma}_{age_{avg}} = 0.3505$	$\hat{\sigma}_{age_{rms}} = 0.4168$
$\hat{\sigma}_{pd_{avg}} = 0.0008$	$\hat{\sigma}_{pd_{rms}} = 0.0007$

from the *Random Traversal* model in the sense that the random selection is **not** guaranteed to select all agents in the world for vivification during any given generation. A random agent is selected for vivification N times per generation where N is the number of cells (hence agents) in the world. The probability of any given agent *not* being selected for vivification within any given generation is $(1-1/N)^N$. As N approaches ∞, Equation 1 arises. Therefore, in the general case, the probability of any given agent being activated at least once in a generation (and hence has a probability of change) is approximately $1-e^{-1}$.

$$\lim_{N \to \infty}\left(1-\frac{1}{N}\right)^N = \frac{1}{e} = e^{-1} \qquad (1)$$

The average age and population density data for this vivification model is shown in Table 2. Though this model results in slightly higher population densities than the random traversal model, the average agent age is approximately double that of random selection without replacement—with a larger, though still relatively small $\hat{\sigma}$. From this data we can see that by simply altering the selection model—even within a generational model—we can introduce significant changes in the dynamics of the overall population. The graph of the data presented in Table 2 can be seen in Figure 2b.

Continuous Model

The "continuous" model represents a bridge between the concept of an agent vivification model with generations and a fully multi-threaded implementation. Here agents simply update themselves continuously in random order. There is no time t where one "generation" starts or ends. As the model runs, data snapshots are taken at consistent intervals. The delay time between agent updates is configurable, but does not impact the overall behavior of the model. This is due to the fact that all agents update themselves atomically, and the delay between atomic updates is irrelevant.

This model is interesting in its own right as it's the only model where static "still-life" structures frequently emerge. In other words, if a still-life world state S is reached at snapshot time t then $St=St+n$ for all $n > 0$. It is interesting to note that, in the trials run, the highest "still-life" density ever achieved was roughly 47%. Of the 15 trials shown in Table 3, all but three reached a still life structure

Table 3. This table summarizes the data from 8 trial runs in the "continuous traversal" model. Only two trials lasted 32,000 snapshots before reaching a "still-life" configuration where no further changes in the world took place. For the trails that did not reach a full 32,000 snapshots, all other columns of data are calculated from the beginning of the trial up to and including the first snapshot that indicated the would was in a "still-life" state. In a still-life state, agents simply continue to age indefinitely.

Snapshots	age_{avg}	age_{rms}	pd_{avg}	pdrms
3687	12.9362	13.4417	0.4317	0.4320
5338	12.9960	13.4752	0.4325	0.4328
7110	13.0392	13.5628	0.4324	0.4327
10162	12.9818	13.4721	0.4324	0.4326
15168	12.9866	13.4789	0.4323	0.4325
16651	12.9581	13.4411	0.4322	0.4325
32000	12.9736	13.4401	0.4322	0.4325
32000	12.7430	13.1830	0.4321	0.4323

$\hat{\sigma}_{age_{avg}} = 0.0679$	$\hat{\sigma}_{age_{rms}} = 0.0844$
$\hat{\sigma}_{pd_{avg}} = 0.0002$	$\hat{\sigma}_{pd_{rms}} = 0.0002$

Figure 3. Figure 3a shows the same type of graph for another trial which only ran for 5042 snapshots before reaching a still-life state. Figure 3b shows Active Agents versus Average Agent Age cluster graph for a trial which ran to completion without reaching a still-life state.

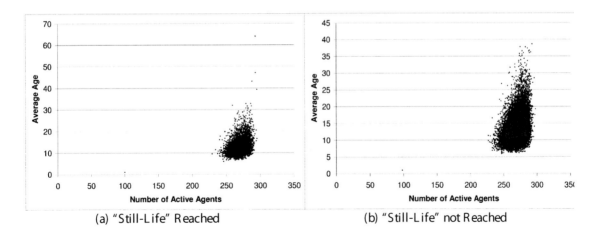

(a) "Still-Life" Reached   (b) "Still-Life" not Reached

before 32,000 snapshots were captured. The "Snapshots" column reflects the number of snapshots taken before reaching any potential still-life state. If 32,000 snapshots were reached, this indicates

that no still-life pattern emerged within the trial run. In no trial did the world ever "collapse" to a population of zero. The cluster graphs in Figure 3 show all data points from two separate trials, one

Table 4. This table is a summary of average age_{avg}, age_{rms}, pd_{avg}, and pd_{rms} gathered from approximately 50 unique trials sorted and grouped by r_{mv}.

rmv	ageavg	agerms	pdavg	pdrms
0.00	4.3575	4.4179	0.4065	0.4070
0.25	4.4734	4.5331	0.4082	0.4088
0.50	4.7333	4.7913	0.4115	0.4119
0.75	5.0794	5.1618	0.4148	0.4153
1.00	5.4556	5.5459	0.4174	0.4178
1.25	5.9317	6.0522	0.4197	0.4201
1.50	6.4028	6.5470	0.4215	0.4219
1.75	6.9438	7.1373	0.4227	0.4231
2.00	7.3821	7.5556	0.4231	0.4235

Figure 4. These graphs depict the vivification variance ratio versus average agent age and density as presented in Table 4.

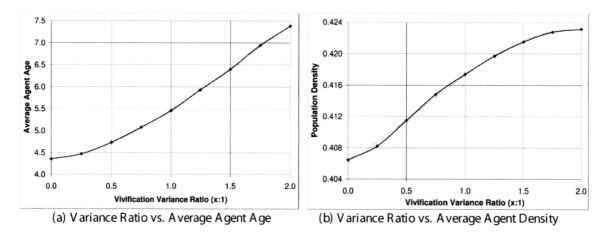

(a) Variance Ratio vs. Average Agent Age

(b) Variance Ratio vs. Average Agent Density

that reached "still-life" early and one that remained dynamic until the end of the trial.

Threaded Model

In the threaded model each agent is controlled by its own thread which activates the agent at varying non-deterministic time intervals. Since every agent acts autonomously, updates are not atomic. In other words, adjacent agents can update themselves simultaneously. This intentional design decision attempts to replicate real-world agent interaction

dynamics as closely as possible. For example, since there exists a finite amount of time between an agent experiencing its environment and then reacting to that environment, reactions may not always reflect the "current" state of an environment.

All agents in the world run with a fixed mean vivification interval within a variable range. For example, the mean vivification interval for a given trial could be fixed at 500ms with a random variance of ±250ms. This would represent a *vivification variance ratio* of 1:1. Trials were conducted with a mean vivification delay time *dm* of 500ms with delay variances *dv* chosen to produce *dm/dv* ratios

Figure 5. Figures 5a-5c illustrate a progression of cluster graphs from R$_{mv}$ of 0.25 to 1.00 and finally to 2.00. Figure 5d is simply a view of average agent age versus time taken from the same trial as shown in Figure 5b. Also notice the spikes in Figure 5d; these spikes directly correspond to the highest—and more isolated—points in Figure 5b.

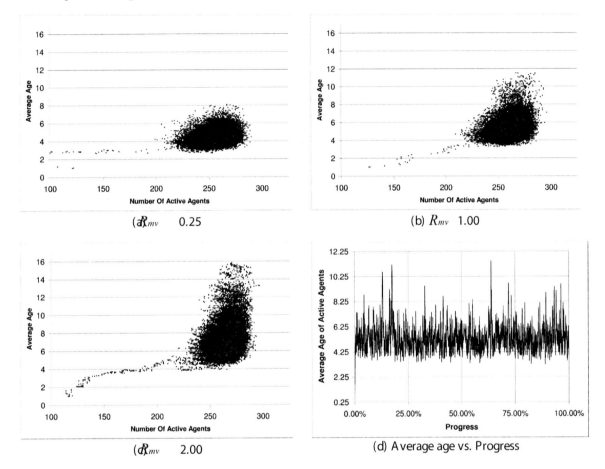

(a) R_{mv} 0.25

(b) R_{mv} 1.00

(c) R_{mv} 2.00

(d) Average age vs. Progress

rmv ranging from 0.0 to 2.0, as summarized in Table 4. To verify our initial hypothesis that *rmv* is the relevant independent variable, several preliminary trials were conducted with *dm* ranging from 250ms to 1000ms while adjusting *dv* holding *rmv* constant. These adjustments produced no statistically significant deviation in our results, so all of our reported trials are run with a *dm* of 500ms for consistency. Table 4 displays the mean values of data gathered from approximately 50 unique trials grouped by *rmv*.

Figures 4a and 4b illustrate *rmv* versus both the agent ages and population densities shown in Table 4. Both graphs depict subtle S-curves for both

the ages and densities of the agent populations as the vivification variance ratios increase. Figure 5 illustrates a progression of age cluster graphs of *rmv* from 0.25 to 1.00 and finally to 2.00. As can be seen, the higher the value of *rmv*, the more snapshot points that extend into the higher regions of the graph. This evidence indicates that higher degrees of timing variability in multi-threaded agent interaction produce greater age variability—and ultimately higher average survival rates—for the population as a whole. The graph in Figure 5d reflects the same age data as presented in Figure 5b, but with respect to time as opposed to population density. From this last graph, it can be seen that the average population age maintained the same level of variability throughout the trial.

CONCLUSION

In this chapter we focused our attention on a Game of Life inspired simulation of agents. In all of our simulations, the agents were spatially embedded within individual cells in a world represented by a two dimensional grid. Furthermore, each agent was only capable of passively examining its immediate neighborhood and then potentially adopting a new state based on the observed states of its neighbors. A series of experiments which gradually decoupled the agents for a globally coordinated world clock ultimately resulted in each agent having complete temporal autonomy. By varying the degree of flexibility of agent's internal timing, we were able to observe the pronounced effect that timing variability has on the overall population dynamics.

Given this relatively simple model of interaction, it is clear that the phenomena exhibited by the introduction of temporal autonomy warrants further study. Thus far, we have shown the local variably in periodicity of passive interrogations of the world state produces a global population effect. Though we suspect that a probabilistic model of agent behavior can be produced, our experimental methodologies are currently focused on an empirical approach. The next chapter in this two part series—*A Simulation of Temporally Variant Agent Interaction via Belief Promulgation*–extends the simulations undertaken in this study and adds the critical component of active agent communication. In the next study we give the agents the ability to actively influence neighboring agents by conveying simple belief representations to the neighborhood. As in this chapter, we will demonstrate that temporal variance plays a significant role in population dynamics.

REFERENCES

Baray, C. (1998). Effects of population size upon emergent group behavior. *Complexity International, 06.*

Berlekamp, E. R., Conway, J. H., & Guy, R. K. (1982). *Winning ways for your mathematical plays* (Vol. 2). Academic Press.

Blok, H. J., & Bergersen, B. (1998, Apr). *Synchronous vs. asynchronous updating in the Game of Life.* Dept. of Physics and Astronomy, University of British Columbia, B.C., Canada, V6T 1Z1: .

Bordini, R., Braubach, L., Dastani, M., Seghrouchni, A. E. F., Gomez-Sanz, J., Leite, J., . (2006). A survey of programming languages and platforms for multi-agent systems. In *Informatica 30* (pp. 33–44).

Conover, A., & Trajkovski, G. (2007, Nov 9–11). Effects of temporally asynchronous interaction on simple multi-agent behavior. In *Emergent agents and socialities: Social and organizational aspects of intelligence. technical report fs-07-04* (pp. 34–41). The American Association for Artificial Intelligence, 445 Burgess Drive, Menlo Park, CA, 94025, USA: AAAI Press.

Conway, J. H. (1976). *On numbers and games.* New York: Academic Press.

Elkies, N. D. (1998). Voronoi's impact on modern science. In (Vol. 1, pp. 228–253). Institute of Math., Kyiv.

Ferber, J. (1999). *Multi-agent systems: An introduction to distributed artificial intelligence.* Addison-Wesley Professional.

Fonseca, S. P., Griss, M. L., & Letsinger, R. (2002, Mar 22). *Agent behavior architectures – A MAS framework comparison* (Tech. Rep. No. HPL-2001-332). : Hewlett Packard Laboratories.

Gardner, M. (1970, Oct). Mathematical games - the fantastic combinations of John Conway's new solitaire game, *Life. Scientific American,* 120–123.

Gosper, W. (1984). Exploiting regularities in large cellular spaces. *Physica-D, 10,* 75–80.

Hautamäki, J. (1997). *A survey of frameworks* (Tech. Rep. No. A-1997-3). : Department of Computer Science, University of Tampere.

Intelligent Artificial Agents, T. F. for. (2007, Nov). *FIPA specifications.*

Lorenz, E. N. (1979). *Predictability: Does the flap of a butterfly's wings in brazil set off a tornado in texas?* (Talk given at the annual meeting of the AAAS December 29, 1979 in Washington). : American Association for the Advancement of Science.

Mitchell, M., Crutchfield, J. P., & Hraber, P. T. (1994). Evolving cellular automata to perform computations: Mechanisms and impediments. *Physica D, 75*(1-3), 361–391.

Schönfisch, B., & Roos, A. M. de. (1999). Synchronous and asynchronous updating in cellular automata. *Biosystems, 51*(3), 123–143.

Varde, A. S., Takahashi, M., Rundensteiner, E. A., Ward, M. O., Maniruzzaman, M., & Jr., R. D. S. (2004). *Apriori algorithm and Game-of-Life for predictive analysis in materials science.*

Wolfram, S. (1994). *Cellular automata and complexity.* Reading, Mass.: Addison-Wesley.

Wolfram, S. (2002). *A new kind of science.* Champaign, IL: Wolfram Media.

Wooldridge, M. (2002). *Introduction to multiagent systems.* John Wiley & Sons.

ADDITIONAL READING

Bersini, H., & Detours, V. (1994, Jul). Asynchrony induces stability in cellular automata based models. In R. A. Brooks & P. Maes (Eds.), *Proceedings of the 4th international workshop on the synthesis and simulation of living systems (artificial life iv)* (pp. 382–387). Cambridge, MA, USA: MIT Press.

Bonabeau, E., & Théraulaz, G. (2000, Mar). Swarm smarts. *Scientific American, 282*(3), 72–79.

Boyd, J. E., Hushlak, G., & Jacob, C. J. (2004). Swarmart: Interactive art from swarm intelligence. In H. Schulzrinne, N. Dimitrova, A. Sasse, S. B. Moon, & R. Lienhart (Eds.), *Proceedings of the 12th ACM international conference on multimedia, october 10-16, 2004, new york, NY, USA* (pp. 628–635). ACM.

Dennett, D. C. (1978). *Brainstorms.* Cambridge, MA: Bradford Books.

Findler, N. V., & Malyankar, R. M. (1995). Emergent behaviour in societies of heterogeneous, interacting agents: Alliances and norms. In N. Gilbert & R. Conte (Eds.), *Artificial societies: The computer simulation of social life* (pp. 212–237). UCL Press: London.

Foner, L. N. (1995). Clustering and information sharing in an ecology of cooperating agents. *the AAAI Spring Workshop on Information Gathering from Distributed, Heterogeneous Environments.*

Franklin, S., & Graesser, A. (1996). Is it an agent, or just a program? : A taxonomy for autonomous agents. In *Intelligent agents III. agent theories, architectures and languages (ATAL'96)* (Vol. 1193). Berlin, Germany: Springer-Verlag.

Gaston, M. E., & desJardins, M. (2005). Agent-organized networks for dynamic team formation. In F. Dignum, V. Dignum, S. Koenig, S. Kraus, M. P. Singh, & M. Wooldridge (Eds.), *4rd international joint conference on autonomous agents and multiagent systems (AAMAS 2005), july 25-29, 2005, utrecht, the netherlands* (pp. 230–237). ACM.

Geire, R. N., & Moffatt, B. (2003, Apr). Distributed cognition: Where the cognitive and the social merge. *Social Studies of Science, 33*(2), 1–10.

Guessoum, Z. (2004). Adaptive agents and multiagent systems. *IEEE Distributed Systems Online, 5*(7).

Gulyás, L., & Kampis, G. (2006, Oct 12–15). Emergence as a relational property in societies of agents. In *Interaction and emergent phenomena in societies of agents* (pp. 1–7). The American Association for Artificial Intelligence, 445 Burgess Drive, Menlo Park, CA, 94025, USA: AAAI Press.

Hofstadter, D. R. (1979). *Gödel, escher, bach: An eternal golden braid.* New York: Vintage Books.

Holland, J. H. (1998). Emergence: From chaos to order. *J. Artificial Societies and Social Simulation, 1*(4).

Huget, MP. (Ed.). (2003). *Communication in multiagent systems: Agent communication languages and conversation policies (lecture notes in computer science / lecture notes in artificial intelligence).* Springer.

Juan, T., & Sterling, L. (2003). A meta-model for intelligent adaptive multi-agent systems in open environments. In *Aamas* (pp. 1024–1025). ACM.

Jung, C. (1999). Emergent mental attitudes in layered agents. *Lecture Notes in Computer Science, 1555*, 195–? ?

Kearney, P. (1994). Experiments in multi-agent dynamics. In C. Castelfranchi & E. Werner (Eds.), *Artificial social systems — selected papers from the fourth european workshop on modelling autonomous agents in a multi-agent world, maamaw-92 (lnai volume 830)* (pp. 24–40). Springer-Verlag: Heidelberg, Germany. (see conclusions)

Kennedy, J., Eberhart, R. C., & Shi, Y. (2001). *Swarm intelligence*. San Francisco: Morgan Kaufman.

Lam, D. N., & Barber, K. S. (2004). Verifying and explaining agent behavior in an implemented agent system. In *Aamas* (pp. 1226–1227). IEEE Computer Society.

Lauer, M. R., Mitchem, P. A., & Gagliano, R. A. (1995). Resource optimization and self interest: Variations on the game of life. *ss, 00*, 136.

Le Strugeon, E., Mandiau, R., & Libert, G. (1994). Towards a dynamic multi-agent organization. *Lecture Notes in Computer Science, 869*, 203–? ?

Lerman, K. (2004). A model of adaptation in collaborative multi-agent systems. *Adaptive Behavior, 12*(3-4), 187–197.

Lewin, R. (1999). *Complexity: Life at the edge of chaos*. University of Chicago Press.

Lu, Q., Korniss, G., & Szymanski, B. K. (2006, Oct 12–15). Naming games in spatially-embedded random networks and emergent phenomena in societies of agents. In *Interaction and emergent phenomena in societies of agents* (pp. 148–155). The American Association for Artificial Intelligence, 445 Burgess Drive, Menlo Park, CA, 94025, USA: AAAI Press.

Lynch, A. (1999). Thought contagion: How belief spreads through society. *J. Artificial Societies and Social Simulation, 2*(2).

Marcenac, P. (1998). Modeling multiagent systems as self-organized critical systems. In *Hicss (5)* (pp. 86–95).

Minsky, M. (1985). *Society of mind*. Simon & Schuster. Paperback.

Parsons, S., Gymtrasiewicz, P., & Wooldridge, M. (Eds.). (2002). *Game theory and decision theory in agent-based systems (multiagent systems, artificial societies, and simulated organizations) (hardcover)*. Springer. Hardcover.

Parunak, H. V. D., Brueckner, S., Sauter, J. A., & Matthews, R. S. (2005). Global convergence of local agent behaviors. In F. Dignum, V. Dignum, S. Koenig, S. Kraus, M. P. Singh, & M. Wooldridge (Eds.), *4rd international joint conference on autonomous agents and multiagent systems (AAMAS 2005), july 25-29, 2005, utrecht, the netherlands* (pp. 305–312). ACM.

Parunak, H. V. D., Brueckner, S., & Savit, R. (2004). Universality in multi-agent systems. In *Aamas* (pp. 930–937). IEEE Computer Society.

Privosnik, M., & Marolt, M. (2001, Sep1–6). The development of emergent properties in massive multi-agent systems. In *Wseas*. Malta: WSEAS.

Schilling, R. (2006, Oct 12–15). A project to develop a distributed, multi-agent communication architecture using message feedback. In *Interaction and emergent phenomena in societies of agents* (pp. 96–103). The American Association for Artificial Intelligence, 445 Burgess Drive, Menlo Park, CA, 94025, USA: AAAI Press.

Servat, D., Perrier, E., Treuil, JP., & Drogoul, A. (1998, Jul). When agents emerge from agents: Introducing multi-scale viewpoints in multi-agent simulations. In J. S. Sichman, R. Conte, & N. Gilbert (Eds.), *Proceedings of the 1st international workshop on multi-agent systems and agent-based simulation (MABS-98)* (Vol. 1534, pp. 183–198). Berlin: Springer.

Simon Parsons, Piotr Gymtrasiewicz, M. W. (Ed.). (2002). *Game theory and decision theory in agent-based systems (multiagent systems, artificial societies, and simulated organizations)*. Springer.

Smith, A. E. (2000). Swarm intelligence: From natural to artificial systems. *IEEE Trans. Evolutionary Computation*, *4*(2), 192–193.

Sørensen, M. H. (2003). *Interactivism at work toward design heuristics for ambient intelligence.* (extended abstract)

Tarasewich, P., & McMullen, P. R. (2002). Swarm intelligence: Power in numbers. *Commun. ACM*, *45*(8), 62–67.

Thrèaulaz, G. (2001). *Swarm intelligence*. San Francisco: Morgan Kaufman.

Trajkovski, G. P. (2001). An imitation-based approach to modeling homogeneous agents societies. *Lecture Notes in Computer Science*, *2258*, 246–??

Trappl, R., Luck, M., Marik, M., & Stepankova, O. (Eds.). (2001). *Multi-agent systems and applications*. Springer.

Wavish, P. (1991, Aug). Exploiting emergent behaviour in multi-agent systems. In *Proc. of the third european workshop on modelling autonomous agents in a multi-agent world* (pp. 297–310). Kaiserslautern, Germany: North-Holland.

Weiss, G. (Ed.). (2000). *Multiagent systems: A modern approach to distributed artificial intelligence*. The MIT Press.

Wolfram, S. (1994). *Cellular automata and complexity*. Reading, Mass.: Addison-Wesley.

Wolfram, S. (2002). *A new kind of science*. Champaign, IL: Wolfram Media.

ENDNOTES

[1]   To ease some visualization and rendering implementation details, the agent age was capped at 64 units. Though infrequent, it is possible for an agent to age beyond this limit. In this case, the age stops incrementing sbut the agent's state is otherwise preserved and continues to follow all other rules. The overall effect is negligible since we are only looking at relative differences between trials.

[2]   "Glider-like" patterns also fall into this category since the total number of live cells does not continue to grow; only the relative position of the cells within the world change.

Chapter VII
Agent Feedback Messaging:
A Messaging Infrastructure for Distributed Message Delivery

Richard Schilling
Cognition Group, Inc., USA

ABSTRACT

This chapter presents a generalized messaging infrastructure that can be used for distributed agent systems. The principle of agent feedback messaging, upon which the infrastructure is built, is presented with examples. Agent feedback messaging allows agents to function as an intelligent agent ecosystem that spans multi-node computing clusters and facilitates agent communications in a way that mimics naturally occurring biofeedback mechanisms. An implementation of agent feedback messaging, AFM, is also described. Biosimulation and a solution to the travelling salesman problem are also presented as examples.

INTRODUCTION

Developing an agent communicatons infrastructure that supports scalable multi agent systems will help accelerate the adoption of intelligent agents within AI specializations and industry alike. Unfortunately, however, relatively little work has been done directly on agent communications infrastructures compared to other challenges and opportunities in agent design. There is a large body of literature documenting the application of intellligent agents to solve higher level problems such as knowledge representation (Picard & Gleizes, 2002), beleivability (Bates, 1997), and distributed content management (Zhang & Lesser, 2004). Multi-agent systems applied to business problems such as supply chain management (Hillersberg et al, 2004) are also fairly common. Approaches to agent communications and agent organization based on newer network architectures such as wireless networks like Shah, Nixon and Ferguson propose (Shah, Nixon, & Ferguson, 2004) are less commonly found. However, in most of the literature researched for this chapter, the agent systems discussed were developed toward a narrowly focused problem. And very little attention was paid toward developing a general messaging framework that utilizes the capabilities of networking technologies developed after the year 2000. Finally, no literature is presently found that makes attempts to simultaneously deal with higher level knowledge representation, agent communication, agent organization, and practical modeling of real world processes. Agent feedback messaging aims to provide a single, multi-agent architecture and communications framework that gives agent developers the means to deal with all of these issues. The resulting multi-agent architecture, agent feedback messaging, meets this goal by separating intelligent agents from their message communication infrastructure.

Agent Feedback Messaging achieves scalability in multi agent systems design by functionally separating intelligent agents from their communications infrastructure at the application level. The task of agent communications is relegated to a communications infrastructure. The communications infrastructure runs in its own thread space at the application layer of the network protocol. Agents are not allowed to control other agents or invoke their methods directly. Each agent resides in its own thread space and communicates with other agents by interacting with the communications infrastructure. Agents also listen for responses (feedback) delivered by other agents. Hence, the name of the architecture, agent feedback messaging

How the communication infrastructure sends messages between hosts is an implementation level detail. The example implementation presented in this chapter uses the Internet Inter-Orb Protocol (IIOP) to transmit messages between hosts. The federation design pattern for agents catalogued by Hayden et al (Hayden, Carrick, & Yang, 1999) is the closest example of a similar approach, however in implementation described below, federation is used only to transmit messages between multiple hosts running agents, and not between agents directly.

Agent feedback messaging is an effective way to develop arbitrary ecosystems of cooperating agents and enforces message delivery characteristics that: a) eliminate dependencies between agents; b) removes the need to include network code in agents such as sockets or datagram programming; and, c) allows the physical layer of the network to change without affecting agent functionality.

This chapter will provde you with an understanding of agent feedback messaging and provide

examples of its usage. An implementation is also presented.

AGENT COMMUNICATIONS AND THE PRINCIPLE OF FEEDBACK

Agent feedback messaging is an approach to agent communications that relies on a message transport mechanism which functions independently from the activities of the agents themselves. The idea, in a nutshell, is to remove the burden of communications management from the agents and relegate it to a reliable message delivery subsystem. At the same time, the message delivery subsystem is built to guarantee that messages between agents are delivered according to a well defined set of rules, so that message delivery is both reliable and predictable.

Another key characteristic of agent feedback messaging is the way it allows agent designers to embody naturally occuring and man made processes. This is done by allowing agent developers to break down processes into communities of agents with varying agent granularity. The phases and steps of a given process can also be changed around at will by simply telling each agent what messages it should respond to and what messages it needs to generate. Even the ordering of code execution in a program can be rearranged by dispursing a large program among multiple agents.

Agent feedback messaging also allows agents to appear and disappear at will throughout the agent community without requiring the multi agent system to be stopped and restarted. That is, an agent can appear and dissappear in the system during runtime without disrupting the functioning of the other agents. And finally, agents are able to operate as both service providers and clients to other agents simultaneously.

Agent Feedback Messaging was inspired by the kinds of "communication" that occurs between organs of a human through the cardiovascular system. Consequently, agent feedback messaging can be made clearer if we compare the approach to the cardiovascular system. The cardiovascular system can be seen as the backbone of a large, complex chemical communications infrastructure. It transports nutrients, minerals and oxygn around the body which can be seen as biological messages.

There are several observations about the cardio-vascular system we can make that will be useful in our disucssion about agent feedabck messaging. As an organ of the body need nutrients (messages) from the blood stream, it extracts them from the part of the blood stream that happens to be passing by at any given moment. Likewise, if a particuar organ needs to send any message to another organ, it simply deposits it into the same blood stream. The cardiovascular system itself:

- Is a closed circular communications system
- Exhibits autonomy: it relies on its own mechanism for managing the speed and direction of messages (the heart).
- Delivers ''messages'' to all parts of the body
- Does not control which organs receive any particular message
- Circulates messages at its own rate.
- Allows organs of the body to "communicate" asynchronously.
- Does not actively manage communications between organs, and does not allow point-to-point nor synchronous messaging.

Likewise, organs can be compared to intelligent agents. Each organ:

- Is attached at only one unique point to the cardiovascular system.
- Communicates with all other organs in the body by inserting messages into the blood stream only at its point of attachment.
- Is only allowed to extract messages in finite amounts at its point of attachment.
- Does not diectly control the speed at which messages are transported (the heart does that).
- Utilizes messages on its own time once it receives them.
- Can only respond, or effect a change in the larger body by reading messages that pass by or by inserting new messages into the blood stream.
- Is exposed to all messages inserted upstream even if the message was not meant for that particular organ.

- Uses the cardiovascular system to communicate with other organs asyncoronously

And to make our comparison complete, the messages (cells and nutrients):

- Can contain resources that are added to or used up by organs (e.g. absorption of oxygen in blood cells).
- Can contain resources that are only partially depleted over time.
- Are not limited to a specific type.
- Generally circulate through the cardiovascular system at one speed. (e.g. a blood cell in the heart does not accelerate to pass another moving blood cell that is in the leg)

When organs interact with each other by using the messaging capabilities provided by the cardiovascular system, a state of homeostasis, or balance, is achieved in the overall body even though the organs are limited to communicating through a messaging infrastructure they have no control over. Likewise, agents using agent feedback messaging are able to achieve a similar state of balance in a community of agents of arbitrary size; a sort of system wide homeostasis.

Table 1 compares the concepts of a cardiovascular system with software concepts that are useful to an implementation of agent feedback messaging infrastructure.

The project to develop agent feedback messaging revealed that certain rules would need to be applied to the agent communications layer. The rules that have been settled upon, as of this writing, allow the agent developer to make some concrete assumptions about how messages are delivered:

1. An agent is never aware of which agents will receive the messages it sends
2. An agent is not required to respond to every message message presented to it.
3. Only the agent that creates a message has the right to destroy it.
4. Any message an agent creates will be delivered to all other agents in the system before being returned to it's creator.
5. A message is presented to all agents in succession, rather than being broadcast.

Table 1. Comparison between the cardiovascular system and agent feedback messaging

Cardiovascular System	Agent Feedback Messaging
blood vessels	shared data structures (FIFO queues)
heart	threads that move messages between shared data structures
organs	intelligent software agents
solutes, nutrients, chemicals, and cells transported through veins	agent messages
homeostasis	functional stabalization of a community of agents as they produce and consume messages
systemic circulation	circular message flow that delivers messages to all agents
diffusion of gases and nutrients to/from particles in the blood stream	read/write policy of agent messages

6. For a given set of active agents the order of agents the message is presented to does not change.
7. For a given agent in a set of active agents, the first agent to receive its messages is unique.
8. A message can be assigned read/write policies, so that agents can add or modify message information as it passes by.
9. The order in which messages are inserted into a stream relative to other messages is maintained.
10. The order in which a given agent sees messages reflects the relative message order in which it was inserted into the message stream.
11. The relative rate of travel between messages in the message stream is zero - messages always travel in the message stream at the same speed.
12. The amount of time it takes for a message to circulate to all agents is independent of the amount of time it takes for any agent to process the message.

Any agent messaging system that imposes these rules on message delivery can also be said to be an agent feedback messaging system.

The benefit of imposing these rules on agent communication can be seen in the design of the agents themselves and is discussed in detail below. From a systems design standpoint, a community of agents can be built up in a part and parcel fashion. Specific communication paths do not need to be hard coded into agent code, which allows the design work to be broken down into manageable sub-elements.

The communications infrastructure underlying agent feedback messaging can be implemented as a software solution, hardware solution, or as a combination of both. The present implementation of agent feedback messaging, discussed below, is built with in Java with an API that can be used by developers who want to build their own implementations. The resulting communications infrastructure is extremely amenable to the development of agent communities of an arbitrary number of agents and promotes the reuse of agent messages for multiple purposes.

Figure 1. Agent feedback messaging architecture

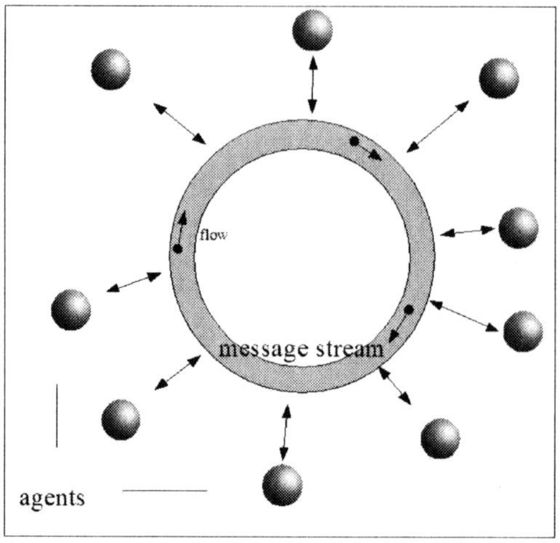

Figure 1 provides a graphical representation of agent feedback messaging. A circular message stream is the central feature of agent feedback messaging. When an agent inserts a message into the message stream it is attempting to incite other agents to perform some activity and, in turn, input their own messages (feedback) into the message stream. The feedback messages are then picked up by the agent that sent the first message. The number of feedback messages created in response to a given message is up to the agent developer. Agent feedback messaging does not require feedback messages to be generated in response to any message.

BENEFITS OF THE APPROACH

The approach to communications taken on the agent feedback messaging project is a marked departure from the traditional agent point-to-point communications. The departure was necessary to avoid problems associated with large scale agent design that are well documented. Becker et al (Becker, Lesser, & Zilberstein 2005) make it clear that when agents are responsible for delivery of messages directly, the resulting myopic communication designs ultimately sacrifice overall system performance. Even when highly scalable federated agent communication approaches using remote method invocation (RMI) are used as in the Cougaar project (Cerys, Rozga,

& Berliner, 2006), the programmer must still manage the complexities of determining which agents communicate with other agents and when. Hayden et al (Hayden, Carrick, & Yang, 1999) properly associate these issues with two desirable features of agent communication systems: a) allowing agents to serve as both client and service-provider, and consequently b) allowing agents to use a complete agent network, a communication network between agents that forms a complete graph.

Agent feedback messaging achieves this feat by completely removing the burden of message addressing and delivery from the sending agent. The only way an agent is allowed to communicate with other agents is by inserting messages blindly into a constantly moving circular message flow, or stream. No destination agent is specified by the sender at any time. It is the responsibility of the receiving agent to detect messages it needs in the message stream and process them. This limits an agent's communication tasks considerably and removes the need to hard-code the destination of a message.

Every agent is assigned its own unique point of interaction with the message stream from which it can read messages from other agents and insert new ones. The circular message stream, operated by its own set of threads, retrieves new messages from all agents simultaneously. Each message is delivered by the message stream to all other agents in succession and is eventually returned to the

Figure 2. Basic agent interaction

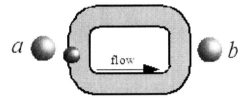

(a) Agent a dispatches a message

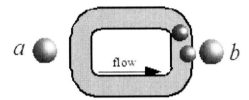

(b) Agent b receives the message and dispatches a response (feedback)

(c) Agent a receives its original message and destroys it. It then receives the response from agent b

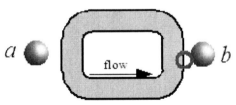

(d) Agent b destroys the response message it created

originating agent. As each agent is presented with a message it determines if the message applies to it before the message stream sends the message to the next agent.

The basic interaction that occurs between all agents is depicted in Figure 2.

Reducing Agent Coding

In terms of writing agent code, the overall effect of the approach described is a dramatic reduction in the coding required of the agent developer. In a system where any agent is allowed to communicate with any other agent, the possible communication paths form a complete directed graph, and can be expressed as

$$p = n (n - 1)$$

where n is the number of agents in the system and p are the possible number of communication paths. If an agent is required to obtain a handle or reference to another agent in order to send a messge, then the possible number of lines of code that must be written for all agents to send one message can be expressed as

$$c = lrn(n - 1)$$

where

c is the total lines of code for all agents.

l is the number of lines of code required for an agent to send one message

r is the number of lines of code requred to detect and read the message.

n is the number of agents in the system.

When agent developers are not required to hard code message destinations into the agents themselves, the overall effect is that the number of lines written for all agents to send one message can be limited to

$$c = lnr$$

The time for a given response to be returned to an agent is undefined, and is viewed as mostly a hardware performance issue. However, the rules imposed on the message delivery infrastructure guarantee that messages and their associated response messages (feedback) are always delivered in the proper order: a message's delivery always preceeds the delivery of feedback messages. It is therefore possible to guarantee that message/feedback delivery occurs in a prescribed order under a simulated timeline.

Modifying Messages While in Transit

Agent feedback messaging also allows for the special case of a message to be modified directly as it is passed from agent to agent. Therefore, all messages have a read/write policy. This is possible because the only time a message is destroyed is when the sending agent determines that it should be, and only after a message has been delivered to all other agents at least once.

Some messages contain data that can be only read (read only policy), while others allow agents to add or change information (read/write policy), and yet other messages require agents to add information (write required policy). Write required policies are used to solicit information from agents that can be supplied immediately, such as the agent's name or the results of a mathematical operation. The read/write policy of a message is determined by the developer of the agent that sends the message.

While other agent communication infrastructures emphasize the delivery of messages between agents in a broadcast fashion (multicast delivery) (Shah, Nixon, & Ferguson, 2004), agent feedback messaging delivers each message to agents one agent at a time (linear delivery). Both approaches have advantages, but I have found that when the combined processing time attributable to message delivery itself, message filtering (deciding if an agent should get a message), message sharing (semaphore locking/unlocking), and response processing (feedback) are taken into account, linear delivery provides advantages that outweigh any percieved loss of performance over multicast delivery. Furthermore, because agent feedback messaging requires each agent to be executed in its own thread space and share data through inter-thread shared memory structures, the complexity associated with managing method call stacks for a large number of agents is reduced.

The designer of an agent determines what messages the agent must respond to. To handle the case where an agent is required to indicate it has no response to a message, the agent can a) create and send another new "no response" message back, or b) add the "no response" data to the message it received, or c) do nothing. The third option, do nothing, is a valid "no response" action because this allows for intentionally delayed responses to occur.

DEPENDENCY ISSUES AND THEIR MANAGEMENT

Before discussing an implementation of agent feedback messaging, it will be helpful to describe how agent feedback messaging can help developers address dependencies in their programs. Although biological simulation was the original intended use for agent feedback messaging, I have also found that it can be used as a general solution to work around dependencies introduced into programs and make code more managable. As Horling (Horling *et al*, 2006) illustrates, the task of managing the code behind agent behavior and communication can increase with the number of distributed autonomous agents involved. Therefore, eliminating dependencies between agents such those that occur when programming logic spans agent boundaries has been a goal of feedback messaging project from the beginnging.

Many of the issues surrounding managability appear to be related to the need to ultimately execute the code behind agents and communicate data between them in a linear fashion, even in the case of instruction pipelining and multi-processor architectures. Parallelism cannot eliminate the fact that on a given processor only one instruction can be run at a time. The best one can hope for is to mitigate the limitations this imposes on agent design.

From the software design standpoint, this could be said to be a side-effect of the Turing model which imposes linear processing. Unfortunately, however applications reducable to a Turing Model do not always map well to higher level processes (biological or human defined) that occur in a non-linear fashion. The Turing Model necessitates that one piece (or block) of code be evaluated before others.

In general, when one block of code is required to be executed before another block of code we can say that the execution of the second block of code is dependent upon the first block. We can call this a dependency.

There are many reasons why dependencies exist, but they can greatly impact how computer code itself is written and maintained, particularly in distributed multi agent systems. Dependencies can be imposed on a program by the the language it is written in as well as the architecture it is executed on, even if the dependency is not required by the programmer. An example would be a single processor machine that can only execute one instruction at a time. Dependencies can also be determined by the higher-level design of the application such as the system's functional policies (e.g. a security requirement), a business process the application must support, or a biological processes the application might simulate.

For the purposes of discussion it is helpful to categorize dependencies into three general categories. These categories, explained below are code dependencies, temporal dependencies, and process dependencies. Whereas process dependencies describe the timing of code execution across application boundaries (in the *macro*-application sense), code and temporal dependencies describe the timing of code execution within a single application (in the micro-application sense).

Code Dependencies

Code dependencies describe the order of execution of code which can be attributed to the design of a computer language or underlying hardware. Programmers always rely on code dependencies to make sure a program executes its instructions in a prescribed order. Code dependencies also exist whenever the order of execution of machine level instructions is enforced simply because the language does not include syntatic features that allow parallel execution of routines. Parallel architectures and pipelining in processors helps alleviate this problem at the machine level, but introducing code dependencies even when they are not necessary is unavoidable in many cases. Giving control of code dependencies to the developer however allows

code blocks to be spread out over multiple agents and multiple hardware hosts. One algorighm, for example can be re-written to be executed on any number of computing nodes.

For example, consider the following three line program

```
int a = firstCalculation();
int b = secondCalculation();
int c = a+b;
```

A code dependency exists between line one and line two for the simple reason that the processor can execute only one function at a time. Since the ability to execcute both functions simultaneously does not exist on a single processor system, and because language itself does not allow the programmer to specify that both functions can be run in simultaneously (in a multi-processor system), the code dependency cannot be reduced unless the first line and the second line executed in two separate agents.

The third line, however is dependent upon the previous two. This code dependency is not imposed by any restrictions of the hardware or language as is the case with the first two lines. This code dependency exists, rather because the programmer chose to write the code that way.

Temporal Dependencies

A temporal dependency is the deliberate ordering of code block execution even though it is not imposed by a code or process dependency (process dependencies are described below). Temporal dependencies exist whenever one part of a program must be executed prior to another part in order to satisfy some design constraint. This type of dependency would most likely occur, for example, when one function is required to be before another to satisfy a system policy. In a real-time system, temporal dependencies are strictly enforced since the functioning of the system relies on the execution of a routine at a pre-defined moment in time.

For example in a non real-time system, temporal dependencies can be created by the timing of code excution to support well defined steps in a single business process (e.g. payroll processing). Temporal dependencies can also be created by simple requirements external to the application. For example, one part of a program may only be allowed to run at night for maintenance purposes, while another part of a program can be run during the day for routine operations.

Process Dependencies

A process dependency (or ``process level'' dependency) is the deliberate ordering of code execution at the application level to correspond with the steps in a process. Process dependencies can also be created to execute one code block (or perhaps an entire appliction) prior to another in order to meet some system policy. Process dependencies, for example, can be imposed to reflect the requirement of one business process (or simulated natural process) to terminate before another starts.

For example, a business may require the execution of a data collection program prior to the execution of an analytics program that operates on the collected data. Or, in a program simulating an ecosystem where a heavy rain causes a river to flood, a process dependency must be created to ensure that a rain simulation starts prior to the execution of a river flood simulation.

Management and Control of Dependencies

The three types of dependencies described above can make agent design and maintenance difficult when a programmer must deal with all three simultaneously. Agent feedback messaging is intended to help alleviate this issue by allowing a developer to focus on the process and temporal dependencies without having to worry about the code dependencies that are imposed by the underlying system. Temporal and Process dependencies are completely controlled by the agent developer through the following means:

a. By specifying which agents produce messages and when
b. By specifying what feedback messages, if any, to generate as responses to messages
c. Determining the order in which agents are assigned on the message stream.

Furthermore, since each agent has its own call stack and runs in its own thread space independent of the other agents and the message communications infrastructure. The developer does not have to worry about returning message results from an agent to the top of a function call stack before delivering it to another agent. Messages are passed, rather, by the communication stream in a producer/consumer fashion through the use of shared memory structures such as shared FIFO queues.

This better control over dependencies and agent feedback messaging's circular message stream helps the development of simulations by providing a way for an agent to dispatch both data and service requests to all other agents without having to keep track of which agents actually receive the message. The agent that sends a message doesn't even need to be the agent that responds to any replies to the message. This allows an agent developer to have complete control over the granularity of agents involed in a simulation.

In their simplest forms, system designs based on agent feedback messaging allow each agent to deliver messages in a "fire and forget" fashion. Messages are created by an agent and completely released into the communications stream. They are only seen again by the agent that created them after all the other agents have seen them. The agent also does not wait for an immediate response, but rather does other processing while it waits for its messages to be returned.

AGENT DESIGN METHODOLOGY

With a generic ``fire and forget'' message delivery system in place agent design methodology can handle scenarios where an agent serves simultaneously as both a client and service provider, even in the case where an agent fills both roles for its *own* requests. This allows for a very straightforward development methodology. In order to develop agents, a basic set of four questions is answered for each agent:

1. What messages are the agent required to listen for?
2. What is the read/write policy of the message?

3. What actions are performed in response to the message?
4. What messages does the agent send, and when does it send them? Recall that the target agent of a message is never defined by the sender.

With these questions answered for each agent, a message delivery matrix can then be developed for an entire system of agents. See Table 2 for an example.

Keeping a master catalogue of agents and agent messages is also useful in the development of systems that use agent feedback messaging. This makes it possible to develop systems that use existing messages and agents designed by other developers independently. When existing agents in the catalogue do not meet a designer's needs, messages from the catalogue can still be used by another developer because they are separate artifacts.

AN IMPLEMENTATION

An implementation of agent feedback messaging is now presented. I will discuss how such a messaging system can be implemented using an arbitrarily defined multi-host compute cluster. I will also discuss how federation of agents can be achieved using CORBA. The passing of messages from host to host using CORBA valuetypes will also be discussed.

AFM: An Implementation of Agent Feedback Messaging

AFM is an implementation of agent feedback messaging and serves to demonstrate how agent feedback messaging can be implemented in a practical solution. AFM has also produced some useful benchmarks which are described below that could be used as a basis of comparison to other agent communication infrastructures.

AFM puts each agent into its own thread space. Each agent utilizes a number of lightweight processes (four threads per agent) that utilize semaphores and shared memory space (FIFO queues) to pass messages from one agent to the next. The agent thread space and mechanisms for moving messages

between agents is depicted in Figure 3.

AFM's design requires each host to pass agent messages exactly one time to all agents on a given host before sending them on to another host. The host that receives each message, in turn sends the message to all agents running on that host, and then passes the message to the next host, and so on. After each message has been presented to all agents running on all other hosts, it is returned to the originating agent.

The passing of messages between hosts is depicted in Figure 4. This design in effect creates a large, circular, multi-host, message stream that all agents have access to. In order to deliver messages between hosts, AFM uses CORBA valuetypes to send marshalled message data via IIOP. CORBA valuetypes are used for two reasons. First, they allow message objects to be passed by value from host to host without involving agents directly in network communications. Second, messages defined as valuetypes support the passing of entire graphs of messages while preserving shared values in the graph. Pages 54 and 55 of the book *Java Programming With CORBA* (Brose, Vogel, & Duddy 2001) describe this mechanism. This approach adds to the AFM implementation the ability to define message heirarchies using both class inheritance and member encapsulation.

The FIPA Agent Messaging Transport Protocol (FIPA, 2008) could be used to transmit messages between hosts as well as long as the use of the protocol is restricted to AFM's communications infrastructure and not programmed directly into agents. Transporting of valuetypes via the existing FIPA Interface Definition Lanaguage (IDL) interface would most likely require some additional work however, such as extensions to the FIPA IDL definition. In addition, parts of the protocol would also be ignored by AFM. That protocol requires in every message the designation of a destination agent to receive the message. In AFM it would not be required to specify the destination agent because it is the responsibility of an agent wishing to receive a message to it. Consequently the field containing the destination agent would be ignored by AFM.

AFM is implemented in Java. There are several features in the Java platform that makes it an attractive platform for implmenting an agent feedback messaging system:

- Robust shared memory object support and semaphores
- Large thread count management with critical sections
- Automatic garbage collection
- Strong support for CORBA interoperability
- Platform independence
- Acceptance in the scientific community

Federated Agent Communications

Federated design architectures make it possible to implement agent feedback messaging as a scalable mesaging infrastructure where hosts running agents can be added and removed to the network dynamically. However, federated approaches have rarely been applied to the realm of intelligent agent communications. The FIPA Abstract Architecture (FIPA, 2006) is the most notable exception.

Agent feedback messaging attempts to open the door to effective federated designs in agent communications. Forslund, et al (Forslund, Smith, & Culpepper, 2000) demonstrate that integrating the functionality of several stand-alone systems through federation is an effective way to integrate network based services across clusters of computing nodes and security domains. Hayden et al (Hayden, Carrick, & Yang, 1999) also document some federated agent design patterns useful for building multi-agent systems. These are the same approaches taken to implement the message communications infrastructure with the present implementation of agent feedback messaging.

Federation on the project to develop AFM was achieved by defining an interface for message communications between hosts using the CORBA IDL. Each host registers itself wth an object request broker so that other hosts can discover the messaging service at runtime. Because standard IIOP is used other non-AFM systems, such as datagram broadcasting systems and peer-to-peer systems can be used in conjunction with AFM.

IIOP is also not the only networking protocol that AFM can be implemented on top of. Since the networking protocol in use is completely transparent to the agents running in the system it can be replaced by something else entirely.

Agent Messaging Benchmarks

The biological simulation dscussed below reveals some usable application wide benchmarks that might be applied to all agent messaging systems.

- **Idle message delivery time**: The time it takes for one message to be delivered to all agents in the system and a result to be returned when the system is idle (no other messages being delivered). Can be expressd in revolutions per unit of time where the dispatch and return of one message is one revolution.
- **Per agent thread count**: The number of threads required per agent.
- **Per agent memory usage**: The average amount of memory used per agent.
- **Messages delivery rate**: The number of messages sent and successfully delivered per unit of time.
- **Message throughput**: The maximum numer of messages the communications infrastructure can deliver per unit of time.

Plotting the se benchmarks against the number of agents in the system provide a useful operating envelope for an agent message delivery system.

TWO EXAMPLES

I will now discuss how some common problems can be solved using agent feedback messaging. I will cover detailed examples of a simple biosimulation and the travelling salesman problem.

Biosimulation

The first test case of AFM was to develop a very simple simulation involving biofeedback. The source code for the simulation is packaged as part of the AFM distribution. The idea to use intelligent agents to simulate natural biofeedback mechanisms was my original inspiration for agent feedback messaging when work to develop the approach started in the early 1990's.

In this simulation, agents are created to simulate the distribution of nutrients throughout the body

Table 2. Biosim message delivery matrix

Agent	StartSimulation	HeartBeat	NeedMoreProtein	NeedMoreNourishment	Eat	ProteinMessage	NourishmentQuantity
Human	S	R			R	S	
Stomach	R	R	S	R		R	S
Heart	R	S		S			R
Left Arm	R	R		S			R
Right Arm	R	R		S			R
Left Leg	R	R		S			R
Right Leg	R	R		S			R
Brain	R	R	R		S		R

Message Purpose

- StartSimulation: Tells all agents to start simulation.
- HeartBeat: Simulates heartbeat to mark the simulation interval.
- NeedMoreProtein: Indicates that more protein is needed.
- NeedMoreNourishment: Indicates that more nourishment is needed.
- Eat: Instructs the person to eat.
- ProteinMessage: Indicates that protein (food) has been eaten.
- NourishmentQuantity: Used to deliver nutrients throughout the body.

S = message sent by organ
R = message received by organ
blank = message ignored by organ

and the interactions that take place between various body parts to signal to a person that he needs to eat more food. Agents represent the brain, heart, stomach, legs, and arms. The decision to eat and the act of eating are both managed by a single ``Human'' agent.

The simulation demonstrates many aspects of agent feedback messaging, however the top five are:

1. No agent knows what agents are responsible for handling messages it sends.
2. All responses to messages can be in the form of other messages generated by different agents (feedback messages).
3. Messages can contain values that get updated as a message is passed from agent to agent (e.g. a message representing a resouce can be "depleated" as it passes between agents).
4. The order in which agents are instantiated in the system can be used to ensure that some agents receive messages prior to others.
5. It is possible to simulate biological processes when all responses to messages are received in a delayed manner (asynchronously).

Table 2 a message delivery matrix, identifies the agents in the simulation and the messages each agent generates and receives.

The simulation starts when the Human agent creates all the other agents and then sends a Start-

Figure 3. Agent thread spaces

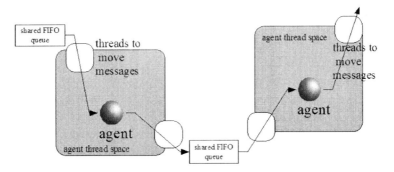

Figure 4. Message passing between hosts

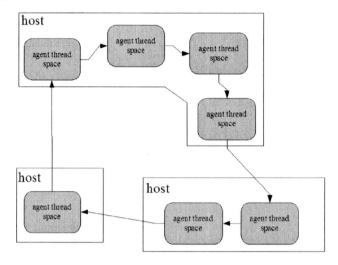

Simulation message. No reply is expected from this message. The Heart agent simulates the passage of time by generating a HeartBeat message at regular intervals. In a real simulation the Heart agent could be programmed to generate a HeartBeat message once it determines that all simulation activity associated with a single heart beat has completed. The Heart agent would determine this by listening to messages produced by other agents.

As time passes, the arms and legs use up nutrients they have stored. Each appendage keeps track of how many nutrients it has stored in its internal state and each uses nutrients at a different rate. As each appendage runs out of nutrients it dispatches a NeedMoreNourishment message requesting more. The feedback appendages expect to receieve at some point in the future is a NourishmentQuantityMessage. Each appendage continuously dispatches NeedMoreNourishment messages until it receives enough NourishmentQuantityMessages to satisfy its internal requirements to have a surplus of nourishment in storage.

The Stomach agent, upon seeing NeedMoreNourishment messages, dispatches a NourishmentQuantityMessage; one for each NeedMoreNourishment message it receives. Stomach keeps track as part of its internal state how much nourishment it can release. As the supply of nourishment in the stomach depletes, the Stomach agent begins to request more protein (which it uses to create nourish-

ment) by dispatching NeedMoreProtein messages. Like the appendages, the Stomach simply expects to see a ProteinMessage at some point in the future, but it does not know when that message will arrive. NeedMoreProtein messages are dispatched in regular intervals until it has the protein it requires.

The Brain agent, which is responsible for listening for NeedMoreProteinMessages, signals that more food must be eaten by dispatching an Eat message. As with all the other body parts, Brain does not know what agent actually is responsible for responding to this message. The more NeedMoreProteinMessages Brain receives, the more Eat messages it dispatches.

The Human agent, an agent that simulates the complicated process of actully eating, responds to Eat messages by dispatching Protein messages. The Stomach agent in turn picks this message up and interprets it as a signal that it should generate more nourishment. Each Protein message the Stomach agent receives causes Stomach to add a specific quantity of nourishment available to its nourishment store, which it can dispatch at a future time whenever it sees a NeedMoreNourishment message.

Agent feedback messaging allows messages to be modified as they are passed from one agent to another. This makes it possible for one message to represent a resource that changes as it circulates among agents. In this simulation, as NourishmentQuantityMessages are read by each agent, the agent "extracts" nutrients from the message by reducing the amount of nutrients the message has. When the NutrientQuantityMessage runs out of nutrients it is no longer valuable and will be ignored by other agents.

The simulation also illustrates that the order of agents on the message stream can be used to enforce priorities in message consumption. Downstream agents closer to the Stomach agent receive NourishmentQuanityMessages first, and therefore have the first opportunity to use the resources in the message prior to downstream messages. Only when the needs of Stomach's nearest downstream neighbors are met will other agents find nourishment available in NourishmentQuantityMessage.

The Travelling Salesman Problem

Solving the travelling salesman problem proved to be one of the more interesting uses of agent feedback messaging. In the setup of the solution, each agent was programmed to act as a single city. In addition to having one agent for each city, an additional agent was used to start and stop the simulation, and keep track of the solution. The message delivery matrix for the agents appears in Table 6.

Another benefit of solving the travelling salesman problem with agent feedback messaging can be illustrated when we look at how it solves cases with more than three cities. For the TSP problem, the AFM approach will enforce the following rule:

For any TSP problem with i cities, and any non-complete path that begins with $X_1,X_2,...X_n$ where n < i, all permutations that begin with $X_1,X_2,...X_n$ will not be searched if $X_1,X_2,...X_n$ forms a path that is more costly than an the best known solution.

The agents solve the problem by simulating the following scenario:

The mayors of all the towns decide to work together to solve the travelling salesman problem. They get together and agree on one randomly picked path of cities as a potential solution. They label the path "The Best Known Path". They assume it's not the best path, but they all agree that whenever they find a path that is better, the new path will become the official "Best Known Path".

The mayor in each town returns to his city, where he immediately hires runners from the town to travel to other cities. Each mayor hires n-1 runners, where n is the number of cities.

Each runner is assigned his own city and travels directly to that city. The runner takes with him a list of all the cities that have been visited before him. On the very first trip at the very beginning of the search, each runner's list only has his hometown on the list.

When a runner arrives at his appointed city, he contacts the mayor of that city and shows him his list of previously visited cities. The list also contains the cost of travelling the entire path to the new city. The mayor then makes a simple decision. If the path of cities on the runner's list more costly than the known shortest solution, he discards the list. Otherwise, the mayor adds his city to the list and copies it. He makes j copies, where j is the number of cities left to visit that are not on the list of previously visited cities. The mayor then sends a new list of cities that have been visited with each new runner.

Table 3. Distance between 3 cities

	A	B	C
A	-	5	8
B		-	3
C			-

Figure 5. Agents created to solve TSP

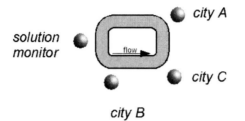

The new group of runners travel to their appointed city and the process repeats.

To demonstrate how to solve this problem using agent feedback messaging a simple problem involving three cities is shown. The problem consists of three cities, A, B, C. The distances between the three cities are shown in Table 3.

Four agents are created: one for each city, and one monitor agent to keep track of the solution. The arrangement of the agents is arbitrary, and they have been randomly connected to the communications infrastructure. Their configuration is shown in Figure 5.

The messages inserted into the message stream by each agent will contain two basic pieces of information: a) the path that makes up the solution, and b) the distance of the path.

As each message visits an agent, the agent will check the message to see if adding itself to the path creates a new path that is longer than the currently known shortest path. If the path is not longer than the shortest path, the agent copies the message, adds itself to the path, updates the distance, and dispatches the new message. If the path is longer than the shortest known path, then the message is ignored. As a result, the only paths that are built up in a message are better than the best known solution. As each message reaches the solution monitor, it is checked to see if it contains a complete path. If it does, and the path is shorter, then the new solution is saved by the solution monitor. The new solution is then dispatched to all the agents in a new message. If the solution is not better, than it is ignored. The only time a complete solution is generated in

a message is if it contains a solution that is better that the currently known solution.

Consequently, as messages are discovered to contain a non-optimal solution they are never copied. The end result is that the solution is able to be calculated without having to perform an exhaustive search of the solution set.

Figure 6 shows the messages that will be generated by each city and how they will propagate to the other cities. City B's message that is sent out at the start of the simulation is shown. There are a few things to note about the messages that are generated because of the message that City B sends out:

1. All permutations of the solution beginning with city B will be generated . Note how message 1 causes two additional messages to be generated: message 2 with path BC and message 3 with path BA

2. Message 2 causes city A to generate message 4 with path BCA.

3. Message 3 will cause city C to generate a fifth message with path BAC (not shown) when the message is moved around to agent city C.

4. Message one will be destroyed by the agent that created it when it reaches the city B agent and will not cause other messages to be created.

Having seen what happens in response to initial message generated by any particular agent, we can take a look at the message generated by all the agents when the simulation starts. The pattern of message generation we see in Figure 6 will be the same for all agents, however, all agents will create and dispatch their messages at the same time.

Figure 6. Message generation created and solution caused by one agent's message

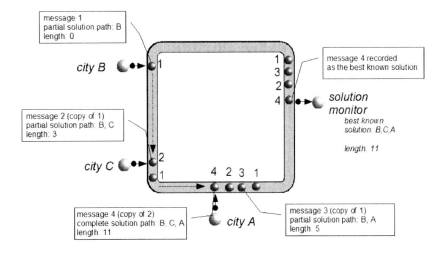

Figure 7. Multiple cities generating the first message

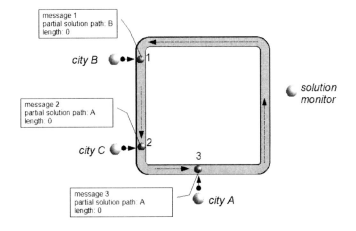

Figure 8. Multiple cities generating subsequent messages; this process is repeated

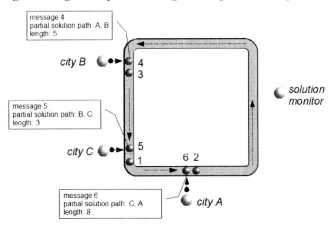

Consequently, the message stream will be much more congested for a period of time. Figures 7 and 8 show how the number of messages grow as they are built up over time.

As the simulation runs, the best known solution will be constantly updated by the solution monitor agent as better solutions are found. The net result is a search algorithm that gets progressively better as the simulation runs.

Consider a problem set with the four cities identified in Table 2. As was mentioned earlier, the strategy used to solfve the TSP involves picking a randomly generated path that is assumed to be non-optimal. Let's assume that for our new five-city problem, the monitor agent arbitrarily picks a solution of A, B, C, D, E. This path is not optimal, but will be used at the start of the simulation as the best known path. Solutions generated by the agents are compared to this path. If at any time an agent gets a partial path, and adding itself to that path creates a solution worse than the monitor's best known path the agent does not generate a copy the partial path, as it knows that it is not possible to result in a better solution that what is already known.

For example, given that A,B,C,D,E is the best known path at the beginning of the simulation, agent A will eventually receive a message with path B,D. Agent A, knowing that the solution needs to be at least shorter than A,B,C,D,E will realize that when it adds itself to B,D it creates a solution with a path that is at least 27. It will not copy the message with path B,D and insert a new message that with a path of B,D,A into the message stream. Consequently, all permutations of the solution that start with B,D,A will not be checked. This will ensure that the agents do not have to search the entire solution domain to find the optimal answer.

The solution C,D,E,B,A will, however eventually be generated by agent A. When it is generated the solution monitor will store that path as the best known path and communicate it to all agents, and all other solutions from that moment on will need to at least be better than C,D,E,B,A. Whatever the optimal path is, it will eventually be generated by an agent and delivered to the solution monitor.

CONCLUSION

The performance of agent feedback messaging, as implemented in AFM, is good enough to begin the creation of large scale simulations of both natural and man-made processes. The number of agents that can be reasonably instantiated on a single computer without a significant loss in overall performance is high enough to attempt agent based simulations of larger models, such as Forrester's production distribution system (Forrester 1962). In addition to continued work on the biosimulation example presented above, work has also begun on simulations of Forrester's production models as well as simulations of a biodiesel manufacturing operation.

Agent feedback messaging also reduces the amout of time managing code dependencies which provides more time for managing the procedural and temporal dependencies that define a given simulation. The granularity of components smulated in a given model can also be manipulated relatively easily, with the number of agents in a simulaton being inversly proportionate the to the size of object in the model being simulated. A large number of agents can be used to simulate the smallest elements in a model (e.g. cells in an animal), or a single agent can be used to simulate one large object (an abstract animal).

Table 4. TSP problem with 5 cities

	A	B	C	D	E
A	-	5	2	4	8
B		-	3	15	2
C			-	1	9
D				-	5
E					-

Table 5. TSP matrix

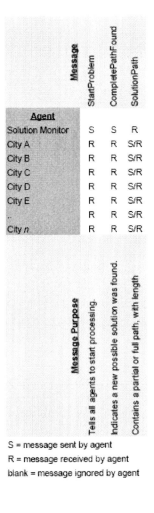

During simulation development, coarse grained agents can be used to validate a simulation against broad parameters. Fine grained sets of agents can then be developed that deal with detailed parameter sets in a model. This provides enough flexibility to pursue bottom-up and top-down approaches to agent design simultaneously.

Efforts to integrate agent feedback messaging with external data sources have also resulted in opportunities to integrate intelligent agents with commonly used Web services technologies.

FUTURE RESEARCH DIRECTIONS

Since agent feedback messaging is a generalized messaging framework for multiagent systems, the possibilities of research where the approach can be useful are unlimited. However, there are a handful of key areas where the current implementation, AFM, can be put to use immediately.

- **Scalabiliy Testing**: One area of critical research that needs will be accomplished as the next order of business will be the measurement of benchmarks of AFM across a large number of nodes.
- **Biological simuation**: Further refinement of the physiological model shown as an example in this chapter. In particular, a proper working physiological model should be built that can at least simulate accurate blood flows and overall functioning of major organs.

Table 6. Some non-optional paths for the five cities

path	*costs*	*total*
CDEBA	1+5+2+5+2	15
ABCDE	5+3+1+5+8	22
BDAEC	15+4+8+9+3	39
CEABD	9+8+5+15+4	41

- **Manufacturing**: Implementation of Forrester's models (1962) as presented in the book in their entirety.
- **Genetic algorithms and genetic programming**: A simple genetic algorithm is planned for development to guage how effectively genetic programming can be carried out using AFM.
- **Semantic Webs and natural language processing:** The building up of Semantic Webs with structured and unstructured data such as that found on Web sites
- **Data fusion**: It is entirely possible to use AFM to accomplish the fusion of data from multiple sensors in a real time environment. The advantage of this research will be to incorporate embedded sensors into agent designs.
- **Robotics**: Developing a robotics control system usin AFM is also a high priority area of research planned for AFM.
- **Emotional Modeling**: Emotional modeling is an underserved area of artificial intelligence.
- **Societies of Agents**: Using agent feedback messaging should lend itself well to the study of phenomena that occur in societies of agents. The scalability of the approach presnted in this chapter should easily allow studies of agent socities that number in the thousands or millions of agents.

REFERENCES

Bates, J. (1997). The role of emotion in believable agents. *Communications of the ACM, 37*(7), 122-125.

Becker, R. & Lesser, V. & Zilberstein, S. (2005). Analyzing myopic approaches for multi-agent communication. In *Proceedings of the 2005 IEEE/WIC/ACM International Conference on Intelligent Agent Technology (IAT 05)*, (pp. 550-557). Compiegne, France: IEEE Computer Society.

Brose, G. & Vogel, A. & Duddy, K. (2001). *Java programming with CORBA, Third Edition*. New York: John Wiley & Sons, Inc.

Cerys, D. & Rozga, A. & Berliner, J. (2006). A cougaar-based logistics modeling tool for highly adaptable military organizations. *Cognitive Agent Architecture (Cougaar)*. Retrieved March 2006 from http://cougaar.org/docman/?group id=17

FIPA (2006). FIPA abstract architecture specification. *Foundation for Intellligent Physical Agents.* Retrieved May 2006, from http://www.fipa.org/specifications

FIPA (2008). FIPA agent message transport protocol for IIOP specification. *Foundation for Intellligent Physical Agents.* Retrieved January 2008 from http://www.fipa.org/specifications

Forrester, J. W. (1962). *Industrial Dynamics*. Cambridge, MA: Massachusetts Institute of Technology (M.I.T.) Press.

Forslund, D. W. & Smith, R. K. & Culpepper, T. C. (2000). Federation of the person identification service between enterprises. In *Proceedings of the AMIA 2000 Symposium*. (pp. 240-244).

Hayden, S. & Carrick, C. & and Yang, Q. (1999). Architectural design patterns for multi-agent coordination.In *Proceedings of the International Conference on Agent Systems '99 (Agents'99)*. Seattle, WA, May 1999. Available WWW . http://citeseer.ist.psu.edu/hayden99architectural.html

Hillersberg, J. & Mooonen, H. & Verduijn, T. & Becker, J. (2004, September). *Agent technology in supply chains and networks*. In *Proceedings of the IEEE/WIC/ACM International Conference on Intelligent Agent Technology (IAT '04)*. Beijing, China.

Horling, B. & Lesser, V. & Vincent, R. & and Wagner, T. (2006). The soft real-time agent control architecture. *Autonomous Agents and Multi-Agent Systems 12*(1), 35-92. An earlier version is available as UMass Computer Science Technical Report 2002-14.

Picard, G. & Gleizes, M. P. (2002). An agent architecture to design self-organizing collectives: Principles and application. In *Proceedings of Adaptive Agents and Multi-Agents Systems (AAMAS) 2001 / 2002*, (pp. 141-158).

Shah, S. W.; & Nixon, P. & Ferguson, R. I. (2004). On the use of IP multicast to facilitate group communication between mobile agents. In *Proceedings of the Intelligent Agent Technology, IEEE/WIC/ACM International Conference,* (pp. 487-490).

Zhang, H. & Lesser, V. (2004). A dynamically Formed hierarchical agent organization for a distributed content sharing system . In *Proceedings of the International Conference on Intelligent Agent Technology (IAT 2004),* (pp. 169-175). Beijing: IEEE Computer Society.

ADDITIONAL READING

Material on intelligent agent commmunication infrastructures tends to be difficult to find at best. The references cited in the body of this chapter were chosen because they seem to form the most relevant material on the subject that can be easily found. However, there are a number of places which can be searched for more information and example implementations:

FIPA (2008). *The Foundation for Intelligent Physial Agents.* Website at www.fipa.org

Cougaar Website (2008). http://cougaar.org

Padgham, Lin & Winikoff, Michael (2004). *Developing intelligent agent systems: A practical guide.* Hoboken, NJ: Wiley and Sons.

Bigus, Joseph P. & Bigus, Jennifer, & Bigus, Joe (2001). *Constructing intelligent agents using Java: Professional developer's guide.* Hoboken, NJ: Wiley and Sons.

Murch, Richard & Johnson, Tony (1998). *Intelligent software agents.* Upper Saddle River, NJ: Prentice Hall PTR.

Woodridge, Michael (1997). *Intelligent Agents II - Agent Theories, Architectures, and Languages: IJCAI'95-ATAL Workshop, Montreal, Canada, August 19-20, 1995.* Proceedings (Lecture Notes in Computer Science). Berlin: Springer-Verlag.

Rehtanz, C (2003). *Autonomous systems and intelligent agents in power system control and operation (power systems).* Kindle Edition. Berlin: Springer-Verlag.

Chapter VIII

Modeling Cognitive Agents for Social Systems and a Simulation in Urban Dynamics

Yu Zhang
Trinity University, USA

Michael Pellon
Trinity University, USA

Mark Lewis
Trinity University, USA

Phil Coleman
Trinity University, USA

Christine Drennon
Trinity University, USA

Jason Leezer
Trinity University, USA

ABSTRACT

Multi-agent systems have been used to model complex social systems in many domains. The entire movement of multi-agent paradigm was spawned, at least in part, by the perceived importance of fostering human-like adjustable autonomy and behaviors in social systems. But, efficient scalable and robust social systems are difficult to engineer. One difficulty exists in the design of how society and agents evolve and the other difficulties exist in how to capture the highly cognitive decision-making process that sometimes follows intuition and bounded rationality. We present a multi-agent architecture called CASE (Cognitive Agents for Social Environments). CASE provides a way to embed agent interactions in a three-dimensional social structure. It also presents a computational model for an individual agent's intuitive and deliberative decision-making process. This chapter also presents our work on creating a multi-agent simulation which can help social and economic scientists use CASE agents to perform their tests. Finally, we test the system in an urban dynamic problem. Our experiment results suggest that intuitive decision-making allows the quick convergence of social strategies, and embedding agent interactions in a three-dimensional social structure speeds up this convergence as well as maintains the system's stability.

INTRODUCTION

In social environments, people interact with each other and form different societies (or organizations or groups). To better understand people's social interactions, researchers have increasingly relied on computational models [16, 40, 41, 42]. A good computational model that takes into consideration both the individual and social behaviors could serve as a viable tool to help researchers analyze or predict the complex phenomena that emerge from the interactions of massive autonomous agents, especially for the domain that often requires a long time to evolve or requires exposing real people to a dangerous environment. However, efficient, scalable, and robust social systems are difficult to engineer [3].

One difficulty exists in modeling the system by holding both the societal view and the individual agent view. The societal view involves the careful design of agent-to-agent interactions so that an individual agent's choices influence and are influenced by the choices made by others within the society. The agent view involves modeling only an individual agent's decision-making processes that sometimes follow intuition and bounded rationality [29]. Previous research in modeling theory of agents and society in a computational framework has taken singly a point of view of society or agent. While the single societal view mainly concentrates on the centralist, static approach to organizational design and specification of social structures and thus limits system dynamics [12, 16, 35], on the other hand, the single agent view focuses on modeling the nested beliefs of the other agents, but this suffers from an explosion in computational complexity as the number of agents in the system grows.

Another difficulty in modeling theory of agent and society exists in quantitative or qualitative modeling of uncertainty and preference. In the case of quantitative modeling, the traditional models like game theory and decision theory have their own limitations. Game theory typically relies on concepts of equilibria that people rarely achieve in an unstructured social setting, and decision theory typically relies on assumptions of rationality that people constantly violate [27]. In the case of qualitative modeling, there are three basic models:

prescriptive, normative and descriptive [31, 37]. A prescriptive model is one which can and should be used by a real decision maker. A normative model requires the decision maker to have perfect rationality, for example, the classical utility function belongs to this category. Many normative theories have been refined over time to better "describe" how humans make decisions. Kahneman and Tversky's Prospect Theory [18, 34] and von Neuman and Morgenstein's Subjective Utility Theory [36] are noted examples of normative theories that have taken on a more descriptive guise. One of the central themes of the descriptive model is the idea of Bounded Rationality [29], i.e., humans don't calculate the utility value for every outcome; instead we use intuition and heuristics to determine if one situation is better than another. However, existing descriptive methods are mostly informal, therefore there is a growing need to study them in a systematic way and provide a qualitative framework in which to compare various possible underlying mechanisms.

Motivated by these observations, we have developed a cognitive agent model called CASE (Cognitive Agent in Social Environment). CASE is designed to achieve two goals. First, it aims to model the "meso-view" of multi-agent interaction by capturing both the societal view and the agent view. On one hand, we keep an individual perspective on the system assumed by the traditional multi-agent models, i.e. an agent is an autonomous entity and has its own goals and beliefs in the environment [5, 43]. On the other hand, we take into account how agent's decisions are influenced by the choices made by others. This is achieved by embedding agents' interactions in three social structures: group, which represents social connections, neighborhood, which represents space connections and network, which span social and space categories. These three structures reproduce the way information and social strategy is passed and therefore the way people influence each other. In our view, social structures are external to individual agent and independent from their goals. However, they constrain the individual's commitment to goals and choices and contribute to the stability, predictability and manageability of the system as a whole.

Our second goal is to provide a computational descriptive decision model of the highly cognitive process wherein an individual agent's decision-making. The descriptive theory assumes agents undergo two fundamental stages when reaching a final decision: an early phase of *editing* and a subsequent phase of *evaluation* [19]. In the editing phase, the agent sets up priorities for how the information will be handled in the subsequent decision-making phase and forms heuristics which will be used during the decision-making process, i.e. the agent only acts with bounded rationality. In the evaluation phase, there exist two generic modes of cognitive function: an *intuitive* mode in which decisions are made automatically and rapidly, and a controlled mode, which is *deliberate* and slower. When making decisions, the agent uses *satisfying* theory [30], i.e. it takes "good enough" options rather than a single "best" option.

The rest of the chapter is organized as follows. Section 2 introduces the related work. In Section 3, we give an overview to cognitive models for social agents, from both the societal view and individual agent view, and introduce preliminary contextual information. Section 4 presents CASE from the perspective of the societal view, i.e. how an agent's decision affects another. Section 5 presents CASE from the perspective of the individual agent's view, i.e. an intuitive and deliberative decision-making mechanism. Section 6 is a simulation supporting CASE agents that provides an integrated environment for researchers to manage, analyze and visualize their data. Section 7 reports the experiments and Section 8 concludes the chapter.

RELATED WORK

Multi-agent systems have been widely used to model human behaviors in social systems from the computational perspective. There have been many successful systems addressing this issue. Due to the lack of space, we limit this discussion to several of the most relevant systems. We review them from two categories: agent modeling and agent simulation.

Agent Modeling

COGnitive agENT (COGENT) [6] is a cognitive agent architecture based on Rasmussen's integrated theory of human information processing [28] and the Recognition Primed Decision (RPD) model [21]. It provides the decision-aiding at multiple levels of information processing, ranging from perceptual processing and situation feature extraction through information filtering and situation assessment, and not a direct process of real human social behaviors.

COgnitive Decision AGEnt (CODAGE) [20] is an agent architecture that derived its decision model from cognitive psychological theories to take bounded rationality into account. However, CODAGE does not consider an agent's influence on other agents and there is no communication between agents. We consider communication important since it permits individuals to expand their spheres of interest beyond the self. Moreover, CODAGE is a centralized system where only one decision maker makes decisions for each agent, while CASE is a distributed system where each agent makes their own decisions.

PsychSim [27] is a multi-agent simulation for human social interaction. In order to represent agents' influence on each other, PsychSim gives each agent full decision models of other agents. In PsychSim, bounded rationality is implemented as three limitations on agents' beliefs: 1) limiting the recursive nested-belief reasoning process to a certain level, 2) limiting the finite horizon of the agents' look-ahead, and 3) allowing the possible error in the agents' belief about others. However, we treat bounded rationality as a human tendency to anchor on one trait or piece of information when making decisions (the detail of this can be found in Section 5).

Construct-Spatial [24] combines an agent's communication and movement simultaneously. It aims to simulate many real world problems that require a mixed model containing both social and spatial features. They integrate two classical models: Sugarscape [7], a multi-agent grid model, and Construct [2], a multi-agent social model, and run virtual experiments to compare the output from the combined space to those from each of the two spaces. Our model is similar in that we also capture multi-dimensional interactions between agents. We embed agents' interactions in three social structures: group, which represents social connections, neighborhood, which represents space connections and network, which span social and space categories. These three structures reproduce the way information and social strategy is passed and therefore the way people influence each other.

Hales and Edmonds [14] introduce an interesting idea of using "tag" mechanisms for the spontaneous self-organization of group level adaptations in order to achieve social rationality. Their idea is to use agents that make decisions based on a simple learning mechanism that imitates other agents who have achieved a higher utility. This research reminds us that sometimes the simplest of techniques can have the most far-reaching results. However, agents in their system need a relatively large number of tag bits (32 tag bits for a population of 100 agents) for all agents to reach a socially rational decision. In this chapter we use a different approach for generating socially rational behaviors. We embed social interaction into three social structures and provide a model for diffusing one agent's strategy to others.

Jiang and Ishida [17] introduce an evolution model about the emergence of the dominance of a social strategy and how this strategy diffuses to other agents. Our model is similar in that it includes multiple groups and allows for diffusion of strategy. But our model differs in two aspects. First is in how the groups are defined. Jiang and Ishida define a one to one relationship between groups and strategies, i.e. for every one strategy there exists one group and each agent belongs to the group that has their strategy. However, in our model, an agent can belong to multiple groups at one time. The second difference exists in whether or not the group's strategy is dynamic. Because Jiang and Ishida define a one to one relationship between groups and strategies, there must always exist one group for every possible strategy. This means group strategies are static and will not change over time. In our model, we model the dynamics between the group and the agent, so both the group's strategy and the agent's may be changed with time.

Agent Simulation

RePast[1], perhaps one of the most feature filled packages, provides templates for easy construction of

behavior for individual agents and integrates GIS (Geographic Information System) support, which is a feature that our simulations will need. It is also fully implemented on all systems. The multi agent system named MASON[2] is a lightweight system with a good amount of functionality. It has the ability to generate videos and snapshots as well as charts and graphs. JADE[3] is a project that we looked at for its ability to be distributed across multiple machines that do not need to be running on the same operating system, which is a feature of our system. It also allows configuration of a distributed model to be controlled by a remote GUI, which is also a feature we implement in our package. Cougaar[4], developed for use by the military is influential in that it allows for huge scaling of projects to simulate many agents working together, which is a very appealing feature for our simulations. JAS[5] (Java Agent based Simulation) library is a package that supports time unit management by allowing the user to specify how a system will operate in terms of hours, minutes or seconds. This is helpful for spatial modeling and simulations. SWARM[6], developed at the Santa Fe Institute, allows for users to write their own software. It also allows for development on a variety of systems. The package is open source and has a large community of developers as well. EcoLab[7] allows for the user to generate histograms and graphs but is only able to be implemented on a limited amount of systems. It provides a scripting language which can access the model's methods and instance variables, allowing experiments to be set up dynamically at runtime. This is good for the user without programming skills. Breve[8] allows the user to define agent behavior in a 3D world. It also allows for extensive use of plug-ins that fit seamlessly with user generated code.

COGNITIVE MODELS FOR SOCIAL AGENTS: AN OVERVIEW

According to social scientists, social behavior is behavior directed towards, or taking place between, agents of the same societies [26]. Understanding the emergence and nature of social behavior is necessary prior to the design of a computational framework. Social behaviors are complex phenomena, which may be better examined at two different levels: the society level and the individual agent level. These two levels are not independent but are intimately related and often overlap.

The Society

Any society is the result of an interaction between agents, and the behavior of the agents is constrained by the assembly of societal structures [9]. For this reason, a society is not necessarily a static structure, that is, an entity with predefined characteristics and actions. If societies such as public institutions or companies possess an individuality of their own which distinguishes them from the assembly created by the individualities of their members, it is not necessarily the same for simpler collective structures such as working groups or herds of animals. Even though societies are considered as being complex, such as colonies of bees or ants, they should not necessarily be considered as individuals in their own right if we wish to understand their organization and the regulation and evolution phenomena prevailing them there. Therefore, in our view, a society is the emergence of properties of individual interactions, without it being necessary to define a specific objective which represents such an outcome[9].

While decision rules were developed for the purpose of understanding decision-making on the individual level, it is not illogical to think that such a theory could be expanded to account for decision-making made by a group of individuals. There are generally two alternative methods of extending interest beyond the self. Both of these ways, however, present some problems.

The first method is to define a notion of social utility to replace individual utilities [4]. Such a concept is problematic, because, as put by Luce and Raiffa, the notion of social rationality is neither a postulate of the model nor does it appear to follow as a logical consequence of individual rationality [22]. Pareto optimality provides a concept of group interest as a direct attribute of the group, but this falls short of a viable solution for the concept of individually rational decision makers since no player would consent to reducing its own satisfaction simply to benefit another – it is not self-enforcing. Adopting this view would require the group to behave as a "super player", who can force agents to conform to a concept of group interest that is not compatible with individual interests. Therefore, there is a clear demand for keeping self-enforcement as the baseline of decision-making for agents behaving under social context [32, 33].

The second method is to incorporate the utility of other agents into the creation of individual utility, such as the RMM (Recursive Modeling Method) model [10]. The problem of this method is that the nesting of these agent models is potentially unbounded. Further, people rarely use such a deep recursive model although infinite nesting is required for modeling rational behavior [19]. Many multi-agent models of human decision-making made reasonable domain specific limitations to the number of nested levels and gains in computational efficiency [27]. But there is an inherent loss of precision. To better understand and quantify how people influence each other, Hogg and Jennings [15] introduce a framework for making socially acceptable decisions, based on social welfare functions which combine social and individual perspectives in a unified manner. It seems that the notion of the social welfare function, which represents the combination of individual and social interests, is especially useful for modeling social influence so that an individual agent's behavior is affected by others but is still able to maintain its individual goal and utility.

The Agent

From a human cognitive psychological perspective, a person's behaviors can be viewed as the outcome of his/her decision-making process [25, 11]. Kahneman and Tversky suggest that a person's decision-making processes follow intuition and bounded rationality [19]. Further, the knowledge that a person has learned through his/her life experience can be viewed as the extension of his/her intuitions [25]. In psychology, intuition has broad meaning encompassing both one's ability to identify valid solutions to problems and to quickly select a workable solution among many potential solutions. For example, the RPD model aims to explain how people can make relatively fast decisions without having to compare options [21], the Prospect Theory captures human intuitive attitudes toward risk, and the Multi-Attri-

Figure 1. Agent-Society Duality

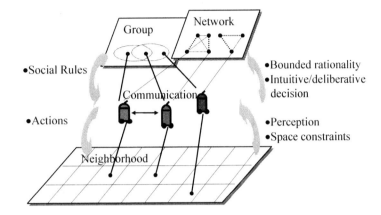

bute Decision-Making model [1, 39] draws intuition in terms of qualitative information.

First introduced by Simon, bounded rationality presents an alternative notion of individual optimization in multi-agent settings to the classic utility theory [29, 23]. Agents are only bounded rationally and use the satisfying theory to make decisions. The idea of the satisfying theory is to reconstruct utility around preferences, rather than actions. It basically states that the only information we can draw from are the preferences of individuals. This concept is an important one, since it reminds us not to ascribe spurious qualities to the individuals studied and abstracted by a utility function; such a function is a mere representation and may contain aspects that do not actually reflect the individual's nature. Stirling's satisfying game theory also shows that people do not judge the utility based off analysis of desired results, but based off their preferences [30].

AGENT-SOCIETY DUALITY

The agent/society duality, shown in Fig. 1, characterizes the processes that take place between the agents and the societies which result from them. We are dealing with dynamic interaction, the logic of which depends simultaneously on the capabilities of individual agents and the dynamic interactions between them. On one hand, agents have their own goals and are capable of performing various actions.

On the other hand, according to social scientists, agents interact with each other and the interactions are embedded in three social structures [13, 26]:

1. **Group:** represents social connections,
2. **Neighborhood:** represents space connections, and
3. **Network:** represents connections that span the social and space categories.

The purpose of these structures is to reproduce the way information and social strategy are passed and the way people influence each other. A group is a collection of agents who "think alike", or make similar decisions. It allows for a diffusion of social strategies through social space. An agent can belong to multiple groups at a time and can change groups over time. Each agent also has its own neighborhood and network. A neighborhood includes the agents whose behaviors this agent can observe within a predefined physical distance. It allows for a diffusion of information through physical space. One agent only has one neighborhood which includes the agents that it can directly observe. However, these neighbors can be different at every step because the agent moves. A network includes the agents that this agent chooses to communicate and interact with. Agents can't choose who is in their neighborhood but they can choose who they want to interact with. Therefore, the network connection allows for selective diffusion of information. Each agent also only has one network but its members can change over time. For example, if the agent has not heard from one agent over a certain step, the communication connection to that agent will be dropped.

Agent-Society Evolvement

Let agent $a \in A$ where A is the set of all agents. Each agent has a social strategy. This social strategy can be either ordinal or cardinal. We denote the social strategy for agent a by S_a.

Let $g \in G$ where G is the set of all groups. Each group also has a social strategy, denoted by S_g. Groups are formulated on the basis of a common preference. Each agent identifies itself with any group such that the agent's strategy falls within some threshold of the group's strategy.

$$\forall a \in A \text{ and } g \in G, \ a \in g \text{ if } \text{diff}(S_a, S_g) < d$$

(1)

where $\text{diff}(S_a, S_g)$ is the difference between the agent's strategy S_a and the group's strategy S_g, and d is the threshold. It can be seen that agent a can belong to more than one group at a time and can belong to different groups over time.

When an agent joins a group they are given a rank in that group. An agent will have one rank for every group they belong to. The agent's rank can be evaluated based on the agent's importance, credibility, popularity, etc. Rank defines how much the agent will influence the group as well as how much the group will influence them. A high-ranking agent influences the group, and therefore its members, more than a low ranking agent and at the same time is influenced more than a low ranking agent. An agent's rank is specific to the domain and may change over time.

Each time step, every group will update their strategy. The update is determined by its members' strategy and the percentage of the total group rank they hold.

Figure 2. Agent execution function

```
/* The function is executed independently by
   each agent, denoted agent a below.*/
execute(KBa, Sa, env, mQueue, t)
   inputs: KBa is the knowledge base for agent a
           Sa, the strategy of agent a
           env, the environment
           mQueue, the message queue for agent a
           t, the current step
   // making decision
       observation(env);
       update(KBa);
       check(mQueue);
       M = situation_assess(KBa);
       action = decision(KBa, Sa, M);
   // performing the output of decision-making
       do(action);
       inform_resource_synchronize(env);
       update(env);
       inform_server_synchronize(masterserver);
   // updating society's strategy
       update_group_strategy();
       update_neighborhood_strategy();
       update_network_strategy();
   // updating agent's strategy
       update_agent_strategy();
   // moving to next step
       t++;
```

$$S_g = \sum\nolimits_{a \in g} S_a \times \frac{R_a^g}{\sum_{b \in g} R_b^g} \qquad (2)$$

where R_a^g denotes agent a's group rank. This allows for groups to be completely dynamic because both their members and their strategy can change each time step.

Just like an agent's rank in it groups, an agent also has a rank in its neighborhood and network. Each agent keeps track of the agents in its neighborhood and the agents it communicates with. Every time an agent observes another agent in his neighborhood, that agent's neighborhood rank will increase. Also, each time an agent communicates with another agent, that agents communication rank increases. Therefore every agent will have a rank value for every agent it interacts with, and a separate rank for every agent he communicates with. When an agent updates its strategy, it will take into account these ranks. Agents with a high rank relative to the other agents will have a stronger influence. Therefore the longer two agents are near each other, the more they will influence each other. The same is true for communications. Below is the update function for the neighborhood's strategy and the network's strategy.

$$S_n = \sum\nolimits_{a \in n} S_a \times \frac{R_a^n}{\sum_{b \in n} R_b^n} \qquad (3)$$

$$S_w = \sum\nolimits_{a \in w} S_a \times \frac{R_a^w}{\sum_{b \in w} R_b^w} \qquad (4)$$

where S_n is the strategy for neighborhood n, P_w is the strategy for network w, R_a^n is agent a's neighborhood rank and R_a^w is agent a's network rank.

Each time step, every agent also updates their strategy. An agent's update function is defined as:

$$S_a^{\,`} = \alpha \times S_a + \beta \times S_g + \gamma \times S_n + \lambda \times S_w \qquad (5)$$

where $\alpha, \beta, \gamma, \lambda \in [0, 1]$ and $\alpha+\beta+\gamma+\lambda = 1$. These values represent what percentage of influence the agent takes from itself, its group, its neighborhood and its network. This allows for multiple agent types. For example, (1, 0, 0, 0) represents a selfish agent because it cares nothing about the whole society, and (0, 0.33, 0.33, 0.34) represents a selfless agent who cares about the three social structures equally. Our system is fully distributed and uses discretized time. At each time step, every agent has an execution cycle, shown in Figure 2.

Figure 3. Two-phase decision-making process

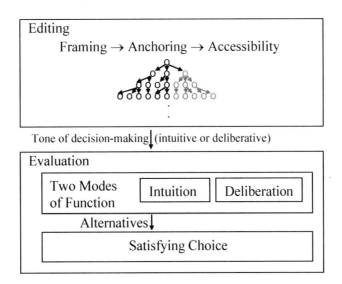

TWO-PHASE DECISION-MAKING PROCESS

Kahneman and Tversky suggest a two-phase decision model for descriptive decision-making: an early phase of editing and a subsequent phase of evaluation. In the editing phase, the decision-maker constructs a representation of the acts, contingencies and outcomes that are relevant to the decision. In the evaluation phase, the agent assesses the value of each alternative and chooses the alternative of highest value. Our decision model incorporates their idea and specifies it by the following five mechanisms:

- Editing
  - **Framing:** The agent frames an outcome or transaction in its mind and the utility it expects to receive.
  - **Anchoring:** The agent's tendency to overly or heavily rely on one trait or piece of information when making decisions.
  - **Accessibility:** The importance of a fact within the selective attention.
- Evaluation
  - **Two modes of function:** Intuition and deliberation.
  - **Satisfying theory:** Being good enough.

Figure 3 shows the two-phase decision-making process. Next we discuss each phase in a sub-section.

Editing Phase

One important feature of the descriptive model is that it is reference based. This notion grew out of another central notion called **framing** where agents subjectively frame an outcome or transaction in their minds and the utility they expect to receive is thus affected. This closely patterns the manner in which humans make rational decisions under conditions of uncertainty.

Framing can lead to another phenomenon referred to as **anchoring**. Anchoring or focalism is a psychological term used to describe the human tendency to overly or heavily rely (*anchor*) on one trait or piece of information when making decisions. A classic example would be a man purchasing an automobile, the client tends to "anchor" his decision on the odometer reading and year of the car rather than the condition of the engine or transmission.

Accessibility is the ease with which particular information come to mind. The concept of accessibility is applied more broadly in this research than in common usage. The different aspects and elements of a situation, the different objects in a scene, and the different attributes of an object, all can be described as more or less accessible for an individual agent exposed to a certain decision situation. As it is used here, the concept of accessibility subsumes the notions of stimulus salience, selective attention, and response activation or priming.

The editing phase gives us the main ideas that have been incorporated practically into the next phase, evaluation, to make quick intuitive decisions.

Evaluation Phase

In the evaluation phase, there exist two modes of cognitive function: an **intuitive** mode in which decisions are made automatically and rapidly, and a **deliberative** mode, which is effortful and slower. The operations of the intuition function are fast, effortless, associative, and difficult to control or modify, while the operations of the deliberation function are slower, serial, and deliberately controlled; they are also relatively flexible and potentially rule governed. Intuitive decisions occupy a position between the automatic operations of perception and the deliberate operations of reasoning.

Intuitions are thoughts and preferences that come to mind quickly and without much reflection. In psychology, intuition can encompass the ability to know valid solutions to problems and decision making. For example, the RPD model aimed to explain how people can make relatively fast decisions without having to compare options [21]. Klein found that under time pressure, high stakes, and changing parameters, experts used their base of experience to identify similar situations and intuitively choose feasible solutions. Thus, the RPD model is a blend of intuition and deliberation. Intuition is the pattern-matching process that quickly suggests feasible courses of action. Deliberation is a conscious reasoning of the courses of action.

We adopted a different approach from the RPD model to handle the intuitive and deliberative decision-making process. For our purpose, what becomes accessible in the current situation is a key issue in determining the tone of decision-making, i.e. intuitive or deliberative. Accessibility is determined in the editing phase by three factors.

- First, an agent utilizes prior knowledge of previous states to frame potential outcomes for its current state. In framing these potential outcomes, an agent ascribes reference based expected utility functions to them. Here, information anchoring or bias becomes a positive force as it leads to the agent's ability to make reference based utilities for each potential outcome.
- Second, when an agent makes decisions, it does not have to search all of its knowledge base. Instead, it concentrates on the relevant and important information.
- Third, a decision which was chosen before receives more attention (or high accessibil-

ity) than other alternatives and tends to be more positively evaluated before it is chosen again.

Based on the above analyses, we compile an information list. In addition to physical properties such as size and distance, the list keeps track of an abstract property called accessibility. The accessibility represents the relevance, similarity or importance of the information. At the beginning, this fact is known to the designer. It will be dynamically updated along with system processing. For example, the deliberation process may increase the accessibility because this information is important; if this information has been used in a previously successful decision, its accessibility will be increased, but if the previous decision was not successful, the accessibility will be decreased. The accessibility of all information is normalized and compared with a threshold for triggering the intuitive function for decision-making.

When making decisions, agents use the **satisfying theory**, i.e. they will take the good enough choice rather than the best one. We model the decision-making as a Multi-Attribute Decision-Making problem [1, 39], which includes a finite discrete set

Figure 4. Two-phase decision-making algorithm

---

decision(KB_a, S_a, M)
   inputs: KB_a, the knowledge base for agent *a*
        S_a, the strategy for agent *a*
        M, the current situation

   //editing phase
   anchors = getAnchor(M);
   topAccessibleMemory = query(KB_a, anchors);

   //evaluation phase
   //intuitive decision-making
   if (topAccessibleMemory is enough)
   rebuild individual tree
      return satisfyingDM(topAccessibleMemory, S_a);

   //deliberative decision-making
   else
      wholeMemory = query(KB_a, M);
      if (wholeMemory is enough)
         return satisfyingDM(wholeMemory, S_a);
      else
         ask(network, anchors);

Figure 5. A three tier SOA diagram

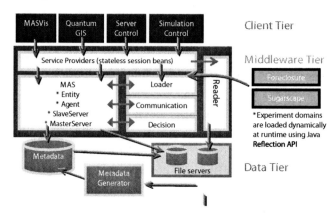

of alternatives which is valued by a finite discrete set of attributes *i*. A classical evaluation of alternatives leads to the aggregation of all criteria into a unique criterion called value function *V* of the form:

$$V(\alpha) = w \cdot v(\alpha) = f_{i \in I}(w_i v_i(\alpha)) \qquad (6)$$

where α is an action, $V(\alpha)$ is the overall value for action α, w_i is a scaling factor to represent the relative importance of the ith attribute, $v_i(\alpha)$ is a single attribute value with respect to attribute index $i \in I$ and *f* is the aggregation function. Function *f* normally is domain dependent, for example, it can be an additive value function for preference independence, a discounted value function when there is reward for different preferences, or a Constant Absolute Risk Aversion function for risk-averse decision-making. The action being finally selected is the first action whose value reaches a predefined desire value D:

$$\varepsilon(\alpha) = \exists \alpha \ s.t. \ V(\alpha) > D \qquad (7)$$

Figure 4 shows the two-phase decision-making algorithm.

A SIMULATION FOR CASE AGENTS

We have developed a simulation for the above agent system. Our system is capable of scaling huge simulations, to be capable of being deployed on many machines with the ability to control what is happening in the simulation through the use of a single GUI running on one machine, and it is able to process large amounts of data and perform operations on that data.

Service-Oriented Architecture

The Service-Oriented Architecture (SOA) [8] is a design pattern commonly used in many large corporations, such as NASA. It provides a flexible and stable architecture for large scale software systems. For this reason we felt it would be a good fit for the distributed multi agent system we were developing.

SOA requires that services should be "loosely coupled", in other words encapsulated and have as few dependencies on other services as possible. This allows for services to be easily swapped and their implementation to be easily upgraded. One service could easily be swapped out for another service that accomplishes the same result.

For our system we use a three tier approach as seen in Figure 5, which consists of:

- The client tier
- The middleware tier
- The data tier

The *client tier* consists of the user interface. As defined by the nature of the SOA design pattern, the

Figure 6. Master/Slave relationship

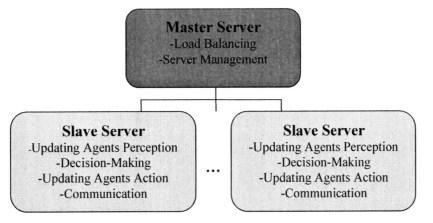

user interface maintains service encapsulation and could theoretically be used with any core system. All that would need to be ensured was that the core followed the service contract as far as how to communicate with the client tier. The first two services that the interface provides are server control and simulation control. This allows the user to set up their own system distribution and experiment. The other two services the interface provides are MAS-Vis and Quantum GIS. MASVis is a data analysis and visualization package we developed for social simulations. It is built on the fundamental design of having data sources that connect through multiple filters to process elements of data and which can be plotted to display the data. Our simulation also supports GIS. The GIS system we use to display our data is Quantum GIS[10]. Quantum GIS is suitable for our needs because it allows for reprogramming. It is quite light and allows for plug-ins so it is easily expandable. It also requires few resources, being able to run on very little RAM and consume little processing power, which is necessary for our simulations since our simulations use the processor heavily. Further, it is completely compatible on all operating systems and has a very large community of active developers. Both MASVis and Quantum GIS are still works in progress.

The *middleware tier* consists of the core CASE agent system as described earlier. The core system is made up of the collection of master and slave servers as well as the CASE agents that occupy them. The middleware tier will also consist of the service providers that help the middleware tier communicate with both the client tier as well as the data tier. We have developed two experimental domains: Sugarscape and Foreclosure. Sugarscape is a classical test-bed for growing agent-based societies [7]. Foreclosure is a domain we developed for helping social scientists to analyze the nationwide "foreclosure crisis" problem (refer to section 4 for more details).

The *data tier* helps encapsulate the data, and stores it separately from the simulation running in the core system; this could entail having the data tier on a separate server. Not only does this help ensure the stability of the data, it also allows for the use of metadata. In our simulation, the data tier records its data using XML specifications specifying important meta information such as date, author, simulation, etc. This allows for a more robust data system, which can easily be searched using filters, such as range of dates or author.

Using these three tiers will help ensure that our simulation is robust enough to allow for any part of it to be updated with little or no difficulty. Also the modular nature of the SOA allows for other researchers to use only the parts of the system that they find to be appropriate for their own project.

Next, we explain in detail the middleware tier which focuses on the system distribution and the client tier which describes the user interface.

Figure 7. A graphical representation of the KD tree

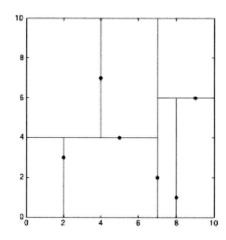

Figure 8. A screenshot of the server control interface

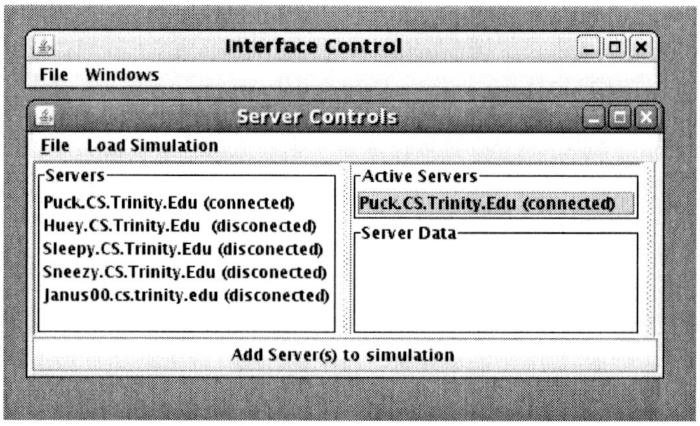

System Distribution

For the system to be effective at dealing with the large number of agents required for social research, it has to be highly distributed both in processing as well as in memory. To achieve this we developed a Master/Slave system, as showed in Figure 6.

The system has a single master server in charge of initializing and synchronizing the other servers (slaves). The master's responsibilities include initializing each step, facilitating agent communication and agent movement from one server to another, and most importantly load balancing all of the servers to ensure optimal performance. The slave is originally initialized with a given bounds and a set of agents. The slave's responsibility is to update all of its agents each step, this is a two step process:

- First it updates all of the agents' knowledge for what they perceived that step
- Secondly it has each of its agents implement its decided action for that step.

The agents are run in the maximum number of threads the server can handle; this ensures optimal performance through parallelization.

To ensure effective load balancing the master keeps track of the rest of the server by using a KD

Figure 9. A screenshot of the Sugarscape Interface

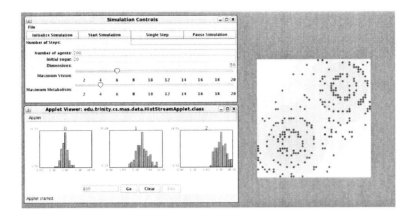

tree. The KD tree works by splitting the bounded region of the simulation on a different axis each time, until there is a single leaf per slave server, as seen in Figure 7. Splitting the region up in this manner allows the master server to go in and shift these splits one way or the other to balance the load between slaves. By shifting a KD split, the master server reduces the amount of the region and the amount of agents that a slave server is responsible for, and by doing so alleviates that server's load. Figure 8 is a screenshot of the server control interface.

User Interface

In creating the user interface, the primary consideration is that users will not be concerned with all of the system's features at once. Furthermore, there will not be enough screen space to conveniently and aesthetically portray all of these features, specifically the settings, server, data, graphical, and simulation windows, at once. To house each element of the system's features in detached windows, able to be hidden and then restored whenever needed, is therefore clearly plausible and arguably necessary for such an open-ended agent simulation. This can be argued for each individual element of the system's features.

Once a user calibrates the appropriate settings for his simulation implementation, he may not need to keep these settings in focus throughout the running of the simulation; rather, the user may be more focused on the system's output and the results of

the simulation. To keep these settings on the screen for the duration of the simulation would force the user to work with cluttered space, constantly having to move windows around in order to see and collect data. To house all of the simulation settings in a detached window, able to be hidden and then restored whenever needed, is, therefore, clearly plausible and arguably necessary for such a wide-breadth multi-agent simulation.

This same logic can apply to the server window, where server hosts can be added, managed, or booted. Clearly, server management is not the primary focus of any type of simulation. While servers need to be added at the beginning of a simulation and monitored and/or booted throughout the duration of the simulation, the server window need not be opened and visible the entire time. Again, the detached and hide-able window system works effectively in this situation.

This detached-window argument can also be applied to output-based elements of the simulation user interface. Consider when a user is focused on only the raw textual data output of a simulation. Clearly, any visual representation of the data in question, whether it is a graphical representation of this data or a step-by-step visualization of the individual agents in the system, would be extraneous and unneeded in the given situation.

Obviously, this scenario can be flipped into a situation in which the user is only focused on visuals, in which case the raw textual data output would be unneeded. Similar to the case of the settings window, housing both graphical data representations and textual data output in detached, escapable and restorable windows, is a necessary feature.

To keep almost every aspect of the simulation in separate, hide-able windows requires the use of a main menu, or a master controller, that cannot be closed. This controller handles not only the core, system-wide commands for MASVis but also the hide and restore functions for all other windows, while still remaining as small as possible and preserving screen space.

Without a doubt, users of MASVis have an advantage with a user interface system with separate, moveable, hide-able windows. Such a system allows for a maximization of the valuable resource of screen real estate and also puts the system's focus on what currently matters to the user. Figure 9 is a screenshot of the Sugarscape interface.

EXPERIMENT

Multi-agent systems are increasingly used to identify and analyze the social and economic problems of urban areas and provide solutions to these problems [9]. We tested the CASE architecture in the urban dynamics field. We did not use the classical benchmarks such as Santa-Fe Artificial Stock Market (SF-ASM) which is commonly used by the Agent-Based Simulation (ABS) community of social science and economics. This is because such classical testing domains were originally designed for game theory, which uses reactive agents and relies on the concept of equilibrium that is rarely seen in

real-world environments, and decision theory, which was grounded on the level of a single individual with a lack of social interests.

Our simulation in urban dynamics focuses on the nationwide "foreclosure crisis" problem. With more than 430,000 foreclosure filings reported nationwide, the nation's rate of foreclosure is at an all time high[11]. This experiment simulated mortgage default in San Antonio, Texas. "San Antonio is dominated by predominately young Hispanic families. In the last decade the city's young and dynamic population has seen median household income grow significantly as childhood poverty declined rapidly. Unemployment remains fairly low, however, due to a lag in higher educational attainment the bulk of the city's households earn only low-to-meddle incomes. Despite this and other factors there was a considerable rise in homeownership as the growing population began to move into neighborhoods in both the metro and suburban areas of the city."[12] By the first quarter 2007, San Antonio's rate of foreclosures is nearly twice the national average and is among the top 20 cities with the highest foreclosure rates in the U.S.[13].

Based on the above observation, we choose to model San Antonio's "foreclosure crisis" as a multi-agent system. This chapter reports our initial experiment. We modeled a simple housing market where agents purchase and sell homes. The agents need to carry out three tasks: selecting a home to purchase, obtaining a loan to purchase that home and making monthly payments on that loan. Each agent selects a home that is feasible for it to purchase based on its individual annual income, credit score

Table 1. Three teams

Team	Feature	Purpose
Reactive Team	•Reactive Agents	The base team
ID Team (Intuition + Deliberation)	•Keep every condition in Reactive Team •Replace Reactive rule by Intuitive & Deliberative decision rule	Test the effectiveness of pure I&D decision rule
IDS Team (Intuition + Deliberation + Society)	•Keep every condition in I&D Team •Add the three social structures to it (group, neighborhood and network)	Test the effectiveness of combined social structure and I&D decision rule

Figure 10. The result of the reactive team

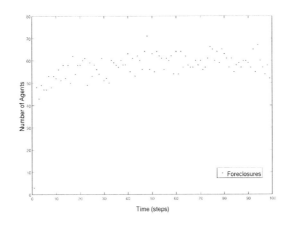

Figure 11. The result of the ID Team

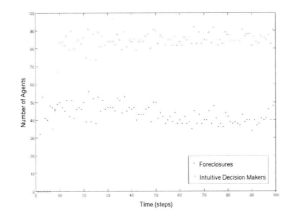

and current interest rates. On the first time step each agent attempts to purchase a home and continues to do so each time step afterwards until it finds a suitable match. Throughout the simulation the interest rates and additional monthly expenses as signed to each agent are subject to change and no agent is given prior knowledge of the schedule or degree of these changes. Once an agent has purchased and occupied a home for one time step, that agent must begin making payments on the loan it initially took out to purchase that home. If during one time step an agent can not make its monthly mortgage payment (i.e. its annual income is less than the sum of its monthly expenses and mortgage payment) then that agent is forced into a situation of default. In remaining time steps that agent may attempt to purchase another home of equal or lesser value but this is made rather difficult as its credit score has dropped significantly. This is done to reflect the difficulty in reality of obtaining a new home after a foreclosure.

The purpose of this simulation is to examine the relationship between an individual agent's strategy, and the diffusion of those strategies to its society (groups, neighborhood and network), and finally the overall foreclosure rate of the city. Our initial simulation used only 100 homeowners (agents) and 100 homes that were both randomly generated within

Figure 12. The result of the IDS team

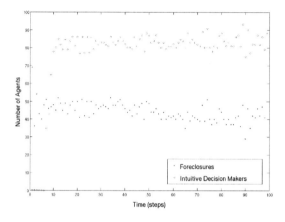

several carefully selected statistical parameters to reflect demographic realities of the city along the following lines: housing values, homeownership history, FICA (Federal Insurance Contributions Act) scores and household income. We ran the system for 100 steps with each single step simulating one month in reality.

We defined two groups of agents within the system: an *aggressive group* and a *conservative group*. Agents that are members of the aggressive group are more adapt to "over-extend" their credit lines and purchase a home that may or may not be within their budget. While agents who are members of the conservative group are more apt to purchase a home that is well within their budget. Initially each agent is given their own strategy that falls within some statistical range of one of the two groups. This initial strategy defines an agent's propensity to join one of the two groups. As time passes, agents are influenced in a variety of ways: either through members of their own groups, their neighbors who may or may not belong to the same group, and their extended social network. An agent's neighborhood is a direct function of its observability, i.e. the amount of agents it can observe at a given time. An agent's network is not a physical construct, but rather a meta-physical medium constructed from the agents it decides to frequently communicate with. Hence as the size of an agent's neighborhood, social network, and group membership grows its strategy becomes more dominant within society as a whole.

We use three teams as defined in Table 1. Except for the decision rules, conditions of all teams were exactly the same.

We report three experiments. Experiment 1 involves only the Reactive Team. These agents do not utilize any social structure (neighborhoods, groups or networks) and hence have no ability to learn through time or adapt to environmental changes. Figure 10 is the result of the reactive team. It shows that the foreclosure rate is extraordinarily high (~%60) and is rather unstable, moving up and down 15 points between some time steps. These large variations in the foreclosure rate are a product of both the agent's simplistic decision making mechanisms and their inability to diffuse successful strategies to other agents. Indicative of the fact that we do not see this high variable of foreclosure rates in reality is the underlying fact that humans utilize a much more complex and sophisticated means for making decisions.

Experiment 2 tests the ID Team. Figure 11 illustrates the results of adding only this intuition and deliberation capability to reactive agents. The upper line shows the number of agents who use intuitive decision-making. At the beginning of the simulation, this number is quite low. But agents are able to quickly learn from the decisions they made before and use them to make new decisions. The low line is the number of foreclosures. It is lower than the Reactive Team in Experiment 1 as the agents are able to recognize recurring instances of potential default and avoid them if possible. However, this adaptability is limited only to an individual agent and there are no mechanisms for one agent to diffuse its successful strategy onto other agents. This limitation is indicated by the presence still of variability in the foreclosure rate. The inability of individual agent leads to decreased stability of the system as a whole.

To further explore this, in experiment 3 we test the IDS Team. We add the three social structures (neighborhood, group and network) on top of the existing individual agent decision-making mechanisms. In doing so we allowed the agents to diffuse their successful strategies through physical (neighborhood) and non-physical (group and social network) space. As Figure 12 indicates, we see the same adaptability present in Experiment 2 as the knowledge base of the individual agents expands, allowing them to better predict future events based on past experiences, in addition to an increased level of stability (measured by less variability in the foreclosure rate) as the successful strategy is diffused through various social structures. Experiments 2 and 3 confirm our hypothesis that human decision-making is "embedded" in a social context.

CONCLUSION

In this paper, we have presented CASE, a multi-agent architecture for supporting human social interaction as well as the intuitive and deliberative decision-making process. This approach allows us to observe a wide range of emergent phenomena of complex social systems and analyze their impact. The chapter also reports our first step in developing a robust and flexible multi-agent simulation that can be used by social scientists and economists.

Within CASE, there are many issues awaiting our research team. We are currently expanding CASE in four directions. The first direction is toward agent modeling. Our current agents use a simple memory structure for intuitive decision-making. The problem with this is it is not very adaptive to the dynamic environment. We are currently analyzing different situation assessment and learning technologies and will incorporate them into our agents. Another on-going project is to theoretically study the emergent patterns in the interplay between the multi-dimen-

sional relations (group, neighborhood and network) in the behavior of agents.

Second, we will add a range of technologies for the simulation. The purpose of the simulation is to provide an integrated environment for social scientists and economists to manage, analyze and visualize their data. Therefore it is important to provide a user friendly interface and a low programming-skill-required environment. We will continue simplifying the task of setting up different testing domains and develop a rich charting package for MASVis that will further simplify the creation of visualizations.

Third, we will continue investigating various data structures and algorithms of load balancing to better distribute CASE agents on clusters of computers or different types of grids. This development will further simplify and speed up the simulation by reducing the computing load and memory load in a single machine.

Fourth, we are also expanding the scale of the foreclosure experiment in order to draw more conclusions to the question regarding the social and economic factors that affect the "foreclosure climate" of a city. The questions that we will investigate include: 1) Where are the foreclosures occurring? 2) Are they clustered or isolated events? 3) Who is being foreclosed upon and do they share common characteristics? 4) What social and economic factors are driving an increase in the foreclosure rate? and 5) Could we predict the likelihood and location of future foreclosures?

REFERENCES

[1]   Ahn, B. S. (2006). Multiattributed Decision Aid with Extended ISMAUT, *IEEE Transactions on Systems, Man and Cyberetics, Part A: Systems and Humans*, 36(3): 507-520.

[2]   Carley, K. M. & Hill, V. (2001). *Structural Change and Learning Within Organizations*, MIT Press/AAAI Press/Live Oak.

[3]   Castelfranchi, C. (2000). Engineering Social Order, *Lecture Notes In Computer Science*; 1972: 1-18.

[4]   Castelfranchi, C. (2001). The Theory of Social Functions: Challenges for Computational Social Science and Multi-Agent Learning, *Cognitive Systems Research*, 2(1): 5-38.

[5]   Coleman, P., Pellon, M. & Zhang, Y. (2007). Towards Human Decision-Making in Multi-Agent Systems, in Proceedings of the *International Conference on Artificial Intelligence*, Monte Carlo Resort, Las Vegas, Nevada.

[6]   Das, S. & Grecu, D. (2000). COGENT: Cognitive Agent to Amplify Human Perception and Cognition. In *Proceedings of 4th International Conference on Autonomous Agents*, Barcelona, Spain, pp. 443-450.

[7]   Epstein, J. & Axtell, R. (1996). *Growing Artificial Societies: Social Science from the Bottom Up*, The MIT Press.

[8]   Erl, T. (2005). Service-Oriented Architecture: Concepts, Technology, and Design, Upper Saddle River: Prentice Hall PTR.

[9]   Ferber, J. (1999). *Multi-Agent System: An Introduction to Distributed Artificial Intelligence*, Harlow: Addison Wesley Longman.

[10]   Gmytrasiewicz, P. J. & Noh, S. (2002). Implementing a Decision-Theoretic Approach to Game Theory for Socially Competent Agents, in Parsons, S., Gmytrasiewicz, P., and Wooldridge, M. (eds.), *Game Theory and Decision Theory in Agent-Based Systems*, pp. 97-118, Kluwer Academic Publishers.

[11]   Goldstone, R., Jones, A., & Roberts, M. E. (2006). Group Path Formation, *IEEE Transactions on Systems, Man, and Cybernetics, Part A: Systems and Humans*, 36(3):611-620.

[12]   Goncalves, B. & Esteves, S. (2006). Cognitive Agents Based Simulation for Decision Regarding Human Team Composition. In *Proceedings of 5th International Conference on Autonomous Agents and Multi-Agent Systems* (AAMAS'06), pp. 34-41.

[13]   Granovetter, M. (1985). Economic Action and Social Structure: the Problem of Embeddedness, *American Journal of Sociology*, 91 (3), 481-510.

[14]   Hales, D. & Edmonds, B. (2003). Evolving Social Rationality for MAS using "Tags". In *Proceedings of 5th International Conference on Autonomous Agents and Multi-Agent Systems* (AAMAS'03), pp. 497-503.

[15]   Hogg, L. & Jennings, N. R. (2001). Socially Intelligent Reasoning for Autonomous Agents, *IEEE Transactions on Systems, Man and Cybernetics - Part A*, 31(5):381-399.

[16]   Hoggendoorn, M. (2007). Adaptation of Organizational Models for Multi-Agent Systems Based on Max Flow Networks , *IJCAI'07*, pp. 1321-1326.

[17]   Jiang, Y. & Ishida T. (2007). A Model for Collective Strategy Diffusion in Agent Social Law Evolution, *IJCAI'07*, pp. 1353-1358.

[18]   Kahneman, D. & Tversky, A. (1979). Prospect Theory: An Analysis of Decision under Risk, *Econometrica*, 47(2): 263-292.

[19]   Kahneman, D. (2002). Maps of Bounded Rationality: A Perspective on Intuitive Judgment and Choice, *Les Prix Nobel*.

[20]   Kant, J. & Thiriot, S. (2006). Modeling One Human Secision Maker with A Multi-agent System: The CODAGE Approach. In *Proceedings of 5th International Conference on Autonomous Agents and Multi-Agent Systems* (AAMAS'06), pp. 50-57.

[21]   Klein, G. (1993). A Recognition-Primed Decision Making Model of Rapid Decision Making, in Klien, G., Orasanu, J., Calderwood, R. and Zsambok, C. (eds.), *Decision Making In Action: Models and Methods*, pp. 138-147.

[22]   Luce, R. D. & Raiffa, H. (1957). *Games and Decisions*, New York, Wiley.

[23]   March, J. (1994). *A Primer on Decision Making: How Decisions Happen*, Free Press, New York.

[24]   Moon, II-C. & Carley, K. M. (2007). Self-Organizing Social and Spatial Networks under What-If Scenarios. In *Proceedings of 6th International Conference on Autonomous Agents and Multi-Agent Systems* (AAMAS'07), pp. 1348-1355.

[25]   Pan, X., Han, C. S., Dauber, K. & Law, K. H. (2005). A Multi-agent Based Framework for

Simulating Human and Social Behaviors during Emergency Evacuations, *Social Intelligence Design*, Stanford University.

[26] Portes, A. and Sensenbrenner, J., Embeddedness and Immigration: Notes on the Social Determinants of Economic Action, *The American Journal of Sociology*, 98(6): 1320-1350, 1993.

[27] Pynadath, D. V. & Marsella, S. C (2005). PsychSim: Modeling Theory of Mind with Decision-Theoretic Agents, *IJCAI'05*, pp. 1181-1186.

[28] Rasmussen, J. (1986). *Information Processing and Human Machine Interaction: An Approach to Cognitive Engineering*, New York, North Holland.

[29] Simon, H. (1957). *A Behavioral Model of Rational Choice, in Models of Man, Social and Rational: Mathematical Essays on Rational Human Behavior in a Social Setting*, New York: Wiley.

[30] Stirling, W. C. (2003). *Satisficing Games and Decision Making: with Applications to Engineering and Computer Science*, Cambridge University Press.

[31] Stanovich, K. E. & West, R. F. (1999). Discrepancies between Normative and Descriptive Models of Decision Making and the Understanding/Acceptance Principle, *Cognitive Psychology*, 38: 349–385.

[32] Stirling, W. C. (2005). Social Utility Functions -part I: Theory, *IEEE Transactions on Systems, Man, and Cybernetics, Part C: Applications and Reviews*, 35(4):522-532.

[33] Stirling, W. C. & Frost, R. L. (2005). Social Utility Functions-part II: Applications, *IEEE Transactions on Systems, Man, and Cybernetics, Part C: Applications and Reviews*, 35(4):533-543.

[34] Tversky, A. & Kahneman, D. (1992). Advances in Prospect Theory: Cumulative Representation of Uncertainty, *Journal of Risk and Uncertainty*, 5: 297-323.

[35] Vazquez-Salceda, J., Dignum, V. & Dignum, F. (2005). Organizing Multiagent Systems, *Autonomous Agents and Multi-Agent Systems*, 11(3): 307-360.

[36] von Neumann, J. & Morgenstern, O. (1947). *Theory of Games and Economic Behavior*, Princeton University Press, second edition.

[37] Weber, E. U. & Coskunoglu, O. (1990). Descriptive and Prescriptive Models of Decision-Making: Implications for the Development of Decision Aids., *IEEE Transactions on Systems, Man and Cybernetics*, 20(2): 310-317.

[38] Yoon, P. K. & Hwang, C. (1995). *Multiple Attribute Decision Making: An Introduction*, Sage Publications.

[39] Zhang, Y., Ioerger, T. R. & Volz, R. A. (2005). Decision-Theoretic Proactive Communication in Multi-Agent Teamwork, in Proceedings of the *IEEE International Conference on Systems, Man and Cybernetics* (SMC'05), Hawaii, pp. 3903-3908.

[40] Zhang, Y. & Volz, R. A. (2005). Modeling Utility for Decision-theoretic Proactive Communication in Agent Team. In Proceedings of the 9th *World Multi-Conference on Systemics, Cybernetics and Informatics*, pp. 266-270, Orlando, FL, July 11-13.

[41] Zhang, Y., Pellon, M. & Coleman, P. (2007). Decision Under Risk in Multi-Agent Systems. In Proceedings of the *International Conference on System of Systems Engineering*, San Antonio, Texas, pp. 133-138.

[42] Zhang, Y., Mark Lewis, Pellon, M. & Coleman, P. (2007). A Preliminary Research on Modeling Cognitive Agents for Social Environments in Multi-Agent Systems. *AAAI 2007 Fall Symposium, Emergent Agents and Socialities: Social and Organizational Aspects of Intelligence*, pp. 116-123.

ENDNOTES

[1]   repast.sourceforge.net

[2]   cs.gmu.edu/~eclab/projects/mason

[3]   jade.tilab.com

[4]   www.cougaar.org

[5]   http://jaslibrary.sourceforge.net/

[6]   http://www.swarm.org/

[7]   http://ecolab.sourceforge.net/

8   http://www.spiderland.org/

9   Conversely, this does not mean that it is impossible or useless to represent societies as entities in their own right. We can of course design a society in the form of an agent, and thus consider MASs as packages of agents and societies, like what has been done in [35].

10   http://www.qgis.org

11   Data provided by Realtytrac. Data Accessed May, 2007.

12   "San Antonio In Focus: A Profile from the Census 2000 " ©2003 Brookings Center on Urban and Metropolitan Policy.

13   Data provided by Realtytrac. Data Accessed May, 2007.

Chapter IX
Developing Relationships Between Autonomous Agents:
Promoting Pro-Social Behaviour Through Virtual Learning Environments Part I

Scott Watson
University of Hertfordshire, UK

Kerstin Dautenhahn
University of Hertfordshire, UK

Wan Ching (Steve) Ho
University of Hertfordshire, UK

Rafal Dawidowicz
University of Hertfordshire, UK

ABSTRACT

This chapter discusses certain issues in the development of Virtual Learning Environments (VLEs) populated by autonomous social agents, with specific reference to existing applications designed to promote pro-social behaviour among children. We begin by describing the ways in which human groups are organised and maintained, and present the primary school class as a particular example of a social network. Contemporary psychological descriptions of bullying are explained, and current anti-bullying interventions are briefly reviewed. Two VLEs are described, which have been designed to counteract the problems inherent in bullying as exemplars of social and educational environments. This chapter concludes in Part II where the requirements for believable, autonomous agents, used in virtual learning environments, are outlined.

INTRODUCTION

Virtual environments have progressed quickly from simple text based interfaces, including internet chat rooms and instant messengers, to more visual and immersive environments (such as IMVU[1]). Furthermore, the popularity of such virtual environments as a medium for interaction has become cemented in recent years for both escapist purposes in the case of online video games (e.g. World of Warcraft, 2004) and also for more 'ordinary' interactions (e.g. Second Life, 2003).

Within these environments users are able to create social networks with other users, whom they may never even meet in the real world. The appeal for such interaction is widespread though, and opens up new questions for developers of artificial intelligences. Virtual autonomous agents are increasingly developed as social agents, i.e. agents can interact not only with objects in their environment, but also with each other, and with users, e.g. Gratch & Marsella (2001), Rickel et al. (2001), Malfaz & Salichs (2006).

Some virtual environments are now also used for educational purposes, and the phrase Virtual *Learning* Environment (VLE) has been coined to describe such applications. Mostly these are internet based environments that are used for uploading teaching materials and information for students (e.g. the University of Hertfordshire's 'StudyNet'[2]), but with powerful computers becoming more readily available, the scope for more sophisticated environments is also increasing. See, for example, the MRE (Mission Rehearsal Exercise) project, which developed a VLE designed to educate American military officers regarding peacekeeping scenarios in the Bosnian conflict (Swartout et al., 2001), and Treasure Hunt which includes empathetic synthetic agents (McQuiggan & Lester, 2006).

This chapter argues that carefully constructed graphical and interactive VLEs populated by socially interactive virtual agents can be an invaluable and innovative educational tool, with the potential to reach a wide audience providing educationally valuable and useful applications for the general public.

Children are an especially approachable audience to reach with VLEs. They are generally open to new and exciting experiences and are becoming much more technology friendly (Clements, 1998). Furthermore, they are usually very honest and direct in voicing their opinions, which can be very useful (if sometimes a little blunt) for software developers (Druin et al., 1998).

Most children of primary school age have already developed an extensive set of cognitive and emotional skills, but it is around this time that children will really begin to experience the social world for a protracted period of time. They will find other children that they like and some that they don't; friendships will be formed and some children will be left alone. At such a critical point in a child's social development life can become very difficult for some children if they are being victimised by their peers. Indeed, these early experiences can shape our social development for many years to come. Given the social nature of this development, interaction with social agents seems a natural way in which to address the issues involved in bullying, victimisation, and how to make friends.

Objectives of this chapter are to describe some of the psychological literature concerning human social networks, with specific reference to primary school classes and the phenomenon of childhood bullying. We will also describe some existing VLEs aimed at helping children's social development, which have been developed by members of the e-CIRCUS project consortium.

GROUPS AND SOCIAL NETWORKS

By his very nature, man is a social animal (Aronson, 1998). Indeed, groups of some kind have existed from mankind's earliest inception if only to guard against threats to their survival (Baron & Byrne, 1996). Group activity is responsible for almost all human achievement from building the physical structures that house us, to developing the moral and legal codes that we live our lives by.

Groups are extremely diverse in nature; they can differ in terms of size, longevity, and purpose. As well as differences between each other, groups can also vary within themselves along a whole range of dimensions including (but not limited to) age, gender, or ethnicity. Take, for example, the differences between a man and woman married for 50 years, a sports team who meet for one hour a week, or a crowd of strangers who stop to watch a street performer for a mere two minutes.

While groups and group dynamics vary greatly, it is also possible to find commonalities that all groups share. In doing so, we can develop a definition of what it is to be a group. Forsyth (1999) suggests that there are five characteristics which are common to most groups: *interaction, structure, cohesion, social identity*, and *goals*.

Within a group there is *interaction* between its individual members. While members will not necessarily interact with *all* other members, they will interact with *some* other members. Such interaction can be physical (in the case of sports teams), verbal, or even textual (e.g. for internet forum contributors). Many such interactions are required to complete tasks, though some interactions also arise from the simple need for interpersonal relationships and peer support.

All groups have a *structure* of some kind. This need not be a formalised structure as in a military hierarchy, but each member of a group will find a clearly defined role for themselves. These roles will, in turn, dictate how members are to behave while conducting group-relevant business. A group's structure and roles leads to the formation of group norms, which lay down the conditions of group membership by illustrating how members should behave in a given situation.

Without a degree of *cohesion* between members, a group would fall apart. Cohesion is maintained on two levels. At a personal level, members must remain drawn to each other through reciprocal liking/respect or emotional ties, for example, after the immediate desire to join a group has passed. At the group level, cohesion reflects the extent to which people feel like they belong together. The more cohesion a group has, the more important it becomes to its members (Cartwright, 1968). Cohesion is maintained through members following group norms – or shared guidelines to behaviour. If an individual member begins to deviate from the group's norms then they may find themselves quickly rejected (Argyle, 1994).

Most people are astutely aware of the groups to which they belong, and are able to recognise other members of their group(s). Such awareness leads us to develop a sense of *social* (or *collective*) *identity*, which may or may not become part of our own self-concept – depending on the importance that we place upon the group (e.g. Tajfel, 1981). We can place ourselves in many different types of social category – from arbitrary group membership (e.g. sports clubs or cliques) to naturally occurring demographic groups (e.g. "I am British").

Groups usually occur in order to achieve a shared *goal*, or to follow some common purpose. Goals can vary immensely, from the serious (e.g. defending a country from attack) to the frivolous (e.g. just meeting to enjoy each other's company). McGrath (1984) has identified four different types of task that groups can perform in order to achieve their goals. These are Generating tasks, Choosing tasks, Negotiating tasks, and Executing tasks. Some groups focus on just one task, while others may carry out all of them at some point.

Groups need to *generate* strategies that can be used to achieve their goals, for example a sports team or army unit will develop new tactics which can be used to outfox their opponents. To solve problems, groups must often *choose* between numerous potential solutions. In doing so, groups will usually need to *negotiate* differences of opinion within their own members. These kinds of tasks are most common for groups responsible for making policy – e.g. business management or government organisations. Finally, most groups *execute* tasks. Sports teams compete against each other, and governments enforce their policies.

School Classes as Social Networks

A specific group of interest for some researchers is that formed by the members of a school class. Clearly, a class of school children legitimately fits Forsyth's (1999) characteristics of a group. Whether it takes the form of working on class projects together or simply asking their neighbour for a pencil, pupils within a class will naturally interact with other. Indeed, teacher and pupils will also interact with each other. Not only is there an obvious hierarchy in a classroom setting whereby the teacher leads the class in activities, but there will also be a sub-structure in terms of which children sit together, and which children are favoured or ignored by their peers. Cohesion for a school class is not governed by mutual appreciation for each other, but rather is enforced by school policy. In this way, cohesion in school classes is created from characteristics such as age and ability, and norms are dictated by the rules laid down by the teacher. As a school class is a fairly rigid social group (membership remains fairly stable after the class is first formed), children can easily form a sense of social identity, a sense of 'belonging' to a certain class. This is often enforced further by school activities (e.g. class performances) or by asking classes to compete against each other (e.g. on sports days). Finally, all members of a school class engage in the same goal – educational activity.

While some groups are formed arbitrarily (e.g. the crowd of people watching a street performer), or determined based upon the member's characteristics (e.g. our school class), yet others may be formed through the pursuit of a specific goal. This kind of a group is often known as a leisure group (Argyle, 1994), or social network. Social networks are formed usually for the explicit purpose of socialising and are often organised around a single common activity or belief, such as dancing, attending church, or simply 'hanging-out' together. There is usually little material reward to the members of these groups and so the social aspect, rather than being a means to an end, becomes an end in itself.

Cairns & Cairns (1994) have shown that members of childhood friendship networks are very similar to each other not only with regards to gender, ethnicity and attitudes towards behavioural norms, but also in terms of prevalence of aggressive and deviant behaviour. Children tend to group themselves with similar peers, and continue to socialize each other in similar directions (e.g. Berndt, 1992).

An interesting example of a social network could be a subset of children from the school class that has already been described. Let us assume that there are six children from our class who all enjoy football (soccer). To follow this common passion, they meet on the school field every lunch time, with a ball, to play their favourite game. This seems like a harmonious union, at first. However, consider that these six children will naturally have different personalities – let us suppose that they differ in terms of how competitive they are towards each other, and how much they like each other. We will return to this scenario at a later point in this chapter.

Aggressive Behaviour

An unfortunate part of human social activity is to act aggressively towards others – either as a group process, or as an individual. Aggression can be confused with assertiveness, ambition, or self-confident behaviour. For example, workers who initiate industrial action to counter poor working conditions could be construed as aggressive. However, in this chapter a more narrow description is used, which implies more malicious intent. Therefore, we will define aggressive behaviour as *behaviour which is directed at causing physical or psychological harm to others* (Aronson, Wilson, & Akert, 1997). An important point to note is the role of *intentionality* in this definition. Behaviour which causes harm is not considered to be aggressive if it occurs accidentally. For example, while being mistakenly hurt in a traffic accident is likely to cause more damage than being punched in a bar-brawl, it is the bar-brawl that is considered aggressive as someone actually holds the intention to cause pain.

Bullying in Schools

Let us now return to our school class. One particular kind of aggressive behaviour that can occur among school children is bullying. Bullying behaviour has been extensively researched, leading to comprehensive estimates of prevalence and future implications. Some reviews show that between 8-46% of children are bullied in primary schools (e.g. Wolke, Woods, Bloomfield & Karstadt, 2006). Other sources show that victimisation at school can lead to issues such as low self-esteem (Matsui, Kakuyama, Tsuzuki, & Onglacto, 1996), anxiety (Salmon, James & Smith, 1998), depression (Craig, 1998), or hyperactivity/behavioural conduct issues (Farrington, 1993).

To be properly classified as bullying, as opposed to one-off aggressive acts, a victim must be the *target of negative action on the part of one or more others*. Furthermore, bullying is a *repeated act, which continues regularly over time* (Olweus, 1999). Bullies also often rely on a real or implied imbalance of strength (Whitney & Smith, 1993).

Most bullying can be classified into one of three categories (Wolke, Woods, Stanford, & Schulz, 2001):

- **Direct physical bullying:** e.g. pushing, hitting, kicking, or stealing belongings.
- **Direct verbal bullying:** e.g. name calling, teasing, or threatening.
- **Indirect (or relational) bullying:** e.g. social exclusion, rumour spreading or withdrawal of friendships.

In general, girls and boys display different styles of aggression whereby boys employ more direct and physical actions, while girls prefer indirect aggression (Björkqvist, 1994). This trend is continued with bullying behaviour – boys use much more physical forms of bullying, while girls tend to use more relational and verbal forms (Crick & Grotpeter, 1995).

Bullying Roles as a Group Process

One particularly successful avenue of research into bullying has uncovered six distinct roles that children can take on in episodes of bullying. Furthermore, these same roles have been confirmed in a number of studies (Salmivalli et al., 1996; Sutton & Smith, 1999; Wolke & Stanford, 1999). These roles (though sometimes labelled differently) are:

- The 'pure' bully who bullies others but is never victimised themselves
- The 'pure' victim who is bullied by others
- The bully-assistant who helps bully, but never initiates the bullying
- The bully-reinforcer who provides positive feedback to the bully, without actually bullying anyone themselves
- The defender who tries to help the victim
- The outsider/bystander who tries not to get involved

On occasion, some children are also classified as bully-victims (Wolke et al 2001). These children are sometimes victims, but they also bully others themselves.

A number of significant trends were found by Salmivalli et al. (1996) through a peer-nomination methodology, whereby children are asked to show which other children in their class fall into the various bullying roles. Of the 573 children in their study, 87% were found to be involved in bullying (i.e. could be reliably assigned to a bullying role). Gender differences showed that girls are more likely than boys to be outsiders (40.2% girls, 7.3% boys) or defenders (30.1% girls, 4.5% boys), while boys are more likely to be a reinforcer (37.3% boys, 1.7% girls) or assistant (12.2% boys, 1.4% girls). More boys than girls were rated as bullies (10.5% boys, 5.9% girls), while the number of victims was similar for both genders (11.8% boys, 11.5% girls).

Figure 1. Example network diagram of a typical school class (Adapted from Salmivalli et al., 1997).

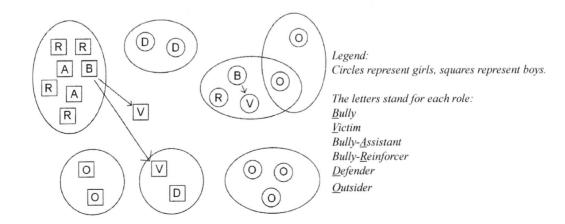

Legend:
Circles represent girls, squares represent boys.

The letters stand for each role:
Bully
Victim
Bully-Assistant
Bully-Reinforcer
Defender
Outsider

It was also shown that victims tend to have a lower social status within their class than any other role, as characterised by low social-acceptance and high social-rejection scores. Male bullies, female reinforcers, and female assistants shared a similar acceptance/rejection pattern, though not to the same extent. The most popular children were defenders (high acceptance, low rejection). This low social status could provide an explanation for why certain children are victimised to begin with. However, Olweus (1991) has pointed out that the ways in which a victim is perceived by their peers can be changed throughout the bullying process. For example – through a process of cognitive dissonance, or as attempt to rationalise one's own bad behaviour, others may (mistakenly) come to feel that a victim 'deserves' to be bullied.

In addition to the evidence above that different bullying roles may be predicted by social status, there is also evidence to suggest that children with similar and complimentary bullying roles tend to form their own social networks. Salmivalli, Huttunen, & Lagerspetz (1997) conducted a large scale review of Finnish school children and found a number of interesting relationships. Firstly, children whose bullying roles were similar or complimentary (e.g. bullies, assistants, and reinforcers) tended to form friendship networks with each. Secondly, bullies and their associates formed larger networks than did defenders and bystanders. Thirdly, children who were not members of friendship networks were more likely to be victims (Figure 1).

The adage "birds of a feather flock together" seems, then, to hold true for children involved in bullying. Children with similar or compatible bullying roles tend to group themselves together and then go on to conflict with others to form varied, but obvious, social networks.

CURRENT ANTI-BULLYING INTERVENTIONS

One of the most important implications of these findings relates to the nature in which interventions should be applied. Far from a dyadic approach which only includes bully and victim, a successful intervention needs to take into account the interplay between the various bullying roles, and needs to reach all children involved in bullying.

Sutton & Smith (1999) suggest that encouraging existing defenders to counter assistants and reinforcers could be a worthwhile course of action – especially since reinforcers are younger (and therefore assumedly more easily impressionable) than outsiders. They also show that defender is a natural secondary role for outsiders, indicating that it would be feasible to promote positive behaviour amongst these children. Indeed, some evidence has already shown that training bystanders to act as a support network for victims can have a positive effect for victims, the peer supporters themselves, and the school environment as a whole (Cowie, 2000).

A number of such interventions already exist in some form. Maines & Robinson (1991) promote the inclusion of observers along with bullies and members of their gang in thinking about ways to reduce victimisation in the "no blame" approach. Some governments have also adopted this position. In England and Wales, for example, the Department for Education advocates a "whole school approach" (DfE, 1994). While popular, Lodge & Frydenberg (2005) have shown that the impact of these holistic approaches unfortunately varies from country to country. In Norway a 50% reduction of bullying was described after a nationwide campaign (Olweus, 1994), while success in the US, Germany, and Belgium has not been so pronounced (Smith, Anadiou, & Cowie, 2003). Other reports show effect sizes of between 15% (Smith & Sharp, 1994) to 30% (Pepler, Craig, Ziegler, & Charach, 1994). Further studies actually show an increase in reports of bullying (Soutter & McKenzie, 2000), though this could be due to increased awareness, leading to increased reports, rather than an actual increase in prevalence. Given the varied success of the traditional interventions above, new ways of tackling bullying in schools are beginning to focus on the use of computers.

Computers in Education

Information and Communication Technology (ICT) is continually playing a more central role in primary education. In the UK, aside from schools updating the delivery medium of classes from the blackboard to the interactive whiteboard, pupils are being encouraged from an early age to use computers. The ICT curriculum in UK focuses not only on teaching children how to use word processors, but also includes spreadsheet/database maintenance, basic statistical analysis, and image editing. A number of specialist resources are also available for less traditional subjects, such as "Kar2ouche", which has a number of modules for PSHE (Personal and Social Health Education) curriculum.

More sophisticated VLEs are now also beginning to be introduced into school systems, again usually to teach less conventional subjects. Scaife & Rogers (2001) discuss a virtual theatre implemented as part of the EU's i3 ESE project 'PUPPET'. One scenario takes place on a virtual farm, where children have to show an autonomous agent (a piglet) how to return to the sty through a user-controlled avatar (the farmer). For use outside of the classroom – but still with an educational purpose – Johnson et al. (1998) describe the NICE (Narrative Immersive Constructionist/Collaborative Environments) project. This project developed a VLE within a CAVE environment in which children create and maintain basic ecosystems. Users interact with other remote users across a network and go on to create stories based on their experiences.

A number of anti-bullying applications already exist and are in operation in some schools. "Text Someone"[3] provides a phone based system which allows children to text or email their concerns to their school. The system records all incoming messages, notifies teachers when a new message has been received, and allows teachers to send replies. "Securus"[4] monitors computer networks and alerts teachers if it detects inappropriate language, or signs of depression, predator grooming, drugs, and harassment. "Vantage Sentinel"[5] is a risk management and incident reporting system similar to Securus, though with wider scope for primary care institutions as well as schools. It should be noted that all these systems are primarily for use by teachers, for the recording of bullying incidences, rather than for use by children. As effective as they may be in this regard, as far as children are concerned these applications can act only as a deterrent while they are using the monitored systems – they do not act at the root cause of bullying, and do not serve to educate children.

Anti-Bullying Virtual Learning Environments

Not only is software an innovative and fun new way to address the issue with children but it seems all the more pertinent given the rise of cyber-bullying via mobile phones and the internet. Kar2ouche, from Immersive Education Ltd, is an anti-bullying software which is aimed at children themselves. Kar2ouche allows users to generate their own storyboards, but is limited in that there is no interaction between user and characters – the users author their own story but

Figure 2. Screenshots of episode and interaction scenes within FearNot!

do not easily learn anything new, without discussion of others' stories. An interactive approach *is* taken by FearNot!, a new VLE that is aimed at promoting pro-social behaviour among children themselves. The authors of this chapter are members of the consortium of the EU Framework 6 project e-CIR-CUS (http://www.e-circus.org), which includes the development and evaluation of FearNot!

FearNot! (*F*un with *E*mpathic *A*gents to achieve *N*ovel *O*utcomes in *T*eaching) is a VLE populated with synthetic characters designed to simulate a primary school setting. FearNot! shows a series of cartoon-like episodes to users, in which an incident of bullying may occur. These episodes are *emergent* in that the characters do not follow a script, but can react dynamically to events in the environment. In between each of these episodes, users are able to interact with the victimised character in order to advise them on how best to cope with the bullying. The victimised character will take this advice on board for the following episode, allowing the user's contribution to guide the path of the story.

Since boys and girls bully in different ways, the episodes in FearNot! have been designed to reflect these differences. The episodes for boys to play include more physical than relational incidences, while the girls episodes are more indirect than physical. The character parameters, implemented with the FAtiMA architecture (Dias, 2005; Dias, Ho, Vogt, Beeckman, Paiva, & André, 2007), have been carefully designed in order to reflect the range of bullying roles encountered in real life. For exam-

ple, bullies and their associates are more confident than victims. It is this architecture, which allows our agents to act autonomously as it includes components representing personality, emotion, mood, motivation, and autobiographical memory.

Users interact with FearNot! individually. This allows for users to engage emotionally with the characters, and to build up an empathic relationship with them. Studies during the development of FearNot! have already shown that the characters are believable (Woods, Hall, Sobral, Dautenhahn, & Wolke, 2003) and successful in eliciting a range of different emotions in users (e.g. Hall et al., 2005; Watson et al, 2007). Individual usage also allows children to deal with a potentially sensitive issue confidentially, and without fear of reprisal from their classmates – this is especially important for children who are being bullied.

Due to the emotional engagement generated by the characters, children are keen to help the victim character and to provide advice. Because children are able to see the consequences of the advice they offer, they are able to learn how to cope with bullying vicariously without having to actually experience it themselves. In this way, FearNot! aims to reduce bullying by promoting onlookers to become defenders and to improve knowledge about bullying and about the best strategies to deal with being bullied.

One of the most successful strategies to deal with bullying in schools is to develop a peer support network – or, in other words, to make friends (Hunter, Boyle, & Warden, 2004). Indeed, as already

Figure 3. Screenshot of C-SoNeS and close-up of agents talking to each other

suggested in this chapter, being a member of a group is the best predictor of *not* being bullied. Therefore, an alternative method to stopping bullying would be to promote the generation of social groups and friendships, thus preventing bullies from finding potential victims in the first place.

This approach is currently under consideration by Dawidowicz, an MPhil student affiliated with the e-CIRCUS project team. Different from FearNot! which has been developed over several years and has already been tested with hundreds of children, this work is an early stage of development. "C-SoNeS" (Children's Social Network Simulation)[6], is designed to teach children potential strategies to make friendships. This VLE currently consists of a simulated playing field, on which six autonomous agents are playing with a ball. The eventual aim for this project is to allow users to control their own avatar in order to learn about how social networks operate. In advance of user-controlled input, however, the network of agents must be able to act as an ecologically valid simulation of real social networks.

The football-like game which agents play in this VLE does not have any rules, and the agents' only goals are to reach and kick the ball – there are no opposing teams and no goal scoring behaviour. Rather, each agent competes against the others in attempting to reach the ball and kick it on again first. Each agent also maintains a record of its relationships with the other agents. At each time-step an agent will perform one behaviour from its repertoire – these behaviours currently include and are limited to: running toward the ball, kicking the ball, obstacle avoidance, going to the field entrance, collecting the ball (when it leaves the playing field), pushing, and talking.

The last of these behaviours, pushing and talking, are most note-worthy as they can affect

Figure 4. Example network diagram, cf. Dawidowicz (2007)

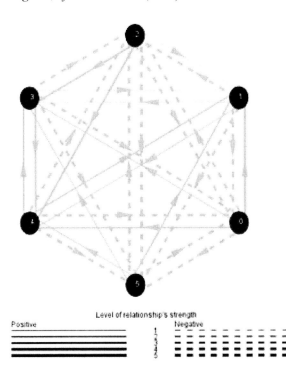

Legend:
Each node represents one agent, while connecting lines represent relationships from one agent towards another. The thickness of each line represents the quality/strength of each relationship.

the relationships between agents (negatively and positively, respectively). If agent A pushes agent B, then the relationship of B towards A decreases. However, agent A's relation towards agent B does not change. In other words if agent A pushes agent B, then B will 'dislike' A, while agent A will not be affected at all. On the other hand, when agents talk to each other, both will improve their relationship towards the other (or 'like' the other) slightly more in a reciprocal fashion. It should be noted that agents only talk in pairs, and that talking only occurs when the ball has been kicked outside of the playing field. Relationships increase or decrease by a fixed integer which is set before each simulation is run. There are no upper or lower thresholds that relationships can reach.

Using this setup, Dawidowicz (2007) ran a series of studies in order to observe the effects of manipulating certain agent parameters, in order to refine these parameters for the VLE to better simulate real life. At the end of each run, the software generated a diagram (see Figure 4) which shows the dyadic relationships between each agent in terms of both negativity/positivity and strength. By examining the network diagram, one can see how the relationships between agents are affected by the various parameter manipulations.

In this way a simple VLE has been developed in which agents can develop basic relationships to each other in a manner in a manner analogous to the social networks which are found in incidences of bullying in primary schools. However, this VLE still requires further development before it is ready to be used as an educational tool. For example, as previously stated, incidences of bullying are not based on simple dyadic relationships, but are reliant on more complex relationships. This is especially true of indirect/relational bullying.

CONCLUSION

This chapter has presented some of the literature concerning social networks and has described the ways in which social groups are organised and maintained. Social networks found between children in primary school classes were the focus, and contemporary psychological perspectives on the nature of bullying among school-age children were outlined. Current anti-bullying interventions and the role of ICT in primary schools were described to provide context for the use of VLEs as anti-bullying interventions. Two VLEs were introduced which have been designed to promote learning and pro-social behaviour among young children, with the help of autonomous social agents.

FearNot! employs emotionally aware agents that model a typical bullying network to educate children about the various coping strategies that can be used to stop bullying. The software has been used in large-scale studies (Hall et al, 2005) where 345 children interacted once with the software. In autumn 2007 we began a longitudinal study, in collaboration with other project partners and schools in UK (University of Warwick) and Germany (University of Würzburg). The study targets around 1200 school children in total and children will interact with the software over several weeks. An alternative VLE, still under development, includes agents which develop their own social network 'from scratch' in order for children to learn how to build and maintain friendships.

Lessons learned from the development of Fear-Not! and C-SoNeS will be presented in Part II of this chapter, along with recommendations for designers of other VLEs. Part II will explain some of the technical and engagement-oriented considerations that need to be made before creating a VLE, and will provide some contemporary methodologies which have been used successfully throughout the e-CIRCUS project.

ACKNOWLEDGMENT

This work was partially supported by the European Community (EC) and is currently funded by the e-CIRCUS project IST-4-027656-STP. The authors are solely responsible for the content of this publication. It does not represent the opinion of the EC, and the EC is not responsible for any use that might be made of data appearing therein.

REFERENCES

Argyle, M. (1994). *The psychology of interpersonal behaviour (5th Ed.)*. St. Ives, UK: Penguin Books.

Aronson, E. (1998). *The social animal (7th Ed.)*. USA: Freeman.

Aronson, E., Wilson, T. D., & Akert, R. M. (1997). *Social psychology (2nd Ed.) (Chapter 12. Aggression: Why we hurt other people)*. USA: Addison-Wesley.

Baron, R. A., & Byrne, D. (1996). *Social psychology (8th Ed.) (Chapter 11. Aggression: Its nature, causes, and control.)* USA: Allyn and Bacon.

Berndt, T.J. (1992). The features and effects of friendship in early adolescence. *Child Development, 53,* 1447-1460.

Björkqvist, K. (1994). Sex differences in physical, verbal, and indirect aggression. *Sex Roles, 30(3/4),* 177-188.

Blizzard Entertainment (developer). World of warcraft. Vivendi Universal (publisher). 2004.

Cairns, R., & Cairns, B. (1994). *Lifelines and risks: Pathways of youth in our time.* Cambridge, UK: Cambridge University Press.

Cartwright, D. (1968). The nature of group-cohesiveness. In D. Cartwright & A. Zander (Eds.), *Group dynamics: Research and theory (3rd Ed.)*. New York, USA: Harper & Row.

Clements, D. (1998, February). *Young children and technology.* Paper presented at the Forum on Early Childhood Science, Mathematics, and Technology Education, Washington DC, USA.

Cowie, H. (2000). Bystanding or standing-by: Gender issues in coping with bullying in English schools. *Aggressive Behaviour, 26,* 85-97.

Craig, W.M. (1998). The relationship among bullying, victimization, depression, anxiety and aggression in elementary school children. *Personality and Individual Differences, 24,* 123-130.

Crick, N.R., & Grotpeter, J.K. (1995). Relational aggression, gender, and social-psychological adjustment. *Child Development, 66,* 710-722.

Dawidowicz, R. (2007). *Social relationships in a multi-agent virtual environment.* MPhil dissertation, University of Hertfordshire, UK.

Department for Education (1994). Don't suffer in silence: An anti-bullying pack for schools. London: HMSO.

Dias, J. (2005). *FearNot!: Creating emotional autonomous synthetic characters for emphatic interactions.* Unpublished doctoral dissertation, Universidade Técnica de Lisboa, Portugal.

Dias, J., Ho, W.C., Vogt, T., Beeckman, N., Paiva, A., & André, E. (2007). I know what I did last summer: Autobiographic memory in synthetic characters. *Conference proceedings ACII 2007.* Berlin, Germany: Springer.

Druin, A., Bederson, B., Boltman, A., Miura, A., Knotts-Callahan, D., Platt, M. (1998). Children as our technology design partners. In Druin, A. (Ed.). *The design of children's technology* (pp. 51-72). San Francisco, USA: Morgan Kaufmann

Farrington, D.P. (1993). Understanding and preventing bullying. In M. Tonry (Ed.), *Crime and justice, Vol. 17.*

Forsyth, D.R. (1999). *Group dynamics (3rd Ed.).* Belmont, USA: Wadsworth Publishing Company.

Gratch, J., & Marsella, S. (2001). Tears and fears: Modelling emotions and emotional behaviours in synthetic agents. *Conference Proceedings AGENTS'01* (pp. 278-285).

Hall, L., Woods, S., Aylett, R., Newall, L., & Paiva, A. (2005). Achieving empathic engagement through affective interaction with synthetic characters. *Conference Proceedings ACII 2005* (pp. 731-738). Berlin, Germany: Springer.

Hunter, S.C., Boyle, J.M.E., & Warden, D. (2004). Help seeking amongst child and adolescent victims of peer-aggression and bullying: The influence of school-stage, gender, victimisation, appraisal, and emotion. *British Journal of Educational Psychology, 74,* 375-390.

Johnson, A., Roussos, M., Leigh, J., Vasilakis, C., Barnes, C., & Moher, T. (1998). The NICE project:

learning together in a virtual world. *Conference Proceedings IEEE 1998* (pp. 176-183).

Linden Research, Inc (developer) Second life. Linden Research, Inc (publisher). 2003.

Lodge, J., & Frydenberg, E. (2005). The role of peer bystanders in school bullying: Positive steps toward promoting peaceful schools. *Theory into Practice, 44(4)*, 329-336.

Maines, B., & Robinson, G. (1991). Don't beat the bullies! *Educational Psychology in Practice, 7*,168-172.

Malfaz, M., & Salichs, M.A. (2006). Learning behaviour-selection algorithms for autonomous social agents living in a role-playing game. *Conference Proceedings AISB'06* (pp. 45-52).

Matsui, T., Kakuyama, T., Tsuzuki, Y., & Onglacto, M.L. (1996). Long-term outcomes of early victimization by peers among Japanese male university students: Models of a vicious cycle. *Psychological Reports, 79,* 711-720.

McGrath, J.E. (1984). *Groups: Interaction and performance.* Englewood Cliffs, USA: Prentice Hall.

McQuiggan, S.W., & Lester, J.C. (2006) Learning empathy: A data-driven framework for modelling empathetic companion agents. *Conference Proceedings AAMAS'06* (pp. 961-968).

Olweus, D. (1991). Bully/victim problems among school children: Basic facts and effects of a school-based intervention program. In K. Rubin, & D. Pepler (Eds.) *The development and treatment of childhood aggression.* New Jersey, USA: Erlbaum.

Olweus, D. (1994). Bullying at school: Long term outcomes for the victims and an effective school based intervention program. In R. Huesmann (Ed.). *Aggressive behaviour. Current perspectives.* New York, USA: Plenum.

Olweus, D. (1999). Norway. In P.K. Smith, Y. Morita, J. Junger-Tas, D. Olweus, R. Catalano, & P. Slee (Eds.), *The nature of school bullying: A cross-national perspective.* London, UK: Routledge.

Pepler, D.J., Craig, W., Ziegler, S., & Charach, A. (1994). An evaluation of an anti-bullying interven-

tion in Toronto schools. *Canadian Journal of Community Mental Health. Special Issue: Prevention: Focus on Children and Youth, 13,* 95-110.

Rickel, J., Gratch, J., Hill, R., Marsella, S., Swartout, W. (2001). Steve goes to Bosnia: Towards a new generation of virtual humans for interactive experiences. *In AAAI Spring Symposium on Artificial Intelligence and Interactive Entertainment.*

Salmivalli, C., Huttunen, A., & Lagerspetz, K.M.J. (1997). Peer networks and bullying in schools. *Scandinavian Journal of Psychology, 38,* 305-312.

Salmivalli, C., Lagerspetz, K., Björkqvist, K., Österman, K., & Kaukainen, A. (1996). Bullying as a group process: Particpant roles and their relations to social status within the group. *Aggressive Behaviour, 22,* 1-15.

Salmon, G., James, A., & Smith, D.M. (1998). Bullying in schools: Self reported anxiety, depression, and self esteem in secondary school children. *British Medical Journal, 317,* 924-925.

Scaife, M., & Rogers, Y. (2001). Informing the design of a virtual environment to support learning in children. *International Journal of Human Computer Studies, 55,* 115-143.

Smith, P., Anadiou, K., & Cowie, H. (2003). Interventions to reduce school bullying. *Canadian Journal of Psychiatry, 48,* 591-599.

Smith, P.K., & Sharp, S. (Eds.). (1994). *School bullying: Insights and perspectives.* London, UK: Routledge.

Soutter, A., & McKenzie, A. (2000). The use and effects of ant bullying and anti-harassment policies in Australian schools. *School Psychology International. Special Issue: Bullies and Victims, 21,* 96-105.

Sutton, J., & Smith, P.K. (1999). Bullying as a group process: An adaptation of the participant role approach. *Aggressive Behaviour, 25,* 97-111.

Swartout, W., Hill, R., Gratch, J., Johnson, W.L., Kyriakakis, C., CLaBore, C., Lindheim, R., Marsella, S., Miraglia, D., Moore, B., Morie, J., Rickel, J., Thiébaux, M., Tuch, L., Whitney, R., & Douglas, J. (2001) Toward the holodeck: Integrating graphics, sound, character and story. *Conference Proceedings AGENT'01* (pp. 409-416).

Tajfel, H. (1981). *Human groups and social categories.* New York, USA: Cambridge University Press.

Watson, S., Vannini, N., Davis, M., Woods, S., Hall, M., Hall, L., & Dautenhahn, K. (2007). FearNot! an anti-Bullying Intervention: Evaluation of an interactive virtual learning environment. *Conference Proceedings AISB'07 (*pp. 446-452).

Whitney, I., & Smith, P.K. (1993). A survey of the nature and extent of bullying in junior/middle and secondary schools. *Educational Research, 35,* 3-25.

Wolke, D., & Stanford, K. (1999). Bullying in school children. In D. Messer & S. Millar (Eds.), *Developmental Psychology.* London, UK: Arnold.

Wolke, D., Woods, S., Bloomfield, L., & Karstadt. (2006). Bullying involvement in primary school and common health problems. *Archives of Disease in Childhood, 85,* 197-201.

Wolke, D., Woods, S., Stanford, K., & Schulz, H. (2001). Bullying and victimisation of primary school children in South England and South Germany: Prevalence and school factors. *British Journal of Psychology, 92,* 673-696.

Woods, S., Hall, L., Sobral, D., Dautenhahn, K., & Wolke, D. (2003) A study into the believability of animated characters in the context of bullying intervention. *Conference Proceedings IVA 2003* (pp. 310-314). Berlin, Germany: Springer.

ADDITIONAL READING

Andreou, E. (2001). Bully/victim problems and their association with coping behaviour in conflictual peer interactions among school-age children. *Educational Psychology, 21(1),* 59-66.

Arsenio, W.F., & Lemerise, E.A. (2001). Varieties of childhood bullying: Values, emotion processes, and social competence. *Social Development, 10(1),* 59-73.

Aylett, R., Louchart, S., Dias, J., Paiva, A., & Vala, M. (2005) FearNot! An experiment in emergent narrative. *Conference Proceedings IVA 2005* (pp. 305-316). Berlin, Germany: Springer.

Aylett, R., Paiva, A., Woods, S., Hall, L., & Zoll, C. (2004). Expressive characters in anti-bullying education. In L. Canamero & R. Aylett (Eds.), *Animating Expressive Characters for Social Interaction.* John Benjamins Publishing Company.

Bates, J., Loyall, A.B., & Reilly, W.S. (1994). An architecture for action, emotion, and social behaviour. *Selected papers from the 4th European Workshop on Modelling Autonomous Agents in a Multi-Agent World, Artificial Social Systems,* 55-68.

Gilbert, N., & Troitzsch, K.G. (2005). *Simulation for the social scientist (2nd Ed.).* Glasgow, UK: Open University Press.

Hall, L., Paiva, A., Aylett, R., & Woods, S. (Unpublished manuscript) Empathy in human computer interaction.

Kanetsuna, T., Smith, P.K., & Morita, Y. (2006). Coping with bullying at school: Children's recommended strategies and attitudes to school-based interventions in Engand and Japan. *Aggressive Behaviour, 32,* 570-580.

Lee, J.J., & Hoadley, C.M. (2006) "Ugly in a world where you can choose to be beautiful": Teaching and learning about diversity via virtual worlds. *Conference Proceedings International Conference on Learning Sciences* (pp. 383-389).

Louchart, S., & Aylett, R. (2004). Narrative theory and emergent interactive narrative. *International Journal of Continuing Engineering Education and Lifelong Learning, 14(6),* 506-518.

Menesini, E., Codecasa, E., Benelli, B., & Cowie, H. (2003). Enhancing children's responsibility to take action aganst bullying: Evaluation of a befriending intervention in Italian middle schools. *Aggressive Behaviour, 29,* 1-14.

Menesini, E., Eslea, M., Smith, P.K., Genta, M.L., Giannetti, E., Fonzi, A., & Constable, A. (1997). Cross-national comparison of children's attitudes towards bully/victim problems in school. *Aggressive Behaviour, 23,* 245-257.

Prendinger, H., & Ishizuka, M. (2001). Social role awareness in animated agents. *Conference Proceedings Autonomous Agents 2001* (pp.270-277).

Solberg, M.E., & Olweus, D. (2003). Prevalence estimation of school bullying with the Olweus bully/victim questionnaire. *Aggressive Behaviour, 29,* 239-268.

Stewart, T.C., West, R.L., & Coplan, R. (2007). Multi-agent models of social dynamics in children. *Cognitive Systems Research, 8,* 1-14.

ENDNOTES

[1] IMVU (Instant Messaging Virtual Universe) is an internet based messenger application with 3D virtual environments and user-controlled personalisable avatars (http://www.imvu.com).

[2] A free demonstration of StudyNet is available here: http://www.studynet1.herts.ac.uk/open_index.html.

[3] Text Someone is provided by Truancy Call Ltd (http://www.textsomeone.com).

[4] Securus is provided by Securus Software (http://www.securus-software.com).

[5] Vantage Sentinel is provided by Vantage Technologies Ltd (http://www.vantage-technologies.co.uk).

[6] For further information about implementation of the C-SoNeS software, please contact the developer: Rafal Dawidowicz, Warszawska 157/50, Kielce, 25-547, Poland, R.P.Dawidowicz@Gmail.com

Chapter X
Construction of Meanings in Biological and Artificial Agents

Martin Takáč
Comenius University in Bratislava, Slovakia

ABSTRACT

In this chapter, we focus on the issue of understanding in various types of agents. Our main goal is to build up notions of meanings and understanding in neutral and non-anthropocentric terms that would not exclude preverbal living organisms and artificial systems by definition. By analyzing the evolutionary context of understanding in living organisms and the representation of meanings in several artificially built systems, we come to design principles for building "understanding" artificial agents and formulate necessary conditions for the presence of inherent meanings. Such meanings should be based on interactional couplings between the agents and their environment, and should help the agents to orient themselves in the environment and to satisfy their goals. We explore mechanisms of action-based meaning construction, horizontal coordination, and vertical transmission of meanings and exemplify them with computational models.

INTRODUCTION

Different kinds of agents—bacteria, animals, humans, some computer programs and robots—have something in common: they all are achieving some goals by sensing and acting in certain (real or virtual) environments (Kelemen, 2003). Some of them can communicate among themselves or even with humans. To what extent can we say that they understand what they do? If they attribute some meanings

to situations and events in their environments, what is the nature of these meanings? Do they use the same meanings when they communicate? Where do these meanings come from? Are they innate (pre-programmed) or learned? These questions are the central focus of this chapter.

Some people may be reluctant to use the terms "understanding" and "meaning" in association with other than human agents. Notions of understanding often presuppose intentionality or consciousness.

However, such notions either exclude some types of agents from consideration by definition, or at least obfuscate the matter even more by reducing the problem to a harder one (as detecting/proving intentionality or consciousness in non-human agents is very problematic). Our approach is different. We will look for as neutral and non-anthropocentric characterizations of meaning and understanding as possible, applicable to preverbal living organisms and artificial agents as well. This is in line with similar efforts to define life and consciousness in such a general way that the human life and human consciousness are just their possible instantiations (Langton, 1989; Holland, 2003).

After providing a formal background, we will start our quest for meaning by drawing lessons from preverbal stages of phylogeny and ontogeny and by studying sensorimotor intelligence of animals and infants. Then we will introduce basic problems with understanding in artificially constructed systems and analyze several examples. The main issue that we will elaborate on is that of the origin of meanings. We will explore possibilities and limits of constructivist approach to meaning by the computational modeling methodology glossed as "understanding by building" (Pfeifer & Scheier, 1999).

The contribution of such an approach is threefold. First, we live in times when human-computer and computer-computer interaction is no longer a science fiction, but a practical engineering problem. We need to design representational formalisms that will allow us to endow machines with ontologies necessary for their successful solving of given tasks and for their mutual coordination/communication. The representation must be sufficiently complex to capture peculiarities of physical and social environments, including their dynamical character. In open environments, the ability to learn and autonomously construct useful representation of relevant meanings is crucial. Second, operationalization of Semantic theories and building relevant computational models can help clarify the notion of "understanding" in artificial systems that has been a source of controversy in Artificial Intelligence for a long time, and provide mechanisms for symbol and language grounding. Last but not least, the computational models can help us better understand ourselves. They can have a backward impact on theories of

learning and language development, and on cognitive science in general.

THEORIES OF MEANING

Philosophers and linguists have studied the big question of "what does it mean to mean something" for many centuries. Nowadays, the study of meaning is mainly in the realm of Semantics and semiotics. In denotational Semantics, linguistic meanings are some objects. Concerning the nature of these objects, the fundamental distinction should be made between the *realist* and *cognitive* (or *conceptualist*) approaches. In the realist approach, meanings are some entities "out there" in the world. In the cognitive approach, meanings are mental entities "in the head". Gärdenfors (2000) characterizes cognitive Semantics by the following six tenets:

1. Meaning is a conceptual structure in a cognitive system (not truth conditions in possible worlds).
2. Conceptual structures are embodied (meaning is not independent of perception or bodily experience).
3. Semantic elements are constructed from geometrical or topological structures (not symbols that can be composed according to some system of rules).
4. Cognitive models are primarily image-schematic (not propositional). Image schemas are transformed by metaphoric and metonymic operations (Lakoff & Johnson, 1980).
5. Semantics is primary to syntax and partly determines it (syntax cannot be described independently of Semantics).
6. Contrary to the Aristotelian paradigm based on necessary and sufficient conditions, concepts show prototype effects (Rosch, 1978).

The first two tenets imply that language understanding cannot be managed by any isolated *language module* (in the sense of Fodor, 1983), but it is an integral part of the very same conceptual system that serves reasoning, orientation and acting in the world (Lakoff, 1987; Barsalou, 1999).

Gärdenfors (2000) represents meanings in

so-called conceptual spaces construed in such a way that representations of similar objects are geometrically close to each other. Other influential cognitive Semantic theories include e.g. Force Dynamics of Talmy (2000), frame Semantics of Fillmore (1982), mental spaces of Fauconnier (1985) and Cognitive Grammar of Langacker (1987, 1991). We will review in more detail a cognitive theory of representation of Šefránek (2002), which aspires to be relevant for real (alive) cognitions in the biological world. This theory is an effort with a declared goal to posit a non-trivial and falsifiable level of analysis of cognition and understanding without the necessity to resort to the brain and neural processes. Rather, this theory focuses on the contents of cognition (meanings). The crucial assumption of this approach is that meanings can be separated from language, i.e. they also exist in animals and preverbal infants. In general, the theory applies to some organisms situated in some environment. The organisms have needs and goals, which they try to satisfy by performing actions (behavior). The organisms possess representations composed of meanings. The theory of meaning is built upon the notion of *identification criteria*. The identification criteria are abstractions of the organism's ability to recognize (identify, distinguish) certain aspects of its (internal or external) environment. Elementary identification criteria recognize objects (individuals), natural kinds of objects, natural properties of objects, and natural relations among objects. More complex criteria, constructed from the elementary ones, recognize situations, rules (types of situations), goals (desired situations), changes in environment, plans (projected changes), methods (successful plans), events and types of events. The construction of the complex criteria is based on the important notion of *transformations of criteria*.

Šefránek (2002) further proposes the way how to move from protoSemantics, protoinference and protocommunication of simple organisms, through 2-word protolanguage, to the full-fledged language with propositional representation and syntax. The ability to understand the complex language is inherently connected with reasoning, more specifically, with hypothetical (non-monotonic) reasoning (Ginsberg, 1987).

FROM PREVERBAL TO LINGUISTIC MEANINGS: AN EVOLUTIONARY VIEW

Within the presented cognitive Semantics views, lexical meanings are a part of the conceptual system that has been shaped by experience with the surrounding world. This implies that understanding does not begin with language; we can also talk about understanding at a preverbal level.

We will start with an evolutionary view on onset of understanding in living organisms. Some scientists, e.g. Goodwin (1978) and Kováč (2000), trace/postulate elementary forms of cognition at very deep levels of the phylogenetic tree, even at bacterial, cellular and molecular levels. Some of the systems that appeared in the course of evolution have persisted, because their structure reflected relevant characteristics of their environment. According to Kováč (2000), biological evolution consists in generation of hypotheses about the nature of the environment, in falsifying these hypotheses, and in maintaining the hypotheses that have not been falsified. Hence, evolutionary adaptations of organisms can be viewed as a form of phylogenetic learning with knowledge being encoded in their structure. The chances of persisting are higher for organisms that actively explore their environment and adapt to it or adjust it by their behavior.

The simplest cognitive systems only consist of mechanisms of sensing and acting on their environment. In the most elementary sense, they attribute meaning to parts of their environment by recognizing, via their sensors and actuators, information useful for achieving their goals (Nehaniv, 2000). Thinking appears at the highest stages of evolution as an abstract action – testing of various motor acts without actually involving the muscles. Deliberation, (short-term) anticipation, proto-planning, and eventually "what-if" thinking (the ability to mentally simulate various scenarios and evaluate their consequences without the necessity to realize them physically) increased the survival chances of organisms and provided them with a significant evolutionary advantage.

Gärdenfors (1996a) distinguishes two kinds of representations required for language to evolve: *cued* and *detached*. A *cued* representation must always be triggered by something present in the current situation. An organism reacting to certain states of its environment in certain ways (e.g. eating objects recognized as food and avoiding objects recognized as predators) performs categorization and possesses cued representations of the respective categories. However, these representations are only activated in the presence of their referents. Cued representations, observable as non-volitional behavioral reactions, are innate and have evolved phylogenetically.

A significant mechanism that enhances the limited memory of an organism consists in putting externalized marks in the environment, for example effluvial marks that help animals in orientation (or a notoriously known knot in the handkerchief as a "don't forget" sign). In these cases, a mark put in the environment later triggers the respective cued representation.

On the contrary, a *detached* representation may stand for objects and events neither present nor triggered by anything in the current situation of the organism. For example, a chimp looking for a (non-present) twig to reach for a banana possesses a detached representation of a twig and its use. It is speculated that the appearance of detached representations in phylogeny co-occurs with the development of neocortex (Gärdenfors, 1996b); in ontogeny it corresponds to object permanence (Piaget & Inhelder, 1966).

Possession of detached representations is a necessary condition for higher cognitive functions such as planning, deception, self-awareness and linguistic communication (Gärdenfors, 1996a). Language is a symbolic sign system that enables externalization and communication of detached representations. Thanks to its detached nature, it enables talking about things not present here and now, even about things that cannot exist physically. According to Gärdenfors (2004), language evolved in order to make cooperation about future goals possible. Language Semantics is grounded in conceptual meanings of various origins. Some of these meanings are innate, if they had been vital for survival on the evolutionary timescale (Fodor, 1981). Other meanings are constructed by observing the environment and consequences of one's own actions (Piaget & Inhelder, 1966; Bloom, 2000). Yet other meanings are transmitted culturally and

are stimulated by the language itself (Whorf, 1956; Waxman, 2004).

MEANINGS IN ARTIFICIAL SYSTEMS

Basic Problems

The appearance of the first artificial systems that could to some extent use natural language, e.g. ELIZA (Weizenbaum, 1966) and SHRDLU (Winograd, 1971), in the early history of AI have raised questions about the nature of understanding in such systems: Do these systems truly understand language or they just manipulate symbols that are meaningless to them? These questions became a subject of many heated debates and controversies. The *Chinese Room Argument* (Searle, 1980) and the *Symbol Grounding Problem* (Harnad, 1990) are examples of attempts to answer, or at least reformulate these questions.

John Searle (1980) has argued that, solely by observing a behavior (the communication, in this case), one cannot determine whether the system truly understands what it is talking about. He proposed a thought experiment, known as the Chinese Room: Let us imagine that a person who does not speak Chinese is locked in the room. People outside the room send into the room questions written in Chinese. In the room, there is a box with Chinese characters and a book of rules for manipulating the characters, enabling to produce answers for questions written with Chinese characters. The person in the room composes the answers entirely by comparing the shapes of the characters with those in the box and by using formal rules. Let us suppose that the person gets so proficient in manipulating the characters that he gives correct answers to the questions. Nobody outside the room can tell that the person doesn't speak a word of Chinese, neither that (s)he understands the content of the communication (s)he is participating in. (S)he has produced answers by manipulating uninterpreted formal symbols.

The Chinese Room Argument led Steven Harnad (1990) to formulate his own version of the problem, known as the Symbol Grounding Problem: "How can the Semantic interpretation of a formal symbol system be made intrinsic to the system, rather than just parasitic on the meanings in our heads? How can the meanings of the meaningless symbol tokens, manipulated solely on the basis of their (arbitrary) shapes, be grounded in anything but other meaningless symbols?" (p. 335).

Hence, internal representations have no intrinsic meaning *per se*. According to Maturana and Varela (1987), they get it via structural coupling with the environment. This coupling has two components: individual and social. The former one, called *Physical Symbol Grounding* (Vogt, 2002), refers to the ability of each individual to create an intrinsic link between world entities and internal representations, while the latter one, called *Social* (or *External*) *Symbol Grounding*, refers to the collective negotiation for the selection of shared symbols and their meanings (Cangelosi, 2006).

In the rest of this section, we briefly review several relevant possibilities of meaning representation in artificial systems and computational models. We analyze them with respect to their expressive power and the ability to cope with the Symbol Grounding Problem.

Discrimination Trees and Prototypes

Now we will describe several models, in which meanings are represented by regions in some geometrical space typically defined over possible sensor values of agents that perceive a shared environment – either a single-sensor one-dimensional space, or in the multidimensional Cartesian product of the sensors' ranges. In these models, meanings are not externally given, but created individually by each agent.

Figure 1. Splitting a discrimination tree. The range of the sensor is repeatedly split into halves (the resulting tree does not have to be balanced)

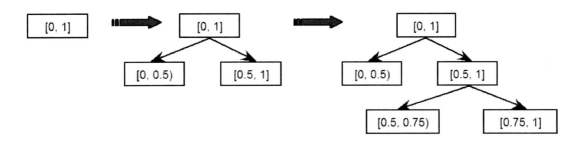

Figure 2. Voronoi tessellation of space to categories generated by prototypes. Round points represent examples of categories, 'x' points are prototypes computed as the centroids of the examples.

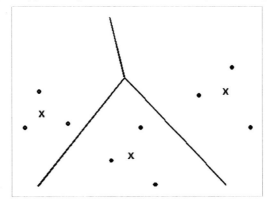

One possibility of partitioning the sensor spaces is via discrimination trees (Steels, 1997), which are used in models of language formation based on computer simulations (Bodík & Takáč, 2003; Smith, 2003, 2005) or on experiments with real robots (de Jong & Vogt, 1998; Steels & Kaplan, 1999; Steels, 1999). For each sensory channel, the agent constructs a separate binary discrimination tree. Nodes of the tree represent subintervals of the corresponding sensor's range. They determine the granularity of the agent's representation: all sensor readings that fall within an interval of some node are treated equal. Initially, each tree only consists of a root that represents the whole range of the corresponding sensor. Trees are adaptively refined by splitting an interval of some node into halves, spawning two subnodes (Figure 1), in the so-called discrimination games (Steels & Kaplan, 1999) played in order to find among the meanings the one that uniquely distinguishes a chosen object (the topic) from all other concurrently present objects (the context). The utility of each split is monitored by recording its use and success in future discriminations; environmentally irrelevant (unused or unsuccessful) distinctions are discarded. Hence, discrimination tasks provide grounding for the constructed meanings.

An alternative, prototype representation of meanings in the sensory space is based on the empirical findings that some exemplars of categories are more representative than others (Rosch, 1978). Such representation of categories is effective, because only the best exemplars (prototypes) need to

be remembered. Each point in the sensory space is considered a member of the category represented by the spatially closest prototype (see Figure 2). Prototypes were used as a representation of meanings in experiments with software agents in a simulated environment (Vogt, 2005; Vogt & Divina, 2007) as well as with real robots (Vogt, 2000, 2002). We will illustrate the use of discrimination trees and prototypes in the section dedicated to computational models of horizontal coordination of lexicon.

Dual-Route Neural Networks

Connectionist models of symbol grounding often employ a dual-route architecture that typically involves both visual input (e.g. retina projection) and linguistic input (e.g. localist or graphemic/phonetic encoding of symbols). The output layer has symbolic units for representing words, and either a categorical representation of input stimuli (e.g. a localist node for each category, or a visual representation of category prototypes) or representation of a desired action (e.g. values of joint angles of an arm). All input and output layers are connected via a shared hidden layer. The route from visual input to symbolic output is used for language production tasks, such as naming of an object represented in the visual scene or its category. The route from linguistic input to visual/categorical/motor output is used for language understanding tasks. The two other possible routes are used for categorization and sensory-based action (the route from visual input to categorical/motor units) and for linguistic imitation

Figure 3. Example of a dual-route neural network used in the experiment of Cangelosi (1999)

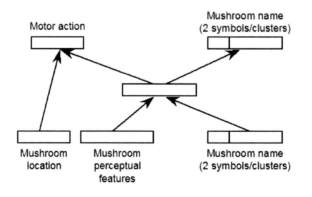

(from linguistic input to symbolic output) (Cangelosi, 2005). Dual-route networks were used e.g. in the models of Cangelosi (1999), Cangelosi and Parisi (2001) and Mirolli and Parisi (2005).

In the model of Cangelosi (1999), a population of 80 organisms lives in a virtual environment that contains three edible and three poisonous types of mushrooms. The model incorporates genetic evolution of organisms. To gain fitness, organisms have to avoid toadstools and identify the type of edible mushrooms and eat them. The behavior of each organism is driven by a dual-route network (Figure 3) that enables performing actions (based on mushroom location and perceptual features and/or linguistic input from other agents) and naming (either as imitation of a linguistic production of another agent or naming the mushroom for another agent based on the mushroom location and its perceptual features). At the beginning, the lexicon is totally random and meaningless. Toward the end of the evolution, the agents are able to evolve shared compositional languages. Although the presented model is deliberately simple, it illustrates a correct connectionist approach to symbol grounding. Meanings, implicitly represented in connection weights of the networks are private and created individually in each organism. The language learning is connected to sensorimotor activities via a shared hidden layer in the dual route architecture.

Corpus-Based Meanings

Although not sufficient for language grounding in the real world (see the Chinese Room Argument), distributional and contextual information is an important cue to word meanings (Li et al., 2004; Bullinaria & Levy, 2007). This is impressively demonstrated by chatbots based on a contextual corpus search. A chatbot is a computer program designed to simulate an intelligent conversation with human users. Many chatbots (like ELIZA) are based on recognizing keywords in the human user's input and answering according to pre-programmed rules. Jabberwacky, made by Rolo Carpenter (2007), is based on different principles: there are no fixed rules programmed into the system and it operates entirely through user interaction. The system maintains a large database of all previous conversations and attempts to use

this information to find the most appropriate response in the current context. The search is based on a complex layered set of heuristics that produce results through analyses of conversational context and a positive feedback (Icogno, 2007).

The success in giving an impression of real thinking depends on a large-enough database. Having been online on the world wide Web since 1997, Jabberwacky has recorded more than 13 million conversations. It reflects back what it had learned from its conversation partners. In this way, it can use jokes, idioms, word games, slang, and even speak foreign languages. Two recent instantiations of Jabberwacky – George and Joan have won the Loebner prize in 2005 and 2006. The Loebner Prize is an annual competition that awards prizes to the chatbot considered by the judges to be the most humanlike of those entered. The format of the competition is that of a standard Turing test (Turing, 1950).

Although Jabberwacky's conversations can be interpreted by humans as having some Semantic content, i.e. as being "about something", this content is extrinsic and Jabberwacky knows nothing about it. Hence, its linguistic knowledge is not grounded in the real world. However, from a different point of view, Jabberwacky is situated in the world of conversational sequences, where it learns from scratch to react appropriately in various contexts. The knowledge of what is "appropriate" is encoded in the recorded history of reactions of the chatbot's human partners. In line with Brooks (1991), we can view Jabberwacky's intelligent behavior as an emergent effect of its interactions, where the knowledge is distributed both in its architecture and the environment.

Other Models

Due to space limitations, our collection of example models cannot be exhaustive. Other interesting approaches to meaning representation and formation include semiotic schemas (Roy, 2005), dynamic maps (Cohen, 1998), redescriptions of co-occurring events (Cohen et al., 1996) and Embodied Construction Grammar (Bergen & Chang, 2003). We refer interested readers to the original literature.

CONSTRUCTION OF MEANINGS

Individual Meanings

The moral of the story told so far is that the presence of understanding/meanings both in the animal kingdom and in the artificial world should be viewed more like a continuum with many degrees ranging from elementary forms to very complex ones, rather than being a subject of yes/no questions. In line with the presented facts, we will now summarize our own perspective on understanding in as non-anthropocentric (and even non-biological) terms as possible.

We will only talk about understanding in agents (biological or artificial) with respect to the environment (real or virtual) they are situated in. A *situated agent* is an autonomous entity that achieves some goals in its environment by sensing and acting (Kelemen, 2003). Note that this definition does not imply or require any consciousness or intentionality: the agent can achieve some goals (or serve some purpose) without "knowing" about it.

Adaptive agents modify themselves to achieve their goals better. We will distinguish phylogenetic (design-time) and ontogenetic (run-time) adaptations. Learning is an ontogenetic adaptation based on a feedback loop between perception and action (or, more generally, input and output). The impact of adaptations on an agent's behavior can be conveniently described in terms of representations regardless of their origin and actual implementation. If an agent categorizes the world by producing different behavioral responses for different classes of inputs, we say that it possesses cued representations, which are the most elementary forms of meanings. More complex cognitive abilities like decision-making and planning require detached representations that can be retained, retrieved and processed independently of external triggers from the current environmental context of the agent.

Socially Shared Meanings

So far, we have talked about subjective or private meanings dependent on each agent's phylogenetic and ontogenetic history. Cooperative planning among agents requires externalization and com-munication of their meanings by exchanging publicly observable signals. We say that a signal is understood as having a Semantic content for an observing agent, if the observer behaves toward it in accordance with this content (van Gulick, 1988). This view is interactionist: private meanings cannot be transferred directly from one agent to another; they can only be inferred from behavioral interactions. However, the communication can only be successful if the private meanings are sufficiently similar. This is granted, if the associations between signals, meanings and their referents are non-arbitrary and had been shaped by the same mechanism, like in the innate signaling systems of animal species or in systems of non-adaptive agents driven by the same preprogrammed code. However, in *symbolic* communication systems, the links between meanings and signals are arbitrary by definition (Chandler, 2007). If they were formed or influenced by individual adaptation, inter-similarity of meanings between different agents cannot be taken for granted. Meanings of individual agents need to be attuned to each other by adaptation in social interactions. Interactions can be unidirectional (vertical), if agent's own representations are adapted to an existing communication system without affecting it (e.g., if an infant learns a language (s)he is exposed to). If the interactions are bidirectional (horizontal), i.e. they result in adaptation on both communicating sides, the whole language behaves as a dynamical system, wherein "public" (negotiated) meanings emerge as (moving) equilibria (Gärdenfors, 2000).

Design Principles for Building "Understanding" Agents

The just-presented interactionist perspective on meanings can be summarized in the criteria of genuine understanding in artificial agents, and design principles for building such agents:

1.   Meanings should stem from interactions of agents with the environment they are situated in. In case of software agents, the environment does not have to be physical: they can "live", i.e. sense and perform actions, in a virtual one, e.g. search in databases or negotiate e-commerce transactions.

2. Non-trivial environments are dynamic and changing in time. Hence, besides static objects and relations, the agents must be capable of capturing/representing dynamic characteristics of the world, such as changes, actions, their consequences and events.

3. Because the environment is open, all possible meanings cannot be anticipated (given beforehand in design time) and the agents should learn. Learning (construction of meanings) should be incremental and continuous.

4. In order to enable mutual understanding in communication, the agents should be endowed with mechanisms for social coordination of individually constructed meanings.

COMPUTATIONAL MODELS

In this section, we will present several computational models that illustrate the above-mentioned design principles. Because of didactic reasons, we selected models that focus on some of the principles or a particular way of their implementation, even if they do not obey all the principles at once.

Individual Sensorimotor Exploration

First, we will present a computational model of individual construction of meanings grounded in sensorimotor interactions (Takáč, 2006a). The model consists of a single agent situated in a simulated environment – a two-dimensional lattice with randomly distributed objects of four types: fruits, toys, furniture and the agent itself. In the beginning, the agent cannot distinguish any types – it just receives information about perceivable properties of objects in its vicinity in the form of frames – sets of <attribute: numeric value> pairs. The attributes encode properties like the position on the lattice, size, weight, color, shape, etc. The time is discrete in the model. In each time step, the agent's perceptual input consists of one frame for each perceivable object. The agent can then select one of the objects for manipulation and try to lift it or put it down. Successful manipulations result in attribute changes of the manipulated object (its vertical position in this case). The actions are

parameterized – the agent can choose the exerted force of lifting and the vertical position of its arm (these parameters are a simplified abstraction of a simulated action – in fact, the agent has neither arm, nor any motors etc.). The maximum force and the arm position are limited by the "construction" of the agent.

The agent can observe consequences of its actions by comparing attribute values of objects in two subsequent time steps. Actual impact of the actions is regulated by the environment simulator based on simplified physical laws, e.g. an attempt to lift an object with a force too little with respect to the object's weight results in no change, otherwise the change in the vertical position of the object is proportional to the vertical position of the agent's arm during lifting.

The agent actively explores its environment by performing random actions and gradually learns to distinguish relevant environmental properties and builds categories of objects, actions and changes similar in some respect. The representation of categories is based on *identification criteria* inspired by the already mentioned cognitive Semantics of Šefránek (2002). Each identification criterion is an activation function that returns, for some input, the degree of the input's membership in the category (Figure 4). The possible inputs include a perceptual frame of one object (in criteria of objects and properties), a ("proprioceptive") frame of action parameters and type (in action criteria), perceptual frames of several objects (in relational criteria), frames of the same object at different times (in change criteria) and output activities of other criteria (in compositional criteria of situations and events). In the beginning, the agent has no criteria – they are gradually constructed from scratch by extracting common statistical properties of encountered examples of categories. For technical details of the representation, see Takáč (2006b; 2007a). If a single action performed on different objects leads to a sufficiently similar outcome (attribute change), all these objects will be considered examples of the same category (with respect to the action and the outcome). A significantly different outcome triggers creation of new categories. The same principle is used for grouping different actions performed upon a single object.

Figure 4. Identification criterion with the multivariate Gaussian activity curve operating in a two-dimensional input space

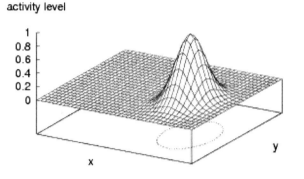

In the computer simulations of our model, we let the agent interact with its environment and measured the utility of the constructed representation for predicting outcomes of the performed actions. The experimental results have confirmed that the proposed mechanism of action-based category formation leads to ecologically relevant categories, i.e. those supporting prediction of results of the agent's own actions. For technical details of the learning algorithm and its evaluation, see Takáč (2006a).

A qualitative analysis of constructed meanings in example simulation runs showed that the agent created object categories that could be interpreted with respect to the associated causal knowledge e.g. as "things too heavy to be lifted" and "things that cannot be put down, because they are already on the ground". Attributes other than weight and vertical position were present in the criteria too, which means that they helped the agent in classification (e.g. if all heavy objects were in the same part of the grid, or had some specific color). Hence, the constructed representation was situated and it also encoded the agent's subjective interactional learning context.

This experiment models activities in the sensorimotor stage of child development (Piaget & Inhelder, 1966), in which, by performing random and uncoordinated movements, infants learn about surrounding objects and possibilities of interacting with them. Repeated causal patterns are recorded, which opens the door for later deliberative planning aimed at satisfying one's goals. An important aspect of the model is that the agent is only endowed with learning mechanisms in design time and all the knowledge about a particular environment the agent is exposed to is only acquired in run time. This enables the agent to be flexible and to adapt to different environments, which are unknown beforehand or which can change during the agent's lifetime (imagine a task of programming a robot that will be sent to a remote planet with unknown conditions).

Looking back at the design principles of understanding agents, this model obeys the principles 1-3. However, the perception/action interface of the model was (deliberately) very abstract and simplified. In embodied systems operating in real environments, the tasks related to perception and processing of noisy analog sensory signal and the effector control (such as servo-motors of mechanical arm, etc.) rank among very hard. As the model only consisted of one agent, there was no social coordination of meanings (principle 4) and no language. We deal with these issues in the following sections.

Horizontal Coordination

In this section, we will present a computational modeling framework of Steels (2000) illustrating the emergence of coordinated communication system from horizontal cultural interactions. Horizontal interactions are bidirectional, which means that both communicating sides try to attune to each other: they change their private associations between externally observable signals, internal meanings and corresponding referents in the world, and also shift the internal meanings themselves.

The adaptation is driven by feedback about success/failure in communication. However, success does not necessarily mean that the communicating agents have identical meanings associated with the same signal. Instead, the success is judged by the pragmatic criteria: as private meanings are not accessible externally, signs should match at the referent level, which is manifested by the agents' behavior. Behavioral criteria are plausible: for example, if I ask someone to give me a pen and (s)he gives me an apple or opens the door instead, I can reasonably suspect that (s)he did not understand me.

In models based on this framework, the agents (simulated or embodied in real robots) play various types of so-called *language games* with various pragmatic goals (Steels & Kaplan, 1999). The games proceed in rounds; in each round, two agents are randomly chosen from the population – one in the role of a speaker and the other in that of a hearer. First, in the *discrimination game*, the speaker tries to uniquely identify and lexicalize a particular object present in the environment, chosen as the topic. Then, in the *guessing game*, the hearer tries to guess the topic from the signal emitted by the speaker.

Agents store their conceptual knowledge (meanings) in discrimination trees, and the lexical knowledge in the form of many-to-many associations between nodes of the trees and signals. The trees and associations are constructed and adapted individually according to success/failure in language games (the acquired associations are adapted by manipulating their numeric-valued strengths).

In case of success in a discrimination game, the speaker tries to lexicalize the selected meaning by using the so-called *introspective obverter strategy* (Smith, 2003): from all signals associated with the meaning, the speaker emits the one that maximizes the estimated probability of being understood properly. The hearer tries to interpret the emitted signal by finding its own internally associated meaning and then to look for a corresponding referent of the meaning among the present objects. Afterwards, the hearer receives a feedback indicating whether its guess was correct or not and adapts the strengths of the involved associations accordingly. In another variant called the observational game (Oliphant, 1997), the hearer receives no feedback. Instead, the speaker narrows down the set of possible referents of the uttered signal by pointing, and the hearer adapts its lexicon by Hebbian learning (if there is more than one candidate, the hearer associates the signal with each of the candidates). Meanings can then be disambiguated cross-situationally (Siskind, 1996; Smith, 2005).

The Talking Heads experiment (Steels, 1999) was a famous physical realization of the guessing game scheme. The experimental setup consisted of two pan-tilt cameras in which different agents could be loaded. The loaded agents could perceive and communicate about a shared environment that consisted of a magnetic white board with various geometric shapes of various colors.

Out of other models that use guessing games, we will mention the one realized by Vogt (2002). In this model, language games were played by two agents embodied in two mobile LOGO robots. The agents used prototype representation of meanings. The goal of the language game was to communicate a name for one of light sources that the robots could detect in their environment.

In both mentioned experiments, the agents successfully arrived at a coordinated grounded lexicon under real physical conditions. The importance of these models is that they demonstrate how a globally coherent communication system can emerge from scratch as a result of local interactions of language users. The agents start with no meanings (undifferentiated sensory channels) and void lexicons and the whole system gets off the ground because of the invention mechanism implemented in the model: in case a speaker lacks a signal to express some meaning, it can emit a random signal. Such a signal would almost surely be misunderstood; nevertheless, the speaker and the hearer record the association between their meanings and the used signal, and can use it in the future. This way, signals may propagate in the population. The agents' tendency to use the signals and meanings that were successfully used in the past creates a positive feedback loop. Variant signals and meanings compete with each other and the successful ones are reinforced. This results in self-organization and the emergence of a coherent communication system. Spontaneous self-organization of language within the time span of one generation with purely cultural horizontal interactions has also been observed among humans in the case of Nicaraguan Sign Language (Kegl et al., 1999).

Looking back at the design principles, the presented models obey the principles 1, 3 and 4. Each agent creates and continuously reshapes its meanings individually, based on interactions with the environment. The meanings are private, not available to other agents and possibly different in each agent. They are attuned to each other so that the agents were able to reach their goals in language games. However, the design principle 2 is violated: agents only communicate about static objects currently present in their vicinity. They have no means to neither represent nor communicate dynamical aspects of their environment. Communication is based on cued representations only.

Learning by Social Instruction

In this section, we will focus on unidirectional interactions between agents and their influence on the meaning adaptation process. A unidirectional adaptation process is an instance of learning, where the unaffected agent is called the *teacher* and the adapting agent is the *learner*. Such learning is a significant part of the language acquisition process occurring between infants and their caregivers. We will present a computational model motivated by the empirical research of Waxman (2004) who studied the influence of verbal instruction (naming) on category formation process. The results of her research suggest that consistent using of the same name for distinct objects motivates the infant to look for similarities and promotes formation of categories.

The computational model (Takáč, in press) consists of two agents situated in a simulated environ-

ment: a teacher describing various aspects of the present situation, and a learner inducing meanings of the teacher's words by noticing cross-situation similarities between their referents. The simulated environment contains planar geometrical shapes characterized by randomly generated numeric attributes such as the number of vertices, coordinates of the centroid of the shape and the size of the bounding rectangle. The environment is dynamic in that randomly selected objects can be resized, moved, or removed from the environment and newly generated objects can be added in each time step (multiple changes can happen simultaneously).

The learner's representation of meanings is based on the already mentioned identification criteria. In the beginning, the learner has no criteria – they can be induced by extracting common statistical properties of presented examples. However, in the course of time, the teacher (an agent with predefined meanings and lexicon) names various aspects of static objects, properties, relations and dynamic changes and the learner has to determine what these names refer to, to create the appropriate criteria and associate them with the words. Along with an uttered expression, the teacher provides a non-verbal hint by "pointing" to an instance of the named category, i.e. the object having the property, being changed or being in the relation.

This simplification is used deliberately, in order to show that even in the absence of the *referent* indeterminacy, the learner has to solve the *sense* indeterminacy, because different words could describe different aspects of the same (known) referent.

The induction of meanings is guided by the *no true synonymy* and *no true homonymy* assumptions. Although natural languages do contain words with multiple meanings (homonyms) and multiple expressions for a single meaning (synonyms), in case of bootstrapping the language and concepts from scratch, it is useful to start with no homonymy and no synonymy.

- **No true synonymy:** Different words have different meanings, even if they share a referent (in that case they express different aspects of the referent). This assumption corresponds to the *Principle of Contrast* (Clark, 1987) known from child language acquisition.

- **No true homonymy:** A single word has a single meaning, even if it is used with more referents. This assumption is crucial for cross-situational disambiguation of the meaning: all the referents of a single word across different situations are considered instances of the same category denoted by the word.

Example: Let us consider an agent that lives in a world of geometric shapes placed on a 50×50 grid with the point coordinates (1, 1) on the bottom left and (50, 50) on the top right. If the agent perceives an object f = {*vertices*: 3; *size*: 18; *color*: 3; *posX*: 1; *posY*: 23} denoted by words "left", "big", "triangle", it creates three identification criteria, which are initially identical and represent the "snapshot" of the perceived object f. The criteria begin to differentiate, when they are updated by more and more instances. E.g., frames of various objects that have all kinds of colors, positions, sizes and other properties, but all have three vertices, will update the „snapshot" criterion associated with the word „triangle". Attributes not common to all instances will be removed from the criterion and others will gain lower importance because of their high variance in the sample. Hence, the property of having three vertices (with zero variance in the sample) will become decisive in the criterion associated with the word "triangle". Also, the word "left" will be heard with many different objects sharing the property of low value of the attribute posX, etc. The more contexts of the word's use, the bigger the probability that the referents will vary in the properties irrelevant for the meaning of the word. However, if e.g. all triangles in the agent's world are big, then having a big size will become part of the meaning of the word "triangle". Hence, the induced representation is situated and contextual.

Computer simulations of this model demonstrated how an existing conceptual system could be culturally transmitted by means of vertical linguistic interactions (Takáč, in press). However, languages are not transmitted as petrified systems, but they themselves undergo changes and evolve in the course of generations (Deacon, 1997), e.g. neologisms appear and archaisms disappear, some elements of syntax simplify and get regularized, etc. The emerging structure of an evolving language is constrained by the ontogenetic process of language

acquisition, which is in turn determined by mostly innate (or preprogrammed) learning mechanisms (Briscoe, 2001). In another experiment reported in Takáč (in press), the *iterated learning framework* of Kirby and Hurford (2001) was applied to study the meaning shifts within iterated vertical transmission.

CONCLUSION

In this chapter, we elaborated the notion of (inherent) meanings. We suggested how artificial agents could individually construct meanings based on interactions with their environment and how their individual meanings could be coordinated collectively. This is especially important in unknown, dynamic and open environments, where all possible meanings cannot be anticipated in design-time.

Regarding communication, we pointed out that mutual understanding does not necessarily require evocation of identical individual meanings; rather, it results in a collectively attuned behavior. This creates an important base for our communication (and co-existence) with artificially built agents. Inherent meanings of the agents that are constructed differently and have different purposes and ecological niches will be different from ours. In spite of that, our communication can be meaningful, provided that we negotiate a common communication system.

FUTURE RESEARCH DIRECTIONS

We illustrated the mechanisms of the individual construction and collective coordination of meanings by several computational models. These models are simplified in many aspects; nevertheless they support the viability of the proposed ideas. First of all, because of methodological reasons, each model deliberately focuses on some of the phenomena in isolation: there is no communication in the model of individual meaning construction, there are no extra-linguistic activities in the models of meaning coordination, etc. Hence, a natural (and more realistic) extension of the models should combine these approaches.

In the model of sensorimotor exploration, the agent had no goals and performed actions randomly.

It was nevertheless able to acquire and represent propositional knowledge about environmental consequences of its actions. The next research step is to endow the agent with needs, need-driven goals and an action planning mechanism.

After integrating a communication level and mechanisms of horizontal and vertical coordination into this model, one can experimentally test whether the goal-achieving autonomous agents profit from exchanging their individually acquired knowledge via the emergent common communication system.

Future research should also consider the expressive power of various types of meaning representation. Meaning representation should capture hierarchic and taxonomic relations and support verb Semantics. In discrimination tree based representation, dynamical aspects of the environment are not captured at all. In identification criteria based Semantics, meanings of verbs are constructed from criteria of one-step changes of attribute values. Representation of larger sequences of changes may be necessary for some verbs. For other verbs, discrete sequences may be insufficient at all and some kind of continuous representation of the dynamics (e.g. phase portraits) may be required.

In the presented models, the language use was always cued by a current situation. However, the primary evolutionary advantage of human language is its detached use, i.e. that it enables talking about things being not here and now. Detached communication would be too ambiguous without some form of grammar that helps to reduce indeterminacy (Gärdenfors, 1996b). Incorporating a grammar to models of language emergence and acquisition is an important future research direction. First steps in this direction have already been taken (Steels, 2004; Steels & Wellens, 2006).

We demonstrated how categorical meanings could be constructed by extracting common statistical properties of examples. However, for construction of more complex meanings, it would be desirable to enhance the model with analysis, synthesis, non-monotonic reasoning and other cognitive operations (Šefránek, 2002).

The final issue is that of the scalability of the presented models. Here we want to refer to a very ambitious project New Ties (from "New and Emergent World Models Through Individual, Evolutionary, and Social learning", http://www.new-ties.org). The project's goal is to evolve a large-size artificial society capable of exploring and understanding its environment through cooperation and interaction (Vogt & Divina, 2005; Gilbert et al., 2006). The very same mechanisms of meaning and language coordination can then open for us the doorway to exploring mixed human-machine societies.

REFERENCES

Bergen, B., & Chang, N. (2003). Embodied construction grammar in simulation-based language understanding. In J. O. Ostman & M. Fried (Eds.), *Construction grammar(s): Cognitive and cross-language dimensions* (pp. 147-190). Amsterdam: Johns Benjamins.

Bloom, P. (2000). *How children learn the meanings of words*. Cambridge, MA: MIT Press.

Bodík, P., & Takáč, M. (2003). Formation of a common spatial lexicon and its change in a community of moving agents. In B. Tessem, P. Ala-Siuru, P. Doherty, & B. Mayoh (Eds.), *Frontiers in AI: Proceedings of the Eighth Scandinavian Conference on Artificial Intelligence SCAI'03* (pp. 37-46). Amsterdam: IOS Press.

Briscoe, T. (Ed.). (2001). *Linguistic evolution through language acquisition: Formal and computational models*. Cambridge, U. K.: Cambridge University Press.

Brooks, R. A. (1991). Intelligence without representation. *Artificial Intelligence, 47* (1-3), 139-159.

Bullinaria, J. A., & Levy, J. P. (2007). Extracting Semantic representations from word co occurrence statistics: A computational study. *Behavior Research Methods, 39*, 510-526.

Cangelosi, A. (1999). Modeling the evolution of communication: From stimulus associations to grounded symbolic associations. In D. Floreano, J. Nicoud, & F. Mondada (Eds.), *Proceedings of the 5th European Conference on Advances in Artificial Life* (pp. 654-663). Berlin: Springer.

Cangelosi, A. (2005). Approaches to grounding symbols in perceptual and sensorimotor categories. In H. Cohen & C. Lefebvre (Eds.), *Handbook of categorization in cognitive science* (pp. 719-737). Amsterdam: Elsevier.

Cangelosi, A. (2006). The grounding and sharing of symbols. *Pragmatics and Cognition, 14* (2), 275-285.

Cangelosi, A., & Parisi, D. (2001). How nouns and verbs differentially affect the behavior of artificial organisms. In J. D. Moore & K. Stenning (Eds.), *Proceedings of the Twenty-third Annual Conference of the Cognitive Science Society* (pp. 170-175). London: Lawrence Erlbaum Associates.

Carpenter, R. (2007). *Jabberwacky – live chatbot.* Retrieved December 8, 2007, from http://www.jabberwacky.com

Chandler, D. (2007). *Semiotics: the basics* (Second ed.). London, New York: Routledge.

Clark, E. (1987). The principle of contrast: A constraint on language acquisition. In B. MacWhinney (Ed.), *Mechanisms of language acquisition* (pp. 1-33). Hillsdale, NJ: Lawrence Erlbaum Associates

Cohen, P. (1998). Dynamic maps as representations of verbs. In *Proceedings of the 13th Biennial European Conference on Artificial Intelligence* (pp. 145-149). New York: John Wiley & Sons.

Cohen, P., Oates, T., Atkin, M., & Beal, C. (1996). Building a baby. In G. W. Cottrell (Ed.), *Proceedings of the Eighteenth Annual Conference of the Cognitive Science Society* (pp. 518-522). Mahwah, NJ: Lawrence Erlbaum Associates.

Deacon, T. W. (1997). *The symbolic species: The co-evolution of language and the brain.* New York: W.W. Norton & Co.

Fauconnier, G. (1985). *Mental spaces: Aspects of meaning construction in natural language.* Cambridge, MA: MIT Press.

Fillmore, C. J. (1982). Frame Semantics. In *Linguistics in the morning calm* (pp. 111-137). Seoul: Hanshin Pub. Co.

Fodor, J. A. (1981). *Representations: Philosophical essays on the foundations of cognitive science.* Cambridge, MA: MIT Press.

Fodor, J. A. (1983). *The modularity of mind.* Bradford Books. Cambridge, MA: MIT Press.

Gärdenfors, P. (1996a). Cued and detached representations in animal cognition. *Behavioral Processes, 35,* 263-273.

Gärdenfors, P. (1996b). Language and the evolution of cognition. In V. Rialle & D. Fisette (Eds.), *Penser l'esprit: Des sciences de la cognition a' une philosophie cognitive* (pp. 151-172). Grenoble: Presses Universitaires de Grenoble.

Gärdenfors, P. (2000). *Conceptual spaces.* Cambridge, MA: MIT Press.

Gärdenfors, P. (2004). Cooperation and the evolution of symbolic communication. In K. Oller & U. Griebel (Eds.), *The evolution of communication systems* (pp. 237-256). Cambridge, MA: MIT Press.

Gilbert, N., Besten, M. den, Bontovics, A., Craenen, B. G. W., Divina, F., Eiben, A. E., Griffioen, R., Hévízi, G., Lörincz, A., Paechter, B., Schuster, S., Schut, M. C., Tzolov, C., Vogt, P., & Yang, L. (2006). Emerging Artificial Societies Through Learning [Electronic version]. *Journal of Artificial Societies and Social Simulation, 9* (2) 9.

Ginsberg, M. (Ed.). (1987). *Readings in nonmonotonic reasoning,* San Mateo, CA: Morgan Kaufmann.

Goodwin, B. C. (1978). A cognitive view of biological process. *Journal of Social and Biological Structures, 1,* 117-125.

Gulick, R. van. (1988). Consciousness, intrinsic intentionality and self-understanding machines. In A. J. Marcel & E. Bisiach (Eds.), *Consciousness in contemporary science* (pp. 78-100). Oxford, U. K.: Clarendon Press.

Harnad, S. (1990). The symbol grounding problem. *Physica, D 42,* 335-346.

Holland, O. (Ed.) (2003). Machine Consciousness [Special Issue]. *Journal of Consciousness Studies, 10* (4-5).

Icogno (2007). *What AI techniques does Jabberwacky use?* Retrieved on December 8, 2007, from http://www.icogno.com/what_ai_techniques.html

Jong, E. de, & Vogt, P. (1998). How should a robot discriminate between objects? A comparison between two methods. In *Proceedings of the Fifth International Conference on Simulation of Adaptive Behavior SAB'98* (pp. 86-91). Cambridge, MA: MIT Press.

Kegl, J., Senghas, A., & Coppola, M. (1999). Creation through contact: Sign language emergence and sign language change in Nicaragua. In M. DeGraff (Ed.), *Language creation and language change: creolization, diachrony, and development.* Cambridge, MA: MIT Press.

Kelemen, J. (2003). The agent paradigm. *Computing and Informatics, 22,* 513-519.

Kirby, S., & Hurford, J. (2001). The emergence of linguistic structure: an overview of the iterated learning model. In D. Parisi & A. Cangelosi (Eds.), *Computational approaches to the evolution of language and communication* (pp. 121-148). Berlin: Springer-Verlag.

Kováč, L. (2000). Fundamental principles of cognitive biology. *Evolution and Cognition, 6,* 51-69.

Lakoff, G. (1987). *Women, fire, and dangerous things: What categories reveal about the mind.* Chicago: University of Chicago Press.

Lakoff, G., & Johnson, M. (1980). *Metaphors we live by.* Chicago, IL: University of Chicago Press.

Langacker, R. W. (1987). *Foundations of cognitive grammar: Theoretical prerequisites* (Vol. 1). Stanford, CA: Stanford University Press.

Langacker, R. W. (1991). *Foundations of cognitive grammar: Descriptive applications* (Vol. 2). Stanford, CA: Stanford University Press.

Langton, C. G. (Ed.). (1989). *Artificial life.* Reading, MA: Addison-Wesley.

Li, P., Farkaš, I., & MacWhinney, B. (2004). Early lexical acquisition in a self-organizing neural network. *Neural Networks, 17* (8-9), 1345-1362.

Maturana, H. R., & Varela, F. J. (1987). *The tree of knowledge: The biological roots of human understanding.* Boston: Shambhala.

Mirolli, M., & Parisi, D. (2005). Language as an aid to categorization: A neural network model of early language acquisition. In *Modelling language, cognition and action: Proceedings of the 9th Neural Computation and Psychology Workshop.* Singapore: World Scientific.

Nehaniv, C. (2000). The making of meaning in societies: Semiotic and information-theoretic background to the evolution of communication. In B. Edmonds & K. Dautenhahn (Eds.), *AISB Symposium: Starting from Society – the application of social analogies to computational systems* (pp. 73-84). Society for the Study of Artificial Intelligence and Adaptive Behaviour.

Oliphant, M. (1997). *Formal approaches to innate and learned communication: Laying the foundation for language.* Unpublished doctoral dissertation, University of California, San Diego, CA.

Pfeifer, R., & Scheier, C. (1999). *Understanding intelligence.* Cambridge, MA: MIT Press.

Piaget, J., & Inhelder, B. (1966). *La psychologie de l'enfant* [The psychology of the child]. Paris: PUF.

Rosch, E. (1978). Principles of categorization. In E. Rosch & B. Lloyd (Eds.), *Cognition and categorization* (pp. 27-48). Hillsdale, NJ: Lawrence Erlbaum Associates.

Roy, D. (2005). Semiotic schemas: a framework for grounding language in action and perception. *Artificial Intelligence, 167* (1-2), 170-205.

Searle, J. R. (1980). Minds, brains, and programs. *Behavioural and Brain Sciences, 3,* 417-457.

Šefránek, J. (2002). Kognícia bez mentálnych procesov [Cognition without mental processes]. In J. Rybár, L. Beňušková, & V. Kvasnička (Eds.), *Kognitívne vedy* (pp. 200-256). Bratislava: Kalligram.

Siskind, J. M. (1996). A computational study of cross-situational techniques for learning word-to-meaning mappings. *Cognition, 61* (1-2), 1-38.

Smith, A. D. M. (2003). *Evolving communication through the inference of meaning.* Unpublished doctoral dissertation, Theoretical and Applied Linguistics, School of Philosophy, Psychology and Language Sciences, The University of Edinburgh.

Smith, A. D. M. (2005). The inferential transmission of language. *Adaptive Behavior, 13* (4), 311-324.

Steels, L. (1997). Constructing and sharing perceptual distinctions. In M. van Someren & G. Widmer (Eds.), *Proceedings of the European Conference on Machine Learning* (pp. 4-13). Berlin: Springer.

Steels, L. (1999). *The Talking Heads experiment. Words and meanings.* (Vol. 1). Antwerpen: Laboratorium.

Steels, L. (2000). Language as a complex adaptive system. In M. Schoenauer (Ed.), *Proceedings of PPSN-VI* (pp. 17-26). Berlin: Springer.

Steels, L. (2004). Constructivist development of grounded construction grammars. In D. Scott, W. Daelemans, & M. Walker (Eds.), *Proceedings Annual Meeting Association for Computational Linguistic Conference* (pp. 9-19). Barcelona.

Steels, L., & Kaplan, F. (1999). Situated grounded word Semantics. In T. Dean (Ed.), *Proceedings of the Sixteenth International Joint Conference on Artificial Intelligence* (pp. 862-867). San Francisco: Morgan Kauffmann.

Steels, L., & Wellens, P. (2006). How grammar emerges to dampen combinatorial search in parsing. In P. Vogt, Y. Sugita, E. Tuci, & C. Nehaniv (Eds.), *Symbol Grounding and Beyond: Proceedings of the Third International Workshop on the Emergence and Evolution of Linguistic Communication* (pp. 76-88). Berlin/Heidelberg: Springer.

Takáč, M. (2006a). Categorization by sensory-motor interaction in artificial agents. In D. Fum, F. Del Missier, & A. Stocco (Eds.), *Proceedings of the 7th International Conference on Cognitive Modeling* (pp. 310-315). Trieste, Italy: Edizioni Goliardiche.

Takáč, M. (2006b). Cognitive Semantics for dynamic environments. In P. Hitzler, H. Schärfe, & P. Øhrstrøm (Eds.), *Contributions to ICCS 2006 – 14th International Conference on Conceptual Structures* (pp. 202-215). Aalborg, Denmark: Aalborg University Press.

Takáč, M. (2007a). *Construction of meanings in living and artificial agents* [Submitted]. Unpublished doctoral dissertation, Comenius University of Bratislava, Slovakia.

Takáč, M. (in press). Autonomous construction of ecologically and socially relevant Semantics. *Cognitive Systems Research.*

Talmy, L. (2000). *Toward a cognitive Semantics.* Cambridge, MA: MIT Press.

Turing, A. M. (1950). Computing machinery and intelligence. *Mind, 59,* 433-460.

Vogt, P. (2000). *Lexicon grounding on mobile robots.* Unpublished doctoral dissertation, Vrije Universiteit Brussel, Belgium.

Vogt, P. (2002). The physical symbol grounding problem. *Cognitive Systems Research, 3* (3), 429-457.

Vogt, P. (2005). The emergence of compositional structures in perceptually grounded language games. *Artificial Intelligence, 167* (1-2), 206-242.

Vogt, P., & Divina, F. (2005). Language evolution in large populations of autonomous agents: issues in scaling. In *Proceedings of AISB 2005: Social Intelligence and Interaction in Animals, Robots and Agents* (pp. 80-87).

Vogt, P., & Divina, F. (2007). Social symbol grounding and language evolution. *Interaction Studies, 8* (1), 31-52.

Waxman, S. R. (2004). Everything had a name, and each name gave birth to a new thought: Links between early word-learning and conceptual organization. In D. G. Hall & S. R. Waxman (Eds.), *Weaving a lexicon* (pp. 295-335). Cambridge, MA: MIT Press.

Weizenbaum, J. (1966). Eliza – a computer program for the study of natural language communication between man and machine. *Communications of the ACM, 9* (1), 36-45.

Whorf, B. L. (1956). *Language, thought and reality: Selected writings of Benjamin Lee Whorf* (J. B. Carrol, Ed.). Cambridge, MA: MIT Press.

Winograd, T. (1971). *Procedures as a representation for data in a computer program for understanding natural language.* Unpublished doctoral dissertation, MIT, Cambridge, MA.

ADDITIONAL READING

Bloom, P. (2000). *How children learn the meanings of words.* Cambridge, MA: MIT Press.

Briscoe, T. (Ed.). (2001). *Linguistic evolution through language acquisition: Formal and computational models.* Cambridge, U. K.: Cambridge University Press.

Cangelosi, A. (2005). Approaches to grounding symbols in perceptual and sensorimotor categories. In H. Cohen & C. Lefebvre (Eds.), *Handbook of categorization in cognitive science* (pp. 719-737). Amsterdam: Elsevier.

Feldman, J. (2006). *From molecule to metaphor: A neural theory of language.* Cambridge, MA: MIT Press.

Gibbs, R. W. (2006). *Embodiment and cognitive science.* Cambridge, U. K.: Cambridge University Press.

Gärdenfors, P. (2000). *Conceptual spaces.* Cambridge, MA: MIT Press.

Gärdenfors, P. (2004). Cooperation and the evolution of symbolic communication. In K. Oller & U. Griebel (Eds.), *The evolution of communication systems* (pp. 237-256). Cambridge, MA: MIT Press.

Kováč, L. (2000). Fundamental principles of cognitive biology. *Evolution and Cognition, 6,* 51-69.

Lakoff, G. (1987). *Women, fire, and dangerous things: What categories reveal about the mind.* Chicago: University of Chicago Press.

Maturana, H. R., & Varela, F. J. (1987). *The tree of knowledge: The biological roots of human understanding.* Boston: Shambhala.

Nehaniv, C. (2000). The making of meaning in societies: Semiotic and information-theoretic background to the evolution of communication. In

B. Edmonds & K. Dautenhahn (Eds.), *AISB Symposium: Starting from Society – the application of social analogies to computational systems* (pp. 73-84). Society for the Study of Artificial Intelligence and Adaptive Behaviour.

Pecher, D., & Zwaan, R. A. (Eds.). (2005). *Grounding cognition: The role of perception and action in memory, language, and thinking.* Cambridge, U. K.: Cambridge University Press.

Pfeifer, R., & Scheier, C. (1999). *Understanding intelligence.* Cambridge, MA: MIT Press.

Roy, D. (2005a). Grounding words in perception and action: computational insights. *Trends in Cognitive Sciences, 9* (8), 389-396.

Roy, D. (2005b). Semiotic schemas: a framework for grounding language in action and perception. *Artificial Intelligence, 167* (1-2), 170-205.

Smith, L., & Gasser, M. (2005). The Development of Embodied Cognition: Six Lessons from Babies. *Artificial Life, 11* (1-2), 13-30.

Steels, L. (2000). Language as a complex adaptive system. In M. Schoenauer (Ed.), *Proceedings of PPSN-VI* (pp. 17-26). Berlin: Springer-Verlag.

Steels, L. (2007). The Symbol Grounding Problem Has Been Solved. So What's Next? In M. De Vega, G. Glennberg, & G. Graesser (Eds.), *Symbols, Embodiment and Meaning.* Oxford, U.K.: Oxford University Press.

Steels, L., & Kaplan, F. (2001a). AIBO's first words: The social learning of language and meaning. *Evolution of Communication, 4* (1), 3-32.

Steels, L., Kaplan, F., McIntyre, A., & Looveren, J. V. (2002). Crucial factors in the origins of word-meaning. In A. Wray (Ed.), *The transition to language* (pp. 252–271). Oxford, U. K.: Oxford University Press.

Vogt, P. (2002). The physical symbol grounding problem. *Cognitive Systems Research, 3* (3), 429-457.

Vogt, P., & Divina, F. (2007). Social symbol grounding and language evolution. *Interaction Studies, 8* (1), 31-52.

Vogt, P., Sugita, Y., Tuci, E., & Nehaniv, C. (Eds.). (2006). *Symbol Grounding and Beyond: Proceedings of the Third International Workshop on the Emergence and Evolution of Linguistic Communication, EELC 2006* (LNAI 4211). Berlin/Heidelberg: Springer.

Weng, J., Hwang, W., Zhang, Y., Yang, C., & Smith, R. (2000). Developmental Humanoids: Humanoids that Develop Skills Automatically. In *Proceedings of the First IEEE-RAS International Conference on Humanoid Robots*. Cambridge, MA.

Ziemke, T. (2001). The construction of 'reality' in the robot: Constructivist perspectives on situated artificial intelligence and adaptive robotics. *Foundations of Science, 6* (1-3), 163-233.

Chapter XI
Training Coordination Proxy Agents Using Reinforcement Learning

Myriam Abramson
Naval Research Laboratory, USA

ABSTRACT

In heterogeneous multi-agent systems, where human and non-human agents coexist, intelligent proxy agents can help smooth out fundamental differences. In this context, delegating the coordination role to proxy agents can improve the overall outcome of a task at the expense of human cognitive overload due to switching subtasks. Stability and commitment are characteristics of human teamwork, but must not prevent the detection of better opportunities. In addition, coordination proxy agents must be trained from examples as a single agent, but must interact with multiple agents. We apply machine learning techniques to the task of learning team preferences from mixed-initiative interactions and compare the outcome results of different simulated user patterns. This chapter introduces a novel approach for the adjustable autonomy of coordination proxies based on the reinforcement learning of abstract actions. In conclusion, some consequences of the symbiotic relationship that such an approach suggests are discussed.

INTRODUCTION

Advances in communication technologies has led to increased agent interactions and increased complexity in the decision-making process. To deal with this added burden, the coordination role is delegated to a proxy agent. Coordination proxy agents [Scerri et al., 2003] are personal agents that take on the coordination role on behalf of a human user (Fig. 1). While the optimization of the global task can be better achieved by the self-organization of proxy agents in dynamic environments, switching roles or teams involves preferences, such as loyalty, boredom, and persistence thresholds, in addition to interpretations that might need to be elicited from the human in the loop. For example, individual drivers differ in their tendency to switch lanes in urban traffic; truck drivers might prefer a less optimal route going through their favorite spots. This chapter addresses issues in determining when switching roles or teams is appropriate to satisfy both the urgency of the subtask relative to the global task, the preferences of the user, and when input from the user is warranted. We hypothesize that a distinct class of agents, proxy agents, will emerge at the junction of the human and non-human worlds that will take on not only decision-making tasks such as coordination, but also the social interactive task and the adaptation task on our behalf. We envision those agents to be embedded in personal mobile devices such as cell phones and personal digital assistants and personalized through a training process.

In this chapter, we claim that through result-driven reinforcement learning, the human can train coordination proxies in a task with examples biasing the way the task is achieved with respect to the outcome of the task in a multiagent system. Similarly, in mixed-initiative planning involving goal selection, directives from the user are obtained interactively in case of plan conflict or provided a priori in the form of plan constraints. Mixed-initiative interactions in multi-agent systems provide a flexible way to harness the cognitive capabilities of the human in the loop in solving a problem while delegating more mundane tasks to the proxy agents. As in the turn-taking problem found in dialog management [Allen, 1999], the key decisions for mixed-initiative

interactions, as applied to the adjustable autonomy of proxy agents, include knowing *when* to ask for help, *when* to ask for more information, and *when* to inform the user of a decision. This chapter claims that learning user preferences is not sufficient for training coordination proxies if those preferences conflict with other agents' preferences and affect the outcome of the task. As long as preferences are inconsistent with each other as evidenced by the outcome of the task, a proxy agent must keep training and continue interacting while suggesting alternatives.

This chapter is organized as follows. A learning approach for training coordination proxies in making decisions is first introduced. We then motivate experiments in the prey/predator canonical coordination domain and present empirical results and an analysis of our evaluation. Finally, we conclude with a summary of related work and extrapolate on the consequences of such interactions. The key contribution of this work is a mixed-initiative approach based on the reinforcement learning of abstract actions and its algorithm scalable to large state space for the adjustable autonomy problem of coordination proxy agents.

Figure 1. Example of coordination proxies helping in traffic by negotiating the road

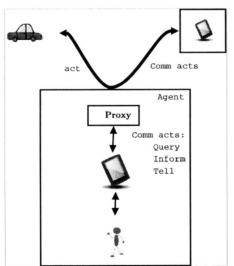

LEARNING APPROACH

A proxy agent can operate in three modes characterizing its dialogue to the user: (a) automatic or no interaction, (b) warn-user and (c) wait-for-user. As the proxy agent learns the preferences of its user, it should evolve to the automatic mode of interaction. ``Warn-user'' is an asynchronous mode of interaction where the opportunity to change roles is given to the human without interrupting the task of the proxy or the human. The ``wait-for-user'' mode is a synchronous mode of interaction that will interrupt the task (subject to timeout). Deciding autonomously which mode to be in for a specific situation constitutes adjustable autonomy [Scerri et al., 2003]. This chapter claims that the urgency to interrupt the human should be based on the ambiguity of a decision reflecting the uncertainty of a situation given the preferences of the user and the expected outcome of the task. As was shown in the Ellsberg paradox [Ellsberg, 1961], ambiguity, as the absence of definitive information, affects behavioral change in a non-rational way.

Our learning approach consists of (1) clustering examples of conflicting goal states to expedite the case-based retrieval of past examples, (2) learning which goal to follow through the reinforcement of user interaction preferences and the outcome of the task and (3) learning alternatives through complementary credit assignments. As a result, preferences will be learned only when they help coordination in some way. Inconsistencies in the user preferences combined with situational ambiguities will trigger mixed-initiative interactions. An approach for detecting decision-making ambiguities is introduced. Those steps can be combined to learn online in an incremental way to adjust to novel situations.

CLUSTERING OF CONFLICTING GOAL STATES

This clustering step quantizes a large continuous state space into a compressed representation that is amenable to tabular reinforcement learning techniques. Clustering as a semi-supervised preprocessing step ensures that distinct states are kept apart and prevents oscillations in state values due to perceptual aliasing when scaling up reinforcement learning to large state space.

A myopic agent with limited perception will not have goal conflicts since only one goal at a time will be perceived. Through communication and shared knowledge an agent might be aware of other goals, increasing the occurrence of decisions or ``choice points.'' To scale up, patterns of observation are generalized and compressed through the competitive Hebbian learning process of self-organizing feature maps (SOFM) [Kohonen, 1997]. A SOFM transforms an input data space $\Re^n$ to a lower-dimensional space (usually two or one) of prototype vectors, the neurons, where each vector, $m_i = (x_1, x_2, ..., x_n) \in \Re^n$, is relatively ordered with respect to its ``neighbors'' preserving the structure of the input space in a lower dimension suitable for visual representation. The update equation of a prototype vector m given a temporally decreasing rate α $(0 < \alpha < 1)$ is as follows:

$$m(t+1) = m(t) + \alpha(t)[x(t) - m(t)] \qquad (1)$$

The granularity of clustering needs to be based on the capability of recognizing goal conflicts. A distance function alone does not guarantee that important distinctions will be recognized. The

Algorithm 1. Clustering of conflicting goals

```
Input: prototype vectors mi
Output: updated prototype vectors mi
Initialize: conflict set W ← {}
REPEAT
    Generate input signals {s, g} from P(s,
    g),  s ∈S, g ∈G
    /* P(s,g) is the joint distribution of
    states s and goals g */
    IF new choice point THEN
        FOREACH w ∈ W
            Update  mw  closer  to sw
        W ← {}
        m ← argmini (distance (s, mi))
            WHILE (conflict ←{m,g'}∈ W and g'≠
g)
                m ← argmini (eligibility (mi))
            eligibility(m) ←1
            W ← W ∪ {s,m,g}
    ENDIF
    Decay eligibilities
UNTIL (stopping criterion met)
```

initial set of prototype vectors also impacts the effectiveness of clustering. A semi-supervised approach is presented here where the ``least recently used'' prototype vector wins if a conflicting goal, $g \in G$, at time t fails to be recognized as distinct (Algorithm 1). This is in accordance to the general principle in using feature maps for pattern recognition that prototype vectors be placed at the class borders to avoid misclassifications [Kohonen, 1997]. An eligibility trace decaying with time indicates the recent usage of a prototype vector. This is a conceptual clustering [Michalski et al., 1983] approach where two data points are put in different clusters regardless of the distance metric because they belong to different concepts and is a way to incorporate domain knowledge.

REINFORCEMENT LEARNING

From Markov Decision Processes (MDP) to Reinforcement Learning

Formally, an MDP is a 4-tuple $\{S,A,T,R\}$ where S is the set of states, A the set of actions, T the transition model specifying the probabilities mapping $S \times A \times S$ to $[0,1]$ and R, the reward function, mapping $S \times A \times S$ to $\Re$. Algorithms in dynamic programming such as value and policy iterations solve MDPs provided T and R. The complete search space of an MDP is exponential in the number of steps required to solve the problem, $\{S \times A\}^n$. Reinforcement learning (RL) approximately solves MDPs without a model of transition probabilities T by directing its search of the state space based on sample return estimates obtained by interacting with the environment [Kaelbling et al., 1996]. Those estimates are encapsulated in the value function $V(s)$ for state s or the action-value function $Q(s, a)$ associating state s to action a. Monte-Carlo methods (Eq. 2) apply to RL when estimating sample returns r based on the outcome of an episode while temporal-difference methods [Sutton and Barto, 1998], such as Q-learning (Eq. 3), are based on the next temporal step s', possibly discounted by a discount factor γ and learning rate α.

$$V(s) = \frac{1}{n}\sum_{0}^{n} r_n \qquad (2)$$

$$V(s) = V(s) + \alpha[r + \gamma \max V(s') - V(s)] \qquad (3)$$

Reinforcement Learning of Abstract Actions

Abstract actions are high-level actions, for example a planning decision, that are implemented by several primitive actions but are temporally abstract. How can credit assignment be given to a high-level action

Figure 2. Non-deterministic HAM controller for goal conflict resolution

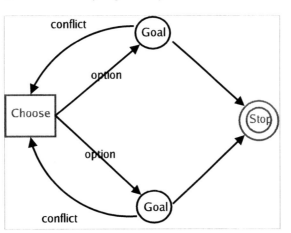

since the external terminal reward might also depend on the successful execution of lower-level actions? High-level actions, such as conflict resolution decisions, occur "offline" and are not temporally part of the execution of a discrete sequence of steps. Similarly, in mixed-initiative strategies involving a human, the high-level decision from the human is not under the control of the coordination proxy agent. The decisions depend only on the current state at certain synchronization points that occur at random time intervals. Consequently, the high-level actions are not completely Markovian since they depend on past temporally selected high-level decisions. In the theory of semi-Markov decision processes (SMDPs), the high-level reward obtained is the mean reward accrued during the time taken to accomplish the goal weighted by the probability of reaching the goal in t time steps [Putterman, 2005]. Given two different temporal scales k and t, Q-learning for SMDPs is defined as follows:

$$Q_{k+1}(s,a) = (1-\alpha_k)Q_k(s,a) + \alpha_k[r_{t+1} + \gamma r_{t+2} + \dots$$
$$+ \gamma \max_{a' \in A} Q_k(s',a')] \qquad (4)$$

Based on the theory of SMDPs, hierarchical abstract machines (HAMs) [Parr and Russell, 1998]

address the issue of combining high-level actions with primitive actions in a Markov decision process. A HAM is a non-deterministic finite state machine specifying valid transitions constraining the underlying temporal MDP. The "HAM-induced" MDP can then be solved more efficiently. It is however possible to learn in the reduced state space of HAMs directly. Figure 2 shows a general HAM for goal conflict resolution. Machine states superimpose to environmental states to identify behavioral states (e.g. explore, hunt, stop, etc.) and choice points. Given an environment statec s, a machine state m, a reward r in the environment state, a past choice point c in a HAM, the accumulated reward r_c since the previous choice point c, and the accumulated discount γ_c ($0 \le \gamma < 1$), since the previous choice point c, HAMQ-learning proceeds as follows:

$$Q([s_c, m_c], a) = (1-\alpha_k)Q([s_c, m_c], a)$$
$$+ \alpha[r_c + \gamma_c V([s,m]) - Q([s_c, m_c], a)] \qquad (5)$$

where $r_c = r_c + \gamma_c r$ and $\gamma_c = \gamma \gamma_c$. The value of the current state $V([s,m])$ is obtained from the underlying temporal MDP as the expected sum of discounted reward $E[\sum_{t=0}^{\infty} \gamma^{t-1} r']$.

Figure 3. Coordination proxy system architecture with interactions from the environment and with other agents

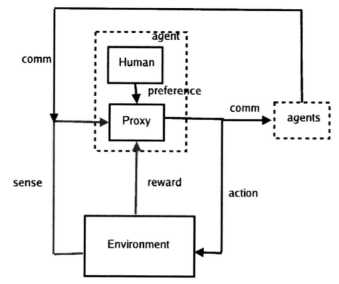

Reinforcement Learning of User Preferences

The compressed patterns of goal states learned in the SOFM preprocessing step described above constitute a proxy agent's internal representation of choice points augmented with HAMQ-learned action values for the two possible actions of selecting or not selecting the goal state. This function approximation approach separates learning the action value function from learning the state representation (but see [Abramson et al., 2003] for a combined approach). The intermediate reward r_c is obtained from the user decision at the choice point while the discounted terminal rewards upon reaching the goal states are obtained from the underlying temporal MDP. Figure 3 describes the architecture of a coordination proxy that learns from reinforcement.

By decomposing the state space into machine states and temporal states, HAMs avoid the looping problem [Papudesi and Huber, 2003] in introducing intermediate rewards based on user preferences, however choice-point rewards can override the outcome if $r_c \gg \gamma_c V([s,m])$ misleading the agent in learning non-optimal preferences for the coordination task. The novel mixed-initiative HAMQ algorithm (Algorithm 3 and Figure 4), based on the credit assignment of choices and alternatives, enables coordination proxies to dynamically adjust their interactions depending on the preferences of their users and the outcome of the task. It is a Monte-Carlo algorithm based on the smooth average of episodic returns of environmental states on the temporal scale combined with Q-learning on the higher-level decision and planning scale. Eligibility traces [Sutton and Barto, 1998] are used here as uncertainty variables modulated by the strength of the pattern matching association of a goal state to a machine state. The complementary credit assignment to alternatives is a key characteristic of this algorithm. The sign of the action value at a choice point determines whether the choice is selectable. Ambiguity arises when more than one option at a choice point is selectable or when none are selectable. The constraints for the fairness and rationality of reward r_a for action $a \in A_c$ at choice point c and actions $a' \in A_c$, $a' \neq a$, are as follows [Papudesi and Huber, 2003]:

$$r_a \leq \gamma_c V([s,m]) \qquad (6)$$

$$r = -\frac{1}{|A_c|-1} r_a \qquad (7)$$

$$\sum_{a \in A} r_a = 0 \qquad (8)$$

Those constraints are extended to the terminal rewards

AMBIGUITY DETECTION

The goal of many human interaction programs is to resolve ambiguity. For example, speech recognition programs resolve the semantic ambiguity of words by the syntactic phrase structure or by the perspective-taking of spatial-visual cues in a multi-modal environment. Recent advances in augmented reality (AR) have to deal with the unambiguous presentation of generated information such as the drawing of coutours and labels of objects of interest. In aligning the graphics with the dynamic physical environment that include the human-in-the-loop, AR systems adapt the granularity of presentation of information to the time-varying estimate of the registration error in deciding whether to push back the disambiguation task to the user [Julier et al., 2003]. Similarly, a proxy agent has to adapt its autonomy to the consistency of the situation and the user patterns.

In a prescriptive approach, such as reinforcement learning, with the human-in-the-loop, it is the absence of ambiguity that is a problem. To detect ambiguity, we first extend the concept of fairness and rationality to model decisions as a zero-sum game against Nature. A decision is a choice to participate in a game between gambles where the price to pay to enter the game is the sum of the expected utility of the gambles. The question is whether this is a fair game. Let a positive utility indicates an acceptable outcome where a betting will be lost if Nature wins, i.e. the goal is not achieved, and a negative utility indicates an unacceptable outcome where a betting in favor of Nature will be lost if the agent wins,

Algorithm 2. Mixed-initiative training (binary choice points)

```
Input: prototype vectors m_c
       eligibility traces e{[m_c]}
Output: a mixed-initiative policy
Parameters: α, γ
Initialize:
       FORALL m_c
              Q([m_c]) = 0
              E([m_c]) = 0
              set usermode
REPEAT
   WHEN choice point c
       C ← {}
       W ← {}
       k ← k + 1
       γ_c ← γ
       FOREACH goal state s ∈ S
         [s, m_c] ← map (s)
              /* each goal state s at a choice
point c
              is mapped to a prototype vector
m */
         C ← C ∪ {[s, m_c]}
         inform user of Q([m_c])
      IF (usermode == WAIT or C is AMBIGUOUS)
THEN
              [s,m_c]← askuser
          ELSE
              [s,m_c]← argmax(C)
          ENDIF
      FORALL m
         Q([m_c]) = (1 - α_k)Q([m_c])+α_kγe([m_c])Q([m
_c])
         e([m_c]) = 0
      FOREACH s'∈ S, s'≠ s
         W ← W ∪ {[s',m_c]}
      obtain reward r_s
      Q([s,m_c]) ← (1 - α_k)Q([s,m_c]) + α_kr_s
      e([s,m_c]) ← similarity (s, m_c)
      FOREACH w ∈ W
         Q([s',m_c]) ← (1 - α_k)Q([s', m_c]) - α_kr_s'
         e([s',m_c]) ← - similarity(s',m_c)
      WHEN goal is attained
         obtain V([s,m])
         FORALL [s,m_c]
            δ = γ_ce([s,m_c])V([s,m])
            Q([s,m_c])← (1 - α_k)Q([s,m_c]) + α_kδ
       γ_c←γγ_c
UNTIL end of episode
```

i.e. achieves the goal. Since only one gamble will be successful, the game is not fair if the gambles bet on the same player. Nature will be sure to win something (Table 1).

Figure 4. Mixed-initiative training flowchart illustration of Algorithm 2

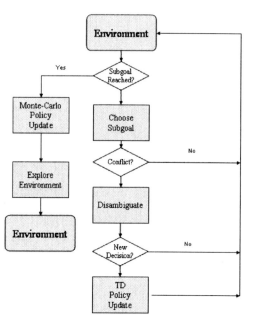

Table 1. Unfair game

	Nature wins	Agent wins
Option 1	Acceptable	Unacceptable
Option 2	Acceptable	Unacceptable

Second, in the case of a clear choice between an acceptable and unacceptable outcome, an ambiguity tolerance threshold reflecting the inconsistency of user preferences needs to be found. Attitudes toward ambiguity, as tolerance of uncertainty, influence preferences on an individual level. Measuring this tolerance gives a way to evaluate whether a choice is really fair in the eye of the user. An ambiguity tolerance factor should "correct" the maximum expected utilities, encapsulated in the Q-values, to account for a user's decision. Following Hurwicz's coefficient [Hurwicz, 1951] α where u_{ij} is the expected utility of action i in state j:

$$\alpha \arg\max_i u_{ij} \leq (1-\alpha)\arg\min_i u_{ij} \qquad (8)$$

The tolerance factor α can be computed during a training phase using objective utilities (such as cost) or evolved online as the most recent linear threshold discriminating between rational and non-rational preferences. As user rewards get incorporated into the Q-value of an action and the expected utilities converge, the less interrupt due to ambiguity should be triggered. Ambiguities are detected when for a given coefficient α,

$$\frac{\arg\min_i u_{ij}}{\arg\max_i u_{ij} + \arg\min_i u_{ij}} \geq \alpha \qquad (9)$$

COMPLEMENTARY CREDIT ASSIGNMENT

What does not work is sometimes more interesting than what works because we can learn from the unexpected. This is the intuition behind complementary credit assignment. Exploration towards more promising state-action pairs can be guided by directly rewarding/penalizing paths not taken. Instead of relying on an explicit exploration strategy such as ε-greedy, the environmental feedback can reach a greater number of state-action pairs through complementary rewards/penalties, thereby quickly reducing the state space. This approach is particularly attractive in mixed-initiative reinforcement learning since we want to quickly bias the search space towards states that were preferred by the human-in-the-loop in achieving the task and not necessarily towards optimal states. In addition, the number of interactions are drastically reduced since alternatives will be automatically taken in case of failure. In our approach, the eligibility trace is manipulated as a marker for credit assignment, weighted by the similarity of the current state to the matched prototype vector and the temporal discount γ, and is extended to state-action pairs in the conflict set (Algorithm 2).

As with eligibility traces, conflicts occur when the state-action pair is revisited again in an episode that might distort the terminal reward [Sutton and Barto, 1998]. Replacing traces [Singh and Sutton, 1996] reset the eligibility trace and avoid this problem. Following this approach, the last visit of each state-action pair between subgoals sets its

eligibility. Subsequent visits reset the eligibility trace for the next subgoal as follows where m is the prototype vector matching the current state s and the decision/action a.

$$e_t(m) = \begin{cases} similarity(s,m) & if \quad a_m = a_{m_t} \\ -similarity(s,m) & if \quad a_m \neq a_m \\ \gamma e_{t-1}(m) & if \quad m \neq m_t \end{cases} \qquad (10)$$

EXPERIMENTAL EVALUATION

Experiments with different simulated patterns of user preferences were conducted: (1) autonomous, (2) conservative, (3) risky, (4) heuristic, and (5) mixed. In an autonomous pattern, the proxy agent learns how and when to switch teams independently of its user. In a conservative pattern, the users initially select a team at random and never switch teams afterwards; in a risky pattern, the users initially select a team at random and always switch teams afterwards; in a heuristic pattern, users have a principled way of selecting a team. In our experiments for a heuristic pattern, agents select the team with the highest sum of preferences and switch teams accordingly. In a mixed pattern, a heuristic, risky or conservative pattern is selected randomly by the proxy agent. This last pattern reflects best the heterogeneity of human users. We show corresponding learning performance results of coordination proxies in the prey/predator domain (introduced below) in terms of autonomously resolving conflicts based on user preferences and the outcome of the task.

PREY/PREDATOR

The prey/predator pursuit game is a canonical example in the teamwork literature [Benda et al., 1985] because one individual predator alone cannot accomplish the task of capturing a prey. Practical applications of the prey/predator pursuit game include, for example, unmanned ground/air vehicles target acquisition and search and rescue operations. Due to the decomposability of the global reward as a sum of local rewards, the original problem can be extended to multiple teams by including additional preys. Prey/predators can sense each other if they are

Figure 5. Prey/Predator on a toroidal grid

in proximity *p* but do not otherwise communicate. Predators communicate with other predators by broadcasting messages to their neighbors according to a communication range *h*. Four predators are needed to capture a prey by filling out four different roles: surround the prey to the north, south, east and west. Those roles are independent of each other and can be started at any time obviating the need for scheduling. The only requirement is that they have to terminate at the same time either successfully when a capture occurs or unsuccessfully if no team can be formed. The predator agents are homogeneous and can assume any role but heterogeneity can be introduced by restricting the role(s) an agent can assume. The prey and predators move concurrently and asynchronously at different time steps. In addition to the four orthogonal navigational steps, the agents can opt to stay in place. Non-determinism is introduced with the modeling of path collisions. In case of collision, the agents are held back to their previous position. The preference u_{ij} of predator agent *i* for a role *j* is inversely proportional to the Manhattan distance *d* required to achieve the role.

The predators move in the direction of their target when assigned a role or explore the space according to a memory-based scheme on the last few steps. The decision space for the role allocation of *P* predators and *p* preys is $O(p^T)$ where *T* is the number

of teams of size *t*. This problem belongs to the most difficult class of problems for constraint satisfaction in multi-agent systems due to the dynamic nature of the environment and the mutually-exclusive property of role allocation. An optimization algorithm can be used in parallel fashion by each agent based on sensed and communicated information from the other agents in the group to autonomously determine which role to assume (Algorithm 3). It is assumed that the other agents reach the same conclusions because they use the same optimization algorithm [Gerkey and Mataric, 2004] and the same payoff function. This type of algorithm degrades gracefully when communication is completely impaired since it does not rely on the communication of intent or preference from the other agents and can rely solely on sensory information. Information necessary to determine the payoff of each role needs to be communicated. Therefore, it is the current local state within the perception range, or augmented with second-hand information, that is communicated to the neighbors instead of the intended role. What is being communicated is a location on the grid. The ``Hungarian'' algorithm [Kuhn, 1955, Papadimitriou and Steiglitz, 1998] based on weighted graph bipartite matching was found to outperform other types of distributed role allocation in dynamic and uncertain environments [Abramson et al., 2005], albeit with the assumption of a homogeneous cost

Algorithm 3. Distributed role allocation

```
Initialize:
    set initial role to explore
    active ← true
REPEAT
    IF (active) THEN
        act according to role
        sense environment
        broadcast local state to neighbors
        active ← false
    ENDIF
    collect neighbors' new information
    estimate possible roles with
        allocation algorithm
    select role
    active ← true
UNTIL (termination condition)
```

Figure 6. Prey/Predator HAM

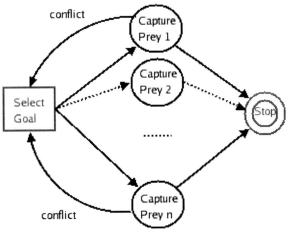

function, and is used here to determine the optimal role for the agent in a team characterized by the prey to pursue as the goal.

Which team to join when multiple preys are present requires a commitment for teamwork beyond role allocation optimization if not enough agents are available to accomplish the overall task. Human users of coordination proxy agents might have vested interest in selecting one team over another such as friendships, trust, loyalty, etc.

Figure 6 describes the HAM for selecting a team with the common goal of capturing a prey. Our state representation of goal conflict consists of 5 features:

the distance of the prey from the agent, the number of agents allocated to the prey, the mean proximity of the agents allocated to the prey, whether the goal is different from the current goal, and the direction of the prey from the agent (4 quadrant values based on the coordinate system: NW, NE, SW, SE) using 1-of-n encoding. Associated with the state representation are two high-level decisions - accept the target or not - determined by the sign of the action value . An ambiguity will occur if the decision values do not uniquely show one acceptable goal or if no goals are acceptable.

Table 2. Cluster granularity for varying communication ranges based on random samples of 2400 choice points in the training set and average error for 400 choice points in the testing set (p = 2, α = 0.07)

Comm Range	Avg Clusters	Avg Err
5	240	0.0137
7	344	0.0182
9	377	0.0287
11	367	0.0268

Table 3. Inconsistency of user patterns (over 100 runs of 5 predators and 2 preys) as number of deviations from greedy moves and minimum ambiguity tolerance threshold (Eq. 9)

User Patterns	Mean	Std	Inconsistency (mean/std)	Ambiguity Tolerance Threshold
Heuristic	0.36	0.17	2.11	0.5
Mixed	0.37	0.14	2.64	0.15
Conservative	0.46	0.15	3.06	0.11
Risky	0.51	0.04	12.75	0.07

EMPIRICAL RESULTS

The experiments were conducted with RePast [North et al., 2006], an agent-based simulation and modeling tool where agents act concurrently in a decentralized manner. Its powerful scheduling mechanism was used to model the asynchronous behavior of the agents in a discrete-event simulation. In addition, its neighborhood mechanism was used to model broadcast communication between neighbors.

Table 2 shows the number of clusters (number of winning neurons) obtained in the preprocessing step (Algorithm 1) of a random sample of 2400 choice points when varying the communication range h of 4 predators and 2 preys on a 30x30 grid and 5% message loss depending on the Manhattan distance. In our implementation only the winning prototype vectors determined by their cosine distance to the input vector were trained. The increase in granularity indicates the increased number of distinct recognizable situations in the training set with increasing h (t-test p-value of 0.003 over 10 runs between clusterings with h=5 and h=11). Results shown are obtained after convergence to a maximum norm correction distance less than 1.E-4 of 1000 initial prototype vectors or 5000 training epochs.

The following experiments were done on a 15x15 grid with 5 predator agents, 2 random preys, and 5% message loss. The agents start at random locations on the grid and the predators are as likely to be slower or faster than the prey. A terminal reward of +1.0 is propagated after each capture or a penalty of -1.0 if no preys are captured after 200 cycles (episode). Each user strategy has a 80-95% success rate to accomplish the task. Table 3 shows the inconsistency of each user pattern with respect to the greedy move in terms of distance to the prey. Learning occurs across 500 episodes. Each agent has a copy of the set of prototype vectors, updated in a pre-clustering step, and will incrementally update the action value associated with each vector through the mixed-initiative HAMQ algorithm (Algorithm 2). Figure 7 compares performance trend results for the different user patterns with refinement of those strategies by the coordination proxies and performance improvement by the proxy agent acting autonomously (with Boltzmann exploration) for catching the first prey. Results for the last prey, although indicative of the overall performance, also include external factors such as exploration to the decision-making process. Duplicate consecutive goal states were eliminated.

Figure 7. Comparative performance of user pattern refinements and autonomous learning of 5 mixed-initiative predator agents in capturing the first prey $h = 7, p = 2, \alpha = 0.07, \gamma = 0.99, r = 4E - 5$

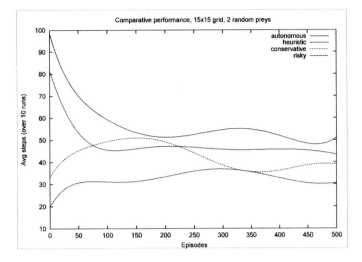

Figure 8. Ambiguity rate for 2 preys

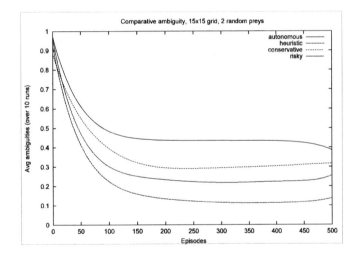

An intermediate reward is allocated when the proxy agent selects the same decision as the user pattern (user precision). Trend results are also shown in terms of ambiguities resulting from this refinement in Figure 8 and in terms of precision to those user patterns in Figure 9.

The results for the different user patterns compared with autonomous learning show clearly that

mixed-initiative HAMQ learning can produce a more stable behavior while reducing interactions due to ambiguities with the human in the loop and increased user precision. Good rational behavior such as the one based on a heuristic did not show a degradation in performance. If an unforeseen situation arises resulting in no selectable goal, the coordination proxy agent will initiate an interac-

Figure 9. User precision rate for 2 preys

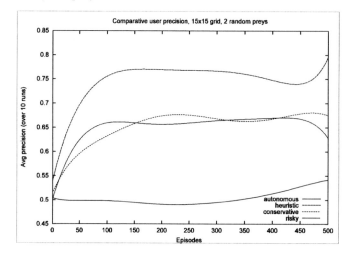

tion with its user. The standard deviations of the learned behaviors over 100 episodes were as follows: (1) autonomous 47.54, (2) heuristic 25.42, (3) risky 43.42 , (4) conservative 34.91, and (5) mixed 35.25. This methodology can also validate user patterns according to their precision rate since successful behavior will most likely be followed. The key factor in reducing the ambiguity rate for all behaviors seems to be in the credit assignment to alternatives which avoids repeating mistakes and implicitly direct exploration towards the most promising actions. Kolmogorov-Smirnov test p-values of average ambiguity rate over 10 runs in ablation studies were (1) autonomous 3.E-5, (2) heuristic 2.E-4, (3) risky 2.E-4 , (4) conservative 2.E-4 and (5) mixed 3.E-5.

RELATED WORK

Previous work on adjustable autonomy [Scerri et al, 2000, Tambe et al., 2002] has concentrated on learning user preferences in isolation without relation to the outcome of the task. Learning co-adaptive predictive models of the exogenous outcome instead of co-adaptive behaviors has been suggested in the context of the El Farol coordination problem where the paradox was that agents could coordinate without communication by not going to the same place, the El Farol Bar, at the same time [Arthur, 1994]. It was

observed that the online adaptation of strategies to recent situations rather than convergence was the key to achieving coordination in a multi-agent system. Other work in this area found that coordination could be achieved with less variance if the agents relied on the accuracy of the same adaptive gradient algorithm [Bell and Sethares, 2001].

Techniques from advice taking [Maclin and Shavlik, 1994, Boicu et al., 2005] where the user preference is explicitly incorporated into the internal representation of the agent are complementary to this approach. Similar to apprenticeship learning [Abbell and Ng, 2005], state-action trajectories are used to refine an existing policy through a reinforcement learning algorithm. In W-learning [Humphrys, 1995], each behavior in a flexible subsumption architecture competes with other behaviors as selfish agents, indirectly collaborating through the communication of the W value and a winner-take-all scheme. In our approach, the user and the result-driven proxy agent interact directly as collaborating agents trying to learn from each other.

Complementary reinforcement learning has been applied in different ways. Optimistic initial values [Sutton and Barto, 1998] indirectly allocate a credit assignment to paths not taken but also do not eliminate the exploration of alternatives and consequently are slower to converge. In complimentary reinforcement back-propagation [Ackley and Littman, 1990] a negative environmental feedback can directly influence the association of state-action pairs by propagating back a complementary output.

CONCLUSION

We have shown how coordination proxies can safely adjust their autonomy in switching teams based on user preferences and taking into account the outcome of the decision. Hierarchies of abstract machines are superimposed to the temporal behavior of the proxy agent to specify the high-level behavior of the human in the loop. The representation of goal states instead of environmental states enables reinforcement learning to scale up and generalize to different situations. The complementary credit assignment to alternatives seems to be a key factor in speeding up the learning process which is critical for user interactions and this hypothesis will be further studied. In addition, more understanding on formalizing ambiguity with respect to mixed-initiative is also desired.

This approach suggests a symbiotic relationship between humans and proxy agents where each agent learns and benefits from each other and is in contrast with anthropomorphic approaches to human-computer interactions. More importantly, this approach does not constrain the development of artificial intelligence but might isolate us from human and non-human agents alike.

ACKNOWLEDGMENT

The author wants to acknowledge useful inputs from Mark Livingstone and Michael Stein.

REFERENCES

Abbeel, P. and Ng, A. Y. (2005). Exploration and apprenticeship learning in reinforcement learning. In *Proceedings of the 22nd International Conference on Machine Learning*.

Abramson, M., Chao, W., and Mittu, R. (2005). Design and evaluation of distributed role allocation algorithms in open environments. In *International Conference on Artificial Intelligence*, Las Vegas, NV.

Abramson, M., Pachowicz, P., and Wechsler, H. (2003). Competitive reinforcement learning for continuous control tasks. In *Proceedings of the International Neural Network Conference*.

Ackley, D. H. and Littman, M. S. (1990). Generalization and scaling in reinforcement learning. In Touretzky, D. S., editor, *Advances in Neural Information Processing Systems*, volume 2, pages 550-557, Denver 1989. Morgan Kaufmann, San Mateo.

Allen, J. F. (1999). Mixed-initiative interaction. *IEEE Intelligent Systems*.

Arthur, W. B. (1994). Inductive reasoning and bounded rationality. *American Economic Review*.

Bell, A. M. and Sethares, W. A. (2001). Avoiding global congestion using decentralized adaptive agents. *IEEE Transactions on Signal Processing*, 49(11).

Benda, M., Jagannathan, V., and Dodhiawalla, R. (1985). On optimal cooperation of knowledge sources. Technical Report BCS-G2010-28, Boeing AI Center, Boeing Computer Services.

Boicu, M., Tecuci, G., and Marcu, D. (2005). Mixed-initiative assistant for modeling expert's reasoning. In *Proceedings of the AAAI-05 Fall Symposium on Mixed-Initiative Problem-Solving Assistants*.

Ellsberg, D. (1961). Risk, ambiguity and the Savage axioms. *Quarterly Journal of Economics*.

Gerkey, B. P. and Mataric, M. J. (2004). *RobotCup 2003*, volume 3020, chapter On Role Allocation in RobotCup. Springer-Verlag Heidelberg.

Humphrys, M. (1995). W-learning: Competition among selfish q-learners. Technical Report 362, University of Cambridge.

Hurwicz, L. (1951). Optimality criteria for decision making under ignorance. In *Cowles Commission Discussion Paper, Statistics*, number 370.

Julier, S., Livingston, M. A., Swan, J. E., Baillot, Y., and Brown, D. (2003). Adaptive user interfaces in augmented reality. In *Proceedings of workshop on Software Technology for Augmented Reality Systems (STARS), 2nd International Symposium on Mixed and Augmented Reality*.

Kohonen, T. (1997). *Self-Organizing Maps*. Springer, 2nd edition.

Kuhn, H. W. (1955). The Hungarian method for the assignment problem. *Naval Research Logistics Quarterly*, 2(83).

Kaelbling, L. P, Littman, M. L., and Moore, A. W. (1996). Reinforcement learning: A survey. *Journal of Artificial Intelligence Research*, 4:237-285.

Maclin, R. and Shavlik, J. W. (1994). Incorporating advice into agents that learns from reinforcements. In *Proceedings of the 1994 American Association of Artificial Intelligence*.

Michalski, R., Stepp, R. E., and Diday, E. (1983). Automated construction of classifications: conceptual clustering versus numerical taxonomy. *IEEE Transactions on Pattern Analysis and Machine Intelligence*, 5(5):396-409.

North, M. J., Collier, N. T., and Vos, J. R. (2006). Experiences creating three implementations of the repast agent modeling toolkit. *ACM Transactions on Modeling and Computer Simulation*, 16(1):1-25.

Papadimitriou, C. H. and Steiglitz, K. (1998). *Combinatorial Optimization: Algorithms and Complexity*. Dover Publications.

Papudesi, V. N. and Huber, M. (2003). Learning from reinforcement and advice using composite reward functions. In *Proceedings of the 16th International FLAIRS Conference*.

Parr, R. and Russell, S. (1998). Reinforcement learning with hierarchies of machines. In *Neural Information Processing Systems*.

Putterman, M. L. (2005). *Markov Decision Processes*. Wiley-Interscience, 2nd edition.

Scerri, P., Pynadath, D., Schurr, N., Farinelli, A., Gandhe, S., and Tambe, M. (2003). Team oriented programming and proxy agents: The next generation. Workshop on Programming MultiAgent Systems, AAMAS 2003.

Scerri, P., Tambe, M., Lee, H., and Pynadath, D. (2000). Don't cancel my barcelona trip: adjusting autonomy of agent proxies in human organizations. In *AAAI Fall Symposium on Socially Intelligent Agents - the Human in the Loop*.

Singh, S. and Sutton, R. S. (1996). Reinforcement learning with replacing eligibility traces. *Machine Learning Journal*, 22:123-158.

Sutton, R. S. and Barto, A. (1998). *Reinforcement Learning: an Introduction*. MIT Press, Cambridge, MA.

Tambe, M., Scerri, P., and Pynadath, D. (2002). Adjustable autonomy for the real world. *Journal of Artificial Intelligence Research*, 17:171-228.

Chapter XII
The Generative Power of Signs:
The Importance of the Autonomous Perception of Tags to the Strong Emergence of Institutions

Deborah V. Duong
OSD/PAE Simulation Analysis Center, USA

ABSTRACT

The first intelligent agent social model, in 1991, used tags with emergent meaning to simulate the emergence of institutions based on the principles of interpretive social science. This symbolic interactionist simulation program existed before Holland's Echo, however, Echo and subsequent programs with tags failed to preserve the autonomy of perception of the agents that displayed and read tags. The only exception is Axtell, Epstein, and Young's program on the emergence of social classes, which was influenced by the symbolic interactionist simulation program. Axtell, Epstein, and Young's program has since been credited for strong emergence. This chapter explains that autonomy of perception is the essential difference in the symbolic interactionist implementation of tags that enables this strong emergence.

In the beginning was the Word, and the Word was with God, and the Word was God. The same was in the beginning with God. All things were made by him; and without him was not any thing made that was made. In him was life; and the life was the light of men. And the light shineth in darkness; and the darkness comprehended it not. (John 1:1-5, KJV)

INTRODUCTION

Holland saw the creative power of the word as important in the formation of living systems when he included the tag as one of the three basic mechanisms of complex adaptive systems. A "tag" is simply a sign, such as a name or a physical trait, which is used to classify an agent. In the social world, a tag may be a social marker, such as skin color, or simply the name of a social group. A tag goes hand in hand with the other two mechanisms Holland thought important to complex adaptive systems, an internal model (whether tacit or explicit) to give meaning to tags, and building blocks to accumulate and recombine the structures that result from those meanings into hierarchical aggregates (Holland 1995).

Holland is commonly thought to be the first to use tags to simulate social phenomena. However, there is another variation on tags, the symbolic interactionist simulation technique, that was developed before Holland's complex adaptive system research program, the Echo project (Duong 1991, Holland 1992). Like Echo, symbolic interactionist simulation recognizes the primacy of signs in the formation of living systems, but differs from Echo in that its agents have autonomous perception of the meaning of signs. The difference is understandable, because the principle of autonomy of perception is more prominent from the social sciences standpoint than from the biological standpoint, even if it exists in biology as well (Maturana, Lettvin, Mcculloch and Pitts. 1960). Many of the ideas in microsociology are inherited from phenomenology and hermeneutics, philosophies that contemplate the mysteries of autonomy, such as the paradox that human beings can only interpret meanings through their individual experiences with their senses, and yet they still come to share meaning (Winograd and Flores 1987). This hermeneutic paradox is core issue of micro-macro integration in sociology from the angle of perception: to solve the hermeneutic paradox is to solve the mystery of the "invisible hand" by which autonomous, selfish agents synchronize their actions into institutions for the good of the whole. Since emergence in agent-based social simulation is fundamentally about solving the micro macro link, symbolic interactionist simulation seeks to solve the hermeneutic paradox. It is by virtue of the preservation of autonomy that symbolic interactionist simulations exhibit strong emergence and constitute minimal social engines.

BACKGROUND

In Holland's Echo program and its successors that simulate the emergence of cooperation in iterated prisoner's dilemma (IPD) programs, tags are implemented with replicator dynamics. Referring to the work of Riolo, Cohen, and Axlerod as well as the work of Hales and Edmonds, Hales discusses the tag implementation: "the models implement evolutionary systems with assumptions along the lines of replicator dynamics (i.e. reproduction into the next generation proportional to utility in the current generation and no 'genetic style' crossover operations but low probability mutations on tags and strategies)." (Hales, 2004). Replicator dynamics do not keep the principle of autonomy of perception: one agent interprets a sign the same way as another agent because they have a common ancestor, not because they both induced the sign separately based on their individual experiences. Simulations of the emergence of common meaning of tags using replicator dynamics exhibit high amounts of genetic linkage (biological or mimetic), so that the relation between the sign and the behavior is an artifact of the method, rather than emergent from the simulation. Any simulation of contagion that explains macro level institututions with micro-level imitation does not exhibit strong emergence: since institutions are behaviors held in common, institutions would be an aggregate of copying behavior rather than emergent phenomena. Micro macro sociologist James Coleman believed that to explain institutions, we must explain the arise of a network of relations in a social system, and not just an aggregate (Coleman, 1994).

Autonomy of perception has been proposed as a necessary requirement for strong emergence in social systems. Bedau (2002) and other philosophers of emergence agree that "emergent properties have irreducible causal power on underlying entities." Downward causation, or "immergence" as Gilbert (1995) called it, is necessary for emergence in the strong sense. Desalles, Galam and Phan (2007) give more details, saying that for strong emergence to occur, agents must be equipped to identify emergent phenomena, and Muller adds that this must be through the physical world, rather than by direct copying of other agent's perceptions (Muller 2004). According to Desalles et al, agents must describe the emergent phenomena they observe in a language other than the language of the lower level process itself, and agents must have a change of behavior that feeds back to the level of observation of the process. This insightful definition of strong emergence acknowledges the importance of autonomy of perception, that is, of not allowing agents to copy each other's internal states, in developing a new emergent language (with tags) to describe emergent phenomena. Immergence, or the ability of the lower level agent to change its behavior based on the emergent social phenomena, opens the door for generative feedback between micro and macro social levels. Such a generative engine, which some social scientists would call a dialectic, characterizes strong emergence.

Luc Steels' research program also addresses the hermeneutic paradox: his agent's signs come to have shared meaning, even though they have autonomous perception. However, his agent's signs were not tags related to social structure as in symbolic interactionist simulation. In Steel's work, arbitrary signs come to have meaning as agents use them to differentiate objects by their features. As individuals make distinctions based on their own perceptions and associations, they come to have shared words to refer to features and shared ontologies of what distinctions to make are important, in an emergence with upper lower feedback (Steels 1996). Ironically, even though these agents may be embodied as robots, they are not truly situated, as they are describing their environment but not applying this description to their utility, or in anyway changing their world with their language. The ontologies these agents use to cut up the world are arbitrary, whereas the ontologies of human languages cut up the world based on utility. Although language is reproduced, culture and the way that the world is manipulated is not.

SYMBOLIC INTERACTIONIST SIMULATION

In symbolic interactionist simulation, the mechanism of autonomous emergence of the meaning of signs facilitates a strong emergence of practical ontologies that coevolve with practical behaviors in symbolic interactionist simulation. Symbolic interacionist agents interpret signs based on utility, so that an interpretation makes sense given the background of the agent's individual experiences. In symbolic interactionist simulation, a sign is interpreted in a certain way because it makes utilitarian sense, and not because it is copied. Agents communicate solely through signs, inducing the meanings of both displayed and read signs. Inductions are based on economic and practical gain, and as a result of these utilitarian interpretations, symbol system and social institutions coevolve.

The first symbolic interactionist simulation (Duong, 1991, Duong and Reilly 1995) was a simulation of a workforce of employers and employees. In some of the runs, for example, there were 3 employers and 50 employees in a society. Each employee had either a high or low level of talent, which the employer could not see until after the employee was hired. However, the employer would look at the signs that an employee displayed to guess whether that it was talented. The prediction was based on the employer's individual past experiences with employees. The employee displayed a fixed sign (such as skin color or race), a sign that costs money (such as a new suit) and a sign that is free (such as a fad). The fixed sign was made to be uncorrelated with talent. Employees obtained money through employment, and thus employees that could stay employed longer could make more money than employees that were fired frequently. A certain percentage of the workforce of each employer was laid off every cycle, but employees that were not talented were laid off in greater proportions. Thus, an employee that is talented has more of a capacity to make money, and the potential to differentiate itself from a non-talented employee using that money. The employees would choose a set of signs to display based on their prediction of whether they would be hired after an employer saw them. This prediction was based on their individual past interviews outcomes. Of course, employees could only display the purchasable signs that they could afford. Both the employer and the employee agents had IAC neural networks to induce the meanings of the signs based on their private experiences with the signs. Even though the signs were arbitrary and autonomously perceived (employers did not consult each other on the meanings of signs, nor did employees), they came to have a shared meaning. Agents learned to buy expensive suits as status symbols, and race often became an issue despite the fact that race was uncorrelated with talent, because it sometimes became correlated with the suit. Races could get into a vicious circle where they could not afford a suit because they were not hired and were not hired because they did not wear a suit, at which time social classes based on race would form.

Axtell, Epstein and Young's model of the emergence of social classes subsequently adapted the autonomy of the symbolic interactionist tag methodology (2000). Desalles et al (2007) took note of the strong emergence Axtell et al achieved by use of autonomously interpreted tags. Axtell et al achieved the emergence of social class based on fixed tags (such as skin color or race) in a one shot bargaining model.

SISTER

Another symbolic inteactionist simulation which uses a one shot bargaining model, SISTER (Symbolic Interactionist Simulation of Trade and Emergent Roles) was prior to and influential on Axtell, Epstein and Young's work on the emergence of social classes (The Economist 1997). SISTER also simulates the coevolution of symbol systems and social structure (Duong 1995, Duong 1996, Duong 2005, Duong and Grefrenstette 2005)

SISTER is a study of the "free tags" of the original model on the emergence of social classes (Duong 1991). The free tags were the equivalent of words in a language, but applied to the identification of people. The dynamics involved in the emergence of meaning of tags are the same for the more general emergence of meaning of words. Symbolic interactionist simulation kept the principles of autonomy and hermeneutics in its study of the emergence of language that subsequent more well known works, such as Steels', did. However, it also addressed critical issues that they did not. Steels and subsequent studies of the emergence of language are separated from studies of the emergence of culture. What is missing are models of language as coevolving with culture, models which capture the coevolutionary dialectic in which language and culture create each other and enable each other to grow. The dynamics of the propagation of signs which start out random is studied, but the dynamics of how they come to denote, hold, and spread new concepts needs more

exploration. SISTER models the emergence of language as a dynamic creator of culture. If we define culture as the knowledge available to a society, both of the objects and the social structure, then SISTER shows how symbols emerge to hold culture and allow it to complexify, and how they enable culture to continue despite the deaths of individuals.

SISTER offers a solution to the hermeneutic paradox as do Steel's models, of how it is that people can only interpret the meaning of signs from the context of their individual life experiences, and yet still come to share meaning. SISTER agents are autonomous because they are closed with respect to meaning: they each have their own private induction mechanisms, and do not copy one another's signs or interpretations of signs, but induce the meanings of the signs from their own experiences alone. SISTER however, is different from Steels' work in that the feedback is directly connected to the utility of the agent. A sign gets a particular interpretation based on what is good for the agent for it to mean, for its survival, rather than from the grunting approval of another agent. SISTER agents see "as the frog sees green" … just as the frog does not observe reality as it is, but constructs it as is beneficial to its survival (Maturana, Lettvin, Mcculloch and Pitts. 1960), so do SISTER agents interpret signs based on whatever it is that gets them the most food. The combination of a direct relation of interpretation to utility along with perceptual autonomy is what makes SISTER agents both embodied and situated. If we do not model the advantage to utility that an interpretation confers at every step, we lose the ability to model important social processes of what becomes popular.

One example of such a process to model is that of the legend. Legends hold deep cultural meaning, often so deep as to be universal. Legends are told and retold orally over many generations. Each time they are retold, the teller contributes to the creation of the legend in small ways. As all the authors of a legend recreate it to meet their needs, it comes to be very good at meeting needs, settling down on a compromise between all needs. Imitation without such modification does not promote cultural products which contribute to the needs of all, deeply intertwined with the rest of the culture. It is not a deep consensus.

The principles of hermeneutics are important to the study of the emergence of language because we can not separate language learning from concept learning, concept creation, and language creation. If we look at language as a passive thing, it does not matter if we include utility or not. If all a word is, is a random sign, and all we are explaining is how one random sign gets chosen over another random sign, then we need look no further than imitation. However, if we look at a word as a holder of a concept, a concept which serves to meet the needs of people within a web of other concepts, and which can only emerge as a word to denote it emerges, then it is appropriate to model the emergence of words in agents which interpret their meanings solely from their individual perspectives and usefulness to their lives. All the interpretations together create words and concepts which best serve the cultural needs of all the individuals. In the study of the emergence of language, it is not the sequence of phonemes that becomes popular that is important, but rather the capturing of the dynamic in which words make possible the ontologies that we use to construct our world. Studies in the emergence of language should address how words make the most practical ontologies, through the contributions of all utterers of words, rather than address the most practical sounds uttered.

SISTER shows that social systems with an emergent symbol system denoting an ontology of roles can enable cultural knowledge to continue despite the deaths of its individual members. The reason that it can continue is that signs denoting roles create expectations of behavior in agents who interact with a role. These expectations serve to train newcomers to the society into the proper behaviors of the role. Each sign for a role is a focal point of a set of social behaviors in a social network, in that the sign means a different thing to different other roles in a social network, and agents of each role have a certain set of expectation for agents of other roles that they interact with. The signs and the set of relations they denote are emergent, and must be emergent if they are going to denote any arbitrary set of behaviors. The knowledge in the society is held in the expectations that signs bring to the different agent's mind. These meanings are all induced by the private inductive mechanisms of agents, and yet the meanings of the signs come to be shared.

SISTER outputs a division of labor and social structure that increases the utility (that is, "satisfaction") of agents. Agent ontologies of roles emerge that guide agents in complex social relations and behaviors needed for survival. SISTER captures the fundamental social process by which macro-level roles emerge from micro-level symbolic interaction. SISTER comprises a multi-agent society in which agents evolve trade and communication strategies over time through the use of tags. The knowledge in

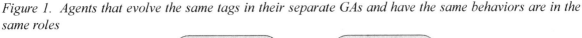

Figure 1. Agents that evolve the same tags in their separate GAs and have the same behaviors are in the same roles

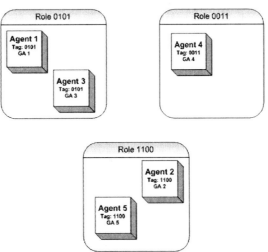

SISTER is held culturally, suspended in the mutual expectations agents have of each other based on the signs (tags) that they read and display. Language emerges and is maintained robustly, despite the stresses of deaths of individual agents. SISTER shows how a complex endogenous communication system can develop to coordinate a complex division of tasking.

SISTER employs coevolution, in which agents each have their own genetic algorithm (GA), whose fitness is dependant on successful interaction with other agents. These GAs evolve tags that come to indicate a set of behaviors associated with a role. Figure 1 illustrates evolved tags indicating agent roles. Roles are nowhere determined in the simulation and exist in no one place, but rather are suspended in the mutual expectations of the coevolving agents. These mutual expectations emerge endogenously and are expressed through signs with emergent meanings. All institutional knowledge is distributed in these subtle mutual expectations.

How SISTER Works

SISTER simulates a differentiation into the roles of a division of labor in an economic system (Duong, 1995, 1996, 2005). In SISTER, initially homogenous agents differentiate into the heterogeneous agents reflecting a division of labor. Roles solve the problem of how agents may work together to increase their utility. Every "day" of the model, agents harvest goods in the morning according to their production plans, trade in a market in the afternoon according to their trade plans, and consume their food at night, judging a single chromosome of plans for the day by their satisfaction in consumption (according to a Cobb-Douglass utility function). Agents are free to devote their efforts to harvesting goods or trading them. The simple economic assumption of economy of scale is built in (it is more efficient to produce a single good than to diversify production), as is a utility function that rewards accumulation of multiple goods. These combine to encourage trade among agents.

Figure 2. Agents must have a corresponding trade plan encoded in their genetic algorithms for a trace to take place. Each chromosome has all the plans of trade and production for a single day, and the plan to display a sign as well (the Passive trader's chromosome tells him to display sign 9, in a section that is not illustrated).

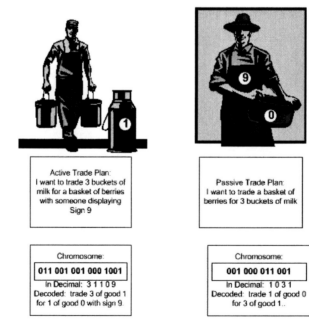

Active Trade Plan:
I want to trade 3 buckets of milk for a basket of berries with someone displaying Sign 9

Passive Trade Plan:
I want to trade a basket of berries for 3 buckets of milk

Chromosome:
011 001 001 000 1001
In Decimal: 3 1 1 0 9
Decoded: trade 3 of good 1 for 1 of good 0 with sign 9.

Chromosome:
001 000 011 001
In Decimal: 1 0 3 1
Decoded: trade 1 of good 0 for 3 of good 1.

SISTER focuses on how agents determine who to trade with. Agents seek trading partners based on a displayed sign. Signs are induced both by the wearer, and by the agent seeking trade. See figure 2 for an example of a trade plan. This "double induction" of a sign is a simulation of Parson's "double contingency" (Parsons, 1951), and facilitates the emergence of a shared symbol system. Signs have no meaning in the beginning of the simulation, but come to have a shared meaning. Agents come to agree on what a sign implies about behavior. As they come to a consensus, a system of roles is developed.

For example, suppose the goods of a simulation run include *berries* and *milk*. Suppose agents coincidently have the trade plan in figure 2, and each agent benefits from the trade. Both agents are satisfied with the trade and the sign: they remember this sign, and repeat it in future trades. The more the trade is repeated in the presence of the original sign, the more it becomes a stable element in the environment and therefore something that other agents can learn. Since an agent with an active trade plan is looking for any agent who displays a particular sign, any agent can get in on the trade just by displaying the appropriate sign. The agents come to believe that the sign means "milk," in the sense that if an agent displays the sign, then other agents will ask him to sell milk. This puts selective pressure on that agent to make and sell milk. If a random agent displays the sign for a composite good (a good composed of other goods, like "berry-flavored milk"), it learns the recipe for the composite good from marketers trying to sell the ingredients for the composite good. Over time, the society divides into roles, with groups of agents displaying the same sign and having the same behavior.

The signs are Berger and Luckmann's "objectivations" that become coercive: if a new agent is inserted into the simulation, then to participate in trade he must learn the sign system already present (Berger and Luckman, 1966). The signs are a guide to his behavior: When he displays a sign, the other agents pressure him to have the corresponding behavior. Thus a sign creates expectations of behavior, in accordance with Parson's ideas of double contingency and Luhmann's model of mutual expectations (Parsons, 1951; Luhmann, 1984).

Figure 3. A scenarios from SISTER representing the trades made in a single day of the simulation. Agents with the same color square have come to have the same role: that is, the same trading behaviors and same sign. The smaller shapes represent goods traded. An arc connecting shapes represents a trade. The stars are composite goods, or goods composed of other goods. Agents have developed complex roles and composite goods.

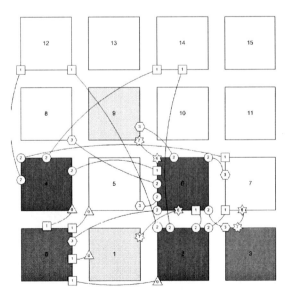

The mutual expectations that the agents have of the roles allows individuals to take advantage of what other individuals have learned in previous interactions. The knowledge of the society is held in the mutual expectations of the symbol system, as in Parsons' and Luhmann's theories (Parsons, 1951; Luhmann, 1984). The reason that role systems can hold more information about how to make cultural products is that agents can replace one another and can learn from the expectations that other agents have of their replacement class. This is how they become trained to do their role. However, this training is not inflexible: what they do is ultimately connected to their utility. They can reject a trade if it is not to their advantage. Thus SISTER agents have the flexibility needed to complexify. Figure 3 illustrates a role based society that is advanced enough to make composite goods, with a relatively high mutual information.

Experiment

In this experiment, agents which display induced signs are compared to a control in which agents are forced to display a unique ID. The use of an ID prevents the formation of a system of roles denoted by the induced signs. We refer to a society where agents read and display signs freely as a "role recognition treatment" and a society where agents are forced to display a unique ID as an "individual recognition treatment." Whether the sign is arbitrary or an ID, an agent seeking a trade has to induce the sign to seek in trade. However, in the role recognition treatment, the displayer of a sign induces the sign it should display at the same time that the agent seeking a trade induces the sign to read. This double induction allows a system of arbitrary symbols to come to have meaning, but there is no double induction in the control. Duong and Grefenstette (2005) contains an experiment where individual recognition is compared to role recognition in the ability to create complex goods. The experiment of this article has both treatments making complex goods, and compares their ability to make them when there is a complete turnover in their population as a result of death and rebirth of agents. Death and birth is added to test the ability of new agents to acquire the language of the existing agents and achieve cultural continuity that is greater than the individual behaviors of members of the culture. The individual recognition treatment and the role recognition treatment are run twenty times each.

In this experiment, three different death rates are applied to each treatment. The average utility of the agents (the number of goods and the evenness of the spread of the goods, measured with a Cobb-Douglas utility function) is compared in each treatment, as well as the mutual information in the symbol systems that have evolved. The higher the correspondence between behavior and the sign displayed, the higher the information content, or mutual information, in the symbol system. Although the signs of the individual recognition treatment are not modifiable by the displayers of the signs, there is still a symbol system whose information may be measured. The individual recognition treatment can reach high values of mutual information if agents displaying different ID's have different behaviors. If a treatment has a higher utility value, then the agents are more successful in trading with each other. If they have higher mutual information, which is correlated with that utility, then it is likely that they are trading better as a result of the information contained in their symbol systems. Thus language makes knowledge and culture possible. They develop a language that is practical for the purposes of setting up networks of trade. If this language can carry these practical recipes for interaction on even through a complete turnover of the population, then language has reproduced culture, and expectation of the meanings of signs have spread knowledge to new members, so that culture continues despite the deaths of members.

The hypothesis of this experiment is: When birth and death are introduced into agent societies, those with role recognition (arbitrary signs) have greater continuity of knowledge of how to make complex goods than societies with only individual recognition.

While the number of agents remains at 16, agents are periodically killed and replaced by randomizing the chromosomes of the private genetic algorithms in each of their heads. When an agent is replaced, it is given a new unique id. The death rate is tested at several values, a 0.001 chance of death resulting

Figure 4. Results for the death scenario. Utility is higher in the role treatment than in the individual treatment. Role mutual information actually increases under the stress of death.

Treatment	Death Rate	Avg Utility	Death Treatment Mutual Information(MI)	No Death MI	CorrellationMI,Utility
Role	.001	145	0.715	0.665	0.43
	.002	133	0.858	0.794	0.36
	.005	125	0.575	0.65	0.5
Individual	.001	127	0	0.14	N/A
	.002	121	0.04	0.27	N/A
	.005	115	0	0.34	N/A

in a complete turnover of agents in about every 1000 cycles, a 0.002 chance of death resulting in a turnover of agents in about every 500 cycles, and a 0.005 chance of death resulting in a turnover of agents in about two hundred cycles. A cycle is defined as a period of 1000 days of trade, after which reproductions in the GAs take place (learning). The tests are all on how well an agent does after one turnover, so the cycle lengths tested are different. Additionally, a 5 bit sign is used to represent the 16 agents rather than a 4 bit sign, in order to give new "names" to the new agents that arise in the system. A 5 bit sign represents 32 different unique names for the individually recognized agents, who must display their unique name in their sign. 32 unique names are needed if all of the agents will die and be replaced about once.

Results

For the parameters of this experiment, 130 is the level of utility where agents have no trade, but have become good at making everything for themselves. Any utility over that level indicates trade, and under that level indicates new agents are having difficulty learning. The average utility is significantly greater in the role recognition treatment, at over the 99% confidence level, than in the individual recognition treatment. Average utilities of the role treatments, for death rates 0.001, 0.002, and 0.005 are 145, 133, and 125. Average utilities of individual treatments are 127, 121, and 115. These show that increasing death rates are harder on both individual and role

utilities at above the 99% confidence level. Figure 11 shows these results in tabular format.

Death flattens the trade and mutual information in all of the treatments for the individuals. The control run (with no death) for the individual treatment does not have much trade, but has more than zero. This is reflected in the average mutual information scores of the 1000 cycle control, 0.14, as compared to the death rate 0.001 treatment, 0; the 500 cycle control , 0.27, as compared to the death rate 0.002 treatment, 0.04; and the 200 cycle control, 0.34 as opposed to the death 0.005 treatment, 0. These decreases in mutual information from the control are all significant above the 98% confidence level. In contrast, the average mutual information in the role recognition runs actually increased from the control; however this increase is not significant. This is reflected in the average mutual information scores of the 1000 cycle control, 0.665, as compared to the death rate 0.001 treatment, 0.715; the 500 cycle control 0.794, as compared to the death rate 0.002 treatment, 0.858; and the 200 cycle control, 0.65 as opposed to the death 0.005 treatment, 0.575. The increase in the average mutual information of the role recognition treatment over the individual recognition treatment is significant above the 99% level.

In the role treatment, average utility is correlated with average mutual information in death rates 0.001, 0.002 and 0.005 at values 0.43, 0.36 and 0.50. These results are significant above the 95% level except for the 0.36 value, which is significant above the 90% level. Individual recognition values are too low to have correlations.

CONCLUSION

This experiment supports the hypothesis that the use of arbitrary symbols helps to preserve the knowledge in society even though individual knowers die. When an agent dies in an individual based recognition society, all the social coordination associated with its place in society is lost. If an agent dies in a role recognition society, even if there is only one agent in that role at a time, other agents in the society or new agents may adjust their sign and receive the selective pressures to adjust their behaviors to the dead agent's niche. The role system exists because of an emergent symbol system to denote it, and is reproduced through the expectations that these symbols bring to mind in the agents. Language acquisition occurs along with concept acquisition, as a result of the pressures of these expectations.

This finding contributes to artificial intelligence, because it shows a way to keep a coevolving society of agents learning new things. When new agents are brought into a society, they can bring change to the society more readily than old agents that have already-converged genetic algorithms directing them. Thus, death is a type of macro level mutation for coevolving systems. Death enables roles in the society to readjust to each other, change as the need arises, and complexify. If role recognition makes agents robust in the face of death, then it can help keep the diversity up in a coevolving system when used in concert with death. This finding further contributes to artificial intelligence in that robot agents in the real world will die by accident, and role based recognition is a way to keep the knowledge that they have accumulated alive socially despite their accidental death.

Role recognition is superior to individual recognition of agents in preserving knowledge because the agents serve as replacements for each other. Roles form robust replacement classes of agents, which enable the preservation of the knowledge of society, even when individual members of a class die. Role classes also promote the creation of knowledge, not only because agents within a role class may learn from each other's experiences. This experiment has shown that role recognition, in conjunction with death, facilitates the creation of knowledge through the diversity that death and

birth bring to a society. Roles coordinate knowledge across generations. These roles are indicated by an ontology in a symbol system, that coevolves with them, and that regenerates them by bringing to mind expectations of behavior, which pressure agents to behave accordingly. Thus, language is generative of culture, and can regenerate it to recover from the deaths of individual members.

FUTURE RESEARCH DIRECTIONS

When Desalles et al praised Axtell et al's strong (symbolic interactionist-style) emergence, Desalles et al noted an immergence, a downward irreducible causation that changed the behavior of the races by means of a tacit, rather than an explicit, understanding of the signs. The signs did not point to something outside of the agent, they point to utility alone as in Maturana et al's frog that sees green. Desalles et al noted that the (symbolic interactionist-style) agent's internal models were not reflexive, that they did not map to the agent's world. However, Desalles along with many other current theorists of "immergence" fail to realize that it is the tacit nature of the model that allows an entire social engine to form, an invisible hand that makes need-filling institutions out of individual selfish actions. Desalle et al proposed an improvement to Axtell et al in which agents can categorize their knowledge into a previously developed ontology. Rather than an improving upon the strong emergence this change would disable the autonomous social engine, because the previously developed ontology is an exogenous and static input. What is needed for true objectivity, the move from tacit as-the-frog-sees-green to explicit, more objective models of the environment that is entirely endogenous is a breakthrough in cognitive science. Since endogenous objectivation is beyond our technical knowledge, tacit knowledge is the only simulatable phenomena that can form an entire need filling engine at this time.

Of course, people cognate detailed models of the environment for their utility just as Maturana et al's frog did, and even though no one person has a complete explicit map of the entire world of thought, these models are more shared than the tacit knowledge of Maturana et al's frog. This objective knowledge is useful in society and to the symbolic interactionist practice of "taking the shoes of another." The technology that could put an agent in the shoes of another would be a technology that could take in correlations that it an agent discovered through induction, and put out a model of cause. Until cognitive science is at the point where it can derive an objective causal simulation from subjective correlative data, programs which purport to simulate immergence must use tacit models. The alternative, considering the state of the science now, is to hard code a representation of the "emergent" property, losing the endogeny necessary for the simulation's fidelity. In the mean time, it is best to, as Holland did, recognize that a tacit model is just as much an internal model as an explicit model.

Endogenously created cognitive maps would go a step farther in simulating the symbolic interactionist paradigm, as reflexivity at the level of getting into the other's shoes is required, and thus the ability to find an objective representation is needed. Further, symbolic interactionist simulations to this point have only covered the first two mechanisms in Holland's recipe for complex adaptive systems: tags and internal models. They have no building blocks, no dynamically recombinable signs that can mean new things to be interpreted during the interaction, as in Garfinkel's ethnomethodology in symbolic interactionism requires (Garfinkel 1967). Endogenous internal causal models from correlated relations and recombinable symbols that are in language are ambitious next steps for not only the symbolic interactionist paradigm, but for cognitive science in general. Maybe the techniques of cognitive science can benefit from the techniques of symbolic interactionism in these next steps for modeling emergent meanings.

REFERENCES

Axtell, R., Epstein, J. & Young, H. (2001). The Emergence of Class Norms in a Multi-Agent Model of Bargaining. In Durlouf and Young (Ed.). *Social Dynamics*. Cambridge: MIT Press

Bedau, M. (2002). Downward Causation and the Autonomy of Weak Emergence *Principia* 6(1),5-50.

Berger, P and Thomas Luckmann (1966). *The Social Construction of Reality* New York: Anchor Books.

Coleman, J (1994). *Foundations of Social Theory*. New York: Belknap.

Dessalles J.L., Müller J.P., Phan D. (2007). "Emergence in multi-agent systems: conceptual and methodological issues" in Phan, Amblard, (Eds) *Agent Based Modelling and Simulations in the Human and Social Sciences*, (pp. 327-356) Oxford: The Bardwell Press,

Duong, D V (1991). "A System of IAC Neural Networks as the Basis for Self Organization in a Sociological Dynamical System Simulation." Masters Thesis, The University of Alabama at Birmingham http://www.scs.gmu.edu/~dduong/behavior.html.

Duong, D V and Kevin D. Reilly (1995). "A System of IAC Neural Networks as the Basis for Self Organization in a Sociological Dynamical System Simulation." *Behavioral Science*, 40,4, 275-303. http://www.scs.gmu.edu/~dduong/behavior.html.

Duong, D V (1995). "Computational Model of Social Learning" *Virtual School* ed. Brad Cox. http://www.virtualschool.edu/mon/Bionomics/TraderNetworkPaper.html.

Duong, D V (1996). "Symbolic Interactionist Modeling: The Coevolution of Symbols and Institutions." *Intelligent Systems: A Semiotic Perspective Proceedings of the 1996 International Multidisciplinary Conference*, Vol 2, pp. 349 - 354. http://www.scs.gmu.edu/~dduong/semiotic.html.

Duong, D V (2004). *SISTER: A Symbolic Interactionist Simulation of Trade and Emergent Roles*. Doctoral Dissertation, George Mason University, Spring.

Duong, D V and John Grefenstette (2005). *SISTER: A Symbolic Interactionist Simulation of Trade and Emergent Roles. Journal of Artificial Societies and Social Simulation,* January 2005. http://jasss.soc.surrey.ac.uk/8/1/1.html.

Duong, D V and John Grefenstette (2005). "The Emulation of Social Institutions as a Method of Coevolution" *GECCO conference proceedings*. http://www.scs.gmu.edu/~dduong/gecco.pdf.

The Economist (1997)."What Boys and Girls are Made Of" March 8, 1997, p. 96. http://www.scs.gmu.edu/~dduong/economist.pdf

Garfinkel, H. (1967). *Studies in Ethnomethodology* Los Angeles: University of California

Gilbert, N. (1995). Emergence in Social Simulations. In Gilbert,N. & Conte, R. (eds) *Artificial Societies: The Computer Simulation of Social Life.* London: UCL Press.

Hales, D. (2004). Tags for All! - Understanding and Engineering Tag Systems. *4th International Conference on Complex Systems (ICCS 2004)* New York: Springer Verlag

Hales, D and Bruce Edmonds (2003). *Can Tags Build Working Systems? From MABS to ESOA.* Working Paper, Center For Policy Modelling, Manchester, UK.

Holland, J H (1975). *Adaptation in Natural and Artificial Systems.* Ann Arbor: University of Michigan Press.

Holland, J. (1993). The *Effects of Lables (Tags) on Social Interactions.* Sante Fe Institute Working Papers. Santa Fe: The Santa Fe Institute.

Luhmann, N (1984). *Social Systems.* Frankfort: Suhrkamp.

Maturana, H., Lettvin, J., McCulloch, W., & Pitts, W. (1960). "Anatomy and physiology of vision in the frog", *Journal of General Physiology*, 43:129--175

Muller, J (2004). The Emergence of Collective Behavior in Problem Solving. *Agents World IV International Workshop* (pp.1-20) New York: Springer Verlag

Parsons, T (1951). *The Social System.* New York: Free Press.

Riolo, R, Michael Cohen and Robert Axelrod (2001). "Evolution of Cooperation without Reciprocity," Nature Vol 414, November.

Steels, L (1996). Emergent Adaptive Lexicons. In Fourth International Conference on Simulation of Adaptive Behavior, Cape Cod. New York: Springer Verlag

Winograd, T. & Flores, F. (1987). *Understanding Computers and Cognition* New York: Addison-Wesley.

Chapter XIII
Propositional Logic Syntax Acquisition Using Induction and Self-Organisation

Josefina Sierra
Universidad Politécnica de Cataluña, Spain

Josefina Santibáñez
Universidad de La Rioja, Spain

ABSTRACT

This chapter addresses the problem of the acquisition of the syntax of propositional logic. An approach based on general purpose cognitive capacities such as invention, adoption, parsing, generation, and induction is proposed. Self-organisation principles are used to show how a shared set of preferred lexical entries and grammatical constructions, that is, a language, can emerge in a population of autonomous agents which do not have any initial linguistic knowledge. Experiments in which a population of autonomous agents constructs a grammar that allows communicating the formulas of a propositional logic language are presented. These experiments extend previous work by considering a larger population and a much larger search space of grammar rules. In particular, the agents are allowed to order the expressions associated with the constituents of a logical formula in arbitrary order. Previous work assumed that the expressions associated with the connectives should be placed in the first position of the sentence.

INTRODUCTION

Recent work in linguistics and artificial intelligence (Steels, 1998, 2000, 2004; Batali, 2002; Kirby 2002) has suggested that some of the complex structure of language may be the result of a quite different process from biological evolution. Interesting experiments showing the emergence of compositional and recursive syntax in populations of agents without initial linguistic knowledge have been presented as evidence in support of alternative explanations. This chapter combines general purpose cognitive capacities (e.g., invention, adoption, parsing, generation and induction) and self-organisation principles proposed as effective mechanisms for syntax acquisition in these experiments in order to address the problem of the acquisition of the syntax of propositional logic.

The important role of logic in knowledge representation and reasoning (McCarthy, 1990) is well known in artificial intelligence. Much of the knowledge used by artificial intelligent agents today is represented in logic, and linguists use it as well for representing the meanings of words and sentences. This chapter differs from previous approaches in using the syntax of logic as the subject of learning. Some could argue that it is not necessary to learn such a syntax, because it is built in the internal knowledge representation formalism used by the agents. We'd argue on the contrary that logical connectives and logical constructions are a fundamental part of natural language, and that it is necessary to understand how an agent can both conceptualise and communicate them to other agents.

The research presented in this chapter assumes previous work on the **conceptualisation of logical connectives** (Piaget, 1985; Santibáñez, 1984, 1988, 1989). In (Sierra 2001, 2002) a grounded approach to the acquisition of logical categories (connectives) based on the **discrimination** of a "subset of objects" from the rest of the objects in a given context is described. The "subset of objects" is characterized by a logical formula constructed from perceptually grounded categories. This formula is satisfied by the objects in the subset and not satisfied by the rest of the objects in the context. In this chapter we only focus on the problem of the acquisition of the syntax of propositional logic, because it is a necessary step to solve the complete problem of the acquisition of a grounded logical language (encompassing the acquisition of both the syntax and the semantics of propositional logic).

The rest of the chapter is organised as follows. First we present the formalism used for representing the grammars constructed by the agents. Then we describe in some detail the language games played by the agents, focusing on the main cognitive processes they use for constructing a shared lexicon and grammar: invention, adoption, induction and self-organisation. Next we report the results of some experiments in which a population of autonomous agents constructs a **shared language** that allows communicating the formulas of a propositional logic language. Finally we summarize some related work and the main contributions of the chapter.

GRAMMATICAL FORMALISM

We use a restricted form of Definite Clause Grammar in which non-terminals have three arguments attached to them. The first argument conveys semantic information. The second is a score in the interval [0, 1] that estimates the usefulness of that association in previous communication. The third argument is a counter that records the number of times the association has been used in previous language games.

Many grammars can be used to express the same meaning. The following holistic grammar can be used to express the propositional formula right∧light.

s([and, right, light]), 0.01) → andrightlight

$$(1)$$

This grammar consists of a single rule which states that 'andrightlight' is a valid sentence meaning right∧light. Notice that we use Prolog grammar rules for describing the grammars. The semantic argument of non-terminals uses Lisp like notation for representing **propositional formulas** (e.g., the Prolog list [and, [not, right], light] is equivalent to ¬right∧light). The third argument (the use counter) of non-terminals is not shown in the examples.

The same formula can be expressed as well using the following compositional, recursive grammar: s is the start symbol, c1 and c2 are the names of two syntactic categories associated with unary and binary connectives, respectively. Like in Prolog, variables start with a capital letter and constants with a lower case letter.

s(light, 0.70) → light	(2)
s(right, 0.25) → right	(3)
s(up, 0.60) → up	(4)
c1(not, 0.80) → not	(5)
s([P, Q],S) → c1(P, S1), s(Q, S2),	
{S is S1∗S2∗0.10}	(6)
c2(or, 0.30) → or	(7)
c2(and, 0.50) → and	(8)
c2(if, 0.90) → if	(9)
c2(iff, 0.60) → iff	(10)

s([P, Q, R],S) → c2(P, S1), s(Q, S2), s(R, S3),
    {S is S1 * S2 * S3 * 0.01}   (11)

This grammar breaks down the sentence 'and-rightlight' into subparts with independent meanings. The whole sentence is constructed concatenating these subparts. The meaning of the sentence is composed combining the meanings of the subparts using the variables *P, Q* and *R*.

The **score of a lexical rule** is the value of the second argument of the left hand side of the rule (e.g., the score of rule 8 is 0.50). The **score of a grammatical rule** is the last number of the arithmetic expression that appears on the right hand side of the rule (e.g., the score of rule 11 is 0.01). The Prolog operator *"is"* allows evaluating the arithmetic expression at its right hand side. The **score of a sentence** generated using a grammatical rule is computed using the arithmetic expression on the right hand side of that rule (e.g., the score of sentence *andrightlight* is 0.50*0.25*0.70*0.01=0.00875).

LANGUAGE GAMES

Syntax acquisition is seen as a collective process by which a population of autonomous agents constructs a *grammar* that allows them to communicate some set of meanings. In order to reach such an agreement the agents interact with each other playing language games. In the experiments described in this chapter a particular type of **language game** called **the guessing game** (Steels 1999, 2002) is played by two agents, a **speaker** and a **hearer**:

1. The speaker chooses a formula from a given propositional language, generates a sentence that **expresses this formula** and communicates that sentence to the hearer.
2. The hearer tries to interpret the sentence generated by the speaker. If it can parse the sentence using its lexicon and grammar, it **extracts a meaning** which can be **logically equivalent or not to the formula intended by the speaker**.
3. The speaker communicates the meaning it had in mind to the hearer and both agents adjust their grammars in order to become successful in future language games.

In a typical experiment hundreds of language games are played by pairs of agents randomly chosen from a population. The goal of the experiment is to observe the evolution of: (1) the communicative success; (2) the internal grammars constructed by the individual agents; and (3) the external language used by the population. The **communicative success** is the average of successful language games in the last ten language games played by the agents. A **language game** is considered **successful** if the hearer can parse the sentence generated by the speaker, and the meaning interpreted by hearer is logically equivalent to the meaning intended by the speaker.

Invention

In the first step of a language game the speaker tries to generate a sentence that expresses a propositional formula.

The agents in the population start with an empty lexicon and grammar. It is not surprising thus that they cannot generate sentences for some meanings at the early stages of a simulation run. In order to allow language to get off the ground, the agents are allowed to invent new words for those meanings they cannot express using their lexicons and grammars. New words are sequences of one, two or three letters randomly chosen from the alphabet.

The invention algorithm is a recursive procedure that invents a sentence E for a meaning M. If M is atomic (not a list), it generates a new word E. If M is a list of elements (i.e., a unary or binary connective followed by one or two formulas, respectively), it tries to generate an expression for each of the elements in M using the agent's grammar. If it cannot generate an expression for an element of M using the agent's grammar, it invents an expression for that element calling itself recursively on that element. Once it has generated an expression for each element in M, it concatenates these expressions randomly in order to construct a sentence E for the whole meaning M.

For example, if an agent tries to generate a sentence for the formula [*and, light, right*], it has an entry in its lexicon that associates the atomic formula *light* with the sequence of letters *'a'*, but it does not have entries for *and* and *right*, then two sequences of letters such as *'en'* and *'rec'* could be invented for expressing the meanings *and* and *right*, respectively. These sequences could be concatenated randomly generating any of the following sentences for the meaning [*and, light, right*]: *'enreca'*, *'enarec'*, *'aenrec'*, *'recena'*, *'arecen'*, *'recaen'*.

As the agents play language games they learn associations between expressions and meanings, and induce linguistic knowledge from such associations in the form of grammatical rules and lexical entries. Once the agents can generate sentences for expressing a particular meaning using their own grammars, they select the sentence with the highest score out of the set of sentences they can generate for expressing that meaning, and communicate that sentence to the hearer. The algorithm used for computing the score of a sentence from the scores of the grammatical rules applied in its generation is explained in detail later.

Adoption

The hearer tries to interpret the sentence generated by the speaker. If it can parse the sentence using its lexicon and grammar, it extracts a meaning which can be logically equivalent or not to the formula intended by the speaker.

As we have explained earlier the agents start with no linguistic knowledge at all. Therefore they cannot parse the sentences generated by the speakers at the early stages of a simulation run. When this happens the speaker communicates the formula it had in mind to the hearer, and the hearer adopts an association between that formula and the sentence used by the speaker.

It is also possible that the grammars and lexicons of speaker and hearer are not consistent, because each agent constructs its own grammar from the linguistic interactions in which it participates, and it is very unlikely that speaker and hearer share the same history of linguistic interactions unless the population consists only of these two agents. When this happens the hearer may be able to parse the sentence generated by the speaker, but its interpretation of that sentence may be different from the meaning the speaker had in mind. In this case the strategy used to coordinate the grammars of speaker and hearer is to decrement the score of the

rules used by speaker and hearer in the processes of generation and parsing, respectively, and allow the hearer to adopt an association between the sentence and the meaning used by the speaker.

The adoption algorithm used in this chapter is very simple. Given a sentence E and a meaning M, the agent checks whether it can parse E and interpret it as meaning M (or MH, where MH is a formula logically equivalent to M). This may happen when the hearer can parse the sentence used by the speaker, but it obtains a different meaning from the one intended by the speaker. In a language game the hearer always chooses the interpretation with the highest score out of the set of all the interpretations it can obtain for a given sentence. So it is possible that the hearer knows the grammatical rules used by the speaker, but the scores of these rules are not higher than the scores of the rules it used for interpretation. If the hearer can interpret sentence E as meaning M, the hearer does not take any action. Otherwise it adopts the association used by the speaker adding a new holistic rule of the form $s(M, 0.01) \rightarrow E$ to its grammar. Observe that the score of the rule is initialized to 0.01. The same initial score value is used for all the rules generated using invention, adoption or induction. The induction algorithm, used to generalise and simplify the agents' grammars, compares this rule with other rules already present in the grammar and replaces it with more general rules whenever it is possible.

Induction

In addition to invent and adopt associations between sentences and meanings, the agents use some **induction mechanisms** to extract generalizations from the grammar rules they have learnt so far (Steels, 2004). The induction rules used in this chapter are based on the rules for chunk and simplification in (Kirby, 2002; Stolcke, 1994) although we have extended them so that they can be applied to grammar rules which have scores attached to them. We use the approach proposed in (Vogt, 2005) for computing the scores of sentences and meanings from the scores of the rules used in their generation.

The induction rules are applied whenever the agents invent or adopt a new association, to avoid redundancy and increase generality in their grammars.

Simplification *Let r1 and r2 be a pair of grammar rules such that the left hand side semantics of r1 contains a subterm m1, r2 is of the form n(m1,S) → e1, and e1 is a substring of the terminals of r1. Then simplification can be applied to r1 replacing it with a new rule that is identical to r1 except that m1 is replaced with a new variable X in the left hand side semantics, and e1 is replaced with n(X, S) on the right hand side. The second argument of the left hand side of r1 is replaced with a new variable SR. If the score of r1 was a constant value c1, an expression of the form {SR is S * 0.01} is added to the right hand side of r1. If the score of r1 was a variable, then the arithmetic expression {SR is S1 * c1} in the right hand side of r1 is replaced with {SR is S *S1 * 0.01}.*

Suppose an agent's grammar contains rules 2, 3 and 4, which it has invented or adopted in previous language games. It plays a language game with another agent, and invents or adopts the following rule.

s([and, light, right], 0.01) → andlightright. (12)

It could apply simplification to rule 12 (using rule 3) and replace it with 13.

s([and, light, R],S) → andlight, s(R, SR),
{S is SR * 0.01} (13)

Rule 13 could be simplified again, replacing it with 14.

s([and, Q, R],S) → and, s(Q, SQ), s(R, SR),
{S is SQ * SR * 0.01} (14)

Suppose the agent plays another language game in which it invents or adopts a holistic rule which associates the formula [or, up, light] with the sentence 'oruplight', and it applies simplification in a similar way. Then the agent's grammar would contain the following rules that are compositional and recursive, but which do not use syntactic categories for unary or binary connectives.

s([and, Q, R],S) → and, s(Q, SQ), s(R, SR),
{S is SQ * SR * 0.01} (15)

s([or, Q, R],S) → or, s(Q, SQ), s(R, SR),
{S is SQ * SR * 0.01} (16)

Chunk I *Let r1 and r2 be a pair of grammar rules with the same left hand side category symbol. If the left hand side semantics of the two rules differ in only one subterm, and there exist two strings of terminals that, if removed, would make the right hand sides of the two rules the same, then chunk can be applied. Let m1 and m2 be the differences in the left hand side semantics of the two rules, and e1 and e2 the strings of terminals that, if removed, would make the right hand sides of the rules the same. A new category n is created and the following two new rules are added to the grammar.*

n(m1, 0.01) → e1
n(m2, 0.01) → e2

*Rules r1 and r2 are replaced by a new rule that is identical to r1 (or r2) except that e1 (or e2) is replaced with n(X, S) on the right hand side, and m1 (or m2) is replaced with a new variable X in the left hand side semantics. The second argument of the left hand side of r1 is replaced with a new variable SR. If the score of r1 was a constant value c1, an expression of the form {SR is S*0.01}is added to the right hand side of r1. If the score of r1 was a variable, then the arithmetic expression {SR is S1 * c1} in the right hand side of r1 is replaced with {SR is S * S1 * 0.01}.*

For example the agent of previous examples, which has rules 15 and 16 for conjunctive and disjunctive formulas in its grammar, could apply chunk I to these rules and create a new syntactic category for binary connectives as follows.

s([P, Q, R], S) → c2(P, S1), s(Q, S2), s(R, S3),
{S is S1 * S2 * S3 * 0.01} (17)
c2(and, 0.01) → and (18)
c2(or, 0.01) → or (19)

Rules 15 and 16 would be replaced with 17, which generalises them because it can be applied to arbitrary formulas constructed using binary connectives, and rules 18 and 19, which state that *and* and *or* belong to c2 (the syntactic category of binary connectives), would be added to the grammar.

Chunk II *If the left hand side semantics of two grammar rules r1 and r2 can be unified applying substitution X/m1 to r1 and there exists a string of terminals e1 in r2 that corresponds to a nonterminal c(X, S) in r1, then chunk can be applied to r2 as follows. Rule r2 is deleted from the grammar and a new rule of the following form c(m1, 0.01) → e1 is added to it.*

Suppose the agent of previous examples adopts or invents the following rule.

$$s([iff, up, right], 0.01) \rightarrow iffupright. \qquad (20)$$

Simplification of rule 20 with rules 4 and 3 leads to replace rule 20 with 21.

$$s([iff, Q, R], S) \rightarrow iff, s(Q, SQ), s(R, SR),$$
$$\{S \text{ is } SQ * SR * 0.01\} \qquad (21)$$

Then chunk II could be applied to rules 21 and 17, replacing rule 21 with rule 22.

$$c2(iff, 0.01) \rightarrow iff \qquad (22)$$

Self-Organisation

The agent in the previous examples has been very lucky, but things are not always that easy. Different agents can invent different words for referring to the same propositional constants or connectives. The invention process uses a random order to concatenate the expressions associated with the components of a given meaning. Thus an agent that has invented or adopted rules 2, 3 and 8 may invent any of the following holistic sentences for communicating the meaning [and,light,right]: lightandright, rightandlight, andrightlight, andlightright, lightrightand, rightlightand.

This has important consequences, because the simplification rule takes into account the order in which the expressions associated with the meaning components appear in the terminals of a rule.

Imagine that the agent has invented or adopted the following holistic rules for expressing the meanings [and,light,right] and [if,light,right].

$$s([and, light, right], 0.01) \rightarrow andlightright$$
$$s([if, light, right], 0.01) \rightarrow ifrightlight$$

The result of simplifying these rules using rules 2 and 3 would be the following rules which cannot be used for constructing a syntactic category for binary connectives, because they do not satisfy the preconditions of chunk I. There do not exist two strings of terminals that, if removed, would make the right hand sides of the rules the same.

$$S([and, X, Y], SC) \rightarrow and, s(X, SX), s(Y, SY), \{SC \text{ is } SX * SY * 0.56\}$$

$$S([if, X, Y], SC) \rightarrow if, s(Y, SY), s(X, SX), \{SC \text{ is } SY * SX * 0.56\}$$

The agents must therefore reach agreements on how to name propositional constants and connectives, and on how to order the expressions associated with the different components of non-atomic meanings. **Self-organisation** principles help to coordinate the agents' grammars in such a way that they prefer to use the rules that are used more often by other agents (Steels 1997, 2004; Batali 2002). The set of rules preferred by most agents for naming atomic meanings, and for ordering the expressions associated with the components of non-atomic meanings constitutes the **external language** spread over the population.

The **goal of the self-organisation process is that the agents in the population be able to construct a shared external language** and that they prefer using the rules in that language over the rest of the rules in their individual grammars.

Coordination takes place at the third stage of a language game, when the speaker communicates the meaning it had in mind to the hearer. Depending on the **outcome of the language game** speaker and hearer take different actions. We have talked about some of them already, such as invention or adoption, but they can also **adjust the scores** of the rules in their grammars to become more successful in future games. First we consider the case in which the speaker can generate a sentence for the meaning using the rules in its grammar. If the speaker can generate several sentences for expressing that meaning, it chooses **the sentence with the highest score**, the rest are called **competing sentences**.

The score of a sentence (or a meaning) is computed at generation (parsing) multiplying the scores of the rules involved (Vorgt, 2005). Consider the generation of a sentence for expressing the meaning [and, right, light] using the following rules.

$$s(light, 0.70) \rightarrow light \qquad (23)$$
$$s(right, 0.25) \rightarrow right \qquad (24)$$
$$c2(and, 0.50) \rightarrow and \qquad (25)$$
$$s([P, Q, R], S) \rightarrow c2(P, S1), s(Q, S2),$$
$$s(R, S3), \{S \text{ is } S1 \cdot S2 \cdot S3 \cdot 0.01\} \qquad (26)$$

The score S of the sentence andrightligth, generated by rule 26, is computed multiplying the score of that rule (0.01) by the scores of the rules 25, 24 and 23 which generate the substrings of that sentence. The score of a lexical rule is the value of the second argument of the left hand side of the rule (e.g., the score of rule 25 is 0.50). The score of a grammatical rule is the last number of the arithmetic expression that appears on the right hand side of the rule (e.g., the score of rule 26 is 0.01). The score of a sentence generated using a grammatical rule is computed using the arithmetic expression on the right hand side of that rule. For example, using the rules above, the score of the sentence andrightlight is 0.50*0.25*0.70*0.01=0.00875.

Suppose that the hearer can interpret the sentence communicated by the speaker. If the hearer can obtain several interpretations (meanings) for that sentence, the **meaning with the highest score** is selected, the rest are called **competing meanings**.

If the meaning interpreted by the hearer is logically equivalent to the meaning the speaker had in mind, the game succeeds and both agents adjust the scores of the rules in their grammars. The speaker increases the scores of the rules it used for generating the sentence communicated to the hearer and decreases the scores of the rules it used for generating competing sentences. The hearer increases the scores of the rules it used for obtaining the meaning the speaker had in mind and decreases the scores of the rules it used for obtaining competing meanings. This way the rules that have been used successfully get **reinforced**. The rules that have been used for generating competing sentences or competing meanings are **inhibited** to avoid ambiguity in future games.

The rules used for updating the scores of grammar rules are the same as those proposed in (Steels, 1999). The rule's original score S is replaced with the result of evaluating expression 27 if the score is increased, and with the result of evaluating expression 28 if the score is decreased. The constant μ is a leaning parameter which is set to 0.1.

$$minimum(1, S + \mu) \qquad (27)$$
$$maximum(0, S - \mu) \qquad (28)$$

If the meaning interpreted by the hearer it is not logically equivalent to the meaning the speaker had in mind, the game fails. Speaker and hearer decrease the scores of the rules they used for generating and interpreting the sentence, respectively. This way the rules that have been used without success are inhibited.

Table 1. Lexicons constructed by the agents after playing 10000 language games about propositional constants in a particular simulation run

Prop Const	a	b	c	l	r	u
Lexicon a1	s(a,l) → c	s(b,l) → v	s(c,l) → hw	s(l,l) → hcm	s(r,l) → l	s(u,l) → zb
Lexicon a2	s(a,l) → c	s(b,l) → v	s(c,l) → hw	s(l,l) → hcm	s(r,l) → l	s(u,l) → zb
Lexicon a3	s(a,l) → c	s(b,l) → v	s(c,l) → hw	s(l,l) → hcm	s(r,l) → l	s(u,l) → zb
Lexicon a4	s(a,l) → c	s(b,l) → v	s(c,l) → hw	s(l,l) → hcm	s(r,l) → l	s(u,l) → zb
Lexicon a5	s(a,l) → c	s(b,l) → v	s(c,l) → hw	s(l,l) → hcm	s(r,l) → l	s(u,l) → zb
Lexicon a6	s(a,l) → c	s(b,l) → v	s(c,l) → hw	s(l,l) → hcm	s(r,l) → l	s(u,l) → zb

Table 2. Grammar rules constructed by every agent for expressing negations (i.e., formulas of the form ¬P) in a particular simulation run

Grammar rules constructed by every agent for expressing negations: ¬P	
Agent a1	s([not, P], R) → 2, zmi, s(P,Q), {R is Q*1}
Agent a2	s([not, P], R) → 2, zmi, s(P,Q), {R is Q*1}
Agent a3	s([not, P], R) → 2, zmi, s(P,Q), {R is Q*1}
Agent a4	s([X,P],R) → 2, c2(X,S), s(P,Q), {R is S*Q*1} c2(not, X) → zmi, {X is 1}
Agent a5	s([X,P],R) → 2, c1(X,S), s(P,Q), {R is S*Q*1} c1(not, X) → zmi, {X is 1}

If the speaker can generate a sentence for the meaning it has in mind, but the hearer cannot interpret that sentence, the hearer adopts a holistic rule associating the meaning and the sentence used by the speaker. This holistic rule can be simplified and chunked later using the rest of the rules in the hearer's grammar.

In order to simplify the agents's grammars and avoid possible sources of ambiguity a mechanism for purging rules that have not been useful in past language games is introduced. Every ten language games the rules which have been used more than thirty times and have scores lower than 0.01 are removed from the agents' grammars.

EXPERIMENTS

We present the results of some experiments in which five agents **construct a shared language** that allows communicating the set of formulas of a propositional language L = {a, b, c, l, r, u} with six propositional constants.

First the agents play **10000 language games** in which they try to communicate **propositional constants**. Then they play **15000 language games** in which they try to communicate **logical formulas** constructed using unary **and binary connectives**. At the end of the first part of a typical simulation run (see table 1) all the agents prefer the same expressions (i.e., words) for referring to the propositional constants of the language L = {a, b, c, l, r, u}.

We describe now the individual **grammar built** by every agent at the end of a particular simulation run. The grammars built by the agents, although

different, are compatible enough to allow total communicative success. That is, the agents always generate sentences that are correctly understood by the other agents. The grammars of all the agents have recursive rules for expressing formulas constructed using unary and binary connectives. Agents a4 and a5 have invented a syntactic category for unary connectives (see table 2). The other agents have specific rules for formulas constructed using negation, which use the same word 'zmi' preferred by the former agents for expressing negation.

The grammar rules used for expressing negation place the word associated with the connective in the second position of the sentence. This is indicated by the number that appears in first place on the right hand side of a grammar rule. Thus the number 1 indicates that the expression associated with the connective is located in the first position of the sentence, the number 2 that it is located in the second position and the number 3 that it is located in the third position. Prolog does not allow the use of left recursive grammar rules. We use this convention thus in order to be able to represent two different types of grammar rules for unary connectives (which place the expression associated with the connective in the first and the second position of the sentence, respectively) and six different types of grammar rules for binary connectives. The induction rules (simplification and chunk) have been extended appropriately to deal with this convention.

But the position of the expression associated with a binary connective in a sentence does not determine uniquely the form of the sentence. It is necessary to specify as well the positions of the expressions associated with the arguments of the connective.

Table 3. Grammar rules constructed by every agent for expressing conjunctions (i.e., formulas of the form Y ∧ Z) in a particular simulation run

Grammar rules constructed by every agent for expressing conjunctions: Y∧Z	
Agent a1	s([and, Y, Z], T) → 2, i, s(Y,Q), s(Z,R), {T is Q*R*1}
Agent a2	s([X, Y, Z], T) → 2, c2(X,P), s(Y,Q), s(Z,R), {T is P*Q*R*1} c2(and, X) → i, {X is 1}
Agent a3	s([X, Y, Z], T) → 2, c1(X,P), s(Z,R), s(Y,Q), {T is P*Q*R*1} c1(and, X) → i, {X is 1}
Agent a4	s([X, Y, Z], T) → 2, c4(X,P), s(Y,Q), s(Z,R), {T is P*Q*R*1} c4(and, X) → i, {X is 1}
Agent a5	s([X, Y, Z], T) → 2, c2(X,P), s(Y,Q), s(Z,R), {T is P*Q*R*1} c2(and, X) → i, {X is 1}

Table 4. Grammar constructed by every agent in a particular simulation run

Grammar a1
s([not, Y], R) → 2, zmi, s(Y,Q), {R is Q*1} s([or, Y, Z], T) → 1, zc, s(Z,Q), s(Y,R), {T is Q*R*1} s([and, Y, Z], T) → 2, i, s(Y,Q), s(Z,R), {T is Q*R*1} s([if, Y, Z], T) → 2, ir, s(Z,Q), s(Y,R), {T is Q*R*1} s([X, Y, Z], T) → 1, c1(X,P), s(Y,Q), s(Z,R), {T is P*Q*R*1} c1(iff, X) → v, {X is 1}

Grammar a2
s([not, Y], R) → 2, zmi, s(Y,Q), {R is Q*1} s([or, Y, Z], T) → 1, zc, s(Z,Q), s(Y,R), {T is Q*R*1} s([if, Y, Z], T) → 2, ir, s(Z,Q), s(Y,R), {T is Q*R*1} s([X, Y, Z], T) → 2, c2(X,P), s(Y,Q), s(Z,R), {T is P*Q*R*1} c2(and, X) → i, {X is 1} s([X, Y, Z], T) → 1, c1(X,P), s(Y,Q), s(Z,R), {T is P*Q*R*1} c1(iff, X) → v, {X is 1}

Grammar a3
s([not, Y], R) → 2, zmi, s(Y,Q), {R is Q*1} s([or, Y, Z], T) → 1, zc, s(Z,Q), s(Y,R), {T is Q*R*1} s([iff, Y, Z], T) → 1, v, s(Y,Q), s(Z,R), {T is Q*R*1} s([X, Y, Z], T) → 2, c1(X,P), s(Z,Q), s(Y,R), {T is P*Q*R*1} c1(and, X) → i, {X is 1} c1(if, X) → ir, {X is 1}

Grammar a4
s([X,Y],R) → 2, c2(X,P), s(Y,Q), {R is P*Q*1} c2(not, X) → zmi, {X is 1} s([if, Y, Z], T) → 2, ir, s(Z,Q), s(Y,R), {T is Q*R*1} s([or, Y, Z], T) → 1, zc, s(Z,Q), s(Y,R), {T is Q*R*1} s([X, Y, Z], T) → 2, c4(X,P), s(Y,Q), s(Z,R), {T is P*Q*R*1} c4(and, X) → i, {X is 1} s([X, Y, Z], T) → 1, c3(X,P), s(Y,Q), s(Z,R), {T is P*Q*R*1} c3(iff, X) → v, {X is 1}

Grammar a5
s([X,Y],R) → 2, c1(X,P), s(Y,Q), {R is P*Q*1} c1(not, X) → zmi, {X is 1} s([or, Y, Z], T) → 1, zc, s(Z,Q), s(Y,R), {T is Q*R*1} s([iff, Y, Z], T) → 1, v, s(Y,Q), s(Z,R), {T is Q*R*1} s([if, Y, Z], T) → 2, ir, s(Z,Q), s(Y,R), {T is Q*R*1} s([X, Y, Z], T) → 2, c2(X,P), s(Y,Q), s(Z,R), {T is P*Q*R*1} c2(and, X) → i, {X is 1}

Figure 1. Evolution of the communicative success in experiments involving a population of five agents. In the first part of the experiment the agents play 10000 language games about atomic formulas (segment [0,1000] in the X-axis). In the second part they play 15000 language games about logical formulas constructed using unary and binary connectives (i.e., ¬, ∧, ∨, → and ↔). The second part of the experiment corresponds to segment [1001,2500] in the X-axis, i.e., to games 10001 to 25000.

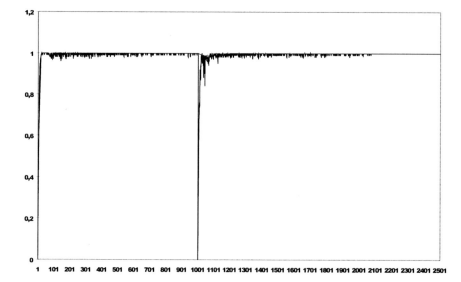

Consider the grammar rules used by agents a2 and a3 for expressing conjunctions (see table 3). Both grammar rules place the expression associated with the connective *and* in the second position of the sentence, but differ in the positions in which they place the expressions associated with the arguments of the conjunction. The grammar rule of agent a2 places the expression associated with the first argument of the connective (variable Y) in the first position of the sentence, and the expression associated with the second argument of the connective (variable Z) in the third position of the sentence. The grammar rule of agent a3 places the expression associated with the first argument of the connective (variable Y) in the third position of the sentence (observe the order in which the nonterminals s(Y,Q) and s(Z,R) appear on the right hand sides of both rules), and the expression associated with the second argument of the connective (variable Z) in the first position of the sentence. Both agents would use thus different sentences for expressing the same formula. For example, agent a2 would use the sentence 'hwizb' for expressing the formula c∧u, while agent a3 would use the sentence 'zbihw' for expressing the same formula. However this will not prevent agent a2 from understanding agent a3 and viceversa, because the formula interpreted by agent a3 after parsing the sentence 'hwizb' would be u∧c which is logically equivalent to the formula c∧u that agent a2 was trying to communicate.

Table 4 shows the grammar rules constructed by every agent at the end of a particular simulation run. It can be observed that all agents have created syntactic categories for binary connectives, although the extent of such categories in the grammars of the individual agents differs depending on the positions in which the expressions associated with the connectives and their arguments are placed in the sentence.

In order to analyze the agents' grammars it is important to distinguish between the grammar rules that are used for expressing formulas constructed with commutative connectives and the grammar rules that are used for expressing formulas constructed with non-commutative connectives. Because if two agents use the same expression to refer to a particular commutative connective and they place such an expression in the same position in the sentence, they will always understand each other correctly, even if they place the expressions associated with the arguments of such a connective in different positions in the sentence. In table 4 we can observe in fact that all agents place in the first position of the sentence the expressions associated with the connectives 'or' and 'iff', and that they use the same words ('zc' and 'v', respectively) for expressing such connectives. As we have explained already, all the agents place the expression associated with the connective 'and' in the second position of the sentence and all of them use the word 'i' for expressing it, although agents a1, a2, a4 and a5 place the expression associated with the first argument of the conjunction in the first position of the sentence, and agent a3 places the expression associated with the first argument of the conjunction in the third position of the sentence.

The positions in which the expressions associated with the arguments of non-commutative connectives are placed in a sentence determine however the meaning of the sentence. We can observe in table 4 that all agents use the word 'ir' for expressing the connective 'if', that they all place it in the second position of the sentence, and that all of them place the expressions associated with the antecedent and the consequent of an implication in the same positions (third and first, respectively) of the **sentence**.

Figure 1 shows the **evolution of the communicative** success in an experiment in which a population of five agents constructs a **shared language (a common lexicon and a grammar)** that allows them to communicate logical formulas from a propositional language with six propositional constants. The communicative success is the average of successful language games in the last ten language games played by the agents.

The agents reach total **communicative success** in 20800 language games. That is, after each agent has played on average 2000 language games about propositional constants and 2160 language games about formulas constructed using unary and binary connectives. The results shown in figure 1 are averaged over ten simulation runs with different initial random seeds.

RELATED WORK

Batali (2002) studies the emergence of recursive communication systems as the result of a process of negotiation among the members of a population. The alternative explored in this research is that learners simply store all of their analyzed observations as exemplars. No rules or principles are induced from them. Instead exemplars are used directly to convey meanings and to interpret signals.

The agents acquire their exemplars by recording observations of other agents expressing meanings. A learner finds the cheapest phrase with the observed string and meaning that can be created by combining or modifying phrases from its existing set of exemplars, creating new tokens and phrases if necessary.

As an agent continues to record learning observations, its exemplar set accumulates redundant and contradictory elements. In order to choose which of a set of alternative exemplars, or modified analyses based on them, will be used in a particular episode the cost of different solution phrases are compared, and a competition process among exemplars based on **reinforcement** and **discouragement** is established. An exemplar is reinforced when it is used in the phrase an agent constructs to record a learning observation, and it is discouraged when it is found to be inconsistent with a learning observation. Reinforcement and discouragement implement therefore a competition among groups of exemplars.

In the computational simulations described in (Batali, 2002) ten agents negotiate communication systems that enable them to accurately convey **meanings** consisting of **sets of 2 to 7 atomic formulas** (constructed from 22 unary and 10 binary predicates) which involve at most 3 different variables, after each agent has made fewer than 10000 learning observations. Each agent acquires several hundred exemplars, of which a few dozen are singleton tokens identical to those of other agents in the population.

The agents express meanings by combining their singleton tokens into **complex phrases** using the order of phrases, as well as the presence and position of empty tokens, to indicate configurations of predicate arguments. Empty tokens are also used to signal the boundaries of constituents, the presence of specific argument maps, and details of the structure of the phrases containing them.

The research presented in (Batali, 2002) addresses the problem of the emergence of recursive communication systems in populations of autonomous agents, as we do. It differs from the work described in the present chapter by focusing on learning exemplars rather than grammar rules. These exemplars have costs, as our grammar rules do, and their costs are reinforced and discouraged using self-organization principles as well. The main challenge for the agents in the experiments described in (Batali, 2002) is to construct a communication system that is capable of naming atomic formulas and, more importantly, marking the equality relations among the arguments of the different atomic formulas that constitute the meaning of a given string of characters. This task is quite different from the learning task proposed in the present chapter which focuses on categorizing propositional sentences and connectives, and marking the scope of each connective using the order of the constituents of a sentence.

Kirby (2002) studies the emergence of basic structural properties of language such as compositionality and recursion as a result of the influence of learning on the complex dynamical process of language transmission over generations. It describes computational simulations of language transmission over generations consisting of only two agents: an adult speaker and a new learner. Each generation in a simulation goes through the following steps: 1.-The speaker is given a set of meanings, and produces a set of utterances for expressing them either using its knowledge of language or by some random process of invention. 2.-The learner takes this set of the utterance-meaning pairs and uses it as input for its induction learning algorithm. 3.-Finally a new generation is created where the old speaker is discarded, the learner becomes the new speaker, and a new individual is added to become a new learner. At the start of a simulation run neither the speaker nor the learner have any grammar at all.

The **induction** algorithm thus proceeds by taking an utterance, incorporating the simplest possible rule that generates that utterance directly, searching then through all pairs of rules in the grammar for possible subsumptions until no further generalisations can be found, and deleting finally any duplicate rules that are left over. The inducer uses **merge** and **chunk** to discover new rules that subsume pairs of rules that have been learnt through simple incorporation, and **simplification** for generalising some rules using other rules that are already in the grammar.

The meaning space of the second experiment described in (Kirby, 2002) consists of **formulas constructed using 5 binary predicates, 5 objects and 5 embedding binary predicates**. Reflexive expressions are not allowed (i.e., the arguments of each predicate must be different). Each speaker tries to produce 50 degree-0 meanings, then 50 degree-1 meanings, and finally 50 degree-2 meanings. The grammar of generation 115 in one of the simulation runs has syntactic categories for nouns, verbs, and verbs that have a subordinating function. It also has a grammar rule that allows expressing degree-0 **sentences using VOS** (verb, object, subject) order, and another recursive rule that allows expressing meanings of degree greater than 0. In the ten simulation runs performed the proportion of meanings of degrees 0, 1 and 2 expressed without invention in generation 1000 is 100%.

The most important difference between our work and that presented in (Kirby, 2002) is that the latter one focusses on language transmission over generations. Rather than studying the emergence of recursive communication systems in a single generation of agents, as we do, it shows that the bottleneck established by language transmission over several generations favors the propagation of compositional and recursive rules because of their compactness and generality. In the experiments described in (Kirby, 2002) the population consists of a single agent of a generation that acts as a teacher and another agent of the following generation that acts as a learner. There is no negotiation process involved, because the learned never has the opportunity to act as a speaker in a single iteration. We consider however populations of five agents which can act both as speakers and hearers during the simulations. Having more than two agents ensures that the interaction histories of the agents are different from each other, in such a way that they have to negotiate in order to reach agreements on how to name and order the constituents of a sentence.

The induction mechanisms used in the present chapter are based on the rules for chunk and simplification in (Kirby, 2002), although we have extended them so that they can be applied to grammar rules which have scores attached to them. Finally the meaning space used in (Kirby, 2002), a restricted form of atomic formulas of second order logic, is different from the meaning space considered in the present chapter, arbitrary formulas from a propositional logic language, although both of them require the use of recursion.

CONCLUSION

This chapter has addressed the problem of the acquisition of the syntax of propositional logic by a population of autonomous agents which do not have any initial linguistic knowledge. An approach based on general purpose cognitive capacities such as invention, adoption, parsing, generation and induction, and on self-organisation mechanisms has been used.

The results of some experiments in which a population of five agents comes up with a common vocabulary and a grammar (i.e., a shared language) that allows communicating all the formulas of a propositional logic language with six propositional constants have been described. This language has a number of interesting properties found in natural languages such as word order dependence and recursion. It includes syntactic categories for propositional sentences and for different types of logical connectives. It contains as well grammatical constructions that determine the particular order in which the expressions associated with the constituents of different types of logical formulas (negations, conjunctions, disjunctions, equivalences and implications) are placed in a sentence. These word order patterns are used therefore to mark the scope of each connective in a sentence.

The experiments described in this chapter extend previous work (Sierra, 2006) by considering a larger population and a much larger search space of grammar rules. In particular the agents are allowed to order the expressions associated with the constituents of a logical formula in arbitrary order. Previous work assumed that the expressions associated with the connectives should be placed in the first position of the sentence. The branching factor

of the search space of grammar rules considered by each agent is extended thus from one to two in the case of formulas constructed using negation, and from two to six in the case of formulas constructed using binary connectives.

ACKNOWLEDGMENT

This work is partially funded by the DGICYT TIN2005-08832-C03-03 project (MOISES-BAR).

REFERENCES

Batali, J. (2002). The negotiation and acquisition of recursive grammars as a result of competition among exemplars. In T. Briscoe (Ed.), *Linguistic Evolution through Language Acquisition: Formal and Computational Models* (pp. 111-172). Cambridge University Press.

Hurford, J. (2000). Social transmission favors linguistic generalization. In C. Knight, M. Studdert-Kennedy and J. Hurford (Eds.), *The Evolutionary Emergence of Language: Social Function and the Origins of Linguistic Form* (pp. 324-352). Cambridge University Press.

Kirby, S. (2002). Learning, bottlenecks and the evolution of recursive syntax. In T. Briscoe (Ed.), *Linguistic Evolution through Language Acquisition: Formal and Computational Models* (pp. 96-109). Cambridge University Press.

McCarthy, J. (1990). *Formalizing Common Sense. Papers by John McCarthy.* Vladimir Lifschitz (Ed.), Ablex.

Piaget, J. (1985). *The Equilibration of Cognitive Structures: The Central Problem of Intellectual Development.* Chicago: University of Chicago Press.

Santibáñez, J. (1984). *Relación del rendimiento escolar en las áreas de lectura y escritura con las aptitudes mentales y el desarrollo visomotor.* Madrid: Universidad Nacional de Educación a Distancia.

Santibáñez, J. (1988). *Variables psicopedagógicas relacionadas con el rendimiento en E.G.B.* Logroño: Instituto de Estudios Riojanos.

Santibáñez, J. (1989) *La evaluación de la escritura: Test de escritura para el ciclo inicial.* Madrid: T.E.C.I. CEPE.

Sierra, J. (2001). Grounded models as a basis for intuitive reasoning. In B. Nebel (Ed.), *Proceedings of the Seventeenth International Joint Conference on Artificial Intelligence* (pp. 401-406). Morgan Kaufmann.

Sierra, J. (2001). Grounded models as a basis for intuitive reasoning: The origins of logical categories. In S. Coradeschi and A. Saffiotti (Eds.), *Papers from AAAI-2001 Fall Symposium on Anchoring Symbols to Sensor Data in Single and Multiple Robot Systems* (pp. 101-108). Technical Report FS-01-01, AAAI Press.

Sierra, J. (2002). Grounded models as a basis for intuitive and deductive reasoning: The acquisition of logical categories. In F. Harmelen (Ed.), *Proceedings of the European Conference on Artificial Intelligence* (pp. 93-97). IOS Press.

Sierra, J. (2006). Propositional logic syntax acquisition. In P. Vogt, Y Sugita, E. Tuci and C. Nehaniv (Eds.), *Symbol Grounding and Beyond* (pp. 128-142). Lecture Notes in Computer Science, volume 4211.

Steels, L. (1997). The synthetic modeling of language origins. *Evolution of Communication* 1(1), 1-35.

Steels, L. (1998). The origins of syntax in visually grounded robotic agents. *Artificial Intelligence,* 103(1-2), 133-156.

Steels, L. (1999). *The Talking Heads Experiment. Volume 1.Words and Meanings.* Antwerpen: Special Pre-edition for LABORATORIUM.

Steels, L. (2000). The emergence of grammar in communicating autonomous robotic agents. In W. Horn (Ed.), *Proceedings of the European Conference on Artificial Intelligence* (pp. 764-769). IOS Press.

Steels, L., Kaplan, F., McIntyre, A., & V Looveren, J. (2002). Crucial factors in the origins of word-meaning. In A. Wray (Ed.), *The Transition to Language* (pp. 252-271). Oxford University Press.

Steels, L. (2004). Constructivist development of grounded construction grammars. In D. Scott (Ed.), *Proc. Annual Meeting of Association for Computational Linguistics* (pp. 9-16). Association for Computational Linguistics

Steels, L. (2004). *Macro-operators for the emergence of construction grammars.* SONY Computer Science Laboratory, Paris.

Steels, L., & Wellens, P. (2006). How grammar emerges to dampen combinatorial search in parsing. In P. Vogt, Y Sugita, E. Tuci and C. Nehaniv (Eds.), *Symbol Grounding and Beyond* (pp. 76-88). Lecture Notes in Computer Science, volume 4211.

Stolcke, A. (1994). *Bayesian Learning of Probabilistic Language Models.* PhD thesis, University of California at Berkeley.

Vogt, P. (2005). The emergence of compositional structures in perceptually grounded language games. *Artificial Intelligence* 167(1-2), 206-242.

Chapter XIV
Hybrid Emotionally Aware Mediated Multiagency

Giovanni Vincenti
Gruppo Vincenti, Italy

James Braman
Towson University, USA

ABSTRACT

Emotions influence our everyday lives, guiding and misguiding us. They lead us to happiness and love, but also to irrational acts. Artificial intelligence aims at constructing agents that can emulate thinking processes, but artificial life still lacks emotions and all the consequences that come from them. This work introduces an emotionally aware framework geared towards multi-agent societies. Basing our model on the shoulders of solid foundations created by pioneers who first explored the coupling of emotions and agency, we extend their ideas to include inter-agent interaction and virtual genetics as key components of an agent's emotive state. We also introduce possible future applications of this framework in consumer products as well as research endeavors.

INTRODUCTION

We as human beings are influenced by many factors as we carry out our daily activities and routines. Emotions in particular play an important role that often provokes biased decisions. Emotion as it influences one's behavior can do so in erratic and unpredictable ways with variations between individuals and circumstances. The unpredictability of emotion based responses can lead to many variations of interaction. This would certainly apply to interactions between humans, but also to interactions

between humans and environmental artifacts and also to human-agent interactions. Decisions biased by a particular emotional state can produce erratic, impulsive or risky decision making behaviors within a given context (Loewenstein, Weber, Hsee, & Welch, 2001). If these states can cause a person to act in a potentially destructive fashion we should investigate ways to limit these effects. Various factors can contribute in eliciting such states and can be influenced by events in the environment, mental defect or disease, genetic disposition, traumatic events, social interactions or based from ones own perceptions. (Selyse & Fortier 1950; Loewenstein et al., 2001; Ohman & Wiens, 2004). Our approach is to use these behaviors and emotional models together with human and non human agents as the foundation for hybrid emotionally aware agent architecture for multiagent systems.

Due to the nature and complications associated with emotions, our aim is not to simulate complex emotional states or conditions within agents themselves, but to investigate how simple emotional simulations can be used to for a variety of purposes. Such phenomena can be modeled within a homogenous multi-agent system composed of emotionally enhanced sets of agents given both a finite set of options and emotional states. Our agents have limited abilities and actions based on their current emotional well being. Following previous experimentation with limited perceptual context for a given agent and its combined effect on understanding and formation of personal goals, we now apply emotion in limiting an agent's perception and motivational attributes (Trajkovski, Collins, Braman & Goldberg, 2006). In experimentations by Trajkovski, a hybrid interaction between human users and non-human agents can form a system that attempts to learn and adapt from each other in various conditions and contexts (2006). Emotions in our framework create a limiting heuristic that is directly associated with an agent's ability to sense and interact within the system.

The current state of an agent is derived from its ability to satisfy its drive to find "goal" locations within the environment. Similar to human behavior, an agent may become distressed or agitated if they fail at their attempts to find these simulated goals. These agents can compute the length of time that has past and/or the number of moves they have made; this compounded with the introduction of obstacles along its path will elicit a angry response as it becomes frustrated at the rise in difficulty or lack of a drive satisfier. In other cases in conjunction to these influences, agents may come into contact with others within the system. Agents in our framework however are limited to perception in a limited sensory field.

We see emotions as both a dynamic and prevailing influence over response mechanisms for an agent. Often emotions are attributed to "clouding" one's ability to make rational decisions which implies

that they have a tendency to interfere with rational thinking and our ability to interpret perceptual information (Artz, 2000). In other situations they can however be extremely useful in making certain decisions "by rapidly reducing the options that one can consider" (Greenberg, 2002). Agents (human or non-human) while working with large amounts of data or available options will want to be able to filter, select and restructure it, with least possible effort (Shneiderman, 2005). In a similar application, emotions can be used in these situations to help filter out certain options. These changes in perception and available options are areas being explored by attributing certain basic states in goal seeking agents and examining its overall consequence.

Often a human emotional response is induced by an event or an "object" that has been given meaning which is part of a particular stimulus. With various stimuli are attributed meanings which are a result of an appraisal process that derives significance to such stimuli or events (Planalp, 1999). Objects, events and interactions are interpreted by each individual agent which contributes to their particular state. Following the distinct emotional conditions established by Elkman & Friesen (1975) which identify six emotional states that are innate across cultures, which are based on facial expressions (Anger, Fear, Sadness, Disgust, Surprise and Joy) we have chosen two emotions in which to focus our research. From these basic states, anger and joy (or happiness) has been selected for this framework. These two states can be attributed to individual factors concerning the achievement of goals (Planalp, 1999).

Generally those who are in a less stressed condition or in a happier state of emotion are less inclined to make riskier judgments. People in a happier state would not wish to take actions with risky or potentially negative outcomes so as not to disrupt their current positive state (Isen, Nygren & Ashby, 1988). An angry person or someone in a "bad" mood is more likely to make poor judgments (Loewenstein et al, 2001). Anger often can influence us to act in ways that are not in our best interest (Borcherdt, 1993). Fear and anxiety often play a role in behavior patterns as one avoids the object or causal of such stress. Depression as related to stressors can also distort judgment and the interpretation of perceived information as obtained from the environment (Gotlib, 1983). We envision the application of these emotional conditions to our artificial agents and apply these concepts as a basis of our experimentation.

Agents in our experiments will be limited to emotions that range between two finite states (anger and happiness) which are based on fuzzy logic. An agent can be in any state between full happiness and complete anger where a numerical value is assigned to denote such state. We propose that each agent's range of perception and actions be limited based of their current emotional condition such that angry agents have the least options available compared to happy agents. In a broader sense we are limiting an angry agent's ability to make poor judgment while giving a happier (thus less influenced) agent more ability and control within the environment. With the simulation of these properties for each agent we investigate the possibility of emergent properties regarding inter-agent interactions.

BACKGROUND

Adding an emotional element into agent architectures is one that has been given much discussion. It is an approach that is useful in modeling certain human-human and human-agent interactions. Bates (1994) first brings up the concept that it is important for an agent to have an emotional component because humans tend to relate more to what is like them. One of the initial papers that come from this area is from research conducted by Damasio (1994). Many resulting projects were spawned after this project as individuals started working on emotional engines that resemble in many ways or at least simulate certain aspects of real life behaviors. It is important to note that there are two schools of thought when it comes to emotional engines for agents. The first incorporates the findings of Damasio (1994) into the models and tries to recreate an environment that is inspired directly by his work. The second instead creates frameworks that may take some concepts from Damasio's work, but are based on independent thinking.

Damasian Frameworks

Although many researchers have followed the steps first left by Damasio (1994), we find in the work by

Sloman (1998) the most interesting interpretation. Groups such as Ventura and Pinto-Ferreira (1998), Velásquez (1997), Gadanho and Hallam (1998) and others focus solely on the Damasio approach, Sloman (1998) focuses on a model that is created through the evolution of the capabilities of life forms through history and pre-history.

Sloman (1998) affirms that there is a need to create control systems that do not rely on a fixed architecture and changing values, but more dynamic frameworks. This idea is motivated by the fact that humans have control structures that are dynamic in nature, both at the conscious as well as unconscious level. Sloman (1998) also states that, within our minds, we have other modules, some of which deal with inputs, others with outputs, and yet others with processing information. This does not necessarily mean that each module has a different architecture and behavior, or that a single module cannot take care of multiple functions. It does mean though that the overall functionality is achieved through the interaction of multiple components.

The model created by Sloman (1998) is the summary of the analysis of several fields unrelated to robotics and agency. He bases his main notions on evolution and the adaptation of the human mind to ever-changing natural conditions. The fields of biology, philosophy, psychology and many more all contributed to the refinement of our understanding of human control modules. The first model that Sloman (1998) analyzes is the reactive model. In this particular model, which characterized many organisms through their evolution, deals with relatively simple reactions based on inputs. This model is characterized by outputs, or actions, that are generated by processes that do not take into consideration ramifications of behaviors and foresight. This means that this particular model lacks a planning module. New behaviors can be learned through positive or negative reinforcement, but they cannot be generated as an internal response to a set of conditions that recall past experiences. The motivations that drive such control mechanisms are instincts, such as hunger, fear or mating. Reactive models are also designed to work in conjunction with other organisms; great examples of such collaborative beings are insects. This model is shown in Figure 1.

The evolution of a reactive model is the addition to this system of deliberative models (Sloman, 1998).

Figure 1. First representation of the model by Sloman (1998)

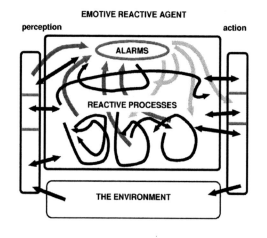

Figure 2. Second representation of the model by Sloman (1998)

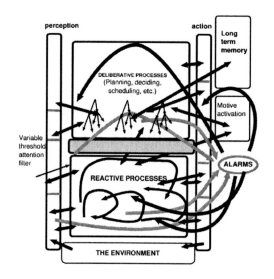

This component elaborates long-term memories and creates new plans and drives, to add to the ones built into the reactive system through evolution and conditioning. Besides a higher processing layer, this particular model requires the presence of reusable memory that can be accessed to store and retrieve information as the controller performs its functions. Sloman (1998) also affirms the necessity for a quick-response module, as careful evaluation of a situation is not always the ideal response to the environment. In dangerous situations, for example, an alarm module would take over and perform the necessary operations to place the organism back into safety, and then higher functions can process the information just received. Figure 2 shows this model.

Damasio (1994) states that there are two kinds of emotions. Primary emotions are generated by external or internal stimulations of sense organs, and secondary emotions instead are generated by the cognitive system. When compared to the deliberative model (Sloman, 1998), we can see some similarities between the emotion system described by Damasio (1994) and Sloman's alarm module. Damasio (1994) also states that secondary emotions always trigger higher cognitive reactions that, in turn, generate psychological changes. This analysis requires a slight modification of the alarm system, which should be divided into a section that deals with emergency situations as the deliberative model, and a second section that deals with similar situations, but interacts only with the deliberative, or cognitive, module (Sloman, 1998). The author compares this new component of the alarm system to the process of growing up and the acquisition of maturity, as also supported by Goleman (1994).

Sloman's proposed architecture involves the controllers discussed so far with the addition of a meta-managegement mechanism (Sloman, 1998). The meta-management process performs functions that work at a higher level compared to the other modules. Such component performs reflective kinds of elaboration, both on events and actions linked to the environment and on the internal state of the agent. Sloman (1998) affirms that, should a robot be given such a module, it may then start reflecting on the concept of "self" and "others". Moreover, this particular system may be overridden by the alarm module in certain cases, thus it may shift the focus

of the operations on other tasks or problems. Sloman (1998) also introduces the idea of tertiary emotions. These emotions are initiated purely cognitively and may or may not trigger other physical changes. For example, a state of infatuation may lead to a decreased level of attention and also sweating and tension. Figure 3 shows this last model.

Non-Damasian Frameworks

The application of Camurri and Coglio (1998), based on the model created by Camurri et al. (1997), works in a setting of the performing arts, introduces a very interesting framework that is not based directly on the work by Damasio (1994). The agent created by the researchers works by observing and being emotionally influenced by a dancer, creating as a consequence outputs of music and rhythm based on its internal emotional state.

This engine is explained in greater detail in Camurri et al. (1997) and is shown in Figure 4. A macroscopic analysis reveals several components of control. There are five active components: Input, Output, Reactive, Rational and Emotional.

The Input component is responsible for either gathering information from the environment or receiving communications from other agents or

Figure 3. Third representation of the model by Sloman (1998)

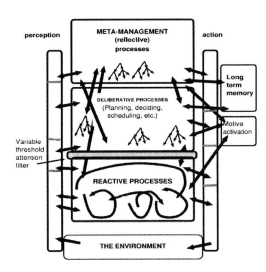

Figure 4. Model by Camurri et al. (1997)

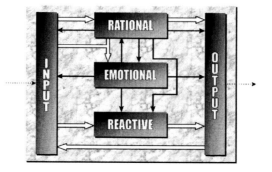

humans. In turn, it will analyze and format it as appropriate to pass on to the Reactive, Rational or Emotional components. Given the responsibility of the Input module to forward the inputs where appropriate, this component is required to access the rational and emotional states. Moreover, the Input component can also receive feedback directly from Output, thus taking also this information into consideration when relaying messages.

The Output component is responsible for creating outputs based on the agent's internal state. The outputs of this module are generated by processing the outputs of the Reactive and Rational components. Although the Emotional component does not feed the Output one directly, it will influence the calculations of the overall output by signaling the agent's emotional state to this last component. The Output component is also responsible for an internal feedback mechanism that affects the Input controller, as reported earlier.

The Reactive module is responsible for the real-time behavior of the agent, which is necessary given its application in the world of music and dance. This component collaborates closely with the Input and Output modules, and its processing is modulated by both the rational as well as the emotional state of the agent.

The Rational component maintains a view of the external world as well as one of the agent, consisting of its goal. This component has no real-time type of operations, leaving it the possibility to perform rather complex operations. This component of the agent interacts with all the other modules in several ways. Perhaps what is most important for this discussion is the role that self-awareness in relation to the goal plays in the overall emotional state of the agent. As the Rational module detects that goals are being accomplished, the emotional state of the agent increments towards a positive attitude, thus creating a better "mood" that will, in turn, affect the rest of the operations.

Finally, the Emotional component is governed by emotional stimuli generated from Input, Reaction and Rational. This module contains an emotional space. Such space is divided into several sectors that identify different emotive states. As the emotional state of the agent changes, it can be traced within this emotional space, which reveals the state of the agent.

INTRODUCTION TO THE HYBRID ARCHITECTURE

Our described architecture was original conceived as a task specific stand-alone multi-agent system described in Vincenti, Braman and Trajkovski (2007). This idea however has been expanded into a broader scope to fit multiple applications. What was once the foundation of a single system can now be adapted and applied in a plethora of situations. Figure 5 illustrates the basic framework of the system as agents processes interact with various internal components before an output or action is computed.

As this framework is designed for flexibility, various modules are utilized to encapsulate functionality and to make future changes easier to implement.

Figure 5. Hybrid emotionally aware mediated agent architecture, with F1 and F2 representing centers of information fusion

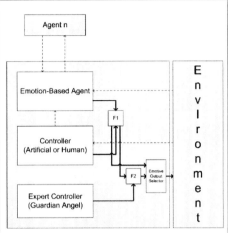

Figure 6. Architecture of the Emotion-Based Agent core

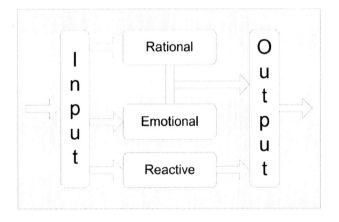

Figure 7. Detailed view of the "Emotional" module

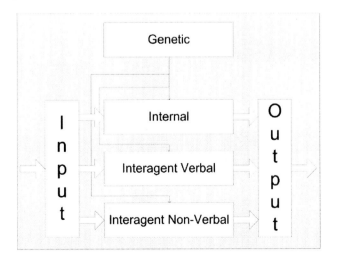

This modular approach also allows particular agents the ability to function on the emotion based engine alone, essentially bypassing other components and the F1, F2 components. As with other agent architecture, other modules can be added with little to no impact on the underlying structure. In some implementations it may be useful for the users of the system to directly interact with an agent or a set of agents without any safeguarding mechanisms in place. The Expert Controller can be bypassed in these cases and data can be sent directly to the output selector module.

Emotion-Based Agent

An essential element to the overall architecture is the Emotion-Based Agent. Each agent has the internal components described in Figure 6 where we have taken a horizontal layering approach with mediated outputs from each component. As this approach focuses on the emotional aspects of each agent, we have not included meta-cognitive states that may also influence behaviors. Adopting and modifying a framework resembling the Camurri architecture (Camurri et al., 1997) each agent discerns input percepts from its environment and makes decisions based on the totality of the inputs from each component. These components include the Rational, Emotional and Reactive modules that are inherent in each emotionally aware agent.

This model allows for direct communication between the emotional module and the output as combined with a rational influence as we believe that the emotional state of an agent should modify the range of actions. Camurri and Coglio (1998) state that, in order to implement an emotional component that evolves over time, it needs to be influenced by external events. We believe an internal component is also crucial, especially when operating in a multi-agent environment, as a corollary to Camurri and Coglio (1998). Therefore we created an elaborate Emotional module, composed of four components: Genetic, Internal, Interagent Verbal and Interagent Non-Verbal. The interaction among these components is shown in Figure 7.

The *Genetic* component of the architecture deals with assigning the associated weights for each subsequent component. These weights represent the level of influence each component has on the final output. We view this component as a way to simulate certain human characteristics of personality and behavioral differences. Some people are easily influences by others, what is said to them (either negative or positive reactions) while other have tendencies of emotional instability. This architecture provides us a mechanism to model some of these behaviors as its influence on other components.

The *Internal* component analyzes information about the agent and elaborates the emotional state. An example of such analysis may be the time elapsed in the simulation, with the agent unable to either find clues or reach the overall goal. As time goes on, the morale of the agent may lower. The rate at which the morale of the agent is affected by internal events is dictated by its genetic predisposition.

The *Interagent Verbal* component instead relies on communications with other agents in order to influence the mood. Communications between agents will consist of clues that they will pass along. Each clue will be dictated by where the agent "believes" the goal is. Along with the belief, there is a weight assigned to the communication. The weight indicates the emotional state of the agent that is communicating the information. The agent will then internalize both the belief as well as the emotional state of the other agent. The emotive component of the communication will affect the agent's own emotional state at a rate dictated by the genetic component.

The *Interagent Non-Verbal* component relies on the concept that, in society, it is often easy to be able to guess what mood a person is in by simply looking at them. Our agents do not only advertise their emotional state through communications, but also visually. When an agent senses the presence of other agents and interacts, this component will analyze and read the apparent emotional state of its peers. Also in this case, the rate at which the agent will internalize emotions is set by the genetic component.

Interfacing the Human and the Artificial Agent

The coupling of the human and the agent happens through direct interaction between the interfaces of the two agents. The interface is based on the notion of an emergent coupling interaction occurring between them. The interface between these agents abstractly is mediation itself. The non-human agent in the system learns from its interactions with the human agent while utilizing its own knowledge about the current situation and building on its previous knowledge. The interface between them is non-invasive and as natural as possible to create a dynamic and adaptable system where each agent can learn and adjust from various forms of interaction. The impact of the coupling process to the emotion based agent and the controller agent is interpreted and sent as output for use in the meditation 1 module labeled F1 (Figure 5). The parameters that are passed to the mediation one module are derived by: 1. The Emotion based agent senses environmental conditions and various input from the human user (or other agents). 2. The human or controller agent generates data by its interaction with the emotional agent and through its actions caused by interpretations of the environment.

The interface between the emotionally enhanced agent and the human user can be accomplished in several ways. First we can view the emotion-based agent as a meta-agent or a leader agent in a multi-agent system of emotionally enhanced set of agents. In this case the multi-agent system itself is the interface between the human user and the meta-agent, of which both becomes part of the multi-agent system itself. Each agent interacts with other agents or the environment collecting data to be interpreted by the meta-agent whose main goal is to understand the interactions and intentions of the human. Using a multi-agent approach to the interface allows us design flexibility on how data is collected and interpreted by the emotion based agent. In a real world setting, implementing a system based on ubiquitous computing strategies would allow for agents to be deployed in multiple locations surrounding the user while remaining transparent to normal everyday functions. The human user would not need to know the state of the multi-agent system composed of ubiquitous devices. Each agent would interact with other agents either wirelessly or in a wired network fashion, while collaborating with the Meta-Agent (Emotional-Based Agent) about the data is collecting on its human subject.

Yet another possible solution is to use direct input into the system such as text, graphical manipulations, or other detectable hardware input

that the system can process. Following previous research conducted with coupling interfaces using simple virtual environments (Trajkovski, Collins, Braman, Goldberg, 2006) we proposed a system where an individual agent and human user coupled collectively to form a multi-agent system where the non-human agent attempts to learn from human input. Depending on the need such human input can be collected directly from physical data manipulations or hardware input (i.e. keyboard, mouse, joystick, steering wheel, break/gas pedals, VR gloves etc.). Input would then drive a simple subsumption architecture where agents would act accordingly in an attempt to learn and react to the human user while actively collaborating with the main Emotional-Agent.

F1

The Fusion one (F1) module is an averaging process that fuses output from both the Emotion based Agent and the human controller as base parameters. The process of which the data is sampled from both agents is dependant on the interface option that was selected for the particular problem domain. This module outputs data to the Fusion two (F2) and to the Emotive output selector. The Emotional based Agent makes decisions based on its own emotional state and from what it senses from the environment and the human user. The averaging of these two outputs are useful because they allow for a equal weighted approach to the decision making process. For example of both agents are "angry" then logically there should be some stressor to both agents for this to occur and we can say that there is a good reason for this emotional state. An "angry" decision made by the human user in this case may be justified and allowed. In contrast if one agent is very happy and the other is very angry then there is some problem in one or the others interpretation of environmental conditions or perhaps there is some underlying internal condition that is cause the emotion. If only the non-human agent is angry or stressed while the human agent is happy, perhaps the human agent in its positive state has failed to detect important environmental conditions. If a multi-agent system approach is being used them there may be an issue in the system itself during the interacting of the agents that have caused extra stress. Averaging the output from both of these agents helps to correct any major differences in emotional states by essentially compromising on a final decision. If the outputs from both agents are similar then outcomes will be relatively equal in control. If output is significantly different then the output is averaged to a mediated outcome.

Expert Controller

The Expert controller serves as a balancing and safe-guarding mechanism for the overall output of the system. This control mechanism serves as a process that mediates the output from the emotionally biased output from the other agents with its own non-biased output. Other agents in the system are influenced by internal and external emotional states whereas the Expert Controller is not. When external percepts are needed by the controller (when internal schemas alone are not sufficient) the Expert controller in a reactive or utility based fashion makes logical deductions for its output. All output from the Expert Controller is directed into the Fusion two module where it is mediated with the results of the Fusion one module.

F2

The second process that fuses inputs into a single, coherent output (F2) is based on the Fuzzy Mediation model by Vincenti and Trajkovski (2007a). This method is based on the evaluation of the absolute difference between inputs of an expert controller and a novice one. The outcome of this algorithm is a single mediated value to be passed on to the object to be controlled.

This mediation will assume that the expert controller process is the expert, and the output of the first fusion is the value generated by the novice one. Fuzzy Mediation functions in three steps.

The first step, analysis of the inputs, evaluates the difference between two inputs, in our case the outcome of the first mediation and the direction that the expert controller computes. The deviation is then translated into a linguistic modifier, chosen from a series of fuzzy sets. A typical breakdown of the numeric range of possible deviations may include the following modifiers: "Similar control", "Slight deviation" and "Wide deviation".

The second step involves the revision of the weight of control. As the two controllers perform

Table 1. Mamdani inference rules

If	Then
Inputs are similar	Shift control to the novice
Inputs are slightly different	Maintain the balance unaltered
Inputs are widely different	Shift control to the expert

Figure 8. Interaction between fusion processes and the emotive output selector

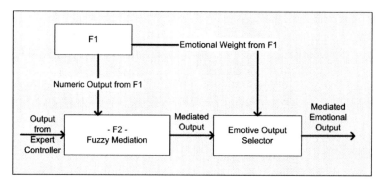

Figure 9. Three levels of agent directionality (In order: Happy State, Normal State and Angry State)

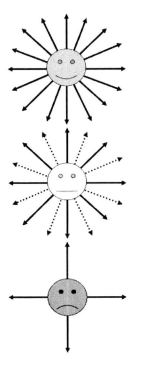

in similar ways, more control is given to the novice. Instead, as the controllers show a wide deviation in the desired direction of the agent, the expert regains control, overriding the weight accumulated by the novice controller. The action taken to modify control is based on the linguistic modifier associated with the deviation found in the first step, and is based on a set of Mamdani-style rules (Mamdani & Assilian, 1975) such as the ones shown in Table 1.

The final step of Fuzzy Mediation is the calculation of the single output. Such value is computed using the formula shown below:

$$MO = \mu T * EI + \mu t * NI$$

where MO is the mediated output, μT and μt refer to the weights of control assigned to the expert (μT) and the novice (μt), and finally EI and NI are the original inputs originated by the expert (EI) and the novice (NI).

Previous studies (Vincenti & Trajkovski, 2006; Vincenti & Trajkovski, 2007a; Vincenti & Trajkovski, 2007b) have shown the validity of this

Figure 10. Fuzzy Sets Representing Emotive States

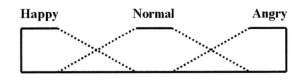

algorithm. In situations where the novice is unable to deal with the situation presented at all, the expert gains full control of the object. On the other hand, as the controllers perform more similarly, Fuzzy Mediation allows the novice to control the object without any interference from the expert.

When operating in this setting, the second fusion will take as inputs the directional outputs from the first fusion and the expert controller process. The single-value output represents the mediated heading of the agent. Figure 8 shows the flow of information and interaction between fusion processes and the emotive output selector.

It is important to note that, although the first fusion outputs both a <direction> and a <emotive state> value, the second fusion utilizes only the <direction> element. The <emotive state> will be used by the Emotive Output Selector for the computation of the final output.

Emotive Output Selector

Our model is based on the notion that the ability of each individual agent is limited by its current level of emotional context. This means that a happy agent has an increased number of options in comparison to an angry agent. Happier agents will have a greater ability to explore due to the enhanced number of available directions. This limitation in capabilities extends to all agents; in a goal-seeking simulation agents are limited no matter their current exploration role or mode.

As shown in Figure 9, a happy agent has sixteen possible movements. An agent that is in a transitional state has at least eight (N,S,E,W,NE,NW,SE,SW) and depending on the transitional status into another emotional state may have one or more or the directional capabilities as denoted by the dashed lines. The amount of these extra directions is based on how far the transition has progressed to the next state (see Figure 10); the particular directions that are chosen from the given set are chosen at random. An agent in an angry state shown at the bottom of Figure 9 is limited to only movements only in the four cardinal directions. We see this limitation on ability tied to that of emotion and motivation where an agent that is happier is more motivated thus having more options available.

Anger can be said to be closely related to that of depression (Pelusi, 2006). We also see this in a wider scope and relate depression with that to a lessening of motivation in agents. It has also been observed in human subjects with depressive disorders that their cognitive flexibility is reduced due to emotional instability and negative thought patterns leading to reduced solutions to given problems. (Deveney & Deldin, 2006). Applying this to agent interactions we have limited the actions and perception of angry agents.

The emotive output selector represents the last level of processing that the data will undergo before being fed to the agent, which will respond by turning to the final heading. The inputs for this module are represented by the <direction> computed by the second fusion and the <emotive state> from the first fusion, as shown in Figure 8. The emotive state will be mapped to the sets shown in Figure 10. Each emotive state will have a set of actions, which may be represented as a greater or lesser possibility of directions, as shown in Figure 9. The output from the second mediation will then be standardized to the closest available direction, based on the ones available.

For example, if the mediated output directs the agent at a heading of 44°, the agent in a "Normal" state may have the range of motion {0°, 45°, 90°, 135°, 180°, 225°, 270°, 315°}, thus standardizing the output to 45°. If, instead, the agent is in an "Angry" state, with an associated range of motions {0°, 90°, 180°, 270°}, the final output will be standardized to a heading of 0°.

In the case of the emotional state being mapped to two sets, then the agent will have at its avail a number of possible headings that is dependent on which emotive state is closest to. So, if the emotive state leans more towards a "Normal" state than a "Happy" state, although it will not have the range of motions associated with "Happy", it will have the ones available to "Angry" and then a portion (chosen randomly) of the ones additionally available with the next emotive state.

THE AGENT AND ITS ENVIRONMENT

During an agent's exploration of the environment it will traverse the environment in either two modes: 1) Traveling and 2) Exploration. In traveling mode agents simply traverse the space within the limitations of their emotional state as it applies to their ability to move. An agent may switch to exploration mode if an object, goal or other agent falls within the sensing layer of their perception (see Figure 11).

If an object is detected within this sphere an

Figure 11. Structure of the agent

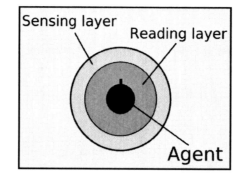

Figure 12. Depiction of the original environment

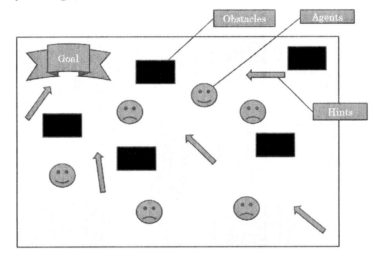

agent may switch from simply traversal, but to an exploration state so that the agent may investigate the type of sensed object. If an obstacle is detected the agent may simply move to avoid it or follow a path around it to continue in a particular direction. If a goal is detected then it may record this event. If another agent is detected it will attempt to communicate with the detected agent. Limitations in the agents mobility based on their emotional state may make such activities more difficult.

The environment in which the agents will operate is shown in Figure 12.

This environment is suitable for this kind of research for several reasons. First, it allows enough room for agents to be isolated. Studying group behaviors entails analyzing both faces of the coin by reviewing how agents interact as they are operating as a group, as well as individually. Then, it allows for clues to point to the goal, with the interruption caused by obstacles that may be on the way. This concept was inspired by the thought of a driver who can see the destination of her/his journey (such as a tall building in a city), but who needs to navigate through complex paths to reach it (as if driving through intricate one-way streets in order to reach the tall building). These hints are built into the environment. After the initial observations, we will allow agents to leave trails of hints that indicate a path that will subsequently lead to the goal, as introduced by Dabirsiaghi and Trajkovski (2006).

CONCLUSION

This framework can be extended into several domains as each agent can be applied to the components of the system to be modeled. One of the first visions of applicability is applying these agents into human assistive devices or utilizing them as interface based agents. One particular example involves agents that restrict menu functionality or security access to certain functions of the interface or program. As previously noted, users in certain emotional conditions may not be best suited to make critical unbiased decisions. If the interface automatically adjusts in limiting key components it would restrict the human user from taking actions that may have a negative impact or one in which he/she would later regret. We see an interface that adjusts to the user's emotional level to provide automatically the best displays and choices as to maximize their efforts. The human element of emotion in interface design is often overlooked. Consider an angry employee with a particularly high level of access or administration rights or an individual that may have access to key financial functions. An emotional driven interface could automatically account for these emotional contexts and shift the user's access to a lower and safer level at which they would be unable to take risky actions without consent from another user or authority figure. It is known that many employees purposely put the goals of a company in jeopardy if they themselves are angry and feel vengeful towards their employer or even may involve themselves in a computer based crime in an attempt to "get even" (Quigley, 2002).

Motor vehicles could also benefit from this type of technology as agents can be imbedded in areas of the vehicles and work together with the human driver. The safety of the passengers would be the goal of the system of agents where sensed input from the environment can be mediated with driver interactions and the expert controller. Road rage as an emotional related safety issue is often is related to anger and aggression on part of the driver (Depasquale et al, 2001). Emotionally aware agents could interpret aggressive responses from the human user and adjust to correct for these behaviors limiting the humans abilities based on the emotional context of the situation. Taking away the ability to accelerate to high dangerous speeds is one such example.

This chapter summarizes the basic framework for our investigation of the effects of emotional states of agents in a multi-agent system. We have also discussed the foundations of the theoretical background that supports the rationale of the project as well as future applications that can be derived from experimentations.

We believe that this approach explores concepts that were so far left unattended in the domain of agency. First of all, we take into consideration a genetic component that directs the inner workings of the emotional state. As a second focal point of this research, we believe that it is important to keep in mind that emotional states dictate the range of options of action that we have available.

FUTURE WORK

Our long term goals of this project include further variations in implementation strategies and several experiments with these agents in different environment types. One such variation on agent cooperation is to utilize some rational-state mechanism where agents can learn areas of the environment where goals are likely to be found. Goals, once found can be removed from the space and relocated at random,

or the agent itself is removed and a new reinitialized agent is placed. Differences in communication mechanisms are another aspect that can be evaluated in this context. If an agents communication module is associated and influenced by the emotional state, how with this effect agent-agent interaction in terms of cooperation? An agent's propensity to communicate with other agents may be a function of its emotion. An angry agent (or shy, mal informed, "genetically damaged") may not be willing to communicate or cooperate with any other agents thus will also decrease the abilities of the individual agent and the team. Angry agents may also have a sharp decrease in its veracity and more prone to communicate false information.

Looking at social aspects of emotional agency we also will be conducting experiments that account for various group dynamics. We find such simulations useful for understanding human-human interactions by looking at emotion based agents in dynamic environments. We plan to demonstrate the combined effects of emotion when the agents are divided into various teams and are in competition with other agents. Will opposing agents frustrate others by conveying misleading and false information to opposing agents? Will frustrations affect the entire team? Will they affect both teams if frustrations propagate throughout the whole system? Competing teams may have a sub-goal to purposely mislead opposing agents with false information or coordinate activities that hinder the efforts of the other team in their own effort to seek a goal.

In future projects we may allow for agents to reproduce and possibly transmit information or "genetic" materials from parent to child agent. From these types of simulations we can also attempt to reproduce several symptoms of certain disorders in a way in which they can be controlled. Several complex models will need to be developed in order to accurately simulate such conditions.

We also plan to investigate the effects of environmental change, inter-agent interaction issues and various internal frustrations as elements that can adversely affect, change or disrupt agent emotional states and how the individual elements impact the multi-agent system itself. The potential of emergent behaviors seem promising within these emotion based simulation.

REFERENCES

Artz, J. (2000). The Role of Emotion in Reason and its Implications for Computer Ethics. *Computers and Society*, 14-16.

Bates, J. (1994). The Role of Emotion in Believable Agents. *Communications of the ACM*, 37(7): 122-125.

Borcherdt, B. (1993) *You Can Control Your Feelings*. Professional Resource Press. Sarasota, Florida.

Camurri, A. & Coglio, A. (1998) An Architecture for E-motional Agents. *Multimedia*, 5(4): 24-33.

Camurri, A., Coglio, A., Coletta, P. & Massucco, C. (1997). An Architecture for Multimodal Environment Agents. *Proceedings of the International Workshop Kansei: Technology of Emotion*, 48-53.

Dabirsiaghi, A. & Trajkovski, G. (2006). Navigational Map Learning by Context Chaining and Abstraction. *2006 Fall AAAI Symposium*. October 12-15, 2006. Arlington, VA. USA.

Damasio, A. (1994). *Descartes' Error – Emotion, Reason, and the Human Brain*. New York, NY: Putnam Book.

Depasquale, J., Geller, S., Clarke, S. & Littleton, L. (2001). Measuring Road Rage: Development of the Propensity for Angry Driving Scale. *Journal of Safety Research*, 32(1): 1-16.

Deveney, C. & Deldin, P. (2006) A Preliminary Investigation of Cognitive Flexibility for Emotional Information in Major Depressive Disorder and Non-Psychiatric Controls. *Emotion*. 2006 Aug, 6(3): 429-37.

Elkman, P. & Friesen, W. (1975). *Unmasking the face*. Englewood Cliffs, NJ: Prentice Hall.

Gadanho, S. & Hallam, J. (1998). Exploring the role of emotions in autonomous robot learning. In Cañamero, D., ed., *Emotional and Intelligent: The Tangled Knot of Cognition*, Menlo Park, CA: AAAI Press.

Goleman, D. (1994). *Emotional Intelligence*. New York, NY: Bantam Dell.

Gotlib, I. (1983). Perception and Recall of Interpersonal Feedback: Negative Bias in Depression. *Cognitive Therapy and Research*, 7(5): 399-412.

Greenberg, L. (2002) *Emotion-focused Therapy: Coaching Clients to Work through Their Feelings*. Washington, DC : American Psychological Association.

Isen, A., Nygren, T. & Ashby, G. (1988). Influence of Positive Affect on the Subjective Utility of Gains and Losses: It Is Just Not Worth the Risk. *Journal of Personality and Social Psychology*, 55(5): 710–717.

Loewenstein, G., Weber, E., Hsee, C. & Welch, N. (2001). Risk as Feelings. The American Psychological Association. *Psychological Bulletin*, 127(2): 267-286.

Mamdani, E. & Assilian S. (1975) An experiment in linguistic synthesis with a fuzzy logic controller. International Journal of Man-Machine Studies, 7(1), 1-13.

Ohman, A. & Wiens, S. (2004). The Concept of an Evolved Fear Module and Cognitive Theories of Anxiety. In Manstead A, Frijda, N, Fischer, A (Eds.), *Feelings and Emotions, The Amsterdam Symposium*. Cambridge, UK: Cambridge University Press.

Pelusi, N. (2003, November 1). Anger, pain, and depression. *Psychology Today*. Retrieved from http://www.psychologytoday.com/

Phanalp, S. (1999) *Communicating Emotion. Social, Moral and Cultural Processes*. Cambridge, UK: Cambridge University Press.

Quigley, A. (2002). Inside job. *netWorker, 6*(1), 20-24.

Selyse H. & Fortier C. (1950). Adaptive reaction to stress. *Psychosomatic Medicine*, 12: 149–57.

Shneiderman, B. & Plaisant, C. (2005). *Designing the user interface. Strategies for effective human-computer Interaction*. University of Maryland, College Park. Addison Wesley.

Sloman, A. (1998). Damasio, Descartes, Alarms and Meta-management. *Proceedings of the IEEE International Conference on Systems, Man, and Cybernetics*, 2652-2657.

Trajkovski, G., Collins, S., Braman J. & Goldberg, M. (2006). Coupling Human and Non-Human Agents. *The AAAI Fall Symposium: Interaction and Emergent Phenomena in Societies of Agents.* Arlington, VA.

Velásquez, J. (1997). *Modeling emotions and other motivations in synthetic agents.* Proceedings of AAAI-97.

Ventura, R. & Pinto-Ferreira, C. (1999). *Emotion-based agents.* Workshop of the Third International Conference on Autonomous Agents.

Vincenti, G., Braman, J. & Trajkovski, G. (2007). Emotion-Based Framework for Multi-Agent Coordination and Individual Performance in a Goal-Directed Environment. *2007 Fall AAAI Symposium.* Arlington, VA. USA.

Vincenti, G. & Trajkovski, G. (2006). Fuzzy Mediation for Online Learning in Autonomous Agents. *2006 Fall AAAI Symposium.* October 12-15, 2006. Arlington, VA. USA.

Vincenti, G. & Trajkovski, G. (2007a). Fuzzy Mediation as a Dynamic Extension to Information Fusion. *Fusion 2007.* July 9-12, 2007. Quebec, Canada.

Vincenti, G. & Trajkovski, G. (2007b). Analysis of Different Mediation Equations and Tightness of Control to Finely Regulate the Exchange of Control Between Expert and Novice Controllers in a Fuzzy Mediation Environment. *2007 Fall AAAI Symposium.* Arlington, VA. USA.

Chapter XV
Mapping Hybrid Agencies Through Multiagent Systems

Samuel G. Collins
Towson University, USA

Goran Trajkovski
Laureate Education Inc., USA

ABSTRACT

In this chapter, we give an overview of the results of a Human-Robot Interaction experiment, in a near zero-context environment. We stimulate the formation of a network joining together human agents and non-human agents, in order to examine emergent conditions and social actions. Human subjects, in teams of three to four, are presented with a task–to coax a robot (by any means) from one side of a table to the other–not knowing with what sensory and motor abilities the robotic structure is equipped. On the one hand, the "goal" of the exercise is to "move" the robot through any linguistic or paralinguistic means. But, from the perspective of the investigators, the goal is both broader and more nebulous–to stimulate any emergent interactions whatsoever between agents, human or non-human. Here we discuss emergent social phenomena in this assemblage of human and machine, in particular, turn-taking and discourse, suggesting (counter-intuitively) that the "transparency" of non-human agents may not be the most effective way to generate multi-agent sociality.

INTRODUCTION

One strand of research in Artificial Intelligence (AI) in general and multiagent systems (MAS) research in particular has been concerned with the simulation of extant life–genetic algorithms, neural nets, ethological simulations like swarming, etc. Another strand (less popular since its zenith in the early 1990s) explores the possibility that artificial agents might themselves constitute a kind of life (Helmreich, 1998; Langdon, 1995). There have been countless insights over the past three decades in AI and cognitive science in general that have hinged upon isomorphisms between these two "phyla": the biological, on the one hand, and the machinic, on the other, with great insights into, say, mirror neurons (on the biological side) and genetic algorithms (on the machine) side, generated by cross-experiments.

All of these, however, ignore the extant to which humans and non-humans together are imbricated in a kind of "second-nature" where nature, machine and human are connected together in complex, mutually constitutive ways, precisely what Deleuze and Guattari (1980) invoke in their conception of "machinic assemblage," the temporary coming-together of heterogeneous elements linked not by filiation but by transformation, an "unnatural participation" that links the human and the non-human.

In other words, defining "humans" and "machines" so as to emulate one with the other may be ontologically problematic when the two are multiply interpenetrated in the first place. In Human-Computer Interaction (HCI) and Human-Robot Interaction (HRI), researchers attempt to accommodate machines to human needs, creating, for example, "socially acceptable" robots for future, human interaction (Koay et al, 2006). But these kinds of interventions are premised on an unchanging human to which non-human agents might be compared.

Our research looks at our cyborg present–a world where acting "human" always already involves machinic practice (Collins, 2007; Trajkovski, 2007). For us, the question in HCI is not to better accommodate non-human agents to humans by more effective "interfaces" better emulating human behavior but to maximize our existing cyborg lives–the bodily hexis, communications, socialities and cultural schema that proliferate in the interstices of the human and the machine.

BACKGROUND

In the following chapter, we report on a series of ongoing experiments involving human agent-non-human agent interaction. In these, we consider the human-robot as our proper object, and the actions of all involved agents as formative of a temporary, shifting, cognitive, social and cultural network. These interactions, we argue, can be considered properly social and, in the Durkheimian sense, emergent, that is, not explicable at the level of the individual agent (Sawyer, 1991). In this, we draw upon synergistic insights from a variety of academic disciplines–AI, cybernetics, cognitive science, science studies, cultural studies and anthropology, each examining the cyborg from a slightly different

perspective. All of them, though, might be said to engage cybernetics, and in particular the "second generation" cybernetics of Humberto Maturana and Francisco Varela (1980). Looking to "autopoietic" systems (literally, systems that make themselves), Maturana and Varela undermined dichotomies of subject and object by focusing on the way that organisms "structurally couple" to their environments, that is, not so much adapting to them as producing them in the course of recursively producing themselves. It is the system itself that is generative of change, rather than some objective reality outside of it. By the 1990s, Varela (1999:48) had extended these insights into autopoeitic systems to more open systems, including human perception itself, describing, for example, vision as "emergent properties of concurrent subnetworks, which have a degree of independence and even anatomical separability, but cross-correlate and work together so that a visual percept is this coherency."

Applying this to HCI means, ultimately, questioning the extent to which action should be most usefully considered first and foremost a product of human intention and, instead, leading us to a model of cognition and social life that arises out of the interaction of a heterogeneity of agents. This is what Michael Woolridge (2002:105) means when he reminds us that "There's no such thing as a single agent system." The strength of cybernetics and multiagent systems research is precisely this radical deconstruction of the Leibnizian monad for models of life that focus less on the "molar" than on the traffic between agencies.

This, we believe, has its philosophic appeal, but this is not our primary reason for enjoining this research; moving to this dynamic, networked model of HCI promises to move us beyond unproductive abstractions ("the human") to real, empirical understandings of humans living in and through their machine worlds (as well as machines "machining" through their human worlds). That is, ultimately (and contrary to the etymology), these approaches gesture towards a more anthropological (and sociological) approach to the study of cyborg lives, implicit in Gregory Bateson's (1972:318) parable: *"Consider a man felling a tree with an axe. Each stroke of the axe is modified or corrected, according to the shape of the cut face of the tree left by the previous stroke. This self-corrective (i.e., mental) process is brought about by a total system, trees-eyes-brain-muscles-axe-stroke-tree; and it is this total system that has the characteristics of immanent mind.''*

The material world around us is, through processes of externalization and sublation, alternately appears as part of an objective outside, or a subjective inside, but the lines between the two are continuously negotiated in the course of daily life. It is a short step from this central insight to a full-blown "cyborg anthropology" that, as Downey, Dumit and Williams (2000:344) explain, holds "that machines and other technologies are attributed agency in the construction of subjectivities and bounded realms of knowledge."

But it would be equally misleading to represent these emergent cyborgs as bounded entities, i.e., simply expanding reified notions of the subject to include that subject's machines. This is the mistake that Dobashi (2005:233) makes in a study of Japanese housewives and keitai (cellular phones). Rejecting a determinist framework where "housewives" and "cell phones" are considered as discrete entities, Dobashi looks instead "to the simultaneous development of both processes into one undividable entity." But this "cyborgification of housewives" (233) is equally flawed, simply substituting "human + machine" for "human," augmenting the human with the non-human, the non-human with the human. The more productive direction would be to see these networks unfolding in time, bringing together multiple agents in temporary communication; that

is, we may be embedded in machinic networks, but to hypostatize their dynamic heterogeneity would be to replace one metaphysics with another.

What we mean (or should mean) by "cyborgification" is something much more shifting and protean–part of the exciting promise of the cyborg is, after all, the possibility of novel ways of thinking and acting. To this we look to the "actor-network theory" (ANT) that examines just such sites of "hybridity," i.e., those complex translations between humans and nonhumans that momentarily coalesce into novel forms before dispersing into other systems. This is Latour's "network", not to be confused with the more static configurations of routers and servers.

THE EXPERIMENT

In the following experiment, we stimulate the formation of a network joining together human agents and non-human agents in order to examine emergent conditions and social actions. 4-5 volunteers drawn from undergraduate anthropology and cultural studies classes, after giving informed consent, were presented with a task: to coax a robot (by any means) from one side of a table to the other.

Carol, a robot built in the Cognitive Agency and Robotics Laboratory (CARoL) was used in these experiments. The basic microcontroller that we use to control our robots in CARoL is Acroname's

Figure 1. Carol, the robot used in the experiments, and its relevant components

Palm Pilot

BrainStem

Sonar

Sonar's servo

Servo

Table 1. The menu implemented in the program of the robot for the second iteration

Position of first obstacle (sonar facing forward)	Side the sonar moves to	Second obstacle	Robot moves
Close (≤6 inches)	Left	Close	Forward
		Far	Forward
		Too Far	Reset
Far (6-12 inches)	Right	Close	Left
		Far	Right
		Too Far	Reset
Too far > 2 inches	Reset menu		

Table 2. Statistics on talking in the first iteration

		Frequency	%	Valid %	Cumulative %
Valid	talk team social	2	1.9	6.5	6.5
	talk robot order	28	27.2	90.3	96.8
	talk robot social	1	1.0	3.2	100.0
	Total	31	30.1	100.0	
Missing	System	72	69.9		
Total		103	100.0		

Table 3. Statistics on movements in the first iteration

		Freq	%	Valid %	Cumulative %t
Valid					
	hand front	20	19.4	27.8	27.8
	hand side	10	9.7	13.9	41.7
	hand back	4	3.9	5.6	47.2
	gesturing	4	3.9	5.6	52.8
	moving position	2	1.9	2.8	55.6
	rotate left	5	4.9	6.9	62.5
	rotate right	6	5.8	8.3	70.8
	move forward	6	5.8	8.3	79.2
	move back	13	12.6	18.1	97.2
	rotate confused/twitch	2	1.9	2.8	100.0
	Total	72	69.9	100.0	
Missing	System	31	30.1		
Total		103	100.0		

BrainStem, The BrainStem is a microcontroller that is supported by various operating systems. Each module can operate as a slave device, run concurrent C-like programs (in a programming language called TEA) and handle reflexive actions automatically. The usefulness of this module is linked to its capability for controlling multiple analog and digital sensors. In addition, the BrainStem can operate up to four servos, which allows it to be used in a multitude of operations.

The BrainStem can be controlled through two programs: the Console and GP. These programs have the ability to control movement and sensor readings, help in debugging, uploading files, and executing reflexes. This platform works well with PalmOS-based PDAs, which we use for expanding the computational and storage power of the basic BrainStem unit. The robot used for these experiments is shown in Figure 1. The experiment uses its two servos for movement of the tracks (left and right track), and another one to move the sonar sensor that is mounted for obstacle detection. The control is hosted on the Palm Pilot on top of the robotic structure.

For the first iteration, Carol was programmed to execute a simple obstacle avoidance program. When the sonar detects an obstacle within its range, it backs up, and scans for obstacles 90 degrees to the left and 90 degrees to the right with its sonar. Afterwards, it either turns full left of full right, depending on which side the farthest obstacle is detected at the time of the sonar scan. In order for the robot to start moving, it needs to detect an obstacle very close to its sonar (a hand movement in front of it would start the program). Initially, the robot is placed on the table in such a way that its axis of movement is at a 45 degree angle with the edges of the table that it is placed on.

For the second iteration of the experiment, we emulated a 2-level menu to control the movements

Table 4. Talking during second iteration

		Freq.	%	Valid %	Cumulative %
Valid					
	talk team strat.	30	13.0	36.1	36.1
	talk team social	18	7.8	21.7	57.8
	talk robot order	21	9.1	25.3	83.1
	talk robot social	14	6.1	16.9	100.0
	Total	83	35.9	100.0	
Missing	System	148	64.1		
Total		231	100.0		

Table 5. Relevant movements during second iteration

		Freq.	%	Valid %	Cumulative %
Valid					
	hand front	42	18.2	28.4	28.4
	hand side	40	17.3	27.0	55.4
	hand back	4	1.7	2.7	58.1
	tapping/snapping	10	4.3	6.8	64.9
	gesturing	1	.4	.7	65.5
	moving position	2	.9	1.4	66.9
	rotate left	27	11.7	18.2	85.1
	move forward	14	6.1	9.5	94.6
	rotate confused/twitch	8	3.5	5.4	100.0
	Total	148	64.1	100.0	
Missing	System	83	35.9		
Total		231	100.0		

of the robot. The menu details are given in Table 1. When the sonar registers an obstacle within 12 inches from it, it evaluates whether it is in the 0-6 or 6-12 inch region, and turns left of right. Depending on whether the next obstacle is close or far, it executes a command. When the obstacle is further than 12 inches, after 10 seconds, the menu resets.

Volunteers were given no information on the robot's programming or sensors. And yet, this is not exactly a "0-context" experiment. On the one hand, the "goal" of the exercise is to "move" the robot through any linguistic or paralinguistic means.

But, from the perspective of the investigators, the goal is both broader and more nebulous: to stimulate any emergent interactions whatsoever between agents, human or non-human.

Of course, this begs the question of the observer, a problem that Hayles (1999) has identified as the most pressing legacy of first-generation cybernetics. Are things "objectively" interesting or emergent, or are they only this way from a given perspective? For Francisco Varela et al (1991:172), this need not lead to solipsism; cognitive categories like colors exist neither wholly "outside" nor "inside" the perceiving agent. For Latour, the observer and the observed form part of "network" enabling the production of facts. As Jan Harris (2005:169) summarizes,

Thus rather than a polarity of a subject and object in which the former, via the methodology of natural science, attains knowledge of the latter, we have a network of 'circulating' references or translations. The objects of the field imply the facts of the laboratory, likewise these facts return us to the field. What is important, then, is neither brute objects nor the incorporeal facts that express them, but the processes

Figure 2. Path covered by the robot in movement in generic distance units, first iteration

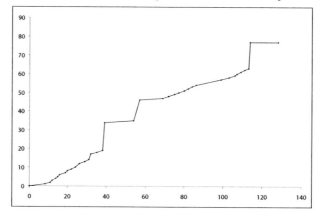

Figure 3. Talking instances, over time, for the first iteration of the experiment

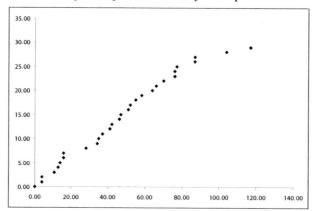

that lead us from one to the other. These processes are a variety of facts of organization, in this manner the order of things revealed by science emerges as the result of an ordering of things.

This insight has methodological significance for our experiment. Rather than take a more computational perspective on multi-agent interaction (using, for example, the robot's programming as the basis for understanding agents' interaction), we have adopted the androcentric perspective of the human observers, examining emergent behaviors through a video camera (itself a part of the actor-network).

Here we present data and analyze two examples of human-robot interaction from our research.

RESULTS

By transcribing speech and actions and coding them, we generate a map of agents' actions as they unfold over time, understood as linguistic actions (after Austin) or paralinguistic actions (movements, gesture); data were also analyzed according to frequency and cross-tabulated. For the first iteration, the summary of the talk and movement are given in Tables 2 and 3 respectively, whereas Tables 4 and 5 summarize the second iteration. Some of the parameters of the interactions sessions derived from the transcripts are shown in Figures 2-5.

Figure 4. Cumulative dynamics (in number of occurrences) of hand movements for all team members over time (in seconds) during the second experiment

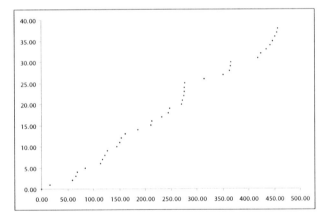

Figure 5. Cumulative dynamics (in number of occurrences) of hand movements for team member A over time (in seconds) during the second experiment

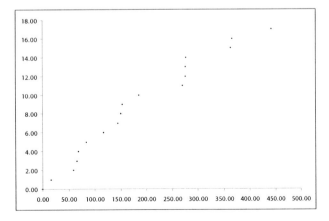

But we also find here examples of emergent socialities. That is, the artifice of the experiment–guiding and coaxing a robot into a goal, both specifies a certain kind of stereotypical structure (a team of human agents working towards a goal) while introducing a potential element of disorder, a non-human agent with which the human agents must interact. The first may not be generative of any particular novelty (as the results of group work in the classroom oftentimes suggests). But the second configuration lays the ground-work for novelty by introducing the confusion of a more complex, 2-level menu. This has the effect of generating more interaction between agents, rather than less, a counter-intuitive finding that we explore more below. In what Michel Serres calls the "parasite," perfectly transparent information–i.e., the perfect identity of speaker and hearer–renders conversation unnecessary. Communication only takes place in the presence of disorder (miscommunication, misapprehension, etc.). As Brown (2002:16-17) writes,

In information terms, the parasite provokes a new form of complexity, it engineers a kind of difference by intercepting relations. All three meanings then coincide to form a 'parasite logic'–analyze (take but do not give), paralyze (interrupt usual functioning), catalyze (force the host to act differently). This parasite, through its interruption, is a catalyst for complexity. It does this by impelling the parties it parasitizes to act in at least two ways. Either they incorporate the parasite into their midst–and thereby accept the new form of communication the parasite inaugurates–or they act together to expel the parasite and transform their own social practices in the course of doing so.

In the following examples, the robot acts the part of the "parasite," interrupting the flat functioning of a team of human agents and forcing it to act differently.

In the first example, we see examples of emergent sociality through turn-taking. The human agents attempt to form what are known as "adjacency pairs" with the non-human agent, initiating a conversational turn (by speech or gesture) that the non-human agent is supposed to complete by moving in the direction of the goal. This is isomorphic to one of the basic "rules" of turn-taking in conversation:

Transcript 1. See text for comments. Roman letters a-d correspond to the human agent's; 'r' to the non-human agent. Text in brackets refers to gesture and movement. The schematics at the top of the transcript show the relative position of the human and the nonhuman subjects on and around the table.

```
b c
-------------------------------r----------- a
d
```

0:52	d	Go straight
0:52	c	Go straight
0:52	r	[Move back]
0:55	d	[left hand in front]
0:55	r	[rotate left]
0:56	d	[left hand in front]
0:56	r	[move back]
0:58	a	[right hand side, then right hand front]
0:58	r	[rotate right]
1:00	c	[right hand in front]
1:00	r	[move forward off table]
1:01	a	[catch falling robot with left hand–reset]
1:02	r	[twitch]
1:04	a	Forward. Go straight.
1:05	c	[let hand in front]
1:05	r	[move back]
1:07	c	[left hand on right side]
1:07	r	[rotate left]
1:08	r	[move forward]
1:09	c	[right hand in front]
1:10	b	Left.
1:11	c	Left!
1:11	c	[point to the left]
1:11	r	[move back]
1:13	b	Left. To the left.
1:14	r	[rotate left]
1:15	r	[move forward]
1:17	b	There we go.

Transcript 2. Excerpt from the second experiment transcript. See text for the comments on this tran-

```
dab
----r-------------------------------------
ecf
```

06.44	a	It it wants to kill itself, who are we to tell it no?
06:47	d	Well I'm here to catch it if it tries to go.
06:48	a	Turn it that way. Turn it.
06:49	d	Hey can we turn it that way? It's getting ready to fall off, dude.
06:50	r	[rotates right, left]
07:00	r	[pi repositions robot]
07:02	c	[Right hand close front; left hand close side]
07:05	c	[right hand close front; left hand close side]
07:05	b	[right hand close front]
07:05	e	Right hand above front
07:06	r	[moves forward, stops]

07:08	b	Female hands?
07:09	b	Right hand front
07:16	r	[rotates left]
07:20	a	It doesn't like you. You're not cussing at it. It does not fear you.
07:21	b	[right hand close front]
07:21	e	[left hand close front, right hand front above]
07:21	c	[left hand side]
07:21	b	We need another hand on that side
07:24	r	[rotates right]
07:24	e	It's moving at least
07:30	r	[Moves forward]
07:31	d	[right hand front]
07:32	d	Not towards me, towards the goal there, come on.
07:35	d	[right hand close front, left hand close side]
07:25	r	[rotate left]
07:42	a	We're cussing it!
07:42	a	You're in the trash if you don't get moving, buddy.
07:46	d	Go that way, the way you were looking before.
07:48	b	Maybe if you guys come over here and . . .

```
fcab
dr----------------------------------------
e
```

If the turn-so-far is so constructed as to involve the use of a 'current speaker selects next' technique, then the party so selected has the right and is obliged to take next turn to speak; no other have such rights or obligations, and transfer occurs at that place. (Sacks et al, 704).

If the nonhuman agent 'r' completes the adjacency pair, then the human agent is entitled to another turn. This is an in-built "bias" in turn-taking, which privileges the "current speaker selects next" turn allocation to the subordinate rule, self-selection (see transcript 1).

And this solves a typical problem–the problem of conversational bias. Sacks et al (1974:712) write:

The 'last as next' bias, however, remains invariant over increases. Not only does this have the effect of stimulating "self-selects" turns in the human agents and, in the comparison to the first examples, increasing the total number of parties – and, with each additional increment in the number of parties, tends progressively to concentrate the distribution of turns among a sub-set of the potential next speakers.

This is confirmed in such stereotypical settings as classroom discourse, where, unless the instructor intervenes, conversation quickly concentrates around a handful of speakers, leaving the rest of the class out of the conversation. Here, the introduction of a non-human agent has the effect of "selecting" another speaker by simply moving down the table–the initial human-agent is not able to take advantage of its prior right to initiate another adjacency pair after the non-human agent has moved out of range. A begins his turn, but quickly remits to B when the robot moves down the table out of range. The non-human agent allows for the 'last as next' bias to be superseded by 'self-select' and, therefore, an engagement with all of the human agents in the robot's trajectory.

The above example shows how the non-human agent intervenes in what might be thought of as an example of ordinary turn-taking, facilitated by the robot's simple obstacle avoidance. Once human agents understand the non-human agent's drive, then forming stereotypical adjacency pairs with it is unproblematic. However, the second case demonstrates what might be thought of as a "conversational anomaly" where the non-human agent fails to complete adjacency pairs altogether.

Here, the non-human agent is unresponsive or, alternately, responds in an undesirable way to the speech and gestures of the human agents. If the nonhuman agent ("r") does not respond, however, then this constitutes a conversation "lapse" and allows another human agent to self-select, initiating her own adjacency pair with the non-human agent. In the case of primary conversation, it means that the current speaker (the human agent) has failed to "select" the next speaker (the non-human agent). As Sacks et al (1974:715) write, "At any transition-place where none of the options to speak has been employed, the possibility of a lapse, and thus discontinuous talk, arises."

Not only does this have the effect of stimulating "self-selects" turns of linguistic and paralinguistic actions in the human agents, but it results in at least two novel behaviors: 1) a level of strategy and metacommentary directed not at the robot, as in the first example, but to the other human agents and 2) the invention of "co-operative" turns, i.e., instances (like in the interval between 7:02-7:05 in Transcript 2, where three human agents train their hands on the nonhuman agent at the same time). This particular example, with human agent "b" suggesting that the robot is moving because of "female hands" is significant in that adjacency pairs up to that point had been dominated by 2 of the male agents, a and d, respectively. As Gibson (2005:135) reminds us,

The second thing we know about conversation is that not everyone is dealt the same hand, in terms of opportunities to speak and be addressed, in terms of what each can hope to say as speaker and hearer as addressee. Conversation, in other words, is a site for the differentiation of persons, perhaps, though not necessarily, along lines established by attributes, personalities, or positions in an encompassing institutional structure.

Thus, here, the non-human agent is not only a catalyst for turn-taking, but is additionally a foil for a challenge to traditional classroom hierarchies which tend to favor males over females. What is counter-intuitively interesting about the second iteration is that the quality of the interaction–the richness of the emergent community–seems inversely related to the expectative fit of the different agents; the total number of instances of talk and movement in the first iteration are 105, compared to the second at 231. If we look at the goal of the system as essentially autopoietic (as opposed to systems that are allopoietic, created from the outside), then the number and quality of the interactions in the second example are more richly differentiated and elaborated. This is the quality of the parasite–that hermetic agent generating difference by creating noise in the system–miscommunications, conversational lapses, misunderstanding, crossed signals.

THE QUASI-OBJECT

In the above experiments, the non-human agent is on one level, subordinate to the human agents. Without their input (and in the absence of another obstacle), the non-human agent goes nowhere. On the other hand, if we look at the these interactions as emergent socialities, the non-human agent has a pivotal role–that of amanuensis for all subsequent social interaction. Without the peregrinations of what Michel Serres has called the "quasi-object",

there is no emergent social interaction to begin with, like the ontological important of a ball for a game of rugby. As he summarizes in a recent interview with Bruno Latour (Serres and Latour, 1995:108),

The ball is played, and the teams place themselves in relation to it, not vice versa. As a quasi-object the ball is the true subject of the game. It is like a track of the fluctuating collectivist around it. The same analysis is valid for the individual: the clumsy person plays with the ball and makes it gravitate around himself; the mean player imagines himself to be a subject by imagining the ball to be an object–the sign of a bad philosopher. On the contrary, the skilled player knows that the ball plays with him or plays off him, in such a way that he gravitates around it and fluidly follows the positions it takes, but especially the relations that it spawns.

That is, the quasi-object is simultaneously quasi-subject (whether human or non-human), taking on aspects of object and subject and in the process weaving a network of relations between agents. In this, the non-human agent would seem to be the sine qua non quasi-object, but humans, too, must accede to the level of quasi-object in order to function in a world of intelligent agents. As Brown (2002:21-22) writes in his summary of Serres's work: "Sociality is neither an automatic adding of individuals, nor an abstract contractual arrangement. It is a collectivist assembled and held together by the circulation of an object."

CONCLUSION

It is now axiomatic that the cognitive world varies considerably from "sense-think-act" cycle of early AI and robotics (Clark, 2001:88). Now, theories of enaction, of interactivism, of emergence, suggest a dynamic, multi-directionality of perception reducible to neither the material nor the ideational world and additionally organized socially as multi-agent systems. What is less studied is the messiness of those multi-agent systems themselves, the way they involve complex "translations " (Latour) between human and non-human agents, or "transcodings" between different representational and discursive modalities. After all, the "machinic" world has the potential to discombobulate: to re-shuffle relationships and practices linking humans to the non-human world. As a corollary of this, we can also say that human participations in the machinic re-forge the machine (Deleuze and Guattari, 1980:398): "It is through the intermediary of assemblages that the phylum selects, qualifies, and even invents the technical elements. Thus one cannot speak of weapons or tools before defining the constituent assemblages they presuppose and enter into."

In our experiment, the assemblage made up of non-human robot and PIs gives way to a new assemblage—a new network—made up of volunteers, PIs and robot. In the process, the robot's "function" shifts. It may have begun with obstacle avoidance, but, by the second iteration, becomes a gesture-machine, a conversation-machine, a turn-taking machine.

It is not too much to say that we can't say in advance of the network's formation what its components may or may not do; this is the obvious legacy of almost three decades of research in distributed cognition, autopoiesis and multi-agent systems. But HRI and HCI still, by and large, construe the human and the computer as ontologically prior to their combination which, as we have argued, is both philosophically problematic and empirically unjustified.

This also has profound implications for the design of human-computer interfaces in the classroom or the company. Is the most "user-friendly" design necessarily the best? Is there any place for resistance in the non-human agent? What do we want the non-human agent for? If it's a phone-tree, than we would want it to confirm existing expectations of human-non-human interaction but if we are in the classroom, than–counter intuitively-- it may be desirable to present a classroom of human agents with anomalous non-human agents.

REFERENCES

Bateson, Gregory (1972). *Steps to an ecology of mind*. NY: Ballantine.

Brown, Steven D. (2002). Michel Serres. *Theory, Culture & Society, 19*(3), 1-27.

Clark, Andy (2001). *Mindware*. New York: Oxford University Press.

Collins, Samuel Gerald (2007). "If I'm not in control, then who is?: The politics of emergence in multiagent aystems." In Goran Trajkovski (Ed.), *An imitation-based approach to modeling homogenous agents societies,* (pp. 93-115). Hershey, PA: IGI Publishing.

Deleuze, Gilles and Felix Guattari (1980). *A thousand plateaus*. Minneapolis: University of Minnesota Press.

Dobashi, Shingo (2005). The gendered ese of *Keitai* in domestic contexts. In Mizuko Ito, Daisuke Okabe and Misa Matsuda (Eds.), *Personal, portable, pedestrian* (pp. 219-236). Cambridge: MIT Press.

Downey, Gary Lee, Joseph Dumit and Sarah Williams (1995). Cyborg anthropology. *Cultural Anthropology 10*(2), 264-269.

Gibson, David (2003). Participation shifts. *Social Forces, 81*(4), 1335-1381.

Harris, Jan (2005). The ordering of things. Supplement to *Sociological Review.*

Hayles, N. Katherine (1999). *How we became post-Human*. Chicago: University of Chicago Press.

Helmreich, Stefan (1998). *Silicon second nature*. Berkeley: University of California Press.

Koay, K.L., K. Dautenhahn, S.N. Woods and M.L. Walters (2006). "Empirical results from using a comfort level device in human-robot interaction studies." In *Proceedings of HRI'06,* Salt Lake City, Utah.

Langdon, Christopher (1995). *Artificial life*. Cambridge: MIT Press.

Maturama, Humberto and Francisco Varela (1980). *Autopoiesis and cognition*. Dordrecht, The Netherlands: Rediel.

Sacks, Harvey, Emanuel Schegloff and Gail Jefferson (1974). A simplest systematics for the organziation of turn-taking for conversation. *Language, 50*(4), 696-735.

Sawyer, Keith (2001). Emergence in sociology. *American Journal of Sociology, 107*(3), 551-86.

Serres, Michel and Bruno Latour (1995). *Conversations on science, culture, and time*. Ann Arbor: University of Michigan Press.

Trajkovski, Goran (2007). *An imitation-based approach to modeling homogenous agents societies*. Hershey, PA: IGI Publishing.

Varela, Fancisco (1999). *Ethical know-how*. Stanford: Stanford University Press.

Varela, Francisco, Evan Thompson and Eleanor Rosch (1991). *The embodied mind*. Cambridge, MA: MIT Press.

Woolridge, Michael (2002). *An introduction to multi-agent systems*. NY: Wiley.

APPENDIX 1. SUMMARY OF KEY TERMS

Actor-Network Theory (ANT): A body of sociological theory originating in the work of Bruno Latour. ANT is a powerful tool allowing social scientists to describe network chains of human and non-human agencies engaging in a variety of practices and discourses, from opening a door to scientific discovery.

Adjacency Pairs: In conversation analysis, sociolinguists (e.g., Harvey Sacks) have examined human speech as a dyadic exchange involving turn-taking. Sociolinguistic phenomena such as "salutations" demand a dyadic exchange for their completion.

Agent: In Multi-agent systems, an "agent" generally refers to either software or robots capable of some degree of autonomy in a designated environment. However: humans can also be considered "agents," although this involves a reduction of the complexities of human behavior and cognition to more machinic drives and expectations.

Assemblage: An "assemblage" is a temporary, shifting concatenation of human- and non-human elements. Initially proposed by Gilles Deleuze and Felix Guattari (1980), including both "machinic" and "animal" elements.

Autopoiesis: Literally "self-making," autopoietic systems organize themselves in an environment through a process of "structural coupling." They were first studied by Humberto Maturana and Francisco Varela. Initially confined to closed systems (e.g., cells), the characteristics of "auopoietic" systems were extended to "allopoetic" systems (e.g., perception and cognition) by Francisco Varela.

Cyborg: "Cyborgs" combine humans and machines. The term originates in NASA proposals for engineering humans for extreme environments.

Hybridity: In our contemporary world, it may be more (empirically) accurate to study humans as combinations of humans and machines. In other words, we have become (and perhaps always were) inseparable from our tools.

Observer: In what has been called "first-generation" cybernetics, the "observer" enjoyed a panoptic view (and perfect knowledge) of the observed system. Subsequent insights in cybernetics and systems theory have located the observer in the system she observes, i.e., imbricated the observer in an ultimately reflexive system where the act of observation and observed phenomena are dialectally linked.

Parasite: The title of a book by the historian of science, Michel Serres, "the parasite" suggests that communication and information exchange might be understood with "parasitic" metaphors and that, furthermore, the "unproductive" parasite (whether in speech or biology) is in some ways constitutive of, rather than extraneous to, the system.

Section III
Second Order Emergences

Chapter XVI
Developing Relationships Between Autonomous Agents:
Promoting Pro-Social Behaviour Through Virtual Learning Environments Part II

Scott Watson
University of Hertfordshire, UK

Kerstin Dautenhahn
University of Hertfordshire, UK

Wan Ching (Steve) Ho
University of Hertfordshire, UK

Rafal Dawidowicz
University of Hertfordshire, UK

ABSTRACT

This chapter is a continuation from Part I, which has described contemporary psychological descriptions of bullying in primary schools and two Virtual Learning Environments (VLEs) designed as anti-bullying interventions. The necessary requirements for believable, autonomous agents used in virtual learning environments are now outlined. In particular, we will describe the technical and engagement-oriented considerations that need to be made. The chapter concludes with recommendations of how to meet these needs and how to design a VLE by including potential users in the development process.

INTRODUCTION

Part I of this chapter has described how human social networks operate, and have focused specifically on the issue of childhood bullying within primary school classes. We also introduced two VLEs (FearNot! And C-SoNeS), which have been created as anti-bullying interventions.

In developing these VLEs, the authors have uncovered a number of issues which needed to be resolved successfully in order that the software was developed to be functionally and pedagogically sound. Many of these issues seem generalisable and pertinent to developers of other VLEs, and so this chapter aims to impart some hard-learned lessons to allow the greater community to prosper from our endeavours.

This chapter intends to show what considerations are necessary when designing an engaging VLE and will outline a number of ways in which these requirements can be met. In this way, it is hoped that future development teams can benefit by drawing from our experiences in the design and implementation of VLEs.

LESSONS TO BE LEARNED FOR THE DEVELOPMENT OF VLES

As part of the development team of FearNot! and C-SoNeS, the authors have learned a number of lessons which are hoped to be of use to future developers of VLEs for young people. Broadly speaking there are two main considerations to make: technical considerations and engagement-oriented considerations.

Technical Considerations

Technical considerations concern the design and implementation of a VLE from a software developer's point of view. The most important aspect here is to ensure that the VLE works and is stable enough when installed on school computers – children will not learn anything from software which does not work! This may not be so much of a concern for VLEs which are not designed for the classroom, such as the NICE system (Johnson

et al, 1998) which uses a CAVE environment, for the simple reason that researchers often have more control over, and access to, the available hardware for development and testing. However, this concern should be carefully considered by developers of systems designed to be used in the classroom, for a number of reasons.

Firstly, programmers will not usually have access to a school's computers during the development of software. This is an issue because schools (at least in the UK), while often possessing relatively new PCs, do not equip their computers to as high a specification as those usually used in a developer's laboratory. It is a simple fact that primary schools do not need as powerful machines as those used in software development, and so prefer to purchase lower specification computers in order to keep their expenditure to a minimum. For example, in installing FearNot! in local primary schools for evaluation, the authors found that most school computers have rather low specifications in terms of slow processors, a lack of RAM, and do not usually have separate graphic cards (rather they share on-board memory between graphics and RAM). While a general survey of the current state of computers in UK primary schools was conducted by the e-CIRCUS project's educational experts, it was almost impossible to determine the precise specification of equipment available in schools. This has caused some problems since the FearNot! application runs in the OGRE 3D[1] graphical engine, and has led to the undesirable situation where some schools who want to take part in the project are unable to because their systems simply do not meet FearNot!'s minimum system requirements.

It is very difficult to determine a general level of computer sophistication in primary schools because there is large variability. Schools are responsible for the purchase of their own computers in the UK, meaning that there is no consistency in terms of the systems installed. There is a wide range of choice available for schools; from laptops to desktops, different suppliers, and different combinations of hardware. This compounds the issue of reduced performance further – not only do developers have to 'scale-down' their applications, but they must also be stable enough to run across many different configurations of low specification machines.

While schools differ from each other in terms of the hardware they purchase, they often also differ in terms of the software installed and ways in which administration rights are managed. Some schools have their own technical support officer, meaning that access to machines is often fairly straightforward (assuming researchers are able to develop a healthy rapport with the school!). Others, however, are maintained centrally by their LEA (Local Education Authority) and so access is 'by arrangement only'; and therefore much more difficult. Some computers run as standalone units, while yet others are governed by one of many different available server-based systems, such as Novell NetWare (http://www.novell.com/products/netware/), or RM's Community Connect 3 system (http://www.rm.com/cc3). Again this creates concerns for developers – should the application run from a server or as on individual machines? Does the user need 'write-access' to save their progress at all?

To summarise, school laboratories are not as well equipped as those developing VLEs, and there is great variation between schools in terms of hardware, software and ease of access for researchers. In designing a school-based VLE, it is recommended that developers perform a thorough survey of the equipment available in their area before they even begin to write their code. Once a developer knows what is available he/she can begin to plan what is technically possible within this framework. It is also recommended that development is carried out on machines representative of those available to schools. This would greatly aid the developer in understanding what is/isn't possible with school machines and will also ease any bug-testing and troubleshooting. While these 'practical' issues raised above seem quite obvious in hindsight, it is very important to be aware of these technical constraints, and even an experienced research team such as the e-Circus consortium had to deal with some of these problems.

Engagement-Oriented Considerations

Let us assume that a development team is capable of meeting the technical constraints above. A successful VLE must also be able to keep the attention of users – without engagement a VLE will not succeed in its attempts to educate users. For deep engagement and the exploration of sensitive personal issues, a VLE needs to be capable of generating empathy between user and agents (Dautenhahn, Bond, Canamero, & Edmonds, 2002).

In essence, empathy is the ability of an observer to react emotionally when he/she recognises that another individual is experiencing a particular emotion (Stotland, Mathews, Sherman, Hannson, & Richardson, 1978). In other words, empathy refers to our ability to understand the emotional state of another (e.g. Wispé, 1987). The two challenges for developers are to create agents which can 1) react empathically themselves ('empathy-feeling agents') and 2) evoke empathy in their users ('empathy-evoking agents') (Paiva et al., 2004). Furthermore, these challenges need to be met by different aspects

Figure 1. Example facial expressions used to convey agent emotional states in FearNot! (figure modified from Paiva et al, 2004)

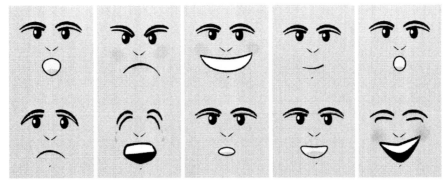

of agent design. Empathy-feeling agents require a carefully implemented internal architecture to allow them to 'feel'[2], while empathy-evoking agents require outward expressions and animations which serve to communicate their 'feelings'.

According to Paiva et al (2004) there are a number of constraints which determine the way in which an architecture must be implemented if an agent is to be able to 'feel' empathy for others. A successful agent architecture must contain the capacity for agents to:

- Recognise the emotional state of other agents
- Communicate with each other agents
- Process emotions (allow situations to trigger emotions in the agent)
- Express emotions (via different modalities)
- Respond to emotions, through different coping strategies

Paiva et al (2004) continue to describe the ways in which agents need to express their internal states if they are to evoke empathy in the user. They suggest three main factors for building empathy: facial and body expressions, situations, and 'proximity'.

As facial and body expressions are one of the main ways in which humans can communicate personal information about their emotions (Russel & Fernández-Dols, 2002), so too can synthetic agents use this outlet to show users how they feel. Naturally, it follows that a user must be able to

perceive and identify the expression displayed by the character – a task for the graphics designer. One way to facilitate understanding is to take a lesson from actors and cartoonists who often use highly stylised and exaggerated gestures to convey their emotions more easily.

In addition, the expression displayed by an agent must also be congruent with how a user would expect the agent to feel at any given time, lest the user becomes confused. Indeed, the situation itself may also be used as a way of communicating empathy. Humans are intuitively empathic, and so will readily understand how a synthetic character *should* feel if placed in a certain situation. In the same way that stylised and exaggerated expressions can create empathy within a user, ensuring that the situations that agents are placed into are similarly unambiguous, can also facilitate the empathic process. This can be done by keeping a character's actions clear and explicit, or by presenting situations with which a user is already familiar.

Familiarity seems key to the creation of empathy. Empathy is stronger among people, who do not know each other, if they consider themselves to be similar to each other. For example, it has been shown that people are comfortable with feeling empathy for cinema and television characters (Tannenbaum & Gaer, 1965; Hoffner & Cantor, 1991), while von Feilitzen & Linne (1975) found that people are more likely to feel sorry for someone (real or imaginary) they perceive as similar to themselves. In order to create an empathic bond between user and agent Paiva et

Figure 2. Mori's Uncanny Valley, cf. MacDorman (2005)

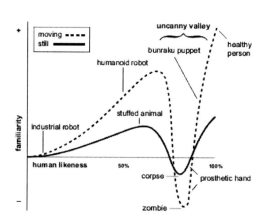

al. (2005) describe the notion of 'proximity' and show how they were able to design environments, characters and situations with which users were familiar and could identify with. Indeed, a number of evaluations of FearNot! have provided evidence that proximity does improve empathic engagement in the manner described here (Hall & Woods, 2004; Watson et al, 2007).

Just because an agent seems to meet the criteria laid out above, empathic engagement will not automatically follow. Even if a character is able to feel empathy, express its emotions, and is similar to the user, it must also be *believable*. Believability is a difficult concept to tie down, but for the purpose of virtual agents has been defined as: a character "that provides the illusion of life thus permitting the audience's suspension of disbelief" (Bates, 1994, p.122). Essentially, character believability can be created through a combination of appearance, autonomy, and expressivity (Paiva et al, 2005).

While evidence has shown that a polished appearance is not necessary to keep a user's attention (Woods et al, 2003; Woods et al., 2005; Watson et al, 2007), it is the first thing that a new user will notice about a VLE and is becoming more important as users often compare VLEs to commercial video games as a familiar reference point. In terms of appearance, level of realism is the key consideration – are realistic looking characters more or less believable than cartoon-like agents, for example? Should characters be designed as human-like, animal-like, or even as aliens? An important consideration is to ensure that whatever direction a developer takes, he/she must be sure to avoid the pitfalls of the 'uncanny valley' (Mori, 1970; MacDorman, 2005).

The uncanny valley theory states that as robots display ever more human-like characteristics, people will react with increasing familiarity until a certain point where subtle flaws in the robot cause people to feel repulsion (also called the 'Zombie effect'). It is this area of repulsion that forms the uncanny valley. However, improving a robot beyond this point can also improve reactions once more until a point is reached where robots are indistinguishable from health human beings.

The uncanny valley theory can also be applied to computer-generated characters, as in the feature films Shrek (2001) and Final Fantasy: The Spirits Within (2001) (Wechsler, 2002), and virtual agents (Gulz & Haake, 2006; Hall et al, 2006). Therefore, the following discussion of robot appearance is also relevant to the design of interactive agents, especially within 3D virtual environments.

Based upon McCloud's (1993) design space of comics, Dautenhahn (2002) has posited a two-dimensional scale (realistic to iconic versus representational to abstract) that can be used to categorise the appearance of different believable social robots. By using this scale, developers can decide on how best to design a robot – simple designs may be better than lifelike designs, and a robot's behaviour and purpose should be taken into account before auto-

Figure 3. Examples of robots with mechanoid, humanoid, and android appearances

Lynx 5 Robotic Arm
(Lynxmotion)
Mechanoid Robot

Asimo
(Honda)
Humanoid Robot

Actroid DER2
(Kokoro & Osaka Uni)
Android Robot

matically deciding on an anthropomorphic form. Indeed, this approach has been used effectively to create a child-sized robot, KASPAR[3], who has been used in a variety of human-robot interaction studies (Blow et al, 2006; Robins et al. 2008).

Robots can also be placed on an anthropomorphic scale from mechanoid through humanoid to android (Walters, 2007). It has been found that mechanical-looking robots have lower expectations of ability placed upon them, and are treated less politely and more subserviently than their more human-like counterparts (Hinds, Roberts & Jones, 2004).

Moreover, Woods, Dautenhahn, & Schulz (2004) have found that the uncanny valley effect holds true when children interact with robots. Children were shown 85 standardised images of robots falling along the mechanoid/android continuum and were asked to rate them on a number of criterion measures (including friendliness, aggressiveness, and some personality characteristics). Both mechanoid and android robots were rated as aggressive, mechanoid robots were considered to be angry, while humanoid robots were seen as most friendly.

Taken with in conjunction with Gulz & Haake's (2006) work, these results show the importance of carefully designing the appearance of robots or virtual agents. Agents do not necessarily need be designed to appear realistic, but their appearance should fit their purpose in a believable manner.

Autonomous characters often seem more believable than their scripted counterparts (take, for example, Tamogotchis, Nintendogs, and the ever increasing use of AI in commercial video games). However, autonomy is not easy to implement with synthetic agents due to the technical difficulties of generating actions and speech, for example, dynamically. Scripted characters can, in some cases, be more believable than autonomous agents – though this requires great effort on the part of developers to pre-empt or limit what users are able to do in the VLE.

For characters to be believable, they must be able to accurately express their current state – their 'mood' or 'feelings' – in the same way that humans can communicate their state through non-verbal channels e.g. facial expressions. This is not just a job for graphical artists who will have to animate characters, but rather is a very difficult task of definition and communication of states. The Disney animators Thomas & Johnston (1981) have described 3 points of interest which should be considered when designing emotionally expressive agents. 1) An agent's emotional state must be clearly defined in a manner which is unambiguous to the observer/user. 2) If the emotional state affects the agent's reasoning then the consequences must be obvious in the agent's subsequent actions. 3) Emotions may need to be exaggerated in order to communicate them effectively to the observer. It is also true that even if an agent is able to effectively communicate it's emotions to the user, that agent must also maintain coherence between its emotions and behaviour – an unpredictable character that lacks temporal and/or cross-situational consistency will not be believable (Moffat, 1997).

The 'Expressivator' (Sengers, 1998) is an interesting system that shows how one can develop agents that are able to express themselves in an ecologically valid manner. Whereas classical architectures view agents as problem solving entities that move quickly form one behaviour to another, the Expressivator supports 'transition behaviours' which can express relations *between* behaviours. These serve to show the user why an agent's behaviour is changing from one state to the next, and therefore provide an explanation of intentionality. In addition, there is a 'sign management' system whereby an agent keeps a record of the behaviours it has shown, and thus can select further behavioural displays not only on internal states, but also on the way in which it's behaviour has already (probably) been perceived.

Empathic engagement and believability go hand-in-hand – it is very difficult to have one without the other. While it may seem straightforward to construct an environment under the guidelines outlined above, the greatest problem that developers face is that the aspects of believability and the empathic notion of proximity can change from one audience to another. To give an example, an early evaluation of FearNot! including children, teachers, and AI experts showed that children responded more positively towards a number of aspects of the software than did teachers or experts, and were also therefore more likely to express empathic reactions (Hall, Woods, Dautenhahn, Sobral, Paiva, Wolke, & Newall, 2004).

To realize that proximity will change between audiences should be obvious. Since proximity refers to the similarity between user and virtual environment, it follows that different users will require different characters with which to empathise. In the same way, different users will also have different concepts of what is believable – of what appearance, amount of character autonomy, and level of expressivity they prefer. This begs the question, then, of how user preferences can be identified. One solution is to simply ask them!

While the role of user as a developer has been challenged with the argument that users are not designers and that their ideas are usually inferior to those of design professionals (Webb, 1996), it is widely accepted in Human Computer Interaction (HCI) that the role of the user as a tool to aid development should not be underestimated. Users are traditionally employed to test or evaluate previously implemented aspects of an interface, which limits their input to purely reactive feedback rather than allowing a proactive role in the original design itself. This, unfortunately, allows that user feedback may be ignored, either because of a developer's reluctance to change their interface, or because deadlines do not allow for a re-design (Scaife, Rogers, Adrich, & Frances, 1997).

An alternative is the 'participatory design' (PD) approach (Schuler & Mamioka, 1993) in which users are treated more as partners in the design process and are given more responsibility than simply feeding back on work already done. Since an application will usually be targeted at a particular user group, it is of the utmost importance to consult with that group at every stage of a VLE's development. This approach has been successful with adults (e.g. Müller, Wildman, & White, 1993) who understand their role and the domain they are operating in, but using children in such a role can be more difficult.

Children can be valuable contributors to a design team as they provide honest opinions and metaphors (Druin & Solomon, 1996) especially as they are becoming quite technologically sophisticated (Oosterholt, Kusano, & de Vries, 1996). Children do require more guidance than adults, however, which means that they are not ideal for a full PD approach. This is why Scaife et al (1997) have adapted the PD approach for children to take the role

of 'native informers'. They describe a framework for 'Informant Design' (ID), which can be useful for developers of software for children. By taking children as informants, Scaife et al (1997) recognise that children may be privy to useful information that designers are not (especially what can encourage learning), whilst also acknowledging that they will not have the skills or time to contribute to a complete PD approach.

It is beyond the scope of this chapter to provide a full description of the ID framework, but it essentially defines four design phases, which users can contribute to each phase, what the contributors input should be, and what methods can be used to elicit these inputs. Under this framework, children are involved in three out of the four design phases and can advise on which aspects of a topic are most difficult to learn, help build a motivational interface, and iteratively evaluate development.

There are a number of methodologies that can be employed by a design team at different stages of development that can yield informative results. Furthermore, these methodologies can also be employed with different groups to uncover various pieces of information. This chapter will now continue to describe some methods that have been used successfully by the e-CIRCUS team, under the ID framework outlined above. The main methods used to date have been questionnaires, design walls, photo-elicitation, mood boards, and focus groups/discussions. It should be noted, though, that this is not meant to be an exhaustive list, and that there are many more HCI methodologies that can be of value (see, for example, Sharp, Rogers, & Preece, 2007 for a recent review).

Questionnaires (e.g. Oppenheim, 1992) are widely used in many different research fields. They are an excellent resource for collecting a large amount of data quickly, and with little effort for the researcher. Usually they will return data of a numerical or quantitative nature, though open-ended questions can allow for qualitative analysis. Questionnaires are ideal for asking about specific aspects of a VLE which is already in development as they allow respondents to quickly show the extent to which they like or dislike part of the VLE with the use of Likert (Likert, 1932) or Guttman (Guttman, 1950) scales, for example. The most common

Figure 4. Photographs of the Design Wall exercise carried out by the e-CIRCUS team in planning the ORI-ENT VLE

way to use questionnaires is to show target users a trailer video of a VLE (e.g. Hall et al, 2004) or allow them to interact with a VLE (e.g. Woods et al, 2003; Hall et al, 2005) before asking them to complete a questionnaire. Alternatively, questionnaires can be used to gauge any changes made to a VLE if, for example, two versions of a VLE are demonstrated before evaluation (e.g. Watson et al, 2007). One potential drawback of a questionnaire-based methodology is the possibility of a novelty effect – that respondents will answer questionnaires more positively than they would do normally as a result of the excitement of trying something new. However, the effects of this bias can be reduced if respondents are given enough time to acclimatise to a new VLE before they are asked to complete a questionnaire. While questionnaires are very useful for asking about a product already in development, because they mostly require fixed responses, they are not as effective when designing a VLE for the first time.

Based loosely upon contextual analysis and affinity diagrams (e.g. Beyer & Holtzblatt, 1999; Raven & Flanders, 1996), 'Design Walls' can be a useful tool at the beginning of a project to identify the themes and issues within a problem that a VLE is to be designed to solve. Usually, this methodology will take experts as its respondents, as they will likely have more knowledge about a specific subject area than the developers of a VLE. Take, as an example, the e-CIRCUS project which was tasked with developing a VLE (named ORIENT) to

educate young people about integration issues faced by immigrants. Few people on the e-CIRCUS team possessed previous experience in this area, and so a workshop was organised to encourage input from experts who were already working with immigrants. The design wall exercise was conducted in order to identify 1) the challenges faced by immigrants, and 2) potential solutions to these challenges. As a result of this exercise, the e-CIRCUS team were able to begin planning their new VLE as the problem area had now been well defined.

'Photo-elicitation' is a relatively new methodology that assists researchers in designing environments with which users will be familiar, and has already been used to good effect with children (Richardson, 2006; Hall et al., 2007). Essentially, the method involves allowing respondents to take photographs of anything they wish. When the photographs are returned to the researcher they can be analysed visually to identify any recurrent themes or images. It is assumed that the more often a theme occurs, the more important it is to the user group, and can therefore be incorporated into a VLE to promote familiarity. The amount of guidance given to the respondents can change the specificity of images returned – for example, by asking respondents to photograph clothes that they like inside a shopping centre developers can gain some insight on how to design the physical appearance of their characters.

Figure 5. Photographs of the (female) Mood Board exercise carried out by the e-CIRCUS team in planning the ORIENT VLE

Another methodology which allows target users to design aspects of a VLE is known as the 'Mood Board', and is especially well suited to designing visual aspects of a VLE, including the interface. Mood boards have been used successfully in a variety of areas including the development of mixed reality systems (Lucero & Martens, 2006) and interface design (Øritsland & Buur, 2003). Indeed, mood boards can also be used as part of an augmented reality system themselves (Martens et al 2006). Under this methodology, potential users are invited to browse through contemporary media (e.g. newspapers/magazines, etc) which are relevant to the user's demographic. They can then select images from the magazines and arrange them in a collage to represent whatever aspect of the VLE they have been asked to focus on. This methodology was also used effectively by the e-CIRCUS team along with the design walls to begin designing interaction modalities and ways in which the ORIENT VLE could move from one scenario to another.

A methodology that is very familiar to computer scientists and psychologists includes interviews or focus groups and discussions. These methods are useful at all stages of a development for a couple of reasons. Firstly, they allow respondents to use their own words, and define their own points of interest – which is useful in early design stages. On the other hand, they also allow researchers the opportunity to ask direct questions about specific aspects of a VLE, while also following-up on new items that respondents may bring to the discussion. Variations of the focus group design, in the shape of 'Classroom Discussion Forums' (CDFs), (Hall, Woods, Dautenhahn, & Wolke, 2004), have been used extensively and effectively by members of the e-CIRCUS team. In this way, the target user group of children and teachers have been continuously involved in the design and development of FearNot! throughout the whole development process. Recent, though unpublished, changes to FearNot! as a result of CDFs include improvements to the graphical appearance, the design of more relevant bullying episodes (e.g. bullying via a mobile phone), and updating of the character's language to include more contemporary and regional phraseology.

By following the principles outlined above, FearNot! has successfully encouraged empathy in the user as a mechanism to generate engagement (e.g. Hall et al., 2005; Watson et al., 2007), and, regarding our work on the development of social networks in VLEs, it is planned to take the elicitation of empathy one step further by including the user as an avatar in the environment itself.

CONCLUSION

This chapter has shown that a VLE needs to be empathically engaging and believable to be successful in educating its users. Some of the ways have been described in which the e-CIRCUS project has been successful in achieving this goal with the FearNot! software. Furthermore, evidence was provided that the facets that combine to make a VLE believable and engaging can, and will, vary between different user-groups. To counteract these issues, it was argued that asking potential users what they want is the best way to ensure the eventual success of a VLE. To that end, a number of user-centred design methodologies were described that have worked well for the e-CIRCUS project team. We explained the use of questionnaires, design walls, photo-elicitation, mood boards, and focus groups/discussions and show how they can be applied in different phases of a VLE's implementation, though do not suggest these to comprise an exhaustive list.

In conclusion, the final message of this chapter is that a VLE's development team should employ a user-centred design methodology as the best way in which to plan, develop and test social agents which are believable, empathically engaging, and educational for the target user group.

FUTURE RESEARCH DIRECTIONS

The technical development and implementation of FearNot! has been completed, and efforts are currently focussed on evaluating the impact that it will have on bullying in primary schools. In a longitudinal study, approximately 350 children from the UK and 250 from Germany will use FearNot! for three weeks, with criteria questionnaires administered once before and twice after the intervention. The same number of children will match this pattern of questionnaires, without the FearNot! intervention, to act as a control condition.

It is hoped that the FearNot! VLE will reduce victimisation and improve knowledge about bullying and the most effective coping strategies. This study will also contribute to the psychological understanding of bullying in primary schools by investigating the efficacy of moral disengagement as a possible predictor variable of bullying behaviour. The study is due for completion in February 2008, and results will be available later that year. Assuming that FearNot! is successful in its aims, the e-CIRCUS project team hopes to make the VLE available to the public for educational purposes.

The e-CIRCUS team is also developing a different, new VLE named ORIENT. This VLE will apply many of the lessons described in this chapter to create an application designed to teach adolescents about the issues faced by immigrants who are attempting to acclimatise to a new host nation. This VLE will take the form of a 3-dimensional landscape, in which users can control their own avatar for navigating through the environment and interaction with the agent population. Users will work in groups, with a number of interaction modalities to be considered, including Nintendo Wii controllers[4], mobile phones equipped with RFID[5] scanners, and a dance mat[6]. Users will be assigned individual but complimentary roles, and will need to work together in order to solve a number of 'engagement scenarios' such as learning the cultural norms and rites that accompany everyday activities (e.g. eating a meal). The synthetic agents in ORIENT will be even more sophisticated than those in FearNot! and will include facets of the FAtiMA and PSI models (Dörner & Hille, 1995), along with a sophisticated autobiographic memory. The agents will play the roles of characters from different cultures, which have their own norms and societies. The technical implementation of ORIENT has already begun in 2007, and evaluations will begin in 2009.

With regards to our work on developing C-SoNeS, the inclusion of 'gossip' between agents may be considered. By implementing such a function, agents will be able to exchange information about other agents in order that relationships can be affected by third-party information. For example, agent could A tell agent B that he has a positive relationship to agent C, thus improving agent B's relationship to agent C. Once 'gossip' between agents had been implemented, users may interact directly with agents in the VLE by controlling their own avatar. In doing so, it is hoped that children will be able to learn about the ways in which social networks develop and will be able to practice making and maintaining friendships.

ACKNOWLEDGMENT

This work was partially supported by the European Community (EC) and is currently funded by the e-CIRCUS project IST-4-027656-STP. The authors are solely responsible for the content of this publication. It does not represent the opinion of the EC, and the EC is not responsible for any use that might be made of data appearing therein.

REFERENCES

Adamson, A., & Jenson, V. (2001). *Shrek.*

Bates, J. (1994). The role of emotion in believable agents. *Communications of the ACM, 37(7),* 122-125.

Beyer, H., & Holtzblatt, K. (1999). Contextual design. *Interactions, 6(1),* 32-42.

Blow, M., Dautenhahn, K., Appleby, A., Nehaniv, C.L., & Lee, D.C. (2006). Perception of robot smiles and dimensions for human-robot interaction design. *Conference Proceedings RO-MAN 2006* (pp. 469-474).

Dautenhahn, K. (2002). Design spaces and niche spaces of believable social robots. *Conference Proceedings International Workshop on Robot and Human Interactive Communication* (pp.192-197).

Dautenhahn, K., Bond, A. H., Canamero, L., & Edmonds, B. (2002). *Socially intelligent agents: Creating relationships with computers and robots.* Massachusetts, USA: Kluwer Academic Publishers.

Dörner, D., & Hille, K. (1995). Artificial souls: Motivated emotional robots. *Conference Proceedings Systems, Man and Cybernetics* (pp. 3828-3832). Institute of Electrical & Electronics Engineering.

Druin, A., & Solomon, C. (1996). *Designing multimedia environments for children: Computers creativity and kids.* New York, USA: John Wiley and Sons.

Guttman, L. (1950). The basis for scalogram analysis. In A. Samuel (Ed.). *Measurement and prediction.* Princeton, USA: Princeton University Press.

Gulz, A., & Haake, M. (2006). Visual design of virtual pedagogical agents: Naturalism versus stylization and static appearance. *Conference Proceedings NordiCHI 2006.*

Hall, L., Jones, S., Hall, M., Richardson, J., & Hodgson, J. (2007). Inspiring design: the use of photo elicitation and lomography in gaining the child's perspective. *Conference Proceedings British HCI 2007.*

Hall, L., Vala, M., Hall, M., Webster, M., Woods, S., Gordon, A., & Aylett, R. (2006). FearNot!'s appearance: Reflecting on children's expectations and perspectives. *Conference Proceedings IVA 2006* (pp. 407-419). Berlin, Germany: Springer.

Hall, L., & Woods, S. (2004). Empathic interaction with synthetic characters: The importance of similarity. *Unpublished Manuscript.*

Hall, L., Woods, S., Aylett, R., Newall, L., & Paiva, A. (2005). Achieving empathic engagement through affective interaction with synthetic characters. *Conference Proceedings ACII 2005* (pp. 731-738). Berlin, Germany: Springer.

Hall, L., Woods, S., Dautenhahn, K., Sobral, D., Paiva, A., Wolke, D., & Newall, L. (2004). Designing empathic agents: Adults vs Kids. *Conference Proceedings ITS 2004* (604-613). Berlin, Germany: Springer.

Hall, L., Woods, S., Dautenhahn, K., & Wolke, D. (2004). FearNot! designing in the classroom. *Conference Proceedings HCI 2004.* London, UK: Springer-Verlaq.

Hinds, P., Roberts, T., & Jones, H. (2004). Whose job is it anyway? A study of human-robot interaction in a collaborative task. *Human Computer Interaction, 19,* 151-181.

Hoffner, C., & Cantor, J. (1991). Perceiving and responding to media characters. In J. Bryant & D. Zillman (Eds.), *Responding to the screen: Reception and reaction processes* (pp. 63-101). Hillsdale, NJ, USA: Erlbaum.

Johnson, A., Roussos, M., Leigh, J., Vasilakis, C., Barnes, C., & Moher, T. (1998). The NICE project: learning together in a virtual world. *Conference Proceedings IEEE 1998* (pp. 176-183).

Likert, R. (1932). *A technique for the measuring of attitudes,* New York, USA: Columbia University Press.

Lucero, A., & Martens, J. (2006). *Mood boards: Industrial designers' perceptions of using mixed reality.* SIGCHI.NL Conference 2005, HCI Close To You.

MacDorman, K.F. (2005). Androids as an experimental apparatus: Why is there an uncanny valley and can we exploit it? *Conference Proceedings CogSci-2005* (pp. 106-118). Stresa, Italy.

Martens, J., Lucero, A., Naalijkens, B., Ekeler, B., Rammeloo, G., van Heist, M., Kwak, M., & Sakovich, M. (2006). *Blue Eye – making mood boards in augmented reality.* HCI 2006, University of London, UK.

McCloud, S. (1993). *Understanding comics: The invisible art.* New York, USA: Harper Collins Publishers Inc.

Moffat, R. (1997). Personality parameters and programs. In R. Trappl, & P. Petta (Eds.). *Creating personality for synthetic actors.* Berlin, Germany: Springer-Verlaq.

Mori, M. (1970). Bukimi no tani: The uncanny valley. *Energy, 7*(4), 33–35.

Müller, M.J., Wildman, D.M., & White, E.A. (1993). 'Equal opportunity' PD using PICTIVE. *Communications of the ACM, 36(6),* 64-65.

Oosterholt, R., Kusano, M., & de Vries, G. (1996). Interaction design and human factors support, in the development of a personal communicator for children. *Conference Proceedings CHI'96* (pp. 557-564).

Oppenheim, A. N. (1992). *Questionnaire design, interviewing, and attitude measurement (2nd Ed.).* London, UK: Pinter.

Øritsland, T.A., & Buur, J. (2003). Interaction styles: A aesthetic sense of direction in interface design. *International Journal of Human-Computer Interaction, 15(1),* 67-85.

Paiva, A., Dias, J., Sobral, D., Aylett, R., Sobreperez, P., Woods, S., Zoll, C. & Hall, L., (2004). Caring for agents and agents that care: Building empathic relations with synthetic agents. *Conference Proceedings AAMAS 2004* (pp. 194-201).

Paiva, A., Dias, J., Sobral, D., Aylett, R., Woods, S., Hall, L., & Zoll, C. (2005).Learning by feeling: evoking empathy with synthetic characters. *Applied Artificial Intelligence, 19,* 235-266.

Raven, M.E., & Flanders, A. (1996). Using contextual inquiry to learn about your audiences. *Journal of Computer Documentation, 20(1),* 1-13.

Richardson, J. (2006). *Designing a water safety environment using lomography.* Unpublished MSc dissertation, University of Sunderland, UK.

Robins, B., Dautenhahn, K., te Boekhorst, R., Nehaniv, C.L. (2008) Behaviour delay and robot expressiveness in child-robot interactions: A user study on interaction kinesics. Accepted for publication in 3rd ACM/IEEE Human-Robot Interaction conference (HRI08).

Russel, J.A., & Fernández-Dols, J.M. (2002). *The psychology of facial expression.* Cambridge, UK: Cambridge University Press.

Sakaguchi, H. (2001). Final Fantasy: The Spirits Within.

Scaife, M., Rogers, Y., Aldrich, F., & Davies, M. (1997). Designing for or designing with? Informant design for interactive learning environments. *Conference Proceedings CHI'97* (pp. 343-350).

Schuler, D., & Mamioka, A. (Eds.). (1993). *Participatory design: Principles and practices.* New Jersey, USA: Lawrence Erlbaum.

Sengers, P. (1998). Do the right thing: An architecture for action-expression. *Conference Proceedings AGENTS'98* (pp. 24-31).

Sharp, Rogers, & Preece (2007). *Interaction Design. Beyond Human Computer Interaction (2nd Ed.).* Chichester, UK: John Wiley and Sons.

Stotland, E., Mathews, K. E., Sherman, S. E., Hannson, R. O., & Richardson, B. Z. (1978). *Empathy, fantasy and helping.* Beverly Hills, USA: Sage.

Tannenbaum, P. H., & Gaer, E. P. (1965). Mood change as a function of stress of protagonist and degree of identification in a film viewing situation. *Journal of Personality and Social Psychology, 2,* 612-616.

Thomas, F., & Johnston, O. (1981). *The illusion of life: Disney animation.* Walt Disney Animation.

von Feilitzen, C., & Linne, O. (1975). Identifying with television characters. *Journal of Communication, 25*(4), 51-55.

Walters, M. (2007). *The design space for robot appearance and behaviour for robot companions.* Unpublished doctoral dissertation, University of Hertfordshire, UK.

Watson, S., Vannini, N., Davis, M., Woods, S., Hall, M., Hall, L., & Dautenhahn, K. (2007). FearNot! an anti-Bullying Intervention: Evaluation of an interactive virtual learning environment. *Conference Proceedings AISB'07 (*pp. 446-452).

Webb, B.R. (1996). The role of users in interactive system design: When computers are theatre, do we want the audience to write the script? *Behaviour and Information Technology, 15(2),* 76-83.

Wechsler, L. (2002). Why is this man smiling? Digital animators are closing in on the complex systems that makes a face come alive. *Wired, 10(6).* Retrieved December 20, 2007, from http://www.wired.com/wired/archive/10.06/face.html

Wispé, L. (1987). A history of the concept of empathy. In N. Eisenberg & J. Strayer (Eds.). *Empathy and its Development.* Cambridge, UK: Cambridge University Press.

Woods, S., Dautenhahn, K., & Schulz, J. (2004). The design space of robots: Investigating children's views. *Conference Proceedings RO-MAN 2004* (pp. 47-52). New Jersey, USA: IEEE.

Woods, S., Hall, L., Sobral, D., Dautenhahn, K., & Wolke, D. (2003) A study into the believability of animated characters in the context of bullying intervention. *Conference Proceedings IVA 2003* (pp. 310-314). Berlin, Germany: Springer.

Woods, S., Hall, L., Sobral, D., Dautenhahn, K., & Wolke, D. (2005). Animated characters in bullying intervention. *Conference Proceedings IVA 2003* (pp.310-314). Berlin, Germany: Springer.

ADDITIONAL READING

Dautenhahn, K. (1998). The art of designing socially intelligent agents - Science, fiction, and the human in the loop. *Applied Artificial Intelligence Journal, 12(7-8)* 573-617.

Druin, A. (Ed.). (1998). *The design of children's technology.* San Francisco, USA: Morgan Kaufmann.

Druin, A. (2002). The role of children in the design of new technology. *Behaviour & Information Technology, 21(1),* 1-25.

Fabri, M., & Moore, D. (2005). The use of emotionally expressive avatars in collaborative virtual environments. *Conference Proceedings AISB 2005.*

Gaver, B., Dunne, T., & Pacenti, E. (1999). Cultural probes. *Interactions, 6(1),* 21-29.

Gilbert, N., & Troitzsch, K.G. (2005). *Simulation for the social scientist (2nd Ed.).* Glasgow, UK: Open University Press.

Hall, L., Paiva, A., Aylett, R., & Woods, S. (Unpublished manuscript) Empathy in human computer interaction.

Hall, L., Woods, S., Dautenhahn, K., & Sobreperez, P. (2004). Using storyboards to guide virtual world design. *Conference Proceedings IDC 2004.*

MacDorman, K.F. (2005). *Androids as an experimental apparatus: Why is there an uncanny valley and can we exploit it?* Workshop Presented at COGSCI 2005, Stresa, Italy.

MacDorman, K.F. & Ishiguro, H. (2006). The uncanny advantage of using androids in cognitive and social science research. *Interaction Studies, 7(3),* 297-337.

Martin, H. & Gaver, B. (2000) Beyond the snapshot from speculation to prototypes in audiophotography. *Conference Proceedings Designing Interactive Systems: Processes, practices, methods, and techniques* (pp. 55-65).

Paiva, A., Dias, J., Sobral, D., Woods, S., & Hall, L. (2004). Building empathic lifelike characters: the proximity factor. *Conference Proceedings AAMAS 2004*

Walters, M., Dautenhahn, K., Woods, S.N., Koay, K.L., Te Boekhorst, R., & Lee, D. (2006). Exploratory studies on social spaces between humans and a mechanical-looking robot. *Connection Science, 18(4)*, 429-439.

Woods, S., Hall, L., Dautenhahn, K., & Wolke, D. (2004). Implications of gender differences for the development of animated characters for the study of bullying behaviour. *Computers in Human Behaviour, 23(1)*, 770-786.

ENDNOTES

[1]   OGRE (Object-Oriented Graphics Rendering Engine) 3D is an open-source, cross platform, 3D graphics engine (http://www.ogre3d. org).

[2]   We do not claim for the purpose of this chapter that the virtual agents are genuinely capable of 'feeling', in the way the term is applied to human and other biological organisms.

[3]   KASPAR (Kinesics And Synchronisation in Personal Assistant Robotics) was developed at the University of Hertfordshire as part of the RobotCub (http://www.robotcub.org/) and Aurora (http://www.aurora-project.com) projects.

[4]   The official Nintendo Wii controllers website can be found here: http://wii.nintendo.com/ controller.jsp.

[5]   RFID (Radio Frequency Identification) technology incorporates a small radio tag which can wirelessly broadcast its identity to a reader/scanner. The scanner is usually able to display the identity of a tag on a screen. For a more detailed description see http://www. rfidc.com/docs/introductiontorfid_technology.htm.

[6]   E.g., Red Octane's Ignition Dance Pad 3.0 (http://www.redoctane.com/ignitionpadv3. html).

Chapter XVII
Reputation:
Social Transmission for Partner Selection

Mario Paolucci
Institute of Cognitive Science and Technology/CNR, Italy

Rosaria Conte
Institute of Cognitive Science and Technology/CNR, Italy

ABSTRACT

This chapter is focused on social reputation as a fundamental mechanism in the diffusion and possibly evolution of socially desirable behaviour (e.g., cooperation, altruism, and norm-abiding behaviour). Reputation is seen as both a property of agents and a process of transmission of beliefs about this property. The main current views and hypotheses about reputation are found to underestimate the importance of the process of transmission. Next, a cognitive analysis of reputation and of its transmission is presented. Hypotheses concerning the transmissibility of reputation are discussed, and checked by means of simulation. Finally, speculations concerning the role of reputation in the evolution of reciprocal altruism are discussed, and ideas for future studies are sketched out.

INTRODUCTION

This chapter will be focussed on the cognitive properties of reputation favouring its transmission. We propose a definition of reputation as socially transmitted (meta-)beliefs (i.e., beliefs about beliefs) concerning properties of agents, namely their attitudes towards some socially desirable behaviour, be it cooperation, reciprocity, or norm-compliance. Such a definition led us to put forward the hypothesis that reputation plays a crucial role in the evolution of these behaviours: reputation transmission allows socially desirable behaviour to emerge and persist even with low probability of repeated interaction.

This role of reputation depends on the extent to which agents are likely to transmit it to one another. In this perspective, we are indebted to contributions from the memetic theory (for a definition of a meme, see Dawkins, 1976; Blackmore, 1999; for a recent collection of contributions on memes and memetics, see Aunger, 2000), especially in its current computational version (see Best and Edmonds, 2001).

Indeed, the cognitive properties of reputation and in particular the reasons why reputation is harboured in the mind help predict its transmissibility (Dawkins, 1976). In turn, transmissibility of reputation bears important consequences for the role of reputation with regard to socially desirable behaviour. This suggestion is supported by findings from several computer simulation studies on norm-abiding behaviour conducted in the last years within our research group. More generally, as will be argued at the end of this chapter, the view of reputation presented here may contribute to the still debated (see the discussion in Nature: Roberts & Sherratt, 2002) problem of reciprocal altruism theory in settings with low probability of repeated interaction.

The chapter is organised as follows. In the next subsection, we will situate the research on reputation in the broader context of the reciprocal interaction of culture and behaviour. Thereafter, the main current views and hypotheses about reputation will be presented and discussed, and found only partially consistent with current experience and observation. Next, our view of a cognitive model of reputation as a socially spreading meta-belief will be presented, and hypotheses about reputation transmissibility will be formulated. Findings from simulation studies about the role of reputation with regard to a special type of socially desirable behaviour, i.e. norm-compliance, will be shown to be consistent with the model provided before and confirm the emphasis laid on reputation transmission. In the following section, speculative hypotheses concerning the utility of the present approach for the theory of reciprocal altruism will be discussed at some length. Finally, a summary and ideas for future studies will be sketched out.

When Does Culture Influence Behaviour?

This question has two different readings: (a) to what extent a given behaviour is influenced by culture as opposed to other factors (genetic, environmental, etc.)—here behaviour is given, and one must find the explanatory factor; (b) whether and to what extent a given cultural input influences behaviour—here culture is given, and one must predict its effect on behaviour.

The first meaning is a classic nurture/nature question: for example, to what extent are gender differences to be explained as an effect of culture rather than nature? This question presupposes a view of culture as less inertial, more dynamic and modifiable than nature.

Personally, we are more interested in the question whether a given behaviour is the result of an evolutionary process -- whether biological or cultural -- or is an accidental and contingent phenomenon. In this respect, the key question is how cultural evolution is possible at all.

The second meaning -- whether and to what extent a given cultural input influences behaviour -- seems more challenging. Two empirical cautions are necessary, though.

First, behaviour is a fundamental component of culture, which is (also) expressed through and by means of behaviour; consequently, it is difficult to isolate cultural phenomena that are not yet behavioural.

Second, cultural phenomena start to exist the moment they influence behaviour, otherwise they are simply products of human activity and thought. In other words, how could one tell that something belongs to culture if it is not reflected upon the behaviours of its members? What is culture, in the end, but the set of human products that affects their behaviours?

Therefore, culture is both an effect and a cause of behaviour and, before, of mental states and processes. (This feedback loop between behaviour and culture shows that the evolutionary process of emergence is not only a bottom-up process of emergence but a multidirectional one.)

Empirically, it is difficult to point out differences between culture and behaviour in nature. Therefore, a *scientific* approach to culture requires that cultural evolutionary processes are not only observed, but that corresponding hypotheses are formulated and *tested*. This is possible by means of artificial data especially if these are compared with natural ones. Artificial societies can help a lot, here, provided *multidirectional emergence* is taken into account in the modelling and implementation. These requirement have effects on the way agents are modelled and implemented: they need not only be adaptive, but also *endowed with mental states* and social cognitive capacities. This is, in our view, what is needed for the feedback loop between culture and behaviour to be explained.

In this chapter, we will argue for this claim using examples from simulation models of *altruism*. In particular, we will try to show the necessity of a social cognitive model of *reputation* as a fundamental evolutionary ingredient of indirect reciprocity, supported by artificial and natural data concerning the role of reputation as a cultural artefact in the emergence of altruism.

BACKGROUND

The extensive literature on reputation is generally focused on the deterrent role of reputation and on learning to reciprocate (see, Ostrom, 2000). Conversely, the evolutionary role of reputation has been relatively underestimated.

In game-theory (Kreps & Wilson, 1982; Raube & Weesie, 1990; Buskens, 1998; Buskens & Weesie, 1999, etc.) and in the sociological literature (Granovetter, 1985; Coleman, 1990; Burt, 1993), reputation is defined as *"... information that agents receive about the behaviour of their partners from third parties and that they use to decide how to behave themselves."* (Buskens, 1998), or as "characteristic or attribute ascribed to one persona... By another... usually represented as a prediction about likely future behavior... however, primarily an empirical statement" (Wilson, 1985). The spread of reputation, from the game theoretic point of view, is essential to the evolution of cooperation in repeated interactions. The emergence of indirect reciprocity with low probability of repeated interaction has been studied (e.g., Nowak & Sigmund, 1998) with repeated interaction being replaced by agents' individual "image", i.e. their attitude towards altruism, by unspecified "tags" (Riolo et al., 2001), that generate similarity-based cooperation, or by costly signaling (Gintis et al, 2001). This is either directly available to anyone, or based upon direct exposition to others' interactions. No attention is paid to the transmission of social beliefs from one agent to another.

According to these definitions, reputation is viewed as a

- **Mechanism acting on interaction:** It concerns agents' attitude toward reciprocity
- **Learned factor**, acquired from third parties that spread it

- **Entering the decision-making of the parts,** initially for forecasting possible future lack of reciprocation
- **Effect-, rather than process-, oriented:** Precisely because it is viewed as acting on exchange, the advantage of reputation is envisaged in its effects (affecting lack of reciprocation, as in contract violation), rather than in the transmission process (gossip).

Everyday life experience suggests that reputation acts not only on exchange, but also on cooperation, altruism and normative behaviour. It is not only a deterrent factor, contributing to social learning, but prior to this, it is a collective self-defensive mechanism: by means of reputation, in an ideal world, the good guys isolate the bad ones, cheaters, transgressors, and free-riders.

Moreover, reputation is often inaccurate: despite of (or thanks to) the high frequency and probability of errors, rumours and gossip about reputation spread very easily in the social environment. In addition, reputation takes effect even while traveling in the social space, and not only once it gets to destination (that is, when it is known to the target or to its partner). Finally, reputation is mainly acquired indirectly. Rather than supporting or implying direct experience of the target, its transmission serves to replace and avoid it. It enters at least two types of decisions:

- How to interact with reputed agents (*social decision*)
- Whether to spread their reputation (*memetic decision*)

Whilst it may be relatively clear what the social decision is based upon, the question as to what are the grounds for the memetic decision, namely whether to transmit rumours and participate in gossip, is less trivial. Why do "third parties" transmit information about others' reputation? What is their utility in doing so? And why is gossip in particular so much fun? In this chapter, we intend to address such questions, and provide a perspective on reputation that might help to answer them.

In substance, our perspective on reputation subsumes the classical game-theoretic and sociological one. Rather than concentrating on the property only, we propose a model of reputation that accounts for its high *transmissibility*. From the game-theoretic (and sociological) hypothesis, according to which reputation allows for exchange with *repeated interaction*, we will move to a memetic hypothesis (cf. Castelfranchi et al., 1998, Conte, 2000), in which the *propagation* of reputation facilitates cooperation (altruism, norm-abiding behaviour) with low probability of repeated interaction. In fact, information travels faster than agents: cheaters are preceded, and rendered inoffensive, by their fame.

A COGNITIVE VIEW OF REPUTATION

We propose here a view of reputation as a complex, multifaceted object, resulting from a process of social transmission (gossip). Therefore, it is both an agent and a population phenomenon.

At the level of the agent, it can be seen as both a factual property and as a mental state, more precisely a meta-belief. As to the former, it is an *objective* and *emergent* property of the reputed agent, the target. It is objective in the sense that it takes effect even independent of the target's beliefs. It is also emergent since agents gradually and unintentionally grow a reputation as a combined effect of their own behaviour, of others' direct and indirect perceptions, actions and of their communication (gossip). As a mental representation of the reputing agents, it is a cognitive social object, concerning not directly the behaviour of the target, but others' explicit evaluations of it. In this sense, reputation is a meta-belief, a belief about others' beliefs. Such a representation may lead the reputing agent to form a corresponding belief of her own. But this step is not necessary for her to act as a third party and pass it on to others. (We will call here third parties the agents receiving and passing information to others without necessarily using it in social decisions concerning the targets of reputation.)

Elsewhere (Conte, 2002), a detailed cognitive model of the epistemic decision to form or not reputation beliefs is presented. Drawing upon that model, we will limit ourselves to call the reader's attention on the difference between forming a belief and a meta-belief. As we shall argue in the next section, the latter does not imply the former although it may favour it.

At the (sub-) population level, reputation is a *meme*. A meme is usually defined as a unit of cultural evolution (Cavalli-Sforza and Feldman, 1981; Dawkins, 1976; Blackmore, 1999; for a collection of views on the field of memetics, see Aunger, 2000). However, a cognitive view of memetics has been proposed (cf. Conte, 2000), where a meme is defined as a representation which succeeds (is stable and frequent) as long as it travels through social minds. As we will endeavour to show, reputation transmissibility may be advantageous even independent of informational accuracy.

The Object

As a mental representation, reputation is a social meta-belief in two senses. At the first level, it concerns other agents' (the target) properties (the target's presumed attitude towards socially desirable behaviour), whether these have been already encountered or not. At the meta-level, it is a belief about others' evaluations of the target against a socially desirable behaviour. Therefore, reputation information may be either directly or indirectly acquired.

At the first level, it is an evaluative information: if "good", it tells that the target is presumed to display a (norm-conforming, socially accepted) behaviour, and if "bad" it tells the opposite. According to Miceli and Castelfranchi (2000), an evaluation is a hybrid representation. An agent has an evaluation when she believes that a given entity is good for, can achieve, a given goal of hers. An agent has a social evaluation when her belief concerns another agent as a means for her goal.

Two different types of decisions are based upon social reputation:

- Social-strategic decision-making, about whether and how to interact with the target. In this decision, informational accuracy is necessary. Errors may either lead the evaluator to trust a cheater and therefore endanger her own resources, or to avoid a good partner and therefore reduce her chances for a useful transaction.

Figure 1. Plan for communication, where g_1 is a means for g_2.

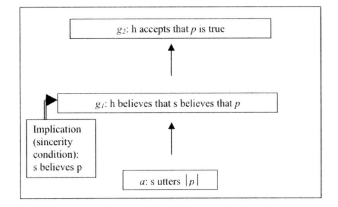

Figure 2. Communicative action is performed to obtain that the hearer believes that t is assigned a given reputation by others, rather than by the speaker herself

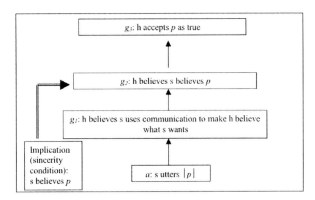

- *Memetic* decision-making, about whether to transmit information to other members of the group, who might benefit from this information. In this decision, accuracy is less crucial, since the evaluator's resources are not (directly) endangered by the output.

Let us see more precisely what are the features of this second, memetic decision.

The Process of Transmission

From a cognitive point of view, a speaker s utters a given sentence p (Castelfranchi, 1992) in order to

- Obtain the goal g_1: hearer h believes that speaker believes that p in order to

- Obtain the goal g_2: hearer accepts that p is true (that is, forms the belief that p).

Figure 1 shows a plan for communication, where g_1 is a means for g_2. However, the figure is still incomplete, since it does not show that both goals, in ordinary communication, are communicative: the speaker wants the hearer to realise that the speaker intended to achieve both effects by means of communication.

In the case of communication about reputation, instead, the communicative action is performed to

- Obtain that the hearer believes that t is assigned a given reputation by others, rather than by the speaker herself (fig. 2: g_2), and to

Figure 3. The communicative action is performed to obtain that the hearer propagates t's reputation (g₄), possibly but not necessarily by having him believe that t is in fact assigned a given reputation (g₃)

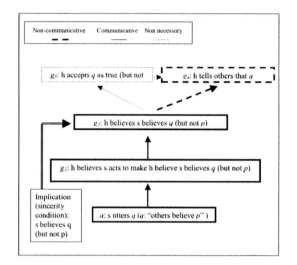

- Obtain that the hearer propagates *t*'s reputation (fig. 3: *g₄*), possibly but not necessarily by having him believe that *t* is in fact assigned a given reputation (fig. 3: *g₃*).

Whilst *g₂* is communicative – the speaker wants the hearer to believe that the speaker used the language to achieve that effect – *g₄* is not. (Indeed, the speaker usually conceals this intention under the opposite communication: "I tell you in confidence, therefore don't spread the news….") To believe that *q* does not imply to believe that *p*. Consequently, communication about reputation is a communication about a meta-belief, i.e. about others' mental attitudes. To communicate *q: "others believe p"* does not bind the speaker to implicitly commit to the truth value of *p*, but only of *q*.

Therefore, unlike ordinary sincere communication, only the acceptance of a meta-belief is required in communication about reputation. And unlike ordinary deception (for a definition of the latter, see Castelfranchi & Poggi, 1998), communication about reputation implies:

- No personal commitment of the speaker with regard to the main content of the information delivered (*p*). If speaker reports on *t*'s bad reputation, he is by no means stating that *t* deserved it.

- No responsibility with regard to the credibility of (the source of) information ("I was told that *t* is a bad guy"). Two aspects ought to be considered here. First, the source of the meta-belief *q* is implicit ("I was told…"). Secondly, the set of agents whom the belief *p* is attributed is non-defined. ("*t* is ill/well-reputed").

Of course, this does not mean that communication about reputation is always sincere. Quite on the contrary, one can and often does deceive about others' reputation. But to be effective, the liar neither commits to the truth of the information transmitted nor takes responsibility with regard to its consequences. If one wants to deceive about reputation, one should report it as a rumour independent of or even despite one's own beliefs!

As a consequence of this analysis, we can derive that unlike other (social) beliefs, reputation may spread even if the majority does not believe it to be deserved. The meta-belief can spread without spreading the belief. More precisely, the cognitive analysis presented above allows some predictions about reputation transmissibility to be made.

Evolutionary Consequences

To further investigate the consequences of our analysis, we move on to inquiring what are the plausible reasons that allowed for reputation to evolve and survive. In this perspective, we are indebted to contributions from the memetic theory (Dawkins, 1976; Blackmore, 1999; Aunger, 2000), especially in its current computational version (see Best and Edmonds, 2001), and to cultural evolution theory (Cavalli-Sforza and Feldman, 1981). In memetics, beliefs may propagate (and therefore contribute to the evolution of social systems) even independent or irrespective of their truth value (see also Doran, 1998). Moreover, it is sometimes the propagation of information itself, rather than its objective content, which provides "added value" to the information in question, and determines its reproductive success. In our view, this is precisely the case of reputation.

In this sense, reputation as a property of an agent affects the environment experienced by that agent, as in the niche construction theory (Feldman, 2003). To show the evolutionary characteristics of reputation, we will now evaluate it with respect to the three components stated in Feldman (2003), i.e., variation, descent, and differential survival. (note: in Conte and Paolucci 2002 we present a similar discussion based on the three original parameters proposed by Dawkins (1976), i.e., fecundity, fidelity, and longevity.)

Starting with descent, in accord with the previous analysis, several factors contribute to *high* fecundity of reputation transmission:

- **Double source.** Source is both direct (one's past experience, and generalization thereof) and indirect (communication from third parties). Obviously this duplicates accessibility to reputation information.
- **No commitment.** The speaker's commitment to the truth of information conveyed is a non-necessary condition for communication about reputation. Hence, the probability that the memetic decision-making leads to communication is higher and the range of reputation transmission is wider.
- **No responsibility.** The costs of the memetic decision about reputation are lower than the costs of other types of communication. Agents will not be considered responsible for circulating rumours and gossip that turned out to be false, provided they circulate them

as such and not as confirmed evidence. Nor will they be held *a fortiori* accountable for the social harm that may follow from such rumours (unless they are found out deliberately to spread around false information). In other words, agents are neither responsible nor accountable for reputation transmission if they transmit meta-belief q, rather than belief p, and if meta-belief is not patently false. However, for the reasons analyzed above, a social meta-belief is less controllable than a belief. Furthermore, whenever it is found to be false, who can be said to be lying in the chain of informants who spread around false reputation? Finally, the more anonymous the set of E whom a given evaluation is attributed, the less a meta-belief can be controlled, and *a fortiori* the less responsible a given "third party" is considered.

About variation, the cognitive analysis does not allow us to harbor high expectations about accuracy in the spread of information about reputation. In fact, on one hand the memetic decision about reputation does not require that the agent is confident about the truth of the information received. On the other, agents will not feel compelled to transmit only information they are certain about, because they are not likely to respond of the effects of reputation transmission. Consequently, errors and false reputation are expected to spread as easily as truthful information. But this lack of accuracy does not necessarily brings a lack in fidelity, that is, from the point of view of the transmitted meme, the probability of being duplicated without modification. Variation in the transmission could result from defective communication, an difficult event if acknowledgment or redundancy mechanisms are implemented, or if a specific agent decides, according to its goals, to modify the information received before transmitting it. It is reasonable to expect that such a decision may be rare, both because of lack of motivation (apart from explicit cheating) and for the interference with the opposite reputation, which is supposed to be spread at some extent in the population.

Lastly, about differential survival, we start from considering that it is our common experience that fame is "sticky". Once you get a given reputation, you are not likely to get rid of it so easily. This is consistent with our cognitive analysis: if reputation accuracy is not checked, it spreads as an unrestrained and uncontrollable flow. But what about the difference between bad and good reputation? Is good reputation as sticky as bad reputation? Are errors in reputation, whether in the positive or in the negative sense, equally likely to spread? Our common intuition is that there is an imbalance here, i.e. a bias for bad reputation. This spreads quicker and sticks to the target more than good reputation, which is more fragile. In our experience calumnies are more fertile and more stable than positive errors. Is this really the case, and if so, why is it so? And what about more subtle reputation aspects that cannot be described by the simple "good/bad" dycothomy?

To propose tentative answers to some of these questions, we resort now to agent-based simulation.

SIMULATION EVIDENCE

Our simulations (Castelfranchi et al., 1998; Paolucci et al., 2000) showed that *repeated interaction is an insufficient condition* for norm-abiding behaviour to compete with cheat. In our studies, agents move on a toroidal grid in search of scarce but self-replenishing food, which they eat as they find it (no accumulation is allowed). Occasionally, an agent may attack another, while this is eating a piece of food. Stronger agents keep ("snatch") the food. Agents' strength increases as an effect of moving around and attacking or receiving attacks. A norm of precedence on food (i.e., not to attack agents eating food marked as "their own") was then implemented in mixed populations of norm-abiders (respecting the norm) and cheaters (not respecting the norm). By definition, to abide the norm may be immediately costly (avoid convenient attacks) and cheat is often a more rational choice for self-interested agents. In mixed population with comparable subpopulation density, these experiments, norm abiders score higher than cheaters on equity (fair distribution of strength on the sub-population), but lower on efficiency (average strength of the sub-population). See (Conte & Paolucci, 2002) for a detailed description of numerical values and strategies used in the experiments.

Things do not improve much when norm-abiders *directly acquire* information about the reputation of cheaters and then punish them by returning illegal attacks (see Fig.4, without exchange of information, left side). In our frame, we found by trial and error that a minimal set of conditions for the normative

Figure 4. Things do not improve much when norm-abiders directly acquire information about the reputation of cheaters and then punish them by returning illegal attacks

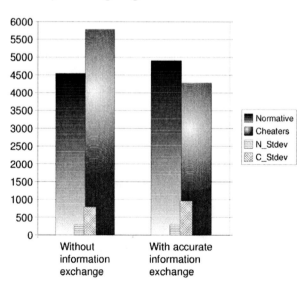

population to overcome inefficiency of the cheating population is composed by:

- Memory of past interactions
- Punishment of cheaters (by cheating them in return)
- Spreading of truthful reputation

Reputation spreading is implemented thanks to an algorithm for information exchange: whenever two norm-abiders meet (they occupy nearby positions), they pass on to one another each its own memory, i.e. a list in which others are recorded as Rs (respectful) or Cs (cheaters). As a result of this exchange, each agent gets a superlist, which contains both the agents' lists.

With information spreading, the average efficiency of the normative strategy is superior. An obvious explanation for these findings can be easily stated. Since reputation transmission is less costly than other actions, included moving around, it travels much faster than agents. It therefore precedes direct experience: agents will punish cheaters even when they did not directly suffer from their misdoing. Hence, agents will profit from reputation information without paying for its acquisition. The transmission process spares agents the cost of knowledge

acquisition, but at the same time renders it accessible to a wider population. Here, what matters is the transmissibility of reputation, and in particular, its fecundity. Thanks to its fecundity, reputation is more efficient and less costly than repeated interaction. In a successive GA-like experiment (Paolucci and Conte, 1999), the norm-abiding behaviour showed a higher reproductive success than cheat, at least when offspring inherited both parents' attitude towards the norm and their reputation.

A follow-up question is now, what if the information transmitted is not accurate? Indeed, informational reciprocity does not prevent errors and deception in reputation transmission. In another experiment (Paolucci, 2000), we have added two sources of inaccuracy: agents may simply make copying errors (communication failures, noise), and there is a tendency to forget information received (memory effect, relaxation rate). While our purpose was mainly of investigating the effects of noise, we serendipitously found that our result can also be classified in terms of the main bias induced by noise. Different combination of noise and relaxation intensities gave rise to two main effects:

- **Inclusive error (courtesy, or social optimism):** A subset of cheaters was erroneously

Figure 5. Summary of simulation findings

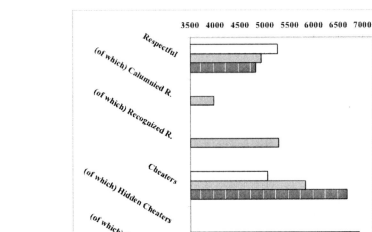

assigned a good reputation (in the recipients' lists of records, some Cs were copied as Rs)

- **Exclusive error (calumny, or social cynicism):** A subset of respectful was erroneously believed to be bad guys (some Rs were copied as Cs).

We had two expectations about findings. First, and consistent with assumptions and results previously obtained by studies on the role of reputation in optimising exchange interactions,, accuracy of information about reputation was expected to be vital for norm-abiders. Errors were expected to benefit cheaters at the expense of the good guys. Secondly, we predicted the two types of errors to produce the same effects. In fact, courtesy was expected to spare cheaters the costs of some deserved retaliation (thereby, producing an absolute benefit for cheaters). Calumny, in turn, was supposed to raise the costs sustained by some unlucky norm-abiders (to the cheaters' relative benefit). An essential *symmetry* of errors in reputation transmission was therefore expected.

Simulation findings (as resumed in fig. 5) point to both some good and some bad news. The good news was that (only) the spread of accurate reputation allowed respectful to out-compete cheaters. This confirmed our expectation that informational accuracy is always preferable for respectful agents

and disadvantageous for cheaters. As is shown by the first set of data, the control or reference condition (in which no errors in reputation transmission were allowed) leads to results far better for respectful agents than either of the error conditions does. Conversely, the results concerning cheaters (see the fourth set of data) show exactly the opposite pattern. Inaccuracy is always preferable for cheaters in either direction.

To check these results, we have run a new set of simulations, in a different framework. All original simulation code has been migrated from C language to Java, with the support of the REPAST (http://repast.sourceforge.net/) framework. The sequence of agent's activation has been modified from contemporary moves to randomly scheduled sequential moves. With our pleasure, the indications coming from reference simulations confirm previous results (Paolucci, 2005).

In this new set of simulations, we model explicitly courtesy and calumny as different algorithms. Instead of adding noise and memory effect, we start by introducing a strength of belief, ranging from 0 to 1, associated with each reputation item. While checking each other's records, agents must make a decision based on their own record (R or C) and the transmitted information (again, R or C), and an update strategy must specify what happens for each possible combination. We examine the following strategies:

Figure 6. The normative strategy remains more efficient with accurate information and no noise

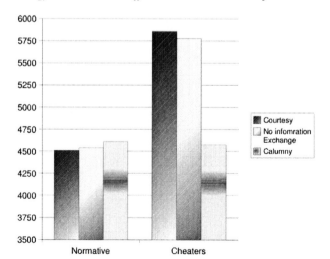

- **Reference strategy:** Only "C" are transmitted, and they are accepted with belief 1.0;
- **Courtesy strategy:** RR and CC cause the belief to be set to the maximum of the two beliefs, while RC and CR cause the receiver to subtract the strength of the transmissed belief from its own.
- **Calumny strategy:** Transmission of C on an R is accepted with strength 1.0: RR and CC cause the belief to be set to the maximum of the two beliefs, while transmission of an R over a C is ignored.

Note the the courtesy strategy is really symmetric with respect to R and C, but since C are more probable (at least with reasonable noise) to be accurate than R, we consider it to be effectively courteous. Simulations are then run with and without noise, defined here as mistakes resulting in faulty transmission. The numerical value given is the probability of error with respect to the single copy. Taking into account the average volume of information exchanges, a rate of 0.0001 causes in average a single copying error each eight turns, that is, about 250 mistakes per 2000-turns run.

Results are summarized in Fig. 6. With accurate information and no noise, the normative strategy remains more efficient. Moreover, the calumny strategy exhibits higher efficiency than the courtesy

strategy. With noise, the situation changes, although not so strongly for the reference and calumny strategies; with very low noise they keep the lead, while for higher noise they are overcome by cheaters' efficiency. What is instead surprising is the effect of noise on the courtesy strategy: even the slightest amount of noise is enough to destroy its equilibrium, and to show a nature of extreme exploitability (note the very high result obtained by cheaters).

The findings confirm the results of the previous experiment, where calumny and courtesy were only a side-effect of noise.

These results point to some interesting news from a social point of view. Unlike expected, errors and biases in propagation are not equivalent. Calumny is by far less detrimental than optimism for respectful agents. Apparently, then, for norm-abiding agents not to be out-competed by cheaters, calumny is preferable over optimism. The expected symmetry in transmission errors does not seem to occur.

Although intrinsically antisocial and aggressive, calumny cooperates with the diffusion of norm-abiding behaviour more than courtesy, which is instead a tolerant, mild, more acceptable behaviour. In the simulations, bad reputation (whether false or not) proved socially disruptive in two distinct senses. On one hand, it ends up with increasing the number of retaliations and hence of aggressions at the population level. On the other, this effect is due to

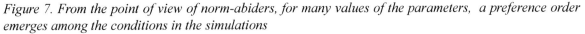

Figure 7. From the point of view of norm-abiders, for many values of the parameters, a preference order emerges among the conditions in the simulations

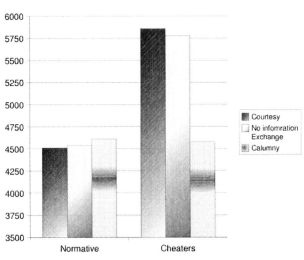

a non-trivial interactive side-effect. Calumny acts as a self-fulfilling prophecy. In fact, its targets will be attacked also by their fellows (other norm-abiders). Hence, these unlucky agents will update their own lists, by "deliberately" turning their attackers, once considered old friends, into Cs (since the old friends now behave as cheaters). Rather than to a retaliatory strategy, this behaviour is due to a fatal chain of misperceptions: the initial error inevitably leads to further misperceptions and consequently to a behavioural adjustment. Much as happens in real life, errors generate further errors.

This renders good reputation intrinsically fragile. An attack which is perceived as undeserved will lead the victim to perceive the attacker as a cheater, whilst this might simply be a good guy, which fell prey to misperception. Unlike bad reputation, good reputation does not act like a self-fulfilling prophecy. Those who are erroneously perceived as honest guys are not induced in an analogous error: they have no reason to modify their records! They will not confirm this misperception by changing their behaviour according to it. Errors towards optimism will not modify effective behaviours, while errors towards cynicism will.

Bad reputation is not only stickier than good reputation. It is also acquired earlier. In our simulations, a fundamental asymmetry occurs also between good and bad reputation, and not only between the two errors implemented. Bad reputation is found out earlier in direct experience. In the simulation, that which is perceived to violate the norm is recorded as a cheater. That which does not, instead, is *not* recorded as a norm-abider, since it might be the case that that violation was contextually inconvenient. Hence, bad reputation spreads faster than good reputation.

Once you get a bad reputation, it will stick to you because

- Others will not revise it immediately even if you don't behave according to your bad reputation (asymmetry)
- Others will have lesser and lesser reasons to revise it because you will increasingly behave according to your bad reputation (self-fulfilling prophecy).

Asymmetry: Threat or Escape?

In some sense, asymmetry in reputation transmission turns into a bias towards bad reputation, and may be interpreted as a threat against accuracy and hence against the fitness of altruism, cooperation, norm-abiding behaviour, etc. If informational accuracy is a necessary condition for norm-abiders not to be out-competed by cheaters, why good reputation is so fragile even when it is true, and bad reputation is so sticky even when it is false?

Here, we can give some preliminary answer on the basis of our simulation, but this question would deserve a rather more complex investigation and should be backed by other, possibly natural data.

Referring again to our data, we can see that not just a stable indication on the superior efficiency of calumny with respect to courtesy appears. From the point of view of norm-abiders, for many values of the parameters (see Fig. 7), a *preference order* emerges among the conditions experimented in our simulations. This preference can be expressed as follows

Accuracy > Calumny > No transmission > Optimism

In other words, whilst truthful information is always preferable for norm-abiders, calumny is the second-best option, preferable not only over optimism but also over no reputation transmission. This hierarchy seems to point to a couple of principles of informational altruism,

- Spread news about others' bad reputation *even if* uncertain (since calumny is preferable to no reputation transmission)
- Do not spread news about good reputation *unless* certain (since no reputation transmission is preferable to optimism).

In sum, despite its disruptive effects at the social level, social cynicism is apparently less dangerous than both social optimism and silence! Doves should act like hawks at the informational level in order not to be invaded by their enemies. This is mirrored by asymmetry in reputation propagation, and in particular by calumny's higher frequency over optimism. Is it this also the reason why calumny is so much fun, in particular more fun than a more discreet, reserved habit in reporting rumours and gossip?

REPUTATION AS INFORMATIONAL RECIPROCAL ALTRUISM

In this section, we will discuss some speculative hypotheses concerning the role reputation as a specific mechanism of partner selection and as an effect of reciprocal altruism which contributed to its stability,.

The focus here is on the evolution of reciprocity. One main problem about the theory of reciprocal altruism, i.e. the evolution of indirect reciprocity (which does not presuppose repeated interaction among donors and recipients) is still in search of an explanation. The main previous attempt by Nowak and Sigmund to solve this problem in terms of an agent property ("image"), will be analyzed. While pointing into the right direction, this attempt will be argued to be is yet unsatisfactory, especially since it does not model reputation as a spreading belief, but only as a property of agents.

The Problem

In sociobiology (Trivers, 1971; Dawkins, 1976), reciprocity may be direct, that is, such that the donor is reciprocated by its recipient (A <-> R), or indirect, such that the donor is reciprocated after several loops by some other recipient than its own (A1 -> A2 -> …->An -> A1).

Direct Reciprocity

In evolutionary game theory, the evolution of cooperation is usually based upon repeated interaction and direct reciprocity (Axelrod, 1997; see also Zeggelink et al., 2000). Obviously, direct reciprocity presupposes individual recognition, and high probability that any two members of the population will meet again after the first encounter. A famous ethological experiment (Wilkinson, 1984) about vampire bats showed that these animals help only individuals coming from the same group, where the probability of repeated encounters is high.

Indirect Reciprocity

Conversely, indirect reciprocity does not require recognition. To reciprocate, the recipient of an altruistic act does not need to re-encounter its previous donor. Indeed, evolutionary game theorists have turned their attention to indirect reciprocity and to the emergence of cooperation in low-density populations. In these conditions, i.e. when donors receive help after several loops, cooperation does not seem to emerge (Boyd and Richerson, 1989) and altruists are bound to die out.

Things improve considerably for altruists if they are allowed to select "trustworthy" partners they have never met before. Nowak and Sigmund (1998) carried out simulation experiments in which donors select recipients according to the extent to which these have helped someone in previous interactions (the authors call this variable "image"). Over time, a strategy called *discriminating cooperation*, in which donors give help to recipients whose image scores are equal or higher than the benefits received, emerges and persists. Nowak and Sigmund show that discriminating cooperation is never invaded by defective strategies (although with increasing size of population and increasing mutation rate multiple strategies tend to co-exist). With a similar approach, (Riolo et al., 2001) uses unspecified "tags" to activate similarity-based cooperation, and (Ginitis et al, 2001) use costly signaling (an altruistic act that evolves to be considered a signal of "high quality") to the same end.

Insufficiency of Image in Partner Selection

Although insightful, the works just described do not show the potential of reputation for indirect reciprocity. Rather than reputation, the authors speak about a "visible" property of agents, immediately and universally (or at least widely) accessible to everybody. No attention is paid to the transmission of social beliefs from one agent to another. No information transmission is at work, and virtually no errors occur.

This solution is not fully satisfactory with regard to the problem of partner selection (see Zeggelink et al., 2001). First, it is poorly realistic. If we could tell altruists so easily, there would be no social dilemma about altruism and cooperation. Secondly, it cannot be a general solution. In Nowak and Sigmund's work, interaction can only be altruistic (if donors don't give help, the interaction has no course), and cheat equals to no help. Consequently, publicity of trustworthiness cannot harm altruists. What would be the case if still unknown cheaters were allowed to act at the expense of altruists, which cannot disguise themselves? If partner selection is based upon public image, it will advantage both sub-populations. An effect that could be assimilated to cheating can be seen in tag structures (Riolo et al., 2001), where agents with zero tolerance can exploit the structure of o group up to its destruction. The periodical formation and collapse of tag groups is apt to model both acceptable phenomena, like fashion changes, and dangerous ones, like social unrest. For the latter, there is a need to understand how exploitation from cheaters can be prevented and controlled.

Rather than upon a public property, therefore, indirect reciprocity ought to rely upon some more selective mechanism, which operates to the advantage of altruists only. This is precisely what reputation does: it consists of the transmission of agents' images among altruists.

Benefits of Reputation

Essentially, we put forward the hypothesis that reputation is a secondary effect of reciprocal altruism. Let us see why.

Being based upon transmission, and not on public display, reputation allows trustworthy partners to be selected and their identities to be kept hidden to cheaters. It kills two birds, selection and secrecy of trustworthy partners.

As with image and tags, reputation transmission allows the number of agents one has information about to exceed the number of agents one interacts with. Therefore, even with low probability of repeated interaction, the number of altruists one helps is higher, and the probability to receive some help is also higher. However, unlike image and tags, reputation allows (un)trustworthy partners to be known only to cooperators or altruists. Consequently, altruists are enabled to select their fellows, but at the same time they cannot be found out so easily by cheaters.

Transmission of reputation points to a second-level reciprocal altruism, i.e. informational altruism. Agents have higher probability of survival and reproduction not only if they provide material help to one another, but also if they provide information about one another's attitude to help, as a means to avoid self-defeating investments. Informational reciprocal altruism (reputation transmission) is here defined as exchange of information that contributes to the reproductive advantage of first-level reciprocal altruism.

One might ask what are the conditions allowing for reciprocity at the informational level, and what happens with cheat at the informational level.

Figure 8. Possible interrelationships the four steps

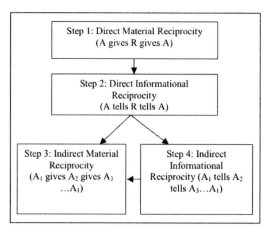

Indeed, it could be objected that if conditions for reciprocity of help are not verified, conditions for reciprocity of information are also not verified.

A couple of considerations seem to attenuate this objection:

• Material help costs are usually higher than the costs of communication. Consequently, incentive to cheat is stronger at the first than at the informational level.

• Material help power is less frequent than information, if only because it does not circulate (memetic effect). Consequently, informational altruism is more likely to occur than material one.

However, a fundamental question arises here. How do altruists select trustworthy partners for information transmission? The most intuitive answer is thanks to direct reciprocity. Exchange of information among known altruists greatly expands the boundaries of help at both levels. If known altruists are trustworthy recipients of both material and informational help (direct reciprocity), they are also credible sources of information. Therefore, also well-reputed agents (known to known altruists) become recipients of material and informational help (indirect reciprocity). Rather than upon personal experience and public image, discriminating cooperation is based upon reputation transmission. Note that there is still space for cheating, but a costly cheating: to be included in informational recirpocal altruism, an agent must cooperate at the material help level, with high immediate costs.

Considering both the dimensions of material and informational help, and of direct and indirect reciprocity, four steps emerge: direct material, direct informational, indirect material and indirect informational reciprocity.

In Figure 8, possible interrelationships among these steps are shown. As argued above, direct material help (step 1) forms a background for direct informational reciprocity (step 2), since known altruists are credible sources and trustworthy recipients of information. Information received by one's fellows works as a mechanism of partner selection for both indirect material and informational reciprocity. Now, agents won't give help only to known altruists,

but also to well-reputed agents, known to known altruists (step 3). Analogously, information will be entrusted to and received by well-reputed agents never met before, but known to known altruists (step 4). The consequent enlargement of information at the agents' disposal will further expand the number of potential trustworthy partners for indirect material reciprocity (from step 4 back to step 3).

SUMMARY AND FUTURE WORK

In this chapter, we have proposed a view of reputation as a complex, multifaceted object both at the agent and at the population level. At the agent level, it is a property of the target which emerges from the propagation of social meta-beliefs, i.e. beliefs about how the target is evaluated by social neighbours.

An analysis of the cognitive features of such meta-belief allows to characterise reputation as an evolutionary process, characterised by efficient transmission (descent), quite stable even if contradicted by experience (with limited variation), and under some hypothesis endowed with differential survival. In particular, reputation spreads quite fast but is often inaccurate, and it a common opinion that bad reputation spreads faster.

Current treatments of reputation (e.g., the game-theoretic one) underestimate the role of transmission, and emphasise the importance of accurate information in repeated exchange. Our simulations studies on the effects of transmission of reputation in artificial populations of norm-abiders and cheaters shed a different light on the subject matter. Due to transmission, reputation plays a role not only in *repeated* encounters, to discourage contract violation, but also in *preventing* interaction with ill-reputed agents. This allowed us to put forward some evolutionary speculations about second-level reciprocal altruism, or reciprocal altruism at the level of information. But what about possible cheat at the level of information?

In our simulations, accuracy results less crucial in reputation transmission (in deciding to pass received information from one to another, agents do not need to check the accuracy of information) than in direct interactions with the target. Initially unforeseen, the exploration on accuracy has given an indication on the difference between a calumny bias and an optimistic bias.

The effects of two different errors in reputation transmission (inclusive, or courtesy, and exclusive, or calumny), showed that, apart from the fact that accurate information is always to be preferred, calumny is preferable both over optimism and over no propagation of reputation.

A further set of simulations showed that norm-abiders are less likely to be out-competed by cheaters if they are alert and spread bad news even at the expense of some of their own members (calumny). The qualitative analysis of simulations highlighted an important feature of calumny, i.e. its antisocial influence. Agents that are mistreated because misperceived will misperceive and mistreat their old friends (self-fulfilling prophecy). This and other qualitative aspects of the simulations contributed to explain a phenomenon frequently observed in social life, i.e. the fragility of good reputation and the stickiness of bad reputation.

These findings seem to encourage further experimental simulation on the subject matter. A follow-up question concerns the social danger consequent to reputation transmission. To what extent, within which limits false reputation is tolerable from a social point of view, and at which point the chain of misperceptions and misbehaviours leads to prejudice, discrimination and social breakdown? Is this a merely quantitative matter, or is there some interesting qualitative phenomenon we should take into account?

To further pursue these research objectives, a research group has been established with the support of EC funding, under the eRep project, that includes in his aims both natural and simulative experiments. Some of the simulative experiments will be performed with the support of a reputation module that distinguishes between image and reputation (Sabater et al., 2006). More details can be found at http://megatron.iiia.csic.es/eRep/.

All our findings points out the direction for a more sound understanding of a well known social phenomenon, gossip as the spread of calumny. Findings are corroborated by the stability they show, even in face of remodeling of the simulation frame: they support our general claim that, in order to tell something about social and cultural phenomena, it is

necessary to include in the modeling explicit mental components in the structure of the agent.

After having stated our point, though, we also want to remind a couple of opposing *caveat*. The first is that modeling *culture* without modeling in some measure the *mind* as a vehicle for the formation, modification and spreading of culture - be it trough tags, signs, semes or memes - is too limited as a position and easily risks to jump to the wrong conclusions. To describe culture, or a part of it, we need to describe also the mind, or part of it. The second starts form the fact that a science of the mind is still far away from being established and widely recognized as something settled, but this should not restrain the scientist from using it while describing culture. Indeed, even the simplest models of the mind can give hints in the description of cultural phenomena - as we have shown for the case of reputation.

ACKNOWLEDGMENT

We gratefully acknowledge Merlin Donald, David Hales, Davide Sparti, and Raimo Tuomela for their useful and interesting comments on a previous version of this chapter. This work has been partially supported by the European Community under the FP6 programme (eRep project, contract number CIT5-028575) and the Italian Ministry of University and Scientific Research under the Firb programme (Socrate project, contract number RBNE03Y338). All mistakes, omissions and misinterpretations that could have happened are, of course, responsibility from the authors only.

REFERENCES

Aunger, R. (ed.) (2000). *Darwinizing Culture: The Status of Memetics as a Science*. Oxford: OUP.

Axelrod, R. (1997). *The Complexity of Cooperation: Agent-Based Models of Competition and Collaboration*. New Jersey: Princeton University Press.

Best, M. & Edmonds, B. (2001). Special Issue on Computational Memetics. *Journal of Memetics, 4*

(2), http://www.cpm.mmu.ac.uk/jom--emit/2001/vol4/index.html#issue2

Blackmore, S. (1999). *The Meme Machine*. Oxford: OUP.

Boyd, R., & Richerson, P. J. (1992). Punishment Allows the Evolution of Cooperation (or Anything Else) in Sizable Groups. *Ethology & Sociobiology,* 13:171-95.

Burt, R.S. (1993). The Social Structure of Competition. In R. Swedberg (Ed.) *Explorations in Economic Sociology*. (pp. 56-103) New York: Russell Sage Foundation.

Buskens, V., & Weesie, J. (1999). Cooperation via Networks. *Analyse und Kritik* 22: 44-74

Buskens, V. (1998). *Social networks and the effect of reputation on cooperation*. ISCORE paper. Mar 1998. 18.

Castelfranchi, C., Conte, R. & Paolucci, M. (1998) Normative reputation and the costs of compliance. *Journal of Artificial Societies and Social Simulation,* vol. 1, no. 3, available at: http://www.soc.surrey.ac.uk/JASSS/1/3/3.html

Castelfranchi, C. (1992). No More Cooperation, Please! In Search of the Social Structure of Verbal Interaction. In A. Ortony, J. Slack & O. Stock (Eds.) *Communication from an Artificial Intelligence Perspective*. Heidelberg, Germany: Springer.

Castelfranchi, C. & Poggi, I. (1998). *Bugie Finzioni e Sotterfugi. Per una scienza dell'inganno*. Roma: Carocci.

Cavalli Sforza, L.L., & Feldman, M.W. (1981). *Cultural Transmission and Evolution*, Princeton: PUP.

Coleman, J.S. (1990). *Foundations of Social Theory*. London: Harvard University Press.

Conte, R. (2000). Memes Through (Social) Minds. In R. Aunger (Ed.)

Conte, R. (2002). Cognitive memetic analysis of reputation. *Cognitive Science Quarterly.*

Conte, R. & Paolucci, M. (2002). *Reputation in Artificial Societies: Social Beliefs for Social Order*. Boston: Kluwer.

Dawkins, R. (1976). *The Selfish Gene*. Oxford: OUP

Doran, J. (1998). Simulating Collective Misbelief. *Journal of Artificial Societies and Social Simulation* vol. 1, no. 1, http://www.soc.surrey.ac.uk/JASSS/1/1/3.html

Feldman, M. W. (2003). Dissent with modification: The science of culture exists. In the *Proceedings of the Conference "Toward a Scientific Concept of Culture."* Stanford University, January 23-26.

Gilbert, N., & Troitzsch, K. (1999). *Simulation for the social scientists*. The Open Univ. Press.

Gintis, H., Smith, E. A., Bowles, S. (2001). Costly Signaling and Cooperation. *J. Theor. Biol.* 213, 103-119

Granovetter, M. (1985). Economic Action and Social Structure: the Problem of Embeddedness. *American Journal of Sociology*, 91: 481-510.

Kreps, D.M. & Wilson, R. (1982). Reputation and Imperfect Information. *Journal of Economic Theory*, 27: 253-279.

Miceli, M., & Castelfranchi, C. (2000). The role of evaluation in cognition and social interaction. In K. Dautenhahn (Ed.), *Human cognition and agent technology*. Amsterdam: Benjamins.

Nowak, M.A., & Sigmund, K. (1998). Evolution of indirect reciprocity by image scoring. *Nature*, 393, 573-577.

Ostrom, E. (2000). Collective Action and the Evolution of Social Norms. *Journal of Economic Perspectives*. 14, 137-158.

Paolucci, M., & Conte, R. (1999). Reproduction of normative agents: A simulation study. *Adaptive Behavior*, special issue on Simulation Models of Social Agents, 7(3), 301-322.

Paolucci, M., Marsero, M., & Conte, R. (2000) What's the use of gossip? A sensitivity analysis of the spreading of normative reputation. In R. Suleiman, K. Troitzsch and N. Gilbert (Eds.) *Tools and Techniques for Social Science MicroSimulation*. Berlin: Springer.

Paolucci, M. (2000). False Reputation in Social Control. In G. Ballot & G. Weisbuch (Eds.), *Applications of Simulation to Social Sciences*. Paris: Hermes.

Paolucci, M. (2005). Reputation as a Complex Cognitive Artefact. Theory, Simulations, Experiments. Unpublished doctoral dissertation, University of Florence, Italy (available at http://150.146.65.191/mario/PaolucciReputationAsACmplxCgntvArtfct.pdf)

Raub, W., & Weesie, J. (1990). Reputation and Efficiency in Social Interactions: An Example of Network Effects. *American Journal of Sociology*, 96, 626-654.

Riolo, R. L., Cohen, M. D. & Axelrod, R. (2001). Evolution of cooperation without reciprocity. *Nature*, *414*, 441-443.

Roberts, G., & Sherratt, T. N. (2002). Does similarity breed cooperation?, *Nature*, *418*, 499-500. Followed by answer from Riolo, Cohen and Axelrod.

Trivers, R. (1971). The evolution of reciprocal altruism. *Quarterly Review of Biology,* 46, 35-56.

Sabater, J., Paolucci, M., & Conte, R. (2006). Repage: REPutation and ImAGE Among Limited Autonomous Partners. *Journal of Artificial Societies and Social Simulation*, 9(2).

Wilson, R., (1985). Reputation in Games and Markets. In A. Roth (Ed.), *Game-Theoretic Models of Bargaining*. Cambridge, CUP

Zeggelink, E.P.H., de Vos, H. & Elsas, D. (2000). Reciprocal altruism and group formation: The degree of segmentation of reciprocal altruists who prefer 'old-helping-partners'. *Journal of Artificial Societies and Social Simulation, 3*(3).

Chapter XVIII
A Simulation of Temporally Variant Agent Interaction via Belief Promulgation

Adam J. Conover
Towson University, USA

ABSTRACT

This chapter concludes a two part series which examines the emergent properties of multi-agent communication in "temporally asynchronous" environments. Many traditional agent and swarm simulation environments divide time into discrete "ticks" where all entity behavior is synchronized to a master "world clock". In other words, all agent behavior is governed by a single timer where all agents act and interact within deterministic time intervals. This discrete timing mechanism produces a somewhat restricted and artificial model of autonomous agent interaction. In addition to the behavioral autonomy normally associated with agents, simulated agents should also have "temporal autonomy" in order to interact realistically. This chapter focuses on the exploration of a grid of specially embedded, message-passing agents, where each message represents the communication of a core "belief". Here, we focus our attention on the how the temporal variance of belief propagation from individual agents induces emergent and dynamic effects on a global population.

INTRODUCTION

In the chapter entitled *A Simulation of Temporally Variant Agent Interaction via Passive Inquiry*, we examined a mechanism of agent interaction where each agent – in a specially embedded two-dimensional grid – periodically examines the states of neighboring agents and modifies its own state according to

an inherent set of rules. In those experiments, the agents did not attempt to actively influence their neighbors in any way. In this chapter, we give agents the ability to send events to neighboring agents in attempt to influence their behavior. Here, we outline two approaches: The first approach extends the previous *Game of Life* simulations by eliminating autonomous agent vivification and replacing it with event triggered vivification. The second approach abandons the *Game of Life* inspired rule-set and instead implements a world of agents, each possessing a simple belief with a corresponding strength. In this last model, agents "compete" to alter the belief of neighboring agents. Finally, we conclude with some details relevant to the implantation of the simulation environment; including a brief overview of agent behavior customization and the data logging techniques used throughout these simulations.

MESSAGE DRIVEN COMMUNICATION

Thus far, we have focused on the exploration of the globally emergent behaviors in passive agent interaction systems. The agents reacted to their environment, but did so in a manner where each agent's vivification was independent of neighboring vivifications. In the message based version of this simulation, the focus shifts from agents behaving passively within the environment into a model where each agent actively attempts to exert influence over the environment. The emergent behaviors observed in previous sections resulted from agents examining their immediate surroundings and updating themselves accordingly. Global behavior arose from the non-deterministic agent vivification order and the asynchronous nature of the updates. In this set of experiments, global emergence is driven by the exchange of messages.

In this section, we expanded our simulation to accommodate *active* agents which directly communicate—albeit in a primitive manner. Information is exchanged as simple messages which are reflective of an agent's internal state. Though agents may take on many states during a simulation, each agent communicates its active state with its spatially embedded neighbors. The active model is divided into two distinct subtypes. The first subtype, discussed in Section "*Message Driven* Game of Life", is a direct extension of the previous "Conway" model; but agents respond to events generated by neighbors rather than vivificating autonomously. The second subtype, discussed in Section "*Fuzzy 'Belief' Promulgation*", is a completely new model based upon temporally variant "belief" interaction. The models in both subtypes display interesting and rather unique behavioral characteristics.

Message Driven *Game of Life*

In this mode, each agent begins in a random Boolean state conforming to the basic "Conway" life/death (active/inactive) rules. As with the threaded model discussed in Section "Threaded Model", the agents behave autonomously within a global mean vivification delay time dm of 500ms with delay variances dv chosen to produce dm/dv ratios rmv ranging from 0.0 to 2.0. However, instead of agents simply examining their neighborhood at intervals which are independent of the environment, the agents

Table 1. This table shows a sampling of data (5 trials for each r_{mv} tested) taken from our complete database of trials for sorted by age_{avg}

r_{mv}	μ_d	μ_a	μ_m	$\hat{\sigma}_d$	$\hat{\sigma}_a$	$\hat{\sigma}_m$
0.15	0.407	4.44	35.5	0.00055	0.030	0.217
0.25	0.409	4.54	36.3	0.00045	0.024	0.217
0.50	0.411	4.72	37.8	0.00055	0.031	0.278
0.75	0.415	5.14	41.1	0.00045	0.059	0.464
1.00	0.417	5.33	42.6	0.00055	0.019	0.167
1.25	0.420	6.00	48.1	0.00045	0.061	0.501
1.50	0.421	6.17	49.3	0.00045	0.066	0.534
1.75	0.423	7.02	56.2	0.00045	0.103	0.850
2.00	0.424	7.12	56.9	0.00110	0.137	1.163

Figure 1. Graphs of the statistics gathered for the experiments conducted in Section "Message Driven Game of Life", along with the plots of the standard deviations for the experimental data

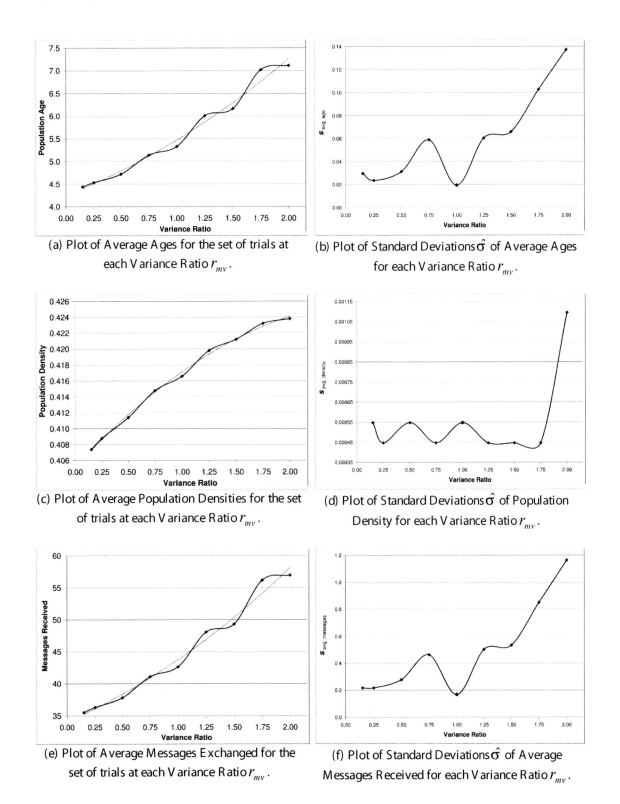

(a) Plot of Average Ages for the set of trials at each Variance Ratio r_{mv}.

(b) Plot of Standard Deviations $\hat{\sigma}$ of Average Ages for each Variance Ratio r_{mv}.

(c) Plot of Average Population Densities for the set of trials at each Variance Ratio r_{mv}.

(d) Plot of Standard Deviations $\hat{\sigma}$ of Population Density for each Variance Ratio r_{mv}.

(e) Plot of Average Messages Exchanged for the set of trials at each Variance Ratio r_{mv}.

(f) Plot of Standard Deviations $\hat{\sigma}$ of Average Messages Received for each Variance Ratio r_{mv}.

now trigger the vivification of their neighbors by sending events. To maintain temporal autonomy, agents still "vivificate" as before, but in lieu of passive examination of neighboring states, the agent queries an internal message queue for the presence of pending notifications received from other agents. If an agent is inactive, it cannot become active until it receives a notification from a live neighbor. Only active agents are capable of sending messages to other agents. When any given agent vivificates, it determines the state of its own environment and sends notifications to all neighbors, if it becomes or remains active. An agent will only send one message to each of its neighboring agents once per vivification regardless of how many messages are in the queue. Once the vivification cycle completes (all neighbors have been notified), the sending agent clears its own message queue and awaits new messages from neighboring agents.

As in Section "Threaded Model", we are primarily interested in the average population density and average population age of the agents as a given trial progresses. However, this time we also examine the number of messages received by each agent between vivifications. A summary of the data gathered in the first set of message based activation trials is shown in Table 1, ordered by r_{mv}. Other values include; the average population density μ_d, the population's average age μ_a, the average number of messages received per agent μ_m, and the standard deviations $\hat{\sigma}_d, \hat{\sigma}_a, \hat{\sigma}_m$, of data in each sample set grouped by r_{mv}.

Fuzzy "Belief" Promulgation

In the "Message Driven" architecture, each agent actively attempts to influence its neighbors' "beliefs" by promulgating belief messages to all adjacent agents upon vivification. Though formal models of agent belief interaction have been studied by others (Cantwell, 2005)(Pasquier & Chaib-draa, 2003), our experimentation requires only a very simplistic model of belief representation. In a similar spirit to work done in dynamic team formation of agents (Gaston & desJardins, 2005) and "Naming Games in Spatially-Embedded Random Networks" (Lu, Korniss, & Szymanski, 2006), our research examines agent clustering driven by agent states. However, we focus on an exploration of the effects

of temporal variance in swarms of agents capable of interacting purely asynchronously.

Every agent participates in a primary active belief which is directly conveyed to each of its spatially embedded neighbors via "belief messages". Agents send and receive messages corresponding to some belief and may adopt a new belief based upon "peer-pressure" from neighboring agents. As agents receive messages, they modify their own active belief in accordance with the messages received from other agents. Loosely speaking, the goal of any individual is to convince its neighbors to become like it. Messages generated by any given agent will affect the beliefs of others in the immediate neighborhood, which in turn will continue to affect other agents farther away. This also introduces feedback into the system, since any agent propagating a message will eventually be affected by its own actions at a later point in time. Ultimately, we see a clustering of agents with the same "beliefs", but whose populations are driven primarily by the "temporal variability" of the actual interactions.

Currently, there are three distinct messages types, each corresponding to an inherent agent belief. Each belief is represented by a unique primary color; RED, GREEN, or BLUE. The experimental reason for having three message types represented by color is for easy real-time visualization of a world with more than just two competing (Boolean) forces, as in the previous model. As agents communicate, their internal state is visually represented by a blending of the colors corresponding to the actual beliefs. Though any agent may be in a "fuzzy" belief state at any given moment, the belief that is communicated is always discrete. In other words, if an agent has been exposed to multiple RED, GREEN, and BLUE messages, it will exist in a state that blends these beliefs, but will always communicate the discrete belief most closely represented.

Though the message produced by any given agent could easily be based purely upon a count of the number of messages received of a given type, we wanted a more flexible system that allowed message types to be weighted or other transformations applied to the fuzzy state. The method used to determine the most appropriate message associated with a belief is based on the color values themselves. The messages are blended into a color in RGB color-space and the

Figure 2. Three snapshots of the clustering of agent types throughout the world; time advances clockwise from the left-most image

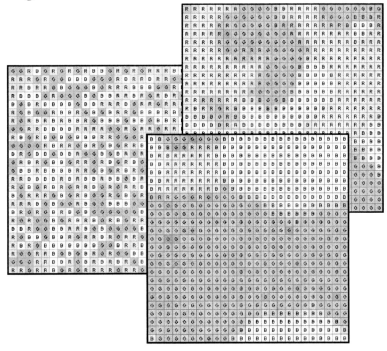

message generation algorithm is derived from the following rules applied in order:

1. If all three RGB color component values are equal, a message type is chosen at random.
2. If there exists an RGB color component that exceeds all others, the message corresponding to the strongest color component is chosen.
3. If any two RGB color values are equal, a random message type corresponding to one of the two equal values is chosen.

Figure 2 is a collage of screen-shots from a running simulation. Each agent is displayed as a cell labeled with a single letter corresponding to the fundamental belief and a color representing the agent's fuzzy belief state. Snapshots of a progressing simulation can be seen while moving clockwise around the figure, starting at the far left. The first image shows the starting state of a simulation with all agents in one of three random states. The second image is further along in a simulation where clustering of beliefs begins to take place. Finally,

the last image shows the near complete clustering of beliefs. A fourth, but omitted, screen-shot would show the one remaining belief once all others have become extinct.

The simulation engine allows for beliefs and message types to carry distinct weights. However, in the experiments outlined here, all beliefs and messages carry the same weight. In other words, the "popularity" of a belief is based solely upon the number of messages exchanged within the environment and not any properties inherent in the beliefs themselves. The only aspect of the simulation we vary during the course of an experiment is the allowable timing variances of each of the three primary message types. In this research effort, the timing variation is always manually controlled[1]. The most striking and readily observable phenomenon is the somewhat non-intuitive effect that timing variance has on population density; the lower the timing variance (the closer zero), the more likely a certain belief is to survive. In other words, the messages being passed with the least amount of timing variation are the messages most likely to influence the beliefs of the recipients.

Figure 3. Population and vivification variance ratios vs. time

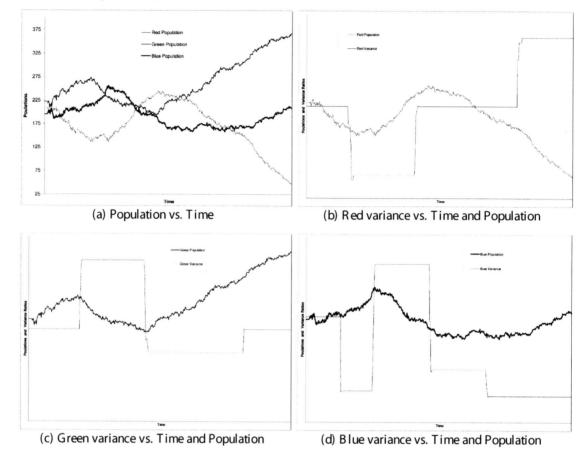

(a) Population vs. Time

(b) Red variance vs. Time and Population

(c) Green variance vs. Time and Population

(d) Blue variance vs. Time and Population

All beliefs b are assigned a unique d_v^b value, which represents the inherent timing variation associated with the dissemination of that particular belief. All agents participating in a given belief adopt the prescribed vivification properties of the belief itself. When an agent adopts a new belief b, its d_v will be updated to match the current d_v^b. For example, an agent participating in a GREEN belief might announce that belief with very regular vivifications; while an agent with a RED belief may announce that belief with an extreme timing variation. A small section of a sample experimental run is shown in Figure 3 which is divided up into four distinct sub-figures. Figure 3a shows a plot of the *relative* population densities for the three message types from the beginning of a trial to an arbitrary point in time within the trial. In this plot, the relative number of agents participating in a given belief

versus time is represented. Figures 8b through 8d require a bit more explanation. The heavier solid line in each of these figures corresponds to one of the lines in Figure 3a and the lighter line represents the d_v of all the agents of a particular belief. As the simulation ran, d_v^b was dynamically altered, affecting the global populations of agents with given beliefs over time.

The plot of the GREEN belief variance (Figure 3c) depicts the total population agents participating in the "GREEN" belief and the correspondin d_v^{GREEN} value over time. The values of d_v^{GREEN} were manually altered over time via the dedicated sliders in the GUI interface (Figure 4) manipulating the overall population. The higher the thin line on the graph, the greater the variance of vivification at that time. The "GREEN" plot clearly illustrates the population of agents participating the in belief changing inversely with the variance level. The "RED" belief plot (Figure 3b) is also interesting to observe since the same effects can be seen, but the population changes lag slightly behind the changes in d_v^{RED}. The "BLUE" belief exhibits this phenomenon as well, though only one of the variance changes produces a clearly discernible response with an immediate change in population; the other responses are more subtly visible.

THE APPLICATION FRAMEWORK

Here we provide a brief overview of the experimentation platform itself. The simulation is a small, custom platform written in Java that uses no "off-the-shelf" agent or swarm simulation frameworks. Though many quality frameworks exist (Bordini et al.., 2006)(Terrence Fong, Illah Nourbakhsh & Dautenhahn, 2003), our intent was certainly not to re-invent the work of others. The rationale for creating a custom platform is twofold. First, the data we are looking for is very specific and narrow in scope, so a full fledged framework would be overkill. Second,

we needed fine grained control over hundreds (and perhaps thousands) of individual threads. Due to the inherent simplicity and versatility of thread management in Java, developing our own mini-platform was the easiest solution that fit the requirements of the experiments we wished to conduct.

Since—in the message based simulations—each agent uses an internal queue to accumulate incoming messages from neighboring agents, a message queuing system is necessary. A full featured message queuing system such as JMS(Sun Microsystems, 2007b)(Henjes, Menth, & Zepfel, 2006) would introduce unnecessary overhead. In our implementation, each agent has its own linked list behaving as a message queue. When an agent sends a message to another agent, the message is added to the target agent's queue. As part of the normal agent vivification cycle, the agent processes all messages in the queue in bulk; processing the entire queue during each vivification. In future, networked versions of the simulation, a system such as JMS will likely become necessary once the need for sophisticated distributed message processing becomes necessary.

Figure 4. Collage of the key interface elements of the temporal variance experimentation platform

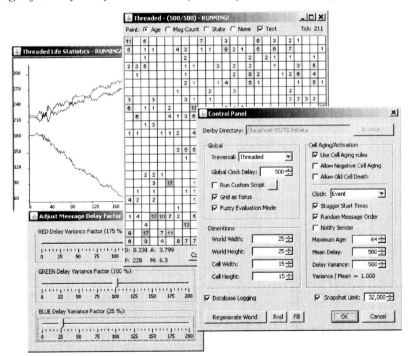

A collage of the full interface to the application with several associated dialog boxes is shown in Figure 4. Though some of the main interface controls in the figure are obscured by other windows, a brief description of the available controls is presented. The "paint" radio buttons across the top of the main application interface configure the display of the age (number of consecutive successful vivifications) of the agents, the number of messages received between successive vivifications, or the agent state. The "tick" value can mean one of two things, depending on the mode of operation. In a globally-clocked simulation, the value represents the number of actual generations the world has been running. In a threaded simulation this value reflects the number of statistical snapshots taken since the simulation began. The lower-left corner of the user interface provides continuous real-time data pertaining to the progress of the simulation. Shown are the population **D**ensity, average population **A**ge, raw **P**opulation, and the average number of number of **M**essages received by each agent per vivification interval. Along the bottom of the main interface window is a "chart" button which displays a real-time graph display provided by the LGPL licensed *JChart2D* library (JChart2D, 2007). On this graph we can watch plots—such as the one shown in the background of Figure 4—in real-time.

The main visualization area itself shows all agent activity as the simulation progresses. Values are only painted on "active" agents and the value displayed is determined by the "paint" setting at the top. Additionally, the color of any given agent will vary depending on the "paint" type. In the simple value types, the agents start out as dark blue and gradually change to yellow as the given value increases. If the "state" is being painted, then the color of the agent is dependant on the actual state of the agent; where specific colors are assigned to specific states. This coloring mechanism provides a clear and intuitive visualization of the agent activity within the world.

Most of the settings for a given simulation are configured in the control panel view shown in Figure 4. Though most of the options on the control panel are self explanatory, we will discus a few options of particular interest. All of the traversal modes discussed in this chapter are selectable from the "Traversal" drop-down list, while the mean vivification time interval is controlled via the "Global Clock Delay" spinner. The world can be configured as either a simple rectangle or a torus via the "Grid as Torus" check-box. "Fuzzy Evaluation Mode" effectively controls the usage of "beliefs" as opposed to simple Boolean messages, which were used in the earlier experiments. "Use Cell Aging Rules" controls the age advancement of the agents within the simulation. "Stagger Start Times" allows all of the agent clocks to have a randomly determined start time, which is useful in simulations with

Figure 5. Javascript code used to implement the Conway Game of Life rules

```
function evaluate(curAge, curStatus, neighborCount) {

    switch (neighborCount) {
        case 0: return 0;
        case 1: return 0;
        case 2: return curStatus;
        case 3: return 1;
        case 4: return 0;
        case 5: return 0;
        case 6: return 0;
        case 7: return 0;
        case 8: return 0;
        default: return 0;
    }

}
```

low delay variances; thus preventing the pseudo-generational like behavior that would occur if all agents attempted to vivificate simultaneously). The "Random Message Order" and "Notify Sender" check-boxes control whether neighbors should be selected in random order and whether the sender of a message should also be included in the recipient list, respectively.

Finally, a few options exist in the control panel which were either not used in any of the trials outlined, or their effects do not impact trial results. "Allow Negative Cell Aging" can force cells to age backwards instead of becoming "inactive" in the *Game of Life*-like simulations. "Allow Old Cell Death" causes any cell which ages past a certain point to automatically become inactive. The ability to run custom rule evaluation scripts is selectable and described briefly below, as is the ability of the simulation to log all snapshots results into an embedded database.

Scripted Rule Evaluation

Java 6 introduced pluggable scripting language engine support. Though this functionality was available in previous versions of Java, it was implemented through non-standard mechanisms. Java 6 implemented "JSR-223" which created a standardized mechanism for the integration and interfacing of scripting environments within the Java platform. *JavaScript* (also known as ECMAScript) is integrated and available by default, but scripting languages such as *Groovy*, *BeanShell*, and even *Scheme* are able to be utilized with little work on the part of the application programmer[2]. The key component of any pluggable scripting language is that Java objects are handled seamlessly by the scripting environment. In other words, Java objects are treated as first class objects in the scripting environment. This allows for nearly unlimited customized control over the behavior of an agent. The major benefit of the scripting is that no code needs to be recompiled (or complicated customization systems implemented) to alter the behavior of the simulation. The framework created for experiments outlined in this chapter utilize this functionality to implement custom rule evaluation methods written in the JavaScript programming language.

Figure 5 illustrates the GUI interface dialog box where the user may enter custom code generate a new state from an existing state and information about the number of adjacent neighbors. Though the parameters here are simple (and not all used in the example), more complicated scripts are possible with little overall performance degradation of the simulation. Shown in this illustration, is the JavaScript code for evaluating the grid based on the *Game of Life* rules.

Derby Database

The *Apache Derby* RDBMS is an embeddable database system derived from *Cloudscape* code donated to the Apache Software Foundation (Zikopolous, Baklarz, & Scott, 2005) by IBM. As of Sun Microsystems' Java 6, Derby now serves as Sun's officially supported embedded RDBMS in the form of *JavaDB* (Sun Microsystems, 2007a). The primary benefit of Apache Derby is that it is capable of running in either network, stand-alone, or embedded modes, making data collection a relatively simple task without the need for a dedicated database server. The simulation framework uses an embedded Derby engine which logs all relevant data for further analysis. Being nearly completely SQL-92 compliant, Derby allows data to be easily queried and/or exported for interpretation by dedicated data analysis and charting tools such as SPSS, R, or Microsoft Excel. ODBC drivers also exist for Derby, which allow straight forward access via nearly any database aware application. Additionally, with the most recent versions of Java[3] and recent JDBC drivers, you are no longer required to *manually* load the database driver class in your code as was previously required[4]. This allows for easy migration to nearly any database system with JDBC drivers and allows the Derby database to be accessed from nearly any JDBC compliant front-end.

HARDWARE/SOFTWARE DETAILS

The simulation environment was programmed using Sun Microsystems' Java 6 Developer Kit and the Netbeans Integrated Development Environment and has been tested on both Windows® XP/Vista and GNU/Linux®. Running on a 2.2Ghz Athlon XP development machine with a 25x25 grid (625 threads) and screen updates disabled, memory usage for the average simulation trial hovered around 60MB with less than 2% overall CPU utilization. Running with visualization (real-time graphs and live visualization) enabled, the CPU utilization jumped to approximately 20%. Profiling confirmed that the dramatic increase in CPU utilization was simply due to Swing[5] paint methods. With real-time visualization disabled, the multi-threaded simulation requires very little system overhead.

Java's threading seems sufficient for medium scale simulations on a single, moderately configured PC. Grids of up to 75x75 (5625 threads) have been implemented successfully, but increasing the thread count much beyond that is likely to generate "Out of Memory" errors due to the excessive thread overhead on the operating system[6]. Later tests on a dual core CPU revealed that a slightly larger number of threads were indeed possible, but the greatest limitation empirically stems from operating system and/or JRE limitations. For significantly larger simulations on a single CPU—which could involve many thousands of concurrent threads—some sort of "thread simulation" would likely be necessary. Such a simulation would involve all agents being under the control of a single master thread which activates agents in a manner which preserves the behavior of a true multi-threaded environment.

Another important implementation decision to note is the intentional lack of "thread safety" in the simulation. The implications of this may seem subtle at first glance but are very significant in the context of creating realistic behavioral models. In any environment where "reaction time" is a factor, there is always the possibly that an agent's environment will change between the time that the environment is sensed and the time that the agent reacts. For example, in the simulation conducted in Section "*Threaded Model*" an agent examines all of its neighbors at time t_i through t_{i+n+tl}, makes a decision as to what state to adopt $t_{i+n+tl+1}$, and finally alters its state accordingly at time $t_{i+n+tl+2}$; where t_i is the initial time at which the agent begins examining its environment, n is the number of neighbors, and tl is a nondeterministic inter-thread latency introduced by the other concurrently executing threads. Since this general timing rule applies to all agents in the

world, an agent may adopt a state at the end of a vivification cycle that is inconsistent with the world as it existed at t_i. This is consistent with the "real-life" actions of physical agents when one considers that reaction time is finite and variable. For example, human agents form *conscious* perceptions of the world by a process Daniel Dennett refers to as "backward projection in time" (Dennett, 1998).

CONCLUSION

Though formal mathematical models of the various results have yet to be completed, the goal of the research presented here is to establish that the manipulation of timing *variability* in temporally autonomous agent systems impacts the emergent population behavior. Throughout this research, two primary phenomena were analyzed. First, the study of the effects of asynchronous updating in the *Game of Life* clearly reveals the fact that simple changes in traversal policies create significant differences in population behavior. Given the nature of the changes, it would seam reasonable to assume that the global behavior of each system would be unique. However, the purpose of these experiments was to establish a progression towards a system that mimicked complete temporal autonomy of a swarm of independent agents. Second, the study of temporal autonomy in agent swarm behavior reveals that altering the timing variability of interacting agents also produces effects in the overarching behavior of the entire system. Emergent clusters of agents participating in independent beliefs are directly affected by the timing variability of their communications. We can see the potential for the foundations of this research to be applicable to any system which models discrete entities acting autonomously in time; such as in vehicular traffic flow modeling, data network communication, neural networks, etc.

Expanded research may also include the ability to connect multiple worlds together over a network. Given Java's ease of network interaction, the implementation mechanics of such a system would be relatively straight forward. However, numerous design decisions would need to be made regarding the nature of the experiments themselves and the topologies of interconnection. For example, six separate simulations could be networked together forming the surface of a cube. Each agent at the boundary of any given world would interact with agents at the boundary of an "adjacent" world. This would preserve the topology of agents acting on a single two-dimensional surface. Another possibly is that of "stacking" simulations on top of each other, where each machine represents a plane of agents which communicate in a virtual three-dimensional space. Regardless of the interconnection topology, the timing variances of agent communication across network connections would be much harder to control and additional elements of experimental uncertainty would be introduced. However, this type of experimentation would be interesting in its own right, as it would be possible to easily simulate the behavior of interacting groups, where the groups each differ in their intra-communication dynamics.

The next immediate and major phase of this ongoing research project is the exploration of an expanded belief system with "belief graphs" that allow for the modeling of interconnected and interrelated belief systems. However, as of this writing the simulation framework is being modified to accommodate dynamically adapting vivification variance ratios. For example, given the desired target ratios of agent populations holding specific beliefs within a swarm, those ratios can be achieved and maintained by controlling the timing variances of the interaction of each belief. For example, suppose we want a world that is 20% "Red", 30% "Green", and 50% "Blue". In a configuration where all beliefs have equal weight and equal timing variances, the most predominant belief will generally prevail and quickly dominate the entire world. However, by dynamically controlling just the vivification delay variances of the agents holding specific target beliefs (leaving the mean message exchange rate and message weights equal), we can establish steady and predictable agent population ratios.

REFERENCES

Bordini, R., Braubach, L., Dastani, M., Seghrouchni, A. E. F., Gomez-Sanz, J., Leite, J., . (2006). A survey of programming languages and platforms for multi-agent systems. In *Informatica 30,* 33-44.

Cantwell, J. (2005). A formal model of multi-agent belief-interaction. *Journal of Logic, Language, and Information, 14*(4), 397-422.

Dennett, D. C. (1998). *Consciousness explained.* Cambridge, Massachusetts: The MIT Press.

Gaston, M. E., & desJardins, M. (2005, July 25-29). Agent-organized networks for dynamic team formation. In F. Dignum, V. Dignum, S. Koenig, S. Kraus, M. P. Singh, & M. Wooldridge (Eds.), *4rd international joint conference on autonomous agents and multiagent systems (AAMAS 2005),* (pp. 230-237). *Utrecht, The Netherlands*: ACM.

Henjes, R., Menth, M., & Zepfel, C. (2006). Throughput performance of Java messaging services using Sun Java System message queue. *High Performance Computing & Simulation Conference (HPC&S), Bonn, Germany.*

JChart2D. (2007). *JChart2D scientific visualization.* (See: http://jchart2d.sourceforge.net)

Lu, Q., Korniss, G., & Szymanski, B. K. (2006, Oct 12–15). Naming games in spatially-embedded random networks and emergent phenomena in societies of agents. In *Interaction and emergent phenomena in societies of agents* (pp. 148-155). The American Association for Artificial Intelligence, Menlo Park, CA: AAAI Press.

Pasquier, P., & Chaib-draa, B. (2003). The cognitive coherence approach for agent communication pragmatics. In *Aamas* (pp. 544-551). ACM.

Sun Microsystems. (2007a, Oct). *Java DB at a glance.* (See: http://developers.sun.com/javadb/)

Sun Microsystems. (2007b, Oct). *Sun Java System message queue.* (See: http://www.sun.com/software/products/message_queue/index.xml)

Terrence Fong, Illah Nourbakhsh, & Dautenhahn, K. (2003). A survey of socially interactive robots. *Robotics and Autonomous Systems, 42,* 143-166.

Zikopolous, P. C., Baklarz, G., & Scott, D. (2005). *Apache derby / IBM cloudscape.* Upper Saddle River, NJ: Prentice Hall PTR.

ADDITIONAL READING

Bersini, H., & Detours, V. (1994, July). Asynchrony induces stability in cellular automata based models. In R. A. Brooks & P. Maes (Eds.), *Proceedings of the 4th International Workshop on the Synthesis and Simulation of Living Systems (Artificial Life iv)* (pp. 382-387). Cambridge, MA: MIT Press.

Bonabeau, E., & Théraulaz, G. (2000, March). Swarm smarts. *Scientific American, 282*(3), 72-79.

Boyd, J. E., Hushlak, G., & Jacob, C. J. (2004, October 10-16). Swarmart: Interactive art from swarm intelligence. In H. Schulzrinne, N. Dimitrova, A. Sasse, S. B. Moon, & R. Lienhart (Eds.), *Proceedings of the 12th ACM International Conference on Multimedia,* (pp. 628–635). New York: ACM.

Dennett, D. C. (1978). *Brainstorms.* Cambridge, MA: Bradford Books.

Findler, N. V., & Malyankar, R. M. (1995). Emergent behaviour in societies of heterogeneous, interacting agents: Alliances and norms. In N. Gilbert & R. Conte (Eds.), *Artificial societies: The computer simulation of social life* (pp. 212-237). UCL Press: London.

Foner, L. N. (1995). Clustering and information sharing in an ecology of cooperating agents. *In Proceedings from the AAAI Spring Workshop on Information Gathering from Distributed, Heterogeneous Environments.*

Franklin, S., & Graesser, A. (1996). Is it an agent, or just a program? : A taxonomy for autonomous agents. In *Intelligent agents III. agent theories, architectures and languages (ATAL'96)* (Vol. 1193). Berlin: Springer-Verlag.

Gaston, M. E., & desJardins, M. (2005, July 25-29). Agent-organized networks for dynamic team formation. In F. Dignum, V. Dignum, S. Koenig, S. Kraus, M. P. Singh, & M. Wooldridge (Eds.), *4th International Joint Conference on Autonomous Agents and Multiagent Systems (AAMAS 2005),* (pp. 230-237). Utrecht, The Netherlands: ACM.

Geire, R. N., & Moffatt, B. (2003, April). Distributed cognition: Where the cognitive and the social merge. *Social Studies of Science, 33*(2), 1-10.

Guessoum, Z. (2004). Adaptive agents and multiagent systems. *IEEE Distributed Systems Online, 5*(7).

Gulyás, L., & Kampis, G. (2006, Oct 12-15). Emergence as a relational property in societies of agents. In *Interaction and emergent phenomena in societies of agents* (pp. 1-7). The American Association for Artificial Intelligence, Menlo Park, CA: AAAI Press.

Hofstadter, D. R. (1979). *Gödel, escher, bach: An eternal golden braid.* New York: Vintage Books.

Holland, J. H. (1998). Emergence: From chaos to order. *J. Artificial Societies and Social Simulation, 1*(4).

Huget, MP. (Ed.). (2003). *Communication in multiagent systems: Agent communication languages and conversation policies* (LNCS/LNAI). Springer.

Juan, T., & Sterling, L. (2003). A meta-model for intelligent adaptive multi-agent systems in open environments. In *Aamas* (pp. 1024-1025). ACM.

Jung, C. (1999). Emergent mental attitudes in layered agents. *Lecture Notes in Computer Science, 1555,* 195.

Kearney, P. (1994). Experiments in multi-agent dynamics. In C. Castelfranchi & E. Werner (Eds.), *Artificial social systems — selected papers from the fourth european workshop on modelling autonomous agents in a multi-agent world, maamaw-92 (lnai volume 830)* (pp. 24–40). Heidelberg, Germany: Springer-Verlag. (see conclusions)

Kennedy, J., Eberhart, R. C., & Shi, Y. (2001). *Swarm intelligence.* San Francisco: Morgan Kaufman.

Lam, D. N., & Barber, K. S. (2004). Verifying and explaining agent behavior in an implemented agent system. In *Aamas* (pp. 1226-1227). IEEE Computer Society.

Lauer, M. R., Mitchem, P. A., & Gagliano, R. A. (1995). Resource optimization and self interest: Variations on the game of life. *ss, 00,* 136.

Le Strugeon, E., Mandiau, R., & Libert, G. (1994). Towards a dynamic multi-agent organization. *Lecture Notes in Computer Science, 869,* 203.

Lerman, K. (2004). A model of adaptation in collaborative multi-agent systems. *Adaptive Behavior*, *12*(3-4), 187-197.

Lewin, R. (1999). *Complexity: Life at the edge of chaos*. University of Chicago Press.

Lu, Q., Korniss, G., & Szymanski, B. K. (2006, Oct 12-15). Naming games in spatially-embedded random networks and emergent phenomena in societies of agents. In *Interaction and emergent phenomena in societies of agents* (pp. 148-155). The American Association for Artificial Intelligence, Menlo Park, CA: AAAI Press.

Lynch, A. (1999). Thought contagion: How belief spreads through society. *Journal of Artificial Societies and Social Simulation, 2*(2).

Marcenac, P. (1998). Modeling multiagent systems as self-organized critical systems. In *Hicss (5)* (pp. 86-95).

Minsky, M. (1985). *Society of mind*. Simon & Schuster.

Parsons, S., Gymtrasiewicz, P., & Wooldridge, M. (Eds.). (2002). *Game theory and decision theory in agent-based systems (multiagent systems, artificial societies, and simulated organizations) (hardcover)*. Springer.

Parunak, H. V. D., Brueckner, S., Sauter, J. A., & Matthews, R. S. (2005, July 25-29). Global convergence of local agent behaviors. In F. Dignum, V. Dignum, S. Koenig, S. Kraus, M. P. Singh, & M. Wooldridge (Eds.), *4th International Joint Conference on Autonomous Agents and Multiagent Systems (AAMAS 2005)*, (pp. 305-312). Utrecht, The Netherlands: ACM.

Parunak, H. V. D., Brueckner, S., & Savit, R. (2004). Universality in multi-agent systems. In *Aamas* (pp. 930-937). IEEE Computer Society.

Privosnik, M., & Marolt, M. (2001, September 1-6). The development of emergent properties in massive multi-agent systems. In *Wseas*. Malta: WSEAS.

Schilling, R. (2006, Oct 12–15). A project to develop a distributed, multi-agent communication architecture using message feedback. In *Interaction and emergent phenomena in societies of agents* (pp.

96-103). The American Association for Artificial Intelligence, Menlo Park, CA: AAAI Press.

Servat, D., Perrier, E., Treuil, JP., & Drogoul, A. (1998, Jul). When agents emerge from agents: Introducing multi-scale viewpoints in multi-agent simulations. In J. S. Sichman, R. Conte, & N. Gilbert (Eds.), *Proceedings of the 1ˢᵗ International Workshop on Multi-Agent Systems and Agent-Based Simulation (MABS-98)* (Vol. 1534, pp. 183-198). Berlin: Springer.

Simon Parsons, Piotr Gymtrasiewicz, M. W. (Ed.). (2002). *Game theory and decision theory in agent-based systems (multiagent systems, artificial societies, and simulated organizations)*. Springer.

Smith, A. E. (2000). Swarm intelligence: From natural to artificial systems. *IEEE Trans. Evolutionary Computation, 4*(2), 192-193.

Sørensen, M. H. (2003). *Interactivism at work toward design heuristics for ambient intelligence*. (extended abstract)

Tarasewich, P., & McMullen, P. R. (2002). Swarm intelligence: Power in numbers. *Communications of the ACM, 45*(8), 62-67.

Thrèaulaz, G. (2001). *Swarm intelligence*. San Francisco: Morgan Kaufman.

Trajkovski, G. P. (2001). *An imitation-based approach to modeling homogeneous agents societies*. (LNCS, 2258, 246).

Trappl, R., Luck, M., Marik, M., & Stepankova, O. (Eds.). (2001). *Multi-agent systems and applications*. Springer.

Wavish, P. (1991, Aug). Exploiting emergent behaviour in multi-agent systems. In *Proceedings of the Third European Workshop on Modelling Autonomous Agents in a Multi-Agent World* (pp. 297-310). Kaiserslautern, Germany: North-Holland.

Weiss, G. (Ed.). (2000). *Multiagent systems: A modern approach to distributed artificial intelligence*. The MIT Press.

Wolfram, S. (1994). *Cellular automata and complexity*. Reading, MA: Addison-Wesley.

Wolfram, S. (2002). *A new kind of science*. Champaign, IL: Wolfram Media.

ENDNOTES

[1]   The simulation engine itself has since been expanded to allow for automated alteration of timing variances.

[2]   See https://scripting.dev.java.net for list of scripting languages that can be integrated into Java.

[3]   JDK 1.6 as of this writing

[4]   For this functionality, the driver must comply with the JDBC 4 specifications.

[5]   "Swing" is the default windowing toolkit included with the official distribution of the Java platform.

[6]   These numbers were determined by trial and error in Windows XP Pro SP2. Preliminary testing on Linux (kernel version 2.4.33) revealed a signifiganly lower maximum thread count. More investigation is needed to determine the cause of this disparity.

Chapter XIX
The Human Mirror Neuron System

David B. Newlin
RTI International, USA

ABSTRACT

Following the discovery in Rhesus monkeys of "mirror neurons" that fire during both execution and observation of motor behavior, human studies have documented a fronto-parietal mirror neuron system (MNS) with apparently similar functions. We discuss some issues related to the human research, including measurement with neuroimaging techniques and recent neurotechnologies for manipulating regional brain function. We note the remarkable overlap between several brain systems studied in people: the MNS, the Theory of Mind (ToM), the "self"-system of the brain, and the neural "default mode." The functional architecture of these systems may have important implications for how the MNS is organized and its functions. We propose that "auto-mirroring" in which self-observation of one's own motor behavior can be either facilitated or blocked, may be a fundamental aspect of the MNS. Finally, the implications of hemispheric asymmetry in the right and left MNS are discussed. Although MNS research is in its infancy, it bears promise to reveal basic aspects of the brain's functional architecture.

Despite impressive gains in understanding the brain, fundamental questions concerning brain organization and function remain unanswered, unresolved, or highly controversial. This is not surprising given the enormous complexity of neural processes. In this discussion we will focus on one brain system that may be particularly important for human functioning: mirror neurons or the mirror neuron system (MNS). The MNS is a fronto-parietal brain system that is activated when an individual performs a specific behavior and observes that same function being performed by another person. In other words, the MNS is sensitive to the "mirroring" of one's behavior in other people. Even though the discovery of mirror neurons is relatively recent (Gallese et al., 1996), there is now a significant body of research, both human and nonhuman primate, providing evidence that the MNS is an important characteristic of brain organization (Gallese & Goldman, 1998; Oberman & Ramachandran, 2007; Rizzolatti & Craighero, 2004).

Discovery. The remarkable discovery of mirror neurons was made in Rhesus monkeys—entirely inadvertently. Gallese et al. (1996) were studying the electrophysiology of the premotor cortex in macaques when they noticed that the same neurons that were active when the monkeys performed simple behaviors were also stimulated when the animals saw other monkeys or humans doing the same thing they were doing. More recent research has extended this finding to the human brain using neuroimaging techniques, primarily functional magnetic resonance imaging (fMRI), electroencephalography (EEG), and neurotechnologies such as transcranial magnetic stimulation (TMS).

The existence of mirror neurons in Rhesus monkeys and the MNS in humans has raised many important questions about the function(s) of this brain system. Ideas about the functions of the MNS have ranged from the neural substrate of imitative learning (in humans), empathy, reciprocity in human relations, the brain's foundation for social interaction, the kernel of language, understanding the intentions of the behavior of others through internal simulation, and even to the nature of consciousness. Of course, these functions are not mutually exclusive. The ultimate limits of the importance of the MNS have not been delineated despite intensive research, both human and animal, over the last decade. However, recent critiques of the human MNS literature (Dinstein et al, 2008; Turella et al., in press), particularly fMRI studies, have raised questions about whether mirror neurons in monkeys are really homologous in function with the MNS in people.

Purpose. The purpose of this discussion is to explore the MNS literature, integrate it with other information concerning brain function, particularly prefrontal executive functions, and begin to develop models of how the MNS may function as part of control systems in the brain. Better understanding of the MNS may inform the design and implementation of control systems for autonomous agents such as robots.

To presage our conclusions, we—as have others—argue that the MNS is particularly important in social processes that involve gauging the intentions of others and predicting their behavior as it relates to our own. This is one of the fundamental functions of the "self" system of the brain. Moreover, it has immediate implications for the design of robotic systems. Autonomous agents may move closer to having a "self" when they incorporate aspects of the MNS in their control systems. The construction of "self" in human and robotic systems has been somewhat of a "Holy Grail" for a long time.

Multi-agent societies. This discussion focuses on intrapsychic processes and dyadic interactions primarily because the literature, whether animal or human, has not progressed beyond this level. Discoveries of mirror neurons and the MNS in humans have broad implications for social interaction in small groups and in larger multi-agent societies. Whether the MNS chiefly supports imitative learning or internal gauging of the motivations and behavioral proclivities of others (or both), these are inherently social processes. These functions can and may provide the foundation for social processes that would be difficult to conceptualize or study without recourse to a system such as the MNS.

The same arguments apply to robotic autonomous agents and their interactions with other robots or with humans. The spread of information in a multi-agent society and the coordination of communication and behavior among autonomous agents require some internal mechanism roughly comparable to the MNS. In fact, MNS-like systems have been incorporated in autonomous agents using neural network software (see Oztop et al., 2006 for a review). One next step is to study social interaction in robotic systems that have simulated MNSs in their control systems. This will require careful consideration of the proposed architecture of the MNS in humans, the limitations and critiques of this literature, and experimentation that is cognizant of these factors.

THE FRONTO-PARIETAL MNS

Mirror neurons have been measured typically with single-cell electrophysiology in monkeys (Gallese & Goldman, 1998). The primary regions of mirror neurons studied in the Rhesus monkey are the ventral premotor cortex (area F5), the superior temporal sulcus (STS), and the rostral part of the inferior parietal lobe (area PF). It has been noted (Fogassi & Ferrari, 2007) that this area of the premotor cortex (F5) in macaques is neuroanatomically homologous to Broca's area on the left side in the human brain. This observation has led to suggestions that mirror neurons may have played a central role in the development of speech functions in ancient humans. This is a social function of profound importance. In contrast to the left hemisphere, it raises the question of what parallel—but different—functions may be controlled by the premotor cortex of the right hemisphere, and how mirror neurons in that area promote that functioning.

Mapping. The MNS has been localized in human brains through neuroimaging techniques, particularly functional magnetic resonance imaging (fMRI). The MNS is more broadly distributed in the human brain than was originally thought. For example, Dinstein et al. (2007) mapped the MNS in humans using fMRI in overlapping brain regions during both executed movements and observed movements (their proposed definition of the MNS). These areas included the ventral premotor cortex and anterior inferior frontal sulcus, and several regions in the parietal lobe (anterior intraparietal sulcus, superior intraparietal sulcus, and posterior intraparietal sulcus), as well as an area within the lateral occipital cortex. This is a large amount of gray matter. This alone speaks to the importance of the MNS for human activity, assuming it is, in fact, a functional system as we and others have proposed. We will discuss criticisms of this assumption in the **Critiques** section below.

Dinstein et al. (2007) used a variant of the "rock-paper-scissors" game to map the MNS. Two factors are important in this paradigm: (i) participants performed actual motor movements using their dominant hands while being scanned, and (ii) they chose the game moves (and corresponding hand movements) themselves; they were not instructed which hand movements to make when. Therefore, the authors overcame an important limitation (discussed below in the **Measurement** section) of the MRI environment by using actual motor behavior, and this behavior was spontaneous, though constrained to three choices in the game. The rock-

paper-scissors experimental paradigm may prove useful in future studies of the MNS.

MEASUREMENT

fMRI. We noted above that the MNS in humans has been studied by a variety of neurotechnologies, including fMRI, EEG, and TMS. While fMRI is a powerful technique for studying brain function, particularly in terms of topographical and temporal resolution, it has some fundamental limitations. Most important in the present context is that the person must be supine (lying on their backs) with their heads in a severely confined magnet structure. Moreover, they must lie perfectly still without moving their heads in the scanner, which emits very loud noises at irregular intervals. The obtrusiveness of fMRI, severe limitations on motor movement, and difficulties in observing the behavior of self and others are primary concerns in studies of the MNS.

EEG. Scalp electrophysiology is a less obtrusive measure than fMRI. Participants in an EEG study are fully able to observe the (mirror) behavior of other people, such as an experimental confederate, an important consideration for studies of the MNS. Also, it is not technically difficult to record EEG in two or more individuals at the same time. This allows interesting studies of MNS activation in social reciprocity.

Despite these advantages, EEG introduces a new set of limitations. Topographical resolution is poor because recording is at the surface, although temporal resolution is superior to or comparable to that of fMRI. Because of these limitations in localizing EEG activity, only gross differences can be ensured between frontal (premotor and motor cortex) and parietal MNS activation, though this is probably the most important neuroanatomical distinction. Secondly, EEG is prone to high-amplitude movement artifacts that can spill into the same frequency range as the brain waves of interest. This places limitations on motor behavior that are much less stringent than fMRI, but significant nonetheless.

Rolandic *mu* suppression. In EEG studies of the human MNS, suppression or desynchronization of the rolandic *mu* rhythm (8-13 Hz. recorded over the sensorimotor cortex; roughly electrode sites C_3 over the left hemisphere, C_z over the vertex of the head, and C_4 over the right hemisphere) has been interpreted as a sensitive measure of MNS activation. The *mu* rhythm is suppressed during both execution and observation of motor movements. Tognoli et al. (2007) also found that while social interaction was important in eliciting MNS activation, *mu* suppression was insensitive to the nature of this interaction. In contrast, parietal *phi* rhythms (9.2 to 11.5 Hz.) recorded over the right hemisphere were strongly related to the degree of coordination or interdependence of their social interaction. If replicated, these findings represent an important advance in understanding the relationship between the frontal and parietal components of the MNS.

TMS. This procedure involves single brief, intense pulses of magnetic energy over certain locations of the motor cortex using an electromagnetic paddle. In this case, there is a motor evoked potential (twitch) in the contralateral limb that can be measured electrophysiologically. Manipulations expected to activate the MNS have been shown to facilitate these evoked potentials in the contralateral hand. Maeda et al (2002) demonstrated specificity of facilitation in the muscles that would be activated to mimic observed hand movement and greater facilitation when the observed hand was shown as if in the participant's perspective. Importantly, facilitation was also greatest when the behavior was goal-directed (e.g., picking up food to eat versus picking up an inedible object).

Correlational measures. The measurements were correlational in all of these cases. They assess the correlation between external manipulations expected to affect the MNS and localized brain activation. They do not manipulate brain function directly. This is an important limitation of the human research. An alternative might be to use neurotechnologies to stimulate or inhibit regional brain activity—presumably of MNS structures or control structures unrelated to the MNS—and determine the effects on cognitive and behavioral functions thought be associated with the MNS.

Two noninvasive neurotechnologies that bear this potential are repetitive TMS (rTMS) and weak transcranial direct current stimulation (tDCS). We are unaware of any applications of rTMS or weak tDCS to study the MNS. This may be a fruitful area for future research because they go well beyond correlational studies. Moreover, research of this type can address concerns raised about the comparability of mirror neurons in Rhesus monkeys and the human MNS (see **Critiques** discussion below).

CONVERGENCE OF HUMAN FUNCTIONS RELATED TO THE MNS

The last decade has witnessed a remarkable convergence of functional brain systems that overlap neuroanatomically with the MNS. This co-localization may indicate the breadth of functions that the MNS subserves. These systems are summarized in **Table 1** as the MNS, the "self" system, the Theory of Mind (ToM), and the "default mode" of the brain when at alert rest. It seems unlikely that this convergence is coincidental, although the degree of integration of these functional systems will be a matter of debate.

The "self" system. It may seem at first far-fetched to argue that the sense of human self is semi-localized within the brain. Certainly there are large areas of the brain whose functions we do not associate with the self. Several authors (e.g., Uddin et al., 2007) have argued that self functions, such as self-recognition, self-other distinction, self-awareness, self-consciousness, etc., are primarily right fronto-parietal. [This does not imply a "homunculus" within the brain, and certainly not a homunculus within a homunculus!]

Uddin et al. (2007) and Wheatley et al. (2007) argued that two different brain systems are primarily related to a person's representation of self: (1) the fronto-parietal MNS and (2) a midline cortical network for social cognition, consisting of superior temporal and medial prefrontal cortex (PFC), fusiform gyrus, posterior cingulate, insula, and amygdala. Note first that these systems taken together include much of the cortex, excluding most primary and secondary sensory areas and more posterior parts of the brain. These authors proposed that the two brain systems, rather than being separate and independent, cooperate closely in constructing self-representation and guiding

Table 1. Summary of brain systems that overlap neuroanatomically with the MNS

Brain System	Definition	Characteristics
Mirror Neuron System (MNS)	brain activity during action execution and observation	used to comprehend the motives and intentions of others by simulating their actions and context
"Self"-System	constellation of functions related to self	self-awareness, self-observation, self-other distinction, self-consciousness, etc.
Theory of Mind (ToM)	recognition that other people have minds similar to our own	fosters "mind-reading" to understand other people's thoughts and affect
Default Mode	brain activity patterns at alert rest	patterns of activation that are negatively correlated between patterns

social interaction (self-other relations). In this scheme, the MNS helps achieve understanding of others by internally simulating their behavior, emotions, and motives. For example, Wheatley et al. (2007) found that observing and imagining moving shapes engaged the MNS, but the midline social network of the brain was activated only when those same moving shapes were reinterpreted as animate (living, moving humans or animals). In terms of recognizing one's own face (Uddin et al., 2005) versus that of others (an important aspect of self-representation), self-face recognition activates right hemisphere MNS structures, while other-face recognition activates only the well-described "default/resting state" brain network, consisting in this case of medial PFC and precuneus. The latter default state is negatively correlated with that noted below (**Default Mode** section) as overlapping substantially with the MNS.

Theory of Mind (ToM). ToM is normally defined as the full awareness that other individuals have minds that are similar to our own (Gallese, 2007). It follows from ToM that other people have motivations, thought processes, and emotions that are also similar to those we possess. ToM is probably something that we take for granted, although it is at least partially species-specific and of inestimable value for survival. Specifically, it allows us to judge and predict the intentions and future behavior of others, a function that is critical to social interaction, control of aggression, and mating systems. Note that this is comparable to our conceptualization of the primary function of the MNS.

To achieve ToM, several more basic functions must be acquired. First, the organism must have a clear distinction between "self" and "other", something that is also prototypical of the foundation for a "self" system in the brain. Following from this, the person or animal must have acquired the capacity for self-recognition, although not necessarily in the visual modality. A third function is the psychological framing of self in relation to others—the "relational self"—whether in terms of social rank, familial relationships, sexual functioning, or other characteristics. Finally, the person or animal must be able to assess social motives, or patterns of behavior in relation to others that are predictive of their future behavior.

This "mind-reading" ability (Gallese, 2007; Gallese & Goldman, 1998; Schulte-Ruther et al., 2007) is a critical component of ToM with clear evolutionary advantages. Whether the 'other' is friend or foe, predator or prey, biological relative or stranger, the need to predict motivations reasonably accurately based on observable information and social context appears critical to survival and reproduction in a social world (Newlin, 2002, 2007). It has been argued that these capacities are based on the human MNS (Agnew et al, 2007). In other words, we can "read the minds" of others by internally simulating their intentions and social context.

Default mode of the brain. Fox and Raichle (2007) summarized evidence that spontaneous brain activity when the person is at rest but alert represents a "default mode" of the brain. This resting activity represents approximately 20% of the total body's energy consumption although the brain is only about 2% of the body's mass. This may be compared with task-related activations, which are energy swings that are usually small relative to this (< 5%). Fox et al.'s (2005) evidence for a default mode is based on several findings: (i) this spontaneous brain activity is topographically and temporally organized, (ii) it shows positively inter-correlated patterns of brain areas with similar functionality, with separate patterns that are negatively correlated with each other, and (iii) it is predictive of task-related activations and the quality of performance on these tasks. The evidence Fox and Raichle (2007) marshal in support of a default mode is impressive, though Morcom and Fletcher (2006) presented a critique of this conclusion.

Our interest in the default mode is that one of these patterns of inter-related brain areas corresponds roughly to the MNS. This "intrinsically defined anti-correlated network" consists primarily of the middle temporal area, frontal eye fields, and the inferior parietal sulcus, a neuroanatomical pattern that at least partially overlaps with the MNS. It is important to recognize that just because the person in the MRI scanner is instructed to "rest," this does not imply they are cognitively or affectively quiescent or "blank." Fox and Raichle (2007) argue quite the contrary. While it is not clear what psychological activity is actually occurring in the default mode, it is a highly organized activity that substantially correlates with the activation produced by cognitive tasks.

Congruence. Taken together, the congruence of these four systems (**Table 1**) is highly interesting, but difficult to interpret. If we assume for the moment that the brain is characterized by hierarchically organized systems that are controlled largely in a top-down manner by prefrontal executive areas (an arguable assumption), then we may ask what system(s) is (normally) superordinate? In other words, is the MNS subordinate to the self-system or to ToM, or is it an executive system (if, in fact, it is a "system" at all) that controls these other systems? Did the MNS evolve relatively recently (in geologic time) as a superordinate system, or as a subordinate processing system that supports language and social interaction? Another possibility is that they are all slightly different manifestations of the same brain system, and that distinctions between them are artificial. There are many other possibilities, of course. For example, the hierarchy of executive systems may shift in relation to environmental demand, so that the MNS may be superordinate at some times and subordinate at others. Our point is that some of the excitement concerning the discovery and elaboration of the MNS is that it may shed light on brain organization that is fundamental to human functioning.

Neuroanatomical localization says little about psychological function, although it does suggest hypotheses about the processes involved. For example, the fact that the MNS includes, among other regions, the premotor area, suggests that praxis is implicated. Recent neuroimaging research emphasizes functional connectivity between different brain regions, as opposed to simply asking what areas are activated during a specific task. The MNS literature has not really advanced to the connectivity stage of analysis. Questions need to be asked about the topographical and temporal connectivity between different regions that are currently subsumed in the MNS. In terms of temporal relations, do anterior or posterior regions of the MNS lead in time, and under what experimental conditions? Following a better understanding of topographical and temporal connectivity within the MNS, the issue of connectivity with other brain systems (i.e., not part of the MNS) can be addressed more fully.

A second issue concerns modularity. Specifically, are there characteristics of the MNS that function as modules? Although beyond the scope of this discussion, this issue is very important in relation to the ideas above concerning overlapping systems. Modularity is a highly controversial area of research, and the question is likely to be a subject of future debate.

AUTO-MIRRORING

One factor that has been unrecognized in MNS research is the simple fact that when a person or Rhesus monkey engages in a behavior (other than facial expressions), they normally observe themselves performing that act, much as they might observe another individual mirroring their behavior. This process represents a feedback loop that we (Newlin, 2007) propose is critically important in how the MNS functions. We were unable to find any consideration in the MNS literature of the role of self-observation in one's own behavior. We refer to this as "auto-mirroring." None of the studies in this literature to date (to our knowledge) have manipulated whether or not the person was able to observe their own motor behavior. Therefore, it is unclear whether auto-mirroring plays a major, minor, or no role at all in the feedback processes that control the MNS.

For example, the rock-paper-scissors game that Dinstein et al. (2007) used to map the MNS could be adapted to study the possible role of self-observation in MNS activation. It would be interesting in terms of visual feedback pathways and self-awareness to manipulate whether or not the participants could see their own hand movements, perhaps using a video camera and monitor and displaying them in real time to the participant while in the scanner. If auto-mirroring were important, then self-observation of their own hand performing the game while in the MRI scanner would be expected to produce significantly greater MNS activation than when they could not see their own hand movements. A second question would be whether self-observation produced greater MNS stimulation than observing the other participant's game moves.

Our rationale for considering auto-mirroring an important factor for MNS operation is based on a number of disparate findings. First, visual and auditory feedback (self-observation) is an integral part of the natural guidance system for praxis in sighted, hearing individuals. In fact, self-observation (Bem, 1967) is a critical component of the "self-system," the constellation of functions (discussed above) that include self-recognition, self-awareness, body image, social context and status in relation to others, self-consciousness, etc. If in fact the self system is related to the MNS, then self-observation of behavior must be considered an important aspect of MNS function. At least, it is a hypothesis that is eminently testable by comparing simple behaviors executed with, versus without, the ability to observe the actions. This basic experiment could be performed in Rhesus monkeys as well. We note that in human studies, an interesting comparison group would be individuals who are blind from birth, as they have likely adapted, at least in part, to having no visual self-observation.

Conditions in which self-observation is disturbed also support our conclusion that this self-observation feedback loop is critical. One example is the clinical phenomenon of unilateral neglect, in which patients who have sustained brain damage, usually to the right parietal area, ignore or even disown the contralateral sides of their own bodies and are inattentive to stimuli presented in the corresponding hemifield. An even more extreme example is the out-of-body experience, which can be elicited by deep electrical stimulation of certain areas of the right temporal-parietal junction (Blanke et al., 2002). Neuroimaging with positron emission tomography in one patient who was stimulated in this same area produced brain activation in the right temporal-parietal junction (De Ridder et al., 2007). The out-of-body experience can also be produced in cleverly designed virtual reality experiments among healthy volunteers (Ehrsson, 2007; Lenggenhager et al., 2007). Moreover, there has been some success in treating "phantom-limb" pain when patients observe a mirror image of their contralateral limb performing basic motor functions (Chan et al., 2007; Guimmarra et al., 2007).

Another important factor, noted above, that bolsters our overarching hypothesis concerning the centrality of auto-mirroring is the remarkable convergence in the neuroimaging literatures concerning (1) the MNS, (2) the ToM, (3) the "self-system", and (4) the "default mode" of the brain (areas active during alert periods of inactivity). All of these systems are fronto-parietal. We hypothesize that auto-mirroring is a basic function of the human MNS that supports and embodies all of these four systems.

HEMISPHERIC ASYMMETRY

There are actually two MNSs (Aziz-Zadeh et al., 2006). These correspond to systems in the right and left hemisphere, connected primarily by fibers in the corpus callosum. It is likely, though unproven, that interconnections between frontal and parietal regions within each MNS are greater than those between the right and left MNSs. These considerations raise a host of questions that the current literature has only begun to address. For example, how specialized are the two MNSs in terms of their function? Is one "dominant" over another? How and when do they interact, and how cohesive are the resulting processes? Are there heuristics that guide the coordinated activities of the right and left MNS? Is auto-mirroring a function of primarily the right rather than the left MNS? What evolutionary advantages in terms of survival or reproduction were conferred by hemispheric specialization of these two systems? In relation to empirical research, what experimental paradigms are well suited to studying these questions?

Table 2. Tentative hemispheric specialization for executive cognitive functions of the prefrontal cortex (PFC). [no strict localizationist assumptions are implied]

LEFT Prefrontal Cortext	
Brain Area	**Function**
BrocaSection 1 s area	• expressive speech
dorsolateral PFC	• verbal working memory • verbal autobiographical memory • deception
ventromedial PFC	• deception • empathy
orbitofrontal PFC	• emotionally laden stimulus processing • social rules • penalty processing • inhibition of negative attitudes
lateral PFC	• updating behavior during cognitive shifting
ventrolateral PFC	• task switching in response to feedback • positive attitudes
RIGHT Prefrontal Cortex	
Brain Area	**Function**
right PFC	• temporal planning • sequence organization
dorsolateral PFC	• visuospatial working memory • contextual autobiographical memory • attention • inhibition of motor responses • negative attitudes
inferior PFC	• inhibitory processes
ventral PFC	• suppression of affect • inhibition of motor responses • stress responses
ventrolateral PFC	• task switching in response to feedback • processing incongruent stimuli • implicit association • affective switching
orbitofrontal PFC	• sustained attention • reward processing • cooperation
lateral PFC	• response to negative feedback
anterior PFC	• semantic monitoring and working memory • deception

At the present time, the primary reason for hypothesizing that the right and left MNS are functionally specialized (and different from each other) is that the structures subsumed in these systems are themselves specialized. For example, we noted above that the premotor area F5 in the macaque frontal cortex is thought to be fully homologous on the left—but not the right—side with Broca's area in humans. Hemispheric specialization—both in the left and right hemisphere—have been well documented for various aspects of human speech.

Executive cognitive functions. **Table 2** lists some (but certainly not all) of the executive cognitive functions that have been related to left, right, and both prefrontal cortices. Much of the underlying research that substantiates this listing is based on neuroimaging studies, specifically fMRI.

Shallice (2004) proposed laterally asymmetric executive functions for the left and right PFC. Rather than the PFC controlling working memory, long an assumption of cognitive neuroscience, he relegated working memory functions to the parietotemporal cortex. He proposed instead that the left PFC exerts supervisory (top-down) control over lower-level systems of the brain, such as working memory and verbal communication. In contrast, the right PFC maintains control over errant mentation and behavior that does not accord with task goals.

Shallice's (2004) analysis, which is specific to the PFC, implies that MNS functions may differ between the right and left hemispheres. Specifically, the formal language functions of the left MNS, which is neuro-anatomically distinct from the right MNS, would be a higher-level system that is controlled by anterior regions of the PFC in the furtherance of current and future goals, i.e., goal-directed motivation. For example, the capacity to form internal representations of the verbal speech of one's self and that of others, particularly as they intersect (mirror or complement each other), would allow more anterior (PFC) supervisory regions of the brain to guide social communication toward goals consistent with enhanced survival and reproductive fitness. At the same time, these internal representations provide "grist for the mill" of the right frontal MNS to detect and correct deviations in communication away from the same goals. A further example is that face recognition, whether it is one's own face or someone else's, is primarily a right frontal function that is part of the MNS (Uddin et al., 2005). It determines social context and whether communication is appropriate to that social situation. The evolutionary advantages of asymmetric supervisory control systems, as proposed by Shallice (2004) are unclear at the present time, but may be important in understanding lateral asymmetry in the MNS.

Functional asymmetry. The early differentiation of cognitive functions that are laterally asymmetric as primarily verbal (left hemisphere) versus visuospatial (right hemisphere) has given way to much more complex notions of hemispheric specialization. This shift was necessitated by results such as those in **Table 2** for prefrontal functions.

Affect. One dimension on which the right and left prefrontal areas differ is affect and motivation.

Table 3. Progression (from top to bottom of table) of conceptualizations of hemispheric differences in psychological functions of the prefrontal cortex

	LEFT Prefrontal	**RIGHT Prefrontal**
Cognition	expressive speech	visuospatial processes
Emotion	positive affect [plus anger]	negative affect [except anger]
Motivation	psychological approach	psychological withdrawal
Supervisory Control	top-down strategic modulation	checking on reaching task goals

This has direct relevance for understanding possible differences between the right and left MNSs. Davidson and his colleagues (Davidson, 1999) first noted, somewhat surprisingly, that negative affective states, such as fear, disgust, or depression, are associated with EEG alpha frequency (centered around 10 Hz.) power asymmetry that indicated right prefrontal specialization for these states. The key assumption in these studies was that alpha reflects an "idling" (relatively quiescent) frequency, while beta (desynchronized high frequency EEG activity) represents brain activation. The corresponding result was that positive emotional states, such as happiness, joy, or contentment, were associated with greater left prefrontal activation (i.e., more beta on the left and alpha on the right). The initial conclusion was that right prefrontal areas were relatively specialized for negative affect, and the left with positive affect. These conceptualizations are listed in **Table 3**.

Motivation. This tentative interpretation proved to be short-lived as evidence mounted that anger—an arguably negative emotion—was associated with greater left prefrontal EEG activation rather than right (Harmon-Jones, 2003). Davidson (2003) then proposed that left prefrontal activation represented a motivational "stance" of psychological approach, or moving toward stimuli. Anger may be viewed as an aggressive emotion for which approach motivation is dominant rather than avoidance or withdrawal motivation (Harmon-Jones, 2003). Conversely, they hypothesized that right prefrontal activity was associated with psychological withdrawal from stimuli, such as when fear, disgust, or depression leads to withdrawal. It is also possible that approach motivation and corresponding left prefrontal activity reflect prosocial affect, while withdrawal motivation and right hemisphere activation represent more antisocial emotions. Therefore, this lateral asymmetry in anterior brain regions can be understood in terms of overarching motivational systems with characteristic affect that is consistent with that orientation (see **Table 3**). Many of the questions raised above about how the different brains interact with each other (see **Congruence** section above) apply equally to this conceptual system.

This major advance in our understanding of lateral asymmetry and emotional systems has direct implications for the two MNSs as the premotor areas on the right and left side are presumably specialized in corresponding ways. For example, expressive speech is strongly related to the left premotor region (Broca's area), and it is a function that is most often used for approach toward social entities and groups. This may be true even for "angry speech." We anticipate that further conceptualizations of prefrontal asymmetry of function, such as that of Shallice (2004), will further our understanding of how the right and left MNS are different and how they are coordinated.

Implications for multi-agent societies. Newlin (2007) suggested that implementation of artificial MNSs in autonomous agents may benefit by dual, semi-independent and specialized control systems modeled after what is now known concerning functions of the right and left prefrontal cortexes of humans. Evolution had millions of years to "develop" these asymmetric systems of the brain and to evolve control systems that coordinate them seamlessly. Genetic algorithms that do not take this long(!) may be useful in finding means of coordination between dual asymmetric control systems in autonomous agents.

Robotic control systems with this degree of sophistication and complexity may be needed to engineer multi-agent societies that interact socially with a semblance of similarity to human societies. Over 100 years of sociology and social psychology attest to the complexity of human social interaction and the difficulties in studying it rigorously. It is likely that artificial multi-agent societies, where the control systems are largely known, may help us understand how specific social processes emerge from the interaction of intelligent systems. These processes include social learning through imitation and the gauging of other agents' intents from internal simulation of their behavior, properties purportedly subserved by the MNS. Whether the MNS, if it exists as a system, has these characteristics is unclear, although there is little doubt that humans readily imitate others and they are able to assess the motivations and intents of others with some degree of accuracy.

Critiques of Human MNS Research. Criticism of human MNS studies is important to temper enthusiasm for this relatively new area of research, to improve the quality of fMRI studies of the MNS, and to highlight areas that are in dire need of further research. Are mirror neurons in the Rhesus macaque truly homologous in function to the MNS in humans? Obviously, the species are different, as are the measurement systems (single unit electrophysiology versus neuroimaging). Because of the clear differences in measuring mirror neuron activity, the manipulations of executed and observed behavior have been different as well. The leap between species may be too great, although we emphasize that if this were the case, the human research to date would still be of great value even if the interpretation in terms of mirror neurons proved to be overly ambitious.

In their critique of the human MNS literature, Dinstein et al., (2008) first noted that the electrophysiological literature upon which the monkey evidence for mirror neurons rests is actually very sparse. In addition to being limited in number, most of the studies in macaques are qualitative rather than quantitative, and in all cases, the percentage of single neurons that exhibited mirror activity was small relative to the number tested. These specific areas have many functions other than "mirroring," so the latter observation is not surprising.

Both Dinstein et al. (2008) and Turella et al. (in press) concluded that most, if not all, neuroimaging studies failed to demonstrate an MNS in humans using criteria adopted from the monkey studies. Many fMRI studies limited their analyses to previously identified MNS structures, an example of circular reasoning that precluded the determination of whether these are, in fact, MNS areas. Both papers (Dinstein et al., 2008 and Turella et al., in press) argued that the essential criterion for assigning MNS status to a brain region is that it responds selectively to both executed and observed action. Moreover, task analysis of the actions used in these fMRI studies indicates that many cognitive-motor functions are necessary for their execution, any one of which could account for their activation in these experimental paradigms rather than mirroring. Neither Dinstein et al. (2008) nor Turella et al. (in press) commented on the fact, noted above, that the dependent measures used in both the monkey studies and the human neuroimaging research are fundamentally correlational. We argue that overcoming

this obstacle by using noninvasive techniques that directly affect brain regions may provide the most persuasive evidence to support or negate the current assumption that the human MNS is homologous to mirror neurons in Rhesus monkeys.

CONCLUSION

We concur that the MNS is an important discovery, with ramifications for many different aspects of human functioning. Whether the MNS is truly homologous with mirror neurons in Rhesus monkeys remains unresolved, but this does not necessarily invalidate the current MNS literature in humans. For example, it is possible that in humans the system evolved somewhat differently, perhaps due to formal language acquisition, greater prefrontal tissue, or some other human characteristic. Also, the use of the term "system" to describe the human MNS remains an debatable issue that can only be resolved by further research. In any case, the MNS studies to date provide a rich database for developing theories that can encompass the existing data, and lead to testable hypotheses to evaluate in future experiments.

We highlight several issues that seem important in deciphering the essential function(s) of the MNS. First, the confluence of conceptually different, but related systems (i.e., MNS, "self"-system, ToM, and the brain's default mode) may suggest theoretical models of how the MNS is organized and its fundamental functionality. Issues concerning hierarchical organization may be paramount here. The notion of auto-mirroring (Newlin, 2007) can spur new research that also bears on these questions. Specifically, what sensory and motor feedback loops are important in MNS architecture? Finally, there is abundant reason to believe that the right and left MNSs are specialized in terms of function. This is a very under-studied area that may prove important in understanding the organization of the MNS. Techniques for studying lateral asymmetry have been well developed over the last few decades. It seems particularly important to determine how the two MNSs are coordinated to achieve cohesive functions.

ACKNOWLEDGMENT

The author would like to thank Goran Trajkovski, Ph.D., for advice and support during the writing of this manuscript. I am indebted to Rachael M. Renton and Jean L. Kuch for technical assistance on this chapter. The author wishes to thank Diana Fishbein for Table 2 (adapted with permission). This work was supported in part by NIAAA grant 1R21AA015704, NIDA grant 1R21DA020592, and RTI International.

REFERENCES

Agnew, Z.K., Bhakoo, K.K. & Puri, B.K. (2007). The human mirror system: A motor resonance theory of mind-reading. *Brain Research Reviews*, *54*(2), 286-293.

Aziz-Zadeh, L., Koski, L., Zaidel, E., Mazziotta, J., & Lacoboni, M. (2006). Lateralization of the human mirror neuron system. *The Journal of Neuroscience*, *26*(11), 2964-2970.

Bem, D.J. (1967). An alternative interpretation of cognitive dissonance phenomena. *Psychological Review*, *74*(3), 183-200.

Blanke, O., Ortigue, S., Landis, T., & Seeck, M. (2002). Stimulating illusory own-body perceptions. *Nature*, *419*(6904), 269-270.

Chan, B. L., Witt, R., Charrow A. P., Magee, A., Howard, R., Pasquina, P. F., Heilman, K. M., & Tsao, J. W. (2007). Mirror therapy for phantom limb pain. *The New England Journal of Medicine*, *357*(21), 2206-2207.

Davidson, R. J. (1999). The functional neuroanatomy of emotion and affective style. *Trends in Cognitive Sciences*, *3*, 11-21.

Davidson, R. J. (2003). Affective neuroscience and psychophysiology: Toward a synthesis. *Psychophysiology*, *40*(5), 655-665.

De Ridder, D., Van Laere, K., Dupont, P., Menovsky, T., & Van de Heyning, P. (2007). Visualizing out-of-body experience in the brain. *The New England Journal of Medicine*, *357*(18), 1829-1833.

Dinstein, I., Hasson, U., Rubin, N., & Heeger, D.J. (2007). Brain areas selective for both observed and executed movements. *Journal of Neurophysiology*, 98, 1415-1427.

Dinstein, I., Thomas, C., Behrmann, M., & Heeger, D.J. (2008). A mirror up to nature. *Current Biology*, *18*(1), R13-R18.

Ehrsson, H.H. (2007). The experimental induction of out-of-body experiences. *Science*, *317*(5841), 1048.

Fogassi, L., & Ferrari, P. F. (2007). Mirror neurons and the evolution of embodied language. *Current Directions in Psychological Science*, *16*(3), 136-141.

Fox, M. D., Snyder, A.Z., Vincent, J. L., Corbetta, M., Van Essen, D. C., & Raichle, M. E. (2005). The human brain is intrinsically organized into dynamic, anticorrelated functional networks. *Proceedings of the National Academy of Sciences of the United States of America*, *102*(27), 9673-9678.

Fox, M.D. & Raichle, M.E. (2007). Spontaneous fluctuations in brain activity observed with functional magnetic resonance imaging. *Nature Reviews Neuroscience*, *8*, 700-711.

Gallese, V., Fadiga, L., Fogassi, L., & Rizzolatti, G. (1996). Action recognition in the premotor cortex. *Brain*, *119*, 593-609.

Gallese, V., & Goldman, A. (1998). Mirror neurons and the simulation theory of mind-reading. *Trends in Cognitive Sciences*, *2*(12), 493-501.

Gallese, V. (2007). Before and below 'Theory of Mind': Embodied simulation and the neural correlates of social cognition. *Philosophical Transactions of the Royal Society B: Biological Sciences*, *362*(1480), 659-669.

Giummarra, M. J., Gibson, S. J., Georgiou-Karistianis, N., & Bradshaw, J. L. (2007). Central mechanisms in phantom limb perception: The past, present and future. *Brain Research Reviews*, *54*(1), 219-232.

Harmon-Jones, E. (2003). Early Career Award. Clarifying the emotive functions of asymmetrical frontal cortical activity. *Psychophysiology*, *40*(6), 838-848.

Lenggenhager, B., Tadi, T., Metzinger, T., & Blanke, O. (2007). Video ergo sum: Manipulating bodily self-consciousness. *Science, 317*(5841), 1096-1099.

Maeda, F., Mazzioatta, J., & Iacoboni, M. (2002). Transcranial magnetic stimulation studies of the human mirror neuron system. *International Congress Series, 1232,* 889-894.

Morcom, A. M., & Flethcher, P. C. (2007). Does the brain have a baseline? Why we should be resisting a rest. *NeuroImage, 34*(7), 1073-1082.

Newlin, D. B. (2002). The self-perceived survival ability and reproductive fitness (SPFit) theory of substance use disorders. *Addiction, 97,* 427-446.

Newlin, D. B. (2006). Self-perceived survival and reproductive fitness (SPFit) theory: Substance use disorders, evolutionary game theory, and the brain. In Platek, S., Keenan, J. P., & Shackelford, T. (Eds.), *Evolutionary Cognitive Neuroscience* (pp. 285-326). Cambridge, Mass.: MIT Press.

Newlin, D.B., (2007, November 9-11). The human mirror neuron system (MNS): Toward a motivated autonomous agent. In *Proceedings of the AAAI Symposium, "Multi-Agent Societies"* (Trajkovski, G., Samuel Collins (Eds). Washington, DC.

Nitsche, M. A., Liebetanz, D., Lang, N., Antal, A., Tergau, F., & Paulus, W. (2003). Safety criteria for transcranial direct current stimulation (tDCS) in humans. *Clinical Neurophysiology,* 114(11), 2220-2222.

Oberman, L.M., & Ramachandran, V.S. (2007). The simulating social mind: The role of the mirror neuron system and simulation in the social and communicative deficits of autism spectrum disorders. *Psychological Bulletin, 133*(2), 310-327.

Oztop, E., Kawato, M., & Arbib, M. (2006). Mirror neurons and imitation: a computational guided review. *Neural Networks, 19,* 254-271.

Rizzolatti, G., & Craighero, L. (2004). The mirror-neuron system. *Annual Review of Neuroscience,* 27, 169-192.

Schulte-Ruther, M., Markowitsch, H. J., Fink, G. R., & Piefke, M. (2007). Mirror neuron and theory of mind mechanisms involved in face-to-face interactions: A functional magnetic resonance imaging approach to empathy. *Journal of Cognitive Neuroscience, 19*(8), 1354-1372.

Shallice, T. (2004). The fractionation of supervisory control. In Gazzaniga, M. S. (Ed.), *The cognitive neurosciences III* (pp. 943-956). Cambridge, Mass.: MIT Press.

Tognoli, E., Lagarde, J., DeGuzman G. C., & Kelso, J. A. S. (2007). The phi complex as a neuromarker of human social coordination. *Proceedings of the National Academy of Sciences of the United States of America, 104*(19), 8190-8195.

Turella, L., Pierno, A. C., Tubaldi, F., & Castiello, U. (in press). Mirror neurons in humans: Consisting or confounding evidence? *Brain and Language.*

Uddin, L. Q., Kaplan, J. T., Molnar-Szakacs, I., Zaidel, E., and Iacoboni, M. (2005). Self-face recognition activates a frontoparietal "mirror" network in the right hemisphere: An event-related fMRI study. *NeuroImage, 25,* 926-935.

Uddin, L. Q., Iacoboni, M., Lange, C., & Keenan, J. P. (2007). The self and social cognition: The role of cortical midline structures and mirror neurons. *Trends in cognitive sciences, 11*(4), 153-157.

Wassermann, E. M. & Grafman, J. (2005). Recharging cognition with DC brain polarization. *Trends in Cognitive Sciences, 9*(11), 503-505.

Wheatley, T., Milleville, S. C., and Martin, A. (2007). Understanding animate agents: Distinct roles for the social network and mirror system. *Psychological Science, 18*(6), 469-474.

Chapter XX
Relationships Between the Processes of Emergence and Abstraction in Societies

Eric Baumer
University of California, Irvine, USA

Bill Tomlinson
University of California, Irvine, USA

ABSTRACT

This chapter presents an argument that the process of emergence is the converse of the process of abstraction. Emergence involves complex behavior resulting from simple rules, while abstraction forming simple rules that describe complex behavior. This converse relationship suggests the possibility that similar mechanisms underlie both processes, and a greater understanding of one can lead to a greater understanding of the other. Especially in the case of human and artificial social systems, the processes of abstraction and emergence are inextricably interconnected; the abstractions that individuals make will determine what behaviors emerge, and the behaviors that emerge in the society determine what abstractions will be made. This relationship between the two processes, which we call the abstraction-emergence loop, can be used to gain a better understanding of both. It is argued that the abstraction-emergence loop functions over various degrees of complexity and levels of detail, and that the loop has the greatest efficacy in certain ranges of detail. This way of understanding the two processes has particular bearing on social interactions; in order to understand macro-level emergent social phenomena, we must also simultaneously understand the micro-level phenomena from which they arise. In considering when emergence occurs, the role of the observer in the emergence abstraction loop is also discussed. In addition to describing various properties of the abstraction-emergence loop, this chapter presents descriptions of several ongoing and future research projects in the creation of autonomous agent societies, and offers pointers to future research directions aimed at exploring and understanding the nature of the abstraction-emergence loop. Such an understanding of the relationship between abstraction and emergence can be helpful in designing communities of autonomous agents that interact socially with each other and with humans, and may also be a helpful step toward understanding the phenomena of emergence and abstraction in general.

INTRODUCTION

A number of different disciplines have taken on the task of studying emergent phenomena, trying to understand how and why they emerge, and delineating what makes emergent phenomena different from other phenomena exhibited by complex systems. Within computer science, much of this work has fallen under the auspices of artificial life (ALife). This subfield focuses on creating computer programs and simulations that exhibit qualities we otherwise attribute to living things, such as the ability to reproduce. A common environment for such work is cellular automata (CA), a grid where each cell on the grid is in a certain state at each tick of a system clock, and each cell's state at the next iteration is determined according to a set of rules that refer to its neighbor's states in the current clock tick (see (Sarkar 2000) for a survey). One of the earliest examples of this is von Neumann's self-replicating machine (von Neumann 1966), the goal of which was to create a theoretical machine capable of universal computation. This CA has the ability to produce any other cellular automaton if given a description in the proper format of the automaton to be produced. If the automaton is given a description of itself, it is thus able to reproduce itself. A reproducing CA was also developed by Christopher Langton (1984), whose goal was not to create a CA capable of universal computation, but rather the simplest possible CA still capable of self-replication. These automata's capacity for reproduction is a well-known example of emergence, in that the high-level phenomenon of reproduction emerging from the low-level rules of the system, where none of the low-level rules explicitly describe the process of reproduction.

Another classic example from ALife is the cellular automaton known as the *Game of Life*, first developed by John Conway (Gardner 1970). The cells in this relatively simple CA have only 2 states, which are called alive and dead. A cell's state at the next iteration is given by three simple rules. Any cell with one or zero live neighbors is dead. Any cell with two or three live neighbors is alive. Any cell with four or more neighbors is dead. From these relatively simple rules, vastly complex patterns emerge. One of the better know is that of the glider (Figure 1), a patter which moves one cell down and one cell to the right every four iterations (the direction of this movement depends on the orientation of the glider pattern). The high-level behavior of a unified pattern moving is not actually built into the system. Indeed, the automaton has no representation of this glider pattern, only the representation of the states of its cells. Rather, the behavior emerges from the interactions between individual cells in the system based on the rules that govern it.

These are a few examples of the types of emergence described in ALife. A system based on fairly simple, low-level rules exhibits some high-level behavior not directly or explicitly built into the system; the high-level behavior emerges from the low-level interactions within the system. It is important to note here that predictability has little to do with whether or not a phenomenon is emergent. As has been noted by Damper (Damper 2000), the property of self-replication exhibited by von Neumann's machine is not only predictable, it was in fact designed into the machine. This does not mean, however, that the property is not emergent. It is still emergent, because the high-level phenomenon of self-replication occurs as a result of interactions between low-level rules that do not explicitly describe the property of self-replication. It can be seen here that as the system exhibits emergent properties, an observer must be present to observe those properties and note that they are indeed emergent. The importance of level of detail and the role of the observer in emergence will be addressed later in this chapter.

Figure 1. A glider from Conway's Game of Life

Emergence, however, does not fall only under the purview of artificial life; a number of other fields have studied emergent phenomena. In a field related to ALife, some researchers in social simulation have tried to describe how certain simulated environments are more suited to the emergence of cultural phenomena (Epstein and Axtell 1996; Gilbert, Schuster et al. 2005). Other disciplines outside the computational sciences are also concerned with emergent phenomena, though sometimes referred to by a different name or with different terminology. For example, some sociologists are interested in how knowledge and meaning are socially constructed (Berger and Luckmann 1966), or how social norms are established, maintained, and fade (Deutch and Gerard 1955; Kelley 1955). Although sociologists do not necessarily self-identify as researchers who study emergent phenomena, from a certain perspective they can be seen as being concerned with how certain social phenomena emerge from the interactions of individual members of a society.

This chapter argues that emergent phenomena in society provide researchers with unique opportunities for studying the process of emergence. In the other cases of emergence mentioned above, simple rules that govern a system give rise to complex behavior, behavior that is not directly or explicitly a part of the simple rules. In society, though, individual members of the society are aware of, and form abstractions about, these emergent patterns, effectively altering the basic rules that govern the system and affecting what further patterns emerge. This cyclic property of societies gives researchers a powerful analytic lens through which to explore the phenomenon of emergence, and it will be one of the main topics of this chapter.

All of the above cited examples of research about emergence have studied emergence in a specific context, that is, emergent properties of a specific system or class of systems. This begs the question, might it be possible to study not emergent social norms or emergent gliders, but to study emergence *per se*? Similar to the way in which physics studies the situationally independent laws that govern the physical universe, might it be possible to study the situationally independent laws that drive emergence? Are emergence in cellular automata and emergence in human societies fundamentally examples of the same underlying phenomenon? Based on current research, answering such a question is quite difficult, if even possible at all. While much research on emergence has been done in emergence in computational systems like CA, relatively little has explored emergence in societies, where the individual actors in the system may be cognizant of, and react to, emergent aspects of the system itself. This chapter argues that, in order to understand the process of emergence fully, we must gain an understand of the ways it operates in various contexts, so that we may ask if it is even the same process at all. Furthermore, social systems provide prime territory for examining the relationships between low-level interactions and high-level phenomena that are at the core of emergence.

DEFINITIONS AND PREVIOUS WORK

Before proceeding in our discussion, it is important to agree upon definitions for terminology that will be used in this chapter. Emergence, abstraction, complexity, and other concepts important are not only somewhat difficult to define but also do not enjoy any sort of consensus about their definition. In addition to surveying and summarizing previous work, this section will also provide working definitions for several terms as they will be used in this chapter.

Emergence

A wide variety of approaches have been taken in trying to define exactly what constitutes emergence, owing partly to the many different disciplines that have addressed the concept. A basic definition, the primary one for this chapter, is that *emergence is the process of complex patterns resulting from simpler rules*. However, approaches to studying this process have been many and varied. Rather than attempt an overview of all such definitions, this section will review some of the major definitions most relevant to the material at hand; for a more encompassing review, see (Damper 2000) or (Cariani 1990).

One major contribution to the study of emergence has been that of Holland's work on constrained generating procedures (cgp) (Holland 1998), which are essentially collections of finite state machines. Using games as an example of systems in which complex properties arise from simple rules, he seeks to use cgp to build emergence out of smaller procedural pieces. The goal is to use constraints to orchestrate the patterns that emerge from these generating procedures. Thus, while Holland's work is a valuable contribution, its value is limited to situations where the conditions under which emergence occur can be explicitly specified and tightly constrained. Furthermore, while the variable version, the cgp-v, can reorganize the connections between its components, Holland does not describe cgp-v's as able to react to, and reorganized in terms of, the emergent behavior they themselves exhibit.

Another more recent contribution has been Wolfram's attempt at mapping the computational universe through investigations of one-dimensional cellular automata (Wolfram 2002). By enumerating and executing all such CAs, Wolfram develops a classification wherein one particular class of CA gives rise to complex behavior that can be described as an instance of emergence. This classification bears resemblance to the λ-parameter developed by Langton (Langton 1991), in that systems with certain λ values are those that exhibit emergent properties. However, both Wolfram's and Langton's both examine systems in which the rules are fixed, while this chapter is more interested in systems where individual components can adapt based on properties of the system as a whole.

Cariani offers a classification system including three different types of emergence (Cariani 1990). The first, computational emergence, "is the view that complex global forms can arise from local computational interactions" (ibid, p. 776). Largely, this is the sort of emergence in which Holland, Wolfram, Langton, and others pursuing similar research programs are interested. The second, thermodynamic emergence, is couched in physical systems, such as the way that chemical bonding emerges from the laws of quantum mechanics. The third, emergence-relative-to-a-model, occurs when the behavior of a system differs from the current model for the system and the model must then be changed to account for the novel behavior. This last definition is the closest to the emergence on which this chapter focuses. However, emergence-relative-to-a-model is a predominantly top-down view of emergence;

it address the way an observer changes its model to reflect the phenomenon being observed, but it also implies a dichotomy between the observer and the phenomenon. This view of emergence does not take into account situations in which the observer is part of the system it is modeling, nor does it take into account situations in which multiple observers are present as distinct parts of the system. In this case, the observer may change its model, which causes it to change its behavior, which in turn causes others to change their models and behaviors, and so on. Societies are an example of such self-referential systems, and for this reason merit study of the unique forms of emergence they may exhibit.

This chapter, though, is certainly not the first to call for exploring the ways in which society may exhibit a case of emergence. Other research in social simulation (Gilbert 1995), artificial societies (Axelrod 2003), and "infosocieties" (Conte 2001) points to the unique opportunities that societies present for studying emergence. Complex systems with the ability to react to their emergent properties have been said to exhibit "second order emergence" (Baas 1993; Steels 1995; Gilbert 2002). Indeed, the concept of second order emergence is similar to the ideas presented in this chapter. Specifically, we aim to come to a better understanding of the relationship between first order emergence and second order emergence, and how we might manipulate one to affect the other.

Abstraction

Abstraction, too, has been given a great deal of consideration, but for the most part not by the same researchers studying emergence. The definition adopted for the purposes of this chapter is that *abstraction is the process of forming simple rules that describe complex phenomena.* We can readily see here a corollary to the definition of emergence; emergence moves from simple rules to complex patterns, while abstraction moves from complex patterns to simple rules. This similarity, which is central to the ideas presented in this chapter, is explored further in the next section.

One common example of abstraction is the mathematical representation of numbers; the concept of the number "five" abstracts away the details of collections of objects and presents a notion of "fiveness" to describe collections of five objects. This type of abstraction is a fundamental aspect of computer science (Abelson 1996); the essence of computation is creating abstract representations that can be manipulated mechanically. Furthermore, a number of methods have been developed to create abstractions automatically. Machine learning algorithms, especially methods like support vector machines and kernel-based methods (Vapnik 1995), reinforcement learning (Kaelbling, Littman et al. 1996), and sequence learning (Berlin 2003) are designed to automatically create abstractions about the series of inputs given them. Each of these techniques is implemented in a different way, is amenable for use in different situations, and produces abstractions that are distinctly different. If, as this chapter argues, abstraction and emergence are converse processes of one another, there may be ways to similarly classify methods of inducing emergent behavior, and thus be able to use specific methods in order to achieve specific desired results.

Abstraction also features prominently in the reductionist approach to scientific inquiry. Under this philosophy, a natural phenomenon may be understood by decomposing the phenomenon into its constituent parts, understanding each part individually, and understanding how these parts interact and combine to produce the whole phenomenon. On the surface, this may seem to contradict the premise of emergence, that complex phenomena can emerge from simple rules that do not directly or explicitly reference the complex phenomenon of which they are a part. However, by taking into account the relationship between abstraction and emergence, we can see that emergence and reductionism are not in opposition but rather complement one another. The abstractions formed in the reductionist approach derive from complex phenomena the simpler principles underlying those phenomena. From the interaction of those principles, we can see the larger, more complex phenomena emerge, just as the principles of quantum mechanics give rise to the phenomenon of chemical bonding. The abstractions we form in the process of applying reductionism will affect the ways in which we perceive that resultant higher-level phenomenon.

Complexity

In the above definitions, emergence and abstraction are described as processes that move in opposite directions along an axis of complexity (Figure 2). This begs the question of how complexity is defined. Once again, there are a number of options; see (Badii and Politi 1997) for a rather comprehensive review. One might use information theory (Shannon 1948) and say that the complexity of a system is based on the amount of information required to fully describe the system. This is feasible, as it means that systems exhibiting emergent properties have the highest levels of complexity, especially in classification schemes similar to Langton's and Wolfram's. However, it becomes difficult to quantify in an information theoretic way just how much information is present in social systems, or what entails a complete description of the system. Another possibility is Kolmogorov complexity (Li and Vitanyi 1997), which measures the complexity of a system based on the length of the description of the mechanism that generates the system. For example, a collection of strings would be only as complex as the length of the regular expression or finite automaton used to generate them. This is not necessarily as useful for our purposes, since emergent properties are by

Figure 2. Emergence and abstraction work in opposite directions along an axis of complexity

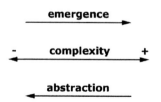

definition far more complex than the mechanism that generates them. Similar problems occur if we attempt to adopt definitions of complexity from formal languages and automata theory. The difficulty is that we need a method to compare the complexity of the rules that define a system to the behavior that the system exhibits. Since it is unclear whether one measure of complexity should be chosen over any other in the study of emergence, it is not claimed that any single method of determining complexity is most applicable to the systems being considered here. Rather, the abstraction-emergence loop, defined in the next section, provides a framework for studying the ways that abstraction and emergence interact. While a single, unified measure of complexity would be of great value to the research program presented here, the development of such a method is beyond the scope of this chapter, and so no authoritative working definition of complexity will be given here.

THE ABSTRACTION-EMERGENCE LOOP

Why do emergent phenomena occur in some situations and not others? What what aspects of certain classes of algorithms examined by Wolfram causes them to exhibit emergent behavior? What aspect of those certain algorithms is lacked by others? Why do certain abstractions serve to very accurately describe complex phenomena while others do not? How can some abstractions lead to more complex behavior than that from which they were originally drawn? Is there perhaps some connection between these two processes that we can use to understand both more fully?

While connections between abstraction and emergence may be at work in many complex systems, these connections are brought to the forefront when the systems involve entities that can observe, take into account, and react to, the emergent patterns to which they are contributing. Social systems are an example of just such a system. Individuals interact with others in a society, form abstractions about their interactions, and those abstractions in turn influence the patterns that emerge from future interactions. We call this cyclic connection of mutual influence the *abstraction-emergence loop;*

the abstractions that individuals make are the basis for the behaviors that emerge in a society, and the behaviors that emerge are the basis for the abstractions that individuals make.

This abstraction-emergence loop bears a great deal of similarity to processes described by various social theorists. For example, Berger and Luckmann (Berger and Luckmann 1966) describe the ways that institutions form based on social patterns. Through habituation and typification, members of a society abstract away the differences between various individuals who may perform a given task to form a role that describes the essence of the task. For example, the role of a judge in a court of law does not include the judge's age, specific facial expressions used by the judge, or the judge's posture while seated at the bench. It does, however, include calling court into session, sustaining or overruling objections, and ensuring that proper procedure is followed. Other members of legal cour room proceedings observe judges and develop a set of expectations, a role, about what constitutes being a judge and how one interacts with a judge. As judges observe one another, they, too, make abstractions about each other's activities. These abstractions serve to influence what individual judges do in their own courts, and thus influences the patterns that emerge across courts in general. The two processes are not separate and distinct, as described here, but rather occur continuously and simultaneously; at the same time that individuals use their abstractions to influence their behavior, they are simultaneously forming or refining their abstractions, which then influence future behavior. Furthermore, the status of judge-ship is being continually both reestablished and redefined by the judges themselves and other interactors in the courtroom.

This draws attention to similarities between the abstraction-emergence loop and Giddens' descriptions of the interactions between individual agency and social structure (Giddens 1979). As an individual acts in society, his or her actions are shaped by the structures inherent in the society of which he or she is a part. Continuing the example above, the individual in the court room respects and defers to the judge as dictated by the relevant social structures. However, the individual also has personal agency, in that the individual's actions also serve to shape social structure. The defendant may decry the judge and biased and refuse to acknowledge the authority of the court, thereby working to establish a new possible structuring of that social interaction. Thus, the individual's actions are both defined by, and serve to define, the structures present in their society. Similarly, an individual's actions both emerge from the abstractions the individual has made and simultaneously serve as actions from which new abstractions are made. While this cyclic nature is the essence of both the abstraction-emergence loop and Giddens' structuration theory, Giddens was more concerned with how social interaction is structured and less with the process of how social structures emerge from individual interactions.

As stated above, the abstraction-emergence loop has some similarity to the concept of second order emergence (Baas 1993; Steels 1995; Gilbert 2002). In first order emergence, emergent properties arise directly from interactions within a system. In second order emergence, parts of the system react to the system's own emergent properties, often changing the nature of the system itself. Although Gilbert sees second order emergence as a specific type of emergence particular to social systems, the position taken here is that the abstraction-emergence loop more accurately captures the nature of the situation than the concept of second order emergence for three main reasons. One, the ways in which parts of a system reacts to its own emergent properties are not described in discussions of second order emergence. The specifics of this reaction are handled as the abstraction portion of the abstraction-emergence loop. Two, the name "second order" implies that there is something distinctly different about this second phase of emergence versus the first or

perhaps a third. The argument here is that, since abstraction and emergence are simultaneous and continuous processes, one cannot divide emergent properties into a series of nth orders. Three, because the approach of second order emergence does not include the process by which the system's components react to its emergent properties, it does not address the ways in which the methods involved in these reactions affect what properties actually emerge. The abstraction-emergence loop places an emphasis on the methods by which reactions occur and their key role in influencing emergence.

Consider that there are a variety of different classes of learning algorithms: vector support machines, reinforcement learning, neural networks, social learning, and others. As described above, such algorithms can be seen as automated, mechanical methods of forming abstractions. Each of these methods includes a broad array of similar algorithms, each method's algorithms have specific strengths and weaknesses, each method is particularly amenable to different types of problems, and each will result in the formation of different types of abstractions. According to the abstraction-emergence loop, giving different agents the ability to form abstractions using these methods should give rise to different emergent phenomena. Such experiments are described in further detail in the future work section below.

LEVELS AND RANGES OF DETAIL

As stated above, abstraction and emergence move in opposite directions along a continuum of complex-

Figure 3. Smaller loops contained within a large abstraction-emergence loop

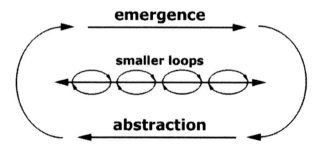

ity; abstractions moves from more complexity to less, emergence from less to more. However, there are not only two levels of complexity, high and low, but an entire spectrum. Within this spectrum, the abstraction-emergence loop can function over many different ranges of complexity and at many different levels of detail.

A range of complexity here refers to the difference in complexity between the complex phenomena and the simpler abstractions, or the difference in complexity between the simple rules and the more complex emergent phenomena. When examining instances of the abstraction-emergence loop, it may be beneficial to consider the range of complexity spanned between the abstractions and the emergent phenomena. It may be the case that the emergent phenomena for one instance of the loop serve as the simple rules for other instances of the loop spanning a range of higher complexity. Thus, a single large loop may actually be composed of many, smaller loops (Figure 3).

For example, the phenomenon of a football game can be seen as one large instance of the abstraction-emergence loop; individuals make abstractions about what it means for an activity to be recognized as a game of football, and these abstractions then affect the way that those individuals go about enacting a game of football. However, this large loop many actually be composed of many, smaller loops. One component of many football games is the crowd of spectators, and participation in the crowd is participation in a smaller abstraction-emergence loop. As individuals participate in the game as spectators, they are drawing on abstractions they have made about what it means to be a spectator at a football game. As they do so, the patterns that emerge from their actions and interactions serve to fuel further abstraction. Simultaneously, the crowd of spectators serves as another component in the definition a football game. As the abstraction-emergence loop alters the nature of the crowd, it simultaneously alters the nature of the football game, because the loop defining and redefining the crowd is a smaller part of the loop that defines and redefines the game as a whole.

The abstraction-emergence loop also functions at different levels of detail. Just as there is a broad spectrum of complexity over which the loop may

operate, it may also operate over many different levels of detail. Consider Conway's *Game of Life*. Depending on the level of detail on which an observer focuses, he or she may see individual cells turning on and off, may see isolated patterns such as gliders moving across the board, may see larger patterns such as glider guns, or may see large overall trends that affect the entire contents of the board. The level of detail at which the observer approaches the system in part determines what that observer recognizes as emergent phenomena. While the subjective nature of emergence is beyond the scope of the current chapter, the important point is that focusing on different levels of detail leads to different emergent phenomena. Furthermore, in different instances, the abstraction-emergence loop operates on different levels of detail.

Consider the minutia of how an individual raises a glass of wine and takes a drink. One might use the right or the left hand. One may swirl, shake, or otherwise agitate the contents of the glass. The glass will reach a specific degree of inclination as it is tilted toward the drinker. One might imbibe the liquid in small sips, in large gulps, or the entire glass in one long draught. The activity might occur in the home, in a bar, at an expensive restaurant, in a park, on a mountain, alone, with a partner, with family, with strangers, or in any number of other situations. Despite these many differences, most observers would be able to abstract away from the lower level of detail to recognize the higher level activity of drinking wine. Because this phenomenon is concerned with only a specific level of detail, we abstract away differences at lower and higher levels of detail to recognize multiple occasions as instances of the same activity.

Before proceeding, it is important to recognize a connection between these concepts and some that have been explored in reinforcement learning. Q-learning (Watkins and Dayan 1992) is a form of reinforcement learning that attempts to correlate states with actions and determine the expected reward, called the Q-value, for taking each action in each state. Hierarchical Q-learning represents an attempt to adapt Q-learning to multiple levels of detail; leaf controllers deal with decisions at a low level, while a selection policy determine which leaf nodes to invoke. For a summary of hierarchical Q-learning and related approaches, see (Berlin 2003). The main difference between these methods and that advocated by the abstraction-emergence loop is that hierarchical Q-learning essentially represents an approach to divide the problem space by decomposing tasks into constituent parts, while the argument here is that tasks can sometimes be decomposed into smaller subtasks. Different levels of decomposition are appropriate for different tasks, based on the range of detail over which abstractions are being made. Also, these algorithms focus on a specific level of detail and degree of decomposition, which may affect the patterns that emerge from the learning process.

Returning to the role of detail in the abstraction-emergence loop, focusing on specific levels and ranges of detail is one of the properties on which social simulation hinges. Sugarscape (Epstein and Axtell 1996) is one somewhat well-known environment for social simulation. Sugarscape is basically a cellular automaton but is more complex than the Game of Life. In sugarscape, there are many individual entities, each one designated as being of a certain race. These entities must use energy to move around a grid; if their energy falls to zero they perish. In order to gain energy, they need to find and consume sugar that occupies some squares of the grid. There is also a valued commodity known as spice, which allows for trade between individuals of different races. An important aspect of this simulation platform is the focus on a certain level of detail. The designers choose not to care about the specifics of a trade might be negotiated between two entities. With humans trading in a market, the customer may haggle with the shopkeeper, the shopkeeper may be pushy and overbearing, and the customer may end up accepting a price higher than might have been preferred. All of these complex details would affect the abstractions an individual makes when developing a notion of the experience of the market and what it is like to trade with a shopkeeper. However, in sugarscape, these low level details of interaction are not the focus; they are omitted, and the trade simply occurs. As Epstein and Axtell demonstrate, this level of detail is more than sufficient to simulate a wide variety of social phenomena. However, this level of detail is not sufficient for describing many phenomena.

Let us return now to the wine and consider trying to determine the difference between an individual tasting wine, in the oenophile sense of tasting, and an individual "just drinking" wine. At a higher level of detail, the actions look very similar; the individual raises a glass containing a liquid derived from the fermented juice of grapes and imbibes some quantity of that liquid. However, wine tasting is an action that can be recognized only by focusing at a lower level of detail. When tasting, one swirls the wine in the glass to open it up and release the flavors, smells the bouquet, holds the wine up to the light to examine its color, tilts it in the glass to examine viscosity, sips a mouthful of the liquid, swishes it around the mouth to explore the flavor, pauses for a moment after swallowing, and often delivers a summary description of the wine and the tasting experience as a whole. Although in many cases social interaction does not occur at this level of detail, there are times in which the minutia of daily interaction becomes integral to the constitution of that interaction (Garfinkel and Sacks 1970). By creating social simulations that do not include this level of detail, researchers automatically exclude the possibility of different higher level phenomena arising from activities with different combinations of these lower level details. While a good deal of the social simulation literature focuses on macro-level emergent phenomena in societies, there is relatively little exploration of micro-level emergent phenomena. Furthermore, there is no exploration of the connections between the two. How does the emergence of low level phenomena affect what higher level phenomena emerge, and how do abstractions about high level phenomena affect the abstractions that individuals make about lower level interactions? In order to understand these connections, we must build social simulations that incorporate a wide range of detail in their interactions. Not only does the abstraction-emergence loop described in this chapter offer one framework for exploring this connection, but such simulations would be a prime method for studying the effects of the abstraction-emergence loop across many varied levels of detail, examining how instances of the loop at different levels interact with and affect one another.

PREDICTION AND CONTROL OF EMERGENCE

One of the main goals of the line of work advocated in this chapter is the ability to predict and control emergent phenomena. A parallel may be drawn to the approach taken by the natural sciences. Based on experimentation, scientists develop laws that describe the workings of the natural universe, for instance, the second law of thermodynamics, or Newton's three laws of motion, or $s = s_0 + v_0 t + 0.5at^2$. Based on these laws, we are able to make predictions about the consequences of certain actions we take, e.g., if my wine glass were to slip from my hands, we could predict its trajectory, its position along that trajectory at any given moment, and the precise moment at which it would strike the floor and shatter. Granted, this would involve significantly more complex formulae than the single one listed above for position, but it could nonetheless be done with quite a good degree of accuracy. Furthermore, we are not only able to make predictions based on these laws, but we can use these predictions to alter the nature of our physical environment. Based on Bernoulli's equations, in conjunction with a number of other principles, engineers are able to manufacture objects that, when traveling forward at a great enough velocity, do not fall towards the earth but actually rise into the air. Just as knowledge of physical laws allows for control and manipulation of the physical environment, knowledge about the laws governing emergence may grant us the ability to control and manipulate emergent phenomena.

The abstraction-emergence loop provides one possible approach to the manipulation of emergent phenomena. In this framework, the abstractions that individuals make are intrinsically connected to the overall patterns that emerge from their behavior. By developing a greater understanding of how this connection actually operates, developers of multiagent systems may be able to predict how different alternative implementations of their individual agents would affect the emergent behaviors of the system, thus enabling them to design certain properties into individual agents that are known to give rise to a certain desired class of emergent phenomena. For example, if a designer wants a market simulation that stabilizes with a high cost of basic goods, perhaps within a certain number of iterations, he or she may choose to implement agents that make abstractions about their exchanges with other agents using a specific type of algorithm, perhaps reinforcement learning. Because of the designer's knowledge of how the abstractions involved in reinforcement learning are connected to the emergent phenomenon of market stabilization, the designer is able to choose a method of abstraction for the individual agents that will give rise to the desired result.

The abstraction-emergence loop may also have implications for the orchestration of large-scale social change. Just as the emergent properties of a

Figure 4. A community of animated agents inhabits a virtual island

multiagent system are intrinsically linked to the abstractions that individual agents make, the emergent properties of human societies are intrinsically linked to the abstractions that individuals make about their interactions with others. With an understanding of just how these individual abstractions are linked to the emergent patterns, if one can get people to change the abstractions they make or the way they go about making them, it may be possible to change the emergent social structures currently in place or cause entirely new structures to emerge. Similarly, with an understanding of how the loop works in both directions, it may be possible to predict just how individuals will make abstractions about these new social structures and thus influence further emergent structures. Some methods for exploring these possibilities are provided in the future work section.

FUTURE WORK

The focus of this chapter has on been describing the abstraction-emergence loop, its properties, and the directions it suggests for possible research on emergence. This section describes a number of future projects intended to explore the abstraction-emergence loop further and determine to what extent it can help us understand, predict, and control emergent phenomena.

Normative Echoes

One of the approaches advocated in this chapter is the development of social simulation that includes not only high level actions, but also the low level details of social interaction. As an initial exploration of this, the authors developed Normative Echoes, an interactive installation which revolves around using the abstraction-emergence loop to allow communities of animated characters to develop patterns of speech based on the patterns of words and phrases spoken by human users. The installation features groups of animated autonomous agents that inhabit stationary computers, which represent islands of virtual space (Figure 4) (Baumer, Tomlinson, et al. 2006). Users interact with agents by speaking into a microphone at either island that serves as the

agents' ears out into the physical world. The words and phrases spoken by participants are recorded as .wav files, which the agents then use to communicate with one another around a central bonfire. Not only do the characters use the words and phrases they learn from participants, but they also use the patterns they learn from each other. Using simple signal processing, the participant's speech is broken up into .wav files based on drops in amplitude of the input. These individual .wav files correspond to the words and phrases that compose the participant's speech, which become the atomic units of which the agents' speech patterns are formed. The agents perform no sophisticated speech-to-text or natural language processing, so there is no Semantic content to their communications. Rather, their communication takes the form of sharing patterns with one another. Initially, agents use the patterns of words and phrases used by participants. For example, if a participant says, "Hi, how's it going?" the agents connect the various sonic components that make up this utterance to form a pattern. These patterns are represented using a language called Scenario ML (Alspaugh 2005), a rich XML-based language developed for describing scenarios in software engineering. As agents communicate with one another, they may alter these patterns. For example, one agent may say "Hi," and another may respond with repeating the greeting "Hi," or may respond with "How's it going?" or even just "....going?" Based on the frequency with which certain patterns are used and what patterns are used as replies to what other patterns, the agents make abstractions about those things that are said and those things that are not said. These abstractions are then used to influence further communication, thus affecting what patterns emerge. It may be the case that every agents often say "Hi" to one another, but rarely say "How's it going?" The system also includes slight random perturbations to keep the communications between the agents from becoming entirely homogeneous and to encourage the development of new structures. Participants may also interact with these characters by moving them between islands with tablet PCs that serve as virtual rafts. In this case, the agents experience a sort of cultural diaspora; the agent that was moved takes with it the vocabulary and patterns it has learned on its island and brings them to the inhabitants of the new island. Simultaneously, the agent that was moved learns the speech patterns that are used on the new island and thus becomes absorbed into that society.

Normative Echoes was shown in the demonstration program of AIIDE-06 (Baumer, Tomlinson, et al. 2006). While there, participants' interactions with the installation were video recorded, and the authors are in the process of analyzing the human participants' interactions with the installation by means of video analysis. The goal of this analysis is in part to understand what happens when human users try to understand the behavior of software that is, in turn, trying to understand them. Importantly, while the animated agents are interacting with one another, they are also interacting with human participants, who are also interacting with one another. While these agents are making abstractions about the humans' and each other's speech patterns and trying to understand them, the humans are simultaneously forming abstractions about the speech patterns of the agents and trying to understand them. In this way, we hope to explore what happens when the abstraction-emergence loop is expanded to include both artificial agents and humans interacting socially. Specifically, the humans and the computational agents use different methods to create abstractions about their interactions with one another. How will the abstractions formed differ? Will these different abstractions cause difficulty in establishing mutual understanding between the humans and computational agents? How will these different abstractions influence the emergence of patterns in the social exchanges within and between the two groups?

Rule-To-Property Complexity

In the above discussion of complexity, a number of different possible complexity measures were discussed for use in measuring the amount of complexity at various points along the abstraction-emergence loop. However, as noted above, there is no single unified complexity measure by which to quantify emergence. Many complexity measures either address the complexity of the system required to produce a phenomenon, such as Kolmogorov complexity (Li and Vitanyi 1997), or address the

complexity of the phenomenon itself, such as information theory (Shannon 1948). The difficulty becomes that, with emergence, we assert that the emergent phenomenon has more complexity than the system from which it arises. While the lack of an objective, quantitative measure has not been an impediment to research on emergence thus far, it would certainly help matters. For instance, if it were possible to measure the complexity of a system and the complexity of the behavior the system exhibits using the same scale, then this quantitative measure of complexity could be used to determine whether or not a phenomenon should be considered emergent by determining if the phenomenon's complexity is significantly higher than the complexity of the system from which it arose. It would also provide a method for measuring the amount of complexity that is being reduced in the process of abstraction by comparing the complex phenomenon to the simple rules being produced. Furthermore, by measuring the amount of complexity in an emergent phenomenon and the amount of complexity in abstractions formed about that phenomenon, one could measure the ranges of complexity over which the abstraction-emergence loop operates, possibly determining variations in its strength in operating over different size ranges. Such a complexity measure would prove extremely useful in exploring emergent phenomena, either via the abstraction-emergence loop or through other approaches.

Social Simulation

Another possible area for research is to further explore social simulations that have a more phenomenological basis. It has already been argued in this chapter that we can benefit from developing social simulations that incorporate not only high level behavior but also the low level details of interaction in order to explore the connections between these low level interactions and the high level phenomena to which they give rise. One method of doing this would be to construct a number of different simulations, each one with agents that form abstractions using different methods, such as kernel-based methods (Vapnik 1995), reinforcement learning (Kaelbling, Littman, et al. 1996), or sequence learning (Berlin 2003). By examining the differences in the emergent phenomena that arise in the system, it may be possible to create generalizations about how different forms of abstraction affect the emergent results, and how those emergent results feed back into future abstractions. For example, all simulations in which agents use reinforcement learning may give rise to a set of emergent phenomena that is classifiably different than the phenomena that arise from simulations using kernel-based methods. A classification system of these emergent phenomena would prove quite useful in advancing a general study of emergence.

Furthermore, it would also be informative to do experiments with simulations where different agents employ different types of abstractions to understand how the different methods of abstraction affect one another. Do the different abstractions that the different agents form affect their interactions? Do different combinations of different methods of abstraction lead to new categories of emergent phenomena? Are the emergent phenomena when different agents use different methods of abstractions any more or less complex than with a system in which all agents use the same methods of abstraction? These are only a few of the many interesting and valuable research questions to be pursued along these lines.

Second Life

In addition to studying artificial social systems, the abstraction-emergence loop can also provide insight when studying human social systems. In another project, the authors are considering the possibility of using the online social world of Second Life (LindenLab 2003) as a test bed to explore the application of the abstraction-emergence loop to the study of human social behavior. There are several rationales behind using Second Life as a means for studying human social interaction. Anthropologists and social scientists are already using online gaming to study social behavior (Boellstorff 2006; Nardi and Harris 2006). In physical reality, recognizing human activities and partitioning them into their constituent parts is a very challenging problem, but in the virtual worlds of online gaming, what constitutes an individual action is determined programmatically by the system. Thus, rather than focusing on the task of activity recognition, the research can

focus on using the abstraction-emergence loop to study the roles of abstraction and emergence in human society. Furthermore, Linden Lab, creators of Second Life, explicitly supports the use of their software for educational purposes. Lastly, much of the content for the game is created by players; there already exist many scripts for performing meta-tasks within the game that the research team may be able to harness.

The actual plan of study consists of two main phases. In the first phase, human participants' Second Life accounts will be instrumented to collect data about their actions and interactions with other players. This data will include what actions are taken by which players, the context of those actions described in terms of who else is present and what other actions are taken, and the temporal relationships between those actions. As with the social simulations described above, a number of different computational methods will be tested to form abstractions from these data that describe the interaction patterns between players. These abstractions will then be used to try to predict what patterns will emerge during player interactions. Based on discrepancies between the predicted and actual actions, the abstractions will be further modified until the abstractions are relatively adequate predictors of player actions. The second phase of the study will involve the validation of those abstractions. The abstractions will be used to guide a simulation where each agent in the simulation is based on one of the characters in the study. Data describing this simulation will be given to human participants, as well as data logs describing actual interactions from the game. The test will be whether or not participants can distinguish between data generated by the simulation and data gathered by the game. According to the abstraction-emergence loop, the types of abstractions individual players make about their interactions will affect what social patterns emerge, and vice versa. If the patterns that emerge from these computational abstractions resemble those that emerge from human social interactions, then the computational abstractions may be an accurate representation of those formed by human players. Furthermore, just as algorithms for creating abstractions may be classified into groups, if the properties of the abstraction-emergence loop hold, then the patterns that emerge from these various classifications of abstraction algorithms will be similarly classifiable. For example, the use of reinforcement learning should lead to the emergence of patterns that are similar to each other and simultaneously different from the patterns emerging from the use of genetic algorithms.

Another, more complex test would be to introduce into the actual game world autonomous characters, or bots, whose behavior is governed by the abstractions acquired during the first phase and used for the simulations described here. The test in this case is if the bots, using the abstraction-emergence loop to continuously modify their behavior, can integrate into the fabric of society within the game. Currently there do not exist well-defined quantitative metrics for measuring this form of membership in the society of a virtual world. Furthermore, the bots would run the risk of deceiving Second Life's paying clientele and betraying their trust that live humans are controlling the characters with whom they interact. Nevertheless, such *in situ* social analysis of the abstraction-emergence loop would be helpful in determining the nature of its effect on human societies.

It could be argued that this process amounts to a Turing test for the social interactions that emerge from the acquired abstractions. As mentioned above, this chapter argues for more phenomenological forms of social simulation, and the tests described here present a way of evaluating the efficacy of interaction-level social simulations in reproducing the details of social exchange. Furthermore, within societies, mutual intelligibility is one of the more important products of the abstraction-emergence loop. Verifying whether such intelligibility can be obtained is core to verifying the effects of the abstraction-emergence loop.

Another question raised by the above methodology is whether the results will have any implications beyond the video gaming domain studied. Early sociological and anthropological work that focused on online interaction often portrayed online social interaction as a method of exploring multiple alternate personalities, or expressing certain otherwise non-dominant facets of one's own personality. For example, some MUD (multi-user dungeon) players have several characters, each with a different personality, and choose which character to play based on their current mood or what facets of their own personality they felt like exploring (Turkle 1995). However, more recent work suggests that people use the Internet not to be someone else but as new ways of being themselves. For example, Trinidadians, for whom connection with family is an important value, use the Internet as a new way to be Trinidadian, such as sending email reminders to their child in London to bring an umbrella because the forecast predicts rain today (Miller and Slater 2000). This later work suggests that social dynamics in an online setting bear very close resemblance to social dynamics at work in offline situations. If the abstraction-emergence loop can be used to analyze, model, and simulate social behavior online, it may be able to do the same for a broader range of human social dynamics.

CONCLUSION

The study of emergent phenomena presents researchers with a number of difficult challenges, not the least of which is developing an overall conceptual approach to the process of emergence. This chapter has presented an argument that the processes of emergence and abstraction are closely related and inextricably connected, and that the study of each can mutually inform the study of the other. This is especially true in the case of social systems, where individuals make abstractions about their interactions that influence what patterns emerge in what was called the abstraction-emergence loop. By drawing parallels to classes of algorithms for automatic creation of abstractions, it was argued that it may be possible to create similar classifications of emergent phenomena. The relationship between the abstraction-emergence loop and level of detail was discussed, and the concept of range of detail was introduced, which can be used to asses the difference between the level of complexity of an emergent phenomenon and abstractions about that phenomenon. Finally, a number of projects were described that are designed to explore the role of the abstraction-emergence loop and its efficacy in helping us understand emergent phenomena.

Why is it important to study emergence? The ultimate goal of this line of work is to understand emergence to the point of being able to manipulate and control it; this chapter focuses on doing so in a number of different computational systems. However, it may be possible to transfer the knowledge gained in understanding emergence in computational systems to other domains. With an understanding of just how abstractions affect emergence, one would be able to predict what patterns would emerge from certain abstractions and thus, in the design of various sorts of complex systems, choose from among a number of alternatives for the system's low level rules, thus enabling the achievement of the desired high level effect from the system. Particularly, this chapter proposes applying this methodology not only to computational systems, but also to social systems. Creating classifications of methods for the mechanical formation of abstractions and complementary classifications of emergent phenomena to which they give rise is not nearly as a great a challenge as creating similar classifications of abstraction and emergence in humans. However, the potential impact on society of understanding the connections involved in the abstraction-emergence loop and of being able to influence the emergence of social structure knowledgeably are substantial.

REFERENCES

Abelson, H. (1996). *Structure and Interpretation of Computer Programs.* Cambridge, MA, MIT Press.

Alspaugh, T. A. (2005). *Temporally Expressive Scenarios in ScenarioML.* Institute for Software Research Technical Report UCI-ISR-05-06. University of California, Irvine.

Axelrod, R. (2003). *Advancing the Art of Simulation in the Social Sciences.* in Journal of the Japanese Society for Management Information Systems **12**(3).

Baas, N. (1993). *Second order emergence.* Oral communication at the second European Conference on Artificial Life, ULB Brussels.

Badii, R. and Politi, A. (1997). *Hierarchical Structures and Scaling in Physics.* Cambridge, Cambridge University Press.

Baumer, E., Tomlinson, B., Yau, M.L., and Alspaugh, T.A. (2006). *Normative Echoes: Use and Manipulation of Player Generated Content by Communities of NPCs.* in AI in Interactive Digital Entertainment (AIIDE-06) Demonstration Program, Marina del Rey, CA, AAAI Press.

Berger, P. L. and Luckmann, T. (1966). *The Social Construction of Reality: A Treatise on the Sociology of Knowledge.* New York, Irvington Publishers, Inc.

Berlin, M. (2003). *Predatory sequence learning for synthetic characters.* Masters Thesis, Media Arts & Sciences. Cambridge, MA, MIT.

Boellstorff, T. (2006). A ludicrous discipline? Ethnography and game studies. *Games and Culture, 1*(1), 29-35.

Cariani, P. (1990). Emergence and artificial life. In *Artificial Life II.* New Mexico: Santa Fe Institute.

Conte, R. (2001). *Emergent (info) institutions. Journal of Cognitive Systems Research, 2,* 97-110.

Damper, R. I. (2000). Editorial for the special issue on 'Emergent properties of complex systems': Emergence and levels of abstraction. *International Journal of Systems Science, 31*(7): 811-818.

Deutch, M. and Gerard, H. B. (1955). A study of normative and informational social influence upon judgment. *Journal of Abnormal and Social Psychology, 51,* 629-636.

Epstein, J. M. and Axtell, R. (1996). *Growing artificial societies from the bottom up.* Cambridge and Washington, MIT Press and Brookings Institution Press.

Gardner, M. (1970). Mathematical Games: The Fantastic Combinations of John Conway's Game of 'Life'. *Scientific American,* 112-117.

Garfinkel, H. and Sacks, H. (1970). Formal structures of practical action. In J. C. McKinney and E. A. Tiryakian (eds.), *Theoretical Sociology.* New York: Appleton Century Crofts.

Giddens, A. (1979). Agency, structure. In A. Giddens, *Central Problems in Social Theory.* Berkeley: University of California Press.

Gilbert, N. (1995). Emergence in social simulation. In N. Gilbert and R. Conte (Eds.), *Artificial societies: The computer simulation of social life,* (pp. 144-156). London, UCL Press.

Gilbert, N. (2002). Varieties of emergence. In *Agent 2002 Conference: Social Agents: Ecology, Exchange, and Evolution.* Chicago.

Gilbert, N., Schuster, S., et al. (2005). Environment design for emerging artificial societies. In *Artificial Intelligence and the Simulation of Behavior 2005 Conference: Social Intelligence and Interaction in Animals, Robots and Agents.* Hatfield, UK.

Holland, J. (1998). *Emergence: from chaos to order.* UK: Oxford University Press.

Kaelbling, L. P., Littman, M. L., et al. (1996). Reinforcement learning: A survey. *Journal of Artificial Intelligence Research 4,* 237-285.

Kelley, H. H. (1955). The two functions of reference groups. In G. E. Swanson, T. M. Newcomb and E. L. Hartley (eds.) *Readings in social psychology,* (pp. 410-414). New York: Holt.

Langton, C. G. (1984). Self-reproduction in cellular automata. *Physica D, 10,* 135-144.

Langton, C. G. (1991). Computation at the edge of chaos: Phase transitions and emergent computation. In S. Forest (ed.), *Emergent computation,* (pp. 12-37). Cambridge, MA: MIT Press.

Li, M. and Vitanyi, P. (1997). *An introduction to Kolmogorov Complexity and its applications.* Berlin: Springer Verlag.

LindenLab (2003). *Second life.* San Francisco.

Miller, D. and Slater, D. (2000). Chapter One - Conclusions. *The Internet: An Ethnographic Approach.* Oxford: Berg.

Nardi, B. A. and Harris, J. (2006). Strangers and friends: Collaborative play in World of Warcraft. In *Computer supported cooperative work.* Banff, Alberta, Canada: ACM Press.

Sarkar, P. (2000). A brief history of cellular automata. *ACM Computing Surveys, 32*(1), 80-107.

Shannon, C. E. (1948). A mathematical theory of communication. *The Bell System Technical Journal 27(July, October, 1948),* 379-423, 623-656.

Steels, L. (1995). The artificial life roots of artificial intelligence. In C. G. Langton (ed.), *Artificial life: An overview.* Cambridge, MA: MIT Press.

Tomlinson, B., Baumer, E., et al. (2006). The island metaphor. In *SIGGRAPH 2006 Posters.* Boston.

Turkle, S. (1995). *Life on the screen: Identity in the age of the Internet.* New York: Simon and Schuster.

Vapnik, V. (1995). *The nature of statistical learning theory.* Berlin Springer-Verlag.

von Neumann, J. (1966). *The theory of self-reproducing automata.* Urbana, IL: University of Illinois Press.

Watkins, C. J. C. H. and Dayan, P. (1992). Technical Note: Q-Learning. In *Machine Learning 8*(3-4), 279-292.

Wolfram, S. (2002). *A new kind of science.* Champaign, IL: Wolfram Media.

ADDITIONAL READING

Axelrod, R. (1984). *The evolution of cooperation.* New York: Basic Books.

Barley, S. R. (1984). Technology as an occasion for structuring: Evidence from observations of CT scanners and the social order of radiology departments. *Administrative Science Quarterly, 31,* 78108

Baumer, E. and Tomlinson, B. (2005). *Institutionalization through reciprocal habitualization and typification.* In Second NASA Workshop on Radical Agent Concepts (WRAC), NASA Goddard Space Flight Center, Greenbelt, MD. (LNCS 3825). Springer.

Boellstorff, T. (2008 (to appear)). *Coming of age in second life: An anthropologist explores the virtually human.* New Jersey: Princeton University Press.

Brooks, R. A. (1990). Elephants don't play chess. *Robotics and Autonomous Systems, 6.*

Cohen, M. D., Riolo, R. L., and Axelrod, R. (1999). *The emergence of social organization in the prisoner's dilemma: How context-preservation and other factors promote cooperation.* Santa Fe Institute Working Paper 99-01-002, Santa Fe, NM.

Cooley, C. H. (1902). *Human nature and the social order.* New York: Charles Scribner's & Sons.

Deffuant, G., Moss, S., and Jager, W. (2006). Dialogues concerning a (possibly) new science. *Journal of Artificial Societies and Social Simulation, 9*(1).

Edmonds, B. and Dautenhahn, K. (1998). The contribution of society to the construction of individual intelligence. In *Workshop on "Socially Situated Intelligence" at Conference of the Society for Adaptive Behavior.* Zurich.

Esteva, M. (2003). *Electronic Institutions: from specification to development.* Dissertation, Artificial Intelligence Research Institute (IIIA), Technical University of Catalonia (UPC), Barcelona.

Garfinkel, H. (1967). *Studies in ethnomethodology.* Englewood-Cliffs, NJ: Prentice-Hall.

Giddens, A. (1984). *The constitution of society: Outline of the theory of structure.* Berkeley: University of California Press.

Goffman, E. (1959). *The presentation of self in everyday life.* New York: Doubleday.

Gilbert, N., Chattoe, E., & Troitzsch, K. G., *The Journal of Artificial Societies and Social Simulation.* http://jasss.soc.surrey.ac.uk/JASSS.html

Hacking, I. (1999). *The social construction of what?* Cambridge, MA: Harvard University Press.

Hales, D., and Edmonds, B. (2003). Evolving social rationality for MAS using "tags". In *Proceedings of the Second International Joint Conference on Autonomous Agents and Multiagent Systems (AAMAS),* 497-503. ACM Press.

Hemelrijk, C. K. (1999). An individual-oriented model of the emergence of despotic and egalitarian

societies. In *Proceedings of the Royal Society of London B, 266,* 361-369.

Hofstadter, D. R. (1979). *Gödel, Escher, Bach: An eternal golden braid.* New York: Basic Books.

Johnson, S. (2002). *Emergence: The connected lives of ants, brains, cities, and software.* New York: Simon & Schuster.

Langton, C. (1995). *Artificial Life: An overview.* Cambridge, MA: MIT Press.

Levy, S. (1992). *Artificial life: A report from the frontier where computers meet biology.* New York: Pantheon.

López y López, F., Luck, M., and d'Inverno, M. (2004). Normative agent reasoning in dynamic societies. *Proceedings of International Conference on Autonomous Agents (AAMAS),* 732-739. ACM Press.

Mead, G. H. (1934). *Mind, self, and society from the perspective of a social behaviorist.* Chicago: University of Chicago Press.

Moss, S. and Edmonds, B. (2005). Towards good social science. *Journal of Artificial Societies and Social Simulation, 8*(4).

Noble, J., Tuci, E., and Todd, P. M. (1999). Social learning and information sharing: An evolutionary simulation model of foraging in Norway rats. *Proceedings of the Fifth European Conference on Artificial Life (ECAL).*

Saussure, F. d. (1916). *Cours de linguistique générale.* Lausanne and Paris: Payot.

Sierra, C., Rodriguez-Aguilar, J. A., Noriega, P., Esteva, M., and Arcos, J. L. (2004). Enginerring multi-agent systems as electronic institutions. *European Journal for the Informatics Professional, 4.*

Tice, D. M. and Wallace, H. M. (2003). The reflected self: Creating yourself as (you think) others see you. *Handbook of Self and Identity.* M. R. Leary and J. P. Tangney (Eds.). New York: The Guilford Press.

Chapter XXI
Emergent Reasoning Structures in Law

Vern R. Walker
Hofstra University, USA

ABSTRACT

In modern legal systems, a large number of autonomous agents can achieve reasonably fair and accurate decisions in tens of thousands of legal cases. In many of those cases, the issues are complicated, the evidence is extensive, and the reasoning is complex. The decision-making process also integrates legal rules and policies with expert and non-expert evidence. This chapter discusses two major types of reasoning that have emerged to help bring about this remarkable social achievement: systems of rule-based deductions and patterns of evidence evaluation. In addition to those emergent structures, second-order reasoning about legal reasoning itself not only coordinates the decision-making, but also promotes the emergence of new reasoning structures. The chapter analyzes these types of reasoning structures using a many-valued, predicate, default logic – the Default-Logic (D-L) Framework. This framework is able to represent legal knowledge and reasoning in actual cases, to integrate and help evaluate expert and non-expert evidence, to coordinate agents working on different legal problems, and to guide the evolution of the knowledge model over time. The D-L Framework is also useful in automating portions of legal reasoning, as evidenced by the Legal Apprentice™ software. The framework therefore facilitates the interaction of human and non-human agents in legal decision-making, and makes it possible for non-human agents to participate in the evolution of legal reasoning in the future. Finally, because the D-L Framework itself is grounded in logic and not on theories peculiar to the legal domain, it is applicable to other knowledge domains that have a complexity similar to that of law and solve problems through default reasoning.

INTRODUCTION

The logical structure of legal reasoning, and especially its second-order reasoning about the reasoning process itself, is a primary mechanism by which new legal rules and new plausibility schemas emerge, and through which such rules and schemas adapt to the nuances of legal cases. This reasoning structure not only coordinates the efforts of numerous autonomous agents, but also promotes the emergence and evolution of new reasoning structures by responding to the tremendous variability provided by individual legal cases. This chapter describes the Default-Logic (D-L) Framework, which accurately models the logical structure of legal reasoning in actual legal cases. Moreover, it is the logical structure of legal reasoning itself, and not any particular set of rules within the legal knowledge domain, that creates this evolutionary mechanism. This means that the evolutionary mechanism captured by the D-L Framework can operate in domestic, foreign and international legal systems; that non-human autonomous agents can participate in this evolution, interacting with human agents; and that similar reasoning structures can operate in many knowledge domains other than law.

Legal reasoning is a distinctive method of reasoning that has emerged because of adherence to the rule of law. The rule of law requires that similar cases should be decided similarly, that each case should be decided on its merits, and that decision-making processes should comply with all applicable legal rules. One safeguard for achieving these fundamental goals is to make the reasoning behind legal decisions transparent and open to scrutiny. If the legal rules and policies are the same between cases, and the evidence and reasoning in particular cases are publicly available and subject to scrutiny, then the legal decisions in those cases are more likely to be evidence-based and consistent. Transparency makes the decisions less likely to be merely subjective, and more likely to have an objective rationale. An important means of achieving the rule of law, therefore, is articulating and scrutinizing the various elements of the reasoning exhibited in legal cases. Such reasoning involves interpreting constitutions, statutes, and regulations, balancing legal principles and policies, adopting and refining legal rules, adapting those rules to particular cases, evaluating the evidence in each case, and making ultimate decisions that are based on all of these elements.

Legal decision-making today requires many agents performing many different tasks. As the number and diversity of legal cases has increased, and the legal issues in those cases have become more specialized, it has become necessary to distribute the functions needed for optimal decision-making over more and more agents. First, these agents include the specialists in the law itself – the lawmakers (legislators, regulators, and judges), the law-appliers (such as judges and administrative personnel), and the advocates using the law (the lawyers representing parties). Such agents, either individually or in groups, establish the legal rules (e.g., by enacting statutes or issuing regulations), clarify their meaning (e.g., when deciding motions), and ensure that the rules are applied in appropriate cases (e.g., by advocating for particular outcomes, rules and policies). Second, there are the agents (witnesses) who supply the evidence needed to apply the legal rules accurately. Some witnesses have personal knowledge of disputed issues of fact. Other witnesses are experts who have scientific, technical, or other specialized knowledge that is relevant in particular cases – for example, knowledge about forensic science, product testing, medical care or engineering. Such agents supply the evidence needed to apply the legal rules accurately. Third, there are agents who act as the "factfinders." Depending upon the nature of the proceeding, a jury, judge, or administrative official listens to the witnesses, reads the relevant documents, evaluates all of the evidence, and decides what that evidence establishes as the "facts" for legal purposes. In modern legal systems, with tens of thousands of legal cases, a very large number of autonomous human agents participate, and they together achieve reasonably fair and accurate decisions. This achievement is possible because the reasoning in those cases is organized and supervised under the rule of law; the law, evidence and reasoning are transparent and publicly available; and the decision-making processes are open to scrutiny.

This chapter examines the logical structure of the reasoning involved in such cases, with particular attention to those structures that have emerged and evolved to help achieve consistency and accuracy. Following a brief background discussion and a summary of the major issues and problems, the chapter describes the elements of the D-L Framework, which has been developed to model the important structures of the reasoning. The next section uses that framework to describe the two basic types of reasoning that have emerged in law: systems of rule-based deductions and patterns of evidence evaluation. The D-L Framework can also model another distinctive feature in legal reasoning: second-order reasoning about the reasoning process itself. The chapter discusses modeling such second-order reasoning using the D-L Framework. This sets up a general discussion of the emergence of reasoning structures or patterns in law. The chapter ends with a conclusion and a suggestion about future research directions.

BACKGROUND

The practical nature of legal reasoning renders traditional deductive logic not particularly useful as a modeling framework. Legal reasoning is fundamentally practical in at least three ways. First, legal reasoning is action-oriented – its purpose is to evaluate the justification for governmental action or inaction. Legal reasoning determines whether a statute has been validly enacted, whether an administrative rule should be enforced, and whether a court should impose a sentence on a criminal defendant or order a civil defendant to pay compensation to a plaintiff. Second, legal reasoning and decision-making occur in real time and are constrained by limited resources, including incomplete information. It is a species of decision-making under uncertainty (Kahneman, Slovic & Tversky 1982; Morgan & Henrion 1990). Within the time and resource constraints, those engaged in legal reasoning must determine the appropriate legal rules, evaluate the evidence, decide whether the evidence is complete enough and the residual uncertainty is acceptable, and arrive at an ultimate decision. Third, legal reasoning is practical in the sense that it must always balance the "epistemic objective" of law against the applicable "non-epistemic objectives" (Walker

2003). The epistemic objective in law is to make findings of fact that are as accurate as possible under the circumstances, while basing those findings on the limited evidence that is available. Law aims at truth, but the findings must be reasonably inferred from the evidence. Weighed against this pursuit of truth are numerous non-epistemic objectives – such as ensuring procedural fairness to parties, improving administrative efficiency, or achieving other governmental goals (e.g., an adequate supply of electric power or economic efficiency within securities markets). Each institution of government balances these objectives differently. Legal reasoning, therefore, is practical because it is oriented toward decisions and actions, it occurs under constraints of limited resources and incomplete information, and because it must always balance epistemic and non-epistemic objectives.

Modeling the distinctive reasoning structures that have emerged within this practical context requires a broad view of "logic" as the study of "correct reasoning," including theories and methods for distinguishing correct from incorrect reasoning (Copi & Cohen 1998). Traditional deductive logic is not a particularly useful framework for modeling legal reasoning because traditional logic is designed to capture the deductive structure of mathematics. More useful in law are recent developments in logic, such as informal logic (Hitchcock & Verheij 2006; Walton 1996, 2002), abductive logic (Josephson & Tanner 1994), and nonmonotonic logic (Brewka, Dix & Konolige 1997; Kyburg & Teng 2001; Levi 1996; Prakken 1997), as well as decision theory, risk-benefit analysis, and risk analysis.

The D-L Framework discussed in this chapter models legal reasoning as an application of default reasoning. Default reasoning uses presumptive inference patterns, together with the available evidence, to warrant defeasible conclusions about possible actions (Besnard 1989; Brachman & Levesque 2004; Brewka, Dix, & Konolige 1997; Josephson & Tanner 1996; Kyburg & Teng 2001; Levi 1996; Pollock 1990; Prakken 1997; Toulmin, Rieke, & Janik 1984; Walton 1996, 2002). Such reasoning patterns possess four important characteristics. First, default reasoning is practical, providing a reasonable basis for decisions and actions. Such reasoning is also dynamic, because the evidence can change over time, as can the degree of support from the evidence to the conclusion. Also, multiple parties can participate interactively in the reasoning process. Third, default reasoning is defeasible, meaning that new evidence or a re-analysis of old evidence can defeat an earlier conclusion or undermine its evidentiary support (Pollock & Cruz 1999; Prakken 1997; Walton 2002). Nevertheless, in the absence of such defeating considerations, default reasoning is presumptively valid – that is, it is reasonable to treat the (provisional) conclusion as being probably true (Walton 2002). The D-L Framework introduced here builds these four characteristics into its logical model.

The D-L Framework also has many points of congruence with the extensive research into legal reasoning from the perspective of artificial intelligence (AI). The prominent role of rules in the D-L Framework is in keeping with the "rule-based reasoning" (RBR) approach in AI research (Branting 2000; Rissland 1990). Other portions of the D-L Framework weigh policy arguments or relevant factors, and are related to the AI interest in reasoning by analogy to case precedents, called "case-based reasoning" (CBR) (Branting 2000; Ashley & Rissland 2003; Rissland 1990). AI researchers have also combined these two approaches into hybrid systems (Branting 2000; Prakken & Sartor 1997; Rissland 1990). Tree structures, which are central to the D-L Framework, are commonly used in AI (Branting 2000; Ashley & Rissland 2003; Prakken, Reed & Walton 2003). Moreover, AI researchers have investigated the use of "argumentation schemes" from informal logic, which bear some loose resemblance to plausibility schemas in the D-L Framework (Prakken & Sartor 2004; Prakken, Reed & Walton 2003; Walton 1996). Plausibility schemas are nevertheless unlike argumentation schemes in important respects (Walker 2007a, 2007c). Finally, the Decision Apprentice™ software developed by Apprentice Systems, Inc. incorporates the D-L Framework and successfully applies it to law in the application called Legal Apprentice™ (for details, visit www.apprenticesystems.com).

There are also isolated pockets of theoretical work on legal reasoning methods that provide useful input to the D-L Framework. For example, within research using traditional legal methods, there are studies of the probative value of the forensic sci-

ences (Faigman, Kaye, Saks & Sanders 2002), and research into general patterns of evidence evaluation (Anderson, Schum & Twining 2005; Kadane & Schum 1996; Schum 1994). There is also extensive case law and commentary on when expert opinions are valid enough to be admissible as evidence – for example, under the U.S. Supreme Court's trilogy of cases, Daubert v. Merrell Dow Pharmaceuticals, Inc., 509 U.S. 579 (1993); General Electric Co. v. Joiner, 522 U.S. 136 (1997); Kumho Tire Co. v. Carmichael, 526 U.S. 137 (1999). Legal reasoning is also examined as such in the context of legal writing (Neumann 2005) and skills training for lawyers (Krieger & Neumann 2003). Moreover, the logic of legal reasoning is studied within particular legal areas, such as tort law (Porat & Stein 2001; Walker 2004) or international trade law (Walker 1998, 2003). Fields outside of law have also studied aspects of legal reasoning, such as psychological research on juries (Hastie 1993) or research in rhetoric (Saunders 2006; Ross 2006). The D-L Framework, however, incorporates insights from these various areas of inquiry into a single, integrated model for legal reasoning as a whole. It also captures the emergent structures of legal reasoning.

Finally, it is essential that the D-L Framework accurately, adequately and efficiently models actual reasoning in actual legal cases. It is the great variety of legal cases, with the hierarchies of legal decision-makers overseeing the reasoning and the extensive documentation of that reasoning, that creates an evolutionary environment. That evolutionary structure refines legal concepts and patterns of reasoning, and adapts them to solving legal problems (Walker 1999, 2007b). These evolutionary forces make it likely that the reasoning patterns that do emerge and evolve are both useful and normative. This evolutionary aspect of legal reasoning necessitates empirical research into the actual balances between epistemic and non-epistemic objectives struck in particular legal areas.

SUMMARY OF MAJOR ISSUES AND PROBLEMS

This chapter models legal knowledge, but the modeling framework is applicable to decisional knowledge in any domain that has similar engineering problems (Russell and Norvig 2003; Singh, Rao, and Georgeff 1999). The major problems in this and similar domains are:

- Accurately capturing the detailed knowledge of the domain, using structures that are suited to that knowledge and to the practice of using that knowledge to solve problems in that domain;
- Integrating expert and non-expert knowledge into a single practical model;
- Applying the knowledge model to solve the next problem;
- Evolving and adapting the knowledge model over time, on the basis of experience with solving problems; and
- Coordinating the use of such knowledge among autonomous agents (both human and non-human) and among different problem sets over time.

The D-L Framework captures the detailed knowledge of the legal domain, and shows how the emergent structures of legal reasoning can help to solve these engineering problems in law and in other knowledge domains.

THE DEFAULT-LOGIC FRAMEWORK

The Syntax, Ontology, and Semantics of the Default-Logic Framework

Because of the highly pragmatic nature of legal reasoning, and because the reasoning structures have emerged and evolved over time within the law, logical models of those structures must be developed empirically. It is important, for example, to empirically abstract the logic of reasoning in particular legal areas, such as tort law (Walker 2004) or international trade disputes (Walker 1998, 2006), or the logic of general concepts found across all legal areas, such as the concept of standard of proof (Walker 1996). Only then can a formal model represent those structures that are actually used and useful, and accurately capture legal reasoning as it

actually occurs in particular cases. The D-L Framework described in this chapter has been developed in this way. It incorporates some but not all of the logical elements found in traditional predicate logic, and also includes additional elements not found in that logic. It includes only those logical structures actually used and useful in legal reasoning.

The knowledge-capture environment of the D-L Framework can be either textual or graphical, but the graphical syntax is very intuitive for human agents to use. The Decision Apprentice™ software uses Microsoft Office Visio™ as a graphical environment for capturing legal rules. The software builds the knowledge model as the user selects, drags, and connects Visio shapes. The software turns these shapes into "smart shapes" that represent the elements of the syntax – objects with various attributes that allow only combinations of elements that are syntactically acceptable. Figure 1 shows representative shapes for the D-L ontology, and illustrates which combinations of shapes are permissible.

The ontology and Semantics for the D-L Framework are as follows:

- **Proposition:** The informational content of a declarative sentence or clause, which can be meaningfully assigned either a truth-value or a plausibility-value. Examples are: "The defendant is a citizen of the United States" and "Jessica Jones is liable to the plaintiff for battery." The Decision Apprentice™ shape representing a proposition is shown in Figure 1. A proposition whose active value in a line of reasoning is its truth-value is called simply a proposition, to distinguish it from an evidentiary assertion. The border of the shape is a solid line. By contrast, a proposition whose active value in a line of reasoning is its plausibility-value is called an "evidentiary assertion" or simply an "assertion," to distinguish it from a proposition whose active value is its a truth-value. The Decision Apprentice™ shape for an evidentiary assertion has as its border a dashed line, to indicate that its operative attribute is its plausibility-value.
  - o The truth-value of a proposition is an attribute taking one of three values: "true / undecided / false."

Figure 1. Illustrative Decision Apprentice™ Shapes for Selected Elements of the D-L Framework

Unanalyzed Proposition:

Analyzed Proposition:

Unanalyzed Assertion:

Most witnesses are truthful under oath.

Analyzed Assertion:

Most members of category A are also members of category B.
Category A
Category B

Implications and Implication Tree (Operating on Truth-Values):

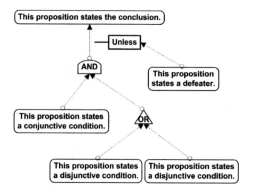

Assertions in a Schema (Operating on Plausibility-Values):

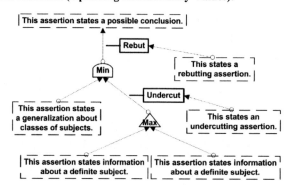

o The plausibility-value of an assertion is an attribute taking a value from a plausibility scale. Plausibility scales can have any number of values, either qualitative or quantitative. For example, a qualitative plausibility scale might be ordinal and have five values (such as "highly plausible / somewhat plausible / undecided / somewhat implausible / highly implausible") or seven values (such as "highly plausible / very plausible / somewhat plausible / undecided / somewhat implausible / very implausible / highly implausible"). By contrast with these qualitative scales, mathematical probability provides an infinite-valued quantitative plausibility scale, using the set of real numbers between zero and one, and having values such as 0.56.

o A proposition or an evidentiary assertion can be either unanalyzed or analyzed into its predicate-subject structure (see Table 1 for illustrations).

- **Subject:** An object, property, situation or event referred to in a proposition, and about which the proposition makes a statement. In the Decision Apprentice™ software, the shape representing a subject can be inserted into a proposition shape, as shown in Figure 1. A "predicate" is not a separate element or shape, but merely the remainder of a proposition excluding its subjects. A predicate functions as a propositional schema that generates meaningful propositions when the appropriate number of subjects are supplied (e.g.: "… is a citizen of … "; "… is liable to … for battery") (Chierchia & McConnell-Ginet 2000; Copi & Cohen 1998; Larson & Segal 1995; Rodes & Pospesel 1997; Saeed 2003; Sainsbury 1991). In the D-L Framework, it may not be useful to identify and represent every subject in a proposition – only those that play an important referring role in the legal analysis.

o A subject can be a definite subject – that is, a specific individual named by a proper name or a definite description (e.g.: Jessica Jones; the defendant).

o A subject can also be a group or class whose members are identified solely by one or more attributes (e.g.: Americans over age 50; tort cases filed this year in U.S. courts).

- **Implication:** A complex proposition (conditional proposition) consisting of one or more propositions as conditions and a single proposition as a conclusion, in which the truth-value of the conclusion is determined by the truth-values of the conditions. In the D-L Framework, the conclusion is placed at the top and its conditions are placed on a lower level, with the conditions connected to the conclusion by "implication arrows" running from the conditions to the conclusion, usually mediated by a truth-value connective (see Table 1 for illustration).

- **Plausible inference:** A complex proposition (conditional assertion) consisting of one or more evidentiary assertions as conditions and a single evidentiary assertion as a conclusion, in which the positive plausibility-value of the conclusion is determined by the plausibility-values of the conditions. In the D-L Framework, the conclusion is placed at the top and its conditions are placed on a lower level, with the conditions connected to the conclusion by "implication arrows" running from the conditions to the conclusion, usually mediated by a plausibility connective.

- **Logical connective:** An operator that mediates between the conditions and conclusion of an implication or plausible inference, and which specifies a formula for assigning a truth-value or plausibility-value to the conclusion as a function of the truth-values or plausibility-values of the conditions (see Table 1 for illustrations). Logical connectives fall into two major categories – those operating on truth-values and those operating on plausibility-values.

- **Truth-value connectives:** The D-L Framework primarily uses three truth-value connectives:

o *Conjunction ("AND"):* A connective specifying that the truth-value of the conclusion is "true" if all of the truth-values of the conjunctive conditions are "true" (Copi & Cohen 1998; Gottwald

2001; Rodes & Pospesel 1997; Sainsbury 1991).

○ *Disjunction ("OR"):* A connective specifying that the truth-value of the conclusion is "true" if at least one of the truth-values of the disjunctive conditions is "true" (Copi & Cohen 1998; Gottwald 2001; Rodes & Pospesel 1997; Sainsbury 1991).

○ *Defeater ("UNLESS"):* A connective specifying that the truth-value of the conclusion is "false" if the truth-value of the defeater condition is "true" (Brewka, Dix, & Konolige 1997; Pollock 1990). The defeater condition may itself consist of either conjunctive conditions or disjunctive conditions.

- **Plausibility connectives:**
  ○ *Minimum ("MIN"):* A connective specifying that the plausibility-value of the conclusion is equal to the lowest plausibility-value possessed by any of its conditions (Gottwald 2001). The MIN plausibility connective is a generalized version of the AND truth-value connective.

  ○ *Maximum ("MAX"):* A connective specifying that the plausibility-value of the conclusion is equal to the highest plausibility-value possessed by any of its conditions (Gottwald 2001). The MAX plausibility connective is a generalized version of the OR truth-value connective.

  ○ *Rebut ("REBUT"):* A type of defeating connective specifying that, if the rebutting condition is plausible to any degree (its plausibility-value is positive), then the plausibility-value of the conclusion is the inverse degree of implausibility (that is, its plausibility-value is negative, and to the same degree as the rebutting condition is positive) (Pollock 1990; Prakken & Sartor 1997, 2004; Prakken, Reed & Walton 2003). For example, if the rebutting condition is "highly plausible" on a seven-point ordinal scale, then the

conclusion is "highly implausible" on the same scale.

○ *Undercut ("UNDERCUT"):* A type of defeating connective specifying that, if the undercutting condition is plausible to any degree (its plausibility-value is positive), then the plausibility-value of the conclusion is whatever it would have been in the absence of the branch of reasoning to which the undercutting defeater is attached (Pollock 1990; Prakken & Sartor 1997, 2004; Prakken, Reed & Walton 2003). An undercutting condition defeats the line of support for the conclusion, whereas a rebutting condition defeats the conclusion itself.

- **Implication tree:** An inverted directed acyclic graph consisting of chained levels of implications, in which a condition of one implication becomes the conclusion of another implication (see Table 1 for illustration).

- **Plausibility schema:** An inverted directed acyclic graph consisting of evidentiary assertions and plausibility connectives (see Figure 1 for illustration), and which functions as a schema producing plausible inferences whenever (1) specific subjects are substituted into the schema, (2) plausibility-values are assigned to the evidentiary conditions of the schema, and (3) the plausibility-values of the evidentiary conditions, mediated by the plausibility-connective of the schema, determine a positive plausibility-value for the schema conclusion. Such an instantiated plausibility schema produces a plausible inference.

- **Inference tree:** An inverted directed acyclic graph consisting of (1) the ultimate conclusion at the top; (2) an implication tree immediately supporting that ultimate conclusion; (3) terminal propositions in each branch of the implication tree, which are supported in turn only by evidentiary assertions; and (4) lower levels of branches (below the terminal propositions) consisting of plausible inferences (instantiated plausibility schemas and perhaps additional evidentiary assertions). See Figure 2 for illustration.

Figure 2. Illustration of a Partial Inference Tree in Decision Apprentice™ Applying Tort Rules for Battery

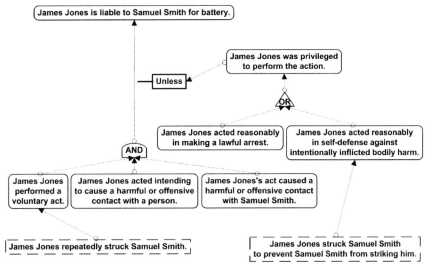

Using the Default-Logic Framework to Model Two Legal Reasoning Structures

The D-L Framework provides the tools for modeling, in any particular legal case, the reasoning that warrants the legal findings, decisions, and actions in that case. The D-L model for the complete reasoning is an inference tree. As discussed above, an inference tree typically has at least two major regions: an implication tree near the top, directly supporting the ultimate conclusion, and plausible inferences below the terminal propositions of the implication tree. Figure 2 illustrates the general structure of an inference tree. The two sub-sections that follow discuss the two major regions of an inference tree – rule-based deductions and evidence evaluation.

Implication Trees As Modeling Systems of Rule-based Deductions in Law

The upper portion of any inference tree is an implication tree, which models all of the implications or lines of reasoning to the ultimate conclusion that are acceptable under the applicable legal rules. The ultimate conclusion at the top is the root node of an inverted "tree" structure because lower-level conditions never depend for their truth-values on a higher-level proposition in the same branch. Implication trees branch downward and outward from a single root conclusion. For example, the rules of tort law for battery, which can justify a court judgment that the defendant must pay damages, can be modeled as one large implication tree that begins as shown in Figure 2. The legal interpretation of this tree is that "the defendant is liable to the plaintiff for battery" (conclusion) if (1) "the defendant performed a voluntary act," (2) "the defendant acted intending to cause a harmful or offensive contact with a person," and (3) "the defendant's act caused a harmful or offensive contact with the plaintiff," unless this line of reasoning is defeated because "the defendant was privileged to perform the action," which would be true if either "the defendant acted reasonably in making a lawful arrest" or "the defendant acted reasonably in self-defense against intentionally inflicted bodily harm" (American Law Institute 1966; Dobbs 2000). In each branch of an implication tree, the conditions of the last rule in that branch are the "terminal propositions" of the rules. In Figure 2, these are the five last propositional shapes (those with solid lines) in the branches. The truth-value of a terminal proposition can be determined to be either "true" or "false" only by stipulation of the parties, by certain types of decisions or rulings by the presiding legal official, or by an evaluation of the evidence by the factfinder. The terminal propositions of an implication tree identify all of the factual issues that are relevant to warranting the ultimate conclusion. The implication tree therefore constrains the evidence and factfinding in the case to what is relevant to deciding the truth-values of the terminal propositions.

Plausibility Schemas as Modeling Patterns of Evidence Evaluation

When decision-making begins in a particular legal case, the truth-values of all of the propositions within the applicable implication tree are "undecided." Evidence evaluation is the process of using evidence to determine whether the truth-values of particular terminal propositions should change from "undecided" to either "true" or "false." Reasoned decision-making involves: producing evidence for the legal record that is relevant to proving one or more of the terminal propositions of the implication tree; organizing that evidence into plausible inferences using plausibility schemas; attaching the schematized evidence to the appropriate terminal propositions; evaluating the plausibility-values of the evidentiary assertions; and using those plausibility-values to assign new truth-values to terminal propositions. The logical connectives can then use those truth-values to propagate truth-values up the implication tree to determine the truth-value of the ultimate conclusion at the top. The topics discussed in this sub-section of the chapter are: the evaluation of the plausibility of single evidentiary assertions, the use of plausibility schemas to organize evidentiary assertions and to make plausible inferences, and the use of instantiated plausibility schemas to determine the truth-value of a terminal proposition.

In a typical legal case, the parties produce witnesses, documents, and other evidence. The witnesses and documents then provide evidentiary assertions "for the legal record," which constitute the bulk of the evidence. The factfinder formulates other evidentiary assertions – for example, in describing the behavior of a witness or in characterizing the results of a medical chart or other exhibit. When evaluating the plausibility of an evidentiary assertion, an agent selects a suitable plausibility scale and assigns a plausibility-value from that scale to the evidentiary assertion. Choosing the best plausibility scale to employ for evaluating any particular evidentiary assertion depends upon the pragmatic context – that is, upon the precision needed in the content and upon the potential for error that is acceptable in assessing plausibility (Walker 2007a). For example, some legal cases might require only a low degree of precision (e.g., measurements of length in inches) and accept even a moderate degree of plausibility (allowing a significant potential for error), with the result that even a single measurement with an ordinary ruler will yield acceptably accurate values. Other cases, by contrast, might require a high degree of precision (e.g., measurements of length in microns) and a high level of quantitative plausibility (e.g., 99.99% confidence that the measurement is accurate to within 2 microns). In general, as the level of required precision increases, the potential for error inherent in assessing plausibility for measurements with that precision also tends to increase. In addition, it often costs some amount of resources to produce additional evidence in an attempt to make the conclusion acceptably plausible. A reasonable decision-maker would therefore use plausibility scales that achieve the least-cost combination of precision and degree of plausibility that will yield acceptably accurate results in the pragmatic context.

The factfinder next organizes individual evidentiary assertions into patterns of reasoning relevant to proving the terminal propositions in the case, using what the D-L Framework calls "plausibility schemas." Plausibility schemas are general patterns of evidentiary reasoning that presumptively warrant plausible inferences, by producing lines of default inference that are plausible but subject to revision. Such schemas also allow the factfinder to strike the appropriate pragmatic balance of acceptable uncertainty. Plausibility schemas consist of evidentiary assertions and plausibility connectives. An evidentiary assertion is a proposition whose active value in a line of reasoning is its plausibility-value (see the ontology above). Plausibility connectives are logical operators that determine the plausibility-value of the assertion that is the schema conclusion as a function of the plausibility-values of the assertions that form the evidentiary conditions of the schema. Four plausibility connectives that occur repeatedly in the patterns of reasoning found in legal cases are MIN, MAX, REBUT and UNDERCUT (defined in the ontology above).

One problem in the operation of plausibility schemas is that factfinding agents may adopt different plausibility scales for evaluating different evidentiary assertions. When this occurs, there must be a rule for operating on a mixture of plausibility scales – for example, where one assertion has a plausibility-value on a seven-point ordinal scale and another in the same plausibility schema has a quantitative value on the real-number scale. For the plausibility connectives of minimum (MIN) and maximum (MAX), the factfinding agent must determine whether a particular value on one scale is lower or higher than a value on another scale. Given such a combined ordering of possible plausibility-values, however, the plausibility-value of the schema conclusion can be determined on the plausibility scale of the critical evidentiary assertion – that is, for MIN, the evidentiary assertion with the lowest plausibility-value, and for MAX, the evidentiary assertion with the highest plausibility-value.

By contrast, the two defeater plausibility connectives, REBUT and UNDERCUT, take single assertions as rebutting or undercutting defeaters, and so do not have this multiple-scale problem (although MIN or MAX connectives under the defeating assertions

may have this problem). In the case of a plausibility rebutter, if the rebutting assertion has a positive plausibility-value, then the connective REBUT assigns to the schema conclusion the degree of plausibility that is the inverse to the plausibility-value of the rebutting assertion. That is, as the degree of plausibility of the rebutting assertion increases, the degree of plausibility of the conclusion decreases (alternatively, the degree of implausibility of the conclusion increases). For example, on the seven-point plausibility scale above, if the plausibility-value of the rebutting assertion is "highly plausible," then the plausibility-value of the schema conclusion would be "highly implausible." On a plausibility scale of mathematical probability, if the rebutter's plausibility-value is 0.56, then the conclusion's plausibility-value would be 0.44 (1 − 0.56).

In the case of a plausibility undercutter, if the undercutting assertion has a positive plausibility-value, then the connective UNDERCUT assigns to the schema conclusion the degree of plausibility that it would have had in the absence of the line of reasoning that is undercut. An undercutter connective can be useful in capturing the logic of an assertion that defeats only one condition of a set of conditions. As illustrated in the schema in Figure 1, a positive undercutting assertion would simply take out of play the right-hand branch below the MIN connec-

Figure 3. Decision Apprentice™ Diagram for the Plausibility Schema for the Statistical Syllogism

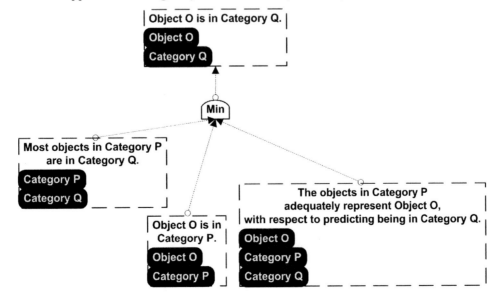

tive of the schema, leaving the plausibility-value of the left-hand assertion under the MIN connective to determine the plausibility-value of the schema conclusion.

An example of a plausibility schema commonly found in actual reasoning is the "statistical syllogism" or "direct-inference" schema, which models one type of presumptive reasoning about a definite subject or specific individual (Walker 2007a, 2007c; Kyburg 1983; Levi 1977, 1981; Pollock 1990; Salmon 1973). Examples of such conclusions are "the tire that caused the accident had a defect" and "the claimant contracted pneumoconiosis," where "the tire" and "the claimant" are definite subjects (for pertinent legal cases, see Kumho Tire Co. Ltd. v. Carmichael, 526 U.S. 137 (1999), and Director, Office of Workers' Compensation Programs, Department of Labor v. Greenwich Collieries, 512 U.S. 267 (1994)). A D-L diagram for the plausibility schema modeling the statistical syllogism is shown in Figure 3 (Walker 2007c, p. 11). The plausibility connective MIN joining the evidentiary conditions of the schema assigns a plausibility-value to the schema conclusion that is equal to the plausibility-value of the least plausible of the three joined assertions. The three conditions state the evidentiary assertions that together render the conclusion plausible. The first evidentiary assertion (from the left) is a generalization asserting that most objects in Category P are also in Category Q. The second evidentiary assertion is that the specific object that is the definite subject of the conclusion (O) is in Category P. The third evidentiary assertion states that the objects in Category P adequately represent Object O, with respect to a sufficient number of variables (attributes) that are predictive of being in Category Q. Thus, a factfinder using this pattern of reasoning to warrant assigning a plausibility-value to such a conclusion must substitute specific values for the three logical subjects ("Category P," "Category Q," and "Object O") and then assign plausibility-values to each of the three evidentiary conditions of the inference. Subject substitution creates an instance of the schema (an instantiated schema). In addition, assigning plausibility-values that generate a positive plausibility-value for the schema conclusion creates a plausible inference.

One component of many plausibility schemas is an assertion that states a generalization (Chierchia and McConnell-Ginet 2000; Copi and Cohen 1998; Kadane and Schum 1996; Rodes and Pospesel 1997; Schum 1994; Toulmin 1958). A generalization is an assertion stating that its description is true of some of the subjects in the class to which it refers (a proper subset of the referenced subject class), but does not assert that it is true of all subjects in the class. Examples of generalizations are: "most witnesses testifying under oath tell the truth"; "one-third of Americans are overweight"; and "60% of the test group in the study developed the disease." These three generalizations have the following logical forms (respectively): "most Ps are Qs"; "X/Y of Ps are Qs"; and "X% of the members of group P are members of group Q." Logicians call group P the "reference class" or "reference group" for the generalization (Kyburg 1990). Two logical attributes of a generalization that can affect its plausibility-value are its degree of quantification and any modal hedge employed. Generalizations imply or explicitly assert a degree of quantification over the reference class – that is, they assert what portion of members of class P is also included in class Q. Moreover, generalizations often contain an explicit modal "hedge" that qualifies the entire assertion. Examples of modal hedges are expressions of frequency (e.g., "sometimes" or "often"), typicality (e.g., "typically" or "normally"), temporal limitation (e.g., "in the past" or "at least for the immediate future"), or degree of confidence of the speaker (e.g., "perhaps" or "almost certainly"). Generalizations may be warranted by scientific, technical or other specialized knowledge, or they may derive from personal experience or "common sense."

Plausibility schemas play an important role in integrating expert evidentiary assertions with non-expert evidentiary assertions into a single line of evidentiary reasoning. For example, the generalization in the statistical-syllogism schema may be supported by either expert or non-expert evidence – statistical or other scientific evidence in one case, but only scattered anecdotal evidence in another case. Regardless of the nature of the support for the generalization, the evidentiary assertion that the definite subject is in Category P may be based upon non-expert eyewitness testimony. The plausibility connective of the schema specifies the algorithm for assigning a plausibility-value to the schema conclusion, regardless of the mixture of expert and non-expert evidence supporting that conclusion. For example, an instantiation of the statistical-syllogism plausibility schema shown in Figure 3 might be the result of a scientific study and have a high level of plausibility, while there may be substantial uncertainty about whether Object O is in fact in Category P. In such a case, the low plausibility-value for the second evidentiary assertion might be the critical minimum value for the instantiated schema, resulting in a correspondingly low plausibility-value for the schema conclusion. The evaluating agent might then consider several strategies for increasing the plausibility-value of that second evidentiary assertion. Alternatively, the agent might rely on a different line of reasoning altogether, using different schemas and evidence, thus bypassing this weak statistical-syllogism line of reasoning.

After the factfinder uses the available evidentiary assertions to instantiate a plausibility schema, the factfinder uses the instantiated schema to determine the truth-value of a terminal proposition in the implication tree. The two primary factors in selecting which plausibility schema to use in reasoning to a particular terminal proposition are (1) the logical form of the terminal proposition and (2) the nature of the evidence available in the case. For example, whether the terminal proposition is a generalization about a group or a proposition about a specific individual will determine what kind of schema conclusion is allowed. Second, different schemas may require different kinds of evidentiary assertions as input. Some schemas might require evidence that is scientific and statistical, while others might not. The agent evaluating the evidence selects a schema that fits the terminal proposition and the evidence in the particular case. In the Legal Apprentice™ software, the user "attaches" the instantiated schema to the terminal proposition to which it is relevant, thus extending the branch of the inference tree out of the rule-based implication tree and into the evidence-evaluation region. The schema instantiated with evidence is specific to the particular case, whereas the implication tree and the plausibility schemas themselves are generic structures for all cases within the knowledge domain.

Finally, in order for an instantiated plausibility schema to provide an inference from plausible evidence to a decision about the ultimate issue at the top of the implication tree, there must be an algorithm for determining the truth-value of a terminal proposition as a function of the plausibility-value of the schematized evidence attached to that proposition. Law calls this rule the applicable "standard of proof" (James, Hazard, and Leubsdorf 1992; Walker 1996). For example, the standard of proof for most issues of fact in civil cases is preponderance of the evidence. Under this rule, if the schematized evidence evaluates as having any plausibility-value other than "undecided," then the preponderance rule assigns the corresponding truth-value to the terminal proposition – that is, it assigns the value "true" to the terminal proposition if the schema evaluates the attached evidence as plausible to any degree, and assigns the value "false" to the terminal proposition if the schema evaluates the attached evidence as implausible to any degree. Standards of proof are the links between the output of schematized, evaluated evidence and the input to an implication tree.

The branches of an instantiated plausibility schema can themselves generate chains of instantiated plausibility schemas, with the evidentiary conditions of a higher-level schema becoming the conclusions of lower-level plausibility schemas. For example, the second evidentiary assertion of the statistical-syllogism schema in Figure 3 is itself an assertion categorizing a definite subject, so in a particular case such an assertion could become the conclusion of an additional statistical-syllogism schema. At some point in any particular branch, of course, the evaluating agent must stipulate plausibility-values for evidentiary assertions – using intuition (human agents), default values (human and non-human agents), sensitivity analysis (all agents), or some other method.

Modeling Second-Order Reasoning About Rules and Evidence

While many instances of legal reasoning employ "substantive" rules of law and the relevant evidence to reach ultimate conclusions, other instances consist of second-order reasoning *about* which rules, evidentiary assertions or plausible inferences are allowed. Such second-order reasoning in law is also rule-based reasoning, but it generally employs "process rules." Process rules in law are traditionally divided into rules of procedure and rules of evidence. Rules of procedure govern the dynamics and timing of default reasoning by authorizing particular procedural decisions under certain conditions. For example, early in a civil proceeding a defendant may move to dismiss the case for lack of jurisdiction; any party may move for summary judgment before trial based on depositions and affidavits; or a party may move for a directed verdict during a trial, based upon the testimony introduced to that point in time (Federal Rules of Civil Procedure; James, Hazard, and Leubsdorf 1992). The presiding official must decide whether to grant a procedural motion or deny it. Implication trees can model the legal rules that govern such decisions, and plausibility schemas can organize the relevant evidence in a particular case.

Evidentiary process rules govern the process of evaluating evidence and making findings about terminal propositions. Evidentiary decisions (rulings on motions) might apply: rules about admissibility (excluding some relevant evidence from the case altogether, or prohibiting its attachment to certain terminal propositions); rules about relevancy (relating particular evidentiary assertions to particular terminal propositions); rules about sufficiency of evidence (deciding whether the totality of evidence attached to a terminal proposition can warrant a finding that the proposition is true); standards of proof (establishing the threshold degree of plausibility required to find a terminal proposition to be true); and rules allocating the burden of persuasion (determining what finding to make when the attached evidence evaluates precisely on the threshold required by the standard of proof). These evidentiary rules govern the presiding official's decisions about the process of evidentiary evaluation in a particular case. An example is the rule admitting an expert opinion into evidence only if it is "scientific, technical, or other specialized knowledge" and it "will assist the trier of fact" (Federal Rule of Evidence 702; Daubert v. Merrell Dow Pharmaceuticals, Inc., 509 U.S. 579 (1993); General Electric Co. v. Joiner, 522 U.S. 136 (1997); Kumho Tire Co. v. Carmichael, 526 U.S. 137 (1999)). Another example is a ruling that the relevant evidence is legally insufficient to warrant a finding of fact by the factfinder. Such a ruling can

directly determine, "as a matter of law," the truth-value of a terminal proposition in an implication tree. Implication trees can model such evidentiary rules, and plausibility schemas can help warrant their application in particular cases.

Process rules therefore apply the rule of law to the process of using implication trees and plausibility schemas in a particular case. More generally, they are rules that govern the dynamics of default reasoning within multiagent systems. Process rules are particularly important in coordinating multiple independent agents to achieve consistent, fair and efficient decision processes. Different participants can play different roles in rule application, evidence production, evidence evaluation, and other decision-making tasks, yet the process rules coordinate and regulate the dynamic process. Legal proceedings consist of many points at which different participants may make different decisions, depending upon the process rules, substantive legal rules and the available evidence. In judicial litigation, for example, the parties, trial judge, jury and appellate court have distinct roles to play, and in administrative rule-makings, the public commenters, expert advisory groups, regulators and reviewing courts have their own distinct roles. Presiding officials oversee the factfinding process by making decisions that are themselves governed by legal rules and the evidence in the record, while reviewing courts oversee the decision-making discretion of the presiding trial official.

A key feature of the D-L Framework, and a key insight into the emergence of reasoning structures, is that no new types of logical structures are required to model legal process rules or their operation. The D-L Framework integrates substantive and process reasoning by attaching process implication trees as branches of the main implication tree in a legal proceeding. For example, a jurisdictional requirement, and its associated implication tree, would be a high-level conjunctive branch for any implication tree for a valid judicial judgment. On the other hand, an evidentiary requirement, and its implication tree, might be a defeater branch connected near a terminal proposition of the main implication tree. This means that the D-L Framework can capture the domain knowledge for evolution and coordination using the same ontology that captures substantive legal rules and the factfinding in particular cases.

THE EMERGENCE OF REASONING STRUCTURES IN LAW

The regime of the rule of law, with its insistence on transparent and documented reasoning, responds to the multiplicity and diversity of legal cases by creating useful logical structures and adapting them to the legal problems they are designed to solve. A system of rule-based deductions captured by an implication tree represents one type of emergent structure. The plausibility schemas recognized in law are such structures as well. Such structures promote consistency among independent legal decision-makers in different cases, while also promoting the principled and consistent evaluation of evidence specific to those cases. But law is not only a domain that happens to have emergent reasoning structures – it is a domain in which these emergent structures promote the emergence and evolution of other structures. In law, the emergence of reasoning structures is not merely a by-product, but rather an intentional product of the system. The reason for this is once again the rule of law. A fundamental value within law is its ability to adapt its rules to new types of situations, and to adapt them in a principled rather than haphazard way. The common law is a particularly good example of a system designed to produce gradual adaptation to new problems through the emergence of new rules and other logical structures. In law, as in ordinary life, the most appropriate new structures generally evolve gradually from successful decisions in past cases.

The adherence to process rules promotes the evolution of new implication trees and new plausibility schemas. Legal systems use process rules to evolve new legal rules from past legal decisions, and to evolve new plausibility schemas from past evaluations of evidence. For example, a motion for summary judgment in a particular civil case might present a novel factual situation, and the arguments by the attorneys might lead the court to decide the motion by instituting a new substantive rule or a new process rule. Such a motion can also lead to a judicial ruling that the available evidence is insufficient for a reasonable factfinder to make a particular finding of fact – a ruling that other courts can apply in similar circumstances. Over time, such rulings can result in the emergence of new plausibil-ity schemas for organizing such evidence. Process rules therefore play an important role in creating emergent reasoning structures in law.

When a reasoned decision is made to adopt a new legal rule (i.e., to modify an implication tree), the reasoning balances "policy rationales" for and against a rule change. Policy rationales can be either epistemic or non-epistemic (Walker 2003, 2004). Epistemic policies have the objective of increasing the accuracy of factual findings, or increasing the number of accurate findings, as well as improving the evidentiary warrant for findings and decisions. An example of an epistemic policy is allocating the burden of producing evidence to the party that is in the best position to produce that type of evidence. Non-epistemic policies pursue non-epistemic objectives (e.g., administrative efficiency and fairness to the parties). The reasoning that justifies a particular rule change ideally balances all of the epistemic and non-epistemic policies that are relevant to the proposed rule.

When a reasoned decision is made to adopt a new plausibility schema, the reasoning also balances the epistemic objective against the appropriate non-epistemic objectives. Plausibility schemas are designed to warrant default inferences to defeasible yet presumptively true conclusions. A major strategy for designing a plausibility schema is to develop a "theory of uncertainty" for the type of inference involved (Walker 2001). A theory of uncertainty explains how the available evidence could be plausible but the conclusion could still be false (or in the case of a plausible defeater, how the conclusion could still be true). It identifies the possible sources of error inherent in the type of inference, and analyzes the sources, types, and degrees of uncertainty associated with drawing the conclusion. In examining the inherent uncertainty, however, a theory of uncertainty also explains why it is reasonable to draw the conclusion in a tentative way, even on the basis of incomplete evidence. Every plausibility schema, therefore, reflects a theory of uncertainty about why the schema's inference is defeasible yet acceptable in the pragmatic legal context. The D-L Framework can assist the evolutionary process by clearly identifying the patterns of reasoning that actually occur in legal cases.

An important advantage of the D-L Framework is the potential it offers to involve non-human autonomous agents in the process of emergence and evolution. To the extent that the D-L Framework can adequately model important aspects of rule-based deduction, evidence evaluation, and second-order process reasoning, non-human agents may be able to make more intelligent searches for relevant reasoning patterns within the vast libraries of legal cases. Second, they may be able to assist human agents by helping them to organize the applicable legal rules into implication trees, or by revising implication trees as new cases are decided. Such agents might be able to play a similar role in designing and maintaining plausibility schemas. Third, such agents might serve a supervisory or quality-assurance function for human decision-makers in new legal cases, especially in legal areas where a high volume of cases must be decided. As these agents try to apply existing rules and schemas to novel issues, they may be able to suggest new rules or schemas, and explore the implications of their adoption by applying them virtually and hypothetically to past cases. The important point is that automation using the D-L Framework makes possible such collaboration between human and non-human agents.

CONCLUSION

The domain of law provides a strategic area for empirically studying multiagent, problem-oriented systems. Legal cases are numerous and complex, and contain reasoning that is extensive and well-documented. The logical structure of legal reasoning, including its second-order reasoning about the process of legal reasoning, is a primary mechanism by which new legal rules and new plausibility schemas emerge, and by which such rules and schemas adapt to the nuances of legal cases. This reasoning structure not only coordinates the efforts of numerous autonomous agents, but also promotes the emergence and evolution of new reasoning structures by responding to the tremendous variability in individual legal cases. The D-L Framework discussed in this chapter successfully captures legal reasoning structures, integrates and evaluates expert and non-expert evidence, and coordinates agents working on different legal problems. It also clarifies how those structures evolve new rules, schemas and structures over time.

In the D-L Framework, a complete inference tree for the reasoning in a particular legal case consists of an implication tree that models all of the applicable substantive and process rules, together with the schematized evidentiary assertions attached to the terminal propositions of that implication tree. The syntax and Semantics of this framework allow the automation of key tasks, and the emergence of dynamic structures for integrating human and non-human agents. Moreover, it is the logical structure of legal reasoning itself, and not any particular set of rules within the legal knowledge domain, that creates this evolutionary mechanism. This means that the evolutionary mechanism applies to domestic, foreign and international legal systems; that non-human autonomous agents can participate in this evolution, interacting with human agents; and that similar reasoning structures can operate in many knowledge domains other than law.

FUTURE RESEARCH DIRECTIONS

The D-L Framework provides a useful, standardized format for empirical research into the reasoning involved in legal cases. Such research has obvious advantages for substantive legal research. The research gains may be just as significant, moreover, for discovering logical structures that allow the interaction of human and non-human agents in evolving reasoning structures in all domains with characteristics similar to law. Several directions for such research present themselves. Research is needed on the reasoning that balances the epistemic objective against non-epistemic objectives to arrive at an appropriate new rule. Such research may discover patterns of rule development that might prove useful in many domains. Research is also needed on the variety of plausibility schemas that are used in different areas of law. Such research would clarify the patterns of default reasoning that human agents have considered valid, and may suggest new structures for developing new schemas. Finally, research is important on the process structures that make emergence and evolution possible. Legal reasoning represents a concerted human effort at principled, adaptive decision-making in the face of incomplete evidence and new situations – a type of problem that confronts society in many domains. In each of these directions, the task is to discover empirically what structures have evolved, and to model and automate those structures to the extent possible, so that emergence and evolution can be more efficient in the future.

ACKNOWLEDGMENT

The author wishes to thank Hofstra University for its research support in preparing this chapter.

REFERENCES

American Law Institute (1966). *Restatement of the law Second, Torts,* Washington, D.C.: American Law Institute.

Anderson, T., Schum, D., & Twining, W. (2005). *Analysis of evidence, Second Edition.* Cambridge, UK: Cambridge University Press.

Ashley, K. D., & Rissland, E. L. (2003). Law, learning and representation. *Artificial Intelligence, 150,* 17-58.

Besnard, P. (1989). *An introduction to default logic.* Berlin: Springer-Verlag.

Brachman, R. J., & Levesque, H. J. (2004). *Knowledge representation and reasoning.* Amsterdam: Elsevier.

Branting, L. K. (2000). *Reasoning with rules and precedents: A computational model of legal analysis.* Dordrecht, The Netherlands: Kluwer Academic Publishers.

Brewka, G., Dix, J., & Konolige, K. (1997). *Nonmonotonic reasoning: An overview.* Stanford, CA: CSLI Publications.

Chierchia, G., & McConnell-Ginet, S. (2000). *Meaning and grammar: An introduction to Semantics.* Cambridge, MA: MIT Press.

Copi, I. M., & Cohen, C. (1998). *Introduction to logic.* Upper Saddle River, NJ: Prentice Hall.

Daubert v. Merrell Dow Pharmaceuticals, Inc., 509 U.S. 579 (1993).

Director, Office of Workers' Compensation Programs, Department of Labor v. Greenwich Collieries, 512 U.S. 267 (1994).

Dobbs, D. R. (2000). *The law of torts.* St. Paul, Minnesota: West.

Faigman, D. L., Kaye, D. H., Saks, M. J., & Sanders, J. (2002). *Science in the Law (3 Vols.).* St. Paul, Minnesota: West Group.

Federal Rules of Civil Procedure (2006).

Federal Rules of Evidence (2006).

General Electric Co. v. Joiner, 522 U.S. 136 (1997).

Gottwald, S. (2001). *A treatise on many-valued logics.* Baldock, England: Research Studies Press.

Hastie, R. (Ed.) (2006). *Inside the juror: The psychology of juror decision making.* Cambridge, UK: Cambridge University Press.

Hitchcock, D. , & Verheij, B. (2006). *Arguing on the Toulmin Model: New essays in argument analysis and evaluation.* Dordrecht, The Netherlands: Springer.

James, Jr., F., Hazard, Jr., G. C., & Leubsdorf, J. (1992). *Civil procedure.* Boston, Toronto, London: Little, Brown.

Josephson, J. R., & Tanner, M. C. (1996). Conceptual analysis of abduction. In Josephson, J. R., & Josephson, S. G. (Eds.), *Abductive inference,* (pp. 5-30). UK: Cambridge University Press.

Kadane, J. B., & Schum, D. A. (1996). *A probabilistic analysis of the Sacco and Vanzetti evidence.* New York: John Wiley & Sons.

Kahneman, D., Slovic, P., & Tversky, A. (Eds.). (1982). *Judgment under uncertainty: heuristics and biases.* UK: Cambridge University Press.

Krieger, S. H., & Neumann, Jr., R. K. (2003). *Essential lawyering skills: Interviewing, counseling, negotiation, and persuasive fact analysis, Second Edition.* New York: Aspen Publishers.

Kumho Tire Co. Ltd. v. Carmichael, 526 U.S. 137 (1999).

Kyburg, Jr., H. E. (1983). The reference class. *Philosophy of Science, 50,* 374-397.

Kyburg, Jr., H. E. (1990). *Science & Reason.* New York: Oxford University Press.

Kyburg, Jr., H. E., & Teng, C. M. (2001). *Uncertain inference.* UK: Cambridge University Press.

Larson, R., & Segal, G. (1995). *Knowledge of meaning: An introduction to Semantic theory.* Cambridge, MA: MIT Press.

Levi, I. (1977). Direct inference. *The Journal of Philosophy, 74,* 5-29.

Levi, I. (1981). Direct inference and confirmational conditionalization. *Philosophy of Science, 48,* 532-552.

Levi, I. (1996). *For the sake of argument.* UK: Cambridge University Press.

Malinowski, G. (1993). *Many-valued logics.* UK: Oxford University Press.

Morgan, M. G., & Henrion, M. (1990). *Uncertainty: A guide to dealing with uncertainty in quantitative risk and policy analysis.* UK: Cambridge University Press.

Neumann, Jr., R. K. (2005). *Legal reasoning and legal writing: Structure, strategy, and style, Fifth Edition.* Boston: Little, Brown and Company.

Pollock, J. L. (1990). *Nomic probability and the foundations of induction.* New York: Oxford University Press.

Porat, A., & Stein, A. (2001). *Tort liability under uncertainty.* UK: Oxford University Press.

Prakken, H. (1997). *Logical tools for modelling legal argument.* Dordrecht, The Netherlands: Kluwer.

Prakken, H., Reed,, C., & Walton, D. (2003). Argumentation schemes and generalisations in reasoning about evidence. In *International Conference of Artificial Intelligence and Law Proceedings '03* (pp. 32-41). New York: ACM.

Prakken, H., & Sartor, G. (1997). Reasoning with precedents in a dialogue game. In *International Conference of Artificial Intelligence and Law Proceedings '97* (pp. 1-9). New York: ACM.

Prakken, H., & Sartor, G. (2004). The three faces of defeasibility in the law. *Ratio Juris, 17(1),* 118-139.

Rissland, E. L. (1990). Artificial intelligence and law: stepping stones to a model of legal reasoning. *Yale Law Journal, 99,* 1957-1981.

Rodes, Jr., R. E., & Pospesel, H. (1997). *Premises and conclusions: Symbolic logic for legal analysis.* Upper Saddle River, NJ: Prentice Hall.

Ross, M. M. (2006). A basis for legal reasoning: logic on appeal. *Journal of the Association of Legal Writing Directors, 3,* 177-189.

Russell, S. J., & Norvig, P. (2003). *Artificial intelligence: A modern approach.* Upper Saddle River, NJ: Prentice Hall.

Saeed, J. I. (2003). *Semantics.* Malden, MA: Blackwell.

Sainsbury, M. (1991). *Logic forms: An introduction to philosophical logic.* Oxford, UK: Basil Blackwell.

Salmon, W. C. (1973). *Logic.* Englewood Cliffs, NJ: Prentice-Hall.

Saunders, K. M. (2006). Law as rhetoric, rhetoric as argument. *Journal of the Association of Legal Writing Directors, 3,* 164-176.

Schum, D. A. (1994). *Evidential foundations of probabilistic reasoning.* New York: John Wiley & Sons.

Singh, M. P., Rao, A. S., & Georgeff, M. P. (1999). Formal methods in DAI: logic-based representation and reasoning. In Weiss, G. (Ed.), *Multiagent systems: A modern approach to distributed artificial intelligence* (pp. 331-376). Cambridge, MA: MIT Press.

Toulmin, S. (1958). *The uses of Argument.* UK: Cambridge University Press.

Toulmin, S., Rieke, R., & Janik, A. (1984). *An introduction to reasoning.* New York: Macmillan.

Walker, V. R. (1996). Preponderance, probability, and warranted factfinding. *Brooklyn Law Review, 62,* 1075-1136.

Walker, V. R. (1998). Keeping the WTO from becoming the "World Trans-Science Organization":

Scientific uncertainty, science policy, and factfinding in the growth hormones dispute. *Cornell International Law Journal, 31(2),* 251-320.

Walker, V. R. (1999). Language, meaning, and warrant: an essay on the use of Bayesian probability systems in legal factfinding. *Jurimetrics, 39,* 391-430.

Walker, V. R. (2001). Theories of uncertainty: explaining the possible sources of error in inferences. *Cardozo Law Review, 22,* 1523-1570.

Walker, V. R. (2003). Epistemic and non-epistemic aspects of the factfinding process in law. *APA Newsletter, 3(1),* 132-136.

Walker, V. R. (2004). Restoring the individual plaintiff to tort law by rejecting "junk logic" about specific causation. *Alabama Law Review, 56,* 381-481.

Walker, V. R. (2006). Transforming science into law: transparency and default reasoning in international trade disputes. In W. Wagner & R. Steinzor (Eds.), *Rescuing science from politics: Regulation and the distortion of scientific research* (pp. 165-192). UK: Cambridge University Press.

Walker, V. R. (2007a). A default-logic paradigm for legal fact-finding. *Jurimetrics, 47,* 193-243.

Walker, V. R. (2007b). Discovering the logic of legal reasoning. *Hofstra Law Review, 35(4),* 1687-1707.

Walker, V. R. (2007c). Visualizing the dynamics around the rule-evidence interface in legal reasoning. *Law, Probability and Risk, 6(1-4),* 5-22.

Walton, D. N. (1996). *Argument schemes for presumptive reasoning.* Mahwah, NJ: Lawrence Erlbaum Associates.

Walton, D. (2002). *Legal argumentation and evidence.* University Park, PA: Pennsylvania State University Press.

ADDITIONAL READING

Anderson, T., Schum, D., & Twining, W. (2005). *Analysis of evidence, second edition.* UK: Cambridge University Press.

Ashley, K. D., & Rissland, E. L. (2003). Law, learning and representation. *Artificial Intelligence, 150,* 17-58.

Brachman, R. J., & Levesque, H. J. (2004). *Knowledge representation and reasoning.* Amsterdam: Elsevier.

Hitchcock, D. , & Verheij, B. (2006). *Arguing on the Toulmin Model: New essays in argument analysis and evaluation.* Dordrecht, The Netherlands: Springer.

Josephson, J. R., & Tanner, M. C. (1996). Conceptual analysis of abduction. In Josephson, J. R., & Josephson, S. G. (Eds.), *Abductive inference* (pp. 5-30). UK: Cambridge University Press.

Kadane, J. B., & Schum, D. A. (1996). *A probabilistic analysis of the Sacco and Vanzetti evidence.* New York: John Wiley & Sons.

Kahneman, D., Slovic, P., & Tversky, A. (Eds.). (1982). *Judgment under uncertainty: heuristics and biases.* UK: Cambridge University Press.

Kyburg, Jr., H. E., & Teng, C. M. (2001). *Uncertain inference.* UK: Cambridge University Press.

Rissland, E. L. (1990). Artificial intelligence and law: stepping stones to a model of legal reasoning. *Yale Law Journal, 99,* 1957-1981.

Rodes, Jr., R. E., & Pospesel, H. (1997). *Premises and conclusions: Symbolic logic for legal analysis.* Upper Saddle River, NJ: Prentice Hall.

Russell, S. J., & Norvig, P. (2003). *Artificial intelligence: A modern approach.* Upper Saddle River, NJ: Prentice Hall.

Schum, D. A. (1994). *Evidential foundations of probabilistic reasoning.* New York: John Wiley & Sons.

Singh, M. P., Rao, A. S., & Georgeff, M. P. (1999). Formal methods in DAI: logic-based representation and reasoning. In Weiss, G. (Ed.), *Multiagent systems: A modern approach to distributed artificial intelligence* (pp. 331-376). Cambridge, MA: MIT Press.

Toulmin, S. (1958). *The uses of argument.* UK: Cambridge University Press.

Toulmin, S., Rieke, R., & Janik, A. (1984). *An introduction to reasoning*. New York: Macmillan.

Walker, V. R. (1999). Language, meaning, and warrant: an essay on the use of Bayesian probability systems in legal factfinding. *Jurimetrics, 39,* 391-430.

Walker, V. R. (2001). Theories of uncertainty: explaining the possible sources of error in inferences. *Cardozo Law Review, 22,* 1523-1570.

Walker, V. R. (2003). Epistemic and non-epistemic aspects of the factfinding process in law. *APA Newsletter, 3(1),* 132-136.

Walker, V. R. (2007a). A default-logic paradigm for legal fact-finding. *Jurimetrics, 47,* 193-243.

Walker, V. R. (2007b). Discovering the logic of legal reasoning. *Hofstra Law Review, 35(4),* 1687-1707.

Walker, V. R. (2007c). Visualizing the dynamics around the rule-evidence interface in legal reasoning. *Law, Probability and Risk, 6(1-4),* 5-22.

Walton, D. N. (1996). *Argument schemes for presumptive reasoning*. Mahwah, NJ: Lawrence Erlbaum Associates.

Walton, D. (2002). *Legal argumentation and evidence*. University Park, PA: Pennsylvania State University Press.

Chapter XXII

Agents in Security:
A Look at the Use of Agents in Host–Based Monitoring and Protection and Network Intrusion Detection

Theodor Richardson
South University, USA

ABSTRACT

Network Intrusion Detection Systems (NIDS) are designed to differentiate malicious traffic, from normal traffic, on a network system to detect the presence of an attack. Traditionally, the approach around which these systems are designed is based upon an assumption made by Dorothy Denning in 1987, stating that malicious traffic should be statistically differentiable from normal traffic. However, this statement was made regarding host systems and was not meant to be extended without adjustment to network systems. It is therefore necessary to change the granularity of this approach to find statistical anomalies per host as well as on the network as a whole. This approach lends itself well to the use of emergent monitoring agents per host, that have a central aggregation point with a visualization of the network as a whole. This chapter will discuss the structure, training, and deployment of such an agent-based intrusion detection system and analyze its viability in comparison to the more traditional anomaly-based approach to intrusion detection.

INTRODUCTION

In what may seem to be a departure from the rest of this work, let us now deviate from agents and consider instead a networking problem that plagues security experts and network administrators alike; namely, the problem of intrusion on a network of machines. In brief, a network can be considered any number of machines connected together in such a manner that they are able to send signals to each other across the connecting medium in blocks of information called packets. Those of you versed in networking may wish to skip to the next paragraph, but for those of you unfamiliar with this particular venue, this is accomplished via protocols, or sets of formal rules governing how information is structured in an exchange either per packet or across several packets; such rules are necessary to allow machines to communicate regardless of operating system. These protocols are common knowledge and therefore, if someone wishing to send unwanted information on a network had access to the physical media, it would be trivial to structure the information to allow it to be transmitted successfully. Considering the fact that most modern networks are connected to the Internet, the question of anyone having access to the network becomes a very moot point. Sending unwanted information on a network is known as an intrusion.

This goal of detecting intrusions on a network presents a complex problem spanning multiple levels of interaction and varied host behavior. The traditional approach to detecting intrusions is to look at network behavior statistically and attempt to determine significant deviations from the expected behavior of the network as a whole. This type of approach, around which these Network Intrusion Detection Systems (NIDS) are designed, is based upon an assumption made by Dorothy Denning in 1987 stating that malicious traffic should be statistically differentiable from normal traffic; however, this statement was made regarding host systems and was not meant to be extended without adjustment to network systems. While this is viable under certain types of attack, such as a botnet attack or slammer worm, it is insufficient to detect more advanced types of attack that may not trigger a statistical amount of errant traffic. Similarly, network traffic is rarely predictable, meaning there will often be false alarms in such statistically based systems. Even if the traffic is broken into seasonality, or predictable periods of expected activity such as higher traffic during the typical nine to five work day, it is unlikely to produce the desired effect. It is therefore necessary to change the granularity of this approach to find statistical anomalies per host as well as on the network as a whole.

To that end, this chapter proposes the use of emergent agents deployed on each host in the network to find a seasonal baseline of activity for the host itself; these hosts will then report in aggregate to a more traditional NIDS device that will compile a view of the network as a whole and determine if there is suspicious activity present on the network as a whole. This combined approach will provide

a comprehensiveness and robustness not currently present in most NIDS systems. This is an example of second emergence, where the emergent behavior is routed back into the system to enhance the emergent result.

The remainder of this chapter is structured to provide an understanding of network intrusion detection systems and how social agents can be applied to this problem. The first section provides an overview of the various approaches to NIDS that currently exist along with a discussion of their relative strengths and weaknesses. The second section presents a formulation of the fundamental problem of determining whether a network has been compromised. The third section describes the methodology used to approach this problem through the use of agent-based monitoring and the socialization. Fourth, the experiments performed to validate the approach are described and Section 5 the final section presents a brief conclusion.

BACKGROUND

Intrusion Detection Systems (IDSs) take many forms and approaches to detection and possibly prevention or recovery, ranging from open source applications such as Snort to extremely expensive dedicated appliances such as Cisco IDS. The fundamental characteristic that defines the two major types of intrusion detection systems is the granularity of the observation: namely, the two types are host-based systems and network-based systems. Both types share many characteristics along with the same fundamental goals but implement them in very different ways.

The essential thing to remember is that there is no silver bullet in security and an IDS of any type should be one line of defense in a multi-tiered strategy. The goal of any such intrusion detection system is to detect anomalous network behavior in an approximation of real time to minimize the damage to the network. Network-based intrusion detection systems (or simply Network Intrusion Detection Systems or NIDS) are used to detect malicious activity across an entire network viewed as a whole. The typical model for this is to have a central aggregation point that collects all traffic sent over the network and runs the analysis on the collected traffic. The majority of NIDS use a signature-based detection method; signatures in this case refer to a particular, detectable pattern of behavior that is known to signify a known or potential attack on the network. In open source applications, such as Snort, these signatures can normally be written by anyone whereas many of the corporate NIDS rely on custom signatures predefined by the issuing company. These signatures are normally constructed to be as broad as possible without causing too many false positives. This type of balance is often sought in statistical methods of security; too many false positives can cause a system administrator to ignore the barrage of alerts and therefore ignore when the alert is signifying a legitimate attack. However, taking the opposite approach and constructing signatures that are too lax may keep the attention of the observing administrator but allow some attacks to pass unnoticed. A signature normally consists of several characteristics including the type of traffic, associated ports, and a small portion of the actual exploit code.

There are several disadvantages of this approach to network intrusion detection systems. One of the most significant is the potential for poor placement within the network itself; in order to be effective, the NIDS needs the ability to see all network traffic, even traffic sent from devices that may require a proxy to route traffic to the NIDS aggregation point. Any blind spots in the network can allow intrusions, or at least part of an intrusion, to pass by without being noticed, thus bypassing any signatures written to capture that specific part of an exploit or at least delaying the detection enough to increase the amount of damage done to the network. Another common problem is with the signatures themselves; either lack of signatures, poorly written signatures, or signatures that have not been updated can cause this approach to fail (Newsome, 2005). While there are many listings of common signatures for NIDS, most of these must be tailored to the network being monitored and must be written by someone with skilled knowledge of the network itself.

This has led to the alternate approach of using anomaly-based detection; where signature based detections fail, anomaly detection excels. Anomaly detection by definition attunes itself to

the network on which it is housed and can excel at detecting previously unknown exploits. Used by itself, though, anomaly detection can be inefficient and noisy. Similar to poorly constructed rules, it produces many false positives when set to an alerting threshold that is too low (Gu, 2007). At a moderate threshold it can detect anomalies on the network, and although it cannot identify the nature of the intrusion, it can alert an administrator that something is wrong, and where the anomaly is located. Anomaly-based detection uses traffic history, seasonality, and percentages to determine what is anomalous and what is permissible.

Anomaly detection also has its own set of shortcomings. Alerting too frequently is one of the most significant problems, and administrators will quickly begin to dread alerts because unlike signature-based systems, the anomaly-based NIDS can only identify that there is a problem without providing a specific reference to the type of problem that is occurring, requiring a network-wide hunt for the source of the problem. Another drawback of anomaly detection is that it will not see intrusions that have already occurred on the network, such as backdoor connections, because they are built into the statistical normal profile. Similarly, attacks that slowly ramp up the amount of traffic used will likely cause the system to simply adopt the traffic as part of the expected profile over time. Finally, intrusions that are very covert and use normal traffic to mask themselves could go completely unnoticed.

The other major category of IDS is Host Intrusion Detection Systems (HIDS), which take a different approach to detecting attacks; specifically, they look at each host independently for signs of attack. HIDS must be deployed on each system that is to be protected. Like NIDS, these host-based intrusion detection systems primarily use signature- and anomaly-based detection (Kodialam, 2003). An advantage to the host-based as opposed to the network-based systems is that the anomaly detection can rely on more detailed analysis and has the opportunity to more closely attune to its respective machine. Finding unknown intrusions in network traffic can be very complex, whereas on a host there are more references to be considered such as processes, network accesses, system calls made, etc. One of the biggest problems of host-based intrusion detection systems is that not every system in the network is capable of supporting one and in general cannot be accomplished via proxy for devices that cannot inherently handle the requisite software. One of the best examples of a HIDS system is OSSEC, an open source IDS that supports multiple platforms and multiple purpose-specific modes of operation such as Web server monitoring. Centralized reporting is also an issue that is not well-addressed by a HIDS system; if a malicious intruder were able to exploit a host and take control before the HIDS could send off an alert, the intruder could prevent that alert from ever being sent, thus blinding the administrators to the intrusion and the lack of communication between HIDS host systems means that the attack can spread without notice.

Host Intrusion Prevention Systems (HIPS) are a slight variation of HIDS; the biggest difference with HIPS is that they try to prevent the intrusion in real time as it is detected. These systems sit inline with network traffic and monitor all traffic that flows through their location. The HIPS can halt what it decides to be a malicious traffic flow while allowing others to continue. They can do this in a number of ways including firewall rules that are added as intrusions are detected (Corman, 2005). They also detect host characteristics such as a buffer overflow to decide if an intrusion has taken place and attempt to stop their progress by halting processes. The first example of a true HIPS is BlackICE developed by a company called NetworkICE; this engine was purchased by IBM and remains part of their Proventia line of products. HIPS suffer from the same problems as most NIDS and HIDS such as false positive rates and tuning; a substantial portion of their monitoring also relies upon protocol analysis as previously discussed. Again, this is because protocols can be predictable and therefore allow errant behavior to be detected quickly (Zheng, 2005).

The final type of IDS is the hybrid system. This means that the system simply combines different components of other types of intrusion detection systems. An example of this is the Prelude system, an open source product for Unix. This is the type of system that will be the focus of the remainder of the chapter. The goal of this work is therefore to create a hybrid intrusion detection system based on an understanding of the fundamental problems necessary to overcome with any intrusion detection mechanisms and demonstrate the successful application of a social agent network to this particular problem.

Alice and Bob at Work

The main difficulty in analyzing network traffic to determine whether an intrusion has occurred is the problem of distinguishing behavior that is uncharacteristic of normal operation. Denning made the now historic assumption for host-based systems that malicious traffic is statistically differentiable from normal activity (Denning, 1987); this assumption was extended without alteration to networks and has been shown to be flawed based on the difficulty of using that mindset to deliver successful NIDS. However, taken with further granularity and put in a proper context, Denning's assumption can still be proven to be correct; essentially, each host in a network will display some behavior errant from its expected function under malicious conditions which may have discernable repercussions on the network environment.

The underlying problem then correlates to the detection of suspicious activity on a host system and propagating the awareness of that activity to the network as a whole. Depending upon the resources available to devote to such monitoring and the level of intervention allowed, the correct monitoring may detect an intrusion early enough to at least minimize the amount of damage that results. However, the use of thresholds and anomaly detection is insufficient in this regard based on the nature of modern computing.

Consider two users, Alice and Bob, the perennial characters of networking scenarios, with different roles within a company environment. If Alice's role is in technical support and Bob's role is in software development, it is expected that, even with the same machine specifications and configuration, their normal machine usage would be significantly different. For example, Alice may need an instant messaging program for online support as well as remote access to other hosts on the network. Bob, on the other hand, would be less likely to be accessing hosts on the network other than perhaps a testing and production environment. Therefore, repeated port scanning from Alice's machine would be less indicative of malicious activity than it would on Bob's machine based on their roles (i.e. a port scan from the instant messaging system that attempts to find a viable session host). Similarly, a large volume of traffic from Alice's machine to a previously unknown host may be part of her normal usage but may indicate compromise of Bob's machine. What this essentially demonstrates is that analyzing host characteristics is entirely insufficient in determining usage and it will be further demonstrated that there is no way to accurately apply a standard that will account for the behavior of the two different users even though the machines on which they operate are exactly the same.

Consider the case of thresholds in the above scenario; if the threshold of acceptable activity was set too high because of Alice's standard and completely benign behavior, Bob's machine could actually be compromised without raising an alarm. If the threshold was set too low, Alice would consistently trigger false positive alarms by transmitting volumes of data to previously un-contacted hosts to resolve issues remotely for other users. Similarly, anomaly detection based on traffic history would be insufficient to handle the nature of Alice's expected normal behavior. While this approach would most likely detect any errant behavior on Bob's machine, whenever Alice contacted a new host, there is a potential for the system to trigger a false positive based on the nature of the new contact, payload size, protocol, etc. Even in a host-based system where the thresholds could be tuned to the respective uses, Alice's normal usage may still appear suspicious, especially given that she will likely be controlling other hosts remotely.

What is therefore necessary is a system capable of adapting dynamically to individual users on a machine and allowing for similar behavior within an environment without using the specific hosts previously seen or contacted under the same application. It is also necessary to allow for the aggregation of alerts to construct a view of the network as a whole and detect any potential repercussions to the compromise of an individual host. The current systems that exist are not capable of this kind of flexibility or granularity of behavior.

Foundationally, what is necessary to begin this new approach is to construct a model of a distributed host-based intrusion detection system with components similar to both NIDS and HIDS for a granular approach to monitoring. Because HIPS address the same fundamental issue with an additional reaction component, they will henceforth be considered beyond the scope of this work. The model therefore begins at the host level with the monitoring of system resources and activity. This approach to intrusion detection differs from a standard HIDS in that data collected will then be shared socially among the various nodes to make a determination on whether or not the behavior should be classified as malicious based on the number of hosts reporting similar suspicious occurrences throughout the network. To address the issue of activity and resource discrepancies across users and machines, the host-based monitoring can be entrusted to learning agents which will develop their own unique model of their environment and adapt as the systems are used. The focus of the agents for this work was to primarily consider the host-based characteristics, such as paging, processes, CPU usage, etc.; in this case, to reduce the scope to a manageable level, the agents will focus on processes and process parents running on the host system. In this manner, the host system is allowed to establish its own baseline of normal behavior without triggering a multitude of false alarms across the network while still detecting malicious activity. By incorporating social aggregate reporting, the system is also designed to address the issue of network-wide attacks or multipoint intrusions, creating an emergent picture of the network in an approximation of real time.

AN INTELLIGENT AGENT BASED APPROACH TO INTRUSION DETECTION

Fortunately, the area of artificial intelligence provides a unique path to achieving these desired ends, particularly intelligent agents able to adapt to their own host environment. With some training, it is possible for an agent deployed on a machine to adapt to the typical usage of an individual user and therefore determine if erratic behavior is occurring. Namely, an agent passively observing the host

Figure 1. Agent Logical Component Layout. The agent module is a standalone executable with access to resource monitoring on the host system and network access through the host. The model an agent constructs and modifies consists of the three lists seen above: allowed, watched, and forbidden processes and associ-

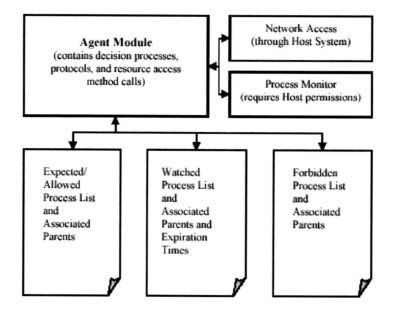

machine in a safe mode of operation (i.e. without a network connection) can gather the information requires allowing it to adaptively monitor the host and determine when it is misbehaving. Similarly, by allowing the agents to socialize within the network, it is possible to determine when activity is erratic based on prior observation. It is also possible in a social environment to determine when a larger scale attack is occurring or to trace the extent of the damage from the compromise of a single host. The remainder of this section will discuss the creation, socialization, and training of an agent for the task of host monitoring. It is worth noting that the agent designed is limited in scope to the observation of the processes running on a host and the parents of those processes. It is entirely feasible to build a more complex model from this idea to allow the monitoring of other resources within the host such that an attack does not have to have a process signature in order to be detected.

Agent Design

An agent deployed on a host machine must have the capability of observing the system usage in terms of ports, processes, applications, and users, which is a concern for the access control mechanisms of the operating system; it is hereafter assumed that the agent has the access privileges necessary to perform its intended operations. The agent must have the ability to create a model of its environment and adapt that model to changing behaviors without raising a large number of false positives and simultaneously recognizing significant deviations from expected behavior. It is also necessary for the agents to socialize in order to determine acceptable behavior across multiple hosts and to communicate any possible malicious behavior between agents. It is also necessary for this socialization to allow agents to query each other with regard to suspicious behavior that they have not previously experienced.

For simplicity, in the scope of this work, the system resources that will be considered will be restricted to processes running on the host system and the associated parent process, which is simply the running process which spawned the new process. From this point forward, whenever a process is considered, it can be assumed for the sake of brevity that this is not only the process but also the parent process that spawned it; for instance, cmd.

exe is not itself a malicious process if spawned by a legitimate parent such as explorer.exe at startup but if it is spawned by malware.exe, it would likely be a risk to the system, so the combined set of the process and its parent must be considered as a single entity. It should be noted, however, that active ports and traffic flow analysis may be a more useful approach to analyzing behavior in a real deployment of this system, lending itself not only to a listing as will be discussed but also a stateful model of particular protocols of concern as in the protocol-based detection approach. It is also assumed that all hosts are capable of supporting the agent, which may not be the case in a real network system. In that case, a proxy would be necessary to at least communicate to surrounding agents that no data is available for the device being contacted such that an active agent does not assume it is contacting a compromised or disabled host.

The agent must therefore have the following capabilities: to store a model of its environment, in this case a set of lists of active processes that may or have been observed on the system along with an associated list of parent processes; to update the existing model over time; and to communicate with agents on other hosts using specified protocols. The model of the environment considered for this work consists of the following: a listing of the processes and associated parent processes that are currently running on the host system; a listing of allowed processes and associated parents that are expected to be seen on the host system; a warning or watch list of processes and parents that are currently under suspicion; and a list of unwanted or forbidden processes and associated parents that should not be running on the host system, as seen in Figure 1. The update of the model will be determined socially by a voting process described later in this section. It is also possible for the agents to report their denied or watched processes to an aggregate server to allow for a network administrator to monitor the state of the network as a whole while the agents handle the majority of the decision making process as to what constitutes suspicious behavior, thereby minimizing the number of false positives that the network administrator would need to handle.

In general, an agent's most complex decision will be when to elevate a process from watched to forbidden status and to reduce the status of a process from watched to acceptable on the host machine. A process is placed on the watch list in two ways: when the process appears and the agent has not seen the process before and when a communicating agent (as discussed in the next part of this section) reports the process as either watched or forbidden on its own respective host. First consider the case of risk elevation from watched to forbidden. This elevation will typically occur in the following manner: a watched process appears on the host system after receiving the process in a notice from a communicating agent, a communicating agent announces the process as forbidden in the result of a vote, a vote called by the host agent results in a majority opposed to allowing the process, or a system administrator issues an override to forbid the process regardless of individual agent decisions. Similarly, a watched process can be reduced in risk from watched to acceptable in the following ways: a communicating agent announces the process as acceptable in the result of a vote, a vote called by the host agent results in a majority in favor of allowing the process, or a system administrator issues an override to allow the process regardless of individual agent decisions. There also exists the case of uncertainty for a watched process in which the process does not elevate or reduce in risk; therefore it is expedient to place an expiration upon the watched process such that if no change in the status of the process occurs during the specified time, the process will be removed from the watch list completely such that a subsequent appearance on the watch list represents a new look at the process without prior prejudice or endorsement.

Agent Socialization

Agents in this environment must communicate with both neighboring agents and foreign agents wishing to contact the host system. It is assumed that each agent will have a listing of the allowed or expected processes on its host system and both a watch list of suspicious processes and a blacklist of forbidden processes along with a view of processes running at the time of communication. When agents communicate, they will engage a handshake protocol to deliver a list of processes that are currently running on their system that are not expected in the scope of the host's normal behavior based upon these two lists. This can alert the contacting agent of processes that should raise an alert if they subsequently appear on the contacting agent's host. The handshake protocol is described below where C represents the contacting agent and R represents the receiving agent and ID represents the network identifier (i.e. the IP or MAC address) of the agent's host:

1. $C \rightarrow R$: Hello(ID_C, ID_R)
2. $R \rightarrow C$: Ack(ID_C)
3. $C \rightarrow R$: ID_C | SusProc(ID_C)
4. $R \rightarrow C$: ID_R | SusProc(ID_R)
5. $C \rightarrow R$: ID_C | Go(ID_R)
6. $R \rightarrow C$: ID_R | Go(ID_C)

The Hello message is simply intended to begin agent communication, wherein the receiving agent can identify that the message is intended for its use. Subsequently the Ack message is to identify whether the receiving agent is active. The Ack message is necessary because there is no guarantee of agent activity on the receiving end based on the nature of the contact, the type of communication (such as a communication to a host that does not have such agents in practice), or the state of the host being contacted. There is a window of time t_a in which the Ack can be accepted by the contacting agent before the receiving agent is assumed to be unresponsive; this is to prevent a self-inflicted Denial-of-Service (DoS) on the contacting host waiting for the receiving host to reply. There are several causes of a lack of response, and t_a should be adjusted such that the contacting agent will wait a sufficient amount of time to account for inherent network delay before assuming that the agent on the receiving host is not going to respond.

It is possible for an agent to die during a malicious intrusion or at least to be silenced from communication even if an agent is installed on the receiving system. Any other agent attempting to contact the deceased agent could assume the lack of response to imply that the agent was not functioning properly and the agent's host should always be suspect in any communication if the receiving host does not respond with an Ack message. If the receiving agent is unresponsive, it is left to the contacting agent to

decide whether or not to continue communication with the host (or in environments in which the agents are given less control, to at least prompt the user that continuing communication could be unsafe). Later, the case will be examined in which agents can report on each other to call for a vote on how to treat the non-responsive agent.

The SusProc message identifies the list of active processes that are either under watch or forbidden on the host system. Given this information, the respective agents can compare the processes against their own list of watched and forbidden processes to determine if communication between the hosts should be allowed. This decision is made by each agent individually. The primary and most simplistic model that will be considered first is the concept that the agent will decide to halt communication if the other agent reports a running process that is forbidden on the host system and merely add the processes to the watch list if it has not previously seen the process reported for each process encountered. Each agent will respectively decide on a response for the Go message. This is a simple yes or no decision on whether to proceed with the communication. Communication will cease (or at least prompt user intervention in a passive implementation) if either Go message returns false.

Even when the communication is allowed to go forward, the list of possibly malicious processes reported by the other agent are subject to watch, meaning that if any of these processes appears on the host system in the duration of time assigned for a process to be under watch, they will immediately be considered malicious and the following actions will be taken: the agent will immediately upgrade the process from the watch list to the forbidden list; the agent will prompt the user, or in automated systems, make a decision as to whether to terminate the process; and the agent will sever the connection (if it remains active) with the host that reported the process.

For the agents to decide on what potentially unacceptable processes should be allowed on a host machine, one approach would be to allow neighborhood voting on processes that occur on the host based on the watch list of the individual agent. Because of this type of periodic socialization, it is necessary for initiating agents to have some way to verify that neighboring agents are alive; a heartbeat, or periodic signal sent by the agent to signify continued activity, is one such possible method. Heartbeats, though, are generally not advisable based on the amount of information about the network that is regularly broadcast (i.e. to an attacker attempting to map the network, there may be sufficient information in the heartbeat transmission to determine the number of hosts on the network at minimum) as well as the implied increase in traffic that this would cause on densely populated networks. Therefore, instead of taking the heartbeat approach, when it is necessary to vote upon a process, the agent calling for the vote will transmit a pulse check which will then prompt an anonymous response of live agents that will participate in voting; an associated time window t_v will then be given for responses which will determine the approximate number of participant responses accepted in the voting process. This number of responses can be used as an upper bound of votes to be counted, but this approach can lead to complications which will be discussed in the next section.

Once the time interval t_v has elapsed, the agent calling for the vote will announce the process (along with the associated parent process) that is in question. Participating voting agents will respond with ALLOW, DENY, or ABSTAIN. If an agent has the process in its model of accepted or expected processes for its respective host, it will vote ALLOW. If the voting agent has denied the process in the past or has the process in its disallowed list of processes, it will vote DENY. If the voting agent has no experience with the process, it will choose to OBSTAIN. The vote is decided by simple majority, and the agent calling for the vote will announce the result, thereby allowing agents without experience with the process to update their tables to either allow or deny it on their own systems without a repeat vote. If there is no majority in either direction, the agent can discard the process from its watch list, allow it to run, and call for a new vote if the process arises again similar to the case in which the process expires from the watch list without a change in status.

Agent Training

Inherently, this system relies upon the socialization of agents contacting other agents when initiating communication or deciding upon what processes are acceptable on the host system. This will allow for a naturally emerging picture of acceptable and forbidden practices on a per host basis within a complex network. However, without training, a model of acceptable behavior will never emerge naturally because no agent will be able to vote with significance on any process presented by another agent. It is therefore necessary to allow a period of acceptance for host behavior. There are two simplistic approaches to this training, each with its own implied advantages and disadvantages.

The first approach to training the agents is to allow the network to run for a period of time in with each agent may safely collect any running process on its host system as acceptable. This is based upon the (potentially unsafe) assumption that, from startup, there is an interval of time T such that any compromise of the network would take greater than T time to achieve (Zhu, 2003). Selecting the time interval, T, safely while allowing significant time for the agents to gather a comprehensive view of the host processes as it behaves on the network is a difficult problem left as open research in the scope of this chapter.

An alternate approach to this assumption is to allow the host system to run without a network connection for a period of time at startup, assuming that the host is running either out of the box or immediately after imaging and has not been previously connected to the network and therefore possibly compromised. During this time, the inherent processes of the host's normal operation will be accepted by the agent; provided that this is not a significant hindrance to the users, it may even be worthwhile to allow the user to startup the normal programs that would be run on the system, still without connecting it to the network. However, this approach means that the behavior of the host as part of the network with its associated users is not captured by the agent and may initially cause a large number of votes to occur to decide on normal processes that may not occur within the host system in isolation. It may also require significant inter-

Figure 2. Logical Layout of the Validation Testing Schema. Each virtual host is physically located on the real host server, which is used as an aggregation point for all of the network-level messages of the system. The router is used to facilitate all communication between agents/hosts.

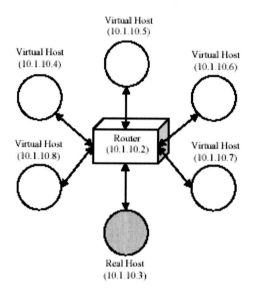

vention of the network administrator to override conservative agents that choose to forbid essential processes that occur as part of the network operation, such as child processes spawned by a network virus scan system such as McAfee or access control mechanism such as Novell.

For the purpose of this work, the method of agent training is chosen as a proof of concept without attempting to address the repercussions of a complex network environment. A combined approach is therefore used. Each agent is allowed to run on the host in isolation for a period of time and then given a very short interval T during which the host is live on the network in order to gather as many native processes as possible and still capture as much network behavior as possible without risking too large an interval and therefore possibly allowing a compromise to become part of the accepted model of the host environment.

The System in Practice

To test the validity of this model, it was decided to target Microsoft Windows XP as a host platform because of its wide adoption in large scale networks.

As previously stated, processes and associated parents were targeted as a key to detecting intrusions because they stay fairly similar across a network except in the event of suspicious activity. Network traffic could also be targeted by such an agent system but network traffic varies greatly, making the detection of anomalies significantly more difficult for an individual agent with a limited view of its context. The approach taken will not detect an attacker that is sophisticated enough to avoid spawning any suspicious processes on the host machine or an attacker who fails to compromise a computer, again spawning no processes to detect. This type of attack requires that an agent have a more complex model of its environment similarly designed to evaluate what is allowed, suspicious, and forbidden for the resource or protocol included.

Arguably the most dangerous type of attacker is one who exploits a computer and then decides to remain on it with a backdoor of some sort that can be used to either compromise another machine and blame the first victim or remain for later use. Fortunately, most backdoors have some sort of process footprint which can then be flagged and denied by the agent. There are several processes which are exposed to the network that are commonly used by backdoors: explorer.exe, iexplore.exe, cmd.exe, services.exe, svchost.exe. These processes can control other processes but can also occur benignly in the routine operation of the host system. Therefore, it is necessary not only to examine the process itself but also the parent process which initiates it. This combination then allows rules to be applied to the process in context without a blanket decision to allow or deny.

The construction of the process monitor for the agent involves finding a way to get a running process list and then determine parent/child relationships; fortunately the Windows API has function calls to provide this information. The process monitor then creates a linked list structure to scan through the results for the relationships among processes and compile them into a list of active processes and associated parents. During the gathering phase, the agent will accept all process tuples present as allowable on the host. After the gathering phase, the agent will add any process and parent that is not already allowed by the current environment model to the watch list if it is reported by another agent. Similarly a new process that spawns on the host machine will prompt the agent to call for a vote if it has had no prior experience with that process.

After each voting process, the agent will compile the results and update its environmental model, which consists of three text files (which can be combined to a single file with annotations if desired) containing allowed processes and parents, denied processes and parents, and watched processes and parents respectively. It should be noted that the agent communication could easily be converted to use a SSL secured connection but was tested using HTTP. The security of the voting process and agent communication is discussed later in this section but for the purposes of validation testing was assumed to be outside of the scope of the implementation model.

Validation testing of the system was performed using five virtual machines. One virtual machine running Windows XP was setup in VMWare and then copied. This allowed for a uniform network similar to what could be found in many corporate configurations despite its size. The agent program was added to each system and the individual agent

results were written to a file in shared memory to evaluate potentially malicious processes in aggregate although no agent was constructed to this purpose, providing a global view of potential threats on the network. The layout of this schema can be seen in Figure 2. The determination of the severity of the potentially malicious processes was made by a parsing script that read the text file and determined threat level based upon the number of times the process was reported. The following extract shows the processes considered to be a risk. It can be seen from the process view of almost any Windows XP system that the majority of the processes were ruled to be safe based solely upon the agent collection and interaction. It should be noted that the agents in this implementation were incredibly verbose, reporting a warning even when a process was added to the watch list in order to observe the behavior of the agents as the test progressed. One malicious use was initiated in one of the virtual machines that would cause Netcat (nc.exe) to spawn a command shell (cmd.exe) and transfer Netcat to another machine and then repeat the process from the new machine, which is a good indicator of malicious activity and in many ways functions as an autonomous worm program would. This process was reported along with several processes that were simply unexpected and missed the collection phase in natural operation; the only user intervention in this case was the use of Netcat so all other processes reported spawned by the native operations of Windows XP Service Pack 2. It can therefore be concluded that the agent system functioned properly in determining a majority of the processes to be safe and acted predictably when encountering new processes that arose on the host system.

```
Process   c:\\windows\\system32\\services.
exe on host 10.1.10.2 is not allowed to have a
child c:\\windows\\system32\\imapi.exe (CLAS-
SIFIED HIGH RISK) Instances Reported: 2
Process   c:\\windows\\system32\\cmd.exe   on
host 10.1.10.2 is not allowed to have a child
c:\\windows\\system32\\ipconfig.exe   (CLAS-
SIFIED HIGH RISK) Instances Reported: 2
Process c:\\windows\\system32\\svchost.exe on
host 10.1.10.2 is not allowed to have a child
c:\\windows\\system32\\dfrgntfs.exe (CLASSI-
FIED MODERATE RISK) Instances Reported: 1
Process   c:\\windows\\system32\\svchost.exe
on host 10.1.10.2 is not allowed to have a
child c:\\windows\\system32\\defrag.exe (CLAS-
```

```
SIFIED MODERATE RISK) Instances Reported: 1
Process c:\\windows\\system32\\svchost.exe on
host 10.1.10.2 is not allowed to have a child
c:\\windows\\system32\\dfrgntfs.exe (CLASSI-
FIED MODERATE RISK) Instances Reported: 1
Process  c:\\windows\\system32\\svchost.exe
on host 10.1.10.2 is not allowed to have a
child c:\\windows\\system32\\defrag.exe (CLAS-
SIFIED MODERATE RISK) Instances Reported: 1
Process c:\\nc.exe on host 10.1.10.2 is not al-
lowed to have a child c:\\windows\\system32\\
cmd.exe (CLASSIFIED HIGH RISK) Instances Re-
ported: 2
```

The reported IP addresses in this case were all identical because of the internal router interface seen by each process as it was writing. In a normal network the IP addresses of the host would be different for each host that is reporting, therefore allowing a network administrator to immediately identify which machine was reporting. There are several processes in this list which are completely valid windows applications, but were not being run on each of the systems yet. Given enough time these processes would be found on all of the systems since the running configurations were identical and as such would be voted acceptable by the agent community.

The one process which was rated as a high risk (i.e. forbidden) that in fact was a backdoor was the process nc.exe. This was the copy of Netcat running on a single system. Netcat itself is simply a tool for constructing network connections and can be used in an entirely legitimate way or it can be used maliciously, just like packet sniffers and scanning. While the risk is successfully classified as forbidden, any attempt to compromise further systems would escalate the threat level at the aggregation point; additionally, the footprint of this exploit could likely be recognized by the network administrator. Even with the successful validation testing of the concept, there are several issues that arise in practice for this approach that are addressed in the remainder of this section.

Vote Tampering

The idea of agent voting is introduced as the primary means of creating an emergent view of the network as a whole. However, there are fundamental issues with the concept of voting as it is simplistically described in previous sections, namely, the issue of participation and security. The true goal of the voting process is to share previously acquired knowledge to allow agents to inform each other of potentially dangerous processes with which they have had prior experience. In a more detailed analysis, it is more effective for agents to participate in voting of they are on a similarly configured host, i.e. an agent on a Windows machine intrinsically has more insight into an agent on another Windows machine that it would insight into an agent deployed on a Macintosh. It is therefore possible for an agent to be active in voting and have no experience with any of the processes being used because they do not occur on the agent's native platform at all or with the same name. This can give rise to the case in which the majority of voting agents abstain. There is a subtle distinction that must be made here in the difference between this type of abstention and an abstention of an agent who could potentially come into contact with that process later and it makes an enormous difference in the validity of the voting process. It is therefore prudent in the initial call for a vote that the agent announces the characteristics of the host, at least in a minimal sense such that agents are voting on the same platform; this requires a substantial size of network, however, in order to assure that there are sufficient voters to make an accurate judgment.

There is also the issue of vote tampering. The idea presented for the voting system assumes that most of the agents which initially respond to the call will participate, but in its current incarnation, there is an opportunity for an agent to vote multiple times or for an adversary to outvote the legitimate agents by flooding the network with votes as soon as the process is announced and blocking legitimate votes because only a certain number of them will actually be accepted. To make this communication secure, each agent would therefore need to be assigned a unique identifier independent of the host's identifying information to ensure that invalid data is not being added to the system which could invalidate the results by an agent voting multiple times. Additional security is also required based on the fact that the identifier could be spoofed or false identifiers could be constructed.

Based on the fact that large networks are unlikely to allow a network map to reside in each agent's model o the network to allow accurate and precise voting, an alternate means of proving identity must be constructed. The most secure way to do this would be through the use of digital signatures using a public key algorithm such as RSA because these would be impossible for an adversary to forge and require only a single key authority for the network. However, this is infeasible given the goal of a lightweight agent that requires minimal processing to operate. Therefore, a compromise to this would be to use the idea of a pre-shared key common to such protocols as WEP and WPA for wireless technology. Each agent upon creation would be installed with the Pre-Shared Key (PSK) for the network, which would be used as part of a cryptographic hash to prove that they are a responding agent that is a legitimate part of the network. Based on the nature of cryptographic hashing and the fact that the PSK is not transmitted, it would be tremendously difficult for an adversary to determine the PSK without compromising an agent. Similarly, the call for a vote should contain this verification to prevent an adversary from clogging the network by spoofing voting calls. The voting protocol would then be multicast to all recipients as follows, with C being the calling agent and R being the responding agent:

1. $C \rightarrow R$: Call(ID_C, S, H[ID_C | S | P])
2. $R \rightarrow C$: Ack(ID_C, ID_R, H[ID_C | ID_R | P])
3. $C \rightarrow R$: ID_C | VoteProc(ID_C, S, H[ID_C | S | P])
4. $R \rightarrow C$: ID_R | VoteRep(ID_C, ID_R, V, H[ID_C | ID_R | S | V | P]))
5. $C \rightarrow R$: ID_C | Dec(ID_C, D, H[ID_C | S | D | P])

In the above protocol, Call is the initial call for respondents; this would be the place to add identifying characteristics for the host to determine which voters should have a vote. S is simply a sequence number to prevent replaying a call or voting to occupy the network and H is a cryptographic hash function to provide integrity checking. The P enclosed within the construction of the hash is the pre-shared key and proves the association with the network. The responding agent will use the ID_C, S, and its own copy of P to validate the match of the hash function before responding.

The message is sent in multicast to all agents within the network or sector of the network assigned; the pre-shared key can also be assigned by sector to limit voting jurisdiction in which all messages that do not have the correct P for integrity verification will simply ignore the voting calls and responses. The reply Ack message sent from each responding agent is merely an acknowledgement that it will participate in the vote; again, the integrity check is placed within the message so that the calling agent can accurately identify, by ID, which agents during the vote will have their votes recorded.

The VoteProc message is the announcement of the suspicious process which is up for voting. Similar credentials to the call for the initial response are used to associate this message with the initial call. The responding agents in this case will rely with their vote V in the VoteRep message, which is included in the hash to prevent vote tampering en route by an adversary. As the calling agent receives these messages, it can assign the votes based on the expected IDs of the agents which initially declared that they would respond. Again, the calling agent will only wait for a specific period of time for a response to avoid the case where a responding agent can stall the calling agent by declaring that it will vote and then never sending its actual vote. The final message is simply the announcement of the decision made by the calling agent based upon all of the respective responses of the voting agents. Here the decision D is included in the hash to prevent tampering. The pre-shared key is not perfect, but it means that an adversary must compromise an agent itself in order to be able to spoof messages in the system; this type of verification is not necessary in the handshake between communicating hosts because there is no assumed trust between agents in that case whereas the voting process is based upon the notion of getting accurate and legitimate votes from agents within the network or neighborhood within the network.

CONCLUSION

This chapter presents the idea of applying the concept of agents in a social environment to approach the security problem of intrusion detection. The fundamental approach is to allow each agent to emerge its own baseline of behavior for the host it monitors. By allowing the agents to decide socially whether a process should be allowed, it will reduce the number of false positives and propagate the denial of decidedly malicious processes. This is then extended to allow reporting to a central collection point to allow a network administrator to see the current threats to the network according to the decisions of the agents. The advantages of this system over the traditional approach to IDS are numerous. This system can detect 0-day attacks because there is no reliance upon signatures but rather a focus on behavioral characteristics. Many of the false positives are also ruled out because of the voting procedure in place. Additionally, this system can also be used to stop users from installing software that is unwanted. User installed software in this case would also be treated as anomalous if it is not widely distributed.

The biggest disadvantage to this approach is the potential for false positives if a network is not uniform. During times where a major network upgrade was occurring, the agents would have many false positives and may require a reset if the voting decided the process should be denied. An additional problem is that an intrusion has already occurred and been successful if the agent detects malicious activity. Therefore, this system is capable of detecting attacks after the fact and preventing their spread, but some amount of damage has occurred already. This threat could be mitigated by allowing the agents to automatically kill processes that are on the forbidden list.

FUTURE RESEARCH DIRECTIONS

This approach to intrusion detection provides a flexible framework for future exploration of more complex analysis of resources present on the network, such as port information or per packet monitoring depending upon the desired granularity. The difficulty in extending this approach to fine grained monitoring is the significant increase in the number of votes necessary to resolve disputes. An additional problem with this system that is not addressed herein is the compromise of an agent in which an agent will

still respond but respond as the attacker wishes it to respond, meaning it would likely vote in opposition to the real decision that should be made. This type of situation would require agents to decide on how much they trust neighboring agents in the voting process or it would require a central authority (which could also be an agent) to make social judgments or require a peer-to-peer negotiation of trust if the agent appears to be misbehaving (Gouda, 2004). This requires an almost hierarchical approach to the agents in terms of voting and negotiating trust, something that would require careful regulation to prevent a corrupt society from shutting out all other agents. Cliques could also form in which agents are only trusting of a few other agents and will not break out of the behavior on their own. However, this agent-based system provides a promising area of research into artificial intelligence and a viable alternative to threshold and signature based systems that currently exist.

REFERENCES

Corman, J. (2005). Defining the Rules for Preemptive Host Protection. Retrieved March 7, 2008, from http://www.iss.net/documents/whitepapers/ISS_Preemptive_Host_Protection_Whitepaper.pdf

Denning, D. (1987). An Intrusion-Detection Model. *IEEE Transactions on Software Engineering, 13*(2), 222-232.

Gouda, M. G., & Liu, X. A. (2004). Firewall Design: Consistency, Completeness, and Compactness. Paper presented at the 24th International Conference on Distributed Computing Systems.

Gu, G., Porras, P., Yegneswaran, V., Fong, M., & Lee, W. (2007). *BotHunter: Detecting Malware Infection Through IDS-Driven Dialog Correlation.* Paper presented at 16th USENIX Security Symposium.

Kodialam, M. & Lakshman, T. V. (2003). *Detecting Network Intrusions via Sampling: A Game Theoretic Approach.* Paper presented at IEEE INFOCOM Conference.

Newsome, J., Karp, B., & Song, D. (2005). *Polygraph: Automatically Generating Signatures for Polymorphic Worms.* Paper presented at IEEE Symposium on Security and Privacy.

Zheng, X., Chen, C., Huang, C. T., Matthews, M. M., & Santhapuri, N. (2005). *A Dual Authentication Protocol for IEEE 802.11 Wireless LANs.* Paper presented at the 2nd International Symposium on Wireless Communication Systems.

Zhu, S., Setia, S. and Jajodia, S. (2003). *LEAP: efficient security mechanisms for large-scale distributed sensor networks.* Paper presented at the Tenth ACM Conference on Computer and Communication Security, Washington, DC.

ADDITIONAL READING

Bleeding Edge Threats. (2007). Retrieved March 7, 2008, from http://www.bleedingthreats.net/

Bleeding Edge Threats Rules. (2007). Retrieved March 7, 2008, from http://www.bleedingthreats.net/rules/bleeding-all.rules

Cid, D. (2008). Welcome to the Home of OSSEC. Retrieved March 7, 2008, from http://www.ossec.net/

Cisco Systems, Inc. (2007). Cisco – Cisco Intrusion Detection. Retrieved March 7, 2008, from http://www.cisco.com/warp/public/cc/pd/sqsw/sqidsz/index.shtml

Giacobbi, G. (2008). The GNU Netcat – Official Homepage. Retrieved March 7, 2008, from http://netcat.sourceforge.net/

Hu, R., & Aloysius K. M. (2004). *Detecting Unknown Massive Mailing Viruses Using Proactive Methods.* Paper presented at the 7th International Symposium on Recent Advances in Intrusion Detection.

IBM Internet Security Systems – BlackICE. (2007). Retrieved March 7, 2008, from http://www.iss.net/blackice/

IEEE Standards Association. (2008). Get IEEE 802.11 LAN/MAN Wireless LANS. Retrieved March 7, 2008, from http://standards.ieee.org/getieee802/802.11.html

Inella, Paul. (2001). The Evolution of Intrusion Detection Systems. Retrieved March 7, 2008, from http://www.securityfocus.com/infocus/1514

Introducing the Proventia Enterprise Security System. (2007). Retrieved March 7, 2008, from http://www.iss.net/proof/preemptiveprotection/index.html

Malgalhaes, Ricky. (2003). Host based IDS vs. Network based IDS. Retrieved March 7, 2008, from http://www.windowsecurity.com/articles/Hids_vs_Nids_Part1.html

McAfee, Inc. (2008). McAfee Antivirus Software and Intrusion Prevention Solutions. Retrieved March 7, 2008, from http://www.mcafee.com/us/

Microsoft Corporation. (2005). Preshared key authentication. Retrieved March 7, 2008, from http://technet2.microsoft.com/windowsserver/en/library/ab62dcc7-a458-48b8-ba72-231b774636b21033.mspx?mfr=true

Netcat is the TCP/IP swiss army knife available since 1996. (1996). Retrieved March 7, 2008, from http://www.vulnwatch.org/netcat/

Novell, Inc. (2008). NOVELL: Worldwide. Retrieved March 7, 2008, from http://www.novell.com/

Prelude-IDS: The Hybrid IDS Framework. (2008). Retrieved March 7, 2008, from http://prelude-ids.org

RSA Securities. (2007). RSA Laboratories – RSA Algorithm. Retrieved March 7, 2008, from http://www.rsa.com/rsalabs/node.asp?id=2146

SANS Institute. (2008). Intrusion Detection FAQ. Retrieved March 7, 2008, from http://www.sans.org/resources/idfaq/

Smirnov, A. (2005). DIRA: Automatic Detection, Identification, and Repair of Control-Hijacking Attacks. Paper presented at DEFCON 13.

Sourcefire, Inc. (2008). Snort – the de facto standard for intrusion detection/prevention. Retrieved March 7, 2008, from http://www.snort.org/

Syverson, P., & Cervesato, I. (2001). The Logic of Authentication Protocols. *Foundations of Security Analysis and Design, Springer Verlag Lecture Notes in Computer Science, 2171.*

Top 5 Intrusion Detection Systems. (2006). Retrieved March 7, 2008, from http://sectools.org/ids.html

Weaver, N., Staniford, S., & Paxson, V. (2004). *Very Fast Containment of Scanning Worms.* Paper presented at the 13th USENIX Security Symposium.

Wi-Fi Alliance. (2007). Knowledge Center - Wi-Fi Protected Access. Retrieved March 7, 2008, from http://www.wi-fi.org/white_papers/whitepaper-042903-wpa/

Winsborough, W. H., & Li, N. (2004). Safety *in Automated Trust Negotiation.* Paper presented at the 2004 IEEE Symposium on Security and Privacy.

Chapter XXIII
Search as a Tool for Emergence

Michael J. North
Argonne National Laboratory, USA
The University of Chicago, USA

Thomas R. Howe
Argonne National Laboratory, USA
The University of Chicago, USA

Nick Collier
Argonne National Laboratory, USA
PantaRei Corporation, USA

Eric Tatara
Argonne National Laboratory, USA

Jonathan Ozik
Argonne National Laboratory, USA
The University of Chicago, USA

Charles Macal
Argonne National Laboratory, USA
The University of Chicago, USA

ABSTRACT

Search has been recognized as an important technology for a wide range of software applications. Agent-based modelers often face search challenges both when looking for agents that need to be connected to one another and when seeking appropriate target agents while defining agent behaviors. This chapter presents an approach to simplifying such search problems and shows examples of its use. The approach presented in this chapter offers both imperative and declarative methods to find sets of agents with particular attributes in particular locales. The imperative approach allows for flexible reactions to the agents that are discovered through querying. The declarative approach builds on the imperative approach and introduces a temporal dimension to the process by explicitly allowing for searches that activate in the future depending on the conditions that obtain in a given model.

INTRODUCTION

Search has been recognized as an important technology for a wide range of software applications.

For example, Internet Society founding member and Google Chief Internet Evangelist Vint Cerf has stated that (Cerf 2007):

*Today's search engines draw the most relevant infor-
mation to our attention, and as more data become
available online, the importance of search engines
will only increase. In the future, people around the
world will likely look for new ways to identify the
authenticity of online information sources.*

According to Ntoulas et al. (2004):

*As the Web grows larger and more diverse, search
engines are becoming the "killer app" of the Web.
Whenever users want to look up information, they
typically go to a search engine, issue queries and
look at the results. Recent studies confirm the growing importance of search engines. According to
(ACNielsen 2004), for example, Web users spend
a total of 13 million hours per month interacting
with Google alone.*

Search technologies are not just used by people
for information retrieval. Software programs within
automated Web services systems are also beginning
to use search technologies to identify other programs
to act as service providers. Liu et al. (2004) elaborate
on this growing trend:

*Web services are self-describing software appli-
cations that can be advertised, located, and used
across the Internet using a set of standards such
as SOAP [Simple Object Access Protocol], WSDL
[Web Services Description Language], and UDDI
[Universal Description Discovery and Integra-
tion] (Papazoglou and Georgakopoulos 2003).
Web services encapsulate application functionality
and information resources, and make them available through standard programmatic interfaces.
Web services are viewed as one of the promising
technologies that could help business entities to
automate their operations on the Web on a large
scale by automatic discovery and consumption of
services. Business-to-Business (B2B) integration
can be achieved on a demand basis by aggregat-
ing multiple services from different providers into
a value-added composite service.*

Liu et al. (2004) also state the following:

*The emerging Service-Oriented Computing (SOC)
paradigm promises to enable businesses and orga-*

*nizations to collaborate in an unprecedented way by
means of standard Web services. To support rapid
and dynamic composition of services in this paradigm, Web services that meet requesters' functional
requirements must be able to be located and bounded
dynamically from a large and constantly changing
number of service providers based on their Quality
of Service (QoS).*

Agent-based modelers and multi-agent simula-
tionists often face similar challenges when specifying searches for groups of agents within models.
This chapter, which builds on the discussion found
in North et al. (October 2006c), addresses this issue
by first considering the kinds of searches commonly found in agent-based models and multi-agent
simulations. It then grounds the need for search
in Holland's properties and features of Complex
Adaptive Systems (CAS) (1995). Building on this
foundation, this chapter then introduces both Repast
Simphony (Repast S) and the Repast S approach to
simplifying many agent-based modeling and multi-
agent simulation search problems. An example
application of the search capability within Repast
S is then provided. Finally, this chapter presents
some conclusions.

BACKGROUND

Several kinds of searches appear to be common in
agent-based models and multi-agent simulations,
including queries for:

- Agents that are to be connected to one another
  either at simulation startup time or later during simulation execution (e.g., finding a set
  of friends with specific properties for each
  person in a social network model);

- Appropriate target agents while defining agent
  behaviors (e.g., finding the set of people that
  are physically near a specific infected person
  at a given point in time in a contagious disease
  propagation model);

- Agents that approach or connect to a given
  agent (e.g., finding students that walk within
  a certain distance of a hall monitor in a elementary school simulation); and

- Agents that change properties, state, or attributes (e.g., alerting a guard when a nearby person unexpectedly draws a weapon in a terrorism simulation).

Are these types of queries needed for systems with emergence and if so, why? If they are needed, how can these queries be efficiently and conveniently embodied in agent-based models and multi-agent simulations? Holland's three properties and four mechanisms common to all CAS suggest an answer to these questions (1995)[1]:

- The *nonlinearity property* is present when components or agents exchange resources or information in ways that are not simply additive (e.g., rumors can be dramatically transformed when retold).
- The *diversity property* is present when agents or groups of agents differentiate from one another over time (e.g., people are unique).
- The *aggregation property* is present when a group of agents is treated as a single agent at a higher level (e.g., people form clubs).
- The *flows mechanism* is present when resources or information are exchanged between agents such that the resources can be repeatedly forwarded from agent to agent (e.g., rumors spread from person to person).
- The *tagging mechanism* is present when there are identifiable flags that let agents attempt to identify the traits of other agents (e.g., a scowling person may be hostile).
- The *internal models mechanism* is present when formal, informal, or implicit representations of the world are embedded within agents (e.g., each person has a view of others in a club).
- The *building blocks mechanism* is present when an agent participates in more than one kind of interaction where each interaction is a building block for larger activities (e.g., a person can be a member of a club and also work in an office).

In principle, every one of these properties and mechanism can make use of searching or querying for agents. For example, returning to Holland's

three properties and four mechanisms common to all CAS (1995):

- The *nonlinearity property* can arise from many sources including the nonlinear results of queries for agent lists (e.g., making lists of the people in each region of a geographical space can produce nonlinear results).
- The *diversity property* can be leveraged by using partial matches in queries for agent lists (e.g., finding all active Artificial Intelligence (AI) researchers in given geographical region).
- The *aggregation property* can arise by grouping agents using queries (e.g., a selected subset of the active AI researchers in a given geographical region might form a professional association for that region).
- The *flows mechanism* can use querying to identify future sources of and targets for flows (e.g., finding a list of AI researchers to notify about a given conference).
- The *tagging mechanism* provides sets of agent attributes for querying (e.g., tagging people as active AI researchers allows them to be candidates to receive AI conference announcements).
- The *internal models mechanism* can use querying as a tool for model building (e.g., people may form ideas about AI by finding and contacting active AI researchers).
- The *building blocks mechanism* can be leveraged much like the diversity property by using partial matches in queries for agent lists (e.g., finding all of the active AI researchers in given geographical region and then contacting them for both a conference announcement and annual association dues).

This discussion suggests that querying can play integral role in CAS. As such, many emergent or potentially emergent behaviors in agent-based models might implicitly leverage, explicitly leverage, or even require search functions. This chapter builds on this idea by offering an approach to simplifying such agent-based modeling and multi-agent simulation search problems. This new approach has been implemented within Repast S.

REPAST S[2]

Repast (ROAD 2007) is a widely used free and open source agent-based modeling and simulation toolkit with four released platforms, namely Repast for Java, Repast for the Microsoft .NET framework, Repast for Python Scripting, and Repast S. North et al. (2005a and 2005b) provide an overview of the Repast S runtime and development environments.

As discussed in North et al. (2005a and 2005b), once a model is designed the Repast S model software design and development is nominally intended to proceed as follows[3]:

- The modeler designs and implements model pieces, as needed, in the form of plain old Java objects (POJOs) or Groovy[4] objects (POGOs), often using automated tools.
- The modeler uses declarative configuration settings to pass the model pieces and legacy software connections to the Repast S runtime system.
- The modeler uses the Repast S runtime system to declaratively tell Repast S how to instantiate and connect model components.
- The Repast S runtime system automatically manages the model pieces based on (1) interactive user input and (2) declarative or imperative requests from the components themselves.

Repast S uses two major types of declarative specifications, namely model and scenario descriptors, to integrate models. Model descriptors define what *can be* in a model such as the allowed agent types, permitted agent relationships. Scenario descriptors define what *actually is* in a model such as agent data sources, visualizations, and logging. Model and scenario descriptors are stored in separate XML files. Model descriptors are created at model development time while scenario descriptors are created at run time. The Repast S development environment provides both a wizard for creating and a point-and-click editor for modifying model descriptors. The Repast S runtime environment includes a point-and-click panel for creating and maintaining scenario descriptors.

Repast S uses Java annotations to declaratively mark code for later operations. Annotations are metadata tags that are compiled into binary class files. Like comments, annotations are not directly executed. Unlike comments, annotations can be stored in the compiled versions of source code[5]. This storage allows executing Java programs such as the Repast S runtime system to read and act on the encoded metadata. This allows Repast S developers to declaratively mark or annotate code at design time for special processing by the Repast S runtime system. This facility is used for tasks such as declaring *watchers* as discussed later.

CONTEXTS AND PROJECTIONS[6]

Repast S represents agent-based modeling and simulation (ABMS) spaces and places through the use of *contexts* and *projections*. Repast S contexts are hierarchically nested named containers that hold model components. The model components can be any type of POJO or POGO, including other contexts, but are often expected to be agent objects. Each model component can be present in as many contexts as the modeler desires. The hierarchical nesting means that a model component that is present in a context is also present in all of that context's parent contexts. Of course, the converse is *not* true in the general case. The hierarchical nesting structure itself can be declaratively or imperatively specified by the modeler. Context membership and structure is completely dynamic and agents can be in any number or combination of contexts at any time. Furthermore, agents can themselves contain any number of contexts and can even be contexts. In addition, the contents of components within contexts (e.g., agent properties) can be declaratively logged at runtime.

In addition to supporting hierarchical nesting, contexts support *projections*. Repast S projections are named sets of relationships defined over the constituents of a context. For example, a Repast S network projection stores a network or graph relationship between the members of its context. The members of this context can then ask who they are linked to and who is linked to them. Similarly, the Repast S grid projection stores a set of Cartesian coordinates for each member of the context. The members of this context can ask where they are.

Each context can support any mixture of projections. Also, projections can be declaratively visualized at runtime as shown in Figure 1. A wide range of projections and projection options are included in Repast S, such as:

- Nnetworks for modeling directed graphs, undirected graphs, trees, and weighted graphs
- Multidimensional discrete grids for modeling toroidal and bounded surfaces
- Multidimensional continuous spaces for modeling toroidal and bounded surfaces
- Geographical information systems (GIS) surfaces

Repast S contexts and projections work with watchers. Repast S watchers are automated listeners or call back procedures that trigger based on complex queries. These queries define what kinds of agents to watch, where to watch for the tracked agents, what to look for in each tracked agent, and when to react to events in the tracked agents. Watchers are typically defined declaratively using Java annotations. Repast S contexts work directly with watchers by allowing watcher queries to use context names and properties to define what and where to watch. Similarly, projections work directly with watchers by allowing watcher queries to use projection names, properties, and relationships.

QUERYING

Simply put, Repast S querying provides support for finding complex subsets of agents. Queries are defined using the following conceptual predicates:

- **Equals:** This predicate determines whether the object is equal to a given object.
- **Property equals:** This predicate determines whether a property in the object is equal to a given value.
- **Property less than:** This predicate determines whether a property in the object is less than a given value.
- **Property greater than:** This predicate determines whether a property in the object is greater than a given value.

Figure 1. The Repast S Runtime System showing a context with two networks and a three dimensional continuous space; the construction of this model is detailed later in this chapter

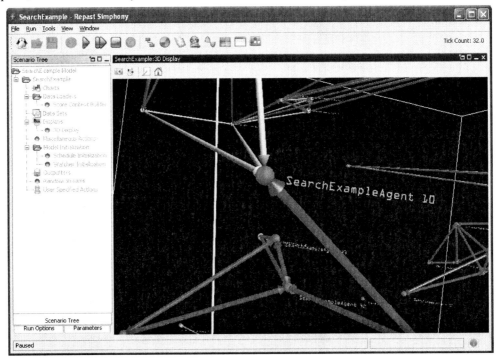

- **Network adjacent:** This predicate determines whether the object is linked to a given object in a specified network.
- **Network successor:** This predicate determines whether the object has an inbound edge from a given object in a specified network.
- **Network predecessor:** This predicate determines whether the object has an outbound edge to a given object in a specified network.
- **Touches:** This GIS predicate determines whether the object touches a given object in space.
- **Contained by:** This GIS predicate determines whether the object is contained by a given object in space.
- **In envelope:** This GIS predicate determines whether the object is within a given envelope (bounding box) in space.
- **And:** This predicate implements intersection.
- **Or:** This predicate implements union.
- **Not:** This predicate implements negation.
- **Von Neumann:** This predicate determines whether an object is within the Von Neumann neighborhood of a given object in a grid.
- **Moore:** This predicate determines whether an object is within the Moore Neighborhood of a given object in a grid.

- **Within distance:** This GIS and non-GIS predicate determines whether the object is within a given distance of a specified object in a GIS space, a non-GIS grid or continuous space, or within a given path length in a network. Concrete subclasses implement specific functions for each projection type.

Searches that utilize these conceptual predicates can also be performed imperatively using Java syntax or declaratively using watcher syntax. Both of these approaches are discussed later in this section. Groovy uses the same syntax as Java for the predicates.

When used in an imperative mode, Repast S queries normally return a list scanning object or *Iterator*. These iterators can be used in programmed agent behaviors to operate on and react to members of the list. An example is shown in Figure 2. In this example, an agent starts a search for an associate who might accept a specific business offer by asking each associate about their interest in the offer. The process begins by creating a network query that returns all of the associates linked to the main agent (i.e., "this"). Each of these linked associates is then asked if they are interested in the offer. If they are, the agent then attempts to negotiate a deal.

A direct approach to the search for a specific associate is shown in Figure 3. Here an agent

Figure 2. An example of an imperative query in Repast S

```
    // Create a network query that lists all of an
agent's associates.
    Query<Associate> netQuery = new NetworkAdjacent
(context, this);
    Iterable<Associate> associates = netQuery.que-
ry();

    // Scan the list of associates that were found.
    for (Associate associate : associates) {

    // Ask the next associate if they are interested
in the offer.
    if (associate.interested(offer)) {

        // Attempt to negotiate a deal.
        this.negotiateDetails(associate);

    }

    }
```

Figure 3. Additional example of an imperative query in Repast S

```
// Create a query that can search the main
content in the simulation.
Query<Associate> query = new AndQuery(
   new PropertyEquals (mainContext, "First
Name", "Chris"),
   new PropertyEquals (mainContext, "Last
Name", "Jones"));

// Find Chris Jones.
Associate chrisJones = query.query().next();
```

Figure 4. Examples of imperative queries incorporating multiple agent relationships

```
// Three kinds of relationships are created,
each by changing one
// line of code.

// These lines create a network query.
Query<Agent>netQuery=new
NetworkAdjacent(context, myAgent);
Iterable<Agent> results = netQuery.query();

// These lines create a grid network query.
Query<Agent> vnQuery = new VNQuery(grid,
myAgent)
results = vnQuery.query();

// These lines create a combination of a grid
and a network query.
Query<Agent> unionQuery = new OrQuery(netQuery,
vnQuery);
results = unionQuery.query();
```

Figure 5. An example of a declarative behavior trigger query in Repast S

```
@Watch(watcheeClassName = "Associate",
    watcheeFieldName = "wealth",
    query = "within 75000 'chicago'"
    triggerCondition = "$watchee.wealth > 10000",
    whenToTrigger = WatcherTriggerSchedule.IMMEDIATE)
    public void salesCall(Associate associate) {

    // Ask the associate if they are interested in the offer.
    if (associate.interested(offer)) {

        // Attempt to negotiate a deal.
        this.negotiateDetails(associate);

    }
}
```

looks for another agent with a specific first and last name. The agent simply creates a query that uniquely specifies the object of the search, "Chris Jones," and then searches for them starting with the main context.

Querying treats grids, networks, GIS, and other environments in a consistent and uniform manner. An imperative example is shown in Figure 4. In this example three projection queries are defined. The first searches a network, the second searches a grid, and the third simultaneously searches both a grid and a network.

Repast S querying also allows agent subsets to be created in a declarative manner. This lays the groundwork for a declarative query language. A simple example that might be used by a salesperson is shown in Figure 5. In this example the salesperson is using a Repast S watcher to keep an eye on the people within 75 kilometers of them in Chicago to see if anyone has enough wealth to afford a specific business offer. If anyone within this 75 kilometer radius becomes a candidate, the salesperson is notified through invocation of the salesCall method. Repast S makes the querying an efficient process since the runtime system uses the listener design pattern to limit checking to only those times and objects for which the watched values change.

AN EXAMPLE SEARCH-BASED APPLICATION

The preceding discussion has considered the kinds of searches commonly found in agent-based models and multi-agent simulations. It then grounded the need for search in Holland's (1995) properties and features of CAS. Subsequently it introduced both Repast S and the Repast S approach to simplifying many agent-based modeling and multi-agent simulation search problems. A few example code extracts were then presented in Figures 2 through 5. The next step is to illustrate the value of such search techniques using a simple, but fully self-contained, example application. A snapshot of the running example application was shown in Figure 1.

The example model contains a set of agents, two networks, and a three dimensional continuous space. The example application was inspired by the widely used Boids model developed by Craig Reynolds (1987, 2001). Reynolds (2001) notes that the Boids "flocking is a particularly evocative example of *emergence*: where complex global behavior can arise from the interaction of simple local rules" (Reynolds 2001).

The example model presented here uses simplified rules combined with search to illustrate the Repast S approach to agent-based modeling and multi-agent simulation search problems. The example model itself is intentionally simple in order to allow readers to focus on the search concepts being discussed. Real search-based models can use the same principles with more complex rules, more sophisticated queries, more types of agents, and more diverse environments.

The example model has four essential components:

1. The model has one agent type, namely the "SearchExampleAgent." Each agent has a speed, a preferred directional heading (i.e., angle) in the XY plane, and a preferred directional heading in the XZ plane. Agents are created and their three attributes are randomly assigned when the model is initialized. Each agent's speed is assigned a double precision uniform random number drawn from the interval [-2.0, 2.0). The agent adjusts its preferred speed over time based on a combination of its influences' speeds and random draws. Each agent's preferred directional headings are assigned a double precision uniform random number drawn from the interval [0.0, 2π). Agent's determine their direction and speed at any given time using a complex query that is discussed later in this chapter.

2. The model has a three dimensional continuous space. All of the agents exist and move around in this space. By default each axis (i.e., X, Y, and Z) ranges in the interval [0.0, 100.0]. The space has periodic boundary conditions so that it forms a torus.

3. The model has a family network that tracks family membership. This network is configured when the model is initialized and remains constant as the simulation progresses. Each agent's family is defined by a query to be the other agents within 25 units at initialization time.

4. The model has a friendship network which tracks friendships. Friendships are formed and broken throughout each simulation run based on several different queries to be discussed later.

Using these components, each run of the model follows these steps:

1. The model is initialized as follows:
    a. A set of 50 agents are created and randomly placed in the continuous space.
    b. Each agent's preferred headings are randomly initialized.
    c. Each agent is connected to its family members and friends using the first query in Table 1. Family members start out as friends but this can change over time as the model runs.

2. Each time step is executed as follows:
    a. Agents find new friends (i.e., agents within 20 units that are not currently friends) using the second query in Table 1. Note that under this definition family members can become, but do not necessarily have to be, friends.

Table 1. Queries used in the example model

Step Name	Construction Step Number	Description	Query
Find Neighbors in 3D	14	This query finds all agents within 25 units of the current agent.	neighbor in (new ContinuousWithin(space, this, 25).query())
Find New Friends	21	This query finds all agents within 20 units of the current agent that are not directly connected in the friendship network.	friend in (new AndQuery(new ContinuousWithin(space, this, 20), new NotQuery(context, new NetPathWithin(friends, this, 1))). query())
Forget Distant Friends	23	This query finds all agents further than 40 units from the current agent that are directly connected in the friendship network.	friend in (new AndQuery(new NotQuery(context, new ContinuousWithin(space, this, 40)), new NetPathWithin(friends, this, 1)). query())
Check Influences	25	This query finds all agents within two steps of the current agent on the family network or within three steps of the current agent on the friendship network.	influence in (new OrQuery(new NetPathWithin(family, this, 2), new NetPathWithin(friends, this, 3)). query())

b. Agents forget distant friends (i.e., current friends over 40 units away) using the third query in Table 1.

c. Agents determine the preferred headings of their influences (i.e., agents within two steps in the family network or within three steps in the friends network) using the fourth query in Table 1.

d. Agents set their next heading as follows:

 i. The next XY angle is set to be the average of their preferred heading and that of their influences. Note that the preferred XY angle is not changed; only a temporary value is calculated.

 ii. The next XZ angle is set to be the average of their preferred heading and that of their influences. Once again, the preferred XZ angle is not changed; only a temporary value is calculated.

 iii. The speed is set to be the average of each agent's preferred heading

and that of their influences plus a uniform random number drawn from the range [-0.5, 0.5]. The speed is bounded to the range [-2.0, 2.0]. Note that unlike the preferred angles, the preferred agent's speed *is* changed.

 iv. The agent moves forward based on its calculated heading.

The example model is created using a series of steps that will now be outlined. These steps assume that the free and open source Repast S system has been downloaded from ROAD (2007) and has been installed as provided for in the installation instructions. It should be noted that there are multiple methods for creating Repast S models. They can be created with pure Java, pure Groovy, pure visual specification, or a mixture of these approaches. The steps presented here represent only one of such possible paths[7]:

1. Create a new Repast S project by selecting the "File" menu's "New" submenu and then "Repast Simphony Project."

2. Set the "project name" to "Search Model" and select "Next" and then "Finish."
3. A new Repast S project will be created and the model descriptor "Score[8]" file editor will open.

As previously discussed, model descriptors define what can be in a model such as the allowed agent types, permitted agent relationships, and watching information. The Score editor presents a hierarchical view of the model descriptor or Score file. The default Score file for a project is automatically initialized by the New Project Wizard to contain a main context named after the model itself (e.g., "SearchModel"). Complete the following steps to create the model in the new project:

4. Add an agent to the file by right clicking on the SearchModel context, selecting the "Create Member" menu then the "Create Member" submenu:
   a. The default agent name will be "Search-ModelAgent."
   b. Open the "SearchModelAgent" tree item.
   c. Right click on the "Attributes" tree item, select the "Create Member" menu, and then select the "Scalar Attribute" menu item
   d. Right click on the new "Scalar Attribute" tree item and select "Show Properties" from the popup menu.
   e. In the properties area, set the "Label" property to "initialCount".
   f. In the properties area, set the "Default Value" property to "50" to automatically create 50 agents.
5. Add a continuous space to the model by right clicking on "SearchModel" context then selecting the "Create Member" menu then "Projection – Continuous Space" submenu:
   a. In the properties area, set the "Label" property to "Space".
   b. In the properties area, set the "Border Rule" property to "PERIODIC".
   c. In the properties area, set the "Dimensionality" property to 3 for a three dimensional space.

d. Open up the "Space" item in the tree view to reveal the "X Extent," "Y Extent," and "Z Extent" items:
   i. Select the "X Extent" item and then set the "Default Value" to "100".
   ii. Select the "Y Extent" item and then set the "Default Value" to "100".
   iii. Select the "Z Extent" item and then set the "Default Value" to "100".
6. Add a family network to the model by right clicking on "SearchModel" context then selecting the "Create Member" menu then "Projection – Network" submenu:
   a. In the properties area, set the "Label" property to "Family".
   b. In the properties area, set the "Directed" property to "true". This means the network does not have to be reflexive (i.e., someone considered a relative may not consider the other person to be related).
7. Add a friendship network to the model by right clicking on "SearchModel" context then selecting the "Create Member" menu then "Projection – Network" submenu:
   a. In the properties area, set the "Label" property to "Friends".
   b. In the properties area, set the "Directed" property to "true". As before, this means the network does not have to be reflexive (i.e., someone considered to be a friend might not return the favor).
8. Save the Score file by selecting the "File" menu's "Save" submenu to store the results.
9. Create a new agent:
   a. Open "Search Model Project" then the "src" directory then the "searchmodel" package.
   b. Right click on the "searchmodel" package and from the menu select the "New" submenu then the "Repast Simphony Agent" submenu.
   c. The New Repast Simphony Agent Wizard will start.
   d. In the properties area, set the "File name" to "SearchModelAgent.agent" then press "Finish."
   e. The visual behavior editor for the "SearchModelAgent.agent" will appear.

10. Add a property for the XY angle:
    a. Set the properties as shown in Figure 6.
    b. Optionally move the label to the upper right corner of the property icon.
11. Repeat step 10 for the XZ angle.
12. Repeat step 10 for the speed property.
13. Add a "Find Family" behavior initiation step and set the properties as shown in Figure 7.
14. Add a "Find the 3D Space" task, set the properties, and link the task as shown in Figure 8. Also see the first query in Table 1.
15. Add a "Find Neighbors in 3D" loop, set the properties, and link the task as shown in Figure 9.
16. Add a "Note a Close Relative" task, set the properties, and link the task as shown in Figure 10.
17. Add and link the ending step to the "Find Neighbors in 3D" task.
18. Add a "Move" behavior initiation step and set the properties as shown in Figure 11.
19. Add a "Find the 3D Space and Network" task, set the properties, and link the task as shown in Figure 12.

20. Add a "Setup Counters" task, set the properties, and link the task as shown in Figure 13.
21. Add a "Find New Friends" loop, set the properties, and link the task as shown in Figure 14. Also see the second query in Table 1.
22. Add a "Make a New Friend" task, set the properties, and link the task as shown in Figure 15.
23. Add a "Forget Distant Friends" loop, set the properties, and link the task as shown in Figure 16. Also see the third query in Table 1.
24. Add a "Forget the Distant Friend" task, set the properties, and link the task as shown in Figure 17.
25. Add a "Check Influences" loop, set the properties, and link the task as shown in Figure 18. Also see the fourth query in Table 1.
26. Add a "Note the Next Influence's Heading" task, set the properties, and link the task as shown in Figure 19.
27. Add a "Finish Moving" task, set the properties, and link the task as shown in Figure 20.
28. Save the new agent by selecting the "File" menu's "Save" submenu to store the final results shown in Figure 21.

Figure 6. The XY Angle properties

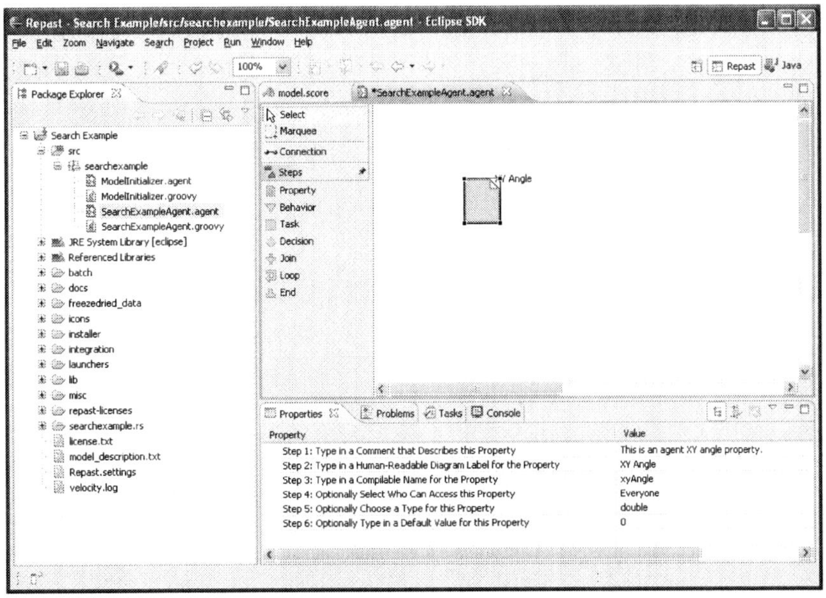

Figure 7. The "Find Family" behavior step

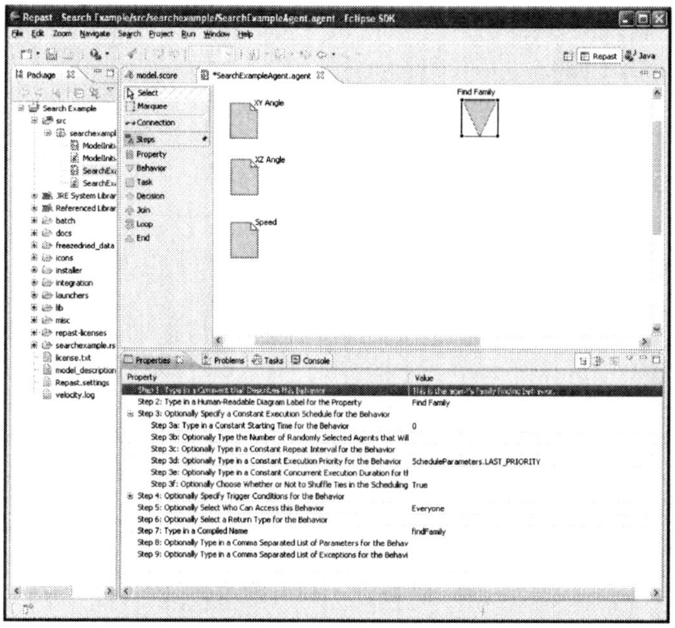

Figure 8. The "Find the 3D Space" task

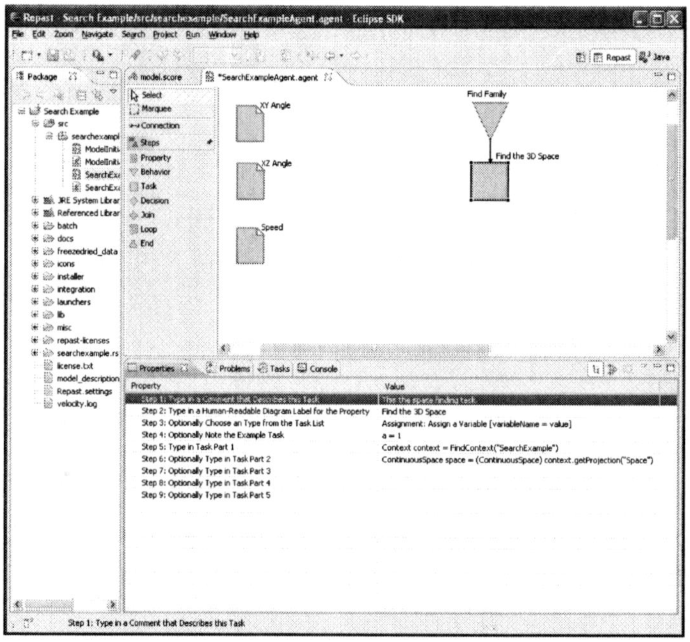

Figure 9. The "Find Neighbors in 3D" loop

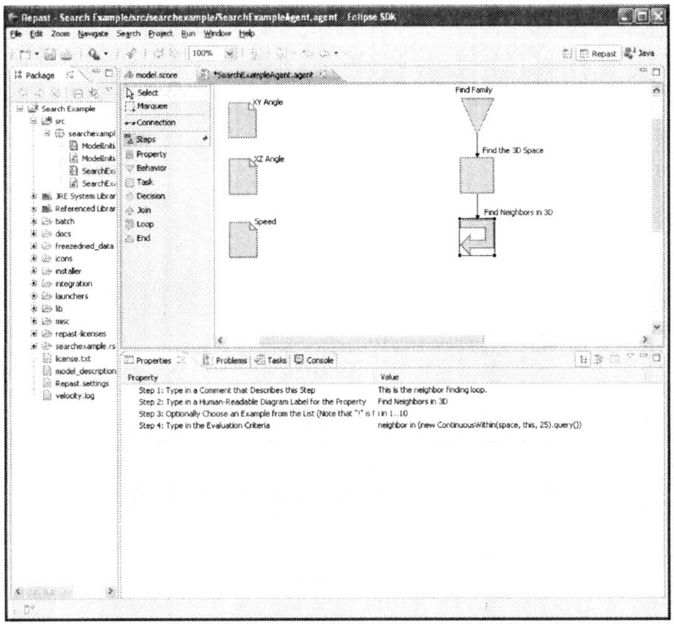

Figure 10. The "Note a Close Relative" task

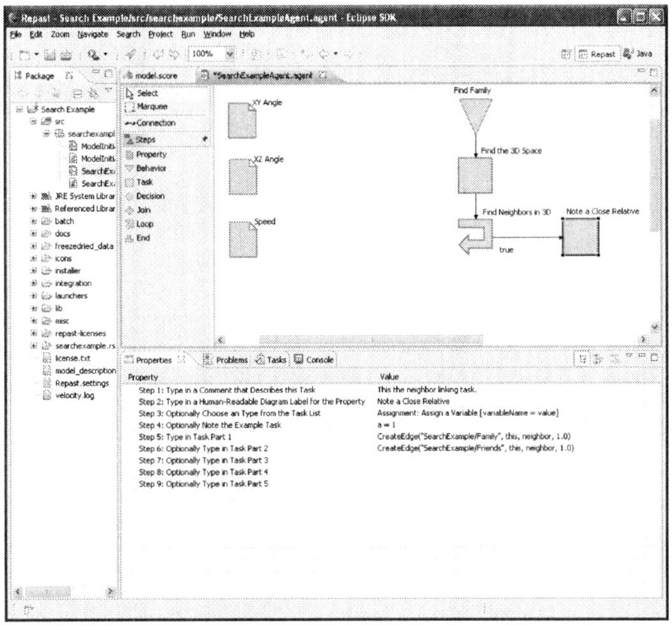

Figure 11. The "Move" task

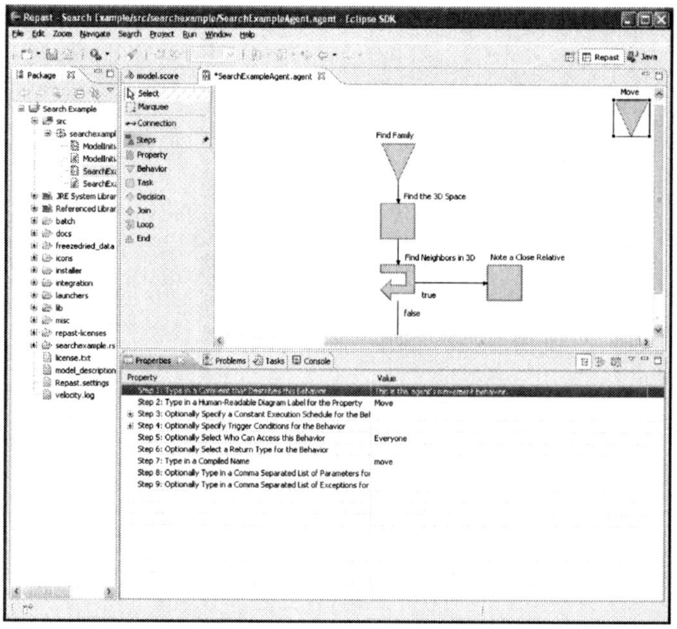

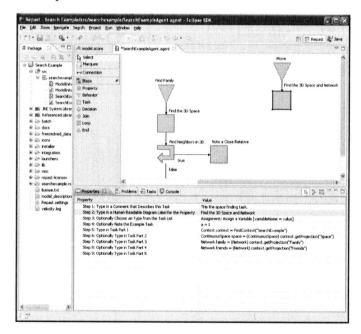

Figure 12. The "Find the 3D Space and Network" task

Figure 13. The "Setup Counters" task

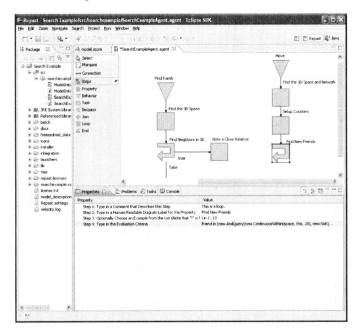

Figure 14. The "Find New Friends" loop

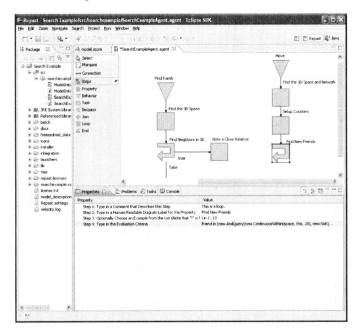

Figure 15. The "Make a New Friend" task

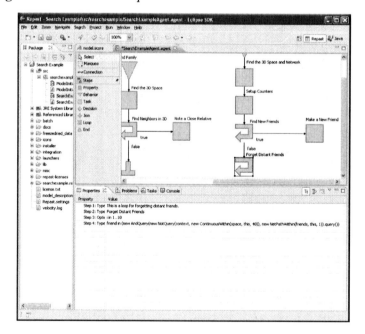

Figure 16. The "Forget Distant Friends" loop

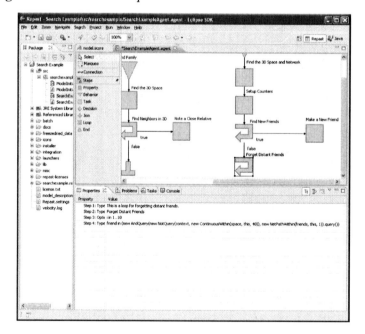

Figure 17. The "Forget the Distant Friend" task

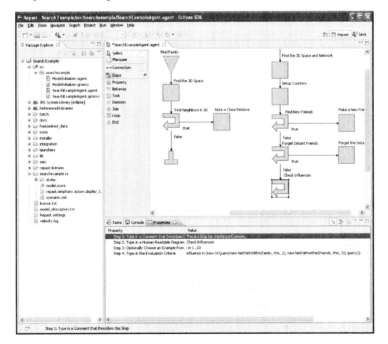

Figure 18. The "Check Influences" loop

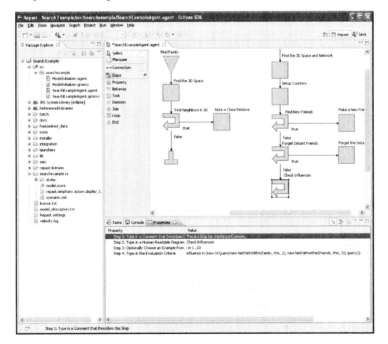

Figure 19. The "Note the Next Influence's Heading" task

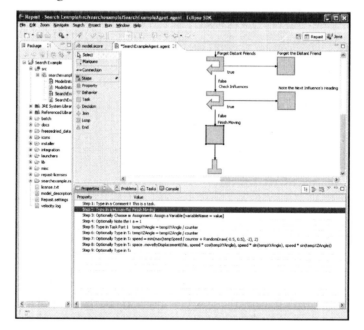

Figure 20. The "Finish Moving" task

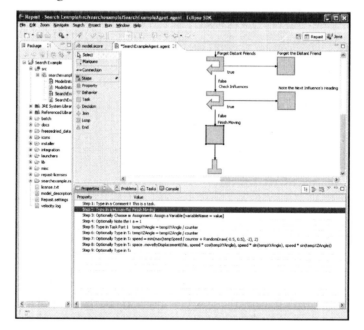

Figure 21. The completed agent

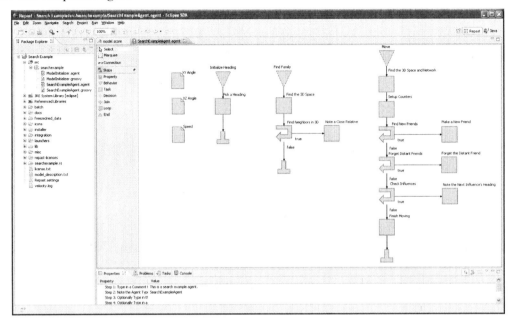

Figure 22. The executing model

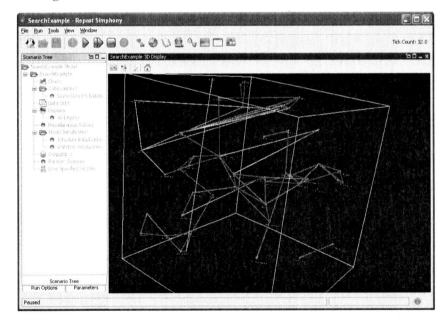

29. Start the model by closing the green activation icon then the "Run Search Example Model" menu option.
30. The "Search Example Model" will load into the Repast S runtime.
31. Setup a 3D display:
    a. Right click on the "Displays" option and then choose "Add Display."
    b. Fill in the "Display Configuration" then click "Next."
    c. Click on the "Edit Style" option on the next wizard page.
    d. Select your choice of style and then click on "OK."
    e. Accept the continuous space style by clicking "Next" on the "Continuous Space Style" wizard page.
    f. Select the "Family" network and then click on the "Edit Style" option on the next wizard page.
    g. Select your choice of style and then click on "OK."
    h. Select the "Friends" network and then click on the "Edit Style" option on the next wizard page.
    i. Select your choice of style and then click on "OK."
    j. Click "Next" on Edge Style wizard page.
    k. Click "Finish" on the "Schedule Details" wizard page.
32. Choose the "Run" forward arrow icon to run the model.
33. The 3D visualization will appear and model will execute as shown in Figure 22.
34. Note the agent's behavior.
35. Run the model for as long as desired and then press the blue "Stop" square when done.

CONCLUSION

Search has been recognized as an important technology for a wide range of software applications. This chapter has demonstrated the relevance of search for agent-based modeling. Approaches to simplifying such search problems and examples of their use were presented. Both imperative and declarative

methods were offered to find sets of agents with particular attributes in particular locales. The imperative approach allows for flexible reactions to the agents that are discovered through querying, while the declarative approach builds on the imperative approach and introduces a temporal dimension to the process by explicitly allowing for searches that activate in the future depending on the conditions that are obtained in a given model.

FUTURE RESEARCH DIRECTIONS

There are a variety of potential next steps for search in agent-based modeling. In the near term these steps include the creation of a language query that matches the watcher style queries; continuing speed and scalability enhancements; and the introduction of additional search predicates. In the longer term, there is a need to develop design patterns for agent-based search much like those for agent-based modeling itself (Coplien 2001, Gamma et al. 1995, North and Macal 2007); and there ultimately is a need to create a theory of how search can be used to underpin emergence in agent-based models and societies of agents.

Queries are currently specified in Repast S using the Java-based approach shown in Figures 2 through 4. This is an efficient and effective way to specify queries which provides a solid foundation for the core implementation. However, it would be advantageous to offer a second method for query specification based on the watcher language shown in Figure 5. This would provide users with a single unified approach for query specification which uses straightforward infix notation rather than the current Java prefix notation.

The current Repast S query and watcher mechanisms are efficient but, naturally, there is room for improvement. It would be good to take advantage of the large and growing body of knowledge on search optimization to enhance the speed and scalability of the Repast S query and watcher mechanisms. In particular, there is potential for great benefits from optimizing multiple nested conjunctive queries (i.e., "and" predicates) that simultaneously search several projections. One important step in this direction is the previously mentioned creation of a watcher-style query language. The creation of such a language will provide the Repast S system with the grist for optimization in the form of a parsed version of each input query and will also allow optimizations to be immediately shared across both queries and watchers.

The introduction of additional search predicates will give users a greater range of ways to search for agents. Of course, any new predicates will need to be added to the watcher query language and then optimized.

Design patterns form a "common vocabulary" describing tried and true solutions for commonly faced software design problems (Coplien 2001). Software design patterns were popularized by Gamma et al. (1995). There is a need to develop design patterns for agent-based search much like those detailed by North and Macal (2007) for agent-based modeling itself. Such design patterns for agent-based search may form the empirical foundation needed to produce a theory of how search can be used to underpin emergence in agent-based models. This theory, combined with the design patterns themselves, might then be used for designing the kinds of queries that are needed to produce various types of emergence in agent-based models and societies of agents

REFERENCES

ACNielsen, *Nielsen NetRatings for Search Engines*. (2004) Available at http://searchenginewatch.com/reports/article.php/2156451

Cerf, V. (2007, August 24). *The Tech Lab: Vint Cerf*. BBC News. Available as http://news.bbc.co.uk/2/hi/technology/6960896.stm

Coplien, J. O. (2001). *Software Patterns Home Page*. Available as http://hillside.net/patterns/

Gamma, E., R. Helm, R. Johnson, & J. Vlissides. (1995). *Design Patterns: Elements of Reusable Object-Oriented Software*. Wokingham, UK: Addison-Wesley.

Holland, J. H. (1995). *Hidden Order: How Adaptation Builds Complexity*, Addison-Wesley, Reading, MA.

König, D., A. Glover, P. King, G. Laforge, & J. Skeet. (2007) *Groovy in action*. Manning Publications.

Liu, Y. A. H. Ngu, & L. Z. Zeng. (2004). "QoS Computation and Policing in Dynamic Web Service Selection." *Proceedings of the 13th International Conference on the World Wide Web*, (pp. 66-73). New York: ACM.

North, M.J., N.T. Collier, & J.R. Vos. (2006, January). "Experiences Creating Three Implementations of the Repast Agent Modeling Toolkit." *ACM Transactions on Modeling and Computer Simulation, 16*(1), 1-25, New York: ACM.

North, M. J., T. R. Howe, N. T. Collier, & J. R.. Vos. (2005a, October). "The Repast Simphony Runtime System," *Agent 2005 Conference on Generative Social Processes, Models, and Mechanisms*. Argonne National Laboratory. Argonne, IL.

North, M. J., T. R. Howe, N. T. Collier, & J. R. Vos. (2005b, October). "The Repast Simphony Development Environment." *Agent 2005 Conference on Generative Social Processes, Models, and Mechanisms*. Argonne National Laboratory. Argonne, IL USA.

North, M. J., T. R. Howe, N. T. Collier, & J. R. Vos. (2006, June) "Spaces, Places, and the Lernaean Hydra of Agent-Based Modeling." *North American Association for Computational Social and Organizational Science 2006 Conference*. Argonne National Laboratory. Argonne, IL USA.

North, M.J., T.R. Howe, N.T. Collier, & J.R. Vos. (2007). "A Declarative Model Assembly Infrastructure for Verification and Validation." in S. Takahashi, D.L. Sallach and J. Rouchier, eds. *Advancing Social Simulation: The First World Congress*. Springer, Heidelberg, FRG.

M.J. North, T.R. Howe, N.T. Collier, & J.R. Vos. (2006c, October). "Demeter, Persephone, and the Search for Emergence in Agent-Based Models." *American Association for the Advancement of Artificial Intelligence 2006 Fall Symposium*. AAAI. Crystal City, VA USA.

North, M.J., & C. M. Macal. (2005, April). "Escaping the Accidents of History: An Overview of Artificial Life Modeling with Repast." in A. Adamatzky and

M. Komosinski, eds. *Artificial Life Models in Software*, pp. 115-141. Springer. Heidelberg, FRG.

North, M.J., & C.M. Macal. (2007, March). *Managing Business Complexity: Discovering Strategic Solutions with Agent-Based Modeling and Simulation*, Oxford, New York, NY USA.

Ntoulas, A., J. Cho, & C. Olston. (2004). "What's New on the Web?: The Evolution of the Web from a Search Engine Perspective." *Proceedings of the 13ᵗʰ International Conference on the World Wide Web*, (pp. 1-12). New York: ACM.

Papazoglou, M.P., & D. Georgakopoulos. (2003). "Service-Oriented Computing." *Communications of the ACM, 46*(10), 24-28.

Reynolds, C. W. (1987) "Flocks, Herds, and Schools: A Distributed Behavioral Model, in Computer Graphics." *SIGGRAPH 1987 Conference Proceedings, 21*(4), 25-34.

Reynolds, C. W. (2001). *Boids (Flocks, Herds, and Schools a Distributed Behavioral Model)*. Available as http://www.red3d.com/cwr/boids/

ROAD, *Repast Home Page*. (2007). Available as http://repast.sourceforge.net/. Repast Organization for Architecture and Design. Chicago.

Viswanath, K. (March 9, 2005) "Java Annotation Facility - A Primer." *Java Developers Journal Online*. Available as http://java.sys-con.com/read/48539.htm. SYS-CON Media

ADDITIONAL READING

Gamma, E., R. Helm, R. Johnson, & J. Vlissides. (1995). *Design Patterns: Elements of Reusable Object-Oriented Software*. Addison-Wesley, Wokingham, U.K..

Holland, J. H. (1995). *Hidden Order: How Adaptation Builds Complexity*. Reading, MA: Addison-Wesley.

North, M.J., N.T. Collier, & J.R. Vos. (2006, January). "Experiences Creating Three Implementations of the Repast Agent Modeling Toolkit." *ACM Transactions on Modeling and Computer Simulation, 16*(1), 1-25.

North, M. J., T. R. Howe, N. T. Collier, & J. R.. Vos. (2005a, October). "The Repast Simphony Runtime System," *Agent 2005 Conference on Generative Social Processes, Models, and Mechanisms*. Argonne National Laboratory. Argonne, IL.

North, M. J., T. R. Howe, N. T. Collier, & J. R. Vos. (2005b, October). "The Repast Simphony Development Environment." *Agent 2005 Conference on Generative Social Processes, Models, and Mechanisms*. Argonne National Laboratory. Argonne, IL.

North, M. J., T. R. Howe, N. T. Collier, & J. R. Vos. (2006, June) "Spaces, Places, and the Lernaean Hydra of Agent-Based Modeling." *North American Association for Computational Social and Organizational Science 2006 Conference*. Argonne National Laboratory. Argonne, IL.

North, M.J., T.R. Howe, N.T. Collier, & J.R. Vos. (2007). "A Declarative Model Assembly Infrastructure for Verification and Validation." in S. Takahashi, D.L. Sallach and J. Rouchier, eds. *Advancing Social Simulation: The First World Congress*. Heidelberg, Germany: Springer.

M.J. North, T.R. Howe, N.T. Collier, & J.R. Vos. (2006c, October). "Demeter, Persephone, and the Search for Emergence in Agent-Based Models." *American Association for the Advancement of Artificial Intelligence 2006 Fall Symposium*. Crystal City, VA: AAAI.

North, M.J., & C.M. Macal. (March 2007). *Managing Business Complexity: Discovering Strategic Solutions with Agent-Based Modeling and Simulation*. New York: Oxford.

ENDNOTES

1.   Please see North and Macal (2005) for further exploration of these ideas relative to artificial life.

2.   This discussion of Repast S follows North, Howe, Collier, and Vos (2005a, 2005b, 2006, and 2007).

3.   To simplify the exposition, this discussion assumes that the model design and implementation are sequential as is found in the waterfall

[4] model of software development. An iterative approach, as described in North and Macal (2007), is recommended for actual agent-based model development.

[4] Groovy (König et al. 2007) is such a dynamic language with the added benefit of tight integration with Java and, hence, the ability to integrate into Repast.

[5] More details on Java annotations can be found in Viswanath (2005).

[6] Contexts and projections are discussed in greater depth in North, Howe, Collier, and Vos (2006).

[7] Continuously numbered bullet points are intentionally used in this example to make it easier for readers to track the model construction process.

[8] The term "Score" as used here refers to the sheet music used to conduct a symphony orchestra.

Compilation of References

Abbeel, P. and Ng, A. Y. (2005). Exploration and apprenticeship learning in reinforcement learning. In *Proceedings of the 22nd International Conference on Machine Learning*.

Abelson, H. (1996). *Structure and Interpretation of Computer Programs*. Cambridge, MA, MIT Press.

Abelson, R. P. (1963). Computer simulation of 'hot' cognition. In S. S. Tomkins & S. Messick (Eds.), *Computer simulation of personality:Frontier of psychological research* (pp. 277-298). New York: John Wiley & Sons.

Ablowitz, R. (1939). The Theory of Emergence. *Philosophy of Science, 6*(1), 16.

Abramson, M., Chao, W., and Mittu, R. (2005). Design and evaluation of distributed role allocation algorithms in open environments. In *International Conference on Artificial Intelligence*, Las Vegas, NV.

Abramson, M., Pachowicz, P., and Wechsler, H. (2003). Competitive reinforcement learning for continuous control tasks. In *Proceedings of the International Neural Network Conference*.

Ackley, D. H. and Littman, M. S. (1990). Generalization and scaling in reinforcement learning. In Touretzky, D. S., editor, *Advances in Neural Information Processing Systems*, volume 2, pages 550-557, Denver 1989. Morgan Kaufmann, San Mateo.

ACNielsen, *Nielsen NetRatings for Search Engines.* (2004) Available at http://searchenginewatch.com/reports/article.php/2156451

Adamson, A., & Jenson, V. (2001). Shrek.

Agnew, Z.K., Bhakoo, K.K. & Puri, B.K. (2007). The human mirror system: A motor resonance theory of mind-reading. *Brain Research Reviews, 54*(2), 286-293.

Ahn, B. S. (2006). Multiattributed Decision Aid with Extended ISMAUT, *IEEE Transactions on Systems, Man and Cyberetics, Part A: Systems and Humans,* 36(3): 507-520.

Allen, J. F. (1999). Mixed-initiative interaction. *IEEE Intelligent Systems.*

Allport, G. W. (1985). The historical background of social psychology. In G. Lindzey & E. Aronson (Eds.), *The handbook of social psychology* (Vol. 1, pp. 1-46). Reading, MA: Addison-Wesley.

Alspaugh, T. A. (2005). *Temporally Expressive Scenarios in ScenarioML*. Institute for Software Research Technical Report UCI-ISR-05-06. University of California, Irvine.

American Law Institute (1966). *Restatement of the law Second, Torts 2d*. Washington, D.C.: American Law Institute.

Anderson, T., Schum, D., & Twining, W. (2005). *Analysis of evidence, Second Edition.* Cambridge, UK: Cambridge University Press.

Archer, M. (1998). Realism in the Social Sciences. In M. Archer, R. Bhaskar, A. Collier, T. Lawson & A. Norrie (Eds.), *Critical Realism: Essential Readings*. London: Routledge.

Argyle, M. (1994). *The psychology of interpersonal behaviour (5th Ed.).* St. Ives, UK: Penguin Books.

Aronson, E. (1998). *The social animal (7th Ed.).* USA: Freeman.

Aronson, E., Wilson, T. D., & Akert, R. M. (1997). *Social psychology (2nd Ed.) (Chapter 12. Aggression: Why we hurt other people).* USA: Addison-Wesley.

Arthur, W. B. (1994). Inductive reasoning and bounded rationality. *American Economic Review.*

Artz, J. (2000). The Role of Emotion in Reason and its Implications for Computer Ethics. *Computers and Society,* 14-16.

Ashley, K. D., & Rissland, E. L. (2003). Law, learning and representation. *Artificial Intelligence, 150,* 17-58.

Aunger, R. (ed.) (2000). *Darwinizing Culture: The Status of Memetics as a Science.* Oxford: OUP.

Axelrod, R. (1984). *The evolution of cooperation.* New York: Basic Books.

Axelrod, R. (1997). *The complexity of cooperation: agent-based models of competition and collaboration.* New Jersey: Princeton University Press.

Axelrod, R. (2003). *Advancing the Art of Simulation in the Social Sciences.* in Journal of the Japanese Society for Management Information Systems *12*(3).

Axtell, R., Epstein, J. & Young, H. (2001). The Emergence of Class Norms in a Multi-Agent Model of Bargaining. In Durlouf and Young (Ed.). *Social Dynamics.* Cambridge: MIT Press

Aziz-Zadeh, L., Koski, L., Zaidel, E., Mazziotta, J., & Lacoboni, M. (2006). Lateralization of the human mirror neuron system. *The Journal of Neuroscience, 26*(11), 2964-2970.

Baas, N. (1993). *Second order emergence.* Oral communication at the second European Conference on Artificial Life, ULB Brussels.

Badii, R. and Politi, A. (1997). *Hierarchical Structures and Scaling in Physics.* Cambridge, Cambridge University Press.

Bainbridge, W. (1995) Neural Network Models of Religious Belief. *Sociological Perspectives,* 38, 483-495.

Bainbridge, W. (2006) *God from the machine: Artificial Intelligence Models of Religious Cognition,* Lanham, MD: Rowman Altamira.

Bainbridge, W., & Stark, R. (1987). *A theory of religion.* New York: Lang.

Bak, P. (1996). *How Nature Works: The Science of Self-Organized criticality.* New York: Copurnicus.

Bandura, A. (1986). *Social foundations of thought and action: a social cognitive theory.* Englewood Cliffs, New Jersey: Prentice-Hall.

Barabasi, A. L. (2003) *Linked: How everything is connected to everything else and what it means for business, science, and everyday life,* Basic Books.

Barandiaran, X. (2005). Behavioral Adaptive Autonomy. A Milestone on the ALife roue to AI? Sansebastian, Spain: Department of Logic and Philosophy of Science, University of the Basque Country.

Baray, C. (1998). Effects of population size upon emergent group behavior. *Complexity International, 06.*

Baron, R. A., & Byrne, D. (1996). *Social psychology (8th Ed.) (Chapter 11. Aggression: Its nature, causes, and control.)* USA: Allyn and Bacon.

Barrett, J. L. & Nyhof, M. (2001). Spreading Non-natural concepts: the role of intuitive conceptual structures in memory and transmission of cultural materials. *Journal of Cognition and Culture,* 1, 69-100.

Batali, J. (2002). The negotiation and acquisition of recursive grammars as a result of competition among exemplars. In T. Briscoe (Ed.), *Linguistic Evolution through Language Acquisition: Formal and Computational Models* (pp. 111-172). Cambridge University Press.

Bates, J. (1994). The Role of Emotion in Believable Agents. *Communications of the ACM*, 37(7): 122-125.

Bateson, Gregory (1972). *Steps to an Ecology of Mind.* NY: Ballantine.

Baumer, E., Tomlinson, B., Yau, M.L., and Alspaugh, T.A. (2006). *Normative Echoes: Use and Manipulation of Player Generated Content by Communities of NPCs.* in AI in Interactive Digital Entertainment (AIIDE-06) Demonstration Program, Marina del Rey, CA, AAAI Press.

Becker, R. & Lesser, V. & Zilberstein, S. (2005). Analyzing Myopic Approaches for Multi-Agent Communication. In *Proceedings of the 2005 IEEE/WIC/ACM International Conference on Intelligent Agent Technology (IAT 05)*, 550– 557. Compiegne, France: IEEE Computer Society.

Bedau, M. (2002). Downward Causation and the Autonomy of Weak Emergence *Principia* 6(1),5-50.

Bednarz, J. (1988). Autopoesis: the Organizational Closure of Social Systems. *Systems Research, 5*(1), 57-64.

Bell, A. M. and Sethares, W. A. (2001). Avoiding global congestion using decentralized adaptive agents. *IEEE Transactions on Signal Processing*, 49(11).

Bem, D.J. (1967). An alternative interpretation of cognitive dissonance phenomena. *Psychological Review, 74*(3), 183-200.

Benda, M., Jagannathan, V., and Dodhiawalla, R. (1985). On optimal cooperation of knowledge sources. Technical Report BCS-G2010-28, Boeing AI Center, Boeing Computer Services.

Bergen, B., & Chang, N. (2003). Embodied construction grammar in simulation-based language understanding. In J. O. Ostman & M. Fried (Eds.), *Construction grammar(s): Cognitive and cross-language dimensions* (pp. 147-190). Amsterdam: Johns Benjamins.

Berger, P. L. and Luckmann, T. (1966). *The Social Construction of Reality: A Treatise on the Sociology of Knowledge.* New York, Irvington Publishers, Inc.

Berlekamp, E. R., Conway, J. H., & Guy, R. K. (1982). *Winning ways for your mathematical plays* (Vol. 2). Academic Press.

Berlin, M. (2003). *Predatory sequence learning for synthetic characters.* Masters Thesis, Media Arts & Sciences. Cambridge, MA, MIT.

Berndt, T.J. (1992). The features and effects of friendship in early adolescence. *Child Development, 53,* 1447-1460.

Berscheid, E., & Reis, H. (1998). Attraction and close relationships. In D. Gilbert, S. Fiske & G. Lindzey (Eds.), *The handbook of social psychology* (pp. 19-281). New York: McGraw-Hill.

Bertalanffy, L. v. (1950). An Outline of General Systems Theory. *British Journal for the Philosophy of Science, 1*(2).

Bertalanffy_von, L. (1968). *General Systems Theory.* New York: Braziller.

Besnard, P. (1989). *An introduction to default logic.* Berlin: Springer-Verlag.

Best, M. & Edmonds, B. (2001). Special Issue on Computational Memetics. *Journal of Memetics,* 4 (2), http://www.cpm.mmu.ac.uk/jom--emit/2001/vol4/index.html#issue2

Beyer, H., & Holtzblatt, K. (1999). Contextual design. *Interactions, 6(1),* 32-42.

Bhaskar, R. (1997). A Realist Theory of Science. In. London: Verso.

Bhaskar, R. (1998). *The Possibility of Naturalism.* London: Routledge.

Bickmore, T. W., & Picard, R. W. (2005). Establishing and maintaining long-term human-computer relationships. *ACM Trans. Comput.-Hum. Interact., 12*(2), 293-327.

Björkqvist, K. (1994). Sex differences in physical, verbal, and indirect aggression. *Sex Roles, 30(3/4),* 177-188.

Blackmore, S. (1999). *The Meme Machine.* Oxford: OUP.

Blanke, O., Ortigue, S., Landis, T., & Seeck, M. (2002). Stimulating illusory own-body perceptions. *Nature, 419*(6904), 269-270.

Blau, P. M. (1977). A macrosociological theory of social structure. *American Journal of Sociology, 83*(1), 26-54.

Blizzard Entertainment (developer). World of warcraft. Vivendi Universal (publisher). 2004.

Bloch, M. (2000) A well-disposed social anthropologist's problems with memes in *Darwinizing Culture: The Status of Memetics As A Science*, pp. 189-203, Oxford, UK: Oxford University Press.

Blok, H. J., & Bergersen, B. (1998, Apr). *Synchronous vs. asynchronous updating in the Game of Life.* Dept. of Physics and Astronomy, University of British Columbia, B.C., Canada, V6T 1Z1: .

Bloom, P. (2000). *How children learn the meanings of words.* Cambridge, MA: MIT Press.

Blow, M., Dautenhahn, K., Appleby, A., Nehaniv, C.L., & Lee, D.C. (2006). Perception of robot smiles and dimensions for human-robot interaction design. *Conference Proceedings RO-MAN 2006* (pp. 469-474).

Blumer, H. (1939). Collective behavior. In R. E. Park (Ed.), *An outline of the principles of sociology* (pp. 219-280). New York: Barnes & Noble.

Bodík, P., & Takáč, M. (2003). Formation of a common spatial lexicon and its change in a community of moving agents. In B. Tessem, P. Ala-Siuru, P. Doherty, & B. Mayoh (Eds.), *Frontiers in AI: Proceedings of the Eighth Scandinavian Conference on Artificial Intelligence SCAI'03* (pp. 37-46). Amsterdam: IOS Press.

Boellstorff, T. (2006). A ludicrous discipline? Ethnography and game studies. *Games and Culture, 1*(1), 29-35.

Boicu, M., Tecuci, G., and Marcu, D. (2005). Mixed-initiative assistant for modeling expert's reasoning. In *Proceedings of the AAAI-05 Fall Symposium on Mixed-Initiative Problem-Solving Assistants.*

Bonabeau, E. (2002). Agent-based modeling: methods and techniques for simulating human systems. *Proceedings of the National Academy of Sciences, 99,* 7280-7287.

Bonabeau, E., Dorigo, M., & Theraulaz, G. (1999). *Swarm intelligence: from natural to artificial systems.* USA: Oxford University Press.

Borcherdt, B. (1993) *You Can Control Your Feelings.* Professional Resource Press. Sarasota, Florida.

Bordini, R., Braubach, L., Dastani, M., Seghrouchni, A. E. F., Gomez-Sanz, J., Leite, J., . (2006). A survey of programming languages and platforms for multi-agent systems. In *Informatica 30,* 33-44.

Boulding, K. E. (1969). Economics as a moral science. *The American Economic Review, 59*(1), 1-12.

Bowles, S. (2001). Comment: Individual behavior and social interactions. *Sociological Methodology, 31,* 89-96.

Boyd, R., & Richerson, P. J. (1992). Punishment Allows the Evolution of Cooperation (or Anything Else) in Sizable Groups. *Ethology & Sociobiology,* 13:171-95.

Boyer, P. & Ramble, C. (2001). Cognitive templates for religious concepts. *Cognitive Science,* 25, 535-564.

Boyer, P. (1994). *The Naturalness of Religious Ideas: A Cognitive Theory of Religion,* Berkeley, CA: University of California Press.

Brachman, R. J., & Levesque, H. J. (2004). *Knowledge representation and reasoning.* Amsterdam: Elsevier.

Branting, L. K. (2000). *Reasoning with rules and precedents: A computational model of legal analysis.* Dordrecht, The Netherlands: Kluwer Academic Publishers.

Breazeal, C. (2002). *Designing sociable robots.* Cambridge, Massachusetts: MIT Press.

Breazeal, C. (2003). Emotion and sociable human robots. *International Journal of Human-Computer Studies, 59,* 119-155.

Breazeal, C., & Scassellatti, B. (2002). Robots that imitate humans. *Trends in Cognitive Sciences, 6*(11), 481-487.

Brehm, S. (1992). *Intimate relationships.* New York: McGraw-Hill.

Brenneis, D. (1984). Grog and gossip in Bhatgaon: Style and substance in Fiji Indian conversation. *American Ethnologist, 11,* 487-506.

Brewka, G., Dix, J., & Konolige, K. (1997). *Nonmonotonic reasoning: An overview.* Stanford, CA: CSLI Publications.

Briscoe, T. (Ed.). (2001). *Linguistic evolution through language acquisition: Formal and computational models.* Cambridge, U. K.: Cambridge University Press.

Brooks, R. A. (1991). Intelligence without representation. *Artificial Intelligence, 47* (1-3), 139-159.

Brooks, R. A. (1991). Intelligence without representation. *Intelligence without reason*(47), 569-595.

Brose, G. & Vogel, A. & Duddy, K. (2001). *Java Programming with CORBA, Third Edition.* New York, NY, USA: John Wiley & Sons, Inc.

Brown, P., & Levinson, S. (1978). Universals in language usage: Politeness phenomena. In E. N. Goody (Ed.), *Questions and politeness: Strategies in social interaction* (pp. 56-289). New York: Cambridge University Press.

Brown, R. (1965). *Social psychology.* New York: Free Press.

Brown, Steven D. (2002). Michel Serres. *Theory, Culture & Society* 19(3):1-27.

Bryson, J. J. (2007). Embodiment vs Memetics. Bath: Artificial Models of Natural Intelligence, University of Bath.

Bryson, J. J. (n.d). Representational Requirements for Evolving Cultural Evolution, *Interdiciplines.*

Bullinaria, J. A., & Levy, J. P. (2007). Extracting semantic representations from word co occurrence statistics: A computational study. *Behavior Research Methods, 39,* 510-526.

Burt, R.S. (1993). The Social Structure of Competition. In R. Swedberg (Ed.) *Explorations in Economic Sociology.* (pp. 56-103) New York: Russell Sage Foundation.

Buskens, V. (1998). *Social networks and the effect of reputation on cooperation.* ISCORE paper. Mar 1998. 18.

Buskens, V., & Weesie, J. (1999). Cooperation via Networks. *Analyse und Kritik* 22: 44-74

Cairns, R., & Cairns, B. (1994). *Lifelines and risks: Pathways of youth in our time.* Cambridge, UK: Cambridge University Press.

Camurri, A. & Coglio, A. (1998) An Architecture for E-motional Agents. *Multimedia,* 5(4): 24-33.

Camurri, A., Coglio, A., Coletta, P. & Massucco, C. (1997). An Architecture for Multimodal Environment Agents. *Proceedings of the International Workshop Kansei: Technology of Emotion,* 48-53.

Cangelosi, A. (1999). Modeling the evolution of communication: From stimulus associations to grounded symbolic associations. In D. Floreano, J. Nicoud, & F. Mondada (Eds.), *Proceedings of the 5th European Conference on Advances in Artificial Life* (pp. 654-663). Berlin: Springer.

Cangelosi, A. (2005). Approaches to grounding symbols in perceptual and sensorimotor categories. In H. Cohen & C. Lefebvre (Eds.), *Handbook of categoriza-*

tion in cognitive science (pp. 719-737). Amsterdam: Elsevier.

Cangelosi, A. (2006). The grounding and sharing of symbols. *Pragmatics and Cognition, 14* (2), 275-285.

Cangelosi, A., & Parisi, D. (2001). How nouns and verbs differentially affect the behavior of artificial organisms. In J. D. Moore & K. Stenning (Eds.), *Proceedings of the Twenty-third Annual Conference of the Cognitive Science Society* (pp. 170-175). London: Lawrence Erlbaum Associates.

Cantwell, J. (2005). A formal model of multi-agent belief-interaction. *Journal of Logic, Language, and Information, 14*(4), 397-422.

Cariani, P. (1990). Emergence and artificial life. In *Artificial Life II*. New Mexico: Santa Fe Institute.

Carley, K. M. & Hill, V. (2001). *Structural Change and Learning Within Organizations*, MIT Press/AAAI Press/Live Oak.

Carpenter, R. (2007). *Jabberwacky – live chatbot.* Retrieved December 8, 2007, from http://www.jabberwacky.com

Carr, W., & Kemmis, S. (1986). *Becoming Critical: Knowing Through Action Research*: Deakin University.

Cartwright, D. (1968). The nature of group-cohesiveness. In D. Cartwright & A. Zander (Eds.), *Group dynamics: Research and theory (3ʳᵈ Ed.)*. New York, USA: Harper & Row.

Carver, C. S., & Scheier, M. F. (1981). *Attention and self-regulation: a control-theory approach to human behavior*. New York: Springer-Verlag.

Castelfranchi, C. & Poggi, I. (1998). *Bugie Finzioni e Sotterfugi. Per una scienza dell'inganno*. Roma: Carocci.

Castelfranchi, C. (1992). No More Cooperation, Please! In Search of the Social Structure of Verbal Interaction. In A. Ortony, J. Slack & O. Stock (Eds.)

Communication from an Artificial Intelligence Perspective. Heidelberg, Germany: Springer.

Castelfranchi, C. (1998). Simulating with Cognitive Agents: The Importance of cognitive emergence. In J. S. Sichman, R. Conte & N. Gilbert (Eds.), *Multi-agent Systems and Agent Based SImulation*. Berlin: Springer.

Castelfranchi, C. (1998). Simulating with Cognitive Agents: The Importance of Cognitive Emergence. In J. S. Sichman, R. Conte & N. Gilbert (Eds.), *Lecture Notes in Artificial Intelligence*. Berlin: Springer Verlag.

Castelfranchi, C. (2000). **Engineering Social Order.** *Lecture Notes In Computer Science; 1972*: 1-18.

Castelfranchi, C. (2001). The Theory of Social Functions: Challenges for Computational Social Science and Multi-Agent Learning, *Cognitive Systems Research*, 2(1): 5-38.

Castelfranchi, C., Conte, R. & Paolucci, M. (1998) Normative reputation and the costs of compliance. *Journal of Artificial Societies and Social Simulation*, vol. 1, no. 3, available at: http://www.soc.surrey.ac.uk/JASSS/1/3/3.html

Cavalli Sforza, L.L., & Feldman, M.W. (1981). *Cultural Transmission and Evolution*, Princeton: PUP.

Cerf, V. (2007, August 24). *The Tech Lab: Vint Cerf.* BBC News. Available as http://news.bbc.co.uk/2/hi/technology/6960896.stm

Cerys, D. & Rozga, A. & Berliner, J. (2006). A cougaar-based logistics modeling tool for highly adaptable military organizations. *Cognitive Agent Architecture (Cougaar)*. Retrieved March 2006 from http://cougaar.org/docman/?group id=17.

Chalmers, D. J. (2006). Strong and Weak Emergence. Canberra: Research School of Social Sciences, Australian National University.

Chan, B. L., Witt, R., Charrow A. P., Magee, A., Howard, R., Pasquina, P. F., Heilman, K. M., & Tsao, J. W. (2007). Mirror therapy for phantom limb pain. *The New England Journal of Medicine*, 357(21), 2206-2207.

Chandler, D. (2007). *Semiotics: the basics* (Second ed.). London, New York: Routledge.

Checkland, P. (1988). *Systems Thinking Systems Practice*. G.B.: John Wiley.

Chierchia, G., & McConnell-Ginet, S. (2000). *Meaning and grammar: An introduction to Semantics*. Cambridge, MA: MIT Press.

Clark, Andy (2001). *Mindware*. New York: Oxford University Press.

Clark, E. (1987). The principle of contrast: A constraint on language acquisition. In B. MacWhinney (Ed.), *Mechanisms of language acquisition* (pp. 1-33). Hillsdale, NJ: Lawrence Erlbaum Associates

Clayton, P. (2006). Conceptual Foundations of Emergence Theory. In P. Clayton & P. Davies (Eds.), *The re-Emergecne of Emergence: The Emergentist Hypothesis from Science to Religion*. Oxford: Oxford University Press.

Clayton, P., & Davies, P. (2006). *The Re-Emergence of Emergence: The Emergentist Hypothesis from Science to Religion*. Oxford: Oxford University Press.

Clements, D. (1998, February). *Young children and technology*. Paper presented at the Forum on Early Childhood Science, Mathematics, and Technology Education, Washington DC, USA.

Cohen, I., Sebe, N., Garg, A., Chen, L. S., & Huang, T. S. (2003). Facial expression recognition from video sequences: temporal and static modeling. *Computer Vision and Image Understanding, 91*, 160-187.

Cohen, P. (1998). Dynamic maps as representations of verbs. In *Proceedings of the 13th Biennial European Conference on Artificial Intelligence* (pp. 145-149). New York: John Wiley & Sons.

Cohen, P., Oates, T., Atkin, M., & Beal, C. (1996). Building a baby. In G. W. Cottrell (Ed.), *Proceedings of the Eighteenth Annual Conference of the Cognitive Science Society* (pp. 518-522). Mahwah, NJ: Lawrence Erlbaum Associates.

Coleman, J. S. (1986). Social theory, social research, and a theory of action. *American Journal of Sociology, 91*(6), 1309-1335.

Coleman, J. S. (1987). Microfoundations and macrosocial behavior. In J. C. Alexander, B. Giesen, R. Münch & N. J. Smelser (Eds.), *The micro-macro link* (pp. 153-173). Berkeley, CA: University of California Press.

Coleman, J. S. (1990). *Foundations of social theory*. Cambridge: Harvard University Press.

Coleman, P., Pellon, M. & Zhang, Y. (2007). Towards Human Decision-Making in Multi-Agent Systems, in Proceedings of the *International Conference on Artificial Intelligence*, Monte Carlo Resort, Las Vegas, Nevada.

Collins, R. (1981). On the microfoundations of macrosociology. *American Journal of Sociology, 86*(5), 984-1014.

Collins, Samuel Gerald (2007). "If I'm Not in Control, Then Who Is?: the Politics of Emergence in Multiagent Systems." In Goran Trajkovski (Ed.), *An Imitation-Based Approach to Modeling Homogenous Agents Societies* (pp. 93-115). Hershey, PA: IDEA Publishing.

Conover, A., & Trajkovski, G. (2007, Nov 9–11). Effects of temporally asynchronous interaction on simple multi-agent behavior. In *Emergent agents and socialities: Social and organizational aspects of intelligence. technical report fs-07-04* (pp. 34–41). The American Association for Artificial Intelligence, 445 Burgess Drive, Menlo Park, CA, 94025, USA: AAAI Press.

Conte, R. & Paolucci, M. (2002). *Reputation in Artificial Societies: Social Beliefs for Social Order*. Boston: Kluwer.

Conte, R. (2000). Memes Through (Social) Minds. In R. Aunger (Ed.)

Conte, R. (2001). *Emergent (info) institutions*. Journal of Cognitive Systems Research, 2, 97-110.

Conte, R. (2002). Cognitive memetic analysis of reputation. *Cognitive Science Quarterly.*

Conte, R., Hegselmann, R., & Terna, P. (1997). *Simulating Social Phenomena.* Berlin: Springer.

Conway, J. H. (1976). *On numbers and games.* New York: Academic Press.

Copi, I. M., & Cohen, C. (1998). *Introduction to logic.* Upper Saddle River, NJ: Prentice Hall.

Coplien, J. O. (2001). *Software Patterns Home Page.* Available as http://hillside.net/patterns/

Corbin, J. M., & Strauss, A. (1990). Grounded theory research: Procedures, canons, and evaluative criteria. *Qualitative Sociology, 13*(1), 18.

Corman, J. (2005). Defining the Rules for Preemptive Host Protection. Retrieved March 7, 2008, from http://www.iss.net/documents/whitepapers/ISS_Preemptive_Host_Protection_Whitepaper.pdf

Cowie, H. (2000). Bystanding or standing-by: Gender issues in coping with bullying in English schools. *Aggressive Behaviour, 26,* 85-97.

Craig, W.M. (1998). The relationship among bullying, victimization, depression, anxiety and aggression in elementary school children. *Personality and Individual Differences, 24,* 123-130.

Crick, N.R., & Grotpeter, J.K. (1995). Relational aggression, gender, and social-psychological adjustment. *Child Development, 66,* 710-722.

Dabirsiaghi, A. & Trajkovski, G. (2006). Navigational Map Learning by Context Chaining and Abstraction. *2006 Fall AAAI Symposium.* October 12-15, 2006. Arlington, VA. USA.

Damasio, A. (1994). *Descartes' Error – Emotion, Reason, and the Human Brain.* New York, NY: Putnam Book.

Damper, R. I. (2000). Editorial for the special issue on 'Emergent properties of complex systems': Emergence and levels of abstraction. *International Journal of Systems Science, 31*(7): 811-818.

Darwin, C. (1872). *The expression of emotions in man and animals.* London: John Murray.

Das, S. & Grecu, D. (2000). **COGENT: Cognitive Agent to Amplify Human Perception and Cognition, in** *Proceedings of 4ᵗʰ International Conference on Autonomous Agents,* Barcelona, Spain, pp. 443-450.

Daubert v. Merrell Dow Pharmaceuticals, Inc., 509 U.S. 579 (1993).

Dautenhahn, K. (2001). The Narrative Intelligence Hypothesis: In Search of the Transactional Format of Narratives in Humans and Other Social Animals. In *Cognitive Technology* (pp. 248-266). Hiedelberg: Springer-Verlag.

Dautenhahn, K. (2002). Design spaces and niche spaces of believable social robots. *Conference Proceedings International Workshop on Robot and Human Interactive Communication* (pp.192-197).

Dautenhahn, K. (2002). The Origins of Narrative. *International Journal of Cognition and Technology, 1*(1), 97-123.

Dautenhahn, K., Bond, A. H., Canamero, L., & Edmonds, B. (2002). *Socially intelligent agents: Creating relationships with computers and robots.* Massachusetts, USA: Kluwer Academic Publishers.

Davidson, R. J. (1999). The functional neuroanatomy of emotion and affective style. *Trends in Cognitive Sciences, 3,* 11-21.

Davidson, R. J. (2003). Affective neuroscience and psychophysiology: Toward a synthesis. *Psycho-physiology, 40*(5), 655-665.

Davies, P. (2006). The Physics of Downward Causation. In P. Clayton & P. Davies (Eds.), *The Re-Emergence of Emergence: The Emergentist Hypothesis from Science to Religion.* Oxford: Oxford University Press.

Dawidowicz, R. (2007). *Social relationships in a multi-agent virtual environment.* Unpublished MPhil dissertation, University of Hertfordshire, UK.

Dawkins, R. (1989). The Selfish Gene, Oxford, UK: Oxford University Press.

De Jaegher, H., & Di Paolo, E. A. (2007). Participatory Sense-making: An enactive approach to Social Cognition. *Phenomenology and the cognitive Sciences, forthcoming.*

De Ridder, D., Van Laere, K., Dupont, P., Menovsky, T., & Van de Heyning, P. (2007). Visualizing out-of-body experience in the brain. *The New England Journal of Medicine, 357*(18), 1829-1833.

Deacon, T. W. (1997). *The symbolic species: The co-evolution of language and the brain.* New York: W.W. Norton & Co.

Deleuze, Gilles and Felix Guattari (1980). *A Thousand Plateaus.* Minneapolis: University of Minnesota Press.

Dennett, D. (1978). *Brainstorms.* Cambridge, Massachusetts: MIT Press.

Dennett, D. (1989). *The intentional stance.* Cambridge, Massachusetts: MIT Press.

Dennett, D. C. (1998). *Consciousness explained.* Cambridge, Massachusetts: The MIT Press.

Denning, D. (1987). An Intrusion-Detection Model. *IEEE Transactions on Software Engineering, 13*(2), 222-232.

Department for Education (1994). Don't suffer in silence: An anti-bullying pack for schools. London: HMSO.

Depasquale, J., Geller, S., Clarke, S. & Littleton, L. (2001). Measuring Road Rage: Development of the Propensity for Angry Driving Scale. *Journal of Safety Research*, 32(1): 1-16.

Dessalles J.L., Müller J.P., Phan D. (2007). "Emergence in multi-agent systems: conceptual and methodological issues" in Phan, Amblard, (Eds) *Agent Based Modelling and Simulations in the Human and Social Sciences,* (pp. 327-356) Oxford:The Bardwell Press,

Deutch, M. and Gerard, H. B. (1955). A study of normative and informational social influence upon judgment. *Journal of Abnormal and Social Psychology, 51,* 629-636.

Deveney, C. & Deldin, P. (2006) A Preliminary Investigation of Cognitive Flexibility for Emotional Information in Major Depressive Disorder and Non-Psychiatric Controls. *Emotion.* 2006 Aug, 6(3): 429-37.

Di Paolo, E. A., & Lizuka, H. (2007). How (not) to Model Autonomous Behaviour. *Biosystems.*

Di Paolo, E. A., Rohde, M., & De Jaegher, H. (2007). Horizons for The Enactive Mind: Values, Social Interaction and Play. In J. Stewart, O. Gapenne & E. A. Di Paolo (Eds.), *Enaction: Towards a New Paradigm for Cognitive Science.* Cambridge MA: MIT Press.

Dias, J. (2005). *FearNot!: Creating emotional autonomous synthetic characters for emphatic interactions.* Unpublished doctoral dissertation, Universidade Técnica de Lisboa, Portugal.

Dias, J., Ho, W.C., Vogt, T., Beeckman, N., Paiva, A., & André, E. (2007). I know what I did last summer: Autobiographic memory in synthetic characters. *Conference proceedings ACII 2007.* Berlin, Germany: Springer.

Dinstein, I., Hasson, U., Rubin, N., & Heeger, D.J. (2007). Brain areas selective for both observed and executed movements. *Journal of Neurophysiology,* 98, 1415-1427.

Dinstein, I., Thomas, C., Behrmann, M., & Heeger, D.J. (2008). A mirror up to nature. *Current Biology, 18*(1), R13-R18.

Director, Office of Workers' Compensation Programs, Department of Labor v. Greenwich Collieries, 512 U.S. 267 (1994).

Dobashi, Shingo (2005). The Gendered Use of *Keitai* in Domestic Contexts. In Mizuko Ito, Daisuke Okabe and Misa Matsuda (Eds.), *Personal, Portable, Pedestrian* (pp. 219-236). Cambridge: MIT Press.

Dobbs, D. R. (2000). *The law of torts*. St. Paul, Minnesota: West.

Doran, J. (1998). Simulating collective misbelieve. *Journal of Artificial Societies and Social Simulation, 1*(1).

Dörner, D., & Hille, K. (1995). Artificial souls: Motivated emotional robots. *Conference Proceedings Systems, Man and Cybernetics* (pp. 3828-3832). Institute of Electrical & Electronics Engineering.

Downey, Gary Lee, Joseph Dumit and Sarah Williams (1995). Cyborg Anthropology. *Cultural Anthropology* 10(2):264-269.

Druin, A., & Solomon, C. (1996). *Designing multimedia environments for children: Computers creativity and kids*. New York, USA: John Wiley and Sons.

Druin, A., Bederson, B., Boltman, A., Miura, A., Knotts-Callahan, D., Platt, M. (1998). Children as our technology design partners. In Druin, A. (Ed.). *The design of children's technology* (pp. 51-72). San Francisco, USA: Morgan Kaufmann

Duong, D V (1991). "A System of IAC Neural Networks as the Basis for Self Organization in a Sociological Dynamical System Simulation." Masters Thesis, The University of Alabama at Birmingham http://www.scs.gmu.edu/~dduong/behavior.html.

Duong, D V (1995). "Computational Model of Social Learning" *Virtual School* ed. Brad Cox. http://www.virtualschool.edu/mon/Bionomics/TraderNetworkPaper.html.

Duong, D V (1996). "Symbolic Interactionist Modeling: The Coevolution of Symbols and Institutions." *Intelligent Systems: A Semiotic Perspective Proceedings of the 1996 International Multidisciplinary Conference*, Vol 2, pp. 349 - 354. http://www.scs.gmu.edu/~dduong/semiotic.html.

Duong, D V (2004). *SISTER: A Symbolic Interactionist Simulation of Trade and Emergent Roles*. Doctoral Dissertation, George Mason University, Spring.

Duong, D V and John Grefenstette (2005). "The Emulation of Social Institutions as a Method of Coevolution" *GECCO conference proceedings*. http://www.scs.gmu.edu/~dduong/gecco.pdf.

Duong, D V and John Grefenstette (2005). *SISTER: A Symbolic Interactionist Simulation of Trade and Emergent Roles. Journal of Artificial Societies and Social Simulation*, January 2005. http://jasss.soc.surrey.ac.uk/8/1/1.html.

Duong, D V and Kevin D. Reilly (1995). "A System of IAC Neural Networks as the Basis for Self Organization in a Sociological Dynamical System Simulation." *Behavioral Science*, 40,4, 275-303. http://www.scs.gmu.edu/~dduong/behavior.html.

Duranti, A., & Goodwin, C. (Eds.). (1992). *Rethinking context: Language as an interactive phenomenon*. New York: Cambridge University Press.

Durlauf, S. N., & Young, H. P. (2001). The new social economics. In S. N. Durlauf & H. P. Young (Eds.), *Social dynamics* (pp. 1-14). Cambridge: MIT Press.

Duval, S., & Wicklund, R. A. (1972). *A theory of objective self-awareness*. New York: Academic Press.

Ehrsson, H.H. (2007). The experimental induction of out-of-body experiences. *Science, 317*(5841), 1048.

Ekman, P. (1965). Communication through nonverbal behavior: a source of information about an interpersonal relationship. In S. S. Tomkins (Ed.), *Affect, cognition, and personality* (pp. 390-442). New York: Springer-Verlag.

Ekman, P., & Friesen, W. V. (1975). *Unmasking the face*. Englewood Cliffs, New Jersey: Prentice-Hall.

Ekman, P., Friesen, W. V., & Ellsworth, P. (1982). What are the similarities and differences in facial behavior across cultures. In P. Ekman (Ed.), *Emotion in the human face* (pp. 56-97). Cambridge, England: Cambridge University Press.

Elkies, N. D. (1998). Voronoi's impact on modern science. In (Vol. 1, pp. 228–253). Institute of Math., Kyiv.

Ellis, G. F. R. (2006). On the Nature of Emergent Reality. In P. Clayton & P. Davies (Eds.), *The Re-Emergence of Emergence: The Emergentist Hypothesis from Science to Religion.* Oxford: Oxford University Press.

Ellsberg, D. (1961). Risk, ambiguity and the Savage axioms. *Quarterly Journal of Economics.*

Engels, F. (1934). *Dialectics of Nature.* Moscow: Progress Publishers.

Epstein, J. & Axtell, R. (1996). *Growing Artificial Societies: Social Science from the Bottom Up,* The MIT Press.

Epstein, J. (2001) Learning to be thoughtless: Social norms and individual computation. *Computational Economics,* 18(1), 9-24.

Epstein, J. M. (1999). Agent-based computational models and generative social science. *Complexity, 4*(5), 41-60.

Epstein, J. M. (2006). *Generative social science: Studies in agent-based computational modeling.* Princeton, NJ: Princeton University Press.

Epstein, J. M., & Axtell, R. (1996). *Growing artificial societies: Social science from the bottom up.* Cambridge, MA: MIT Press.

Erl, T. (2005). *Service-Oriented Architecture:Concepts, Technology, and Design, Upper Saddle River: Prentice Hall PTR.*

Eronen, M. (2004). *Emergence in the Philosophy of Mind.* University of Helsinki, Helsinki.

Etzioni, A. (1991). Socio-economics: A budding challenge. In A. Etzioni & P. R. Lawrence (Eds.), *Socio-economics: Toward a new synthesis* (pp. 3-7). Armonk, NY: M. E. Sharpe, Inc.

Evans, R. R. (Ed.). (1969). *Readings in collective behavior.* Chicago: Rand McNally & Company.

Faigman, D. L., Kaye, D. H., Saks, M. J., & Sanders, J. (2002). *Science in the Law (3 Vols.).* St. Paul, Minnesota: West Group.

Farrington, D.P. (1993). Understanding and preventing bullying. In M. Tonry (Ed.), *Crime and justice, Vol. 17.*

Fauconnier, G. (1985). *Mental spaces: Aspects of meaning construction in natural language.* Cambridge, MA: MIT Press.

Federal Rules of Civil Procedure (2006).

Federal Rules of Evidence (2006).

Feldman, M. W. (2003). Dissent with modification: The science of culture exists. In the *Proceedings of the Conference "Toward a Scientific Concept of Culture."* Stanford University, January 23-26.

Ferber, J. (1999). *Multi-Agent System: An Introduction to Distributed Artificial Intelligence,* Harlow: Addison Wesley Longman.

Fillmore, C. J. (1982). Frame semantics. In *Linguistics in the morning calm* (pp. 111-137). Seoul: Hanshin Pub. Co.

FIPA (2006). FIPA abstract architecture specification. *Foundation for Intellligent Physical Agents.* Retrieved May 2006 from http://www.fipa.org/specifications.

FIPA (2008). FIPA agent message transport protocol for IIOP specification. *Foundation for Intellligent Physical Agents.* Retrieved January 2008 from http://www.fipa.org/specifications.

Fodor, J. A. (1974). Special; Sciences or The Disunity of Science as a Working Hypothesis. *Synthese, 28,* 18.

Fodor, J. A. (1981). *Representations: Philosophical essays on the foundations of cognitive science.* Cambridge, MA: MIT Press.

Fodor, J. A. (1983). *The modularity of mind.* Bradford Books. Cambridge, MA: MIT Press.

Fogassi, L., & Ferrari, P. F. (2007). Mirror neurons and the evolution of embodied language. *Current Directions in Psychological Science, 16*(3), 136-141.

Fonseca, S. P., Griss, M. L., & Letsinger, R. (2002, Mar 22). *Agent behavior architectures – A MAS frame-*

work comparison (Tech. Rep. No. HPL-2001-332). : Hewlett Packard Laboratories.

Forrester, J. W. (1962). *Industrial Dynamics*. Massachusetts Institute of Technology (M.I.T.) Press. Cambridge, MA.

Forslund, D. W. & Smith, R. K. & Culpepper, T. C. (2000). Federation of the person identification service between enterprises. *Proceedings of the AMIA 2000 Symposium*. Pages 240-244.

Forsyth, D.R. (1999). *Group dynamics (3ʳᵈ Ed.)*. Belmont, USA: Wadsworth Publishing Company.

Fox, M. D., Snyder, A.Z., Vincent, J. L., Corbetta, M., Van Essen, D. C., & Raichle, M. E. (2005). The human brain is intrinsically organized into dynamic, anticorrelated functional networks. *Proceedings of the National Academy of Sciences of the United States of America, 102*(27), 9673-9678.

Fox, M.D. & Raichle, M.E. (2007). Spontaneous fluctuations in brain activity observed with functional magnetic resonance imaging. *Nature Reviews Neuroscience, 8*, 700-711.

Franklin, S. (1998). *Artificial Minds*. London: MIT press.

Frijda, N. Emotions are functional, most of the time. In P. Ekman & R. Davidson (Eds.), The nature of emotion (pp. 11-122). New York: Oxford University Press.

Froesea, T., Virgo, N., & Izquierdo, E. (2007). Autonomy: a review and a reappraisal. Brighton Uk: University of Sussex.

Fuchs, C., & Hofkirchner, W. (2005). The Dialectic of Bottom-up and Top-down Emergence in Social Systems. *tripleC 1*(1), 22.

Gadanho, S. & Hallam, J. (1998). Exploring the role of emotions in autonomous robot learning. In Cañamero, D., ed., *Emotional and Intelligent: The Tangled Knot of Cognition*, Menlo Park, CA: AAAI Press.

Gallese, V. (2007). Before and below 'Theory of Mind': Embodied simulation and the neural correlates of social cognition. *Philosophical Transactions of the Royal Society B: Biological Sciences, 362*(1480), 659-669.

Gallese, V., & Goldman, A. (1998). Mirror neurons and the simulation theory of mind-reading. *Trends in Cognitive Sciences, 2*(12), 493-501.

Gallese, V., Fadiga, L., Fogassi, L., & Rizzolatti, G. (1996). Action recognition in the premotor cortex. *Brain, 119*, 593-609.

Gamma, E., R. Helm, R. Johnson, & J. Vlissides. (1995). *Design Patterns: Elements of Reusable Object-Oriented Software*. Wokingham, UK: Addison-Wesley.

Gärdenfors, P. (1996a). Cued and detached representations in animal cognition. *Behavioral Processes, 35*, 263-273.

Gärdenfors, P. (1996b). Language and the evolution of cognition. In V. Rialle & D. Fisette (Eds.), *Penser l'esprit: Des sciences de la cognition a' une philosophie cognitive* (pp. 151-172). Grenoble: Presses Universitaires de Grenoble.

Gärdenfors, P. (2000). *Conceptual spaces*. Cambridge, MA: MIT Press.

Gärdenfors, P. (2004). Cooperation and the evolution of symbolic communication. In K. Oller & U. Griebel (Eds.), *The evolution of communication systems* (pp. 237-256). Cambridge, MA: MIT Press.

Gardenfors, P. (2006). *How Homo became Sapiens: On the evolution of Thinking*. Oxford: Oxford University Press.

Gardner, M. (1970). Mathematical Games: The Fantastic Combinations of John Conway's Game of 'Life'. *Scientific American,* 112-117.

Garfinkel, H. (1967). *Studies in Ethnomethodology* Los Angeles: University of California

Garfinkel, H. and Sacks, H. (1970). Formal structures of practical action. In J. C. McKinney and E. A. Tiryakian (eds.), *Theoretical Sociology*. New York: Appleton Century Crofts.

Gaston, M. E., & desJardins, M. (2005, July 25-29). Agent-organized networks for dynamic team formation. In F. Dignum, V. Dignum, S. Koenig, S. Kraus, M. P. Singh, & M. Wooldridge (Eds.), *4rd international joint conference on autonomous agents and multiagent systems (AAMAS 2005)*, (pp. 230-237). *Utrecht, The Netherlands*: ACM.

Gell-Mann, M. (1995). *The Quark and the Jaguar: Adventures in the simple and the complex.* Great Britain: Abacus.

General Electric Co. v. Joiner, 522 U.S. 136 (1997).

Gerkey, B. P. and Mataric, M. J. (2004). *RobotCup 2003*, volume 3020, chapter On Role Allocation in RobotCup. Springer-Verlag Heidelberg.

Gibson, David (2003). Participation Shifts. *Social Forces* 81(4):1335-1381.

Giddens, A. (1979). Agency, structure. In A. Giddens, *Central Problems in Social Theory.* Berkeley: University of California Press.

Giddens, A. (1984). *The constitution of society: Outline of the theory of structuration.* Berkeley: University of California Press.

Gilbert, N. & Conte, R. (1995) *Artificial Societies: The Computer Simulation of Social Life*, London, UK: UCL Press.

Gilbert, N. (1995). Emergence in social simulation. In N. Gilbert and R. Conte (Eds.), *Artificial societies: The computer simulation of social life,* (pp. 144-156). London, UCL Press.

Gilbert, N. (2002). *Varieties of Emergence.* Paper presented at the Social Agents: Ecology, Exchange, and Evolution Conference Chicago.

Gilbert, N., & Troitzsch, K. (1999). *Simulation for the social scientists.* The Open Univ. Press.

Gilbert, N., Besten, M. den, Bontovics, A., Craenen, B. G. W., Divina, F., Eiben, A. E., Griffioen, R., Hévízi, G., Lörincz, A., Paechter, B., Schuster, S., Schut, M. C., Tzolov, C., Vogt, P., & Yang, L. (2006). Emerging Artificial Societies Through Learning [Electronic version]. *Journal of Artificial Societies and Social Simulation, 9* (2) 9.

Gilbert, N., Schuster, S., et al. (2005). Environment design for emerging artificial societies. In *Artificial Intelligence and the Simulation of Behavior 2005 Conference: Social Intelligence and Interaction in Animals, Robots and Agents.* Hatfield, UK.

Ginsberg, M. (Ed.). (1987). *Readings in nonmonotonic reasoning*, San Mateo, CA: Morgan Kaufmann.

Gintis, H., Smith, E. A., Bowles, S. (2001). Costly Signaling and Cooperation. *J. Theor. Biol.* 213, 103-119

Giummarra, M. J., Gibson, S. J., Georgiou-Karistianis, N., & Bradshaw, J. L. (2007). Central mechanisms in phantom limb perception: The past, present and future. *Brain Research Reviews, 54*(1), 219-232.

Glushko, R., J. Tenenbaum, & B. Meltzer. (1999). An XML Framework for Agent-based E-commerce. *Communications of the ACM, 42*(3).

Gmytrasiewicz, P. J. & Noh, S. (2002). Implementing a Decision-Theoretic Approach to Game Theory for Socially Competent Agents, in Parsons, S., Gmytrasiewicz, P., and Wooldridge, M. (eds.), *Game Theory and Decision Theory in Agent-Based Systems*, pp. 97-118, Kluwer Academic Publishers.

Goldspink, C. (2000). *Social Attractors: An Examination of the Applicability of Complexity theory to Social and Organisational Analysis.* Unpublished PhD, University Western Sydney, Richmond.

Goldspink, C., & Kay, R. (2003). Organizations as Self Organizing and Sustaining Systems: A Complex and Autopoietic Systems Perspective. *International Journal General Systems, 32*(5), 459-474.

Goldspink, C., & Kay, R. (2004). Bridging the Micro-Macro Divide: a new basis for social science. *Human Relations, 57* (5), 597-618.

Goldstone, R., Jones, A., & Roberts, M. E. (2006). Group Path Formation, *IEEE Transactions on Systems, Man, and Cybernetics, Part A: Systems and Humans,* 36(3):611-620.

Goleman, D. (1994). *Emotional Intelligence*. New York, NY: Bantam Dell.

Goncalves, B. & Esteves, S. (2006). Cognitive Agents Based Simulation for Decision Regarding Human Team Composition, in *Proceedings of 5ᵗʰ International Conference on Autonomous Agents and Multi-Agent Systems* **(AAMAS'06), pp. 34-41.**

Gonce, L. Upal, M., Slone, J. Tweney, R. (2006) Role of Context in the Recall of Counterintuitive Concepts, *Journal of Cognition and Culture*, 6 (3-4), 521-547.

Gong, T., Ke, J., Minett, J. W., & Wang, W. S. (2004). A Computational Framework to Simulate the co-evolution of language and social structure.

Goodwin, B. C. (1978). A cognitive view of biological process. *Journal of Social and Biological Structures, 1*, 117-125.

Gosper, W. (1984). Exploiting regularities in large cellular spaces. *Physica-D, 10*, 75–80.

Gotlib, I. (1983). Perception and Recall of Interpersonal Feedback: Negative Bias in Depression. *Cognitive Therapy and Research*, 7(5): 399-412.

Gottwald, S. (2001). *A treatise on many-valued logics*. Baldock, England: Research Studies Press.

Gouda, M. G., & Liu, X. A. (2004). Firewall Design: Consistency, Completeness, and Compactness. Paper presented at the 24th International Conference on Distributed Computing Systems.

Granovetter, M. (1985). Economic action and social structure: The problem of embeddedness. *American Journal of Sociology, 91*(3), 481-510.

Granovetter, M. (1990). The old and the new economic sociology: A history and an agenda. In R. Friedland & A. F. Robertson (Eds.), *Beyond the marketplace: Rethinking economy and society* (pp. 89-112). New York: Aldine de Gruyter.

Granovetter, M., & Swedberg, R. (Eds.). (1992). *The sociology of economic life*. Boulder, CO: Westview.

Gratch, J., & Marsella, S. (2001). Tears and fears: Modelling emotions and emotional behaviours in synthetic agents. *Conference Proceedings AGENTS'01* (pp. 278-285).

Greenberg, L. (2002) *Emotion-focused Therapy: Coaching Clients to Work through Their Feelings*. Washington, DC : American Psychological Association.

Grice, P. (1969). "Utterer's Meaning and Intention," *The Philosophical Review* 78: 147-77

Gu, G., Porras, P., Yegneswaran, V., Fong, M., & Lee, W. (2007). *BotHunter: Detecting Malware Infection Through IDS-Driven Dialog Correlation*. Paper presented at 16th USENIX Security Symposium.

Gulick, R. van. (1988). Consciousness, intrinsic intentionality and self-understanding machines. In A. J. Marcel & E. Bisiach (Eds.), *Consciousness in contemporary science* (pp. 78-100). Oxford, U. K.: Clarendon Press.

Gulz, A., & Haake, M. (2006). Visual design of virtual pedagogical agents: Naturalism versus stylization and static appearance. *Conference Proceedings NordiCHI 2006*.

Guttman, L. (1950). The basis for scalogram analysis. In A. Samuel (Ed.). *Measurement and prediction*. Princeton, USA: Princeton University Press.

Hales, D and Bruce Edmonds (2003). *Can Tags Build Working Systems? From MABS to ESOA*. Working Paper, Center For Policy Modelling, Manchester, UK.

Hales, D. & Edmonds, B. (2003). Evolving Social Rationality for MAS using "Tags", in *Proceedings of 5ᵗʰ International Conference on Autonomous Agents and Multi-Agent Systems* (AAMAS'03), pp. 497-503.

Hales, D. (2004). Tags for All! - Understanding and Engineering Tag Systems. *4th International Conference on Complex Systems (ICCS 2004)* New York: Springer Verlag

Hall, L., & Woods, S. (2004). Empathic interaction with synthetic characters: The importance of similarity. *Unpublished Manuscript*.

Hall, L., Jones, S., Hall, M., Richardson, J., & Hodgson, J. (2007). Inspiring design: the use of photo elicitation and lomography in gaining the child's perspective. *Conference Proceedings British HCI 2007.*

Hall, L., Vala, M., Hall, M., Webster, M., Woods, S., Gordon, A., & Aylett, R. (2006). FearNot!'s appearance: Reflecting on children's expectations and perspectives. *Conference Proceedings IVA 2006* (pp. 407-419). Berlin, Germany: Springer.

Hall, L., Woods, S., Aylett, R., Newall, L., & Paiva, A. (2005). Achieving empathic engagement through affective interaction with synthetic characters. *Conference Proceedings ACII 2005* (pp. 731-738). Berlin, Germany: Springer.

Hall, L., Woods, S., Dautenhahn, K., & Wolke, D. (2004). FearNot! designing in the classroom. *Conference Proceedings HCI 2004.* London, UK: Springer-Verlaq.

Hall, L., Woods, S., Dautenhahn, K., Sobral, D., Paiva, A., Wolke, D., & Newall, L. (2004). Designing empathic agents: Adults vs Kids. *Conference Proceedings ITS 2004* (604-613). Berlin, Germany: Springer.

Harmon-Jones, E. (2003). Early Career Award. Clarifying the emotive functions of asymmetrical frontal cortical activity. *Psychophysiology, 40*(6), 838-848.

Harnad, S. (1990). The Symbol Grounding Problem. *Physica, 42,* 335-346.

Harris, Jan (2005). The Ordering of Things. Supplement to *Sociological Review.*

Hastie, R. (Ed.) (2006). *Inside the juror: The psychology of juror decision making.* Cambridge, UK: Cambridge University Press.

Hautamäki, J. (1997). *A survey of frameworks* (Tech. Rep. No. A-1997-3). : Department of Computer Science, University of Tampere.

Hayden, S. & Carrick, C. & and Yang, Q. (1999). Architectural design patterns for multi-agent coordination. *Proceedings of the International Conference on Agent Systems '99 (Agents'99).* Seattle, WA,

May 1999. Available WWW . http://citeseer.ist.psu.edu/hayden99architectural.html

Hayles, N. Katherine (1999). *How We Became Post-Human.* Chicago: University of Chicago Press.

He, M. (2004). Designing Bidding Strategies for Autonomous Trading Agents. *Thesis, University of Southampton.*

Hedström, P. (2005). *Dissecting the social: On the principles of analytic sociology.* Cambridge, UK: Cambridge University Press.

Hedström, P., & Swedberg, R. (Eds.). (1998). *Social mechanisms: An analytical approach to social theory.* New York: Cambridge University Press.

Heider, F. (1958). *The psychology of interpersonal relations.* New York: John Wiley & Sons.

Helal A., A. Jagatheesan, & M. Wang. (2001). Service-Centric Brokering in Dynamic E-Business Agent Communities. *Journal of Electronic Commerce Research (JECR),* Baltzer Science Publishers.

Helmreich, Stefan (1998). *Silicon Second Nature.* Berkeley: University of California Press.

Henjes, R., Menth, M., & Zepfel, C. (2006). Throughput performance of Java messaging services using Sun Java System message queue. *High Performance Computing & Simulation Conference (HPC&S), Bonn, Germany.*

Hillersberg, J. & Mooonen, H. & Verduijn, T. & Becker, J. (2004). *Agent technology in supply chains and networks.* In Proceedings of the IEEE/WIC/ACM International Conference on Intelligent Agent Technology (IAT '04). Beijing, China, September 2004.

Hinds, P., Roberts, T., & Jones, H. (2004). Whose job is it anyway? A study of human-robot interaction in a collaborative task. *Human Computer Interaction, 19,* 151-181.

Hirshleifer, J. (1985). The expanding domain of economics. *American Economic Review, 75*(6), 53-68.

Hitchcock, D. , & Verheij, B. (2006). *Arguing on the Toulmin Model: New essays in argument analysis and evaluation.* Dordrecht, The Netherlands: Springer.

Hoffner, C., & Cantor, J. (1991). Perceiving and responding to media characters. In J. Bryant & D. Zillman (Eds.), *Responding to the screen: Reception and reaction processes* (pp. 63-101). Hillsdale, NJ, USA: Erlbaum.

Hofstadter, D. R. (2007). I am a Strange Loop. In: Basic Books.

Hofstede, G. (1994) *Cultures and Organizations*, New York, NY: McGraw-Hill.

Hogg, L. & Jennings, N. R. (2001). Socially Intelligent Reasoning for Autonomous Agents, *IEEE Transactions on Systems, Man and Cybernetics - Part A*, 31(5):381-399.

Hoggendoorn, M. (2007). Adaptation of Organizational Models for Multi-Agent Systems Based on Max Flow Networks , *IJCAI'07*, pp. 1321-1326.

Holland, J H (1975). *Adaptation in Natural and Artificial Systems.* Ann Arbor: University of Michigan Press.

Holland, J. (1993). The *Effects of Lables (Tags) on Social Interactions.* Sante Fe Institute Working Papers. Santa Fe: The Santa Fe Institute.

Holland, J. (1998). *Emergence: from chaos to order.* UK: Oxford University Press.

Holland, J. H. (1995). *Hidden Order: How Adaptation Builds Complexity*, Addison-Wesley, Reading, MA.

Holland, O. (Ed.) (2003). Machine Consciousness [Special Issue]. *Journal of Consciousness Studies, 10* (4-5).

Horling, B. & Lesser, V. & Vincent, R. & and Wagner, T. (2006). The Soft Real-Time Agent Control Architecture. *Autonomous Agents and Multi-Agent Systems* 12(1):35–92. An earlier version is available as UMass Computer Science Technical Report 2002-14.

Howell, S. R., & Becker, S. (n.d). Modelling Language Aquisition: Grammar from the Lexicon?

Humphrys, M. (1995). W-learning: Competition among selfish q-learners. Technical Report 362, University of Cambridge.

Hunter, S.C., Boyle, J.M.E., & Warden, D. (2004). Help seeking amongst child and adolescent victims of peer-aggression and bullying: The influence of school-stage, gender, victimisation, appraisal, and emotion. *British Journal of Educational Psychology, 74*, 375-390.

Hurford, J. (2000). Social transmission favors linguistic generalization. In C. Knight, M. Studdert-Kennedy and J. Hurford (Eds.), *The Evolutionary Emergence of Language: Social Function and the Origins of Linguistic Form* (pp. 324-352). Cambridge University Press.

Hurwicz, L. (1951). Optimality criteria for decision making under ignorance. In *Cowles Commission Discussion Paper, Statistics*, number 370.

Hutchins, E., & Hazlehurst, B. (1995). How to invent a lexicon: the development of shared symbols. In N. Gilbert & R. Conte (Eds.), *Artificial Societies.* London: UCL Press.

Icogno (2007). *What AI techniques does Jabberwacky use?* Retrieved on December 8, 2007, from http://www.icogno.com/what_ai_techniques.html

Intelligent Artificial Agents, T. F. for. (2007, Nov). *FIPA specifications.*

Irvine, J. T. (1974). Strategies of status manipulation in the Wolof greeting. In R. Bauman & J. Sherzer (Eds.), *Explorations in the ethnography of speaking* (pp. 167-191). New York: Cambridge University Press.

Isen, A., Nygren, T. & Ashby, G. (1988). Influence of Positive Affect on the Subjective Utility of Gains and Losses: It Is Just Not Worth the Risk. *Journal of Personality and Social Psychology*, 55(5): 710–717.

Izard, C. (1977). *Human emotions.* New York: Plenum Press.

Jackson, M. C. (2000). *Systems Approaches to Management*. London: Kluwer Academic.

James, Jr., F., Hazard, Jr., G. C., & Leubsdorf, J. (1992). *Civil procedure*. Boston, Toronto, London: Little, Brown.

JChart2D. (2007). *JChart2D scientific visualization*. (See: http://jchart2d.sourceforge.net)

Jiang, Y. & Ishida T. (2007). A Model for Collective Strategy Diffusion in Agent Social Law Evolution, *IJCAI'07*, pp. 1353-1358.

Johnson, A., Roussos, M., Leigh, J., Vasilakis, C., Barnes, C., & Moher, T. (1998). The NICE project: learning together in a virtual world. *Conference Proceedings IEEE 1998* (pp. 176-183).

Johnson, M. (1990). *The Body in the Mind: The Bodily Basis of Meaning, Imagination and Reason*. Chicago: The University of Chicago Press.

Jones, E. E. (1990). *Interpersonal perception*. New York: Freeman.

Jones, E. E., & Davis, K. E. (1965). From acts to dispositions: the attribution process in social psychology. In L. Berkowitz (Ed.), *Advances in experimental social psychology* (Vol. 2, pp. 219-266). New York: Academic Press.

Jones, E. E., & Harris, V. A. (1967). The attribution of attitudes. *Journal of Experimental Social Psychology, 3*, 1-24.

Jong, E. de, & Vogt, P. (1998). How should a robot discriminate between objects? A comparison between two methods. In *Proceedings of the Fifth International Conference on Simulation of Adaptive Behavior SAB'98* (pp. 86-91). Cambridge, MA: MIT Press.

Josephson, J. R., & Tanner, M. C. (1996). Conceptual analysis of abduction. In Josephson, J. R., & Josephson, S. G. (Eds.), *Abductive inference,* (pp. 5-30). UK: Cambridge University Press.

Julier, S., Livingston, M. A., Swan, J. E., Baillot, Y., and Brown, D. (2003). Adaptive user interfaces in augmented reality. In *Proceedings of workshop on Software Technology for Augmented Reality Systems (STARS), 2nd International Symposium on Mixed and Augmented Reality*.

Kadane, J. B., & Schum, D. A. (1996). *A probabilistic analysis of the Sacco and Vanzetti evidence*. New York: John Wiley & Sons.

Kaelbling, L. P., Littman, M. L., et al. (1996). Reinforcement learning: A survey. *Journal of Artificial Intelligence Research 4*, 237-285.

Kahneman, D. & Tversky, A. (1979). Prospect Theory: An Analysis of Decision under Risk, *Econometrica*, 47(2): 263-292.

Kahneman, D. (2002). Maps of Bounded Rationality: A Perspective on Intuitive Judgment and Choice, *Les Prix Nobel*.

Kahneman, D., Slovic, P., & Tversky, A. (Eds.). (1982). *Judgment under uncertainty: heuristics and biases*. UK: Cambridge University Press.

Kalakota, R., & M. Robinson. (1999). E-Business: Roadmap for Success. *Addison-Wesley Information Technology Series*, Addison-Wesley, Reading, MA.

Kant, J. & Thiriot, S. (2006). Modeling One Human Secision Maker with A Multi-agent System: The COD-AGE Approach, in *Proceedings of 5th International Conference on Autonomous Agents and Multi-Agent Systems* (AAMAS'06), pp. 50-57.

Kapoor, A., & Picard, R. W. (2005). *Multimodal affect recognition in learning environments*. Paper presented at ACM international conference on Multimedia, Singapore.

Kauffman, S. (2000). *Investigations*. New York: Oxford.

Kauffman, S. A. (1993). *The Origins of Order: Self Organization and Selection in Evolution*: Oxford University Press.

Kauffman, S. A. (1996). *At home in the Universe: The Search for Laws of Complexity*. London: Penguin.

Kay, R. (1999). *Towards an autopoietic perspective on knowledge and organisation.* Unpublished PhD, University of Western Sydney, Richmond.

Keeney, B. P. (1987). *Aesthetics of change*: Guilford.

Kegl, J., Senghas, A., & Coppola, M. (1999). Creation through contact: Sign language emergence and sign language change in Nicaragua. In M. DeGraff (Ed.), *Language creation and language change: creolization, diachrony, and development.* Cambridge, MA: MIT Press.

Kelemen, J. (2003). The agent paradigm. *Computing and Informatics, 22,* 513-519.

Kelley, H. H. (1955). The two functions of reference groups. In G. E. Swanson, T. M. Newcomb and E. L. Hartley (eds.) *Readings in social psychology,* (pp. 410-414). New York: Holt.

Kelley, H. H. (1967). Attribution theory in social psychology. In D. Levine (Ed.), *Nebraska symposium on motivation* (Vol. 15, pp. 192-238). Lincoln: University of Nebraska Press.

Kelley, H. H., & Thibaut, J. W. (1978). *Interpersonal relations: a theory of interdependence.* New York: John Wiley & Sons.

Kennedy, J., & Eberhart, R. C. (2001). *Swarm Intelligence* (1 ed.). London: Academic Press.

Khosla, R., & Dillon, T. S. (1998). Welding Symbolic AI with Neural Networks and their applications. *IEEE Transactions on Evolutionary Computation.*

Kirby, S. (2002). Learning, bottlenecks and the evolution of recursive syntax. In T. Briscoe (Ed.), *Linguistic Evolution through Language Acquisition: Formal and Computational Models* (pp. 96-109). Cambridge University Press.

Kirby, S., & Hurford, J. (2001). The emergence of linguistic structure: an overview of the iterated learning model. In D. Parisi & A. Cangelosi (Eds.), *Computational approaches to the evolution of language and communication* (pp. 121-148). Berlin: Springer-Verlag.

Klein, G. (1993). A Recognition-Primed Decision Making Model of Rapid Decision Making, in Klien, G., Orasanu, J., Calderwood, R. and Zsambok, C. (eds.), *Decision Making In Action: Models and Methods,* pp. 138-147.

Koay, K.L., K. Dautenhahn, S.N. Woods and M.L. Walters (2006). "Empirical Results from Using a Comfort Level Device in Human-Robot Interaction Studies." Proceedings of *HRI'06*, Salt Lake City, Utah.

Kodialam, M. & Lakshman, T. V. (2003). *Detecting Network Intrusions via Sampling: A Game Theoretic Approach.* Paper presented at IEEE INFOCOM Conference.

Kohonen, T. (1997). *Self-Organizing Maps.* Springer, 2nd edition.

König, D., A. Glover, P. King, G. Laforge, & J. Skeet. (2007) *Groovy in action.* Manning Publications.

Kováč, L. (2000). Fundamental principles of cognitive biology. *Evolution and Cognition, 6,* 51-69.

Kreps, D.M. & Wilson, R. (1982). Reputation and Imperfect Information. *Journal of Economic Theory,* 27: 253-279.

Krieger, S. H., & Neumann, Jr., R. K. (2003). *Essential lawyering skills: Interviewing, counseling, negotiation, and persuasive fact analysis, Second Edition.* New York: Aspen Publishers.

Krier, D. (1999). Assessing the new synthesis of economics and sociology: Promising themes for contemporary analysts of economic life. *American Journal of Economics and Sociology, 58*(4), 669-696.

Kroeber, A. L. & Kluckhohn, C. (1952) *Culture: A Critical Review of Concepts and Definitions.* Cambridge, MA: Peabody Museum.

Kuhn, H. W. (1955). The Hungarian method for the assignment problem. *Naval Research Logistics Quarterly,* 2(83).

Kumho Tire Co. Ltd. v. Carmichael, 526 U.S. 137 (1999).

Kyburg, Jr., H. E. (1983). The reference class. *Philosophy of Science, 50,* 374-397.

Kyburg, Jr., H. E. (1990). *Science & Reason.* New York: Oxford University Press.

Kyburg, Jr., H. E., & Teng, C. M. (2001). *Uncertain inference.* UK: Cambridge University Press.

Laird, J. D., & Bresler, C. (1992). The process of emotional feeling: a self-perception theory. In M. Clark (Ed.), *Emotion: Review of Personality and Social Psychology* (Vol. 13, pp. 223-234). Newbury Park, CA: Sage.

Lakoff, G. (1987). *Women, fire, and dangerous things: What categories reveal about the mind.* Chicago: University of Chicago Press.

Lakoff, G., & Johnson, M. (1980). *Metaphors we live by.* Chicago, IL: University of Chicago Press.

Lakoff, G., & Johnson, M. (1999). *Philosophy in the flesh: The embodied mind and its challenge to Western thought.* New York: Basic Books.

Laland, & Odling-Smee (2000) The Evolution of the Meme in *Darwinizing Culture: The Status of Memetics As A Science*, pp. 122-141, Oxford, UK: Oxford University Press.

Lang, K., & Lang, G. E. (1961). *Collective dynamics.* New York: Thomas Y. Crowell Company.

Langacker, R. W. (1987). *Foundations of cognitive grammar: Theoretical prerequisites* (Vol. 1). Stanford, CA: Stanford University Press.

Langdon, Christopher (1995). *Artificial Life.* Cambridge: MIT Press.

Langton, C. G. (1984). Self-reproduction in cellular automata. *Physica D, 10,* 135-144.

Langton, C. G. (1991). Computation at the edge of chaos: Phase transitions and emergent computation. In S. Forest (ed.), *Emergent computation,* (pp. 12-37). Cambridge, MA: MIT Press.

Langton, C. G. (Ed.). (1989). *Artificial life.* Reading, MA: Addison-Wesley.

Larson, R., & Segal, G. (1995). *Knowledge of meaning: An introduction to Semantic theory.* Cambridge, MA: MIT Press.

Lawler, E. J., Ridgeway, C., & Markovsky, B. (1993). Structural social psychology and the micro-macro problem. *Sociological Theory, 11*(3), 268-290.

Lenggenhager, B., Tadi, T., Metzinger, T., & Blanke, O. (2007). Video ergo sum: Manipulating bodily self-consciousness. *Science, 317*(5841), 1096-1099.

Leont'ev, A. N. (1978). *Activity, Consciousness and Personality.* Engelwood Cliffs: Prentice Hall.

Levesque, H. J., Cohen, P. R., & Nunes, J. H. T. (1990, July 29-August 3). *On acting together.* Paper presented at the Eighth National Conference on Artificial Intelligence (AAAI-90), Boston, MA.

Levi, I. (1977). Direct inference. *The Journal of Philosophy, 74,* 5-29.

Levi, I. (1981). Direct inference and confirmational conditionalization. *Philosophy of Science, 48,* 532-552.

Levi, I. (1996). *For the sake of argument.* UK: Cambridge University Press.

Li, M. and Vitanyi, P. (1997). *An introduction to Kolmogorov Complexity and its applications.* Berlin: Springer Verlag.

Li, P., Farkaš, I., & MacWhinney, B. (2004). Early lexical acquisition in a self-organizing neural network. *Neural Networks, 17* (8-9), 1345-1362.

Likert, R. (1932). *A technique for the measuring of attitudes,* New York, USA: Columbia University Press.

LindenLab (2003). *Second life.* San Francisco.

Liu, Y. A. H. Ngu, & L. Z. Zeng. (2004). "QoS Computation and Policing in Dynamic Web Service Selection." *Proceedings of the 13th International Conference on the World Wide Web,* (pp. 66-73). New York: ACM.

Lodge, J., & Frydenberg, E. (2005). The role of peer bystanders in school bullying: Positive steps toward promoting peaceful schools. *Theory into Practice, 44(4),* 329-336.

Loewenstein, G., Weber, E., Hsee, C. & Welch, N. (2001). Risk as Feelings. The American Psychological Association. *Psychological Bulletin,* 127(2): 267-286.

Lorenz, E. N. (1979). *Predictability: Does the flap of a butterfly's wings in brazil set off a tornado in texas?* (Talk given at the annual meeting of the AAAS December 29, 1979 in Washington). : American Association for the Advancement of Science.

Lorenz, E. N. (2001). *The Essence of Chaos* (4 ed.). Seattle: University of Washington Press.

Lorenz, K. (1961). *King solomon's ring.* London: Methuen.

Lu, Q., Korniss, G., & Szymanski, B. K. (2006, Oct 12–15). Naming games in spatially-embedded random networks and emergent phenomena in societies of agents. In *Interaction and emergent phenomena in societies of agents* (pp. 148-155). The American Association for Artificial Intelligence, Menlo Park, CA: AAAI Press.

Luce, R. D. & Raiffa, H. (1957). *Games and Decisions,* New York, Wiley.

Lucero, A., & Martens, J. (2006). *Mood boards: Industrial designers' perceptions of using mixed reality.* SIGCHI.NL Conference 2005, HCI Close To You.

Luhmann, N (1984). *Social Systems.* Frankfort: Suhrkamp.

Luhmann, N. (1990). *Essays on Self Reference.* New York: Columbia University Press.

Luhmann, N. (1995). *Social Systems.* Stanford: Stanford University Press.

M.J. North, T.R. Howe, N.T. Collier, & J.R. Vos. (2006c, October). "Demeter, Persephone, and the Search for Emergence in Agent-Based Models." *American*

Association for the Advancement of Artificial Intelligence 2006 Fall Symposium. AAAI. Crystal City, VA USA.

MacDorman, K.F. (2005). Androids as an experimental apparatus: Why is there an uncanny valley and can we exploit it? *Conference Proceedings CogSci-2005* (pp. 106-118). Stresa, Italy.

Maclin, R. and Shavlik, J. W. (1994). Incorporating advice into agents that learns from reinforcements. In *Proceedings of the 1994 American Association of Artificial Intelligence.*

Maeda, F., Mazzioatta, J., & Iacoboni, M. (2002). Transcranial magnetic stimulation studies of the human mirror neuron system. *International Congress Series, 1232,* 889-894.

Maes, P. (1994). Agents that Reduce Work and Information Overload, Communications of the ACM, 37(7).

Maes, P. (1995). Intelligent software. *Scientific American, 273,* 84-86.

Maines, B., & Robinson, G. (1991). Don't beat the bullies! *Educational Psychology in Practice, 7,*168-172.

Malfaz, M., & Salichs, M.A. (2006). Learning behaviour-selection algorithms for autonomous social agents living in a role-playing game. *Conference Proceedings AISB'06* (pp. 45-52).

Malinowski, G. (1993). *Many-valued logics.* UK: Oxford University Press.

Mamdani, E. & Assilian S. (1975) An experiment in linguistic synthesis with a fuzzy logic controller. International Journal of Man-Machine Studies, 7(1), 1-13.

March, J. (1994). *A Primer on Decision Making: How Decisions Happen,* Free Press, New York.

Martens, J., Lucero, A., Naalijkens, B., Ekeler, B., Rammeloo, G., van Heist, M., Kwak, M., & Sakovich, M. (2006). *Blue Eye – making mood boards in augmented reality.* HCI 2006, University of London, UK.

Matsui, T., Kakuyama, T., Tsuzuki, Y., & Onglacto, M.L. (1996). Long-term outcomes of early victimization by peers among Japanese male university students: Models of a vicious cycle. *Psychological Reports, 79*, 711-720.

Maturana, H. R., & Varela, F. J. (1987). *The tree of knowledge: The biological roots of human understanding.* Boston: Shambhala.

Maturana, H., & Varela, F. (1980). *Autopoiesis and Cognition: The Realization of the Living* (Vol. 42). Boston: D. Reidel.

Maturana, H., Lettvin, J., McCulloch, W., & Pitts, W. (1960). "Anatomy and physiology of vision in the frog", *Journal of General Physiology*, 43:129--175

McBreen, H., & M. Jack. (2000). Animated Conversational Agents in E-Commerce Enterprises. *Proceedings of the Third Workshop on Human-Computer Conversation*, pp.112-117.

McCarthy, J. (1990). *Formalizing Common Sense. Papers by John McCarthy.* Vladimir Lifschitz (Ed.), Ablex.

McCloud, S. (1993). *Understanding comics: The invisible art.* New York, USA: Harper Collins Publishers Inc.

McGee, K. (2005). Enactive Cognitive Science. Part 1: Background and Research Themes. *Constructivist Foundations, 1*(1), 15.

McGee, K. (2005). Enactive Cognitive Science. Part 2: Methods, Insights, and Potential. *Constructivist Foundations, 1*(2), 9.

McGrath, J.E. (1984). *Groups: Interaction and performance.* Englewood Cliffs, USA: Prentice Hall.

McKelvey. (1997). Quasi-Natural Organisation Science. *Organization Science, 8*, 351-380.

McMullin, B., & Grob, D. (2001). Towards the Implementation of Evolving Autopoietic Artificial Agents, *6th European Conference on Artificial Life ECAL 2001*. University of Economics, Prague.

McQuiggan, S.W., & Lester, J.C. (2006) Learning empathy: A data-driven framework for modelling empathetic companion agents. *Conference Proceedings AAMAS'06* (pp. 961-968).

Meltzoff, A. N., & Decety, J. (2003). What imitation tells us about social cognition: a rapprochement between developmental psychology and cognitive neuroscience. *Philosophical Transactions of the Royal Society of London, 358*, 491-500.

Meltzoff, A. N., & Moore, M. K. (1989). Imitation in newborn infants:exploring the range of gestures imitated and the underlying mechanisms. *Developmental Psychology, 25*, 954-962.

Mesenbourg, T. (2000). Measuring Electronic Business, Definitions and Underlying Concepts. *United States Census Bureau*, September 2000.

Metta, G., Vernon, D., & Sandini, G. (2005). *The Robotcup Approach to the Development of Cognition.* Paper presented at the Fifth International Workshop on Epigenetic Robotics: Modeling Cognitive Development in Robotic Systems Lund University Cognitive Studies, .

Miceli, M., & Castelfranchi, C. (2000). The role of evaluation in cognition and social interaction. In K. Dautenhahn (Ed.), *Human cognition and agent technology.* Amsterdam: Benjamins.

Michalski, R., Stepp, R. E., and Diday, E. (1983). Automated construction of classifications: conceptual clustering versus numerical taxonomy. *IEEE Transactions on Pattern Analysis and Machine Intelligence*, 5(5):396-409.

Miklosi, A. (1999). The ethological analysis of imitation. *Biological Reviews, 74*, 347-374.

Miller, D. and Slater, D. (2000). Chapter One - Conclusions. *The Internet: An Ethnographic Approach.* Oxford: Berg.

Mingers, J. (2002). Are Social Systems Autopoietic? Assessing Luhmanns Social Theory. *Sociological review, 50*(2).

Mingers, J. (2004). Can Social Systems be Autopoietic? Bhaskar's and Giddens' Social Theories. *Journal for the Theory of Social Behaviour, 34*(4), 25.

Minsky, M. (2006). *The emotion machine: commonsense thinking, artificial intelligence, and the future of the human mind.* New York: Simon & Schuster.

Mirolli, M., & Parisi, D. (2005). Language as an aid to categorization: A neural network model of early language acquisition. In *Modelling language, cognition and action: Proceedings of the 9th Neural Computation and Psychology Workshop.* Singapore: World Scientific.

Mitchell, M., Crutchfield, J. P., & Hraber, P. T. (1994). Evolving cellular automata to perform computations: Mechanisms and impediments. *Physica D, 75*(1-3), 361–391.

Moffat, R. (1997). Personality parameters and programs. In R. Trappl, & P. Petta (Eds.). *Creating personality for synthetic actors.* Berlin, Germany: Springer-Verlaq.

Moon, II-C. & Carley, K. M. (2007). Self-Organizing Social and Spatial Networks under What-If Scenarios, **in** *Proceedings of 6ᵗʰ International Conference on Autonomous Agents and Multi-Agent Systems* **(AAMAS'07), pp. 1348-1355.**

Morcom, A. M., & Flethcher, P. C. (2007). Does the brain have a baseline? Why we should be resisting a rest. *NeuroImage, 34*(7), 1073-1082.

Moreno, A., & Etxeberria, A. (1995). Agency in natural and artificial systems. San Sabastian, Spain: Department of Logic and Philosophy of Science University of the Basque Country.

Moreno, A., Umerez, J., & Ibanes, J. (1997). Cognition and Life. *Brain and Cognition, 34*, 107-129.

Morgan, M. G., & Henrion, M. (1990). *Uncertainty: A guide to dealing with uncertainty in quantitative risk and policy analysis.* UK: Cambridge University Press.

Mori, M. (1970). Bukimi no tani: The uncanny valley. *Energy, 7*(4), 33–35.

Muller, J (2004). The Emergence of Collective Behavior in Problem Solving. *Agents World IV International Workshop* (pp.1-20) New York: Springer Verlag

Müller, M.J., Wildman, D.M., & White, E.A. (1993). 'Equal opportunity' PD using PICTIVE. *Communications of the ACM, 36(6)*, 64-65.

Nardi, B. A. and Harris, J. (2006). Strangers and friends: Collaborative play in World of Warcraft. In *Computer supported cooperative work.* Banff, Alberta, Canada: ACM Press.

Nehaniv, C. (2000). The making of meaning in societies: Semiotic and information-theoretic background to the evolution of communication. In B. Edmonds & K. Dautenhahn (Eds.), *AISB Symposium: Starting from Society – the application of social analogies to computational systems* (pp. 73-84). Society for the Study of Artificial Intelligence and Adaptive Behaviour.

Neumann, Jr., R. K. (2005). *Legal reasoning and legal writing: Structure, strategy, and style, Fifth Edition.* Boston: Little, Brown and Company.

Newlin, D. B. (2002). The self-perceived survival ability and reproductive fitness (SPFit) theory of substance use disorders. *Addiction, 97*, 427-446.

Newlin, D. B. (2006). Self-perceived survival and reproductive fitness (SPFit) theory: Substance use disorders, evolutionary game theory, and the brain. In Platek, S., Keenan, J. P., & Shackelford, T. (Eds.), *Evolutionary Cognitive Neuroscience* (pp. 285-326). Cambridge, Mass.: MIT Press.

Newlin, D.B., (2007, November 9-11). The human mirror neuron system (MNS): Toward a motivated autonomous agent. In *Proceedings of the AAAI Symposium, "Multi-Agent Societies"* (Trajkovski, G., Samuel Collins (Eds). Washington, DC.

Newsome, J., Karp, B., & Song, D. (2005). *Polygraph: Automatically Generating Signatures for Polymorphic Worms.* Paper presented at IEEE Symposium on Security and Privacy.

Nitsche, M. A., Liebetanz, D., Lang, N., Antal, A., Tergau, F., & Paulus, W. (2003). Safety criteria for transcranial direct current stimulation (tDCS) in humans. *Clinical Neurophysiology*, 114(11), 2220-2222.

North, M. J., & C. M. Macal. (2005, April). "Escaping the Accidents of History: An Overview of Artificial Life Modeling with Repast." in A. Adamatzky and M. Komosinski, eds. *Artificial Life Models in Software*, pp. 115-141. Springer. Heidelberg, FRG.

North, M. J., T. R. Howe, N. T. Collier, & J. R. Vos. (2005, October). "The Repast Simphony Development Environment." *Agent 2005 Conference on Generative Social Processes, Models, and Mechanisms*. Argonne National Laboratory. Argonne, IL USA.

North, M. J., T. R. Howe, N. T. Collier, & J. R. Vos. (2006, June) "Spaces, Places, and the Lernaean Hydra of Agent-Based Modeling." *North American Association for Computational Social and Organizational Science 2006 Conference*. Argonne National Laboratory. Argonne, IL USA.

North, M. J., Collier, N. T., and Vos, J. R. (2006). Experiences creating three implementations of the repast agent modeling toolkit. *ACM Transactions on Modeling and Computer Simulation*, 16(1):1-25.

North, M.J., & C.M. Macal. (2007, March). *Managing Business Complexity: Discovering Strategic Solutions with Agent-Based Modeling and Simulation*, Oxford, New York, NY USA.

North, M.J., T.R. Howe, N.T. Collier, & J.R. Vos. (2007). "A Declarative Model Assembly Infrastructure for Verification and Validation." in S. Takahashi, D.L. Sallach and J. Rouchier, eds. *Advancing Social Simulation: The First World Congress*. Springer, Heidelberg, FRG.

Nowak, M.A., & Sigmund, K. (1998). Evolution of indirect reciprocity by image scoring. *Nature*, 393, 573-577.

Ntoulas, A., J. Cho, & C. Olston. (2004). "What's New on the Web?: The Evolution of the Web from a Search Engine Perspective." *Proceedings of the 13th*

International Conference on the World Wide Web, (pp. 1-12). New York: ACM.

Oberman, L.M., & Ramachandran, V.S. (2007). The simulating social mind: The role of the mirror neuron system and simulation in the social and communicative deficits of autism spectrum disorders. *Psychological Bulletin*, 133(2), 310-327.

Ohman, A. & Wiens, S. (2004). The Concept of an Evolved Fear Module and Cognitive Theories of Anxiety. In Manstead A, Frijda, N, Fischer, A (Eds.), *Feelings and Emotions, The Amsterdam Symposium*. Cambridge, UK: Cambridge University Press.

Oliphant, M. (1997). *Formal approaches to innate and learned communication: Laying the foundation for language*. Unpublished doctoral dissertation, University of California, San Diego, CA.

Olweus, D. (1991). Bully/victim problems among school children: Basic facts and effects of a school-based intervention program. In K. Rubin, & D. Pepler (Eds.) *The development and treatment of childhood aggression*. New Jersey, USA: Erlbaum.

Olweus, D. (1994). Bullying at school: Long term outcomes for the victims and an effective school based intervention program. In R. Huesmann (Ed.). *Aggressive behaviour. Current perspectives*. New York, USA: Plenum.

Olweus, D. (1999). Norway. In P.K. Smith, Y. Morita, J. Junger-Tas, D. Olweus, R. Catalano, & P. Slee (Eds.), *The nature of school bullying: A cross-national perspective*. London, UK: Routledge.

Oosterholt, R., Kusano, M., & de Vries, G. (1996). Interaction design and human factors support, in the development of a personal communicator for children. *Conference Proceedings CHI'96* (pp. 557-564).

Oppenheim, A. N. (1992). *Questionnaire design, interviewing, and attitude measurement (2nd Ed.)*. London, UK: Pinter.

Øritsland, T.A., & Buur, J. (2003). Interaction styles: A aesthetic sense of direction in interface design.

International Journal of Human-Computer Interaction, 15(1), 67-85.

Ostrom, E. (2000). Collective Action and the Evolution of Social Norms. *Journal of Economic Perspectives.* 14, 137-158.

Oyama, S. (2000). *The Ontogeny of Information: Developmental Systems and Evolution.* Duke University Press.

Oztop, E., Kawato, M., & Arbib, M. (2006). Mirror neurons and imitation: a computational guided review. *Neural Networks, 19*, 254-271.

Paiva, A., Dias, J., Sobral, D., Aylett, R., Sobreperez, P., Woods, S., Zoll, C. & Hall, L., (2004). Caring for agents and agents that care: Building empathic relations with synthetic agents. *Conference Proceedings AAMAS 2004* (pp. 194-201).

Paiva, A., Dias, J., Sobral, D., Aylett, R., Woods, S., Hall, L., & Zoll, C. (2005).Learning by feeling: evoking empathy with synthetic characters. *Applied Artificial Intelligence, 19,* 235-266.

Pan, X., Han, C. S., Dauber, K. & Law, K. H. (2005). A Multi-agent Based Framework for Simulating Human and Social Behaviors during Emergency Evacuations, *Social Intelligence Design*, Stanford University.

Paolucci, M. (2000). False Reputation in Social Control. In G. Ballot & G. Weisbuch (Eds.), *Applications of Simulation to Social Sciences.* Paris: Hermes.

Paolucci, M. (2005). Reputation as a Complex Cognitive Artefact. Theory, Simulations, Experiments. Unpublished doctoral dissertation, University of Florence, Italy (available at http://150.146.65.191/mario/PaolucciReputationAsACmplxCgntvArtfct.pdf)

Paolucci, M., & Conte, R. (1999). Reproduction of normative agents: A simulation study. *Adaptive Behavior*, special issue on Simulation Models of Social Agents, 7(3), 301-322.

Paolucci, M., Marsero, M., & Conte, R. (2000) What's the use of gossip? A sensitivity analysis of the spreading of normative reputation. In R. Suleiman, K. Troitzsch and N. Gilbert (Eds.) *Tools and Techniques for Social Science MicroSimulation.* Berlin: Springer.

Papadimitriou, C. H. and Steiglitz, K. (1998). *Combinatorial Optimization: Algorithms and Complexity.* Dover Publications.

Papazoglou, M.P., & D. Georgakopoulos. (2003). "Service-Oriented Computing." *Communications of the ACM, 46*(10), 24-28.

Papudesi, V. N. and Huber, M. (2003). Learning from reinforcement and advice using composite reward functions. In *Proceedings of the 16th International FLAIRS Conference.*

Park, R. E., & Burgess, E. W. (1921). *Introduction to the science of sociology.* Chicago: University of Chicago Press.

Parr, R. and Russell, S. (1998). Reinforcement learning with hierarchies of machines. In *Neural Information Processing Systems.*

Parsons, T (1951). *The Social System.* New York: Free Press.

Pasquier, P., & Chaib-draa, B. (2003). The cognitive coherence approach for agent communication pragmatics. In *Aamas* (pp. 544-551). ACM.

Pepler, D.J., Craig, W., Ziegler, S., & Charach, A. (1994). An evaluation of an anti-bullying intervention in Toronto schools. *Canadian Journal of Community Mental Health. Special Issue: Prevention: Focus on Children and Youth, 13,* 95-110.

Peterson, G. R. (2006). Species of Emergence. *Zygon, 41*(3), 22.

Pfeifer, R., & Scheier, C. (1999). *Understanding intelligence.* Cambridge, MA: MIT Press.

Phanalp, S. (1999) *Communicating Emotion. Social, Moral and Cultural Processes.* Cambridge, UK: Cambridge University Press.

Piaget, J. (1985). *The Equilibration of Cognitive Structures: The Central Problem of Intellectual Development.* Chicago: University of Chicago Press.

Piaget, J., & Inhelder, B. (1966). *La psychologie de l'enfant* [The psychology of the child]. Paris: PUF.

Picard, G. & Gleizes, M. P. (2002). *An agent architecture to design self-organizing collectives: Principles and application*. In Proceedings of Adaptive Agents and Multi-Agents Systems (AAMAS) 2001 / 2002, pages 141–158

Picard, R. (1997). *Affective computing*. Cambridge, Massachusetts: MIT Press.

Plutchik, R. *The emotions*. Lanham, MD: University Press of America.

Pollock, J. L. (1990). *Nomic probability and the foundations of induction*. New York: Oxford University Press.

Porat, A., & Stein, A. (2001). *Tort liability under uncertainty*. UK: Oxford University Press.

Portes, A. and Sensenbrenner, J., Embeddedness and Immigration: Notes on the Social Determinants of Economic Action, *The American Journal of Sociology*, 98(6): 1320-1350, 1993.

Prakken, H. (1997). *Logical yools for modelling legal argument*. Dordrecht, The Netherlands: Kluwer.

Prakken, H., & Sartor, G. (1997). Reasoning with precedents in a dialogue game. In *International Conference of Artificial Intelligence and Law Proceedings '97* (pp. 1-9). New York: ACM.

Prakken, H., & Sartor, G. (2004). The three faces of defeasibility in the law. *Ratio Juris, 17(1)*, 118-139.

Prakken, H., Reed,, C., & Walton, D. (2003). Argumentation schemes and generalisations in reasoning about evidence. In *International Conference of Artificial Intelligence and Law Proceedings '03* (pp. 32-41). New York: ACM.

Prigogine, I. (1997). *The End of Certainty: Time, Chaos and the New Laws of Nature*. New York: The Free Press.

Prigogine, I., & Stengers, I. (1985). *Order out of Chaos: Man's New Dialogue with Nature*: Flamingo.

Putterman, M. L. (2005). *Markov Decision Processes*. Wiley-Interscience, 2nd edition.

Pynadath, D. V. & Marsella, S. C (2005). PsychSim: Modeling Theory of Mind with Decision-Theoretic Agents, *IJCAI'05*, pp. 1181-1186.

Radnitzky, G. (1992). The economic approach. In G. Radnitzky & A. M. Weinberg (Eds.), *Universal economics: Assessing the achievements of the economic approach* (pp. 1-68). New York: Paragon House.

Radnitzky, G., & Bernholz, P. (Eds.). (1987). *Economic imperialism: The economic approach applied outside the field of economics*. New York: Paragon House Publishers.

Rasmussen, J. (1986). *Information Processing and Human Machine Interaction: An Approach to Cognitive Engineering*, New York, North Holland.

Raub, W., & Weesie, J. (1990). Reputation and Efficiency in Social Interactions: An Example of Network Effects. *American Journal of Sociology*, 96, 626-654.

Raven, M.E., & Flanders, A. (1996). Using contextual inquiry to learn about your audiences. *Journal of Computer Documentation, 20(1)*, 1-13.

Reeves, B., & Nass, C. (1996). *The media equation: how people treat computers, television, and new media like real people and places*. Stanford, CA: Center for the Study of Language and Information.

Reynolds, C. W. (1987) "Flocks, Herds, and Schools: A Distributed Behavioral Model, in Computer Graphics." *SIGGRAPH 1987 Conference Proceedings, 21*(4), 25-34.

Reynolds, C. W. (2001). *Boids (Flocks, Herds, and Schools a Distributed Behavioral Model)*. Available as http://www.red3d.com/cwr/boids/

Richardson, J. (2006). *Designing a water safety environment using lomography*. Unpublished MSc dissertation, University of Sunderland, UK.

Richardson, K. A. (2002). Methodological Implications

of a Complex Systems Approach to Sociality: Some further remarks. *Journal of Artificial Societies and Social Simulation, 5*(2).

Richardson, K. A. (2002). *On the Limits of Bottom Up Computer Simulation: Towards a Non-linear Modeling Culture.* Paper presented at the 36th Hawaii International Conference on Systems Science, Hawaii.

Rickel, J., Gratch, J., Hill, R., Marsella, S., Swartout, W. (2001). Steve goes to Bosnia: Towards a new generation of virtual humans for interactive experiences. *In AAAI Spring Symposium on Artificial Intelligence and Interactive Entertainment.*

Riolo, R. L., Cohen, M. D. & Axelrod, R. (2001). Evolution of cooperation without reciprocity. *Nature, 414,* 441-443.

Rissland, E. L. (1990). Artificial intelligence and law: stepping stones to a model of legal reasoning. *Yale Law Journal, 99,* 1957-1981.

Rizzolatti, G., & Craighero, L. (2004). The mirror-neuron system. *Annual Review of Neuroscience,* 27, 169-192.

ROAD, *Repast Home Page.* (2007). Available as http://repast.sourceforge.net/. Repast Organization for Architecture and Design. Chicago.

Roberts, G., & Sherratt, T. N. (2002). Does similarity breed cooperation?, *Nature, 418,* 499-500. Followed by answer from Riolo, Cohen and Axelrod.

Robins, B., Dautenhahn, K., te Boekhorst, R., Nehaniv, C.L. (2008) Behaviour delay and robot expressiveness in child-robot interactions: A user study on interaction kinesics. Accepted for publication in 3rd ACM/IEEE Human-Robot Interaction conference (HRI08).

Rocha, L. M. (1998). Selected Self-Organization: and the semiotics of evolutionary systems In S. Salthe, G. Van de Vijver & M. Delpos (Eds.), *Evolutionary Systems: Biological and Epistemological Perspectives on Selection and Self-Organization* (pp. 341-358): Kluwer Academic Publishers.

Rodes, Jr., R. E., & Pospesel, H. (1997). *Premises and conclusions: Symbolic logic for legal analysis.* Upper Saddle River, NJ: Prentice Hall.

Rogers, C. (1951). *Client centered therapy.* Boston: Houghton-Mifflin.

Rosch, E. (1978). Principles of categorization. In E. Rosch & B. Lloyd (Eds.), *Cognition and categorization* (pp. 27-48). Hillsdale, NJ: Lawrence Erlbaum Associates.

Ross, L., & Nisbett, R. (1991). *The person and the situation.* New York: McGraw-Hill.

Ross, M. M. (2006). A basis for legal reasoning: logic on appeal. *Journal of the Association of Legal Writing Directors, 3,* 177-189.

Roy, D. (2005). Semiotic schemas: a framework for grounding language in action and perception. *Artificial Intelligence, 167* (1-2), 170-205.

Rudrauf, D., Lutz , A., Cosmelli, D., Lachaux , J.-P., & Le Van Quyen, M. (2003). From Autopoiesis to Neurophenomenology: Francisco Varela's exploration of the biophysics of being. *Biol. Res, 36,* 27-65.

Russel, J.A., & Fernández-Dols, J.M. (2002). *The psychology of facial expression.* Cambridge, UK: Cambridge University Press.

Russell, S. J., & Norvig, P. (2003). *Artificial intelligence: A modern approach.* Upper Saddle River, NJ: Prentice Hall.

Saam, N. J. (1999). Simulating the micro-macro link: New approaches to an old problem and an application to military coups. *Sociological Methodology, 29,* 43-79.

Sabater, J., Paolucci, M., & Conte, R. (2006). Repage: REPutation and ImAGE Among Limited Autonomous Partners. *Journal of Artificial Societies and Social Simulation,* 9(2).

Sacks, Harvey, Emanuel Schegloff and Gail Jefferson (1974). A Simplest Systematics for the Organziation of Turn-Taking for Conversation. *Language* 50(4):696-735.

Saeed, J. I. (2003). *Semantics*. Malden, MA: Blackwell.

Sainsbury, M. (1991). *Logic forms: An introduction to philosophical logic*. Oxford, UK: Basil Blackwell.

Sakaguchi, H. (2001). Final Fantasy: The Spirits Within.

Salmivalli, C., Huttunen, A., & Lagerspetz, K.M.J. (1997). Peer networks and bullying in schools. *Scandinavian Journal of Psychology, 38*, 305-312.

Salmivalli, C., Lagerspetz, K., Björkqvist, K., Österman, K., & Kaukainen, A. (1996). Bullying as a group process: Particpant roles and their relations to social status within the group. *Aggressive Behaviour, 22*, 1-15.

Salmon, G., James, A., & Smith, D.M. (1998). Bullying in schools: Self reported anxiety, depression, and self esteem in secondary school children. *British Medical Journal, 317*, 924-925.

Salmon, W. C. (1973). *Logic*. Englewood Cliffs, NJ: Prentice-Hall.

Santibáñez, J. (1984). *Relación del rendimiento escolar en las áreas de lectura y escritura con las aptitudes mentales y el desarrollo visomotor*. Madrid: Universidad Nacional de Educación a Distancia.

Santibáñez, J. (1988). *Variables psicopedagógicas relacionadas con el rendimiento en E.G.B.* Logroño: Instituto de Estudios Riojanos.

Santibáñez, J. (1989) *La evaluación de la escritura: Test de escritura para el ciclo inicial*. Madrid: T.E.C.I. CEPE.

Sarkar, P. (2000). A brief history of cellular automata. *ACM Computing Surveys, 32*(1), 80-107.

Saunders, K. M. (2006). Law as rhetoric, rhetoric as argument. *Journal of the Association of Legal Writing Directors, 3*, 164-176.

Sawyer, K. R. (2001). Emergence in Sociology: Contemporary Philosophy of Mind and Some Implications for Sociology Theory. *American Journal of Sociology, 107*(3), 551-585.

Sawyer, K. R. (2003). Artificial Societies: Multiagent Systems and the Micro-macro Link in Sociological Theory. *Sociological Methods & Research, 31*, 38.

Sawyer, R. K. (2003). *Group creativity: Music, theater, collaboration*. Mahwah, NJ: Erlbaum.

Sawyer, R. K. (2003). *Improvised dialogues: Emergence and creativity in conversation*. Westport, CT: Greenwood.

Sawyer, R. K. (2004). The mechanisms of emergence. *Philosophy of the Social Sciences, 34*(2), 260-282.

Sawyer, R. K. (2004). Social explanation and computational simulation. *Philosophical Explorations, 7*(3), 219-231.

Sawyer, R. K. (2005). *Social emergence: Societies as complex systems*. New York: Cambridge.

Scaife, M., & Rogers, Y. (2001). Informing the design of a virtual environment to support learning in children. *International Journal of Human Computer Studies, 55*, 115-143.

Scaife, M., Rogers, Y., Aldrich, F., & Davies, M. (1997). Designing for or designing with? Informant design for interactive learning environments. *Conference Proceedings CHI'97* (pp. 343-350).

Scassellati, B. (2000). *Foundations for a theory of mind for a humanoid robot*. Unpublished Ph.D. Thesis, MIT, Cambridge, Massachusetts.

Scerri, P., Pynadath, D., Schurr, N., Farinelli, A., Gandhe, S., and Tambe, M. (2003). Team oriented programming and proxy agents: The next generation. Workshop on Programming MultiAgent Systems, AAMAS 2003.

Scerri, P., Tambe, M., Lee, H., and Pynadath, D. (2000). Don't cancel my Barcelona trip: adjusting autonomy of agent proxies in human organizations. In *AAAI Fall Symposium on Socially Intelligent Agents - the Human in the Loop*.

Schank, R. (1979) Interestingness: Controlling Inferences, *Artificial Intelligence*, 12: 273–297.

Schelling, T. (1977) Dynamic models of segregation. *Journal of Mathematical Sociology*, 1, 143-186 (1977).

Schelling, T. (1978). *Micromotives and macrobehavior* New York: Norton.

Schönfisch, B., & Roos, A. M. de. (1999). Synchronous and asynchronous updating in cellular automata. *Biosystems*, 51(3), 123–143.

Schuler, D., & Mamioka, A. (Eds.). (1993). *Participatory design: Principles and practices.* New Jersey, USA: Lawrence Erlbaum.

Schulte-Ruther, M., Markowitsch, H. J., Fink, G. R., & Piefke, M. (2007). Mirror neuron and theory of mind mechanisms involved in face-to-face interactions: A functional magnetic resonance imaging approach to empathy. *Journal of Cognitive Neuroscience*, 19(8), 1354-1372.

Schum, D. A. (1994). *Evidential foundations of probabilistic reasoning.* New York: John Wiley & Sons.

Searle, J. R. (1980). Minds, brains, and programs. *Behavioural and Brain Sciences, 3*, 417-457.

Šefránek, J. (2002). Kognícia bez mentálnych procesov [Cognition without mental processes]. In J. Rybár, L. Beňušková, & V. Kvasnička (Eds.), *Kognitívne vedy* (pp. 200-256). Bratislava: Kalligram.

Selyse H. & Fortier C. (1950). Adaptive reaction to stress. *Psychosomatic Medicine*, 12: 149–57.

Sengers, P. (1998). Do the right thing: An architecture for action-expression. *Conference Proceedings AGENTS'98* (pp. 24-31).

Serres, Michel and Bruno Latour (1995). *Conversations on Science, Culture, and Time.* Ann Arbor: University of Michigan Press.

Shah, S. W.; & Nixon, P. & Ferguson, R. I. (2004). *On the use of IP multicast to facilitate group communication between mobile agents.* In proceedings of the Intelligent Agent Technology, IEEE/WIC/ACM International Conference, pages 487-490.

Shallice, T. (2004). The fractionation of supervisory control. In Gazzaniga, M. S. (Ed.), *The cognitive neurosciences III* (pp. 943-956). Cambridge, Mass.: MIT Press.

Shannon, C. E. (1948). A mathematical theory of communication. *The Bell System Technical Journal 27(July, October, 1948),* 379-423, 623-656.

Sharp, Rogers, & Preece (2007). *Interaction Design. Beyond Human Computer Interaction (2ⁿᵈ Ed.).* Chichester, UK: John Wiley and Sons.

Shneiderman, B. & Plaisant, C. (2005). *Designing the user interface. Strategies for effective human-computer Interaction.* University of Maryland, College Park. Addison Wesley.

Shrader, W. E. (2005). *The Metapysics of Ontological Emergence.* University of Notre Dame.

Sierra, J. (2001). Grounded models as a basis for intuitive reasoning. In B. Nebel (Ed.), *Proceedings of the Seventeenth International Joint Conference on Artificial Intelligence* (pp. 401-406). Morgan Kaufmann.

Sierra, J. (2002). Grounded models as a basis for intuitive and deductive reasoning: The acquisition of logical categories. In F. Harmelen (Ed.), *Proceedings of the European Conference on Artificial Intelligence* (pp. 93-97). IOS Press.

Sierra, J. (2006). Propositional logic syntax acquisition. In P. Vogt, Y Sugita, E. Tuci and C. Nehaniv (Eds.), *Symbol Grounding and Beyond* (pp. 128-142). Lecture Notes in Computer Science, volume 4211.

Simon, H. (1957). *A Behavioral Model of Rational Choice, in Models of Man, Social and Rational: Mathematical Essays on Rational Human Behavior in a Social Setting*, New York: Wiley.

Singh, M. P., Rao, A. S., & Georgeff, M. P. (1999). Formal methods in DAI: logic-based representation and reasoning. In Weiss, G. (Ed.), *Multiagent systems: A modern approach to distributed artificial intelligence* (pp. 331-376). Cambridge, MA: MIT Press.

Singh, S. and Sutton, R. S. (1996). Reinforcement learning with replacing eligibility traces. *Machine Learning Journal*, 22:123-158.

Siskind, J. M. (1996). A computational study of cross-situational techniques for learning word-to-meaning mappings. *Cognition, 61* (1-2), 1-38.

Sloman, A. (1998). Damasio, Descartes, Alarms and Meta-management. *Proceedings of the IEEE International Conference on Systems, Man, and Cybernetics*, 2652-2657.

Smelser, N. J., & Swedberg, R. (Eds.). (1994). *The handbook of economic sociology*. Princeton, NJ: Princeton University Press.

Smith, A. D. M. (2003). *Evolving communication through the inference of meaning*. Unpublished doctoral dissertation, Theoretical and Applied Linguistics, School of Philosophy, Psychology and Language Sciences, The University of Edinburgh.

Smith, A. D. M. (2005). The inferential transmission of language. *Adaptive Behavior*, 13 (4), 311-324.

Smith, E. R., & Conrey, F. R. (2007). Agent-based modeling: a new approach for theory building in social psychology. *Personality and Social Psychology Review, 11*(1), 87-104.

Smith, L.: Sects and Death in the Middle East. *The Weekly Standard*, (2006).

Smith, P., Anadiou, K., & Cowie, H. (2003). Interventions to reduce school bullying. *Canadian Journal of Psychiatry, 48,* 591-599.

Smith, P.K., & Sharp, S. (Eds.). (1994). *School bullying: Insights and perspectives*. London, UK: Routledge.

Soutter, A., & McKenzie, A. (2000). The use and effects of ant bullying and anti-harassment policies in Australian schools. *School Psychology International. Special Issue: Bullies and Victims, 21,* 96-105.

Sperber, D. (2000) An Objection to the Memetic Approach to Culture, in *Darwinizing Culture: The Status of Memetics As A Science*, pp. 122-141, Oxford, UK: Oxford University Press.

Sperber, D. 1996. Explaining Culture: A Naturalistic Approach, Malden, MA: Blackwell Publishers.

Stanford Encyclopedia of Philosophy. (2006). Emergent Properties, *Stanford Encyclopedia of Philosophy.*

Stanovich, K. E. & West, R. F. (1999). Discrepancies between Normative and Descriptive Models of Decision Making and the Understanding/Acceptance Principle, *Cognitive Psychology*, 38: 349–385.

Steels, L. (1995). The artificial life roots of artificial intelligence. In C. G. Langton (ed.), *Artificial life: An overview*. Cambridge, MA: MIT Press.

Steels, L (1996). Emergent Adaptive Lexicons. In Fourth International Conference on Simulation of Adaptive Behavior, Cape Cod. New York: Springer Verlag

Steels, L. (1997). Constructing and sharing perceptual distinctions. In M. van Someren & G. Widmer (Eds.), *Proceedings of the European Conference on Machine Learning* (pp. 4-13). Berlin: Springer.

Steels, L. (1997). The synthetic modeling of language origins. *Evolution of Communication* 1(1), 1-35.

Steels, L. (1998). *Structural coupling of cognitive memories through adaptive language games*. Paper presented at the The fifth international conference on simulation of adaptive behavior on From animals to animats 5, Univ. of Zurich, Zurich, Switzerland.

Steels, L. (1998). The origins of syntax in visually grounded robotic agents. *Artificial Intelligence,* 103(1-2), 133-156.

Steels, L. (1999). *The Talking Heads Experiment. Volume 1. Words and Meanings*. Antwerpen: Special Pre-edition for LABORATORIUM.

Steels, L. (2000). Language as a complex adaptive system. In M. Schoenauer (Ed.), *Proceedings of PPSN-VI* (pp. 17-26). Berlin: Springer.

Steels, L. (2000). The emergence of grammar in communicating autonomous robotic agents. In W. Horn (Ed.), *Proceedings of the European Conference on Artificial Intelligence* (pp. 764-769). IOS Press.

Steels, L. (2004). Constructivist development of grounded construction grammars. In D. Scott (Ed.), *Proc. Annual Meeting of Association for Computational Linguistics* (pp. 9-16). Association for Computational Linguistics

Steels, L. (2004). *Macro-operators for the emergence of construction grammars.* SONY Computer Science Laboratory, Paris.

Steels, L. (2005). The emergence and evolution of linguistic structure: from lexical to grammatical communication systems. *Connection Science, 17*(3 & 4), 17.

Steels, L., & Kaplan, F. (1998). Stochasticity as a Source of Innovation in Kanguage Games. In C. Adami, R. K. Belew, H. Kitano & C. Taylor (Eds.), *Artificial Life VI.* Cambridge, MA: MIT Press.

Steels, L., & Kaplan, F. (1999). Bootstrapping grounded word semantics. In T. Briscoe (Ed.), *Linguistic evolution through language acquisition: formal and computational models,* . Cambridge, UK: Cambridge University Press.

Steels, L., & Kaplan, F. (1999). Situated grounded word semantics. In T. Dean (Ed.), *Proceedings of the Sixteenth International Joint Conference on Artificial Intelligence* (pp. 862-867). San Francisco: Morgan Kauffmann.

Steels, L., & Wellens, P. (2006). How grammar emerges to dampen combinatorial search in parsing. In P. Vogt, Y. Sugita, E. Tuci, & C. Nehaniv (Eds.), *Symbol Grounding and Beyond: Proceedings of the Third International Workshop on the Emergence and Evolution of Linguistic Communication* (pp. 76-88). Berlin/Heidelberg: Springer.

Steels, L., Kaplan, F., McIntyre, A., & V Looveren, J. (2002). Crucial factors in the origins of word-meaning.

In A. Wray (Ed.), *The Transition to Language* (pp. 252-271). Oxford University Press.

Stewart, I. (1990). *Does God Play Dice - The New Mathematics of Chaos*: Penguin.

Stioica-Kluver, C., & Kluver, J. (2006). Interacting Neural Networks and ther Emergence of Social Structure. *Complexity, 12*(3), 11.

Stirling, W. C. & Frost, R. L. (2005). Social Utility Functions-part II: Applications, *IEEE Transactions on Systems, Man, and Cybernetics, Part C: Applications and Reviews*, 35(4):533-543.

Stirling, W. C. (2003). *Satisficing Games and Decision Making: with Applications to Engineering and Computer Science*, Cambridge University Press.

Stirling, W. C. (2005). Social Utility Functions -part I: Theory, *IEEE Transactions on Systems, Man, and Cybernetics, Part C: Applications and Reviews*, 35(4):522-532.

Stolcke, A. (1994). *Bayesian Learning of Probabilistic Language Models.* PhD thesis, University of California at Berkeley.

Stotland, E., Mathews, K. E., Sherman, S. E., Hannson, R. O., & Richardson, B. Z. (1978). *Empathy, fantasy and helping.* Beverly Hills, USA: Sage.

Sun Microsystems. (2007, Oct). *Java DB at a glance.* (See: http://developers.sun.com/javadb/)

Sun Microsystems. (2007, Oct). *Sun Java System message queue.* (See: http://www.sun.com/software/products/message_queue/index.xml)

Sutton, J., & Smith, P.K. (1999). Bullying as a group process: An adaptation of the participant role approach. *Aggressive Behaviour, 25,* 97-111.

Sutton, R. S. and Barto, A. (1998). *Reinforcement Learning: an Introduction.* MIT Press, Cambridge, MA.

Swartout, W., Hill, R., Gratch, J., Johnson, W.L., Kyriakakis, C., CLaBore, C., Lindheim, R., Marsella, S., Miraglia, D., Moore, B., Morie, J., Rickel, J.,

Thiébaux, M., Tuch, L., Whitney, R., & Douglas, J. (2001) Toward the holodeck: Integrating graphics, sound, character and story. *Conference Proceedings AGENT'01* (pp. 409-416).

Tajfel, H. (1981). *Human groups and social categories.* New York, USA: Cambridge University Press.

Takáč, M. (2006). Categorization by sensory-motor interaction in artificial agents. In D. Fum, F. Del Missier, & A. Stocco (Eds.), *Proceedings of the 7th International Conference on Cognitive Modeling* (pp. 310-315). Trieste, Italy: Edizioni Goliardiche.

Takáč, M. (2006b). Cognitive semantics for dynamic environments. In P. Hitzler, H. Schärfe, & P. Øhrstrøm (Eds.), *Contributions to ICCS 2006 – 14th International Conference on Conceptual Structures* (pp. 202-215). Aalborg, Denmark: Aalborg University Press.

Takáč, M. (2007). *Construction of meanings in living and artificial agents* [Submitted]. Unpublished doctoral dissertation, Comenius University of Bratislava, Slovakia.

Takáč, M. (in press). Autonomous construction of ecologically and socially relevant semantics. *Cognitive Systems Research.*

Talmy, L. (2000). *Toward a cognitive semantics.* Cambridge, MA: MIT Press.

Tambe, M. (1997). Towards flexible teamwork. *Journal of Artificial Intelligence Research, 7,* 83-124.

Tambe, M., Scerri, P., and Pynadath, D. (2002). Adjustable autonomy for the real world. *Journal of Artificial Intelligence Research,* 17:171-228.

Tannen, D. (Ed.). (1993). *Framing in discourse.* New York: Oxford University Press.

Tannenbaum, P. H., & Gaer, E. P. (1965). Mood change as a function of stress of protagonist and degree of identification in a film viewing situation. *Journal of Personality and Social Psychology, 2,* 612-616.

Terrence Fong, Illah Nourbakhsh, & Dautenhahn, K. (2003). A survey of socially interactive robots. *Robotics and Autonomous Systems, 42,* 143-166.

The Economist (1997)."What Boys and Girls are Made Of" March 8, 1997, p. 96. http://www.scs.gmu.edu/~dduong/economist.pdf

Thomas, F., & Johnston, O. (1981). *The illusion of life: Disney animation.* Walt Disney Animation.

Thompson, E., & Varela, F. J. (2001). Radical Embodiment: neural dynamics and consciousness. *TRENDS in Cognitive Sciences, 5*(10), 418-425.

Tinbergen, N. (1951). *The study of instinct.* New York: Oxford University Press.

Tognoli, E., Lagarde, J., DeGuzman G. C., & Kelso, J. A. S. (2007). The phi complex as a neuromarker of human social coordination. *Proceedings of the National Academy of Sciences of the United States of America, 104*(19), 8190-8195.

Tomlinson, B., Baumer, E., et al. (2006). The island metaphor. In *SIGGRAPH 2006 Posters.* Boston.

Toulmin, S. (1958). *The uses of Argument.* UK: Cambridge University Press.

Toulmin, S., Rieke, R., & Janik, A. (1984). *An introduction to reasoning.* New York: Macmillan.

Trajkovski, G., Collins, S., Braman J. & Goldberg, M. (2006). Coupling Human and Non-Human Agents. *The AAAI Fall Symposium: Interaction and Emergent Phenomena in Societies of Agents.* Arlington, VA.

Trajkovski, Goran (2007). *An Imitation-Based Approach to Modeling Homogenous Agents Societies.* Hershey, PA: IDEA Publishing.

Trivers, R. (1971). The evolution of reciprocal altruism. *Quarterly Review of Biology, 46,* 35-56.

Tullock, G. (1972). Economic imperialism. In J. M. Buchanan & R. D. Tollison (Eds.), *Theory of public choice: Political applications of economics* (pp. 317-329). Ann Arbor, MI: The University of Michigan Press.

Turella, L., Pierno, A. C., Tubaldi, F., & Castiello, U. (in press). Mirror neurons in humans: Consisting or confounding evidence? *Brain and Language.*

Turing, A. M. (1950). Computing machinery and intelligence. *Mind, 59*, 433-460.

Turkle, S. (1995). *Life on the screen: Identity in the age of the Internet.* New York: Simon and Schuster.

Tversky, A. & Kahneman, D. (1992). Advances in Prospect Theory: Cumulative Representation of Uncertainty, *Journal of Risk and Uncertainty*, 5: 297-323.

Uddin, L. Q., Iacoboni, M., Lange, C., & Keenan, J. P. (2007). The self and social cognition: The role of cortical midline structures and mirror neurons. *Trends in cognitive sciences, 11*(4), 153-157.

Uddin, L. Q., Kaplan, J. T., Molnar-Szakacs, I., Zaidel, E., and Iacoboni, M. (2005). Self-face recognition activates a frontoparietal "mirror" network in the right hemisphere: An event-related fMRI study. *NeuroImage, 25*, 926-935.

Upal, M. (2005) Role of Context in Memorability of Intuitive and Counterintuitive Concepts, in *Proceedings of the 27th Annual Meeting of the Cognitive Science Society*, pages 2224-2229, Mahwah, NJ: Lawrence Earlbaum.

Upal, M. (2005) Towards a cognitive science of new religious movements, *Cognition and Culture*, 5(2), 214-239.

Upal, M. (2007) The structure of false social beliefs, in *Proceedings of the First IEEE International Symposium on Artificial Life*, 282-286, Piscataway, NJ: IEEE Press.

Upal, M. (2008) *The Layers of Culture*, forthcoming.

Upal, M., Gonce, R., Tweney, R., & Slone, J. (2007) Contextualizing Counterintuitiveness: How context affects comprehension and memorability of counterintuitive concepts, *Cognitive Science*, 31, 1-25.

Upal, M.A., & Sama, R. (2007): Effect of Communication on the Distribution of False Social Beliefs, in *Proceedings of the International Conference on Cognitive Modeling.*

Vapnik, V. (1995). *The nature of statistical learning theory.* Berlin Springer-Verlag.

Varde, A. S., Takahashi, M., Rundensteiner, E. A., Ward, M. O., Maniruzzaman, M., & Jr., R. D. S. (2004). *Apriori algorithm and Game-of-Life for predictive analysis in materials science.*

Varela, F. (1979). *Principles of Biological Autonomy.* New York: Elsevier-North Holland.

Varela, F. (1997). Patterns of Life: Intertwining Identity and Cognition. *Brain and Cognition, 34*, 72-87.

Varela, F., Maturana, H., & Uribe, R. (1974). Autopoiesis: The Organization of Living Systems, Its Characterization and a Model. *Biosystems, 5*, 187-196.

Varela, Fancisco (1999). *Ethical Know-How.* Stanford: Stanford University Press.

Varela, Francisco, Evan Thompson and Eleanor Rosch (1991). *The Embodied Mind.* Cambridge, MA: MIT Press.

Vazquez-Salceda, J., Dignum, V. & Dignum, F. (2005). Organizing Multiagent Systems, *Autonomous Agents and Multi-Agent Systems*, 11(3): 307-360.

Velásquez, J. (1997). *Modeling emotions and other motivations in synthetic agents.* Proceedings of AAAI-97.

Ventura, R. & Pinto-Ferreira, C. (1999). *Emotion-based agents.* Workshop of the Third International Conference on Autonomous Agents.

Vincenti, G. & Trajkovski, G. (2006). Fuzzy Mediation for Online Learning in Autonomous Agents. *2006 Fall AAAI Symposium.* October 12-15, 2006. Arlington, VA. USA.

Vincenti, G. & Trajkovski, G. (2007). Fuzzy Mediation as a Dynamic Extension to Information Fusion. *Fusion 2007.* July 9-12, 2007. Quebec, Canada.

Vincenti, G. & Trajkovski, G. (2007). Analysis of Different Mediation Equations and Tightness of Control to Finely Regulate the Exchange of Control Between Expert and Novice Controllers in a Fuzzy Mediation

Environment. *2007 Fall AAAI Symposium.* Arlington, VA. USA.

Vincenti, G., Braman, J. & Trajkovski, G. (2007). Emotion-Based Framework for Multi-Agent Coordination and Individual Performance in a Goal-Directed Environment. *2007 Fall AAAI Symposium.* Arlington, VA. USA.

Viswanath, K. (March 9, 2005) "Java Annotation Facility - A Primer." *Java Developers Journal Online.* Available as http://java.sys-con.com/read/48539.htm. SYS-CON Media

Vogt, P. (2000). *Lexicon grounding on mobile robots.* Unpublished doctoral dissertation, Vrije Universiteit Brussel, Belgium.

Vogt, P. (2002). The physical symbol grounding problem. *Cognitive Systems Research, 3* (3), 429-457.

Vogt, P. (2005). The emergence of compositional structures in perceptually grounded language games. *Artificial Intelligence, 167* (1-2), 206-242.

Vogt, P. (n.d). Group Size Effects on the Emergence of Compositional Structures in Language. Tilburg, Netherlands: Tilburg University.

Vogt, P., & Divina, F. (2005). Language evolution in large populations of autonomous agents: issues in scaling. In *Proceedings of AISB 2005: Social Intelligence and Interaction in Animals, Robots and Agents* (pp. 80-87).

Vogt, P., & Divina, F. (2007). Social symbol grounding and language evolution. *Interaction Studies, 8* (1), 31-52.

von Feilitzen, C., & Linne, O. (1975). Identifying with television characters. *Journal of Communication, 25*(4), 51-55.

von Neumann, J. & Morgenstern, O. (1947). *Theory of Games and Economic Behavior,* Princeton University Press, second edition.

von Neumann, J. (1966). *The theory of self-reproducing automata.* Urbana, IL: University of Illinois Press.

von_Krogh, G., & Roos, J. (1995). *Organizational Epistemology.* London: St Martins Press.

Vygotsky, L. S. (1962). *Thought and Language.* Cambridge, Mass: MIT Press.

Walker, V. R. (1996). Preponderance, probability, and warranted factfinding. *Brooklyn Law Review, 62,* 1075-1136.

Walker, V. R. (1998). Keeping the WTO from becoming the "World Trans-Science Organization": Scientific uncertainty, science policy, and factfinding in the growth hormones dispute. *Cornell International Law Journal, 31(2),* 251-320.

Walker, V. R. (1999). Language, meaning, and warrant: an essay on the use of Bayesian probability systems in legal factfinding. *Jurimetrics, 39,* 391-430.

Walker, V. R. (2001). Theories of uncertainty: explaining the possible sources of error in inferences. *Cardozo Law Review, 22,* 1523-1570.

Walker, V. R. (2003). Epistemic and non-epistemic aspects of the factfinding process in law. *APA Newsletter, 3(1),* 132-136.

Walker, V. R. (2004). Restoring the individual plaintiff to tort law by rejecting "junk logic" about specific causation. *Alabama Law Review, 56,* 381-481.

Walker, V. R. (2006). Transforming science into law: transparency and default reasoning in international trade disputes. In W. Wagner & R. Steinzor (Eds.), *Rescuing science from politics: Regulation and the distortion of scientific research* (pp. 165-192). UK: Cambridge University Press.

Walker, V. R. (2007). A default-logic paradigm for legal fact-finding. *Jurimetrics, 47,* 193-243.

Walker, V. R. (2007). Discovering the logic of legal reasoning. *Hofstra Law Review, 35(4),* 1687-1707.

Walker, V. R. (2007). Visualizing the dynamics around the rule-evidence interface in legal reasoning. *Law, Probability and Risk, 6(1-4),* 5-22.

Walters, M. (2007). *The design space for robot appearance and behaviour for robot companions.* Unpublished doctoral dissertation, University of Hertfordshire, UK.

Walton, D. (2002). *Legal argumentation and evidence.* University Park, PA: Pennsylvania State University Press.

Walton, D. N. (1996). *Argument schemes for presumptive reasoning.* Mahwah, NJ: Lawrence Erlbaum Associates.

Wassermann, E. M. & Grafman, J. (2005). Recharging cognition with DC brain polarization. *Trends in Cognitive Sciences, 9*(11), 503-505.

Watkins, C. J. C. H. and Dayan, P. (1992). Technical Note: Q-Learning. In *Machine Learning 8*(3-4), 279-292.

Watson, S., Vannini, N., Davis, M., Woods, S., Hall, M., Hall, L., & Dautenhahn, K. (2007). FearNot! an anti-Bullying Intervention: Evaluation of an interactive virtual learning environment. *Conference Proceedings AISB'07 (*pp. 446-452).

Watson, S., Vannini, N., Davis, M., Woods, S., Hall, M., Hall, L., & Dautenhahn, K. (2007). FearNot! an anti-Bullying Intervention: Evaluation of an interactive virtual learning environment. *Conference Proceedings AISB'07 (*pp. 446-452).

Watts, D (2002) A simple model of global cascades on random networks. in *Proceedings of the National Academy of Sciences,* 5766-5771.

Waxman, S. R. (2004). Everything had a name, and each name gave birth to a new thought: Links between early word-learning and conceptual organization. In D. G. Hall & S. R. Waxman (Eds.), *Weaving a lexicon* (pp. 295-335). Cambridge, MA: MIT Press.

Webb, B.R. (1996). The role of users in interactive system design: When computers are theatre, do we want the audience to write the script? *Behaviour and Information Technology, 15(2),* 76-83.

Weber, E. U. & Coskunoglu, O. (1990). **Descriptive and Prescriptive Models of Decision-Making: Implications for the Development of Decision Aids,** *IEEE Transactions on Systems, Man and Cybernetics,* 20(2): 310-317.

Wechsler, L. (2002). Why is this man smiling? Digital animators are closing in on the complex systems that makes a face come alive. *Wired, 10(6).* Retrieved December 20, 2007, from http://www.wired.com/wired/archive/10.06/face.html

Weiss, M. (2001). Patterns for e-business Agent Architectures: Using Agents as Delegates. *Pattern Languages of Programming* (PLoP-01).

Weizenbaum, J. (1966). Eliza – a computer program for the study of natural language communication between man and machine. *Communications of the ACM, 9* (1), 36-45.

Weizenbaum, J. (1976). *Computer power and human reason* W.H. Freeman & Company.

Wheatley, T., Milleville, S. C., and Martin, A. (2007). Understanding animate agents: Distinct roles for the social network and mirror system. *Psychological Science, 18*(6), 469-474.

Whitney, I., & Smith, P.K. (1993). A survey of the nature and extent of bullying in junior/middle and secondary schools. *Educational Research, 35,* 3-25.

Whorf, B. L. (1956). *Language, thought and reality: Selected writings of Benjamin Lee Whorf* (J. B. Carrol, Ed.). Cambridge, MA: MIT Press.

Williams, G. P. (1997). *Chaos Theory Tamed.* Washington D.C: Joseph Henry Press.

Wilson, R., (1985). Reputation in Games and Markets. In A. Roth (Ed.), *Game-Theoretic Models of Bargaining.* Cambridge, CUP

Winograd, T. & Flores, F. (1987). *Understanding Computers and Cognition* New York: Addison-Wesley.

Winograd, T. (1971). *Procedures as a representation for data in a computer program for understanding natural language.* Unpublished doctoral dissertation, MIT, Cambridge, MA.

Wispé, L. (1987). A history of the concept of empathy. In N. Eisenberg & J. Strayer (Eds.). *Empathy and its Development.* Cambridge, UK: Cambridge University Press.

Wolfram, S. (1994). *Cellular automata and complexity.* Reading, Mass.: Addison-Wesley.

Wolfram, S. (2002). *A new kind of science.* Champaign, IL: Wolfram Media.

Wolke, D., & Stanford, K. (1999). Bullying in school children. In D. Messer & S. Millar (Eds.), *Developmental Psychology.* London, UK: Arnold.

Wolke, D., Woods, S., Bloomfield, L., & Karstadt. (2006). Bullying involvement in primary school and common health problems. *Archives of Disease in Childhood, 85,* 197-201.

Wolke, D., Woods, S., Stanford, K., & Schulz, H. (2001). Bullying and victimisation of primary school children in South England and South Germany: Prevalence and school factors. *British Journal of Psychology, 92,* 673-696.

Woods, S., Dautenhahn, K., & Schulz, J. (2004). The design space of robots: Investigating children's views. *Conference Proceedings RO-MAN 2004* (pp. 47-52). New Jersey, USA: IEEE.

Woods, S., Hall, L., Sobral, D., Dautenhahn, K., & Wolke, D. (2003) A study into the believability of animated characters in the context of bullying intervention. *Conference Proceedings IVA 2003* (pp. 310-314). Berlin, Germany: Springer.

Woods, S., Hall, L., Sobral, D., Dautenhahn, K., & Wolke, D. (2005). Animated characters in bullying intervention. *Conference Proceedings IVA 2003* (pp.310-314). Berlin, Germany: Springer.

Wooldridge, M. (2002). *Introduction to multiagent systems.* John Wiley & Sons.

Yoon, P. K. & Hwang, C. (1995). *Multiple Attribute Decision Making: An Introduction,* Sage Publications.

Zafirovsky, M. (1999). Economic sociology in retrospect and prospect: In search of its identity within economics and sociology. *American Journal of Economics and Sociology, 58*(4), 583-627.

Zeggelink, E.P.H., de Vos, H. & Elsas, D. (2000). Reciprocal altruism and group formation: The degree of segmentation of reciprocal altruists who prefer 'old-helping-partners', *Journal of Artificial Societies and Social Simulation, 3*(3).

Zeleny, M. (1991). *Autopoiesis: A Theory of Living Organization.* New York: North Holland.

Zhang, H. & Lesser, V. (2004). A Dynamically Formed Hierarchical Agent Organization for a Distributed Content Sharing System . In *Proceedings of the International Conference on Intelligent Agent Technology (IAT 2004),* 169– 175. Beijing: IEEE Computer Society.

Zhang, Y. & Volz, R. A. (2005). Modeling Utility for Decision-theoretic Proactive Communication in Agent Team, in Proceedings of the 9th *World Multi-Conference on Systemics, Cybernetics and Informatics,* pp. 266-270, Orlando, FL, July 11-13.

Zhang, Y., Ioerger, T. R. & Volz, R. A. (2005). Decision-Theoretic Proactive Communication in Multi-Agent Teamwork, in Proceedings of the *IEEE International Conference on Systems, Man and Cybernetics* (SMC'05), Hawaii, pp. 3903-3908.

Zhang, Y., Mark Lewis, Pellon, M. & Coleman, P. (2007). A Preliminary Research on Modeling Cognitive Agents for Social Environments in Multi-Agent Systems, *AAAI 2007 Fall Symposium, Emergent Agents and Socialities: Social and Organizational Aspects of Intelligence,* pp. 116-123.

Zhang, Y., Pellon, M. & Coleman, P. (2007). Decision Under Risk in Multi-Agent Systems, in Proceedings of the *International Conference on System of Systems Engineering,* San Antonio, Texas, pp. 133-138.

Zheng, X., Chen, C., Huang, C. T., Matthews, M. M., & Santhapuri, N. (2005). *A Dual Authentication Protocol for IEEE 802.11 Wireless LANs.* Paper presented at the 2nd International Symposium on Wireless Communication Systems.

Zhu, S., Setia, S. and Jajodia, S. (2003). *LEAP: efficient security mechanisms for large-scale distributed sensor networks.* Paper presented at the Tenth ACM Conference on Computer and Communication Security, Washington, DC.

Zikopolous, P. C., Baklarz, G., & Scott, D. (2005). *Apache derby / IBM cloudscape.* Upper Saddle River, NJ: Prentice Hall PTR.

About the Contributors

Goran Trajkovski is director of Product Design at the Laureate Higher Education Group, Inc, Baltimore, MD, USA. Before going into consulting, as the CEO of Algoco e-Learning Solutions, Trajkovski was the chair of the Department of Information Technologies of South University and associate professor of IT at its Savannah, GA campus. He was previously the founding director of the Cognitive Agency and Robotics Laboratory (CARoL) at Towson University, Towson, MD, USA. The virtual version of CARoL now exists in SecondLife. He also taught at Towson University, West Virginia University, Parkersburg, WV, USA, and the University "SS Cyril and Methodius, Skopje, Macedonia. His research focuses on cognitive and developmental robotics, and interaction and emergent phenomena in agent societies. He is an affiliate of the Institute for Interactivist Studies at Lehigh University, and a member of the organizing committee of the biannual Interactivist Summer Institutes. He has authored over 200 publications, including ten books and edited volumes. He has chaired two symposia for the Association for Advancement of artificial intelligence. Dr Trajkovski is the founding Editor-in-Chief of the *International Journal of Agent Technologies and Systems*. His work has been funded by NSF, the National Academies of the Sciences, and OWASP (Open Web Application Security Project). Dr Trajkovski holds a BSc in applied informatics, MSc in mathematical and computer sciences, and PhD in computer sciences from the University "Ss Cyril and Methodius," Skopje, Macedonia.

Samuel Collins is associate professor of Anthropology at Towson University. His research includes cybernetics, information society, globalization and the future, both in the United States and in South Korea. He is the author of *All Tomorrow's Cultures: Anthropological Engagements with the Future and Library of Walls: The Library of Congress and the Contradictions of Information Society.*

* * *

Myriam Abramson is a computer scientist at the US Naval Research Laboratory in Washington, DC. She obtained her PhD in information technology at George Mason University in 2003 in the area of artificial intelligence. Her dissertation investigated learning coordination strategies through self-organized and distributed reinforcement learning coupling Kohonen maps and algorithms for temporal difference learning. She has conducted research in cooperative multi-agent systems and developed coordination algorithms in open and uncertain environments. Currently, she is involved in the requirements of a DIME/PMESII framework including cultural and societal modeling. In this context, she is doing research in cognitive maps as a representation for mental models.

Eric Baumer is a graduate student in the Department of Informatics at the University of Califorian, Irvine. His research includes human-computer interaction, social computing, computational linguistics, and multi-agent systems. He has published a number of scholarly papers about the incorporation of ideas from sociology, anthropology, and social science, in the development of multi-agent systems. His current research is exploring the use of computational identification of conceptual metaphor to engender critical reflection. He earned his BSc magna cum laude in computer science with a minor in music at the University of Central Florida, where his honors thesis focused on the development of an emotion-like state generator for a robotic office assistant, as well as a MSc in computer and information sciences at UC Irvine.

James Braman is a lecturer for the Computer and Information Science Department at Towson University, Towson, MD, USA. He is also a doctoral candidate in applied information technology and holds a master's degree in computer science from Towson University. His current research focus includes intelligent agents, simulated emotions and education in virtual and immersive environments.

Joseph Bullington is a assistant professor in the Department of Information Systems at Georgia Southern University in Statesboro, GA, USA. His background includes a PhD in social psychology from the University of California at Davis, and a love of computing. His areas of research interest include social cognition and its relationship to human computer interaction, affective computing, the psychological foundations of risk and decision-making, and issues in the foundations of cognitive science. He has been crisscrossing the line between psychology and computing since graduate school.

Phil Coleman is a computer science student at Trinity University. His research interests are distributed multi-agent systems. He has co-authored over 10 conference papers in this area. He was the recipient of the 2008 Charles Babbage Award, which is given to the top computer science graduate each year.

Nick Collier began his work with complex adaptive systems in 1998 with Social Science Research Computing at the University of Chicago, IL, USA where he was a co-designer and the first developer of the Repast framework for creating agent based simulations. Since 2003 Dr. Collier has worked for Argonne National Laboratory on Repast Simphony, a next generation agent simulation framework, environmental visualization software, GIS based modeling and analysis systems, and a variety of simulations. Dr. Collier has a PhD in philosophy of religions from the University of Chicago.

Adam J. Conover is a lecturer in applied information technology at Towson University. He has a BS and MS in computer science, and a DSc in applied information technology and approximately twelve years of experience in professional software engineering and technical consulting. Conover's initial experience in software engineering was as a developer of educational software for a leading producer of software based text-book supplements, curriculum support, classroom management, and distance learning internet applications. For the past several years, he has been teaching fundamentals of programming in Java and various information systems courses. His research topics have ranged from object-oriented software engineering to agent and swarm simulation. Currently, it is focused on studying the effects of timing instability in swarms of inter-communicating agents.

Rosaria Conte is president of AISC, Italian Association of Cognitive Science, vice-president of ESSA, the European Association of Social Simulation, and head of the LABSS (Laboratory of Agent Based Social Simulation) at the ISTC (Institute for Cognitive Science and Technology), and teaches Social Psychology at the Univ. of Siena. She is the scientific coordinator of the FP6 EMIL "Emergence In the Loop: Simulating the two way dynamics of norm innovation" project. She is a cognitive and social scientist, with a special interest for the study of positive social action (altruism, cooperation and social norms), and reputation-based social regulation. Quite active in the MAS field, she contributed to launch the field of social simulation in Europe by organising amongst the main events held in the last ten years or so, editing collective volumes and coordinating a EU-funded Special Interest Group on agent-based social simulation. She has been member of several European research projects and Networks of Excellence. She has published about 120 among scientific articles and books on cognitive social agents, norms representation and reasoning, and agent-based simulation. Her research interests range from agent theory to multi agent systems, from agent-based social simulation and cultural evolution to info-societies and virtual markets.

Kerstin Dautenhahn received her PhD degree from the Department of Biological Cybernetics at University of Bielefeld, Germany. She is professor of artificial intelligence in the School of Computer Science at University of Hertfordshire where she coordinates the Adaptive Systems Research Group. She has published more than 150 research articles on social robotics, robot learning, human-robot interaction and assistive technology. Prof. Dautenhahn has edited several books and frequently organises international research workshops and conferences including hosting the AISB05 convention and general chair of IEEE RO-MAN 2006. Currently she is a general chair of HRI08, the 3rd ACM/IEEE International Conference on Human-Robot Interaction. She is involved in several FP6 and FP7 European projects (Cogniron, Robotcub, Iromec, eCircus, LIREC, I-Talk) and is Editor-in-Chief of the *Journal Interaction Studies: Social Behaviour and Communication in Biological and Artificial Systems.*

Rafal Dawidowicz received a First Class BSc (Hons) computer science degree in June 2005 from the University of Hertfordshire (UK). In February 2008 he finalized his MPhil degree in the area of social robotics, at the University of Hertfordshire. From May 2007 he worked as a junior software developer in Deltavista in Poland with headquarters in Krakow. Mainly, his tasks are Web-services oriented. His responsibility is data processing and data usage in the risk assessment for credit protection.

Christine Drennon has been teaching at Trinity University for six years. Although she is an associate professor in the Department of Sociology and Anthropology, her PhD is in geography, and her major contribution to the university is in the Urban Studies Program. Her previous research has been on the political landscape of the city, and most importantly, how political boundaries impact residential diversity by sorting communities by socioeconomic group, thus creating homogeneous groupings with very little interaction between neighboring communities. Dr. Drennon was the recipient of Trinity Junior Faculty Distinguished Teaching and Research Award in 2006. She is the director of the Geographic Information Systems Laboratory at Trinity University. Dr. Drennon's current research integrates multi-agent systems and GIS to model the urban investment environment.

Deborah V. Duong is a senior computational social scientist at the Office of the Secretary Defense. She works there as a contractor for SAIC. She received her PhD from George Mason University Computational Sciences and Informatics, with a major in computational social science. Her BS is in sociology/anthropology. Her specialty is the simulation of interpretive social phenomena, using the symbolic interactionist simulation technique, in which agents institutions. She also works on coevolutionary systems, genetic algorithms, neural nets/fuzzy systems, expert systems, game theory, ontologies, and natural language processing.

Chris Goldspink has twenty years experience as an internal and external consultant in organization and management improvement. His background is diverse and includes experience with information technology, education, organizational management and public sector reform. He has senior and middle management experience and maintains an interest in practical management in both the public and private sectors, teaching and consulting in both. He teaches in areas including strategic management, leadership and marketing as well as public management reform, the Australian system of Government and in systems derived research methodologies. His research interests include the applicability of complex systems theory to social and organizational analysis, computer simulation of social phenomena and issues in cross cultural education.

Wan Ching Ho received his first BSc and PhD degrees from University of Hertfordshire in 2002 and 2005 respectively. The title of his PhD thesis is *Computational Memory Architectures for Autobiographic and Narrative Virtual Agents*. He is now working as a full-time post-doc research fellow in the Adaptive Systems Research Group in the same university. His research mainly focuses on developing control architectures for narrative and autobiographic virtual agents for an EU Framework 6 funded project e-CIRCUS. Wan Ching Ho's research interests are interdisciplinary, including: applying theories from cognitive science and psychology to computational agent control architectures, developing narrative and autobiographic agents for educational software and computer games. The common aim of these is to increase the agents' believability and the interactivity of the software application.

Thomas Howe received his MS in computer science in 2007 from the University of Chicago, IL, USA. He began his career with Social Science Research Computing at the University of Chicago where he was the maintenance developer of the Repast framework for creating agent based simulations. In 2004 he started work for Argonne National Laboratory on Repast Simphony, a next generation agent simulation framework, environmental visualization software, GIS based modeling and analysis systems, and a variety of simulations. In 2007, he left the Repast project to head back to the University of Chicago, where he is now a developer for the Globus grid computing framework.

Robert Kay is cofounder of Incept Labs, a firm specializing in strategic innovation and commercialization services. Formerly Robert was the head of strategic innovation at Westpac Banking Corporation. This role involved the integration of various systems theories into the innovation processes of the bank. He has also performed as a senior lecturer in Information Systems at the University of Technology, Sydney (UTS), and lectured at the University of Western Sydney; the International Graduate School of Management, University of South Australia; and University of New South Wales. His central research interest is in the application of autopoietic and complexity theory to understanding organizational sustainability and change.

Jason Leezer is a computer science student at Trinity University. His research interests are multi-agent systems. Jason was awarded the Outstanding Sophomore Research award and the Outstanding Junior Research award. He was also awarded the Mach Fellowship.

Mark Lewis completed his MS in computer science and PhD in astrophysics and planetary science at the University of Colorado at Boulder working on large scale numerical simulations of planetary rings. Since joining the faculty of the computer science department at Trinity University, his work has focused on simulation methodologies for large-scale, spatial simulations and on the analysis and visualization of simulation results.

Charles M. Macal, PhD, PE, has over twenty five years of experience applying agent-based modeling and simulation, discrete event simulation, mathematical programming, operations research methods, and artificial intelligence techniques to government and business decision problems. Dr. Macal is the director of the Center for Complex Adaptive Agent Systems Simulation within the Decision and Information Sciences Division of Argonne National Laboratory. In this role, Dr. Macal directs an interdisciplinary team of modelers, operations researchers, systems analysts, social scientists, engineers, and computer programmers. From 1987 to the present, Dr. Macal published widely and has obtained over $50 million in project funding.

David Newlin, PhD, is a psychophysiologist/psychopharmacologist at RTI International. He was a research psychologist at NIH's National Institute on Drug Abuse – Intramural Research Program for 16 years before coming to RTI. His work has focused on the psychopharmacology of drugs of abuse, risk factors for alcoholism, and the psychophysiology of alcohol.

Michael J. North, MBA, PhD, is the deputy director of the Center for Complex Adaptive Agent Systems Simulation within the Decision and Information Sciences Division of Argonne National Laboratory and is a senior fellow in the Joint Computation Institute of Argonne and the University of Chicago. Dr. North has over fifteen years of experience developing and applying advanced modeling and simulation applications for various branches of the U.S. federal government; state government; several international agencies; private industry; and academia. Dr. North is the lead author of the book *Managing Business Complexity: Discovering Strategic Solutions with Agent-Based Modeling and Simulation* (Oxford 2007) and has published over forty journal articles and conference papers. Dr. North holds ten college degrees, including a PhD in computer science from the Illinois Institute of Technology.

Jonathan Ozik has spent the last three years as a postdoctoral fellow at Argonne National Laboratory and a visiting scholar at the University of Chicago. His research revolves around the modeling of predominantly social complex systems for the purpose of improving understanding of the various mechanisms at play at the multiple spatio-temporal levels that are often required to encapsulate system behavior and the often counterintuitive emergent macro patterns that such systems can exhibit. As part of the Joint Threat Anticipation Center (JTAC), a collaborative project of the University of Chicago and Argonne National Laboratory, he has been engaged in the designing and building of social computational models for better anticipating long-term threats to international security arising from social, behavioral, economic and cultural processes. Jonathan is also involved in the development of agent-based social modeling computational tools. Jonathan received his PhD in physics from the Chaos and Nonlinear Dynamics Group at the University of Maryland in 2005.

Mario Paolucci is a researcher LABSS (Laboratory of Agent Based Social Simulation, http://labss.istc.cnr.it) at ISTC/CNR (Institute for Cognitive Science and Technology), Rome. He studies and applies multiagent-based social simulation and agent theory to understand social artefacts, in particular norms, reputation, responsibility, and the cultural evolutionary mechanisms that support them. His publications include a book on Reputation with Rosaria Conte and articles on JASSS and adaptive behavior. He is the scientific coordinator of the eRep "Social Knowledge for e-Governance" FP6 project. He is unit coordinator for the FIRB-Socrate project. I'm also currently participating to the EMIL project on norm innovation. He has chaired the RASTA '02 and '03 workshops, the RAS '04 workshop, and the MABS 2007 workshop. He has has participated in the program committee of several conferences and worshops, including the MABS series. He currently teaches a course on social simulation at the University of Bologna. He's been teaching Java language at the University Of Perugia and Data Bases at the University of Rome 1.

Mike Pellon is a computer science student at Trinity University. His research interests are artificial intelligence and multi-agent systems. He has published over 10 conference papers in this area. He was the awarded the Outstanding Junior Research award and the Outstanding Senior Research award at Trinity.

Theodor Richardson is an assistant professor at South University. He has earned his terminal degree along with a National Security Agency Certificate of Information Assurance and Security in network security at the University of South Carolina, Columbia, SC, USA. He specializes in protocol construction and security and has published several conference papers in the field of network security in wireless networks and intrusion detections.

Jorge A. Romero has a PhD in management science and also holds an MBA from The University of Texas at Dallas, TX, USA. He has expertise in market measures of firm performance, and accounting information systems. He currently works as assistant professor of Management at Towson University, after having gained experience from industry in both the U.S. and Latin America.

Josefina Santibáñez is an associate professor at the Education Department of the University of La Rioja, Spain. She has been interested in the problem of language acquisition since her PhD research which focused on the relation between the process of learning to read and to write, and the mental aptitudes and the visual-motor development. She has published several books in the areas of pedagogy, teacher education, and information and communication technologies applied to education. She has an extensive teaching experience, first as a school teacher, and then as a teacher training professor at the Education Department of the University of La Rioja. Her broad research interests have led her to direct and participate in several international and national research projects in the areas on education, teacher education and new technologies applied to education. She has written more than a hundred papers in scientific journals, edited volumes and major conferences in the areas of teacher education, didactics, learning and new technologies applied to education.

R. Keith Sawyer is associate professor of education, psychology, and business at Washington University in St. Louis. His 2005 book, *Social Emergence: Societies as Complex Systems* (Cambridge) draws on philosophy of science to develop a new theoretical framework with which to understand emergence theories, and then uses that framework to describe and analyze the various approaches to emergence in the social sciences and in computational modeling. Sawyer's theoretical work developed out of a series of empirical studies of small group interaction that he has published in several books, including *Pretend Play as Improvisation* (1997, Erlbaum), *Creating Conversations* (2001, Hampton), and *Improvised Dialogues: Emergence and Creativity in Conversation* (2003, Greenwood). Sawyer is also known for his studies of group creativity; his most recent book is *Group Genius: The Creative Power of Collaboration* (2007, Basic Books).

Josefina Sierra is associate professor at the Software Department of the Technical University of Cataluña, Spain. She worked for several years as an associated researcher at the Formal Reasoning Group at Stanford University. The formalization of common sense knowledge and reasoning, and specifically the declarative formalization of heuristics were the main research areas she worked on during that period. She has been interested in areas of logic, artificial intelligence, and knowledge representation and reasoning both as a researcher and as an instructor She has published papers on the declarative formalization of heuristics and its application to planning and in the origins of logical categories, both from a semantic and a syntactic point of view.

Richard Schilling completed his undergraduate degree in computer science, with an artificial intelligence specialization, in 1996 at Central Washington University in Ellensburg, Washington. He also completed his MBA in 2002 at City University in Bellevue, Washington. From 1996 until 2008 Richard worked in health care as a senior software developer and technical project manager. In 2002 he started his own consulting firm, Cognition Group, an open source development services and business consulting company. Richard has also served on standards development committees at ASTM, X12, and OMG. Presently, he continues his research into intelligent agents, and actively works on robotics projects involving embedded agent designs.

Martin Takáč has graduated from the Comenius University in Bratislava, Slovakia in 1997, where he received RNDr (Doctor of Natural Sciences) degree in 2001. His thesis focused on how artificial agents can autonomously acquire and represent knowledge of their environment. His research interests include cognitive semantics and computational modeling of sensory-motor intelligence, categorization, language and ontology acquisition in single-agent and multi-agent scenarios. He has held a lecturer position in artificial intelligence and cognitive science at the Comenius University since 1999 and is the author of more than twenty scientific publications including one textbook and four book chapters.

Eric Tatara received his PhD in chemical engineering from Illinois Institute of Technology in 2005. Dr. Tatara has published over 40 journal articles and conference papers in his primary research fields which include industrial process modeling, supervision and control, agent-based simulation, analysis and simulation of nonlinear dynamical systems, military operations research, and biomedical engineering applications.

Bill Tomlinson is assistant professor of Informatics at the University of California, Irvine, CA, USA and a researcher in the California Institute for Telecommunications and Information Technology. He studies the fields of multi-agent systems, human-computer interaction, real time graphics and environmental technologies. He has authored more than thirty scholarly publications. In 2007, he received an NSF CAREER award. His animated film, *Shaft of Light*, was screened at the Sundance Film Festival and was distributed by the Anti-Defamation League in its Anti-Bias/Diversity Catalog. He holds an AB in Biology from Harvard College, an M.F.A. in Experimental Animation from CalArts, and S.M. and PhD degrees from the MIT Media Lab.

M. Afzal Upal is assistant professor of Cognitive Science and director of the Cognition and Culture Laboratory at Occidental College in Los Angeles and an adjunct professor of Psychology at Bowling Green State University. He has published over two dozen technical articles on cognitive science, artificial intelligence, agent-based simulations, and cognitive modeling. He was the chair of the CogSci-07 Workshop on Cognition and Culture, AAAI-06 Workshop of Cognitive Modeling and Agent-based Social Simulations, the 2006 Annual Meeting of the North American Association of Computational, Social and Organizational Sciences, and the 1999 Canadian Workshop on Soft Computing. He is interested in computational approaches to the study of cognition and culture, in particular, those involving cognitive foundations of religion and religious movements. His research has been funded by AFRL, DARPA, OBOR, and MDA.

Giovanni Vincenti, DSc, is in charge of research and development at Gruppo Vincenti, Rome, Italy. His main areas of research include fuzzy mediation, information fusion, emotionally-aware agent frameworks and robotics. He held several positions at Towson University, including a lecturership with the Department of Computer and Information Sciences. He also taught courses for the Center of Applied Information Technology, also at Towson University. He is the author of many publications, and the father of the concept of fuzzy mediation, as applied to the field of information fusion.

Vern R. Walker is professor of Law at Hofstra University School of Law in Hempstead, New York. He received his PhD in philosophy from the University of Notre Dame and his JD in law from Yale Law School. Professor Walker specializes in the study of legal reasoning, with particular focus on the fact-finding processes employed in law. He has also helped to design software to automate portions of the legal reasoning process. Professor Walker teaches courses in the areas of scientific evidence, torts, administrative law, and European Union law. He has published extensively on the design of governmental fact-finding processes, on the use of scientific evidence in legal proceedings, and on the topics of risk assessment, risk management and scientific uncertainty. He has been a consultant on these topics to both private and governmental institutions. He is co-author of the book *Product Risk Reduction in the Chemical Industry*; is on the editorial board of the Oxford University Press journal *Law, Probability and Risk*; and is a past president of the Risk Assessment and Policy Association. Prior to joining the Hofstra faculty, Professor Walker was a partner in the Washington, D.C., law firm of Swidler & Berlin.

Scott Watson graduated from the University of Lincoln (UK) in 2000 with a degree in psychology, and from the University of Hertfordshire (UK) with a MSc in research methodology for psychology. As an associate lecturer he taught personality, statistics, and research methods in the School of Psychology at the University of Hertfordshire for three years. In 2005 he became a research assistant on the EU Framework 6 project e-CIRCUS (Education through Characters with emotional-Intelligence and Role-playing Capabilities that Understand Social interaction). In this project he is responsible for the recruitment of schools, administration of a large-scale longitudinal evaluation of the FearNot! anti-bullying software, and analysis and publication of data from these evaluations. He is also investigating the efficacy of a computational model of autobiographic memory, developed alongside Dr. Wan Ching Ho. His professional interests lie within personality theory, human-computer/ robot interaction, and the development of ecologically valid models of artificial intelligence. Moreover, he enjoys applying rigorous psychological principles and methodologies to the HCI/HRI field.

Yu Zhang completed her PhD in computer science at Texas A&M University in 2005. She obtained her BS and MS in computer science from Central South University, China in 1995 and 1998 respectively. She is currently an assistant professor in the Department of Computer Science at Trinity University and the director of the Laboratory for Distributed Intelligent Agent Systems. Dr. Zhang's research falls within AI and multi-agent systems. Her research is funded by NSF, ACS (Association of Colleges in South), CUR (Council on Undergraduate Research) and Trinity University. She is in the editorial board and program committee for over 30 journals, conferences and technical groups.

Index